Political

THE BUSINESS ENVIRONMENT

Themes and Issues in a Globalizing World

Social

Technological

Legal

Environmental
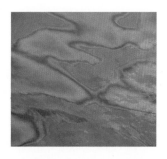

Ethical

THE BUSINESS ENVIRONMENT

Themes and Issues in a Globalizing World

THIRD EDITION

**Paul Wetherly and
Dorron Otter**

OXFORD
UNIVERSITY PRESS

Great Clarendon Street, Oxford, OX2 6DP,
United Kingdom

Oxford University Press is a department of the University of Oxford.
It furthers the University's objective of excellence in research, scholarship,
and education by publishing worldwide. Oxford is a registered trade mark of
Oxford University Press in the UK and in certain other countries

First edition 2008

Second edition 2011

Impression: 1

Published in the United States of America by Oxford University Press
198 Madison Avenue, New York, NY 10016, United States of America

British Library Cataloguing in Publication Data

Data available

Library of Congress Control Number: 2013955310

ISBN 978–0–19–966138–1

Printed in Great Britain by
Bell & Bain Ltd, Glasgow

To the memory of Bill and Chris (PW)

To Ingrid, Søren, Fredie, and Ferdy (DO)

NEW TO THIS EDITION

This edition has been updated throughout, with a large proportion of new case and illustrative material added.

The chapters have been re-structured so that seven 'environments' of business are now included in the first part, adding the 'ethical environment' and the 'natural environment'.

For this edition the business environment has been reconceptualized to enable readers to think critically about the claim that we are living in a 'globalizing world' and to understand the implications for business.

CONTENTS

DETAILED CONTENTS

Lecturer's guide

Finding stimulating ways of reinforcing students' understanding of the Business Environment can be difficult. A helpful chapter-by-chapter Lecturer's guide has been provided by the authors to assist instructors in their teaching of Business Environment modules. This includes the rationale for each chapter, how it links with other chapters within the book, suggestions for seminar activities, and exam questions.

Figures and tables from the text

All figures and tables from the text have been provided in high resolution format to download to your lecture presentations and include in handouts.

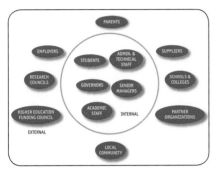

■ For students

Multiple choice questions

Ten online multiple choice questions for each chapter provide a quick and easy way to test your understanding during revision. These self-marking questions give you instant feedback and provide page references to the textbook to help you focus on areas that need further study.

Podcasts

To complement this text we are featuring podcasts to accompany each chapter, summarizing the content and pulling out important issues raised.

ACKNOWLEDGEMENTS

There are many people we would like to thank for their help during the production of this book, not least our families for their patience in dealing with the opportunity costs of our spending the time necessary to complete the book!

We are indebted to all at OUP for their terrific support, especially Lucy Hyde and Tom Randall for keeping us on track with our writing schedule, and to Joanna Hardern for all her help in the production process. We would also like to wish Francesca Griffin all the best and thank her for all her support in the early discussions for this third edition.

We would like to thank all of the authors, both those who have been part of the team on the previous editions and those who have joined us for this third edition. We would also like to extend this thanks to Howard Vane for his contribution to the previous editions. There are many of our colleagues here at Leeds Met who have contributed to this book in ways it is not always easy to quantify, but in particular we would like to thank our colleagues in Economics and International Business and in Politics and Applied Global Ethics. We would also like to extend our thanks to all the reviewers who have commented upon the revised draft chapters and reflected on their experiences of using the book with their students.

As always we would like to thank all of our students who have helped us in developing our approach to exploring the Business Environment.

INTRODUCTION

1 'Business' and its 'environment' in a 'globalizing world'
Paul Wetherly and Dorron Otter

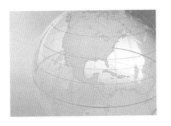

housing, and other necessities. More specifically, international tourism has been facilitated by technological developments lowering the cost of travel. Along with communications technologies, it can be argued that transportation is one of the principal facilitators of globalization. In the 19th century British people took advantage of the new technology of steam trains to go on excursions to the seaside. In the late 20th century they took advantage of the new technology of passenger airlines to holiday overseas. Mass foreign travel is a fairly recent phenomenon in rich countries like the UK—we might think of the growth of package holidays to European destinations, such as Spain, in the 1960s and 1970s as a watershed. Since then foreign travel has become a more normal experience of British people and they are travelling further afield: destinations that were once 'exotic' become normal. Citizens of the rich countries are now being joined in rapidly growing numbers by people from fast-developing BRIC economies (Brazil, Russia, India, and China).

Hence the world is 'globalizing' in the sense that European, and now Russian and Chinese, people have increasingly global horizons when it comes to tourism. Tourism, in other words, is increasingly international or cross-border and creates interconnections and interdependence between the world's economies. The most obvious way it does this is through the dependence of the many and diverse companies and their employees that are part of the tourism sector on revenues generated by foreign visitors. Thus, UK economic performance is dependent in part on the country's success in attracting foreign tourists. The payments they make are equivalent, in terms of the balance of payments, to revenues earned by the export of goods. This interconnectedness is the essence of what we mean by a 'globalizing world'.

⯈ **VALUES** International tourism is not new, but the *volume* of cross-border movement is increasing. It is also still confined largely to travel between the rich countries of the world, yet people from the rich countries are travelling to more destinations and foreign visits from developing BRIC countries are growing fast. Hence, globalization is extending in geographical *reach* as well. (Still, we are a very long way from foreign travel being part of the lifestyle of all people in the world, and it is questionable whether such an outcome would be feasible or desirable. Again, what counts as success from a business point of view—more customers, revenue and profit—and from the point of view of individual customers—more affordable foreign travel—might be undesirable from the viewpoint of societal or environmental impact, such as damaging areas of natural beauty or contributing to global warming.)

If people are increasingly taking part in a globalizing world then the same can be said of business. Indeed, it can be argued that globalization is fundamentally an economic phenomenon, driven by the profit motive and competitive pressures in the market. We can see this from the tourism example: although companies cannot make people undertake foreign visits against their will, the rise of international tourism has been powered by companies continually seeking new products and markets and promoting them through marketing.

A globalizing world involves the increasing volume and reach of cross-border movement and consequent interconnectedness. These movements include people, trade, and international investment. Globalization is both driven by business and constitutes the environment in which it operates. Thus, it is essential to our understanding of 'business' in its 'environments'.

▥ **What is business? Broad and narrow definitions**

⯈ **DIVERSITY** One way in which it is common to think about business is in terms of *a specific business organization* with which we are familiar, such as Amazon. It is this meaning that is being used when we refer to 'starting a business' or 'managing the business'. But there are a number of other, related, ways in which we might answer the question 'what is business?' To pursue the Amazon example a little further, we can see that two other answers are implied. One is to think of business in terms of *a specific activity*, which is what we refer to in answer to the question what 'line of business' an individual or organization is in. In this sense, Amazon is an online retail business selling CDs, DVDs, books, and much else. (It is worth noting here that large global corporations are often conglomerates, engaged in several business activities.) Amazon is also an example of a *specific legal form* of business—it is a PLC (public limited company) which is a form of private ownership and part of the 'private sector' of the economy. As a private sector business, Amazon strives to operate profitably through sales of its products in competition with other companies in the same market. For example, Amazon competes not only with other internet retailers but also businesses engaged in retail sales of books and music in specialized stores and supermarkets. The particular market in which a business operates is clearly a key aspect of its environment, the arena in which businesses compete.

▶ **SPATIAL LEVELS** But it is also important to think more broadly in terms of the character of *the business system* as a whole. We might refer to this using terms such as 'the market system' or 'capitalism', but we should think of it not just in terms of economic organizations such as businesses but the whole range of organizations that interact to shape the pattern of economic activity, including trade unions, professional bodies, consumer groups, regulatory agencies, and other governmental bodies. It is customary to think of the business system in terms of a national economy, such as the UK, but in a globalizing world we need to recognize the ways in which the system operates across borders and creates the interconnectedness of nations. Thus, we may refer to the international (or even global) business system.

A further meaning of business is invoked when we refer to *the* 'business community' or perhaps 'business class'. This suggests that businesses constitute a distinctive group within society and that, for some purposes, individual business organizations may find it advantageous to work together to pursue shared interests or goals. For example, there may be a desire within the business community to present a common position in order to influence some aspect of government economic policy, such as a decision on taxation, interest rates, or business regulation. Such a common position might be presented by a collective business organization like the Confederation of British Industry (CBI). The business community may also now be thought of as spanning national borders, such as in the form of the annual meetings of the World Economic Forum (WEF) at Davos. However, there are often conflicting interests within the business community, for example, between renewable energy companies and oil producers in relation to carbon pricing.

Ways of thinking about 'business'

- A specific business organization or firm
- Type of economic activity engaged in—type of goods or services produced
- Legal form
- The business system
- The business community.

Everybody would agree that Amazon is an example of a business organization, but there would be much less agreement on whether the term applies also to the police force. Thinking about these two examples can help us to clarify the meaning of business and to distinguish narrow and broad definitions. The reason for thinking that the police force is not a business arises from the common association between business, paying customers, competition, and the profit motive. Citizens do not pay for policing services in the form of a market price that is set at a level to yield a profit, and the police do not face any competitors for customers (indeed the direct recipients of police services, crime suspects, are not really 'customers' at all in the sense of choosing to use the service). But this is a narrow view of business that equates it with a specific legal form and the private sector.

A broad view of business is based on thinking of business as an activity. If we step back from the particular line of business that Amazon is in we can describe business in general terms as the activity of production—the transformation of various inputs (or 'factors of production') into diverse outputs in the form of goods and services to meet particular wants or needs of people in society. Amazon and the police are both engaged in this generic activity, using particular inputs (employees with particular skills and knowledge, particular types of equipment and technology) to produce particular services. They are both, in this broad sense, business organizations, and it is not relevant to this definition that Amazon is part of the private sector and the police service is part of the state or public sector.

▶ **DIVERSITY** In this book a broad definition of business is used. A key advantage of this definition is that it reminds us that there is more than one business model available, and the advantages and disadvantages of different models are at the centre of controversy about the nature of business and its role in society. Why is Amazon in the private sector and the police in the public sector? In the latter case, a large part of the answer is that we regard protection of the public as a primary duty of government and a right of citizens rather than something that should depend on their ability to pay, whereas in the former case, we are generally happy that consumption of books and CDs can be left to individual choice and ability to pay. But, if we look a little more closely, we can see that even these apparently straightforward cases involve some degree of controversy. It is clear that governments cannot guarantee to protect their citizens from threats to their lives and property, and there is a large range of private sector businesses operating in the field of security. Many large stores employ their own security guards, so the protection of their property does depend, to some extent, on ability to pay. Although the market is very good at meeting most people's wants for books and CDs, if you are poor and cannot afford to buy books, Amazon will not respond to your wants or needs. That is a large part of the argument for public libraries and a reason why there is concern over their future. So, in both of these cases there is a mix of public and private provision, and a broad definition of business allows us to analyse this mix.

Dealing with the problem of scarcity

This broad definition of business in terms of production can be related to the need of all societies to decide how to allocate the available productive resources between all the possible types of production of goods and services for which they can be used. What economists call the **basic economic problem** is scarcity—resources are limited and the large, and even open-ended, set of wants, needs, and goals that make demands on those resources can't all be satisfied at once (see Chapter 2). The broad definition of business recognizes that there is more than one way of dealing with this problem.

❱❱ **VALUES** All societies have to develop and agree rules and institutions which provide the framework or system within which resources are allocated; that is, rules governing the operation of business in the broad sense. In any society such rules and institutions are likely to remain a constant focus of controversy and debate, because they might work more to the advantage of some members of society than others, and because there are competing values at stake. There is never likely to be unanimous agreement, hence the nature of the business system is always an intensely political issue. For example, the global economic recession, initially triggered by problems in the financial sector in 2008, has reignited fierce political controversy over the need for government intervention to limit the recession and whether new forms of regulation of the market, particularly the banking sector, are needed to prevent a recurrence in the future. This is a debate not only about the role of national governments but also the need for international action (see Chapter 9). The business model that was widely supported in the 1980s and early 1990s is now open to question.

❱❱ **DIVERSITY** What alternatives are available to society in deciding a framework of rules and institutions within which business operates? In the real world societies differ from each other in complex ways, but it is possible to identify some broad principles and mechanisms. To start with we can distinguish between centralized and decentralized systems. Centralized allocation of resources is undertaken by government or the state, whereas the market is a decentralized mechanism. Other decentralized mechanisms are: voluntary agencies and charities (third sector), and the 'informal economy'. These alternatives can be illustrated through the example of healthcare.

The market or capitalist system operates on the basis of private property, voluntary exchange, competition, and the profit motive. In a market for healthcare, services are offered by private companies which compete with one another for sales to paying customers, and the main purpose of business is to make a profit. In a pure market, individuals have to be self-reliant in meeting their own needs for healthcare through their ability to pay. The level of resources allocated to healthcare and the mix of services is determined by the decentralized interaction of buyers and sellers.

Government or the state provides an alternative mechanism to the market for allocating resources. Government can use its tax-raising powers to provide public services to citizens on the basis of criteria other than ability to pay. For example, the UK National Health Service (NHS) is essentially a tax-funded system that operates on the basis of equal treatment for equal need, and medical need replaces profit as the purpose of the business. In effect, taxpayers contribute to a common fund and all citizens are able to draw on the fund in the form of medical treatment on the basis of need, irrespective of the amount they have paid in. The level of resources allocated to healthcare is determined in a centralized way through government budget decisions, and the mix of services is determined by a central regulatory body coupled with decentralized assessments of clinical need by medical practitioners.

The voluntary, or third, sector provides an alternative decentralized mechanism for allocating resources where the purpose is to meet certain categories of need rather than to make a profit. Funding is provided by voluntary donations and sometimes by government grants, and services are provided often on a last resort basis where individuals have no access to services provided through the market or government. For example MSF (Médecins Sans Frontières) provides emergency medical assistance in circumstances of civil conflict or natural disaster, usually in poor countries. However, there is a role for the voluntary provision of health services even in one of the richest countries in the world, the US, because of the shortcomings of both the market and government in meeting the needs of the poor in that society.

The **informal** economy includes both paid and unpaid work. Informal paid work can be defined as 'the paid production and sale of goods or services which are unregistered by, or hidden from the state for tax, benefit and/or labour law purposes, but which are legal in all other respects' (Katungi, Neal, and Barbour 2006), such as businesses supplying goods and services and/or hiring workers on a cash-in-hand basis. Informal unpaid work includes informal care provided within the household or community. Although the informal sector is not included in government measures of economic activity, and therefore its size is difficult to determine, it is clear that it encompasses important areas of production of goods and services and constitutes a significant element of social and economic life. For example, 'The 2011 Census shows there are approximately 5.8 million people providing unpaid care in England and Wales, representing just over one tenth of the population (10.3 per cent). … Of these … 1.4 million provide 50 hours or more unpaid care' (White 2013, p. 2).

❯❯ **STAKEHOLDERS** We can see that, aside from the informal economy, there are three basic models of business: the market, government, and the third sector. Remember that we are including these in our broad definition of business because they are all engaged in the activity of production of goods and services of some kind. We can add to this that in each model of business outputs are produced for 'consumers' (customers, users, or clients) and in response to their requirements, wants, or needs; and this is an intrinsic aspect of business. The important point is that the success of business is always bound up to some degree with consumers' requirements and expectations. These three models never exist in a pure form but may be combined or interact in various ways that shape the overall character of the business system within society. On an international level, there are important differences between countries in the ways these models combine and interact. Most obviously, these differences can be seen in the size of the public sector and the role played by government in economic life. The boundaries between these sectors are not fixed but shift as a result, most notably, of government policy. For example, the scope of the private sector and market has been expanded in the UK since the 1970s through a policy of privatization, as part of a move towards a more 'free market' business model. However, outside the pages of economics textbooks there is no such thing as a pure market system or free market, because markets everywhere have developed in conjunction with government, the third sector, and, more generally, the wider society.

A broad definition of business

Business is a mechanism for deciding the allocation of the resources available to society between various possible uses (or competing wants and needs), the methods of production, and the distribution of the output (who gets what), in a situation of scarcity where not all wants can be satisfied. The three basic forms of business are the market (private sector), government (public sector), and the third sector. In each case business success is bound up with meeting the requirements of consumers (though these are not the only stakeholders). The character of the business system is determined by the changing way in which the three forms are combined and interact.

▒ The private sector of business

❯❯ **STAKEHOLDERS** ❯❯ **DIVERSITY** The private sector is made up of business organizations that are owned and controlled as forms of private property. 'Private property' is a legal concept, but it includes a variety of legal forms. The largest businesses take the form of public limited companies (PLCs) which are owned by their shareholders. These shareholders can be private individuals, although a majority of shares is owned by pension funds, insurance companies, and financial institutions (Office for National Statistics 2012). Private sector businesses can take other legal forms, such as sole traders, partnerships, mutual organizations, and private limited companies (see Chapter 5). Private ownership is the thread connecting all these types. However, the private sector is characterized by further specific features:

- production of goods and services for sale
- the profit motive
- competition.

Private sector businesses produce goods and services for sale to customers in a context of competition with other firms in the market and with the principal purpose of making a profit. We will examine in more detail how markets operate in Chapter 2, but here we can look more closely at these features and see that they are not straightforward.

Free market vs. regulation?

The basic idea of private business is that firms are free to manage their own affairs and use their own resources as they choose. In this way, private ownership of business may be likened to other forms of private property where the whole point of owning something is to use it as we please and for our own benefit or self-interest. In business terms this means that businesses should be managed in the interests of their owners, and this means making a profit. It might be added to this that businesses are best able to judge for themselves how to manage their affairs efficiently, and that by being left to do this there is benefit for the wider public through the resulting innovation and economic growth. However, in reality there is no such thing as a **free market** in the sense of businesses being left entirely free to make decisions for themselves. In all market systems the law is used more-or-less extensively to regulate various aspects of business decisions and behaviour (see Chapters 4 and 5).

❱❱ **VALUES** One of the prime reasons for using the law to regulate business is a recognition that a free market would have undesirable consequences for certain groups in society, including some of the stakeholders within firms. Consumers and employees would be at a disadvantage in their dealings with business without various protections afforded by law. In other words, although business pursuing its self-interest produces substantial public benefit such as greater prosperity, there are many ways in which business self-interest and the public interest clash. What is good for business is not always good for society.

For example, the Minimum Wage Act, requiring all businesses in the UK to pay a **minimum wage**, ensures that profit-seeking businesses facing competitive pressures do not harm vulnerable groups of employees by forcing wages down below a decent level. Paying a minimum wage may be seen as a social obligation that business must fulfil. More fundamentally, this example raises the question of how we define business and what is good for business. If we equate a business that was paying below the minimum wage (e.g. a contract cleaning company) solely with the managers and shareholders then the minimum wage might be seen as bad for business by raising costs and therefore potentially squeezing the profit margin. However, the office cleaners are stakeholders within the business so the increase in pay resulting from the minimum wage means the company is operating more successfully from their point of view. Thus, the example reveals the conflicts of interest between the different stakeholders that make up a business (Chang 2013, pp. 190–8).

It is clear that although we refer to private ownership of business, decisions about managing those businesses are never purely private ones since they involve certain restrictions and obligations defined by law. And law is the outcome of a political process that involves collective decision-making and reflects, in some way, values within society. Thus, the operation of business in the market involves an interaction of private and public decisions.

Mini-Case 1.1 Guiding the 'hidden hand'—the minimum wage and the 'living wage'

》 VALUES 》 STAKEHOLDERS The idea of the 'hidden hand' is a metaphor for the way the market system, though based on millions of independent decisions and not subject to an overall plan or control by any actual hand, does not degenerate into chaos but operates in a highly coordinated way. It is *as if* a hidden hand is guiding it.

Adam Smith argued in the 18th century that even though businesses may be concerned only with their self-interest (profit) they would be guided, by and large, to serve the public good. This seems like a paradox—promoting the common good by acting selfishly. Smith's argument was that it would only be by serving the needs of others (customers) that businesses would be able to make a profit. When businesses throughout the economy act in this way the result is that the supply of goods and services matches consumer demand.

The hidden hand of the market operates through the price mechanism. The price adjusts until balance is achieved between supply and demand. For example, if supply exceeds demand the price will tend to fall, and vice versa.

However, the hidden hand can produce outcomes that are not socially desirable or fair. In a market system profit-seeking businesses respond to ability to pay—it is not their purpose to act like charities. The problem is that the price determined by the hidden hand might be one that not everyone can afford to pay because of differences in levels of household income. Perhaps it doesn't matter that not everyone can afford a BMW, but it is more serious if some people cannot afford healthcare when they need it.

In labour markets price is the wage or salary that people receive for the jobs they perform. In this case the problem is that for some low-paid occupations this price might not be sufficient to enable people to have a decent standard of life.

One solution to this problem is to use the law to guide the hidden hand through price controls. The UK Labour government introduced a National Minimum Wage (NMW) in 1999. The then Department for Trade and Industry explained the rationale of the NMW in terms of fairness and creating a level playing field on which businesses compete:

The national minimum wage is an important cornerstone of government strategy aimed at providing employees with decent minimum standards and fairness in the workplace.

It applies to nearly all workers and sets hourly rates below which pay must not be allowed to fall. It helps business by ensuring companies will be able to compete on the basis of quality of the goods and services they provide and not on low prices based predominantly on low rates of pay.

There are different levels of NMW, depending on age, and these rates are reviewed annually by the Low Pay Commission, taking account of economic circumstances.

From 1 October 2012 the NMW rates were:

Adult Rate (for workers aged 21+)	Development Rate (for workers aged 18-20)	16-17 Year Olds Rate	Apprentice Rate
£6.19	£4.98	£3.68	£2.65

Source: Low Pay Commission (<**http://www.lowpay.gov.uk/lowpay/index.shtml**>. Accessed 14 February 2013)

In its 2012 report, the Low Pay Commission stated that the increase in the adult rate of the NMW since its introduction (by nearly 69%) had been greater than both average earnings and prices, thus improving the position of low-paid workers both in real terms and in relation to the average. By 2011 the NMW was 52% of median earnings, compared to 46% in 1999. The report also states that the NMW has had 'little or no significant adverse impact ... on employment' (Low Pay Commission 2012).

》 VALUES Although controversial when first introduced, being supported by the trade unions and opposed by the Conservative party and business, the minimum wage has now become an accepted part of the business landscape in the UK supported by all the main political parties.

A 'living wage'—an idea whose time has come?

The minimum wage does not, by itself, protect against poverty (defined as 60% of median income). Does fairness in the job market require something more? In 2013 Citizens UK launched a campaign in support of cleaners employed at John Lewis stores on the minimum wage. John Lewis is a partnership in which all employees receive a share of the profits in the form of an annual bonus (John Lewis

Partnership). In 2013 the bonus was 17% for all employees, from the highest to the lowest paid within the partnership. But the cleaners did not get a bonus because they were not partners as they were employed by a contract cleaning company. Some people felt this arrangement was unfair and not in keeping with the ethos of the partnership. After all, a cleaner who had worked for the whole year had contributed to the success of the business in just the same way as a partner working as a sales assistant or in any other role. Citizens UK, an alliance of community groups including London Citizens, was campaigning for John Lewis to pay the cleaners a living wage (Rajan 2013; Citizens UK). This is a rate of pay that is higher than the NMW, set independently of government and with no statutory force, that is calculated as 'the minimum pay rate required for a worker to provide their family with the essentials of life' (Citizens UK). In London in 2013 the rate was set at £8.55 per hour, and £7.45 outside London, significantly above the NMW (*The Guardian* 2012).

The living wage is supported by all three main political parties, and was described by David Cameron as 'an idea whose time has come'. It is an idea that the 'going rate' for a job, as determined by the market, and fairness are different things; and that paying a living wage should be seen as a social obligation on the part of business. Citizens UK campaigns to persuade John Lewis and all other employers to agree to pay the living wage, with the ultimate goal that no worker in the country should be paid less. There is some way to go: a study by KPMG in 2012 found that 4.82 million workers in Britain (about one-fifth of the workforce) are paid less than a living wage (Weaver 2012).

How does the UK minimum wage compare to other nations?

》 SPATIAL LEVEL Minimum wage policies have been implemented in many other countries, including developing countries such as Brazil, India, and China (International Labour Organization 2013). Table 1.1 shows how the UK minimum wage compares with a number of other developed countries. The calculation, using purchasing power parities (PPPs), is designed to be a more realistic comparison of what the minimum wage can purchase in the different countries. In broad terms, it might be expected that the minimum wage would reflect the level of average income (Gross National Income, or GNI, per capita) in particular countries (because richer countries are able to pay a higher minimum wage), but Table 1.1 shows that the US has a relatively low minimum wage (ranking 9 of 13) despite being one of the world's richest countries. This shows that the minimum wage also reflects national political judgements about the appropriate level, which can be more or less generous.

Thus, the US comes towards the bottom of the sample of countries (rank 11) in terms of the generosity of the minimum wage as a share of median earnings. France has the most generous minimum wage both in terms of purchasing power and

Table 1.1 Comparison of adult minimum wages by country, using exchange rates and purchasing power parities (PPPs) (2011) and relative to full-time median earnings (2010).

	In UK£ (at Sept. 2011 exchange rates)	In UK£ (PPPs, at Sept. 2011)	PPP Rank order	Relative to full-time median earnings (mid-2010)	Rank order relative to median earnings
Australia	10.05	7.73	2	51.8	4
Belgium	7.12	6.98	4	51.7	5
Canada	6.20	5.90	8	45.0	8
France	8.01	7.86	1	60.1	1
Greece	3.66	4.16	11	41.9	10
Ireland	7.54	6.86	5	51.9	3
Japan	6.08	4.83	10	37.0	13
Netherlands	7.22	7.37	3	43.6	9
New Zealand	6.69	6.31	6	59.1	2
Portugal	2.44	2.87	13	48.0	6
Spain	3.23	3.62	12	37.6	12
UK	6.08	6.08	7	46.1	7
US	4.59	5.67	9	38.8	11

Source: Low Pay Commission 2012, p. 174 Table A3.1 and p. 175 Table A3.2.

share of median earnings. The least generous country (relative to median earnings) is Japan: although workers on the minimum wage in Japan are better off in purchasing power terms than their counterparts in Portugal, they are likely to compare themselves with those on median earnings in their own country and, on this measure, the Japanese are worse off than the Portuguese. The UK is middle-ranked both in terms of the purchasing power of the minimum wage and its share of median earnings.

What is fair in poor countries?

Table 1.1 suggests that what is regarded as fair varies from one country to another. It might be argued that what is fair has to be related to the average wages and living standards in a country because they influence the prevailing ideas or norms in that society about what constitutes a decent life. On this basis a fair minimum wage in a rich country would be higher than in a developing country with a lower standard of living, such as India. Even between countries with comparable income levels, such as in Table 1.1, it might be argued further that different nations decide for themselves what is fair based on their own values. On this basis France has a more generous minimum wage than the US because it has a different culture with a different idea of fairness. For example, a more individualistic culture in the US might translate into support for the idea that it is fair for incomes to be determined by how well people do on the basis of their own efforts in the market.

In a globalizing world national minimum wage policies increasingly take on an international dimension. This is partly because minimum wages have to take into account the potential economic impact in terms of competitiveness and employment in firms producing internationally traded outputs. The consideration here is of a trade-off between fairness and competitiveness. Another aspect of a globalizing world is the growing awareness of income disparities between countries, and particularly of global poverty. In this context international and global ideas of fairness are coming to the fore. For example, although minimum wage policies in the European Union are the preserve of member states to decide for themselves (e.g., Germany has no minimum wage), it is also debated at the European level. The European Commission has expressed the view that 'setting minimum wages at appropriate levels can help prevent growing in-work poverty and is an important factor in ensuring decent job quality' (see European Commission 2012, p. 9). British workers on the minimum wage might wonder why EU membership shouldn't mean that they are treated as generously as their French counterparts.

Within the EU there is a tension between the idea that member states should decide their own minimum wage policies for themselves on the basis of their levels of productivity and competitiveness and their own ideas about fairness,

and the integrationist idea that all workers in the EU should benefit from the same protections. What about a developing country such as Bangladesh with which the UK has no such relationship? Should we be concerned about the level of wages and minimum wage protections in such countries? In a globalizing world such concerns have grown, partly because in a world of instant communication people in the West have become much more aware of global disparities in living standards and wish to 'make poverty history' (to use Oxfam's campaign slogan). We increasingly regard the poor in developing countries who we see on our TV screens as 'people like us' and we share their concerns. People in rich countries are also increasingly aware of the interconnections between rich and poor countries through trade and global supply chains managed by western companies. For example, when cheap clothes in the West are made possible by low wages in poor countries we might feel that western companies sourcing their products from low-cost producers in countries like Bangladesh have a responsibility for the plight of the low-paid workers in their supply chains, and that we share that responsibility as customers. These considerations were brought to the fore in 2013 by the deaths of more than one thousand Bangladeshi garment workers in the collapsed Rana Plaza factory building (BBC 2013b).

It could be argued that western companies are not responsible for low wages in the developing world, since workers are being paid the 'going rate' as determined by economic conditions in those countries. It is simply rational behaviour for companies in competitive global markets to source their products from the cheapest suppliers. Furthermore, workers in manufacturing may have higher incomes than those in the agricultural sector. However, the problem is that the price set in the market—the 'going rate' for factory work—is insufficient to provide a decent standard of life. One way of defining a decent standard is to use an international measure of poverty. For this purpose households with daily per capita income below US$1.25 or US$2 (calculated on PPP basis) are classed respectively as in extreme or moderate poverty (International Labour Organization (ILO) 2013). The ILO estimates that 'out of a total number of approximately 209 million wage earners ... in ... 32 developing countries at different points in time from 1997 to 2006, about 23 million were earning below US$1.25 a day and 64 million were earning less than US$2 per day. This indicates that minimum wages ... remain a relevant tool for poverty reduction' (2013 p. 38). Therefore 'the ILO encourages member States to adopt a minimum wage to reduce working poverty and provide social protection for vulnerable employees' (2013).

Some developing countries have minimum wage policies, but these are not always adequately enforced or set at a sufficient level to tackle working poverty. The charity War on Want campaigns for a living wage for all workers. A study of the Bangladeshi garment industry reveals the low pay and poor working conditions experienced by the mainly female workers employed as sewing operators and helpers, the lowest paid jobs in the industry. Under the country's minimum wage law the monthly pay of sewing operators starts at £32 per month but this is often paid only if production targets are met, and meeting the targets requires the women to work excessive hours. In any case, the minimum wage falls well short of the living wage, calculated at £42 per month, an amount intended to 'enable workers and their dependants to meet their needs for nutritious food and clean water, shelter, clothes, education, health care and transport, as well as allowing for some discretionary spending' (War on Want 2012).

According to War on Want, working poverty in the Bangladeshi garment industry can be attributed to the business model used by British and other western companies:

Many British companies source their clothes from Bangladesh because the country boasts lower labour costs than anywhere else in the world. High street retailers such as Primark, Tesco and Asda have long benefited from these cheap prices, in the full knowledge that workers in the Bangladeshi garment industry are regularly denied their basic rights. The huge profits made by these retailers depend on the exploitation of the women who make their clothes (War on Want 2011).

The charity also names a further 26 high street brands which do not ensure a living wage is paid to workers in their supply chains (2012).

Questions

1. How does the NMW affect the private ownership of business?

2. Is it good for business, or bad for business? If you were an employer, would you support the NMW?

3. Do western companies have a responsibility to ensure that workers in their supply chains in developing countries benefit from a living wage?

Competition vs. market power?

So private ownership turns out not to be a straightforward idea. The same can be said of competition and **profit**. Competition is a key aspect of the environment in which businesses in a market system operate, and we will look at it more closely in Chapter 2. It is competition that keeps businesses responsive to consumers since they have the option of going elsewhere if they are not satisfied. This reasoning is behind the claim that consumers are 'sovereign', meaning that they exercise power in markets since it is their preferences to which firms must respond. The other side of this is the idea that firms have little or no power in the market themselves. However, it seems clear that firms do not all face the same amount of competitive pressure and that some firms exercise more market power than others, particularly in the case of 'big business'.

》 VALUES 》 SPATIAL LEVELS It seems clear that firms have more power when they face no or few competitors and less power when they face a large number of rivals. In particular they may be able to engage in anti-competitive behaviour, most notably in the form of price-fixing. Such concerns are often raised in relation to prices in markets dominated by a small number of producers or suppliers, such as petrol prices (BBC 2103a). Giant corporations, especially multinational corporations that have created powerful global brands, may exercise power over consumers through persuasive advertising. Concern is sometimes also expressed about the political influence of such companies (see Chapter 11).

Profit vs. social responsibility?

》 VALUES 》 STAKEHOLDERS At the start of this chapter it was stated that whether a business manages to operate successfully within its environment depends on the criteria used to judge success. We have also seen that, for all forms of business, success is bound up with meeting the requirements of consumers. The performance of business in the private sector is conventionally measured in terms of profitability (and, relatedly, share value) because this is seen as the prime motive—why else put money into a business if not to make more money? As we have seen, meeting the requirements of consumers is really a means to an end—businesses that do not produce goods or services that customers want (or can be persuaded) to buy are not profitable. However, the notion of business 'success' is not quite so straightforward, and this goes to the heart of debates about the role of private sector business in society.

First, it can be argued that the idea of the single-minded profit-maximizing business is an oversimplification that ignores the possibility that businesses may themselves have other **non-profit objectives**. There is no doubt that private sector businesses exist to make profits, but the question here is whether this primary motive is the only purpose that they set for themselves. Indeed, John Kay has argued that there is a 'profit-seeking paradox: the most profitable companies are not the most profit-oriented' (Kay 2004a). The claim is that profitability arises indirectly from pursuing other goals, such as managing a pharmaceutical company with a mission that 'medicine is for the people'. Thus, the goal of making a profit is best approached obliquely. Second, in any case, other groups in society increasingly demand or expect business performance and success to be measured by criteria other than just profit. These groups—including employees, customers, suppliers, the wider community, or society—may be seen as **stakeholders** who are affected by, and therefore have an interest or 'stake' in, business decisions.

Thus, thinking about the success of business requires us to think about the criteria that are used as a basis for judgement, and this raises questions about whose interests are taken into account and who makes these judgements. If we see profit as the sole criterion, this involves, on the face of it, only taking into account the self-interest of business owners and might therefore ignore the interests of other stakeholders. Thus, the profit motive may be counterposed to some notion of wider social responsibility, which involves the argument that business success needs to be judged in terms of a wider set of social benefits and obligations (see Mini-Case 1.2 and Chapter 7).

Other sectors of business—the public sector and the third sector

» DIVERSITY The private sector is the dominant element within the UK and other capitalist or market economies—most of the goods and services that we consume on a daily basis are purchased from private sector businesses, and most employees work in the private sector. Yet if we think in terms of our broad definition—transforming inputs into outputs of goods and services to meet the needs and wants of consumers—it is clear that other types of organization are also involved in business. These are not-for-profit organizations operating in both:

- the **public sector** and
- the 'third' sector of voluntary organizations.

» DYNAMIC Although these organizations make up a relatively small part of the business or economic life of the country, they are involved in the production of some key services, such as healthcare and education. It is also important to note that the boundaries between these sectors are not fixed but can, and do, shift, largely as a result of political decisions. For example, in the recent past in the UK, mainly under Conservative governments in the 1980s and 1990s, a programme of **privatization** transferred businesses that had operated for many years as parts of the public sector—such as British Telecommunications, British Gas, and British Rail—into the private sector. Within these sectors business organizations are also diverse when considered, for example, in terms of the type of output they produce, their legal status, and size.

Mini-Case 1.2 What is business for?

VALUES The profit-maximizing view of business may be defended on the following grounds:

1. It can be argued that private property is a basic principle of western societies and the whole point is that private property brings benefits to its owners. It is, therefore, not reasonable to expect people to use their private property other than for their own benefit.

2. Of course, individuals may choose to use some of their own property to benefit others by donations to charity or other means. But there are two reasons why it might not be reasonable to expect a business to act like this. First, the purpose of business is to make profit, whereas decisions about charitable giving should be left to the owners of the business in deciding for themselves how they use the distributed profits. Second, it can be argued that in a competitive market environment firms are under continual pressure to maximize profit in order to secure long-term survival. This is because profit can be used for reinvestment in the business to sustain or improve competitiveness, and because profitability is key to the ability of a firm to raise external finance. Firms which are less profitable than their rivals will tend to fall behind in the competitive struggle.

3. Third, it can be argued that through the single-minded pursuit of profit businesses simultaneously create benefit for society and thereby, far from ignoring the interests of other stakeholders, fully discharge their social responsibility. This is the 'hidden hand' argument, and the key idea is that firms only make profit by serving the needs and wants of customers. At the same time, profit-seeking businesses create employment and generate economic growth.

However, all of these arguments can be contested. As we have already seen, a problem with the hidden hand argument is that, even if customers are well-served by business, the good deals that they enjoy might rely upon low paid jobs. How do we balance the interests of consumers with those of low paid workers? The national minimum wage and arguments for a living wage can be seen as attempts to strike such a balance.

The hidden hand also tends to create social costs or externalities such as environmental pollution (see Chapter 2).

INTERNAL/EXTERNAL The argument that firms are forced by competition to maximize profit in order to secure long-term survival is questionable because it suggests that businesses have no discretion in terms of their conduct. This is a simplistic model of the market and is contradicted by observations of business decisions. It is clearly not the case that western fashion retailers are powerless to improve the pay and conditions of workers in the Bangladeshi garment industry.

It is true that private property is a basic principle or value of western societies for which there is strong public support. But private property is a legal arrangement which can be judged on the basis of whether it serves the common good of society as a whole. On this basis all western societies impose certain restrictions on private property. There are some things that people are not allowed to own (e.g. harmful drugs or guns) and restrictions on how property may be used (such as not being allowed to drive my car as fast as I like). Very few people would say that individuals should be able to drive their cars just as they please because that is the whole point of owning your own car. Most would agree that the likely harms to the community in the shape of road accidents from such a free-for-all outweigh the benefits to the car owners. Similarly, it is reasonable to say that we should judge the private ownership of business on the basis of the common good and not just that it allows the owners to do what they want with their own property.

Questions

Do you think that the sole purpose of business is, or should be, to make as much profit as possible?

If your answer is 'no', would you think differently if you were a shareholder?

If your answer is 'yes', do you think that the pursuit of profit leads business to serve the public interest or common good?

Differences between the private and public sectors

Public and private sector organizations differ in important respects. However, there is disagreement over how far these differences are real and whether the two sectors ought to be more alike. For example, reforms of the public sector since the 1980s have attempted to make the public sector more like the private sector in some important respects (see Chapter 14).

- *Revenue.* Public sector organizations like schools and NHS hospitals are largely financed through taxation rather than sales revenue generated by customers paying a price in

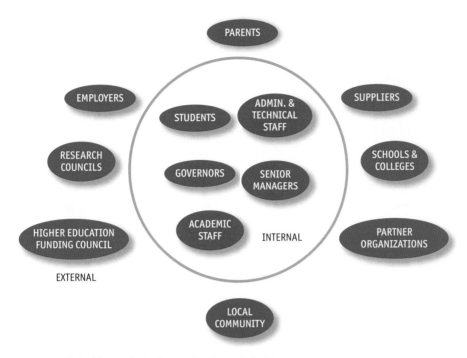

Figure 1.1 Stakeholder analysis—key university stakeholders

contrasted with the traditional view of the firm as primarily or solely concerned with profit. Firms may themselves have different views about the desirability of stakeholder engagement. In terms of environmental analysis, businesses need to have an understanding of:

- who their stakeholders are
- the nature and level of their interest in the business
- their power to exert influence.

A stakeholder map is shown in Figure 1.1.

For each of the internal and external stakeholders shown:

a) Identify the nature of their interests (e.g. the interests of students might include high quality teaching).

b) Consider whether there are any conflicts between the interests of different stakeholders (e.g. Do students and academics have the same interests?).

c) Consider in what way, and to what extent, each stakeholder exercises power or influence (e.g. Do you have any influence over university decisions? Should you have?).

> *Stop and Think*
> ....
> Can you explain what is meant by each of the four terms that constitute the PEST framework: political, economic, social, technological?

Summary

- Business as an activity can be defined broadly as the transformation of inputs (or factors of production) into diverse outputs (goods and services) to meet the needs and wants of consumers. Business is a mechanism for deciding the allocation of the scarce resources available to society between various possible uses (or competing wants) in a situation of scarcity where not all wants can be satisfied.

- In a narrow sense, business is often used to refer to the private sector and the key characteristics of private ownership, competition, and profit. The broad meaning of business includes organizations in the public and third sectors.

- Market or capitalist economic systems, such as the UK, are dominated by the private sector. However, the boundary between the private, public, and third sectors is not fixed. The private sector is very diverse.

- The primary motivation of business in the private sector is profit. However, this is not the only measure of the purpose or success of business. In particular, it can be argued that business should fulfil wider obligations to society.

- Businesses can be understood as open systems interacting with their environments. Each business operates within an environment that is, to some extent, unique.

- The external environment is complex or multi-faceted, dynamic, and must be analysed in terms of a variety of spatial levels or scales, from the local to the global.

- It is important for business to engage in monitoring and analysis of the environment. A variety of techniques is available. However, business can never have complete knowledge of the environment or how it will change.

Case Study: Tax avoidance in a globalizing world—managing costs efficiently or acting immorally?

VALUES Tax avoidance: 'using tax law to gain a tax advantage not intended by Parliament' (House of Commons Committee of Public Accounts 2013, p. 3).

It may be argued that it is rational for profit-seeking companies to take steps to limit their tax liabilities, and tax avoidance may be seen as an obligation to their shareholders. Minimizing the tax bill enables companies to protect shareholder interests through paying a higher dividend or investing retained earnings in the business in order to sustain its competitiveness. Why pay more taxes than you have to? This is the logic of tax planning or legal tax avoidance measures (as contrasted with illegal tax evasion). In this view, the limit of a company's obligation to society is to obey the tax laws.

SPATIAL LEVEL One way in which MNCs can manage their tax liabilities is by locating production facilities in countries which have low rates of corporation tax (i.e. tax on profit). The tax rate is one of a range of factors that determine the locational advantage companies may gain from different countries. For this reason national governments may try to set corporation tax at a 'competitive' (i.e. low) rate in order to advertise their country as the 'best place to do business' and thereby attract and retain investment. This approach has been adopted quite vigorously by the UK government (Chapter 4). It can be argued that this can lead to a higher tax *yield* because it encourages business activity. However it also shows that the globalization of business enables large corporations to play governments off against each other in a competition to attract investment and, therefore, makes it hard for governments to tax business effectively.

If governments want to attract business through low taxes it makes it hard for them to state that they are going to 'get tough' on tax avoidance since this might be interpreted as hostile to business and unreasonable (since the avoidance is not illegal). Yet the UK and other governments have found themselves facing both directions at once. In the 2013 budget George Osborne announced a reduction in corporation tax to 20% to come into effect in 2015, this being the third consecutive cut under the coalition government from the inherited rate of 28% (see Chapter 4). But in the 2012 Autumn State-ment he also referred to measures to tackle tax avoidance:

We want the most competitive corporate tax system of any major economy in the world, but we expect those corporate taxes to be paid. So today we are confirming that we will put more resources into ensuring multinational companies pay their proper share of taxes. And we are leading the international effort to prevent artificial transfers of profits to tax havens. ... we have asked the OECD to take this work forward and we will make it an impor-tant priority of our G8 Presidency next year (HM Treasury 2012).

Similarly, Prime Minister David Cameron stated that

there are some forms of avoidance that have become so aggressive that I think it is right to say these raise ethical issues, and it is time to call for more responsibility and for governments to act accord-ingly. ... Individuals and businesses must pay their fair share. And businesses who think they can carry on dodging that fair share ... need to wake up and smell the coffee, because the public who buy from them have had enough (Cameron 2013).

Cameron's remarks, and Osborne's budget statement, fol-lowed a report by the House of Commons Public Accounts Committee which highlighted tax avoidance by MNCs with business activities located in the UK. Cameron's reference to 'smelling the coffee' appears to be directed at Starbucks, which was one of three American companies (the others being Google and Amazon) investigated by the Committee. The report states that

international companies are able to exploit national and international tax structures to minimise corporation tax on the economic activity they conduct in the UK. The outcome is that they do not pay their fair share (House of Commons Public Accounts Committee 2012).

MNCs are able to exploit tax laws by shifting profits to low-tax jurisdictions. They can do this by locating part of the business in a country with a low rate of corporation tax and by making transfers to that unit through devices such as royalty payments and internal prices. In this way, the profit is declared in the low-tax jurisdiction, away from the country where the eco-nomic activity took place. Starbucks claimed that it had made a loss in every year of its fifteen years of UK operations, except for one taxable year of profitability, despite reporting its UK business as successful to its shareholders. It had paid £8.6 mil-lion in tax from revenue of £3.1 billion. The Committee did not believe that Starbucks was making a loss in the UK (why would it carry on these operations if that were the case?) and claimed that UK profits were being shifted to the Netherlands and Switzerland where they were subject to a much lower rate of tax. Similarly, the Committee's investigation showed how Google and Amazon avoid UK tax by shifting profits to low-tax jurisdictions, respectively in Ireland and Luxembourg.

These are not isolated cases, and the chair of the Com-mittee claimed that they are widespread. Such practices may be seen as pervasive among multinational companies, and it is not just rich countries like the UK which are losing out on tax revenues. Associated British Foods (ABF) is one of the world's largest food multinationals. The charity Ac-tionAid investigated the operations of one of its subsidiaries in Zambia, Zambia Sugar plc. Zambia is a lower-middle in-come country in which, according to ActionAid, two thirds of the population live on less that $2 per day, the interna-tionally recognized poverty line. ActionAid's investigation reveals that:

ABF's Zambian subsidiary uses an array of transactions that have seen over a third of the company's pre-tax profits – over US$13.8 million ... a year – paid out of Zambia, into and via tax haven sister companies in Ireland, Mauritius and the Nether-lands. ... Thanks to this financial engineering, ... Zambia has lost tax revenues of some US$17.7 million since 2007, when ABF took over the Illovo sugar group (ActionAid 2013).

The problem for governments in the UK, Zambia and else-where is that corporate tax avoidance involves erosion of the tax base and creates a 'tax gap' between the revenues that are expected and those that are actually collected. This compro-mises the ability of the government to finance public services (including those that are important for business). It means that other taxpayers have to pay more, giving tax avoiders an unfair competitive advantage over firms that do pay their taxes, and this can undermine public confidence in the tax system and the willingness to pay tax. The head of the OECD has stated:

Companies have a responsibility to pay corporation tax in the jurisdictions where they operate. Citizens are already losing faith in their banks and the financial system. If big corporations fail to pay tax and leave it to SMEs and middle income groups, it will undermine democracy. This is about the survival of democracy (Gurria, quoted in Inman 2013; see also OECD 2013).

In this case, what's good for individual businesses is not good for government, business as a whole, or society. But is it 'unfair' or 'immoral'? In evidence to the House of Com-mons Public Accounts Committee, Google's Vice President for Sales and Operations in Northern and Central Europe stated that companies 'are required to do two things. One is to play by the rules ... Secondly, we are required to manage our costs efficiently in order to satisfy our shareholders.' In this view minimizing tax through avoidance is 'not unfair to British taxpayers. We pay all the tax you require us to pay in the UK'. Against this view the chair of the committee stated, 'We are not accusing you of being illegal; we are accusing you of being immoral' (House of Commons Public Accounts Committee 2012).

Google's view appears to be that morality stretches no further than obeying the law—a company's duty is to satisfy its shareholders within the law and nothing more should be asked of it. However, this view does not appear to be shared among the wider public. It was reported that '[m]ore than 100,000 people have signed a petition launched by an independent bookseller calling on Amazon "to pay their fair share of tax in the UK"' (Flood 2013), and Starbucks became the target of a consumer boycott. This shows that 'managing costs efficiently' through tax avoidance has the potential to backfire through reputational damage and loss of sales. Google's view has also been challenged by the Confederation of British Industry (CBI) which lobbies on behalf of the business community as a whole. The director-general of the CBI supported action against tax avoidance: 'The majority of businesses pay the right amount of tax, and for the small minority which do not, times are getting

tougher, and rightly so' (quoted in Elliott and Stewart 2013). Against Google's view it can be argued that acting morally requires us not merely to obey the letter of the law while looking for loopholes in it, but to behave in a way consistent with the spirit of the law, in other words paying the taxes that Parliament intended.

Questions

1. To what extent is tax avoidance an inevitable consequence of a globalizing world?

2. Is corporate tax avoidance moral, or do companies have a moral obligation to pay the taxes intended by law-makers? (If you were in charge of Starbucks what would you do?)

3. To what extent is the problem of companies 'gaming' tax regimes merely a consequence of governments playing a game of tax competition?

Review and discussion questions

1. How does the idea of a 'globalizing world' help us to understand the business environment?

2. To what extent do you agree that the only social responsibility of private sector business is to maximize profits?

3. 'There is no such thing as a free market.' Explain what is meant by this statement.

4. What is the rationale for a broad definition of business, including the public sector and third sector? Compare and contrast the characteristics of the public and private sectors.

5. Give examples of the ways in which the external environment affects business decisions and behaviour, and the ways in which businesses may influence their environments.

Assignments

1. Investigate annual reports for two FTSE companies and analyse the extent to which they incorporate non-profit objectives and measures of performance.

2. Use the Internet to identify four recent newspaper reports that relate to factors in the external business environment under the PEST headings. Use a PEST grid to show the sources of the reports and to provide a brief bullet-pointed summary of each.

3. Imagine you report to a senior executive of Google or Amazon who has been called to appear before the Public Accounts Committee of the House of Commons. Write a briefing paper to provide arguments justifying measures taken by the company to avoid UK corporation tax.

Further reading

Sutherland, J. and Canwell, D. (2004) *Key Concepts in Business Practice* (Basingstoke: Palgrave Macmillan).

ESRC (2012) *Britain in 2013: the nation in focus*, annual magazine of the Economic and Social Research Council,

published 19 November 2012.I <http://www.esrc.ac.uk/news-and-events/press-releases/24197/britain-in-2013the-nation-in-focus.aspx>

online resource centre

Test your understanding of this chapter with online questions and answers, explore the subject further through web exercises, and use the web links to provide a quick resource for further research. Go to the Online Resource Centre at <www.oxfordtextbooks.co.uk/orc/wetherly_otter/2>

Useful websites

<http://www.bized.co.uk/>

<http://www.cbi.org.uk/>
Confederation of British Industry (CBI)

<http://www.tuc.org.uk/>
Trades Union Congress (TUC)

<http://www.bis.gov.uk/>
Department for Business, Innovation and Skills

<http://www.statistics.gov.uk/default.asp>
Office for National Statistics

<http://www.ifs.org.uk/>
Institute for Fiscal Studies

<http://www.oecd.org/>
Organisation for Economic Co-operation and Development (OECD)

<http://epp.eurostat.ec.europa.eu/portal/page/portal/eurostat/home/>
Eurostat

<http://www.weforum.org/>
World Economic Forum

References

ActionAid (2013) 'Sweet nothings: The human cost of a British sugar giant avoiding taxes in southern Africa' <http://www.actionaid.org/sites/files/actionaid/sweet_nothings.pdf>

BBC (2013) 'Chilly 2012 boosts profits for British Gas' <http://www.bbc.co.uk/news/business-21598740>

BBC (2013a) 'OFT says UK petrol market is working well' <http://www.bbc.co.uk/news/business-21258809>

BBC (2013b) 'Bangladesh building collapse death toll passes 700' <http://www.bbc.co.uk/news/world-asia-22431151>

Cameron, D. (2013) 'Prime Minister David Cameron's speech to the World Economic Forum', 24 January2013, Davos-Klosters, Switzerland. <http://www.number10.gov.uk/news/prime-minister-david-camerons-speech-to-the-world-economic-forum-in-davos/>

Chang, H.-J. (2103) *23 Things They Don't Tell You About Capitalism.* (Harmondsworth: Penguin).

Citizens UK, <http://www.citizensuk.org/2013/03/john-lewis-cleaners-miss-out-on-bonus-the-living-wage/>

Elliott, L. and Stewart, H. (2013) 'David Cameron makes swipe at Starbucks as he promises focus on tax', *The Guardian,* 24 January. <http://www.guardian.co.uk/politics/2013/jan/24/david-cameron-starbucks-focus-tax?INTCMP=SRCH>

Flood, A. (2013) 'Amazon tax petition hits 100,000 signatures', *The Guardian,* 22 March. <http://www.guardian.co.uk/books/2013/mar/22/amazon-tax-petition-signatures?INTCMP=SRCH>

The Guardian (2012) 'Boris Johnson announces rise in London living wage', *The Guardian,* 5 November 2012. <http://www.guardian.co.uk/politics/2012/nov/05/boris-johnson-london-living-wage>

HM Treasury (2012) 'Autumn Statement 2012 to the House of Commons by the Rt Hon. George Osborne, MP, Chancellor of the Exchequer', 5 December 2012. <http://www.hm-treasury.gov.uk/as2012_statement.htm>

House of Commons Public Accounts Committee (2012) *Nineteenth Report - HM Revenue and Customs: Annual Report and Accounts* (London: House of Commons). <http://www.publications.parliament.uk/pa/cm201213/cmselect/cmpubacc/716/71602.htm>

House of Commons Committee of Public Accounts (2013) *29th Report: Tax avoidance: tackling Marketed avoidance schemes* (London: House of Commons). <http://www.publications.parliament.uk/pa/cm201213/cmselect/cmpubacc/788/788.pdf>

Inman, P. (2013) 'OECD calls for crackdown on tax avoidance by multinationals', *The Guardian,* 12 February2013. <http://www.guardian.co.uk/business/2013/feb/12/oecd-crackdown-tax-avoidance-multinationals>

International Labour Office (2013) *Global Wage Report 2012/13: Wages and equitable growth* (Geneva: International Labour Office). <http://www.ilo.org/wcmsp5/groups/public/--dgreports/--dcomm/--publ/documents/publication/wcms_194843.pdf>

Katungi, D., Neal, E., and Barbour, A. (2006) *People in Low-paid Informal Work* (Joseph Rowntree Foundation). <http://www.jrf.org.uk/publications/people-low-paid-informal-work>

Kay, J. (2004) *The Truth About Markets* (London: Penguin).

Kay, J (2004a) 'Oliquity', *Financial Times*, 17 January 2004 (available at: <http://www.johnkay.com/2004/01/17/obliquity>).

Hopkins, K. (2008) 'Child labour: Primark caught out', *The Guardian*, 23 June 2008.

John Lewis Partnership, <http://www.johnlewispartnership.co.uk/about.html>

Low Pay Commission (2012) *National Minimum Wage: Low Pay Commission Report 2012* (The Secretary of State for Business, Innovation and Skills). (<http://www.lowpay.gov.uk/lowpay/report/pdf/8990-BIS-Low%20Pay_Tagged.pdf>)

OECD (2013) *Action Plan on Base Erosion and Profit Shifting* (<http://www.oecd.org/tax/beps.htm>)

Office for National Statistics (2012) *Ownership of UK Quoted Shares, 2010* (Office for National Statistics). <http://www.ons.gov.uk/ons/dcp171778_257476.pdf>

Rajan, A. (2013) 'Congratulations to John Lewis on record profits, but why not give cleaners a share too?', *The Independent*, 7 March 2013. <http://www.independent.co.uk/voices/comment/congratulations-to-john-lewis-on-record-profits-but-why-not-give-cleaners-a-share-too-8524476.html>

Urquhart, C. (2013) 'How the influx of new global elites is changing the face of Europe', *The Observer*, 10 March 2013. <http://www.guardian.co.uk/world/2013/mar/09/global-elites-change-face-of-europe?INTCMP=SRCH>

War on Want (2011) *Stitched Up: Women Workers in the Bangladeshi garment sector*. <http://www.waronwant.org/attachments/Stitched%20Up.pdf>

War on Want (2012) '"Pay living wage everywhere" call to British firms'. <http://www.waronwant.org/news/press-releases/17724-pay-living-wage-everywhere-call-to-british-firms>

Weaver, M. (2012) 'Almost five million British workers paid less than the living wage', *The Observer*, 29 October 2012. <http://www.guardian.co.uk/society/2012/oct/29/five-million-britons-living-wage>

White, C. (2013) *2011 Census Analysis: Unpaid care in England and Wales, 2011 and comparison with 2001* (Office for National Statistics). <http://www.ons.gov.uk/ons/dcp171766_300039.pdf>

PART ONE
ENVIRONMENTS

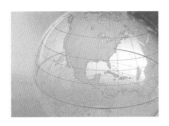

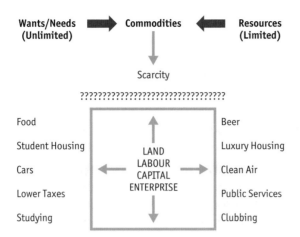

Figure 2.1 The business in its environment

The concept of opportunity cost is a fundamental economic concept. Decisions mean selecting between alternatives. When any decision is being made about resource use, the full range of options has to be considered. Whenever a business decision is made there is an opportunity cost in terms of the opportunities that have been lost as a result of this decision.

So how can we judge if allocative decisions are taken correctly? How can we construct an economic environment that ensures that the 'right' commodities are produced? In other words how can we ensure that we achieve 'allocative efficiency'?

The production problem

How does the economy organize the production of the chosen commodity? Given that resources are scarce businesses should produce the maximum output of the highest quality for the minimum resource use or input. This is referred to as productive efficiency. If resource costs are minimized so must be the opportunity costs.

Any firm is being productively efficient if it produces a level of output at which the cost of all units, the average cost, is minimized. We need to carefully examine the ideal economic environment that would lead to such productive efficiency.

The distribution problem

⫸ **VALUES** When the economy has decided what to produce, and how, it must decide who gets it.

This means that we ought to have a clear set of criteria for judging distributive efficiency or what can be variously described as equity, fairness, or justice. In reality our views are influenced by our value judgements. As we shall see, very often there can appear to be a conflict between efficiency in allocation and production and people's views as to appropriate distributive justice.

⫸ **COMPLEXITY** This then makes any assessment of the role of business in the wider economic environment complex. If we are to judge business efficiency in its wider context we must relate it to these three aspects of efficiency, and it is likely that businesses operating in different environments will have different goals which may conflict with certain aspects of efficiency.

In an economic environment in which businesses are predominately privately owned the emphasis may be placed on customer satisfaction and cutting costs to maximize profits but there may well be a conflict between how the business views its efficient operation and how society judges it. 'People before profit' is a cry often heard from critics of business with popular campaigns against the perceived irresponsible behaviour of businesses. Chapter 7 explores this in more detail. In the public sector the lack of a profit motive may lead to a lack of incentives to cut costs and encourage wasteful use of resources.

The economic problem then is easily defined but incredibly complex to solve. Every day millions of economic decisions have to be made regarding allocation, production, and distribution. A crucial decision has to be made as to the best way to organize economic activity.

▦ **Perspectives on the economic environment**

⟩ **VALUES** There are fierce debates regarding the best way to structure the economic environment and these could be seen to stem from the different ways in which scarcity is viewed.

Consider Figure 2.2: What do you see? Some of you will see a picture of a young woman, some an old one. Some of you will see both. Some of you will wonder why these images have been included. The same picture but four different responses: those of you that see the young woman will not be able to immediately understand why people are seeing an old woman and vice versa; those of you that see both will smile knowingly; and those of you who can't see the point will wonder what this has to do with the economic environment! The same factual information is presented and yet we have four different perspectives!

Figure 2.2 Young/old woman

This famous figure was published in 1915 in *Puck*, an American humour magazine, and is credited to British cartoonist W. E. Hill. It is likely though that he adapted this from an image that was popularly used on trading cards in the 18th and 19th centuries.

Source: Hill, W. E., 'My wife and my mother-in-law'. *Puck*, 10 (11) Nov. 1915.

- *Primary*: mining, fuel extraction, farming, forestry
- *Secondary*: manufacturing
- *Services*: retailing, marketing, finance, travel.

In general, as economies grow the proportion of income spent on primary goods tends to decrease and that spent on manufacturing and services, especially, tends to increase. This can make life difficult for primary producers unless they can find ways of increasing market power through restricting competition.

We are witnessing for the first time in history a significant change in where people live in the world. We are now seeing the proportion of people living in urban areas increasing ahead of those in rural areas. For most of human history the majority of people have been agricultural workers. Rural producers face enormous structural problems in markets and are often the poorest members of society in the absence of government intervention. A major cause of their problems is to be found in the fact that both the price elasticity of demand and income elasticity of demand for agricultural products is very low.

To solve this problem agricultural policy in America and Europe has been designed to provide minimum prices for farmers (in Europe through the Common Agricultural Policy). For many farmers in the developing world their governments lack the funds to undertake similar support policies.

In the longer term, as economic growth raises living standards, people spend proportionally less on agricultural goods and more on manufactured or service goods. The income elasticity of demand for agricultural goods gets more inelastic over time. This means that farmers need help to diversify and, in some cases, to move out of agriculture altogether. Again, in the developed world such assistance is available for farmers but this is not the case in the poorer countries.

Macroeconomic instability

Macroeconomics is the study of markets at the aggregate level and we explore this in Chapter 9. At the aggregate level fluctuations in economic activity mean that the processes of economic growth is far from smooth in the way that Smith assumed would occur in individual markets. We will see in this chapter that the smooth uninterrupted process of growth that Smith predicted in the 18th century did not occur and, in fact, the development of economies lurched from periods of boom to slump. There seemed to be something about the way in which economies performed at the aggregate level which could prove problematic to growth as a whole.

Distribution

⟫ **VALUES** Perhaps the greatest problem of all in market systems is that, if left alone they tend to lead to great inequalities of income and wealth. The reasons for this are hotly contested. For those with a belief in the innate capacity of markets to bring about prosperity this is the result of the natural distribution of skills and ability in the population. It is inevitable that rewards will be heavily skewed, with some people gaining vast incomes as a result of their exceptional skills and ability to have correctly anticipated risks and uncertainty. While the argument for provision of merit and public goods is accepted, this world view insists that such social provision must be kept to a minimum to avoid the need for high taxes which will undermine the incentives for risk taking and enterprise.

However, these inequalities may not reflect the rewards earned by people in their productive capacity but may reflect self-perpetuating social inequalities and barriers. One reason may be the persistence of inheritance and the class system or the power of certain groups to discriminate over others. Another could be that poor people may lack access to the basic education and health provision so vital to progressing up the ladder of economic achievement.

Furthermore, in this view inequality distorts the whole basis of the economic system. The economic problem becomes circular with the demands of the rich determining what should be produced. A free market system will then reinforce inequality and make it difficult for the less advantaged to either get what they need or make their way in society.

Competing perspectives–social reform and socialism

Smith's prediction in the 18th century was that the emergent market system would bring about sustained economic growth and that this would bring about harmony in society with all people benefiting from this economic growth.

By the 19th century however, while the huge energy of the Industrial Revolution was unleashed with the rise of the factory system and the development of steam power and a whole range of inventions and innovations, the harmony predicted by Smith did not appear. Working and living conditions for ordinary workers were truly dreadful and workers sought to gain improvements by forming trades unions to demand reforms. A range of social reformers began to question not only the moral values of capitalism but also the real effect it was having on people. Initially, help for the poor came from charities and religious institutions as well as enlightened philanthropic businesses such as Rowntree in Britain (see Chapter 7) and Andrew Carnegie in the US. However, increasingly the structural weaknesses in the areas of market activity we have already highlighted were now apparent and, especially in areas of social reform, it was argued that there needed to be government provision of poor relief, old age protection, public health, sanitation, and education. Legislation was passed to try to improve working conditions in factories and, as well as important changes in the economic institutions, there were pressures to widen political power by extending the franchise more widely.

Friedrich Engels had recorded the appalling conditions faced by working people in England in 1844 (Engels 2009) and it was his friend, Karl Marx, who set out to explore the reasons why capitalism seemed to have two faces; the power, on the one hand, to radically transform the economic environment by dramatic increases in economic growth, and, on the other, to create a highly unequal and unjust society based on extreme levels of inequality. While it appeared that capitalists were making their money from exploiting markets, in reality the profits were being made out of the blood, sweat, and toil of the workers. Marx argued that the growing class divisions between the capitalists and workers would eventually cause severe unrest resulting in a revolution. Since the root of the exploitation lay in the institution of private property, he argued that if businesses were commonly owned then the profits generated could be more fairly distributed. He did not, however, show how this new world of socialism would work as he simply felt that capitalism had to fail given its inner contradictions. It would be up to the post-revolutionary generation to build that socialist environment and it would be pressure from working class people that would lead to this change. (For a summary of Marx's ideas see Callinicos (2011).)

The development of global capitalism in the 20th century

》 DYNAMIC While Britain had been the first country to industrialize and was thus able to establish a very strong international competitive advantage, it was soon followed by many European countries, especially France, Germany, Italy, Holland, and Belgium and of course by the US. This was the Age of Imperialism whereby European countries colonized large parts of the world and then used the colonies as a source of cheap resources as well as exploiting the larger markets that they provided. The same debates that were taking place about the nature of the domestic business environment were transposed to the nature of imperialism. In the classical view, all international trade does is allow a much greater development of markets which should see the fruits of capitalism being spread internationally. For critics of imperialism it was argued that the benefits flowed largely one way to enrich the imperial country and create powerful minority elites in the colonies who derived their wealth from exploiting the cheap labour and natural resources.

》 SPATIAL The growth of international trade was not accompanied by the development of international laws to regulate this trade and in the competitive scramble for new territories conflicts over spheres of economic and political influence culminated in the horror of the First World War.

The history of the 20th century can be seen as the gradual and, in some cases, painful development of modern political and economic systems with each country working out its own specific ways of combining the state and the market economy. In 1917 the Russian Revolution brought about an attempt to dramatically re-shape the business environment by developing the Soviet model of state planning and what was to become known as 'real existing socialism'. In Western Europe and the US, as already noted, there was a range of social reforms to try to help the poor.

In the first half of the 20th century the deep problems that faced the continued growth in the western capitalist world were seen to be primarily a failure to appreciate the importance of governments' role in ensuring economic efficiency at the national level, and in promoting effective economic and political relations between countries. The pivotal moments in the history of western capitalism were the outbreak of the Great War of 1914–18 followed by the onset of the Great Depression brought on by the Wall Street Crash of 1929.

The Great Depression lasted for much of the 1920s and 1930s and caused persistent unemployment and rising poverty across Europe and the US. Economic policy-makers were frozen into inaction as they believed that in response to the depression, wages, interest rates, and prices would all fall and eventually markets would ensure that demand picked up thus allowing supply to follow. This simply did not happen. In the US the New Deal was launched to try to cope with social distress through welfare benefits and government spending on infrastructure programmes to provide employment. In Britain, John Maynard Keynes argued not that capitalism was broken, but that there was a need to develop a new macroeconomic analysis that could explain why unemployment could be persistent and economic recovery take a long time. We will explore this in more detail in Chapter 9. Governments across Europe increasingly felt that there was a need for government intervention to restore economic stability. In the midst of all this economic turmoil the second great war of the 20th century broke out.

The domestic business environment

》 DIVERSITY 》 SPATIAL LEVELS At the domestic level, after the disaster of the Great Depression and the Second World War, developed capitalist economies adopted a different approach to managing their economies. This involved a much greater role for the state in providing welfare

Mini-Case 2.3   Capitalism with many faces?

Often a distinction is drawn between the American and, increasingly, British forms of Anglo-Saxon capitalism and the more 'coordinated' economies such as Germany, Japan, and the Nordic countries. The heart of the distinction is seen as their differing approaches to how to best manage the trade-off between social fairness and efficiency, as defined by business profitability and the relative reliance on market liberal approaches and supporting organizational structures.

In Germany it is argued that there is much more reliance on non-market mechanisms involving cooperation between government, business, and employees. There is a widespread system of vocational training involving close collaboration between businesses and education institutions and there are high levels of social protection. A distinctive feature of the German economic environment is the *Mittelstand* which comprises a very large number of small and medium enterprises with a focus often on niche products and with a predominance of family ownership. Ninety-nine per cent of all

German business is in the *Mittelstand*. Funding for the companies is based on long term equity and they are responsible for taking on over 80% of all trainees. The government plays a vital role in supporting the *Mittelstand* through support for research and development, investment, and advice over business start ups and hand overs.

Source: Federal Ministry of Economics and Technology (2012) German Mittelstand: Engine of the German Economy accessed at: <http://www.bmwi.de/English/Redaktion/Pdf/factbook-german-mittelstand,property=pdf,bereich=bmwi,sprache=en,rwb=true.pdf>

Questions

1. What are the common ingredients that are found in a capitalist economic environment?

2. How might the German model of capitalism address some of the problems associated with free market capitalism?

systems, supporting industry, and overseeing the macroeconomic environment. In Britain this has been called the 'Keynesian welfare consensus' and in Western Europe, the 'social market'. There was a widespread acceptance of the need for governments to intervene both at the macro- and microeconomic levels as well as directly taking responsibility for social transformation in the fields of education, health, and social security. Indeed, particularly in Europe, many key industries were taken into state ownership. For many commentators, the period between 1945 and the mid-1970s in the first world was the 'Golden Era', with an unprecedented period of economic growth. There was a general rise in prosperity, and the big gains in productivity brought about by the increase in mass production techniques and constant technological improvement meant that there were reductions in the prices of household goods. This, coupled with rising wages, meant that people could fill their houses with a range of consumer goods. Two countries performed spectacularly well during this period, namely the two losers of the Second World War, Japan and Germany. In the case of Japan, the key was in the way it had based its development on new technologies as well as changing the nature of the production process itself. In the case of Germany, it was argued that its tripartite partnership of government, business, and trade unions coupled with the strength of its manufacturing *Mittlestand* (small and medium-sized enterprises) was at the heart of its *Wirtschaftswunder* (Economic Miracle), (see Mini-Case 2.3). What they had in common though was their huge strength as exporting countries.

■ The global business environment—one world economy or three?

The global order after 1945 could be characterized as consisting of three different worlds. The 'first world' was composed of the western industrial nations led by the US, and the 'second world' was the communist countries of the USSR, the countries of Eastern Europe, which adopted (or were forced depending on your point of view) this model, and the Peoples' Republic of China, which was created in 1949.

In the post-war period many of the former colonies of the Western European powers, e.g. India and many countries in Africa and the Far East, fought for and gained independence, and now their policy-makers had a choice to make: to pursue the first world capitalist economic model or the second world of communism. In the optimism of the birth of new nations anything seemed possible and many countries argued for a 'third world' model. The use of the term 'third world' did not mean to imply inferiority. Far from it. It was the belief that by studying how other countries had developed, the new developing countries could copy their successes, avoid their failures, and recognize that in trying to develop now the circumstances they faced were very different and, therefore, required different approaches. Crucially, there was a belief amongst many of these countries that if they were to develop rapidly they would need to protect themselves in terms of world trade, whilst seeking to exploit their huge advantages in terms of cheap labour and primary resources. It was also felt that in order to grow quickly such countries would need more direct forms of government intervention.

While there were clear differences in the ways in which countries in these three worlds sought to organize their business environments, at the time each group of countries was optimistic that their system would work in their individual context.

In 1944 the negotiations for the future of the western political and economic system took place in the US in the small New Hampshire town of Bretton Woods. At the political level there was a desire amongst the western nations to rebuild their economies as quickly as possible. They sought to integrate as both an economic and political block to resist the rise of the 'second world' of communism in the Soviet Union and its satellite countries in Eastern Europe. These countries were not involved in the Bretton Woods talks and sought to stay within their own communist bloc.

Given the instability of the inter-war period, there was a desire amongst national policymakers in the 'first world' to devise a system of international rules which would prevent protectionist trading policies and thereby help build national and world economic trade, development, and growth whilst avoiding political conflict. As the US was the strongest country after the Second World War, its policy-makers were determined to create a future world where international trade could take place to secure markets for its output. However, there were strong economic arguments (coming especially from Keynes) that recognition was needed that countries, especially the war-ravaged countries of Western Europe, required help in building up their national economies so that they could compete on a world scale. In order for them to do so they might need the help of trade protection in the short term. The vision was that over time and through a progressive series of trade negotiations (or rounds of trade talks) trade barriers would eventually be removed and trade would be free of restrictions. At the heart of this was the 1947 General Agreement on Tariffs and Trade which became the World Trade Organization (WTO) in 1995. It was felt that, by allowing countries time to build up their competitive strengths and by getting them to sign up to targets for tariff reduction, eventually all countries would be able to trade freely. International agreements and promises would prevent individual countries trying to 'go it alone' and return to the protectionist policies of the inter-war period.

▶ SPATIAL In 1945, in order to develop a stable global financial system to support the development of this world economic system, the International Monetary Fund was established. Its aim was to help countries who experience balance of payments problems by lending them money to help finance their debts whilst adopting policies to improve their international competitiveness. Just as it was accepted that Europe would need inflows of capital (especially from the US), either as foreign direct investment or in the form of official aid (the Marshall Plan), so it was accepted that many of the poorer countries of the world would need development assistance if they too were going to be in a position to compete in the new world economic order. At the same time, the International Bank for Reconstruction and Development or, as it is most often called, the World Bank, was established for this purpose.

At the global level, trade expanded rapidly both in terms of volume and its importance to the world economy, as measured by ratio of world merchandise exports to world GDP. However, the pattern of trade was highly influenced by this division within the world economy. Developing countries exported mainly primary products, agricultural goods, and minerals, while Europe and North America exported manufactured goods and, increasingly, a range of services and high technology goods. The system of trade rules, whilst allowing for the gradual reduction of tariffs across a wide range of manufactured goods and services, also allowed persistently high tariffs to protect the agricultural goods produced by European and North American farmers. Communist countries stayed out of this system and formed their own trading alliances.

The rise of the neoclassical (neoliberal) perspective–from three worlds to one?

The optimism of the 1950s and 1960s was knocked by the severe economic crisis that many countries across the world experienced in the 1970s. In the developed countries the type of balances that had been struck between the state in intervening in the economy and the market appeared now not to be working. Increasingly, unemployment levels began to rise and growth slowed down while many economies also began to experience a rapid rise in inflation rates. Keynesian analysis could not explain how economies could experience both inflation and unemployment at the same time. In addition, the oil price rises of the 1970s posed great strains on these economies. This sudden and unexpected rise in oil prices was a result of oil producers' willingness, especially in the Middle East, to exert their political and economic power. This brought into stark view the degree to which oil underpins the technologies that create the economic prosperity of the developed world.

Across the range of developed economies government budgets were under severe strain. In the communist world, especially the Soviet Union and Eastern Europe, it was increasingly recognized that the systems were suffering from economic stagnation and that a policy change was needed. In the developing countries, against a backdrop of spiralling debt problems (especially in Latin America) and falls in living standards in Africa, it appeared that their attempts to adopt a different model of development had failed.

This period at the end of the 1970s and into the 1980s saw a change in ideas about the policies that should be adopted across the world at national level and in the thinking that took place at the supranational level. The right wing of the political spectrum and the neoclassical school of economic thought believed the lesson that needed to be learned was that there is no substitute for the free market at both the national and global level.

It was felt that the role of government had simply become too large and wherever you looked it was this that could explain the economic slowdown across the world. In the developed world excessive spending on welfare benefits had encouraged a 'dependency culture' and the high taxes to provide for such spending was undermining the incentives needed to create an 'entrepreneurial culture'. Too much economic activity had been taken out of the market and, where industries had been nationalized, they now needed to be returned to the private sector through privatization. Excessive government regulations, especially in financial markets, needed to be removed to enable credit to flow more readily both within and between countries. Finally, it was felt that the desire to reduce inequalities in society had resulted in too many social protection measures for workers and, coupled with the rise of organized labour's power, too much of the wealth was going to workers and not enough was being retained as profits.

In this analysis the best way to create an ideal business environment was to go back to the basic economic principles based on free markets. In the US this approach to economic policy was called Reaganomics after the then President Ronald Reagan and, in the UK, Thatcherism after Prime Minister Margaret Thatcher. In many Western European countries too, especially West Germany, there was a move towards more emphasis on the market although there was a view that this should be done with a little more caution than in the Anglo-American vision of the new capitalist model. Meanwhile countries such as Sweden, Denmark, and Norway, which had developed a particular Nordic model of capitalism, were less willing to dismantle their social democratic structures.

However, not all parts of the three worlds were suffering this slowdown. It was clear many of the countries in Southeast Asia were industrializing very rapidly. These so called 'Asian Tigers' (e.g. Hong-Kong, Taiwan, Singapore, South Korea, and Thailand) were experiencing very rapid growth, and at the same time were exporting a range of manufactured and high technology goods. The lesson appeared obvious from these regions that the path to growth lay down the route of globalization and that this meant rapid trade liberalization. A recent convert to this economic policy was China with a move to 'an open door' policy in the late 1970s.

The adoption of new economic policies based on the liberalization of markets in the developed world spread to the developing world, especially in Latin America and India. In the late 1980s the collapse of the Soviet Union and rapid changes in Eastern Europe saw these countries eager to effect a transition from state planning to market liberalization. These new free market based economic policies came to be called the 'Washington Consensus'. Here enterprise, competition, free trade, and technological change are key. We will explore this in Chapter 9 and further in Chapter 10.

By the end of the 1980s people began to talk about the triumph of the market and express the view that all economic success could be reduced to a set of universal economic principles as embodied in the Washington Consensus. At first this restoration of a more market orientated environment caused economic turmoil but as the 1980s gave way to the 1990s economic growth rates began to pick up in the developed world and, increasingly, in some of the countries of the former Soviet Bloc. Coupled with the success of East Asian economies and other developing countries, the world business environment appeared in robust health. Of course the developing country that was now leading the way was China, but while purporting to be communist it was using unashamedly capitalist methods to open up its economy. China was not alone and in 2001 Jim O'Neill of Goldman Sachs (a major global merchant bank) developed the term 'the BRICS' to highlight the success of Brazil, Russia, India, China and South Africa.

However, there was one looming problem that began to emerge. It was not only the constant issue of inequality that market reforms seem to lead to, but the sheer rate of the widening of this inequality and the very high incomes being earned by people at the top of global corporations as well as in the increasingly global financial markets. There was reluctance by governments to interfere in these areas. After all, the success of these global companies and the financial sector was fuelling the steady growth rates experienced across the developed world. In particular, the economies of the UK and USA were heavily reliant on their financial sectors. Not only were 'The City' and 'Wall Street' responsible for bringing in large amounts of export earnings as they served as the financial centres of the global economy, but they provided governments with large taxation revenues from their profits and salaries. Businesses and consumers also benefited as the seemingly never-ending rise of the financial sector allowed large increases in credit which in turn fuelled growth.

However, the experiment in the restoration of free market policies itself has recently come under attack from structuralist and Marxist/socialist critics. The actual experience of implementing these policies appeared not to be so simple. The Credit Crunch of 2008 and the onset of the second biggest global economic crisis since the Great Depression has called for yet another reappraisal of how we can best create that illusive environment which will ensure growth and prosperity.

The world economic problems caused by the banking crisis have led to a reassessment of the need for greater government involvement, both at the national and global levels to regulate the banking sector and provide cooperation to ensure a stable global economic environment. We explore this in the case study 'The 2008 Credit Crunch and the Future of Capitalism' at the end of this chapter.

◼ Looking ahead

There now exists a substantial body of research on the conditions needed to produce successful economies. Acemoglu (2012) seeks to review this literature and evaluate the evidence. For Acemoglu, it is not simply markets or entrepreneurs that are the key to innovation and growth but what is crucial is that governments help create the correct mix of institutions that can direct entrepreneurs' energies toward seeking gain from innovation and then developing the markets to realize that gain. He distinguishes between 'inclusive institutions' such as secure property rights, low barriers to entry to ensure competition, equal opportunities, efficient public services and infrastructure, and the existence of democratic states which can maintain effective law and order and 'extractive institutions' which will distort growth. We will explore this further in Chapters 3 and 10.

It is better not to talk of capitalism as such but as a variety of capitalisms across the world, linked together through trade, and with various attempts to regulate this trading system both nationally and internationally. Nationally, capitalism differs from country to country with each system trying to manage the mix between market and state in its own way.

The global economic crisis that began in 2008 has created an ongoing debate about the future of capitalism. This has intensified the debates between those who instinctively feel that the clues to economic success lie in less, not more, state regulation and those who argue that, far from governments being inimical to the creation of a favourable economic environment, they are instrumental in achieving it.

◼ Summary

- The economic environment is created by the existence of scarcity. The study of business from an economic standpoint is the study of the role that businesses play in efficiently resolving the economic problems of allocation, production, and distribution.

- There are a range of competing perspectives as to the best type of economic system to encourage businesses to be economically efficient.

- Markets play a significant role in setting the economic environment of business in modern economies and all economies are involved in trying to better develop these market systems.

- It is clear that markets can often fail both at the microeconomic and macroeconomic levels. So, any examination of the economic environment must involve a close examination of the role of government in correcting these problems.

Case Study: The 2008 Credit Crunch and the Future of Capitalism

From the mid-1990s up until the publication of the first edition of this book (January 2008) the economic environment across much of the world had appeared to be stable and there was every hope that prosperity and growth would continue. While acknowledging this, we wrote in the 'Looking Ahead' chapter,

The one certain thing that we can say about the economic environment is to prepare for the unexpected.

(Wetherly and Otter 2008)

We discussed the ongoing battles between those who favoured a broadly free market approach and those who were becoming increasingly concerned about growing inequality, the power of big business, and the need to improve global governance. We argued,

The issue of how best to ensure that businesses do not abuse their global market positions and operate in a globally responsible way will be very important

and

The distribution of income and rewards is skewed in a very particular way. There is a very small group of very rich people and particular concern is expressed about the gap between executive pay and the rest of the working population. The British newspapers are full of the stories of how the large annual bonuses earned by city brokers are spent.

(Wetherly and Otter 2008)

The financial services sector occupies a vital intermediary position in the business environment. The function of financial institutions is to act as a way of channelling the individual savings of businesses and/or households, enabling businesses to invest and households to borrow to buy long terms assets such as housing and consumer durable goods. Banks make money through the ability to issue credit on the basis of the assets they accumulate from the deposits they receive. This primary retailing function of banks is supplemented by their ability to use some of their assets to engage in more speculative activities in the wholesale or investment banking sector.

At the heart of the banking sector lies the need for savers and depositors to have confidence in their ability to withdraw their money should they wish to do so. Banks have the ability to issue credit based on their initial deposits to many times the value of the original deposits. There is nothing wrong in their doing this as on a day-to-day to basis only a fraction of the deposits they receive will ever be withdrawn, and their ability to issue credit is vital if modern economies are to function.

However, the potential risk of a loss of confidence in a bank and an ensuing rush on that bank causing a more general banking crisis has meant that countries have developed a whole host of rules and regulations, as well as state intervention in the form of strong central banks that can act as 'lenders of last resort' to prevent banking collapses. As the global economy has expanded, this need for regulation has led to the development of global financial institutions, such as the IMF, to coordinate international financial flows.

During the 1970s and 1980s it was felt that these regulations had become far too constrictive and that if the financial system was to flourish then many of them needed to be relaxed. This would allow much more credit to flow, releasing the funds vital for investment and allowing banks to both compete globally and fuel economic expansion.

In 2008 the world economic environment was thrown into turmoil by the crisis that first started in the banking sectors of the US and UK as a result of a growing realization that many loans that had been made were not going to be paid back. It became clear that the root cause of the 'credit crunch' was that bankers, in their desire to earn ever higher annual bonuses, were doing all they could to lend more and more money and were not paying due care and attention to the risk of these loans not being repaid. This was part of a wider risk culture that involved individual brokers in a range of financial markets effectively gambling with the assets of their institutions in order to try to make speculative profits in the knowledge that if their institutions were to get into trouble, the government, in order to retain the stability of the economy, would have to step in and save them. In other words, 'banks were too big to fail'.

Alan Greenspan, who as the former US Federal Reserve Chairman had resisted calls for regulation in financial markets, in a Congressional Hearing in 2008 to explore the reasons for the crisis admitted that he had 'found a flaw' in the free market ideology he had adhered to all his life and had outlined in the annual Adam Smith lecture in 2005 (see Mini-Case 2.2). He explained, 'I made a mistake in presuming that the self-interests of organizations, specifically banks and others, were such that they were best capable of protecting their own shareholders and their equity in the firms' (Clark and Treanor 2008).

Across the globe, other banks found themselves embroiled in this general panic and they themselves were soon found to have been dealing in highly risky operations. The world financial system was thrown into turmoil and governments found themselves having to 'bail out' or, in other words, take direct or part ownership of many prestigious financial institutions. This global financial crisis meant that credit all but dried up, businesses found themselves suffering large reductions in demand for their goods, and the world was engulfed in recession.

At domestic levels there has been huge short-term intervention by governments in the financial systems. But while there is a widespread recognition that more controls over the financial sector need to be considered, fault lines have appeared regarding both the extent of and the urgency with which these changes can be effected. In the US and Britain the strength and influence of finance is strong and politicians are more reluctant to frame rules to constrain the power of banks (HM Treasury 2013). In the European Union there has been a recognition that in order to keep the economic union together there needs to be a strengthening of economic co-operation but Britain has been reluctant to agree to certain aspects of this. The BRICS countries have suffered from the drop in exports and have drawn the lesson that it is dangerous simply to rely on exports to developed countries as the base of their growth. They are seeking to rebalance their economies to build up domestic demand and find ways of working together to form their own trading network. What has emerged from this crisis is the recognition that the global nature of the crisis requires a globally coordinated policy response involving a greater role for the state at the domestic, regional, and global levels (IMF 2013).

(*Sources*: IMF (2013), WEF (2013), HM Treasury (2013))

Questions

1. Why do some people argue that individuals should be free to earn whatever the market pays them? What are the economic arguments for big differences in earnings?

2. Why was it argued that the pursuit of individual remuneration by many people in the investment banking sector created the economic conditions that caused the global recession from 2008 onwards?

3. How might governments intervene in financial markets to make them more efficient?

Review and discussion questions

1. What is meant by the economic problem and its three constituent parts? Why do we need to consider these three parts when assessing the efficiency of business behaviour?

2. How and why might the private goals of a business conflict with the threefold definition of efficiency as outlined in the chapter?

3. How will an economic recession generally impact on businesses and which businesses will be likely to cope best in such difficult trading times?

4. a) Identify the opportunity costs of the resources that will be used to enable you to pursue your studies.

   b) What are the benefits of you studying?

   c) Who should pay for giving you the opportunity of studying?

5. Why might businesses prefer to operate in markets where the demand is relatively price inelastic and how can they seek to create such market conditions?

6. What do you feel are the essential legal, social, and political institutions needed to ensure that we minimize the problems markets can cause and maximize the benefits they can bring?

Assignments

1. Write an essay which addresses the following question: Critically examine the extent to which university students should be asked to pay full fees to cover all the tuition and associated living costs of undertaking an undergraduate programme. Is there a case for government support for students, and in what other ways might governments have a legitimate interest in shaping the business environment in which universities operate?

2. As a business consultant you have been asked by the CEO of a major FTSE company to prepare a report which outlines the main features in the global business environment that are likely to impact on the performance of the business in the next five years.

Further reading

Dasgupta, P. (2007) *Economics: A Very Short Introduction* (Oxford: Oxford University Press). *A concise introduction to key economic concepts.*

Gillespie, A. (2013) *Business Economics* (Oxford: Oxford University Press). *An excellent textbook which introduces business students to how economics is used in business.*

Heilbronner, R. and Milberg, W. (2001) *The Making of Economic Society* (Harlow: Pearson). *A very good explanation of the development of and perspectives applied to modern economic systems.*

Mulhearn, C. and Vane, H. (2011) *Economics for Business* (Basingstoke: Palgrave Macmillan). *A clear and accessible introductory economics text which explicitly relates economics to the business context and is written by one of the authors of Chapter 9.*

Stiglitz, J. (2010) *Freefall and the Sinking of the Global Economy* (London: Allen Lane). *An analysis of the current global economic crisis from an ex-chief economist of the World Bank. He argues that this has been the result of too much faith being invested in free markets and that the balance between state and markets should be restored.*

online resource centre

Test your understanding of this chapter with online questions and answers, explore the subject further through web exercises, and use the weblinks to provide a quick resource for further research. Go to the Online Resource Centre at <www.oxfordtextbooks.co.uk/orc/wetherly_otter/2>

Useful websites

<www.bbc.co.uk/programmes/p00fvhj7>
This is the BBC World Service World Business Report site that profiles the big issues that affect business and the environment.

<www.ft.com>
The website of the *Financial Times*.

<www.mckinsey.com/insights>
A website operated by McKinsey and Company, one of the world's leading management consultancy firms which profiles leading themes and issues that affect global businesses.

<www.wsj.com>
The website of the *Wall Street Journal*.

<www.economicsnetwork.ac.uk>
Managed by the UK Economics Network, this site contains many useful resources and links.

<www.hm-treasury.gov.uk>
This site is the main site for the UK government treasury.

<www.bized.co.uk>
An invaluable website for business studies and economics students run by the Institute for Learning and Research Technology.

References

Acemoglu, D. (2012) 'The world our grandchildren will inherit: the rights revolution and beyond', in Palacios-Huerta, I. (ed.), *Economic Possibilities for Our Grandchildren* (MIT Press).

Browne, J. (2010) *Securing a Sustainable Future for Higher Education–An independent Review of Higher Education Funding and Student Finance* (accessed 4 April 2013) <**http://www.bis. gov.uk/assets/biscore/corporate/docs/s/10-1208-securing-sustainable-higher-education-browne-report.pdf**>

Callinicos, A. (2011) *The Revolutionary Ideas of Karl Marx* (Chicago: Harvester Books).

Collini, S. (2012) *What are Universities For?* (London: Penguin).

Engels, F. (2009) *The Condition of the English Working Class* (Oxford: Oxford University Press).

Clark, A. and Treanor, J. (2008) *Greenspan: I was wrong about the economy. Sort of.* (accessed 21 May 2013) <http://www.guardian.co.uk/business/2008/oct/24/economics-creditcrunch-federal-reserve-greenspan>

Federal Ministry of Economics and Technology (2012) *German Mittelstand: Engine of the German Economy* (accessed 4 April 2013) <http://www.bmwi.de/English/Redaktion/Pdf/factbook-german-mittelstand,property=pdf,bereich=bmwi,sprache=en,rwb=true.pdf>

International Monetary Fund (2013) *World Economic Outlook Update: Gradual Upturn in Global Growth During 2013* (accessed 20 March 2013) <http://www.imf.org/external/pubs/ft/weo/2013/update/01/>

OECD (2012) *Education at a Glance 2012; OECD Indicators* (accessed 20 March 2013) <http://www.oecd.org/edu/eag2012.htm>

Smith, A. (1976) [1776] *An Inquiry into the Nature and Causes of the Wealth of Nations* (Chicago: University of Chicago Press).

Treasury Committee (2010) *Minutes of Evidence - Too Important to Fail - too Important to Ignore* (accessed 4 May 2010) <http://www.publications.parliament.uk/pa/cm200910/cmselect/cmtreasy/261/10012606.htm>

World Economic Forum (2013) *Global Agenda Outlook 2013* (accessed 20 March 2013) <http://www3.weforum.org/docs/WEF_GAC_GlobalAgendaOutlook_2013.pdf>

HM Treasury (2013) *Banking Reform: A New Structure for Stability and Growth* (accessed 21 March 2013) <http://www.official-documents.gov.uk/document/cm85/8545/8545.pdf>

Chapter 3
The technological environment

Dorron Otter

Learning objectives

When you have completed this chapter you will able to:

- Explain the meaning of technology and its impact on business.
- Examine the conditions that need to exist for the creation of an effective innovation environment.
- Critically evaluate the role of technology and its impact on business performance as well its contribution to economic growth.
- Debate the ethical dimensions of the impact of technology.

THEMES

The following themes of the book are especially relevant to this chapter

》 **INTERNAL/EXTERNAL**

The focus of this chapter is on the external environments that are conducive to the development and implementation of technological improvement but we will also explore how this shapes business strategy.

》 **COMPLEXITY** OF THE ENVIRONMENT

There is a range of political, economic and social conditions that need to be present in the external environment if technological change is to be supported.

》 **VARIETY** OF SPATIAL LEVELS

Globalization is rapidly combining with the new technologies to transform the external business environment.

》 **DYNAMIC** ENVIRONMENT

We live in a world where technological change is rapid and no business can afford to stand still in the face of this change.

》 **VALUES**

Technology alters the business environment by providing new opportunities. However, while we are all fascinated by its potential there are fears that there may also be harmful consequences.

Introduction

In this chapter we will define the different meanings of technology and the sources of technological change that can occur within business. The focus of the chapter is primarily on the best environments in which technology can flourish. We will explore the advantages of technological change, not only within individual businesses, but also in relation to its wider impact on the nature of economic growth and on society as a whole. However, we will see that, as outlined in Chapter 2, there are competing views about both the nature of the technological environment and its impact. Inevitably, since technological change is so all-pervasive, and in many cases has such a transformative effect on all our lives, there are ethical dimensions that need to be explored.

What is technology?

Technology is the application of knowledge to production and this can happen in a variety of ways. **Invention** occurs when completely new ideas about products or ways of producing things arise. However, technological advances are fuelled by the process of innovation, which improves or enhances original inventions (**product innovation**) or develops production processes (**process innovation**) that enable the original inventions to be developed into more marketable and/or more profitable products and services. The technological environment can be seen as encompassing both the creation of new knowledge and its application to improve business efficiency and, in so doing, improve the standards of living and quality of life of us all.

» INTERACTION It is how this technology is used or applied that is important, and that fundamentally depends on the wider political, economic, and socio-cultural environment and the way in which people within business seek to exploit its commercial potential.

While the original inventor or innovator is fundamental to the creation of potential future products and services, it is the function of business that will transform those ideas into actual value. Often a long road is travelled before the idea or prototype is converted into the finished commodity. The effort, work, and initiative of many other people are involved between the original spark of the inventor and the point when the final product emerges.

The World Wide Web is a good example of this. The Web has allowed the Internet to take off. The basis for this explosion was developed out of the scientific work at the CERN particle lab which is aiming to discover the building blocks of matter. This involves cooperation of scientists across the globe and in 1989, Tim Berners-Lee, a scientist at CERN, invented the World Wide Web as a means of enabling better communication between these science communities. The Web brings together the developing technologies of personal computers, their ability to be networked, and the new language of hypertext to produce an instant global information system (for more information see <http://info.cern.ch/>).

It is the way in which businesses and users have sought to use the Internet that has opened opportunities for its commercial exploitation. Without the Internet the world of information and communication technology (ICT) and the 'Digital Age' would not have been able to have expanded so exponentially. The Internet has had a major influence on shaping the process of globalization as communication across the world has been speeded up so rapidly.

Stop and Think

Which technological developments most affect you and in what way?

Mini-Case 3.1 From local to global? The rise of the supermarket

Across the developing world the main form of retail outlet is the small specialist shop: local markets for food or small family owned grocery shops. As economic growth increases in the newly industrialized countries, and with a rise in the numbers of 'time poor' but 'income rich' middle class consumers, there is evidence that the shape and form of retail outlets is beginning to change with the advent of large shopping malls and supermarkets that are so prevalent in the developed world.

In 2012 the Indian government announced that foreign supermarket chains such as Tesco and Walmart would now be welcome to establish outlets in India. This provoked intense opposition within India. It was argued that India's 600 million farmers would be adversely affected by the stranglehold that such large businesses might have and by the potential loss of employment of the millions of small shopkeepers which are so much a part of the Indian way of life (Virmani 2012).

These criticisms reflect the long-standing fears in the developed world as epitomized in Britain by the debate about the decline of the British high street and whether this was something to be concerned about. In 2012 the UK government commissioned Mary Portas to undertake a review into the future of the high street (Portas 2011).

Supermarkets have transformed the face of many localities and this has been made possible by the rapidly changing technology across all parts of the food production chain. Agriculture is now a highly technical activity with the application of scientific techniques, pesticides and fertilizer, and machinery. Food distribution has been transformed by road transport and international transportation changes mean that food can be conveyed across the globe. For advocates of foreign supermarket expansion in developing countries it is argued that these changes can only benefit suppliers and consumers alike. The nature of the food we eat has been altered beyond all recognition with food processing and food technology driving a reduction in food costs and new product development seeking ever more fanciful ways of producing products to tempt us. Supermarkets enable vast economies of scale to be produced, and new technologies in-store, such as bar coding and electronic point of sales, seem to be making shopping a much more efficient process. The ICT technologies have brought huge advantages in terms of procurement, supply chain management, knowledge management, and customer relationship management.

The next supermarket innovation now lies in the rapid development of online retailing. The Portas Review reported that in the UK Internet sales accounted for 10% of all retail sales but between 2003 and 2010 it is estimated that half the growth in retail sales was either through e- or m-commerce, and the annual sales through these media is predicted to be £40 billion by 2015. '[N]ew technological developments now mean that the Internet is one of the key threats to retail on our high streets' (Portas 2011).

De Kare Silver highlights the huge impact that Digital Technology is having on business and in relation to retailing he argues that it is 'gradually ceasing to be a bricks and mortar world' (De Kare Silver 2011).

In the UK for every £1 spent in retail 50% is on food and grocery and there are 8000 supermarkets accounting for 97% of all grocery sales (ONS 2011 Retail Sales). Increasingly, the supermarkets are diversifying into providing a whole range of other goods and services such as financial services, health and beauty, flowers, clothing and household goods. However, there are anxieties about the effect that such a transformation has ranging from fears about the loss of community, the driving out of business of many local businesses and the increasing power that supermarkets now have over suppliers and consumers alike (see Simms 2007).

(*Sources:* Portas 2011, De Kare Silver 2011, Virmani 2012, Simms 2007, ONS 2011)

Questions

1. What have been the key changes in the political, social, and economic environment that have encouraged the growth of supermarkets?

2. What are the possible advantages and disadvantages of supermarket shopping? Think about this in relation to food suppliers, consumers, the government, the environment, and the nature of community life?

3. What are the relative advantages and disadvantages of the move of foreign supermarkets into developing countries such as India?

▥ The impact of technology on business and the implications for business strategy

▶ SPATIAL LEVELS ▶ INTERACTION Perhaps the classic statement of the advantages of technology to a business is provided by Michael Porter (Porter 1985). He emphasizes the importance of technology in creating the competitive environment at the level of the individual firm. He also emphasizes the danger of seeing technology as a goal in itself. All too often it is easy to assume that any technological change is good and, further, that the more costly and sophisticated the investment in technology the better it will be. However, technological change does not have to be so costly and complicated. Using the concept of the **value chain**, Porter shows how every activity of a business in combining inputs into outputs has the potential to use technology to alter the production process and add value. In practice, a firm is a collection of different technologies that can be applied, enhanced, or implemented across all the different activities of the business.

A value chain can be seen as consisting of the following functions and processes:

- *Horizontal* functions or support services of a business in terms of its basic infrastructure (finance, planning, information systems, office technology), human resources (training and development), technology development, and purchasing departments.

- *Vertical* or primary business operations in terms of inbound logistics (transport, handling, storage, information systems), production operations (process, materials, machines, packaging, design, and testing), outbound logistics, marketing and sales, and finally service.

These activities comprise the value chain and each operation involves the use of technology to combine inputs into outputs so there is the opportunity for technological improvement across the range of activities to improve the profit margins of the business. One technology that occurs across the range of activities is that of ICT. The use of e-mail and other forms of communication devices such as Skype and video-conference facilities has enabled communication across all ranges of the business to be vastly improved, meaning that information can be rapidly shared and networks more easily established.

In relation to production, there is now the widespread use of computer aided manufacturing to improve both the speed and quality of production. In many cases, this has resulted in computer integrated manufacturing across the production chain, as in the case of the use of robotic technology in car manufacturing. Computer aided design has radically altered the design process and this has been given a further boost by the development of 3D design technologies.

Across retailing the development of electronic point of sales (EPOS) and EFTPOS (electronic funds transfer at point of sale) technologies has both reduced the running costs for businesses as well as improving the speed and quality of service. They also allow retail outlets to keep an accurate record of stock levels and indicate what consumers are buying, which in turn can then feed into customer relationship marketing (CRM) techniques such as the use of loyalty cards.

E-commerce (purchasing via a computer) and increasingly m-commerce (purchasing via a mobile device) are increasing at a rapid rate. By 2015 it is estimated that the total e-commerce and m-commerce market will account for £40 billion of retail sales. Currently in the UK 10% of all retail sales are being accounted for via on-line purchasing, and between 2003 and 2010 it has been estimated that half of the growth in retail sales has come from e-commerce, with m-commerce rising by over 500% in the last two years (Portas 2011).

The increase in the use of the Internet to search for information and the use of social media has vastly increased the potential for businesses to mine this data to analyse customer behaviour and also use technology to develop CRM across sales, marketing, customer service and technical support. It is argued that we are just at the start of the 'Big Data' era. Our individual use of the Internet has generated and will generate at an exponential rate collectively enormous amounts of information about ourselves and our lifestyles. Through analysing this data, which in itself will require the ever more sophisticated data analysis techniques now made possible through ever increasing computing power, new products will be developed.

In sum, the impact of technology in a business potentially can reduce costs, improve quality and productivity, and enable new products to be developed and/or differentiated. Ultimately, the incentive for firms to develop a technology strategy is to improve their competitiveness and add value to the firm. It is to the strategic implications that we will now turn.

Technology strategy

DYNAMIC Technological change can improve the competitiveness of the firm if it either reduces costs or allows a business to differentiate its products or services from that of its rivals. Changes in the external market can create the possibility of untapped economies of scale that in turn call for a technological response to boosting production. Individual businesses are intimately linked to technological changes in other businesses and in other industries. If competitors gain a technological advantage a business needs to respond or else lose out. Changes in the technology of suppliers may impact on the business and, if there are technological advances in related support industries, a business needs to adapt. Furthermore, a technical change in one part of the activities of a business might well call for changes in technologies elsewhere.

Technology cannot be ignored by business and it can either boost a firm's individual position or improve the profitability of the industry in which it operates. Conversely, it can lead to a business declining as its competitors develop a technological advantage or a technological change boosts alternative industries. If it is likely that a business would be able to maintain the technological advantage over time then there is an incentive for firms to innovate and/or develop new products. This can be the case where firms are able to assert their intellectual property rights through patents or where the cost of the research and development is so high as to deter competitors. Some firms may try to simply outspend their rivals and hope that the market appeal of such products allows costs to be more than recouped. The rapid pace of technology, though, means there is always the prospect of a rival using alternative cheaper technology.

It is important for a business to adopt a technology strategy that enables it to respond to external changes as well as one which allows it to develop a consistent approach in relation to its goals. A major decision businesses need to make is whether to be a technology leader or technology follower. In general terms, this requires a balance of risks. Moving first can mean that a business is able to establish a reputation that survives even when alternative competitors enter the market. Being first can mean that a business can develop a strong lead, be in a position to set industry standards, or develop favourable channels of distribution. Conversely, there is a huge risk in going first. Considerable sums of money can be expended and there is the risk that someone else will learn from your mistakes and develop a leaner and fitter product.

In terms of risk, there is the obvious cost of the investment of resources in technological research. Here we can distinguish between two types of research:

Basic or **experimental research:** research which attempts to discover completely new ideas and knowledge. This is sometimes referred to as 'blue-skies thinking'.

Applied research: research which seeks to find the best ways to develop these ideas into commercial commodities.

Only a tiny fraction of original ideas stand a chance of being developed into successful products or services. While a lot of this research does take place within business there is the obvious problem that businesses might not be in a position to risk investment in basic research where the prospect of an eventual return on the initial outlay is slim. There are many cases where the estimated private returns on investment in research might be less than the future possible social returns of the research. In such cases of potential market failure it is often argued that governments should fund such research either directly or indirectly by subsidizing research within companies or by allowing companies a high degree of monopoly power to preserve the future commercial rights of the products they have helped to develop.

Mini-Case 3.2 I'll see you on Facebook!

Mark Zuckerburg initially developed Facebook as a site solely for his fellow Harvard University students in 2004. However, it quickly had established itself as the leading global social networking site. Social networking sites have been made possible by the widespread penetration of the Internet through faster broadband and the development of IT skills in the wider population as well as the increase in the number of ways of accessing the Internet through handheld smart phones and tablets.

Prior to Facebook there were other social networking sites, such as Bebo and Myspace, but Facebook has quickly come to dominate the social networking market in the developed world. By 2010 there were 400 million members of the Facebook community and by 2013 there were over 1 billion users.

For a networking site to prosper and grow it needs to establish itself as a large network and ensure that its users stick with it. Sites such as Myspace and Bebo have suffered from users jumping ship. The strength of Facebook's business model lies in its ability to create networks, its ability to use the information that its users give to customize adverts and potentially other applications, as well as its sheer market reach.

While there would appear to be no potential rival to usurp Facebook, it does face some strategic problems. The basic problem for Facebook is that users access it for free. This means that its main source of income is from hosting adverts and, in turn, this means that if the company is to grow its revenues it needs to keep expanding its customer base or find other ways of generating income. While it is clear that

Facebook's rise has been rapid, businesses in the IT sector can fall as dramatically as they can rise. The 'dot-com' bubble between 1997 and 2000 showed the dangers of getting carried away.

As a platform for hosting adverts Facebook faces severe competition from many other rivals. There is always the possibility that a new competitor will appear offering something that Facebook currently does not. There is also the potential for users to feel that the adverts are cluttering up the site and that concerns over privacy will turn them away.

It is clear that Facebook's strategy is to constantly expand its customer base, but it faces problems with existing social network sites in countries such as China and Russia (where government regulation can prohibit what information is allowed). In Africa, lack of access to personal computers can be a barrier, although the rapid expansion of mobile phones does provide opportunities for expansion through this medium.

Questions

1. Why have social networking sites grown so much in the last decade?

2. What have been the reasons for the success of these sites and others such as Myspace and LinkedIn and why have others such as Bebo not been so successful?

3. What are the potential threats to the continued success of Facebook and how might Facebook respond to these?

The evolution of technological change

》 INTERNAL/EXTERNAL The Industrial Revolution from the 18th century onwards started not with new products but with new processes to produce existing ones. Before an industrial revolution is possible it is important that there are increases in the productivity of agriculture so that food supplies can increase. These are necessary so that people can be 'freed' from the land to work in factories. In England it has been estimated that it took 1,000 years for agricultural production to boost food yields from 0.5 tonnes per hectare to 2 tonnes, but in the 18th century it took only 40 years to raise this to 6 tonnes.

As discussed in Chapter 2 these changes came about not as the result of the application of capital intensive techniques or scientific changes. For centuries landowners primarily earned their wealth not from taking a direct interest in their land, but by simply collecting rents from impoverished farmers who worked their land. These farmers aimed to produce food for their own needs. In order to minimize the risk of climate and pests and to ensure some sort of variety of food, they would seek to produce a range of produce. Any surplus could either be stored or sold at market to provide the occasional 'luxury'. Under this system there was little incentive for farmers to produce surpluses as they knew that all that would happen is that landlords would raise the rents.

Capitalism and the increase in markets changed this system of agriculture. Now the landlords saw that they could make more money by directly selling produce themselves in the marketplace. They sought to specialize in the use of their land and sell the products on the market. Farmers were now either forced to specialize in the production of certain marketable foods or products or were evicted from the land to allow an increase in the scale of the production by combining farms and benefiting from economies of scale.

One of the first marketable products identified was wool. Vast tracts of land were given over to sheep rearing and the wool was then transformed into woven cloth through the process of spinning and weaving. Initially this was achieved through small scale 'cottage' industries where wool was largely spun at home by 'spinsters' and then woven into cloth in small scale weaving factories. However, in the 18th century industrialists began to develop the large scale modern factory systems powered initially by water and then steam. In these modern factory systems a clear division of labour took place with the introduction of new and vastly more productive machinery such as Hargreaves' 'Spinning Jenny', the water frame developed by Richard Arkwright, often regarded as the person who first developed the modern factory system, and then the combination of these two processes in the form of Crompton's 'mule'. However, these innovations in themselves were not scientifically complex but made use of simple ideas and mechanical devices and yet with spectacular results in terms of output.

However, it was cotton that was the first major industrial product. The production of cotton entailed the creation of a global market both in terms of sourcing the raw material and in terms of expanding the world market for this. The British had first learned about the possibility of manufacturing cotton by discovering the quality of Indian textiles. The Empire now ensured cheap and plentiful supplies of cotton especially from America where slavery meant that cotton was cheap. Techniques developed to produce woollen cloth more cheaply were now used to spur the development of cotton. Developments in steam power to work the textile mills, and then, of course, for transportation of goods via the railways and on steam ships, further served to reduce costs dramatically as well as expand world trade. Finally, the move to transporting goods via roads brought in the development of the container as a way of cutting transport times and costs (see Mini-Case 3.3).

Mini-Case 3.3 Containerization

On 6 November 2012 the *Marco Polo* operated by the French CMA CGM transportation group became the world's biggest container ship with a capacity of 16,000 containers (**<www.cmacgm-marcopolo.com>**). The previous world record holder had been the *Emma Maersk* owned by the Danish A.P Moller-Maersk Group who are now planning to launch a new series of Triple E vessels which will carry 18,000 containers (**<www.maerskline.com>**). It is the South Korean shipbuilder, Daewoo, that has been responsible for the construction of all these ships (**<www.dsme.co.kr>**). The new ships will be so large that were all the containers of one ship to be stacked one on top of the other they would reach the stratosphere at 29 miles above the earth, or if unloaded onto a train it would need to be 69 miles long (Neate 2013)! While the Triple E vessels look set to be the world leaders from their expected 2013 launch, Neate quotes David Tozer, the global manager for container ships at Lloyds Register group, as follows, 'The Technology is there to get bigger and bigger. It is absolutely massive business'. Without container ships the expansion of global trade that is at the heart of globalization would not be possible, and yet it is the simple technology of the containers they carry that has done so much to transform the world in which we live.

The container is simply a steel box in which goods can be placed to be transported. The simplicity of the container is that it can be carried on a multi-modal basis, i.e. on a lorry, by rail, by sea, or air. However, it has revolutionized the logistics of transporting goods to such an extent that to all intents and purposes it has reduced transport costs to an almost negligible level.

In essence the reason for this is simple. Economies of scale mean that by doubling the dimensions of a box you expand the storage capacity of this box many more times meaning that more goods can be placed into one container. Previously, the container loading and unloading goods for freight by sea was highly labour intensive and goods were in individual crates of different sizes and shapes that then had to be manually lifted and stowed in the holds of ships. Whilst the longshoremen involved in this were skilled at packing in the cases, the odd shapes meant that great care had to be paid to how the crates went in and not all available space could be used. There was the real risk that badly loaded cargo would shift when at sea and lead to breakages or even the capsizing of the vessel.

Upon unloading, this cargo had to be sorted and transferred onto vehicles en route to the final destinations. Containerization did many things: firstly, it made it much easier to stack containers, requiring far fewer workers; secondly, it made it much easier to load and unload the containers. Each container is simply lifted onto a lorry and then off it goes.

The container ports of today are much more capital and technologically intensive compared to the docklands of old. Marc Levinson charts the conditions that led to the development and the huge impact the container has had on the world (Levinson 2006). In making shipping cheap the container also made it possible to have a world economy. Cheap transportation has revolutionized the supply chain for businesses. Firms no longer need to locate near to ports or locate different parts of the supply chain close together but can split it up and locate each production stage where costs are lowest. Firms could thus be truly international and in many ways are forced to go global as competitor firms exploit their global reach.

While containers had been in limited use as one way of transporting goods by sea, it was in the 1950s that the American McLean Trucking Corporation really appreciated the revolutionary potential of containerization and that this, if used widely, would radically transform the whole transportation industry. McLean's first venture into containerization was to avoid the road congestion along the Eastern seaboard interstate highways (his first ship, the Ideal X, carried just 58 containers!). Trucks would deposit containers onto ships for these then to be sent by sea to destinations along the seaboard and then off loaded onto other trucks to be taken to the final destination. What McClean did was to see the potential in integrating shipping and road transportation and the huge economies of scale that could be derived from converting ships into container ships and the necessary changes that would need to be made to the trucks that would pull them and the way in which docks would operate in the future.

(*Sources:* Levinson 2006, **<www.worldshipping.org/about-the-industry/history-of-containerization>**, **<www.emma-maersk.info/>**, Neate 2013)

Question

What is containerization and how did the innovative use of containers transform the global distribution of goods?

The countries of Europe, North America, and Australasia were able, through rapid industrialization and the production of thousands of new goods, to bring about big improvements in the social welfare of their people in the fields of health and education and poverty reduction. Not only did increases in productivity increase standards of living, in turn they led to the development of new industries and associated processes. The next most influential change was that brought to production as a result of the developments in the motor car industry with the mass production techniques pioneered by Henry Ford being transferred to the production of a wide array of other goods. Some commentators indeed refer to this external business environment as being one of Fordism, which it is argued pre-dated the Second World War but found its greatest expression in providing the technological backdrop for the rapid economic growth in the developed world in the post Second World War period. Human development is also in turn an important influence on technological development. Higher levels of education mean that people have the skills and are able to develop the knowledge to promote new products and processes. Higher education can produce the skilled personnel to pioneer new developments but a general increase in educational skills allows people at all levels in organizations to adapt to change and master new techniques.

In the latter part of the 20th and now into the 21st century it has been, of course, the rise of the new technologies, especially the digital and information technologies, that have driven economic growth. Information and communications technology (ICT) is seen as ushering in a new paradigm of never ending growth as communication networks increase the spatial integration of business beyond geographical limits. The development of the World Wide Web as a means of navigating the Internet and the explosion in computing power as well as the corresponding software programmes to develop the potential uses of these new communication and information possibilities, have led to a massive increase in invention and innovation. This combination of the new information technologies and globalization has created the modern network age and this has had a huge impact on the way in which we now do business.

E-commerce embraces a whole host of activities that we now take for granted and yet which are relatively new. The first mobile phone was only produced in prototype in 1986, we have seen that Tim Berners-Lee introduced the World Wide Web in 1989 and Facebook only launched in 2005. Texting, social networking, online banking, online shopping, e-ticketing, and e-mail are all a fundamental part of daily life and yet are all relatively new products. However, the simple assertion that technology will always be at the root of economic growth is not accepted by all.

▪ Perspectives on the creation of favourable technological environments

▶ COMPLEXITY ▶ INTERNAL/EXTERNAL Chapter 2 outlined the broad competing views as to the best way of organizing economic activity. The same broad views can be distinguished when it comes to the sources of technological change.

For Adam Smith it was the development of widespread markets that allowed the conditions for the rapid improvements in productivity that led to the rapid advance of capitalism. The greatest source of technological advance lay not in the sophisticated application of science or complex new technologies. It was the expansion of markets that propelled businesses to reorganize production to meet these new market opportunities in their pursuit of profit. The crucial change in production techniques was in developing production processes that utilized the division of labour and specialization. Taking the example of an industrial product, a 'pin' (or nail) in the *Wealth of Nations*, Smith showed how huge gains in productivity could be obtained by a simple change in the organization of the production process to allow a greater division of labour. Smith demonstrated how specialization or the splitting of production into separate tasks allowed great gains in productivity of 'pins' to be gained.

On the back of this increase in the 'wealth of nations' it is clear that from the profits generated new ways of producing could be sought, but these technological advances are independent of the initial growth in markets that made these profits possible. In this sense, technology can be seen as 'exogenous' to the process of growth. In other words, technology can give growth in business profits an added boost but it is not the primary source of the profits.

This could be seen as a strong endorsement of the neoclassical view of a world in which the role of the private entrepreneur and free markets are pivotal for economic success. An important element in propelling the technological change is the response of the business so we need to look at the entrepreneurial activity within the business (see Chapter 15). How do such entrepreneurs behave and what are the conditions that are most likely to exploit technology?

However, as we have seen, Smith was well aware of the wider structural or institutional factors that would be needed to support the market. It took changes in the political and social structure to allow the expansion of trade and a robust legal system to provide the rules to both protect the rights of businesses as well as the wider society from the possible exploitation by business. While the roles of the entrepreneur and markets are critical, so are these wider institutional and structural ingredients in the external business environment and we will explore these later.

For Karl Marx, technology is indeed seen as being vital for the competitive strategy within a business as the capitalist constantly strives to boost profits. However, as with Smith, it is not the primary source of value, as for Marx, all value comes from the ability of the capitalist to exploit labour. Marx is fulsome in his praise for the extent to which this can potentially transform and improve well-being but for him the problem lies in precisely the disjunction between the potential social benefits of technological change and the private motivation of the capitalist desires to pursue individual profit. The main benefit of technology to the capitalist is that it enables an increase in the productivity of labour, thus enabling more value to be squeezed from the labourer and into the balance sheets of the business. This expansion of technology also has many other consequences including the inevitable 'concentration and centralization' (monopoly control and widening inequality in society) of business and the constant pressure on profit rates as more and more resources are devoted to the 'accumulation of capital' (investment in technology). Ultimately, Marx argued, this process of capitalist accumulation will result in an inevitable crisis in capitalism when the workers, who are the true source of all the wealth, will rise up and transform private ownership into common ownership so that industry is set to work for the social good rather than private profit. However, for Marx the implication is clear. Businesses have no choice but to constantly seek to invest in new technology but, in the process, the share of income going to the workers will fall in relation to that going to the owners of capital.

Writing in the early years of the 20th century, Joseph Schumpeter was the first person to develop a formal theory of the centrality of innovation to explain the development of capitalism. In other words, for Schumpeter, technology itself is the driver of capitalist growth but technology emerges from within business organizations and the competitive environment. In economic terms, this is an **endogenous** theory of growth, or in other words, stems from the internal processes within businesses themselves. For Schumpeter, the origins of capitalist growth lie in the important function of the entrepreneur but, as business organizations began to develop and grow, it was clear that this entrepreneurial function was moving away from the initial individual pioneers of the early Industrial Revolution to the specialist research and development personnel within businesses. In response to Marx's belief that capitalism as an economic system would fail as a result of crisis, Schumpeter argued that indeed capitalism would constantly renew itself as technologies first rose and then fell through what he saw as a process of 'creative destruction'. For Schumpeter this theoretical view of change very much tied in with the empirical observations of the Russian economist, Nikolai Kondratiev, who had explained the succession of booms and slumps in the business cycle (see Chapter 9) that occurred in capitalism from the late 18th century to the early 20th century as being explained by waves of successive technological development. It was Schumpeter who coined the term 'Kondratieff Waves' in his honour (Schumpeter 1942).

Many people have indeed explained the subsequent development of capitalism in this way. Freeman and Louçã trace the development of the modern world in a series of five Kondratieff waves from the start of Industrial Revolution of the late 18th to early 19th century: 'The Age of Cotton, Iron, and Water Power'; 'The Age of Iron Railways, Steam Power, and Mechaniza-tion' from the early 19th century to late 19th century; 'The Age of Steel, Heavy Engineering, and Electrification' from the early 20th century through to 'The Age of Oil, Automobiles, Motorization, and Mass Production' that formed the main part of the 20th century. Of course, we are now in the fifth 'Age of Information and Communication Technology' (Freeman and Louçã 2002).

More recently, Robert Gordon has sought to compress the history of the development of capitalism into three periods. IR1 comprised developments in steam, cotton and rail. IR2 saw the development of the internal combustion engine, electricity, and highways but also he in-cludes a range of technologies that enabled a huge reallocation of labour (especially female labour) from the home to the workplace. Chief amongst these was indoor plumbing, running water, and a range of domestic household appliances. We are now in IR3 which is, of course, characterized by the use of the computer and Internet. For Gordon, the IR1 and IR2 periods enabled the effects on economic growth rates to be felt for approximately 100 years before diminishing returns occur (Gordon 2013).

After the Second World War and in response to the economic recession that occurred in the developed world between the wars, and the relative state of backwardness of many developing countries, much attention focused on the role of government in actively encouraging growth. To many the Great Depression of the 1920s and 1930s seemed to confirm Marx's predictions of the inevitable decline of capitalism, not least because the slow-down of growth in the West could be contrasted with the spectacular growth rates on the Soviet Union where the govern-ment had assumed responsibility for industrial production and capital investment.

As we shall see in Chapter 9, in Western Europe and North America countries adopted the policy proposals of John Maynard Keynes. In the Keynesian framework, governments through spending on capital infrastructure such as roads, schools, and welfare services could both act to boost demand at the macro-level and improve the human capital of the people through investment in education and skills and training. If the private sector was reassured that the economy was stable this would give them the confidence to borrow and invest. Public investment in research and development would also ensure that adequate research investment was made and provide the pool of skilled research personnel required. There was an implicit belief that capital growth would lead to economic growth. Despite initial successes in both the developed and developing world, growth rates slowed markedly in the 1970s and many countries found that government borrowing had spiralled out of control. For free market thinkers this was the inevitable result of forgetting that the secret to eco-nomic growth lay in the creation and development of new markets and that the key to this was private enterprise.

■ Is the world becoming flat?

One of the most influential theories of growth which also appeared to fit very closely with the thinking outlined above has been a result of the work of Solow. It was Solow, in 1956, who first argued that whilst a focus on capital growth and savings were important in order for growth not to slow, it was technological improvement that was important. Economists seek to measure the extent of increases in productivity through the use of total factor productivity. This is the residual increase in total output having allowed for the increase in the inputs of labour and capital. For Solow, technology is the explanation for this additional growth. If technology, then, is the key, what causes this?

❯❯ INTERNAL/EXTERNAL This theory is most commonly known by the rather clumsy title **neoclassical endogenous growth theory**. Technology is the result of individuals or firms seeking profits through research and developing and adapting existing technologies. Also of importance is the openness to trade between countries, with technology flowing across frontiers referred to as technology transfer, as well as across businesses within one country. In this view, technology will itself allow increases in productivity and decreases in costs. A vital role is played by human capital, i.e. the ability of people to learn and improve. As people learn they constantly improve on ideas and techniques and the returns to human capital can be increasing. Thus the causes of economic growth can be seen as being the following: trade openness with the addition of diffusion of technology through education, research, and development.

❯❯ SPATIAL While it is the case that much of technological progress is 'endogenous' it is equally clear that political institutions and structures to support and promote this technological progress are vital as well as ensuring that the owners of the human capital that had resulted in the new products or processes have the ability to benefit from their intellectual labour. It is important to have clearly defined property rights to protect technological leaders from having their ideas stolen.

Globally, it is not necessary for all countries to be world leaders in technological improvement. All that is needed is for a few countries to be technological leaders with other countries being technological followers able to adapt and learn from the leaders. Through technology transfer it will be possible for less developed regions of the world to 'catch up' with the already developed ones.

❯❯ INTERACTION We shall see in Chapter 12, there is a fierce debate about the impact of globalization on poorer less-developed countries and whether the development of trade and investment across country borders will be beneficial to both rich and poor countries alike.

Technology has traditionally flowed from rich countries to poor countries, with multinational corporations seeking to enhance their global competitive advantage. Technology transfer can occur directly through joint ventures or strategic alliances, or through the issuing of licences to domestic firms to operate on behalf of the MNC. Trade itself does allow the possibility for domestic firms in less developed countries to 'reverse engineer' products to explore whether they can be improved. For Solow, this technology transfer is at the heart of the growth of the newly industrializing countries and should lead to convergence between rich and poor countries to everyone's benefit.

Of course there is every danger that products and ideas might be copied and counterfeited, so companies seek global protection through patents and through trade related property rights. While patents can be relatively easily enforced within countries and even in some cases regions, it is less easy to do this globally (see for example the websites of the European Patent Office at **<http://www.epo.org/>** and the World Intellectual Property Organization at **<http://www.wipo.int/about-wipo/en>**).

The influential American journalist Thomas Friedman places technology firmly at the centre of globalization. For Friedman, the ability of less developed countries to exploit technology through the use of relatively low cost but well educated labour forces will mean that, far from being at a disadvantage compared to the developed world, developing countries will be able to exploit their comparative advantages in lower cost labour with the emerging new digital and information technologies. Friedman starts his influential book, *The World is Flat,* in Bangalore, India—the centre of the Indian software industry. For Friedman, what he saw in Bangalore reflects the wider changes that are occurring in economic systems, especially in the developing world, as a result of developments in the new information technologies. These technologies have allowed ICT to be applied across the whole value chain referred to above and have acted as a platform to unleash a whole series of 'flattening' tendencies. Fundamentally, the ability of computers to talk together through common software protocols such as HTML has allowed businesses to go global. This has allowed greater controls over supply chains so production can be situated where costs are lower or nearer to markets. It has enabled outsourcing of both manufacturing and service activities (e.g. call centres), and countries such as India and China have been at the forefront. Above all, the development of these platforms has enabled the rapid sharing of information and made collaboration online so much easier.

We will explore the impact of globalization in Chapter 12. Friedman argues that initially globalization was powered by the expansion of governments and countries and he refers to this as the globalization 1.0 era. In globalization 2.0, multinational companies were the motor force, but now in globalization 3.0, it is the ICT technologies that are driving globalization and allowing the flattening of the world, both in terms of spatial proximity and in terms of living standards, as developing countries quickly converge with the developed ones (Friedman 2007).

David Landes outlines what he sees as the reasons some countries are able to grow and prosper and others don't (Landes 1998). For Landes, while invention is indeed exogenous, what is needed is the endogenous use of inventions and innovations through institutions, markets, and property rights.

There now exists a substantial body of research on the causes of economic growth and the role of technology. In Chapter 2 we reviewed the recent contribution of Acemoglu which distinguishes between those economies based in inclusive institutions, which would provide a conducive environment for risk taking and innovation, and those on extractive institutions where technological progress will be blocked (Acemoglu 2012).

There is debate about the precise way in which governments can foster the environment for technology. It is generally agreed that governments have a vital role in developing human capital through education. Indirect policies such as competition policy and regulation through guaranteeing patents are necessary to encourage incentives to innovate. However, there are many cases where the future potential returns to society might be greater than the private returns of the investment required. In these cases it might be argued that governments should subsidize research and development either within companies or through government research bodies and grants to universities. However, such action by governments can cause problems in relation to international trade agreements when one country adopts a more generous stance to subsidies than another (see Mini-Case 3.4).

Mini-Case 3.4 Solar power: global technology strategy

In response to the prospect of global climate change, which we explore in Chapter 8, one possible strategy is for countries to develop alternative sources of energy that do not cause the emissions of the greenhouse gases that lead to global warming.

There is potentially a huge benefit to society of moving to these alternative green technologies (such as wind, tidal, and solar), but the problem for the private companies involved in developing solar panels is that the cost of developing the technology is considerable and currently the price of power generated by such sources is relatively high compared to conventional energy sources.

In 2000 global solar power generating capacity was 1,000 MW; but by 2011 it was 50,000 MW; and there is global competition between companies to both increase the total market as well as increase market share.

In recent years there has been a fierce argument between Chinese and American producers of solar panels. In 2006 there were 2 Chinese companies in the top 10 global manufacturers of solar panels, but in 2013 there were 6.

At current levels of demand, production potentially is outstripping demand. But in China the government has set ambitious targets for solar power capacity to rise from 3 GW in 2011 to 10 GW in 2013 and then to an impressive 40 GW by 2015.

Chinese manufacturers are able to secure cheap long term loans from the China Development Bank which, while a private bank, nevertheless is closely associated with the government and the government is seeking to encourage a process of mergers and acquisitions among Chinese producers to consolidate the number of firms in the industry. As a result of this investment and strategy it is likely that the cost of solar panels will fall.

In the US solar power businesses have complained that this is unfair competition. The chief marketing officer for the American solar cell firm, Suniva is quoted as saying, 'The Chinese Strategy is very clear. They are engaging in predatory financing and they're trying to drive everyone else out of the market' (Lacey 2011). In 2013 the US raised its tariffs on Chinese solar panel imports and China lodged a complaint with the World Trade Organization.

(*Sources:* Ma 2013, Lacey 2011, BBC News Business 2013)

Questions

1. How might the Chinese solar panel manufacturers justify their technology strategy?

2. How might American and European solar power firms develop a technology strategy to compete with the Chinese?

3. What role should governments play in developing green technologies?

All too often throughout history and still to this day in many parts of the world it is 'extractive institutions' that are the norm. Here narrow elites control the resources available and monopoly power predominates. In such circumstances, while wealth is created it is done through narrow elites of the rich and the powerful exploiting labour forces and natural resources through their economic and political power.

> Technological change and hence growth, is much more likely to take place under inclusive institutions because they provide opportunities and incentives for a larger segment of the population. In fact extractive institutions often explicitly block technological innovation because it is regarded as destabilizing for the regime in charge, or because it runs against the interests of a narrow elite controlling power.
>
> (Acemoglu 2012)

In these environments, while technology undoubtedly leads to impressive increases in quantitative growth, the qualitative nature of this growth is distorted. In particular it is argued that the impact of technology transferring over from the developed world to the developing will exacerbate the tendency for income inequality to widen in the developing countries as profits rise relative to wages (Acemoglu and Robinson 2012).

In this way paradoxically the growth that has occurred in societies founded on rights based inclusive institutions has allowed growth to increase in countries not characterized by democracy and with extractive institutions which benefit small elites who are able to exploit the labour and natural resources of their countries. This is especially the case in many parts of the developing world where democratic institutions are not well developed. In this case, it is argued that the fruits of economic growth often are underpinned by the development of export industries reliant on imported technology from the developed world. The American Marxist Paul Baran referred to this type of capitalism as being 'comprador capitalism.' His explanation for the lack of development in many 'backward' countries is that the structure of the economies was geared to export production controlled through foreign corporations in cooperation with indigenous elites. This type of extractive growth would lead to widening income inequality both within and between countries as opposed to the type of inclusive growth envisaged by neoclassical theorists. We will explore this further in Chapter 10.

As we shall see, it is also argued that there is a danger that the development of the new technologies may well act to undermine the nature of the inclusive institutions in the developed world themselves, with technology creating an ever richer elite.

As in the supermarkets case discussed in Mini-Case 3.1, many people are concerned that the adoption of western technologically advanced methods might not be appropriate to the structural conditions that exist in many parts of the developing world. Here there is a feeling that what is needed is the development of *appropriate* technology as an alternative to transfers of expensive capital intensive technology that may result in disruption of traditional industries and unemployment.

As we shall see later in this chapter, other critics fear that imported technology in the developed world will lead to exacerbating the big income gaps between rich and poor and that what is needed is 'Bottom of the Pyramid' models of development and the use of Frugal Innovation. Frugal innovation involves stripping away the complexity of products so that poor consumers in the developing world can both produce them and afford them. Examples of such products are the solar powered wind-up radio, the Nokia 1100 mobile phone, which is a basic form of mobile phone allowing text and voice, and the Tata Nano car in India. In Africa Internet penetration is low and computers are expensive to buy but there are now more than 650 million mobile phone subscribers using basic mobile phones. These phones enable businesses to communicate much more easily. Farmers in remote areas can get instant access to price information putting them in a stronger position when negotiating deals. In Africa where banking infrastructure is underdeveloped increasingly people are able to use their phones to conduct financial transactions.

It is often argued that the expense of ICT will lead to a 'digital divide' between rich and poor countries but the ability to access information through mobile phones counters that. Jensen, in a study of fisherman in South India argued that the use of mobiles has resulted in a 'digital provide' with fishermen able to negotiate better prices for their catches and that there has been a measurable increase in living standards in these communities (Jensen 2007).

Prahalad and Hart both argue that, instead of seeing poor people as passive victims of economic neglect, what is needed is for investors to see them as potential creative entrepreneurs and consumers. If foreign multinationals, governments, and aid agencies encourages the potential at the base of the pyramid, in the long run poverty will be reduced as the poor exploit their entrepreneurial potential in their own local environments (Prahalad 2010, Hart 2010). Hart has developed the 'base of the pyramid' protocol to encourage multinational corporations to meet the needs of the poor rather than the narrow range of affluent consumers in the developing world. The Project Overview for the Protocol states that:

> The MNC has become synonymous with global inequality and Westernization, increasingly becoming the target of choice for multinational anti-globalization movements. Recently, however, it has been proposed that MNCs possess the resources and wherewithal to deploy business models capable of serving the needs of the billions of people in the developing world, many of whom earn less than $5 dollars a day.
>
> (Base of the Pyramid Protocol 2006)

Stop and Think

Why might it be in the interests of businesses in the developed world to actively engage in the process of technology transfer to the developed world?

■ The great innovation debate

In recent times sceptical views have been expressed about the simple formulation that technology does indeed lead inevitably to increased growth and productivity at the national level. *The Economist* magazine profiled this debate under the theme of 'The Great Innovation Debate' in January 2013 (*The Economist* 2013). While technology undoubtedly changes the nature of many aspects of the business process as, we have seen above, to what extent is this reflected in the growth figures?

This debate has especially been directed at the effects of the digital age and stemmed from the following observation by Solow himself in an article in the *New York Times* in 1987, 'We can see the computers everywhere except in the productivity statistics' (Solow 1987). This so called 'IT productivity paradox' has been developed by notable economists such as Ha Joon Chang at the University of Cambridge and Robert Gordon (see above).

For Gordon the productivity effects of IR1 and IR2 both lasted 100 years before **diminishing returns** set in but with IR3 starting in 1960 the peak of the effects was in the 1970s and 1980s culminating in the dot.com boom and bust in the 1990s. In the US average growth rates between 1891 and 1972 were 2.3% but from 1972 to 1996 this had slowed to 1.4%. For Gordon, the effects of ICT now is reduced to a range of entertainment and communication devices which '[d]o not fundamentally change labour productivity or the standard of living in the way that electric light, motor cars or indoor plumbing changed it' (Gordon 2012).

In similar vein, Ha Joon Chang argues that the invention of the washing machine did more to fundamentally affect economic growth than the computer. He argues that in every age the new inventions are the ones that attract the awe and admiration but that often it is the old technologies that have done most to transform the world. The washing machine was one of a range of household devices that enabled women to enter the workforce transforming not only economic performance in general but their lives and the lives of their families in particular (Chang 2011, chapter 4).

Gordon reinforces this view by arguing, '[t]here was no more important event that liberated women than the invention of running water and indoor plumbing, which happened in urban America between 1890 and 1930' (Gordon 2012).

Cowen seeks to explain the apparent technological plateau that appears to have been reached in America and other developed nations. He argues that in the US there is now what he terms a 'great stagnation'. Initially, America was able to exploit the 'low hanging fruit' of extensive discoveries of new natural resources, taking advantage of the influx of waves of new immigrants and also bringing education up to secondary level for all citizens as well as dramatically improving access to higher education for many. However, eventually these productivity gains have begun to diminish. In relation to technology, he too argues that the major innovations of the 18th and 19th century have essentially slowed and that, while we continue to improve and enhance these, there have been no fundamental breakthroughs as before. In relation to ICT, while this has undoubtedly improved peoples' lives especially in relation to communication and entertainment, there is little evidence that this has increased productivity (Cowen 2011).

In terms of the development of new ideas it has been argued that, given the huge amount of knowledge that there is now to know, it takes even our most potentially innovative people a long time to reach the position where they can attain the scientific or technical knowledge required to be in a position to innovate. This has been referred to as 'the burden of knowledge' (Jones 2012). The implication of this is that over time it becomes increasingly harder to maintain increases in economic growth through technological change.

This 'innovation pessimism' was highlighted by *The Economist*. Asking the question 'Has the ideas machine broken down?', it profiled the work of Cowen and cited research by Azoulay and Jones which shows that the contribution to total factor productivity of a R&D worker in 1950 was seven times that of such a worker in 2000.

Reviewing the growth data in the US, Brynjolfsson (1993) and Stressman (1997) initially confirmed that there was indeed this IT paradox, but in recent years Brynjolfsson has come to the view that the reason for the paradox is simply that the future huge potential of the new technologies has yet to be unlocked (Brynjolffson and Hitt 1998). For Brynjolffson, while it is true that the link between productivity and traditional innovation inputs has weakened, the surge in ICT investment will lead to an increase in productivity.

In 1965 the co-founder of Intel, Gordon E. Moore, predicted that the number of transistors on a chip would double every two years and this has turned out to be an accurate prediction. To put this into terms that non IT people will understand the Intel website asks its viewers to picture a standard music hall with a capacity of 2,300 people in 1970 and then shows that if this was a computer chip 1.3 billion people would fit in it by 2011 (Intel 2013).

In particular, it is digitization that will have the biggest effect as it will change the way that innovation itself is done and will enable businesses to escape the 'burden of knowledge'. A concept that is similar to Moore's Law is 'the second half of the chessboard'. There is a fable that the inventor of chess was asked by the Emperor to name his reward for developing this new game. The inventor asked the Emperor to pay him in rice grains starting with one grain on the first square of the chessboard and then doubling the amount on the next and so on until all the squares were filled. Initially this doubling of the amount of rice on each successive square is quite modest but as we move into the second half of the chessboard the amounts of rice rise exponentially. Kurzweil applied this concept to the world of technology strategy arguing that as we move onto the second half of the chessboard each technological leap will be staggering (Kurzweil 2000, Brynjolfsson and McAfee 2011 and 2012).

Stop and Think

On a calculator work out how many gains of rice will be on the 64th square of the chessboard if, starting with 1 grain on square 1, you then double the amount on the next one and then keep doubling the amount of grains on each successive square compared to the previous one! (The answer is more grains of rice than the world produces every year!)

While research might be multiplying beyond the ability of humans to absorb this knowledge, cognitive computing technologies will enable us to master the machines. Brynjolfsson argues that this will happen 'through innovations in management techniques, business models, work processes and human resource practices'. He asserts that digitization will transform innovation in four ways:

1. Improved real-time measurement of business activities: this is especially the case in the e-economy where the use of computers to control and monitor information means that most businesses now sit on vast tracts of data which they can now use to improve business processes across the value chain, e.g. data on Internet searches can be gathered to gain insights into consumer behaviour, inventories and supplies can be monitored with the use of RFID (Radio-frequency identification) tags to make business processes more efficient.

2. Faster and cheaper business experimentation: digitization enables businesses to speed up the testing of new ideas and products.

3. More widespread and easier sharing of ideas: since it is the case that most new innovations stem from the work of often complex teams within businesses, digitization can speed up the sharing of data and make sharing this data so much easier.

4. The ability to replicate innovations more quickly and accurately: digitization enables new ideas to be scaled up and of course to encourage much more rapid innovation. Indeed, citing the software industry itself, Brynjolffson argues that the process of 'creative destruction' is heightened as new competitors rise up to supplant the old (Brynjolfsson 2011).

It is clear that technology has a dramatic transformative effect on individual businesses in terms of enabling them to both increase profits and develop a competitive advantage. However, there is a fierce debate about the impact of the digital age in terms of its aggregate effects in terms of boosting economic growth rates overall.

This scepticism about the impact of technology is also voiced in relation to the effect that technological change has on raising aggregate living standards both within and between countries.

■ Looking ahead

❱ **VALUES** ❱ **STAKEHOLDERS** It is not just the way that technology affects business performance and growth that causes debate, but questions are also asked about the effect that technology has on our well-being.

The evolution of the factory system brought about the rise of the industrial world and in turn the rates of growth which enabled living standards to increase. Electricity has literally brought light into the darkness and further fuelled industrial growth. Transport costs have fallen dramatically and with this the expansion of markets both nationally and now globally. However, each technological change has had its fierce critics with people fearful of the impact and being labelled 'Luddites' or 'techno-phobes'. The term 'Luddite' has come to mean anyone who is opposed to technology. The Luddite movement had its biggest influence in the early 19th century and was concentrated in the North Midlands and particularly in Lancashire and West Yorkshire. The Luddites were mostly traditional workers in the textile industry who were suffering from the lower prices of wool and cotton that were made possible by the introduction of the new stocking frames and from the prospect of being made unemployed as capital replaced labour. Their response was to break into factories at night and attempt to smash the new machines. Their resentment of the new technologies was rooted in the fact that for them, the new technology would result simply in a loss of their livelihoods. The containerization case, discussed in Mini-Case 3.3, also showed that technological change has not been a universal benefit. The structural unemployment in the traditional ports of Liverpool and London created long term economic and social problems that are only now being overcome. On top of all this is the environmental cost of transporting these containers by sea and rail but especially by road and air. Ironically, given that many of our roads are now choked with the fumes of ever larger articulated lorries, Levinson argues that it was to avoid road congestion that the first commercial venture into containerization was developed in the US in the 1950s.

Technology is not always welcome. Not only can many technologies be used in a way to promote interests of certain groups at the expense of others but it is part and parcel of many technologies that there are costs and benefits. The fears of the Luddites echo in modern day criticism of the effect that the new technologies of communication have on the ability of businesses to outsource their call centres or production to areas of the globe where costs are cheaper. It also shows that the effects of technology cannot be seen in isolation from other forces in the external environment.

There has been a recent upsurge in this type of technological pessimism, especially in the US. Paul Krugman agrees with the view that technology will grow apace with developments in robotics and digitization but he warns that

> Smart machines may make higher GDP possible but also reduce the demand for people—including smart people. So we could be looking at a society that grows ever richer but in which all the gains in wealth accrue to whoever owns the robots.
>
> (Krugman 2012)

Technology optimists, such as Brynjolfsson and McAfee, do warn about the potential problems that can arise if public policy does not address these. They do see possible a future in which humans are involved in a 'race against the machine' and see evidence that this is indeed happening. In the US while profits are booming in the new technological industries, most people are not sharing in the gains and it is clear that that the top 1% of income earners are moving away from everyone else. In particular this is due to the rise of corporate profits at the expense of the share in total income going to the labour force.

Lynn and Longman argue that across the developed world, and in the US in particular, the reason for this lies in the increasing concentration of monopoly power especially in banking, manufacturing and retail and there is the danger that big business will lack the incentive to innovate but will strangle the competition, often by a strategy of 'innovation through acquisition' (Lynn and Longman 2010, and Lynn 2010). For Lynn and Longman, Schumpeter was right to focus on the role of entrepreneurship in the process of 'creative destruction' but he didn't pay sufficient attention to the problems that monopoly power would create.

Krugman sees that there is indeed a potential problem of big companies coming to dominate the development of technology and seeking to swallow up the more innovative small companies. He warns,

> I think our eyes have been averted from the capital/labour dimension of inequality for several reasons. It didn't seem crucial back then in the 1990s and not many people (me included) have looked up to notice that things have changed. It has echoes of old fashioned Marxism—which shouldn't be a reason to ignore facts, but too often is, and it has really uncomfortable implications. But I think we had better start paying attention to those implications.
>
> (Krugman 2012)

However, Brynjolfsson and McAfee argue that the answer will lie in the ability of businesses to create what they term a 'race with the machine strategy'. They argue that digital technologies will enable a large number of new entrepreneurs to come to the fore and that the nature of the technology means the organizational structure of businesses will change.

> While the archetypal 20th-century multinational was one of a small number of megafirms with huge fixed costs and thousands of employees, the coming century will give birth to thousands of small multinationals with low fixed costs and a small number of employees each. Both models can conceivably employ similar numbers of people overall, but the latter one is likely to be more flexible.
>
> (Brynjolfsson and McAfee 2012)

Citing Hal Varian, Chief Economist at Google, they refer to these new businesses as being 'micromultinationals', small companies employing fewer than a dozen employees but which sell worldwide and use global supplier and partner networks (Brynjolfsson and McAfee 2012).

In 2004 the editor of *Wired* magazine, Chris Anderson, predicted that in the future we would move away from a business structure dominated by the 'Head' of mainstream products and markets to a world of the 'long tail' of millions of small niche markets made possible by the cheaper production costs brought about by technology and the ease of global distribution through the Internet. He subsequently developed this idea into a book (Anderson 2004). We will explore the implications of this in Chapter 16.

Stop and Think

Are you a technological optimist or pessimist?

■ Summary

- Successful use of technology improves the performance of business both in terms of performance and productivity.

- For technological change to be successful it is a combination of entrepreneurial endeavour and factors in the external environment that are important. This is vital for national competitive advantage. For businesses to be successful there are key strategies that need to be pursued at the national level and so public policy is important. Increasingly as business goes global these strategies also need to be coordinated at the supra-national level.

- Despite the undoubted benefits to individual business profitability, the aggregate effects of technology to overall economic growth are disputed. Technological optimists are confident that the digital age will truly revolutionize business and society to benefit of all but pessimists question how extensive these changes really will be and are argue that the gains from technology will be concentrated in the hands of fewer and fewer businesses.

Case Study: Just Google it!

With its informal slogan of 'Don't be Evil', Google has rapidly become a global business giant. It was founded by two self-confessed 'geeks', Sergei Brin and Larry Page. They can be seen as examples of true genius who have reaped vast personal fortunes from their idea of meeting consumer demands for a highly effective and efficient search engine with which to navigate the billions of available web pages. Google did not invent search engines but recognized the value of having web pages ranked in terms of their importance to each individual user and the need to deliver these to the user as quickly as possible. This first innovation was called PageRank (after Larry Page).

Brin and Page met as computer engineering graduate students at Stanford University and both had a formidable grasp and recognition of the potential power of using algorithms when organizing searches. The initial development of the company owed much to the lessons that they learned as graduate students of the need for the consumer to come first in the application of information technology and their ability to use the IT infrastructure of Stanford, which was needed to process the growing number of searches that they were seeking to handle. They drew heavily on the pool of talented graduates from Stanford and other US universities. The business culture of Google has been well documented. Google does everything it can to attract the brightest staff and rewards them well. Staff are encouraged to dress casually and are provided with free healthy meals, massages, and 20% of their time to think 'blue sky' thoughts (Levy 2011).

Initially, they had no idea of how to 'monetize' their unique approach to organizing web searches. They were determined that they would not allow page selections to be determined by how much money advertisers would be prepared to pay. Other search engines placed search results in a ranking order dependent on advertising income offered for these sites. Their overriding ambition was to put the consumer first in the belief that this would produce the most effective searches.

Auletta charts how the founders only very slowly and with all sorts of reservations about being infected by the values of traditional money making business models, began to recognize that there was a need for strategic business expertise to work together with the creative engineering driving force of Google and in 2001 Eric Schmidt was appointed as CEO to help develop the business strategy for the business (Auletta 2010).

The development of their two major income earners 'Adwords' and 'Adsense' have meant that Google has now become a dominant force in commanding huge revenues from advertising revenue and a huge competitive threat to the existing advertising media companies. In contrast to previous methods of advertising on the Internet, whereby advertisers simply paid for the placement of an advert on a particular site and had no real idea if users were actually clicking on the link to view content, Google introduced three innovations. First, with Adwords, Google introduced the technology to measure how many times a particular link was clicked on and allows advertisers to access that information directly. Secondly, advertisers bid for the right to have their ads placed on the search results generated by particular key words. Rankings on the list of adverts that appear depend on the bids. Google makes its revenues from the advertisers every time users click on a link. Finally, Brin and Page, using advice gleaned from

the newspaper industry, decided that the adverts appearing on result pages would be grouped together, away from the results of the searches themselves. Adsense operates as an effective partnership between website designers, advertisers and Google. Using Google as an intermediary, web designers can conduct auctions between advertisers to carry links on their sites. They then share the revenue generated with Google. Google's increasing dominance in Internet advertising revenue was reinforced by its 2007 acquisition of Double-Click, which had been the leading digital marketing company up to that point.

In an interview in 2008, Schmidt argued that the main implication for businesses of the Internet was that it would dramatically alter the way products are sold, that change would be faster as a result of network effects and that internally organizational structures too would become networked and move away from separate departments and divisions controlled from the top. In terms of global expansion he foresaw the problems of a global strategy coming up against different regulatory requirements and the need for Google to have legal expertise in each of its national markets. While accepting that there was a lot of energy and potential in 'the long tail' as envisaged by Anderson (see Looking ahead section), he was adamant that the real revenue potential of the Internet lay in 'the Head'. He said, '[a]nd, in fact, it's probable that the Internet will lead to larger blockbusters and more concentration of brands' (Manyika 2008).

Schmidt's view was that, in fact, the Business of the Internet had now become dominated by the big four companies of Google, Apple, Amazon and Facebook. But despite its ever rising revenues and profits (Google's total revenue was over $50 billion in 2012) Google faces some challenges not least of which stems the overwhelming reliance of its revenues and profits coming from advertising revenues. In 2012 95% of its revenues came from advertising revenue (Google 2013a).

It has been increasingly embroiled in a number of legal and regulatory issues. Google's main unique selling point is on search and the ability to tailor adverts to the end user and so Google is keen to make use of the vast amount of personal information that people seem willing to post up on the Internet. This has raised many privacy concerns and attracted the attention of the regulators. In terms of global expansion Google was forced to pull out of mainland China and relocate to Hong Kong as a result of the Chinese government's desire to censor search results. In the US and Europe there have been accusations that Google is downgrading the services of its competitors on its search engine and there have been a number of disputes over patent infringements.

As competition for attracting advertising revenues increases, the income per click has been falling and so Google needs to continually try to increase the amount of searches occurring. Furthermore the increasing use of smart phones to access the Internet has reduced the amount of clicks as mobile users are less likely to click on adverts.

As a result of these potential pressures Google has not been slow to diversify its business by a process of acquisitions of venture capital companies for example, YouTube in 2006. Its Android operating system is expanding fast and in 2011 it made its largest acquisition when it took over Motorola. At the heart of its strategy though is a constant search for developing new technologies that will improve the ability of people to search the Internet. As well as this it continues to develop a range of new products such as Gmail, its web browser, Google Chrome, its own social networking service, Google+ launched in 2011 and in 2013 it is due to launch Google Glass which will be the first wearable computer (Google 2013b).

Questions

1. What have been the main technological developments that have enabled Google to grow so dramatically?

2. How has Google developed such a successful technology strategy?

3. What features within the external environment have been necessary to enable Google to develop in the way in which it has?

4. What criticisms have been voiced about some aspects of the activities of Google?

5. What are the potential threats to Google's continued growth?

Review and discussion questions

1. How does technology potentially increase productivity and allow a business to establish competitive advantage?

2. What are the main conditions in the external national business environment that it is argued are necessary for technological change to increase economic growth?

3. Explain what is meant by the 'Productivity Paradox' in the context of the impact of technology and critically examine the competing views that seek to explain this

4. What are the main general disadvantages associated with technological change?

5. What are going to be the main technological advances in the future?

Assignments

1. Research and then outline the main technological changes that have allowed supermarkets to become the dominant players in the grocery industry in the past fifty years. What have been the effects of these changes on the producers and other stakeholders during this time? On balance is the global expansion of supermarkets inevitable and is this something that everyone should welcome?

2. Prepare a market evaluation report which explains both the rise of one of the following global technology companies: Google, Apple, Amazon or Facebook and critically examines the way in which the technological environment has impacted on and been influenced by your chosen company.

Further reading

Brynjolfsson, E. and McAfee, A. (2011) *Race Against the Machine: How the Digital Revolution is Accelerating Innovation, Driving Productivity and Irreversibly Transforming Employment and the Economy* (Lexington, MA: Digital Frontier Press). *The authors argue that technological progress will accelerate and that this has profound implications for how business and society need to respond.*

Lanier, J. (2013) *Who Owns the Future* (London: Allen Lane). *Lanier argues that unless we change the way in which we*

value the information that we give up for free, the benefits of the data revolution will all accrue to a concentrated minority of businesses, and that wealth will become concentrated while technology will vastly increase the amount of people who are unemployed.

Schmidt, E. and Cohen, J. (2013) *The New Digital Age: Reshaping the Future of People, Nations and Business* (New York: Alfred A. Knopf). *Written by the former CEO of Google and an eminent social scientist, this book profiles the likely* interconnections between the physical and virtual worlds and what needs to be done if we are to take full advantage of the new digital technologies being developed.

Mayer-Schönberger, V. and Cukier, K. (2013) *Big Data: A Revolution That Will Transform How We Live, Work and*

Think (London: John Murray). *This book predicts how businesses, government, and individuals will be able to use data to improve all aspects of our lives.*

online resource centre

Test your understanding of this chapter with online questions and answers, explore the subject further through web exercises, and use the web links to provide a quick resource for further research. Go to the Online Resource Centre at <www.oxfordtextbooks.co.uk/orc/wetherly_otter/2>

Useful websites

These websites profile the latest debates and trends in technology:
<www.bbc.co.uk/technology>
<http://www.guardian.co.uk/business/technology>

References

Acemoglu, D. (2012) 'The world our grandchildren will inherit: the rights revolution and beyond' in Palacios-Huerta, I. (2012) *Economic Possibilities for Our Grandchildren* (MIT Press).

Acemoglu, D. and Robinson, J. A. (2012) *Why Nations Fail: The Origins of Power, Prosperity and Poverty* (New York: Crown Publishers).

Anderson (2004) 'The Long Tail', *Wired Magazine*, Issue 12.10, Conde Nast Digital (accessed on 15 March 2013) <www.wired/archive/12.10/tail.html> or see <http://changethis.com/manifesto/10.LongTail/pdf/10.LongTail.pdf>

Auletta, K. (2010) *Googled: The End of the World As We Know It* (London: Penguin).

Base of the Pyramid Protocol (2006) 'Project Overview' (accessed May 12 2013) <www.bop-protocol.org/about>

BBC News Business (2013) 'EU to investigate Chinese Solar panel subsidies' (accessed at <www.bbc.co.uk/news/business-20249003>

Brynjolfsson, E. (1993) 'The Productivity Paradox of IT', *Communications of the ACM* 36 (12) pp. 7-77.

Brynjolffson, E. and Hitt, L. (1998) 'Beyond the Productivity Paradox' *Communications of the ACM* 41(8) pp. 49-55.

Brynjolfsson, E. (2011) 'ICT, innovation and the e-economy', *EIB Papers*, ISSN 0257-7755, Vol. 16, Iss. 2, pp. 60-76 (accessed on 15 March 2013) <http://hdl.handle.net/10419/54668>

Brynjolfsson, E. and McAfee, A. (2011) *Race Against the Machine: How the Digital Revolution is Accelerating Innovation, Driving Productivity and Irreversibly Transforming Employment and the Economy* (Lexington, Massachusetts: Digital Frontier Press).

Brynjolfsson, E. and McAfee, A. (2012) *Research Brief Race Against the Machine: How the Digital Revolution is Accelerating*

Innovation, Driving Productivity and Irreversibly Transforming Employment and the Economy, MIT Sloan Management (accessed on May 14 2013 <www.ebusiness.mit.edu/research/Briefs/Brynjolfsson_McAfee_Race_Against_the_Machine.pdf>

Chang, Ha Joon (2011) *23 Myths of Capitalism* (London: Penguin).

Cowen, T. (2011) *The Great Stagnation: How America Ate All the Low-Hanging Fruit of Modern History, Got Sick and Will (eventually) Feel Better* (New York: Dutton).

De Kare Silver, M. (2011) *e-shock 2020: How the Digital Technology Revolution is Changing Business and All Our Lives* (Basingstoke: Palgrave Macmillan).

Engels, F. (1989) *The Condition of the English Working Class*, edited by Kiernan, V. G. (London: Penguin).

Freeman, C. and Louça, F. (2002) *As Time Goes By: From the Industrial Revolutions to the Information Revolution* (Oxford: Oxford University Press).

Friedman, T. (2007) *The World is Flat* (London: Penguin).

Google (2013a) *2013 Financial Tables, Google Investor Relations* (accessed 14 May 2013) <http://investor.google.com/financial/tables.html>

Google (2013b) 'Google's Mission is to Organize the World's Information and make it Universally Accessible and Useful' (accessed 14 May 2013) <http://www.google.com/about/company/>

Gordon, R. J. (2013) 'Is US Economic Growth Over? Faltering Innovation Confronts the Six Headwinds' (accessed 2 March 2013) <www.cepr.org/pubs/PolicyInsights/policyInsight63.pdf>

Hart, S. L. (2010) *Capitalism at the Crossroads: Aligning Business, Earth and Humanity* (New Jersey: Pearson).

Intel (2013) 'Moore's Law Inspires Intel Innovation' (accessed 13 May 2013) <www.intel.com/content/www/us/en/silicon-innovations/moores-law-technology.html>.

Jensen, R. (2007) 'The Digital Provide: Information Technology and Welfare in the South Indian Fisheries Sector', *Quarterly Journal of Economics* Vol CXXII, Issue 3, pp. 879-924.

Jones, B. F. (2012) 'The Burden of Knowledge and the Death of Renaissance Man: Is Innovation Getting Harder?', *The Review of Economic Studies* Vol 76, Issue 1, pp. 283-317.

Krugman, P. (2012) 'Is Growth Over? The Conscience of A Liberal', *New York Times* 26 December 2012 (accessed on March 15 2013) <http://krugmanblogs.nytimes.com/2012/12/26/is-growth-over/>

Kurzweil, R. (2000) *The Age of Spiritual Machines* (London: Penguin).

Landes, D. (1998) *The Wealth and Poverty and Nations* (London: Abacus).

Lacey, S. (2011) 'How China Dominates Solar Power', *Guardian Environment Network* (accessed May 13 2013) <http://www.guardian.co.uk/environment/2011/sep/12/how-china-dominates-solar-power>

Levinson, M. (2006) *The Box—How the Shipping Container Made the World Smaller and the World Economy Bigger* (Oxford: Princeton University Press).

Levy, S. (2011) *In the Plex: How Google Thinks, Works and Shapes Our Lives* (New York: Simon & Schuster).

Lynn, B. C. and Longman, P. (2010) 'Who Broke America's Jobs Machine?', *Washington Monthly* March/April 2010 (Accessed 15 March 2013) <http://www.washingtonmonthly.com/features/2010/1003.lynn-longman.html>

Lynn, B. C. (2010) *Cornered: The New Monopoly Capitalism and the Economics of Destruction* (New Jersey: John Wiley and Sons).

Ma, W. (2013) 'China Plans to Ramp Up Solar Power Capacity', *Wall Street Journal* 8 January 2013 (accessed 10 March 2013) <online.wsj.com/article/SB10001424127887323706704578229570073217326.html>

Manyika, J. (2008) 'Google's view on the Future of Business: An Interview with CEO Eric Schmidt', *McKinsey Quarterly* September 2008 (accessed 12 May 2013) <http://www.mckinseyquarterly.com/Business_Technology/BT_Strategy/Googles_view_on_the_future_of_business_An_interview_with_CEO_Eric_Schmidt_2229>

Neate, R. (2013) 'Giants of the Sea Force Ports to Grow', *The Guardian* 7 March 2013, p. 33.

ONS (2011) *Retail Sales*, Office for National Statistics (accessed March 4 2013) <www.ons.gov.uk/ons/rel/rsi/retail-sales/index.html>

Portas, M. (2011) 'The Portas Review: an Independent Review into the future of our High Streets' (accessed 4 March 2013) <www.maryportas.com/wp-content-uploads/The_Portas_Review.pdf>

Porter, M. E. (1985) *Competitive Advantage—Creating and Sustaining Superior Performance* (London: Collier Macmillan).

Porter, M. E. (1998) *Competitive Advantage of Nations* (New York: Free Press).

Prahalad, C. K. (2010) *The Fortune at the Bottom of the Pyramid* (New Jersey: Pearson).

Schumpeter, J. (1942) *Capitalism, Socialism and Democracy* (New York: Harper Row).

Simms (2007) *Tescopoly: How one Shop came out on Top and Why it Matters* (London: Constable).

Smith, A. (1976) [1776] *An Inquiry into the Nature and Causes of the Wealth of Nations* (Chicago: University of Chicago Press).

Solow, A. (1987) 'We'd Better Watch Out', *New York Times Book Review* 12 July 1987, p. 36.

Stressman, P. (1997) *The Squandered Computer* (New Caanan, CT: Information Economics Press).

The Economist (2013) 'The Great Innovation Debate' (accessed 12 March 2013) <www.economist.com/news/leaders/21569393-fears-innovation-slowing-are-exaggerated-governments-need-help-it-along-great>

Vise, D. A. and Malseed, M. (2008) *The Google Story—For Google's 10th Birthday* (New York: Delacorte Press).

Virmani, P. (2012) 'Co-operatives not Multinational Supermarkets best for Farmers in India', *Guardian Poverty Matters Blog* 21 December 2012 (accessed on March 10 2013) <www.guardian.co.uk/globaldevelopment/poverty-matters/2012/dec/21/cooperatives-multinationals-supermarkets-farmers-india>

employment rights for shares in a company. In our opinion, these proposals represent an unjustified attack on employment rights. The government argues these measures will provide increased flexibility for businesses and give 'employee owners' an increased stake in their company. In practice, the proposals will strip employees of basic workplace rights. Employee will lose out on protection from unfair dismissal and the rights to redundancy pay, making it easier and cheaper for employers to sack them. ... These provisions flout the basic principle that it should not be possible to contract out of basic statutory rights, even in return for money. Since the 1970s, UK employment legislation has included provisions preventing the contracting out of rights. These provisions were included in the legislation to reflect the imbalance of power which exists between employers and employees (TUC 2012).

Question

Is George Osborne right to claim that 'Owners, workers, and the taxman [are] all in it together'?

■ Creating the 'best place to do business'

》 VALUES 》 INTERACTION In a speech to the annual conference of the Confederation of British Industry in 2011, Prime Minister David Cameron declared:

> If we are to build a new model of growth, we need to give a massive boost to enterprise, entrepreneurship and business creation. Put simply Britain must become one of the best places to do business on the planet. That's why we are working with business to track down pointless or harmful red tape that holds business back – sector by sector – and getting rid of it. That's why we are cutting the time it takes to set up a business, creating the most competitive corporate tax regime in the G20 and cutting corporation tax to 23 per cent – the lowest in the G7.
>
> (Cameron 2011)

This ambition to make the country the best place to do business has been expressed many times by politicians of differing political persuasions. Barack Obama, President of the United States, declared in his 2011 State of Union Address:

> We know what it takes to compete for the jobs and industries of our time. We need to out-innovate, out-educate, and out-build the rest of the world. We have to make America the best place on Earth to do business. We need to take responsibility for our deficit and reform our government. That's how our people will prosper. That's how we'll win the future.
>
> (Obama 2011)

Similarly, Gordon Brown, as Chancellor of the Exchequer in the Labour government in 2005, spoke at a conference of business leaders about an 'opportunity to create a consensus on tax as well as stability to make Britain the best place to do business' (in Tempest 2005).

It seems clear that there is a consensus among governments that one of their prime responsibilities is to make their country 'the best place to do business', meaning creating the best environment for private sector businesses to flourish. In other words, governments are keen to present themselves as friends of business. This agreement on the role of government may seem unremarkable as it reflects a broad political consensus about the desirability of the market system as a way of organizing economic life that is a feature of our times and has held together despite cracks caused by the financial crisis and its recessionary aftermath.

》 SPATIAL LEVEL Of course it is logically impossible for all governments to succeed in making their own country the best place for business, and Obama's statement expresses the perception that in a globalizing world governments are in competition with each other and, more specifically, that America's position as the world's leading economy cannot be taken for granted. America, he says, has to compete with the rest of the world through, for example, achieving better educational outcomes that will feed into economic advantage. This sense of global competition between nations was also expressed, in very stark terms, by David Cameron in his speech as leader of the Conservative Party to its 2012 annual conference.

> All of my adult life, whatever the difficulties, the British people have at least been confident about one thing. We have thought we can pay our way. That we can earn our living as a major industrial country—and we will always remain one. It has fallen to us to say—we cannot assume that any longer. Unless we act, unless we take difficult, painful decisions, unless we show determination and imagination, Britain may not be in the future what it has been in the past. Because the truth is this. We are in a global race today. And that means an hour of reckoning for countries like ours. Sink or swim. Do or decline. [Thus it is the responsibility of government to set out] how we compete and thrive in this world—how we can make sure in this century, like the ones before, Britain is on the rise. Nothing matters more. Every battle we fight, every plan we make, every decision we take is to achieve that end—Britain on the rise.

(Cameron 2012)

Whether Cameron's language exaggerates the threat to Britain is debatable, and we will see in the chapter on globalization that there are competing views of its nature and implications (Chapter 10). But for the moment we can see how governments think about their role in supporting business in the context of a 'global race'. It is clear that governments seek to support business not only because it is in the interests of business for them to do so but also because business success is seen as good for society as a whole. Creating a favourable business environment is imperative in order to generate growth and jobs and because '[t]hat's how our people will prosper' (Obama). And the perceived success of governments in achieving prosperity is a key factor in determining whether the people, as voters, will continue to support them and return them to power. Thus, there is a relationship of interdependence between government and business.

However, the problem for governments is not only that they cannot all win the 'global race' but that there is disagreement about how to be the best place to do business, and how to balance this goal with other responsibilities of government. Does being the best place to do business mean that governments should do more or that they should do less? Or, more of some things and less of others? A difference of approach is apparent in the words of Cameron and Obama: Cameron suggests that government should do less in the way of regulation ('red tape') and taxation of business, whereas Obama suggests a more active role for government in terms of innovation, education and building (e.g. investing in transport infrastructure). Even though supporting business can lead to greater prosperity that benefits society, specific measures to support business can conflict with the interests and values of other groups. For example, Cameron's call for deregulation is reflected in Osborne's proposal to remove employers' duties in relation to unfair dismissal but, as we have seen, critics argue that employee protection measures are too important to be surrendered for business advantage.

■ The interdependence of business and government

》 INTERACTION In order to think about how government might act to create a favourable environment for business it is useful to set out the types of relationship that are possible. Government involvement in economic life is a feature of all capitalist economies, though its precise nature and scope vary considerably between different societies. Politics and business are not separate but *interdependent*—in some ways business depends on government, and government in some ways depends on business. In all capitalist or market-based economies

However, despite the 'global race', the political environment of business varies between countries. For example, in 2013 there was great variation in corporation tax rates among the 34 OECD member countries, ranging from a low of 12.5% in Ireland to a high of 39% in the United States (reputedly the home of 'free enterprise'). The rate was 30% or higher in eight countries, including France and Germany (OECD Tax Database). To understand the political environment in a globalizing world therefore requires knowing something about different types of political system and their implications for business. If we were to look closely at political systems in different countries we would find that they differ in many details and so to some extent each country is unique. However, we can classify political systems into broad types to allow us to see the most important differences and group countries with similar political systems together. One of the reasons for doing this is that it allows us to think about which is the best type of political system, particularly in terms of business, but more generally in relation to the whole society and principles of 'good governance'. What's good for business might not always be good for society, and vice-versa, so evaluating good governance is not straightforward. A basic distinction can be made between **liberal democracies** such as the UK and **non-democratic** systems.

Liberal democracy

Government exercises a unique form of power—to make and enforce the rules under which we live—and good governance matters to all members of society. Among western capitalist societies some variant of **liberal democracy** has become the predominant framework governing who rules and the law-making process. A liberal democracy is a form of government that combines democratic procedures with forms of individual freedom and equality that have been championed in the liberal political tradition, hence 'liberal + democratic'. Liberalism sees **individual freedom** as the most important value and the hallmark of a good society, and holds that ensuring freedom is one of the primary purposes of government. This means protecting people from each other so that they can go about their daily business and live their lives as they choose, for example protecting individuals from theft or violence. But in the liberal view it also means that government has to be kept in check so that it does not interfere in people's lives more than is necessary. This certainly means preventing government using its power in a manner that is oppressive, but some liberals have also argued more generally for government to play a minimal role in economic and social life.

Historically, two of the most important ways of keeping government in check in western societies have been by creating a framework of individual rights, such as freedom of speech, and through the principle of the **rule of law**. The rule of law means that all citizens are equal before the law and have to obey it, but also that the actions of government must be lawful. For this reason the 'rule of law' is often contrasted with the 'rule of men' since state officials can only act within their lawful powers, and so the rule of law prevents arbitrary government.

A third way of keeping government in check is through democracy. The basic principle of democracy is 'rule by the people' or popular sovereignty, meaning that political power is in the hands of the people as a whole. In liberal democracies the people rule indirectly by electing representatives to act on their behalf (hence the term representative democracy). The basic features of a democracy include the following:

- universal suffrage (all adults have the right to vote, thus involving formal political equality)
- regular elections (the UK now has fixed-term parliaments of five years)

- choice of candidates (usually standing for election as members of a political party in a multi-party system, e.g. as a Conservative or Labour candidate)
- civil liberties or rights (such as freedom of speech), media organizations that are independent from government, and a culture that accepts diversity of lifestyles, values and beliefs.

Having the right to vote is of little value unless elections are held at regular intervals and voters can choose between candidates offering alternative policies or programmes for government. Thus, political parties campaign on the basis of competing proposals for running the country, with prominence given to policies dealing with business and the economy. Civil liberties or rights, such as freedom of speech and association, are important conditions for political participation as they enable the free exchange of ideas through media organizations that are independent of government and through expanding 'social media', and allow people to criticize the government (or business) and engage in protest.

In essence democracy is supposed to ensure good government because the people choose their law-makers. If the current set of law-makers are doing a bad job—such as mismanaging the economy—democracy provides a peaceful and orderly mechanism (elections) for replacing them with a different set. Of course, this does not mean that democratic politics always produces especially competent governments with high public approval ratings. On the contrary, opinion surveys often reveal low, or negative, approval ratings for politicians in the UK. It seems that people are in favour of the idea of democracy but sceptical or even cynical about the actual practice of democratic politics.

Variants of liberal democracy

Today western societies are characterized by a combination of capitalist economic system and liberal democratic political system, as exemplified by the member states of the EU.

In some important ways there is a good 'fit' between capitalism and liberal democracy. The liberal commitment to freedom and rights can be seen as embodied in a capitalist economy through property rights which are a foundation of private enterprise, and freedoms to set up a business and to buy and sell. Indeed, supporters of free markets often express their arguments in terms of freedom: a market is portrayed as a system of voluntary exchanges into which each party—buyer and seller—enters freely on the basis of a calculation of their own self-interest. This view is often linked to the argument that government should play a minimal role in markets and leave people free to make decisions for themselves as far as possible. Democracy can be a good fit for capitalism in so far as it is associated with the rule of law, political stability, effective government, and peaceful transfers of power between governments through elections, but also because business is able to have an effective political voice.

However, operating in a liberal democracy also involves challenges for business because it allows for an ongoing process of competition between rival views and interests and therefore can create uncertainty about the policy environment. Policy victories under one government can be overturned under the next. Much then depends on whether business can rely on government being responsive to its interests and avoiding policies that it regards as unfavourable. It can be argued that business can generally rely on this responsiveness because there is a high level of political consensus about the desirability of the market system, and because business is able to exercise an influence over government that is unrivalled by other groups in society (Chapter 11). Indeed it can be argued that there is a tension between capitalism and cannot be handled effectively at a national level. In this way governance also operates at an international scale—across borders. Multi-level governance is an aspect of the globalizing world and an increasingly important dimension of the business environment.

The idea of **multi-level governance** points to the way political decisions are made at a variety of levels or spatial scales:

- sub-national, i.e. a level of political authority below or within the nation-state (e.g. local government)
- national, i.e. the nation-state
- supra-national, i.e. a level of political authority above the nation-state, of which the EU is the most important example.

In all democratic states the division of political power between national and sub-national (local and regional) tiers is an important question, and important aspects of business and economic development policy can be decided at the sub-national level, reflecting local needs and priorities. Britain is distinctive in its tradition of highly centralized government and relatively weak local government. That tradition was criticized in Lord Heseltine's report *No Stone Unturned* which makes the case for 'a major rebalancing of responsibilities for economic development between central and local government' and sets out proposals to enhance the economic potential of England's regions and cities (Department for Business, Innovation & Skills 2013). In its response to the review the government announced the creation of a growth fund from 2015 which local enterprise partnerships (LEPs) would be able to bid for (BBC 2013a, Department for Business, Innovation & Skills 2013). 'LEPs are partnerships between local authorities and businesses. They decide what the priorities should be for investment in roads, buildings and facilities in the area' (Department for Communities and Local Government 2013).

A major revision to Britain's centralized system of government has been the creation of a Scottish Parliament and Welsh Assembly with limited legislative powers, and the achievement of devolved government in Northern Ireland. The UK and Scottish governments agreed to hold a referendum of the Scottish people on full independence for Scotland in 2014. This would be a significant change in the business environment, raising questions about the economic prospects of an independent Scotland and the management of economic policy. For example, George Osborne raised doubts about whether an independent Scotland would be able to retain sterling as its currency (BBC 2013b).

Supra-national governance—the European Union

The most important example of supra-national governance is the European Union (EU). UK membership of the EU represents a substantial revision of parliamentary sovereignty, for EU law takes precedence over national law. In other words, EU law can be seen as the supreme law of the UK (and all other member states).

> The Community constitutes a new legal order for whose benefit the states have limited their sovereign rights, albeit within limited fields, and the subjects of which comprise not only the member states, but also their nationals.
>
> (Ruling of the European Court 1963, in Dearlove and Saunders 2000, p. 717)

The 'limited fields' are those governed by EU treaty—in other areas member states retain their ability to make their own laws (their 'sovereign rights'). Some commentators see this legal order as involving a straightforward loss of sovereignty, but others see it as a pooling or sharing of sovereignty because the EU is a form of inter-governmentalism through which each member participates in developing laws by which all are bound (see Chapter 13).

Reluctant Europeans?

▶ **STAKEHOLDERS** Britain is often seen as a 'reluctant European', joining late (1973) and often resisting closer integration (e.g. not joining the single currency). British debate on EU membership has been marked by a strong strain of 'Euro-scepticism'. This scepticism has often reflected economic concerns—to maintain our own (felt to be superior) 'model of capitalism' and to fit economic policies to the requirements of the national economy. Yet the development of the EU has been driven largely by economic considerations, and Britain's entry reflected a desire to share the economic benefits. Chief among these are the gains in efficiency, competitiveness, and growth that flow from the creation of a single market. By removing barriers to cross-border investment, trade and migration businesses can shift activities to the most advantageous locations and have unfettered access to a vastly expanded market on a 'level playing field', and competitive pressures will drive up efficiency. For this reason the EU can be viewed as pro-market, but some commentators have also seen in the EU the opportunity for more effective regulation of business in order to afford stronger protections to other stakeholders such as employees and consumers (see Chapter 13).

In the 2010 general election in the UK the 'Euro-scepticism' of the Conservatives was one of the principal dividing lines with the other main parties, and the Conservative Prime Minister, David Cameron, subsequently pledged to renegotiate the terms of Britain's membership of the EU and hold an in–out referendum on the basis of the new settlement if the Conservatives were to win the general election in 2015. However, Cameron emphasized his preference for Britain to remain a member of the EU, not least for the economic benefits derived from the single market. In 2013 Cameron advocated an EU-US trade agreement which would, he argued, bring substantial benefits to the UK (BBC 2013). The benefit of EU membership in this case is that a trade agreement can be negotiated by the EU as a whole whereas it would be difficult for the UK to negotiate effectively on its own. Representing the views of business, the CBI has also endorsed Britain's continuing membership of the EU, arguing: 'It's essential we stay at the table to bang the drum for businesses and defend our national interest'. Rejecting the argument for withdrawal the CBI stated: 'Businesses don't want the baby thrown out with the bathwater—not with 50% of our exports heading to Europe'. Advocating a trade agreement with the US, the CBI argued: 'we pack a bigger punch in securing trade deals inside the EU than outside. The US wants the big prize—access to a market of 500 million customers across the EU, not just 60 million on our own shores. So the best way of getting the right deal for the UK is on an EU-wide basis. The EU must be the launchpad for UK business to trade with the rest of the world, carving out a new global role for ourselves' (CBI 2012a).

▓ **Looking ahead**

The political environment in the UK and Europe will continue to be dominated by the aftermath of the financial crisis and economic recession and the politics of 'austerity'. There is likely to be a resumption of economic growth in the UK, though it is difficult to predict how quickly the economy will 'bounce back'. It will take a number of years for national output, and therefore living standards, to get back to the pre-crisis level.

The prospects for growth will depend on whether the UK government continues on its path of deficit reduction through public spending cuts. This has been the central question in British politics since 2010 and will continue to be at the top of the agenda. In 2013 the government was resisting calls from the IMF and others to moderate the austerity programme. Much will depend on the outcome of the 2015 general election. If the Labour party is returned to government it might alter policy on the basis of its consistent criticism that the pace of deficit reduction has been 'too fast'. Whichever party is in power, the objective of deficit reduction will act as a constraint on public spending. However, the debate about the role of government in a market system will continue at the heart of politics. How can the best environment for business be created, balancing with other interests and goals? And what is the most desirable mix of tax, spending, and regulation?

The political environment of business in Britain could be fundamentally altered by the resolution of two constitutional questions: the future of the union with Scotland, and Britain's relationship with the EU. A referendum on Scottish independence will take place in 2014. If a Conservative government is returned in 2015 renegotiation of the terms of Britain's membership of the EU has been promised, to be followed by an in–out referendum by 2017.

At a global level, the business environment is changing as a result of democratic and market reforms and rapid economic growth in some countries and regions, notably the BRIC nations. The western model of a capitalist economy and democratic government is becoming more prevalent, a new global balance of economic power is emerging, and a new pattern of interdependence between nations through trade and investment is developing.

Because the world is divided into nation-states, each will seek to pursue its own national interest in a 'global race', particularly by trying to create favourable conditions for business. However, countries will also seek to cooperate to solve common problems and achieve mutual benefits. For example, an important change in the business environment could result from progress in EU-US trade negotiations.

■ Summary

- Politics is concerned with decisions and choices that affect the whole society: determining the rules under which we live together and creating a 'good society'.

- Politics is a key element of the business environment. There is interdependence between business and government. One of the key questions in political debate concerns the nature and responsibilities of business and the type of capitalist economy we want to live in. In other words, business is politically controversial.

- The UK political system is a liberal democracy based on the principle of rule by the people. Government exercises a unique form of power in society—to make and enforce rules. However, rule is no longer the main function of modern states—they have become responsible for a range of public services and steering social and economic development.

- The UK has a combination of a democratic political system with a market or capitalist economy. On a global scale these economic and political forms have become more prevalent in recent decades. However, the world is characterized by great disparities in economic development and democratization. There is a close relationship between level of development and democracy: all of the large high income OECD countries are democracies (either 'full' or 'flawed'), and almost all full democracies are high income OECD countries.

- Politics is not conducted just at a national level but is characterized by multi-level governance. The EU is the most important example of supra-national politics in the modern world.

Case Study: The rise (and fall?) of big government

Arguments for and against 'big government', and the ways in which they have been embodied in economic and social policies, have shaped the world we live in today and the political choices we now face. We can identify both a broad pattern of development and change at an international level and important differences between countries in how the pattern has taken shape.

- *Growth of the state*. If the market and private enterprise, left to their own devices, cannot produce the outcomes that society views as desirable, the principal means to rectify these failings is through government action of some kind. Thus, political debate centres on the desirable balance or mix between the market and the state. In the 20th century this debate shifted from one side to the other on two occasions, as exemplified by the British experience. In broad terms the early part of the century was characterized by the dominance of free market and minimal government ideas. Although the beginnings of the growth of the state can be traced to the early years of the century, the decisive shift occurred after the Second World War with the expansion of government spending and public sector employment associated particularly with the **welfare state**. In the post-war years, particularly the 1950s and 1960s, the commitment to 'big government' was the basis of political consensus under both Labour and Conservative governments in the UK. However, this consensus fragmented in the 1970s under the strain of economic difficulties and was firmly rejected in the 1980s and 1990s by Conservative governments which defined their central purpose in terms of 'rolling back the state'. It can be argued that this period established a new consensus so that free market ideas still dominate political debate and government policy today. Yet , looked at as a whole, the growth of the state still appears as a striking transformation during the 20th century: public spending in the UK, for example, has remained around the post-war 'big state' level despite the attempts to 'roll back' the state. However, the austerity programme of the coalition government involves unprecedented reductions in public spending and can be seen as a renewal of the 'small government' agenda.

- *Models of capitalism*. The growth of the state in the 20th century was not confined to Britain but was, to varying degrees, an international phenomenon among the advanced capitalist economies. Britain is sometimes seen as an originator and international leader of welfare state reforms, but in fact the involvement of the state in the provision of welfare services has been developed much further in other European societies, notably Sweden. The general picture though is of a general growth of the state but with variation between countries

in the level of public spending and in the specific pattern of institutions and policies developed. This variance in the relationship between state and society, and more specifically in the economic role of the state, has given rise to the identification of distinct 'models' of capitalism.

We can gain a clearer idea of the historical and comparative variance in the role of government by looking first at the UK experience in a little more detail and then placing the UK in an international context. In essence, the growth of the state in the post-war years reflected the acceptance by governments of a wider range of responsibilities in relation to social and economic problems and, by the same token, a belief that these problems could not be resolved by leaving things to the market. The inability of the market to produce socially desirable outcomes is referred to as 'market failure'. While the market would remain the principal mechanism for allocating resources and most economic activity would remain in the private sector, a 'good society' required an extensive programme of reforms and an expanded public sector. These reforms can be seen as designed to create a different kind, or model, of capitalism. In the UK what is sometimes referred to as the **Keynesian welfare consensus** comprised the following elements:

- Keynesian macroeconomic policy, to provide economic stability (i.e. to counter the cycle of boom and recession) and ensure 'full employment'.

- Provision by government of a range of public services broadly concerned with ensuring the welfare of citizens, including health, education, and income maintenance (e.g. cash benefits for people who are unemployed, sick or retired)—the 'welfare state'

- Public ownership (nationalization) of some basic industries, such as transport and energy, establishing a 'mixed economy' of private and public sectors.

- Acceptance of the legitimate role of trade unions as stakeholders in bargaining with employers and negotiating with government.

- The use of law to regulate business decisions and behaviour, often with the aim of protecting the interests of other groups in society such as consumers and employees.

During the 1980s this consensus came under attack from a **neoliberal** perspective that was sceptical of government as a force for good, and aimed to 'roll back' the state (i.e. reduce its size). This anti-statist approach was justified in terms of the idea that reducing the role of government would restore greater freedom for individuals, but the main emphasis was on disengaging the state from the economy, creating a free market and reducing state interference in business. The idea of 'government failure' referred to the idea that interference in the market, however well-intentioned, often does not work and undermines economic performance—government is the problem, not the solution. In a reversal of the post-war consensus the main elements of the neoliberal approach were:

- A switch from Keynesian policy to monetarism, renouncing full employment as a responsibility of government in favour of a focus on the control of inflation through monetary policy (money supply and interest rates).

- A critique of the commitment to high public spending and taxation necessitated by the welfare state. In the neoliberal view taxation should be minimized so that people can decide for themselves how to spend their own money, as a key aspect of individual freedom, but also to reduce the tax 'burden' on business. Public services were regarded as inherently inefficient and unresponsive to users because of the absence of competition and the profit motive, and therefore attempts were made to improve efficiency by introducing competitive pressures and choice, or through privatization. Welfare payments to the unemployed were seen as undermining self-reliance and creating a culture of 'dependency' (where claimants become dependent on benefits and become 'scroungers').

- Privatization of the publicly owned industries, again based on the argument that they were poorly managed in the public sector and that the profit motive would drive improvements in efficiency and customer responsiveness.

- A legislative attack on trade union rights and 'immunities' in the workplace on the grounds that trade unions were too powerful and had become an obstacle to businesses improving their competitiveness. The aim was to restore the 'right to manage'.

- An emphasis on deregulation, seeking to reduce the costs of compliance (e.g. in terms of managerial attention and loss of flexibility) imposed on business by regulatory requirements.

Thus, in the second half of the last century the UK has implemented experiments with two quite distinct models of capitalism, involving different ideas about the relationship between the state and the market in a good society.

UK public spending as a share of national income: historical and comparative perspective

Public spending as a share of GDP fluctuates due to changes in government spending plans and the rate of growth of GDP (the economic cycle). Over the sixty year period from the late 1940s to the late 2000s spending by the public sector in the UK increased in real terms at an average annual rate of 3.4% (Institute for Fiscal Studies 2009). Public spending peaked at 47.4% of national income in 2009/10 and is projected to fall to 39.5% by 2017/18 under the government's austerity programme involving an unprecedented reduction of public spending in real terms (Institute for Fiscal Studies 2013). However, 39.5% will be a reversion to the norm and the same share of GDP as in 2003/4. Within that total, Figure 4.1 shows the composition of public spending and how this is projected to have changed between 2003/4 and 2017/18.

In international terms the share of public spending in national income in the UK in 2010/11 was sixth highest among

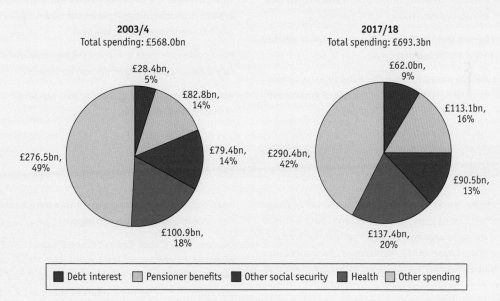

Figure 4.1 UK public spending in real terms, 2003/4 to 2017/18

Source: Institute for Fiscal Studies, 2013.

Table 4.4 General government expenditure as a share of GDP—selected European countries

	2001 (%)	2001 (Rank)	2011 (%)	2011 (Rank)
Belgium	49.1	4	53.3	3
Denmark	53.7	2	58.0	1
France	51.7	3	56.0	2
Germany	45.1	7	45.3	9
Greece	47.1	5	50.1	5
Ireland	31.2	11	48.7	7
Italy	45.9	6	49.9	6
Norway	42.3	8	44.5	10
Spain	39.2	9	44.1	11
Sweden	55.1	1	51.3	4
UK	36.8	10	48.7	7

Source: OECD 2013.

the 28 OECD member countries. This was a consequence of relatively rapid growth of public spending in the UK in the 2000s, moving the UK up from a position of 22 out of 28 in 1997/8 (Institute for Fiscal Studies 2010). Table 4.4 shows public spending as a share of GDP in the UK compared to a selection of other European countries.

Questions

1. Is government in the UK a big spender in international terms?

2. What are the main changes in the projected composition of public spending in 2017/8 compared to 2003/4?

Review and discussion questions

1. Explain the nature of politics, and consider whether it is possible or desirable to keep politics out of business.

2. With reference to the UK political system, explain what is meant by the term liberal democracy.

3. Explain the differences between the minimal, developmental and social democratic models of the role of government. Where does the UK fit in this classification?

4. To what extent are countries involved in a 'global race' to achieve economic success? From the data in this chapter, which countries are winning this race?

5. What evidence is there to support the argument that democracy is the best political environment for business?

6. With reference to the UK political system, explain the concept of multi-level governance.

Assignments

1. Research the 'shares for rights' policy of the UK coalition government. Using government, CBI and TUC websites present the main arguments for and against the measure. Analyse the passage of the legislation in Parliament and identify how the policy was amended as a result of political debate.

2. Examine Lord Heseltine's review *No Stone Unturned*. What criticisms does it make of the UK political environment, and

what measures does it propose to enhance the economic performance of England's cities and regions?

3. Examine 'The Global Competitiveness Report 2012-2013' produced by the World Economic Forum (WEF). Identify the 12 'pillars of competitiveness' described in the report, and examine how far these pillars exist in the UK (<**http://www3.weforum.org/docs/WEF_GlobalCompetitivenessReport_2012-13.pdf**>).

Further reading

Heywood (2007) and Jones, B. et al. (2007); *both provide introductions to the study of politics and political systems. Heywood has useful discussions of different types of economic system and political regimes.*

Wilson (2003) and Moran (2009) *provide extended discussions of the relationship between business and politics. Wilson discusses a number of countries in a comparative study. Moran focuses on the UK and the US.*

Chang (2010) *challenges a number of ideas about how capitalism works as false, and provides numerous insights into the role of government in capitalist economies. Both Chang and Kay (2004) challenge 'free market' or 'minimal state' thinking.*

World Economic Forum (2012) *sets out 12 'pillars of competitiveness'. This can be read as a statement of the characteristics of the best environment for business.*

online resource centre

Test your understanding of this chapter with online questions and answers, explore the subject further through web exercises, and use the web links to provide a quick resource for further research. Go to the Online Resource Centre at <www.oxfordtextbooks.co.uk/orc/wetherly_otter/2>

Useful websites

<http://news.bbc.co.uk>
The BBC website is a useful source for reports on contemporary politics and current affairs.

Parliament website

10 Downing Street

Look on the political party websites for information on policies relating to the economy and business:

The Labour party – <www.labour.org.uk/home>

The Conservative party –

The Liberal Democrats –

<http://www.oecd.org>
Organisation for Economic Cooperation and Development (OECD)

<http://www.worldbank.org/>
World Bank

<http://www.cbi.org.uk/>
Confederation of British Industry (CBI)

<http://www.ifs.org.uk/>
Institute for Fiscal Studies

<http://www.weforum.org/>
World Economic Forum

References

BBC (2013) 'EU shadow over David Cameron's US agenda', 13 May 2013. <http://www.bbc.co.uk/news/uk-politics-22507594>

BBC (2013a) 'Have ministers really embraced Heseltine's revolution?', 22 March 2013. <http://www.bbc.co.uk/news/uk-england-21899897>

BBC (2013b) 'Scottish independence: SNP dismisses threat to banknotes as "scaremongering"', 22 April 2013. <http://www.bbc.co.uk/news/uk-scotland-scotland-politics-22246176>

CBI (2012) 'CBI responds to George Osborne's speech to Conservative Party Conference', Confederation of British Industry, 8 October 2012. <http://www.cbi.org.uk/media-centre/press-releases/2012/10/cbi-responds-to-george-osbornes-speech-to-conservative-party-conference/>

CBI (2012a) 'UK must carve out a new trading role in the world for 2013, urges CBI Director-General', Confederation of British Industry, 31 December 2012. <http://www.cbi.org.uk/media-centre/press-releases/2012/12/uk-must-carve-out-a-new-trading-role-in-the-world-for-2013-cbi/>

Cameron, D. (2011) Speech to the CBI: 'We need to go for growth', 21 November 2011. **<https://www.gov.uk/government/speeches/we-need-to-go-for-growth>**

Cameron, D. (2012) Speech to the Conservative party conference, 10 October 2012. **<http://www.conservatives.com/News/Speeches/2012/10/David_Cameron_Conference_2012.aspx>**

Chang, H.-J. (2010) *23 Things they don't tell you about Capitalism* (Harmondsworth: Penguin).

Dearlove, J. and Saunders, P. (2000) *Introduction to British Politics* (Cambridge: Polity Press).

Department for Business, Innovation & Skills (2013) *No Stone Unturned: in Pursuit of Growth* [Lord Heseltine review] Ref: BIS/12/1213. **<https://www.gov.uk/government/publications/no-stone-unturned-in-pursuit-of-growth>**

Department for Communities and Local Government (2013) 'Supporting economic growth through local enterprise partnerships and enterprise zones'. **<https://www.gov.uk/government/policies/supporting-economic-growth-through-local-enterprise-partnerships-and-enterprise-zones/supporting-pages/local-enterprise-partnerships>**

Economist Intelligence Unit (2011) *Democracy Index 2011: Democracy under Stress.* **<http://www.sida.se/Global/About%20Sida/S%c3%a5%20arbetar%20vi/EIU_Democracy_Index_Dec2011.pdf>**

Heywood, A. (2007) *Politics* (Basingstoke: Palgrave-Macmillan).

Institute for Fiscal Studies (2009) *A Survey of Public Spending in the UK,* IFS Briefing Note BN43, September 2009. **<http://www.ifs.org.uk/bns/bn43.pdf>**

Institute for Fiscal Studies (2010) Public spending under Labour: IFS Election Briefing Note No. 5 (IFS BN92), 2010. **<http://www.ifs.org.uk/bns/bn92.pdf>**

Institute for Fiscal Studies (2013) 'The rapidly changing state' March 2013. **<http://www.ifs.org.uk/publications/6642>**

Jones, B. et al. (2007) *Politics UK* (Harlow: Pearson).

Kay, J. (2004) *The Truth About Markets* (London: Penguin).

HM Treasury (2012) Autumn Statement 2012: Chancellor's statement, 5 December 2012. **<https://www.gov.uk/government/speeches/autumn-statement-2012-chancellors-statement>**

Moran, M. (2009) *Business, Politics and Society: an Anglo-American Comparison* (Oxford: Oxford University Press).

OECD Tax Database (no date). **<http://www.oecd.org/tax/tax-policy/oecdtaxdatabase.htm#C_CorporateCaptial>**

OECD (2013), 'Government expenditures, revenues and deficits', in *OECD Factbook 2013: Economic, Environmental and Social Statistics,* OECD Publishing. **<http://dx.doi.org/10.1787/factbook-2013-81-en>**

Obama, B. (2011) 'Remarks by the President in State of Union Address', 25 January 2011. **<http://www.whitehouse.gov/the-press-office/2011/01/25/remarks-president-state-union-address>**

Osborne, G. (2012) Speech to the Conservative Party Conference on 8 October 2012. **<http://www.conservatives.com/News/Speeches/2012/10/George_Osborne_Conference_2012.aspx>**

TUC (2012) 'Trading rights for shares: TUC response to BIS consultation on "employee owner status"'. **<http://www.tuc.org.uk/tucfiles/438/Trading-rights-for-shares-TUC-response-2012.pdf>**

Tempest, M. (2005) 'Brown offers clues to pre-election budget plans', *The Guardian,* 4 February 2005. **<http://www.guardian.co.uk/politics/2005/feb/04/economy.uk?INTCMP=SRCH>**

Wilson, G. K. (2003) *Business and Politics* (Basingstoke: Palgrave).

World Economic Forum (2012) *The Global Competitiveness Report 2012–2013.* **<http://www3.weforum.org/docs/WEF_GlobalCompetitivenessReport_2012-13.pdf>**

Chapter 5
The legal environment

David Amos

Learning objectives

When you have completed this chapter you will be able to:

- Outline the different sources of law.
- Understand the relevance and working of European Union law as an example of international law.
- Identify the different legal structures that businesses can adopt and understand how that can have an effect on their development and decision-making.
- Identify and appreciate the different competing interests that will influence the law.
- Explore the different arguments for and against legal intervention in business.

THE LEGAL ENVIRONMENT AND THE THEMES OF THE BOOK

⏩ DIVERSITY

In this chapter we will look at the different legal structures that a business can adopt. These may vary according to the size, nature, and history of the business and can change as it develops. As we will see, the legal structure a business adopts can affect its decision-making.

⏩ INTERNAL/EXTERNAL

The legal structure of a business also affects its internal and external relationships. For companies in particular there are a number of internal stakeholders. The relationship between these stakeholders is heavily regulated.

That is not to say that a business has a free hand in their external relationships. Again, these are regulated in a whole series of ways. The success of a business can be determined by how it manages the legal requirements imposed on it.

⏩ COMPLEXITY

The law is shaped by a number of factors—social, economic, and political. To fully understand the law and the direction it is taking it is, therefore, necessary to understand the broader context within which it is made. In this way, the legal environment encapsulates many of the major themes within this book.

⏩ SPATIAL LEVELS

Legal systems operate within geographical boundaries or jurisdictions. The law in different nation-states will therefore vary. However, the legal environment is an area where the impact of globalization has been felt strongly with law increasingly being made at an international level.

Therefore, law that is made outside of a national legal system can be central to the law within it and, as we shall see, international agreements known as **treaties** form one of the sources of law. To illustrate the impact of international law we will look at the European Union.

》 DYNAMIC ENVIRONMENT

The legal environment is an extremely dynamic part of the business environment. The law changes on a daily basis and adds to the complexity of the business environment. At the same time, this reflects the different influences that there are on the law. The law isn't changed for the sake of it but is altered in line with broader changes in society.

》 INTERACTION

The law is a balance between different competing interests of which business is just one. As we have seen in Chapter 4, business has an active role to play in influencing government policy (and therefore the law) so that it is sensitive to its needs. As we shall see, the legal environment determines the parameters within which businesses can operate.

》 STAKEHOLDERS

Within the legal environment there are a whole series of different stakeholders, as the law affects us all. In this chapter we will consider how different competing interests can influence what the law is. More specifically, we will look at the different stakeholders connected to business organizations and how the law regulates their relationships.

》 VALUES

Given its all-embracing nature, law is inevitably influenced by the prevailing values within society. However, neither values nor the law exist in a vacuum but represent the views of important social groups. In this chapter we will look at the impact that these groups, and the ideologies they espouse, have on the law.

▨ Introduction

This chapter will consider the role of law in society and, in particular, the way that the law impacts on business activity. It will consider the effect that the law has on businesses in shaping both their internal workings and the external environment in which they operate.[1]

We will start with the basic question of what is the law and go on to look at various aspects of the infrastructure of the law such as the court system and the different sources from which the law is derived. It is clear that the structure of the law has been affected by changes in the political environment and globalization. Therefore, we will look briefly at the international position, particularly the role of the European Union (EU).

Having sketched out the overall legal framework, we will then consider issues that are more specific to businesses. In particular, we will look at the different legal structures that businesses can adopt and how those structures can affect and even determine how businesses operate.

It will be apparent from this discussion that the law is not a static entity, and its direction may be altered by broader changes in society and any one of many competing interests. We will look more closely in Chapter 11 at the way in which businesses can exert their influence on politics and the law.

---

[1] The law in this chapter is as at 1 February 2013.

We will conclude this chapter by weighing up the arguments for and against legal intervention and indeed regulation in its wider forms, considering the competing interests that need to be balanced and the tension between business freedom and the authority of the law. This discussion will reflect the ideological divides that are dealt with elsewhere in this book (see Chapters 2 and 4).

▧ **What is the law?**

Our starting point has to be to think about what law is. This is not a straightforward question and there are many different views on this. At a superficial level, law is simply what both judges and governments decide. However, that does not tell us why some situations are covered by the law and others are not.

If we think a little more deeply, we can see that laws are made to help govern the numerous relationships that we have with other individuals and organizations. The assumption behind this is that people will adjust their behaviour to comply with the law. It is clear that this does not always happen—otherwise prisons would be empty. Sometimes, breaking the law may simply be a result of ignorance, but more often it reflects the fact that people's behaviour is governed by other considerations than the law. Indeed, many of the rules which determine how we act are not part of the law at all.

❱ **VALUES** Some of these rules arise from our moral beliefs or accepted standards of behaviour rather than being determined by any law. It is perhaps more accurate to call these norms, rather than rules, as they prescribe how situations should be and how things should happen.

At a very simple level, it is not illegal to pick your nose and eat what you pull out, although it is generally considered socially unacceptable to do so. However, if you were to punch someone else on the nose you would most likely find yourself facing a criminal charge and possibly also having to pay damages to your victim.

The issue of what is legal but generally socially unacceptable is not always so clear cut. It is legal in England to have sex with whoever you wish even if they are married to someone else or are the same gender as you, provided they consent and are old enough. However, this may not be socially acceptable to all.

On the other hand, in other countries which have different belief systems sexual behaviour is more regulated. Thus under Islamic law adultery is considered a crime whilst homosexuality is illegal in at least 70 countries. Indeed it is punishable by death in some places.

This helps to illustrate the relationship that there is between society more generally and the law. Marxists such as Cohen (1978) argue that the form that law takes is determined by the economic basis of society. A capitalist society would therefore have different legal relationships and forms of government than those that are seen under feudalism.

Although the Marxist view is not widely accepted, it does help answer the question of why some situations are dealt with legally. Law is one of the mechanisms used to preserve order within society and will be shaped by the interests of those in power. The law will also reflect broader movements within society and the interests of influential sectors such as business.

Law is therefore formed as the result of the interaction between a whole series of different factors. These can be economic, political, social, and ethical. Often there are quite important material interests involved and those who make laws have to balance the needs of these different interests.

▪ Sources of the law

In this section we will concentrate on the sources from which the law derives in England and Wales, although the picture we describe here is similar to most other jurisdictions. Until recently these have been twofold:

- Case law/precedent
- Legislation

However, the passing of the Human Rights Act has had a huge influence on these main sources. The role of international law, particularly within the EU, has also now become central. As we shall see, the foundation of the EU is a series of treaties.

Treaties are agreements between states on particular issues and constitute the highest form of international law. In many countries, treaties become part of domestic law as soon as they are ratified by the nation-state. This allows citizens to use the provisions of a treaty in court action. However, in countries such as England and Wales, although the state becomes bound by a treaty when it is approved, separate domestic legislation is required before a citizen can rely upon it. Nevertheless, in every jurisdiction treaties are an important source of the law.

Case law/precedent

England and Wales operate under what is known as a common law system. This means that the law can be developed by the courts through the system of **precedent**. Under this system a court must follow the decision made by an earlier court. On the face of it, this would lend itself to a great deal of certainty, as to find out the law all you have to do is to refer to an earlier similar case.

However, there are various qualifications to this basic rule and indeed the Supreme Court does have the option to overturn one of its previous decisions. The system of precedent is therefore not entirely satisfactory as it leaves many grey areas.

Codes

It should be noted that most of continental Europe, and indeed Central and South America, operate under a completely different system known as codified or Civil law. Here the basic law is contained in a series of detailed codes which judges must simply apply to the situation that faces them. There is therefore no system of binding precedent. The law of the EU borrows heavily from such systems.

Legislation

This is now the primary source of law in the UK and is divided between Acts of Parliament and what is known as delegated legislation. Acts of Parliament go through a detailed system of scrutiny within Parliament before they are passed. Once they are approved, however, they are the highest form of law except where they are overridden by EU law.

No less important is delegated legislation, so called as the power to make the law is often delegated to the relevant ministers or authority. This is usually published in the form of what are known as statutory instruments.

This legislation is also subject to scrutiny but such monitoring is limited. There are normally in excess of 3,000 statutory instruments a year as against around thirty Acts. Most legislation is therefore passed with little comment. Despite this lack of monitoring, important areas of the law are passed in this way as, for example, with the Companies (Model Articles) Regulations 2008 which set out a standard set of articles for a company which effectively act as its internal rule book.

It is the case that there is a vestige of judicial control over legislation, in so far as a court can issue what is known as a declaration of incompatibility if the legislation does not comply with the Human Rights Act 1998. The courts can also interpret legislation if there are ambiguities within it. However, technically Parliament is supreme and thus the courts should simply apply the legislation that it has enacted.

One by-product of the supremacy of Parliament is that legislation is subject to influence that can be exerted on government and MPs by pressure groups and lobbyists (see Chapter 11). Indeed, many MPs have relationships, paid or otherwise, with outside bodies. There is therefore a much greater interrelationship between this branch of law-making and the political environment that businesses operate in.

Constitution

The doctrine of parliamentary supremacy derives from the constitution. A constitution can serve a number of purposes; in particular, it can outline the structure of the state and its powers, set out the principles on which the state is based, and confer rights on citizens.

In Britain there is no core document which forms the constitution. However, in other countries, most notably the US, the constitution is contained in either one or a small number of core documents. Typically such constitutions are drawn up following a change in power such as the American and French revolutions. With the change in power comes a change in values which is reflected in the constitution. Whilst these are legal documents their content is therefore determined by political considerations. Again, this is a good example of the interaction between the legal and political environment.

> *Stop and Think*
> ....
> In this section we noted that legislation is now the primary source of law and that Parliament is supreme.
>   What is meant by this?
>   Why do you think that this is an important principle?

Structure of the courts

We mentioned earlier how the system of binding precedent was one of the two main sources of domestic law in England and Wales. In order to fully understand how this operates we need to look at the structure of the courts. To help you understand this section you should look at Figure 5.1.

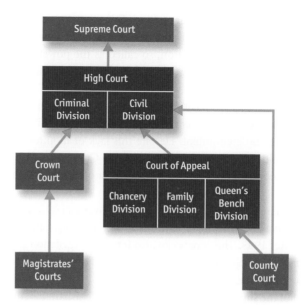

Figure 5.1 Simple outline of the structure of the courts in England and Wales

The court that a case is heard in is largely determined by the type of issue that is being dealt with. The primary split in the UK in this regard is between Civil and Criminal Courts. However, there has been the advent recently of more specialist courts such as those dealing with technology and construction cases and commercial disputes.

Criminal cases

Criminal cases will always start in the Magistrates Court. Less serious matters, such as most driving offences, will stay in that court with more serious cases being referred to the Crown Court.

If a party is unhappy with the decision made by the Magistrates Court they can appeal and have the matter reconsidered in either the Crown Court or the High Court depending on the nature of the appeal. In turn, if a party is dissatisfied with the decision in the Crown Court they would generally appeal to the Criminal Division of the Court of Appeal.

Any appeal from the Court of Appeal would be to the Supreme Court. For the purposes of considering precedent the Supreme Court is the highest authority. Any decision made there would therefore bind the Court of Appeal, and so on down the line.

Although businesses might be involved in criminal cases less frequently than civil matters nevertheless they can still be prosecuted, for example when they breach health and safety legislation.

Civil claims

As for civil disputes, such as an argument over a contract or a personal injury compensation claim, where the case starts can vary according to the value and complexity of the claim. Traditionally the lower value and less complex claims would start in the County Court.

The High Court has three divisions which deal with different types of case. These are: Family, Chancery, and Queen's Bench. For businesses, the latter two are the most important as they contain within them separate Companies and Commercial Courts.

As with criminal matters, parties can appeal to the Court of Appeal—in this case the Civil Division. Again, from there the final recourse domestically is to the Supreme Court with this being the highest authority for the purposes of precedent.

The European Court of Justice

In line with developments in the political and economic sphere, the EU now has an overarching role to play in the structure of the courts in England and Wales. National courts have a responsibility to protect and apply EU law and the European Court of Justice is the highest court when there is a European dimension to a case.

Tribunals and alternative dispute resolution

Aside from the system outlined above there are less formal fora for resolving disputes. An example of these which is important for businesses is the Employment Tribunal (ET) which can be used to deal with breakdowns in the employment relationship.

There has also been a rise in what is known as alternative dispute resolution (ADR). This takes different forms but the basic principle is that parties to a dispute should try to resolve it in their own way without the formalities, costs, and delays inherent within the court system. Indeed, such an approach is suggested in the rules governing the Civil Courts which have been reinforced by a number of important court decisions.

Comparison of court systems

Whilst the system described above is specific to England and Wales, the core features of this system are common to most jurisdictions. In France, for example, the primary divide in the court system is between administrative and judicial courts which, in turn, reflect the division between public and private law in that country. However, within these courts there are specialist courts for criminal, civil, and other matters. Similarly, there is a hierarchy of courts which allows for review and appeal of decisions.

In the US, the court system reflects the constitutional divide between the federal/national government and the state governments. The courts therefore have jurisdiction over the matters that the government they are linked to has power over. Again, however, there are specialist courts and the core hierarchy of first instance court, intermediate appellate court, and highest court remains the same.

Stop and Think

In this section we have looked at the different courts that cases can be heard in. Why do you think that in all systems there are courts that parties can appeal to?

■ The European Union

⟫ SPATIAL LEVELS So far we have concentrated on national legal systems but there are a number of worldwide bodies and agreements which have an influence on international business, such as the United Nations, World Trade Organization, International Monetary Fund (IMF), and World Bank. A good example of a 'supra-national' legal order can be seen in the development of the EU (see Chapters 4 and 13).

The first thing to appreciate about the EU is that although it is a union it is, in fact, still a collection of sovereign independent states. At the same time, each member state has to surrender elements of its sovereignty. In particular, EU law becomes an integral part of that country's domestic law. It is therefore essential to have some knowledge of EU law particularly as it has a tremendous impact on how and where businesses can operate within the EU.

Sources of European law

Primary sources

The primary sources of European Law are the **Treaty** on European Union (TEU) and the Treaty on the Functioning of the European Union (TFEU), both 2010. The clauses in these treaties are called articles and, as we shall see, these can confer rights on individuals as well as institutions.

Secondary sources

Article 288 of the TFEU sets out the five types of secondary European Community law:

- Regulations
- Directives
- Decisions
- Recommendations
- Opinions.

Regulations have general application and therefore bind all of the member states. They do not need to be put in force by national legislation and are intended to achieve uniformity of law across the union. An example of this is Regulation 2679/98 on the functioning of the internal market.

Directives are addressed to specific member states and are not directly applicable. Instead they will direct that members enact appropriate national legislation to achieve a set aim by a set date. They are therefore aimed at achieving harmonization rather than uniformity of the law so that, whilst all member states will be expected to achieve the same result, they have flexibility as to the means by which they do so. Prominent Directives include Directive 2003/88 on the regulation of working time (which we shall consider at the end of the chapter) and Directive 93/98 on the protection of copyright.

Decisions represent a sort of hybrid of the above two. Like directives these are addressed to specific bodies although these can be institutions and individuals as well as member states. However, like regulations they are directly applicable and therefore do not require legislation at a national level. They are frequently used by the European Commission to grant companies import or export licences and to notify member states of their Common Agricultural Policy and Structural Funds allocations.

Recommendations and opinions are not legally binding but should be taken into account by national courts. These are sometimes known as soft law—a term which covers other items such as codes of conduct issued by Community institutions. It is still necessary to be aware of these as whilst they may not have direct legal force they still constitute part of the regulatory regime that companies operate under.

As in the UK, legislation is supplemented by the work of the courts, in this instance the European Court of Justice. This court is made up of one judge per member state.

In terms of secondary sources the influence of the court has been twofold. Firstly, it has set out a number of general principles of Community law to assist in considering Community legislation. The principles are necessarily widely drawn and include equality, fundamental human rights, and legal certainty.

More specifically, the case law of the court has helped develop understanding of European law. Probably the most striking example of this came with the development of the principles of 'direct effect' and supremacy which we will consider later.

Who makes European law?

Having seen what the different sources of the law are in the EU it is instructive to briefly consider who makes the law in the EU, particularly as the system is different to that which operates in the UK and is therefore subject to influence in a different way.

Essentially there are three separate entities which have an input into the legislative process:

1. the Commission, the representative organ of the general interests of the Community;

2. the Council of the European Union (or the Council of Ministers as it is popularly known), the representative institution of the member state governments; and

3. the European Parliament, the representative body of the peoples of Europe.

In terms of the composition of these bodies, there are 27 Commissioners—one from each member state. Once appointed, a Commissioner's responsibility is to the EU as a whole. They therefore have to be approved by the European Parliament and take an oath to act in the interests of the EU rather than their national government.

The Council meanwhile is made up of one representative from each member state who is authorized to bind the government of that state. The personnel of the Council will change depending on the subject being discussed, so for example if the issue at hand is farming then the agriculture minister will attend.

As with the UK Parliament, the European Parliament consists of directly elected representatives.

It is beyond the scope of this chapter to consider exactly how EU legislation is made. However, there is an opportunity for the Parliament, Council, and Commission to each have an input into the process. Essentially, it is the Commission which initiates legislation but it is the Parliament and Council which adopt it. The Commission and the member states will then implement the measures that have been adopted.

In addition to the above bodies, in 2009 the European Council became one of the EU's official institutions. This body is made up of the Heads of State and the President of the Commission. The Council now has its own President, Herman Van Rompuy and a High Representative of Foreign Affairs. Its role is more strategic in that it sets out the general political direction and development of the EU.

Who enforces European law?

There are two main institutions which play a role here: The European Court of Justice and the Commission. The Court has two functions. Firstly, it decides whether the Commission, Council, or national governments are operating in a way that is compatible with Treaty obligations. Such actions can be brought before it by any EU institution, national government, individual, or organization. Secondly, as noted above, national courts can request authoritative rulings on points of EU law.

As for the Commission, its role is essentially twofold. Firstly, it can bring before the European Court of Justice a member state which is not fulfilling its obligations. Secondly, it ensures that the community rules on competition, which are of direct relevance to businesses, are adhered to.

It is important to note that EU laws do allow rights for individual citizens which can be enforced through their own national courts. It does this through the concept of 'direct effect'. This principle was first elucidated by the European Court of Justice in the *Van Gend En Loos* case 26/62 (1963) E.C.R. 1 (see Mini-Case 5.1).

Mini-Case 5.1 Van Gend En Loos and direct effect

In September 1960 Van Gend En Loos imported a chemical product called unreformaldehyde from Germany into the Netherlands. They were charged a duty of 8%. This was 5% higher than the duty which operated when the 1957 EC Treaty came into force.

Van Gend En Loos sought to recover the difference between the two rates. They therefore took the matter to the *Tariefcommisie*; the administrative tribunal having jurisdiction over customs duties in the Netherlands. In turn, the *Tariefcommisie* referred the matter to the European Court.

The case was based on Article 12 of the Treaty of Rome which dealt with fiscal barriers to trade. (This is now Article 30 TFEU.) The imposition of the additional tariff was argued to be in breach of this article.

In order to be successful in their case Van Gend En Loos had to show first of all that Article 12 had 'direct effect'. This means that it gave them individual rights that they could rely on in the court in the Netherlands.

In considering this issue the court argued that the Treaty didn't only create obligations between nations but covered individuals as well. Indeed, they pointed out that the preamble to the treaty 'refers not only to governments but to peoples'.

As a result the court concluded:

the Community constitutes a new legal order of international law for the benefit of which the states have limited their sovereign rights ... and the subjects of which comprise not only Member States but also their nationals ... Community law, therefore, not only imposes obligations on individuals but is also intended to confer upon them rights.

The rights and obligations of EC law could therefore be enforced by individual parties in national courts. This, along with the concept of the supremacy of EU law established in the Costa (6/64) case, has worked to ensure the uniform application of EU law across all of the member states. It has therefore been central to ensuring the effectiveness of the European legal system and the attainment of the aims of European integration.

There are certain criteria to be fulfilled for direct effect to apply and therefore it does not cover all EU legislation. There have also been various refinements to the general principle. However, it does show the importance that the EU has now assumed in the legal environment.

Question

In this mini-case study, we have looked at how, under the principle of direct effect, individuals have been given rights to enforce certain elements of EU law in their own national courts. Why do you think that this principle is important?

EU law is therefore a central component of the legal environment. Indeed, the EU plays a fundamental role in determining the parameters within which a company can operate. In particular, in order to achieve its aim of a single market the EU has established rights for the free movement of:

- goods (established in Article 34 TFEU and the *Cassis de Dijon* (120/78) case)
- persons (found in Article 45 TFEU)
- services (laid down in Article 56 TFEU).

Allied to these is the right to freedom of establishment (Article 49 TFEU) which allows individuals and companies to set up businesses in other member states under the same conditions as citizens/companies of the host state. These positive rights are supplemented by measures to control anti-competitive practices such as agreements between companies to share markets or price fixing (see Articles 101 and 102 TFEU).

The extensive powers of the Commission in this regard were seen in 2012 when it imposed a fine of over €1.4 billion on a number of companies, including Phillips, LG, and Panasonic, for price fixing and dividing markets between them (Chee 2012). One notable feature of this case was that it involved companies who weren't primarily based in the EU. It therefore illustrates that companies which trade internationally have to take account of the legal position in the jurisdiction in which they are working. It should be noted that at the time of writing the fines were subject to appeal.

Business organizations

▶ DIVERSITY ▶ INTERNAL/EXTERNAL So far we have looked purely at the external legal environment. Businesses clearly have to be aware of this as it can have a huge impact on the decisions they make. However, in order to understand fully how businesses operate and make decisions we have to look internally, particularly at the different legal structures that businesses can adopt:

- Sole traders
- Partnership
- Limited Liability Partnerships
- Companies.

Again in this section we will focus, by way of illustration, on the law in England and Wales. The core features of the different types of business organization are largely the same throughout the world. However, as we illustrate in Mini-Case 5.2, the precise form may vary according to the context within which the company operates.

Mini-Case 5.2 Company structures and their environment

While looking at the legal issues surrounding the different business forms it may help to briefly consider the history of two major companies to see how their structure was influenced by their development and the context they operated within.

A company that adopted the main different legal structures described in this section was the chocolate manufacturer, Cadbury. The company started in 1824 with John Cadbury setting up on his own in a shop in Birmingham. His business was sufficiently successful for him to rent a small factory in 1831. However, in 1847 John Cadbury went into partnership with his brother Benjamin and rented a larger factory in the centre of Birmingham. The company continued to grow, expanding its range of products and the size of its manufacturing base so that by 1899 Cadbury Brothers incorporated as a limited company.

Cadbury listed on the London Stock Exchange in 1969 in the same year as it merged with Schweppes, who had a similar organizational history. However, although the company enjoyed success—becoming the world leader in sugar and functional confectionery—it demerged with Schweppes in 2008. In 2010, Cadbury was taken over by Kraft after a high-profile hostile bid which was reported to be in the region of £12 billion (see, for example, Sibun 2010).

At the time this takeover was a controversial step, and Unite, the union which represents Cadbury employees, called for a 'Cadbury Law'. Under such a law hostile takeovers of British companies would be banned (Inman 2010). However, while a committee of MPs who investigated the matter welcomed moves to consider a review of the rules and legislation concerning takeovers in the UK, they did not feel any changes should be directed specifically against foreign companies.

Not all governments take a similar view, as we shall see in the case of LG, one of the world largest electrical companies. LG has its roots in the chaebols, which are a group of largely family-owned conglomerates based in South Korea. The company was formed as Goldstar in the late 1958 by Koo In-Hwoi to produce the first domestically produced radio in Korea.

Whilst not an immediate success, the company benefited from various changes in Korean government policy. Initially, they were able to expand as a result of the government's move to supply radios to rural areas. More fundamentally, in the 1960s a series of plans were announced by the government to grow Korean industry, with Goldstar expanding alongside the implementation of the electrical industry development plan. Under these plans the government supported export-led industrialization and gave various forms of financial support to companies engaged in that process (see Powers 2010).

Goldstar grew to such an extent that in 1969, it was able to set up a series of subsidiary divisions. This use of subsidiary companies aided its development internationally, and by the mid 1990s a new vehicle was adopted to oversee this development as Goldstar became LG electronics. Nevertheless, the structure of the ownership of the firm meant that there was a complicated system of shareholding which helped to maintain the position of the Koo family who founded the firm.

This system was simplified when LG became a holding company in 2003, as the group sought to ensure that its model of governance met the diverse needs of its subsidiaries which currently number over 100 worldwide. However, there is still a strong interrelationship between the different companies, and the Koo family remain at the heart of the organization.

Question

Explain what factors you think might influence businesses such as Cadbury and LG to adopt different legal structures over time.

Sole traders

Here an individual is the sole proprietor of the business. They therefore have sole control over the business and can take all the profit from it. However, at law they also have unlimited personal liability. What this means is that they are responsible for any debts and losses.

In terms of setting up the business, as the sole owner they have to finance it themselves, although of course they can take out a loan to do so. Legally there are virtually no formalities involved in starting such a business, although they do have to keep the necessary financial records for tax purposes.

This freedom from regulatory constraint may be an incentive for an individual to set up such a business although becoming a sole trader may not always be a positive choice. In some industries, such as the building trade, it may benefit larger companies to classify people who are in effect employees as self-employed. This is because it may allow them to avoid certain elements of the legislation governing employment.

Partnership

Partnerships are also characterized by a relatively light regulatory touch. They are governed by the Partnership Act 1890 which defines the relationship as one 'which subsists between persons carrying on business in common with a view to profit' (s1(1)). Usually when a partnership is formed the partners will draw up a document called a deed which is in effect a constitution for the partnership. This will deal with issues such as who provides the capital for the organization, the management structure, and the allocation of the profits.

However, it is not essential to have such a document, as the Partnership Act will govern the relationship in the absence of the necessary provisions. Under the Act there is an assumption of equality between the partners. Thus, in the absence of any agreement to the contrary, partners are deemed to have equal rights to manage the business. In addition, they will be entitled to an equal share of the profits but will contribute in equal share to any losses.

As with sole traders, most partnerships have unlimited liability. However, as there is more than one person involved the liability is joint and several. This means that whilst each partner is jointly responsible for all of the debts a debtor can choose to recover the money from only one partner. If that did happen, the partner who paid the debt could recover the money they had paid out from the other partners.

The necessary corollary of this is that any partner can bind the firm. They can therefore enter into contracts on behalf of the firm, sign cheques, hire employees, and other such matters. A partnership can remove this power but has to notify people outside the partnership that it has done so. The partnership relationship does therefore involve an element of trust as the individual's business identity is not separate but bound up in their membership of the partnership.

The finance for partnerships comes from the partners themselves. Whilst they can take out loans, this means that there is a limit to the amount of capital they will have access to and therefore the size of undertakings that they can pursue.

The other factor which can inhibit the size of partnerships is the problems associated with unlimited liability. The bigger the partnership, the greater the risk is for the individual partners. This problem has recently been addressed with the advent of limited liability partnerships.

Limited Liability Partnerships

As a form of business organization, Limited Liability Partnerships (LLPs) are a relatively new innovation being allowed for under the Limited Liability Partnerships Act 2000. They are something of a hybrid. Whilst they are still technically partnerships, they share many of the central features of companies, so, for example, the owners are called members rather than partners.

As their name suggests the main advantage of such an organization is that a member's liability will be limited. This means that their responsibility for any debts of the LLP would be restricted to the amount that they invested. At the same time, they have a **separate legal personality**. We shall discuss this in more detail in relation to companies but essentially this means that any legal action will be taken against the organization rather than the individual partners.

On the downside, LLPs are regulated more closely than a traditional partnership as they have to abide by many of the rules which cover companies.

Companies

⟫ INTERNAL/EXTERNAL Despite its merits the LLP does not solve the other issue that tends to inhibit the size of undertaking that a partnership can contemplate: access to large amounts of capital. Companies, of whatever type, have managed to resolve this problem by allowing unlimited numbers of people to invest capital in the business. The number and size of the investments are controlled by the company itself which can issue what are known as shares to the value of the capital that they require.

Having large numbers of investors does pose problems over who runs the company. Clearly it would cause difficulties if thousands of investors wanted to have a say on every minute aspect of the company's operation. This issue has been resolved by separating the people who own the business (shareholders) from those who run it on a day-to-day basis (directors and company secretary).

The reality for many small companies is that this separation may be illusory as the shareholders will also be directors (see Chapter 15). For larger and thus economically more important companies this separation is often central to their existence.

Public vs. private companies

To some extent the size and method of operation of a company is reflected in the regulatory regime that governs it. Smaller companies will typically be classified as private companies, whilst

Figure 5.2 Company structure

larger companies tend to be Public Limited Companies (PLCs) with shares that are traded on either the London Stock Exchange or the Alternative Investment Market.

Under the Companies Act 2006 there are more relaxed requirements on private companies in relation to auditing, the holding of meetings, and the requirements for a Company Secretary. The running of larger public companies also tends to come under greater scrutiny.

The distinction between such companies has become more important with the rise of private equity companies. These companies will invest in other companies where they see a prospect for growth and therefore a high return for their investment. Such investments have included high profile companies such as RJR Nabisco and Alliance Boots.

There have, however, been criticisms of the way that such firms operate. Firstly, they often use high levels of debt to fund their transactions, although the capital can come from other investors. Secondly, it is felt that in order to achieve high returns they are quick to cut staff costs and 'asset strip' firms they have taken over. Lastly, there has been concern about the secrecy of such firms. This last point led to a high profile report being prepared by Sir David Walker, a prominent British banker. The report resulted in a series of voluntary guidelines on transparency and disclosure in the private equity industry which are overseen by the Walker Guidelines Monitoring Group (<http://www.walker-gmg.co.uk/>).

Whatever the size or designation of a company, there are still common components to it, even in businesses with complicated structures such as LG. To understand how these work in practice we need to look at the different individuals involved in such organizations and what their roles are. You should consider Figure 5.2, showing the structure of a company, to help you grasp the interrelationship between the different bodies and individuals concerned.

Separate legal personality

▶▶ COMPLEXITY The starting point for considering a company's structure is the idea that the company itself has a *separate legal personality* as this provides the context within which to place the various elements of a company's organization.

The notion that a company should be a separate legal entity was first established in the case of *Salomon* v *Salomon* (1897) AC 22 (see Mini-Case 5.3).

Mini-Case 5.3 *Salomon* v *Salomon* and separate legal personality

For many years Aron Salomon had successfully traded on his own as a leather merchant and bootmaker. It was a family business and four of his sons worked with him. His sons pressed him to give them a share of his business and in 1892 Mr Salomon set up a company to carry their wishes into effect.

The shareholders of the company were Mr Salomon, his wife, and his four sons. The company bought the business from Mr Salomon for £40,000; £10,000 of which was financed by a loan given by Mr Salomon to the company which was secured on the company's assets (this is known as a debenture). Despite the sale, Mr. Salomon retained a majority interest in the company and was one of its directors—the other two directors being his sons.

Unfortunately, the company hit hard times as a result of both a downturn in the footwear trade and a series of strikes. Mr Salomon obtained a loan for the company from a Mr Broderip by using his debenture as a security. However, the interest payments on this loan were not met and Mr Broderip wound up the company. The company's assets were sold which paid off Mr Broderip and left some money available for other creditors.

Mr Salomon sought to recover this money to pay off the debenture/loan that he had secured over the company's assets. The other (unsecured) creditors objected to this on various grounds but argued, in particular, that the company never in reality had an independent existence. It was, in effect, Mr Salomon under another name and he could not owe money to himself.

The House of Lords (now the Supreme Court) roundly rejected this argument. The company had complied with the necessary legal formalities to be properly incorporated. It therefore had an entirely separate legal identity and so could be in debt to Mr Salomon. As his loan was secured he therefore took precedence over the creditors.

Questions

1. When you look at the facts of this case can it really be said that the company was separate from Mr Salomon?

2. Do you think the court's decision was a fair one for the unsecured creditors?

3. Assume your answer was no to one or both of these questions, how do you think you could justify this decision?

▪ Effect of separate legal personality

As we saw with LLPs, separate legal personality means that individuals within a company are largely protected from legal action which has to be taken against the company rather than individuals within it. The concept does also mean that a company can enter into contractual relationships with its shareholders/members. Most obviously, a shareholder can be an employee of the company and can take action against it if the contract of employment is breached.

▪ Shareholders/members

❯ STAKEHOLDERS ❯ INTERNAL/EXTERNAL The designation of the company as a separate legal entity also has an impact on the nature and role of the different individuals within it. These are the people who provide one of the two sources of finance for the company, the other being loans. They are essentially people who make an investment in the company in the hope of making some gain on the money they have put into it. They are generally a mix of large institutions, such as pension funds and individuals, although this does depend on the size and type of the company. As noted above, when we discussed private equity, some firms largely exist to invest in other companies whilst, as we saw in relation to LG, companies within the same group can invest in each other.

Although technically these investors are known as members, they are commonly referred to as shareholders. This is because the capital of the company is divided into shares with those who have invested in the company being given certificates recording the amount of capital that they have. The liability that a member will have for any debts of the company is limited to the extent of the shareholding that they possess.

The shares provide the potential profit that a member can make on their investment. Firstly, the share itself is a form of property and can thus be bought or sold as with any other form of property. For many larger companies the price of their shares is quoted on a stock exchange. Secondly, if the company is doing well it can give its shareholders a sum of money called a dividend. This will be calculated according to the size of holding that a member possesses.

The shareholders are the owners of the company and although they may not run it on a day-to-day basis they do have some control over what happens within it. This control can be exercised internally at a General Meeting or externally through court action. The most notable example of this in recent times came with the so-called 'shareholder spring' in 2012. Disputes over directors' pay and corporate performance led to investors voting against remuneration packages for senior executives with prominent individuals across large companies stepping down.

Directors

The people who do have hands-on control of the company are the directors. They are collectively known as the board and are given the opportunity to discuss the operation of the company at board meetings. Their role has been subject to much scrutiny in recent years with a series of reports including Cadbury (1992), Greenbury (1995), Hampel (1998), Higgs (2003), and Smith (2003) being prepared.

These reports looked at various aspects of the running of companies and led to the evolution of a code of best practice known as the UK Corporate Governance Code with similar codes operating in countries other than the UK. Amongst other things, the Code covers the make-up and operation of the board, directors' pay, accountability and auditing, and relationships with shareholders.

One important area that the Code looks at is the different types of directors. These will have more or less involvement with the running of the company and indeed some directors may not be members of the board. We need to look in particular at:

- the managing director
- executive directors
- non-executive directors.

The managing director (otherwise known as the chair of the board) is central to the running of the company, providing a link between the board and the senior executives within the company who will implement the board's decisions. The Code clearly sets out that there should be a division between the running of the board and the running of the company. This is to avoid any one individual becoming too powerful and not subject to sufficient checks on their actions.

Executive directors are working directors who are employees of the company. They will generally have responsibility for a particular function within the company such as production or marketing.

Non-executive directors are less engaged with the running of the company on an ongoing basis but are no less important. They may well be part time and will often be appointed for their expertise outside of the company. The reason for this is bound up with the role that they play. Firstly, they can act as monitors of the performance of the company. Secondly, on a more long-term basis they can have an input into the strategic direction of the company.

Non-executive directors therefore have an important supervisory role to play which is recognized in the Code. It suggests that, except in smaller companies, at least half the board should be non-executive directors, whilst in smaller companies there should be at least two directors of this type (see Section B.1 UK Corporate Governance Code 2012 pp. 11–12). The Code also places store on the independence of non-executive directors from the firm. Independence here is considered largely in financial terms—although of course non-executive directors will still be paid by the firm.

Directors' legal duties

As can be seen from the above, the directors hold a powerful position within the company. It is they who act on its behalf, concluding contracts, taking out loans, and other such matters. Given that they are in effect dealing with other people's money, there are some protections built into the system.

Specifically, part 10 of the Companies Act 2006 provides the legislative framework within which directors work, and it sets out their central duties. These duties are a mixture of the general and the specific. A director must therefore manage the company with reasonable diligence, care, and skill; and exercise independent judgement. As a result, they should avoid conflicts of interest and not accept benefits from third parties.

As noted above, directors are powerful individuals and to help limit that power the Act specifically requires them to act in accordance with their company's constitution. Whatever they do, s172 of the Act makes it clear that they must promote the success of the company. What is success for the company may be a matter of debate (see Chapter 1), but it is clear that the company's best interests must be central to what a director does. This statutory requirement is reinforced by the Code.

It should be noted that if the directors breach their statutory duties legal action can be taken against them.

Company secretary/auditor

The other two main elements within the organization are the company secretary and the auditors. Since the 2006 Act, private companies are not obliged to have a company secretary but most of them will do so. Those companies that do have a secretary can decide whether or not they are a director and have flexibility in determining their precise role. However, normally this will be largely administrative and will involve issues such as convening meetings, keeping company records, and accounts.

The auditors have a more important role in monitoring the company's activities in relation to financial matters. The Companies Act 2006 requires both private and public companies to appoint professionally qualified and independent auditors who will review and approve the company's accounts. They will then report to the members on the accounts. This process is subject to some discretion on behalf of the directors and, again, there is a lighter regulatory touch for small private companies.

In theory, the auditors can act as an important check on any financial abuses. However, high profile cases in the US have exposed weaknesses in the system with the auditors, Arthur Andersen, being implicated in the scandals surrounding Enron and WorldCom. In both of these cases the companies concerned grossly misrepresented their financial position.

There was widespread concern after these scandals broke that they represented a deeper systemic problem with the auditing of companies (see, for example, the documentary *Bigger Than Enron* at **<http://blip.tv/ecn220/bigger-than-enron-pbs-video-business-ethics-5957955>**). As a result, legislation was passed in both America and Britain which imposed stricter controls on auditors.

However, it is not clear how effective this has been, as is illustrated by the collapse in 2008 of Lehman Brothers—an event which helped bring about a worldwide financial crisis. In a report[2] prepared in March 2010 as part of the court proceedings arising out of the collapse it was alleged that the company removed $50 billion from its balance sheet by use of an accounting device known as Repo 105. It was also alleged that the company's auditors were aware of the use of this device but did nothing to question its use and the failure to disclose it. It should be noted that the auditors for the company defended their position and no prosecutions arose out of the report. However, as Anton Valukas, who compiled the report, commented, 'If there's anything I've learned, being both in the government as a prosecutor and on the civil side as a defense attorney, is that it's effective regulation that prevents it from happening in the first place, which is the critical part of the process' (Harris 2012).

Stop and Think

....

In this section we have looked at the different parties involved in the structure of a company and have highlighted the role played by non-executive directors and auditors.

Why do you think it is important to have independent scrutiny of what a company is doing?

General Meetings and written resolutions

▶ **STAKEHOLDERS** ▶ **INTERNAL/EXTERNAL** Having looked at the different entities and the roles that they play we now need to consider the arenas where the different entities come together and the owners of the company (the shareholders) can exercise some vestige of control. This is one area where, at least in law, there is quite a big difference between private and public companies.

Private companies can dispense with the need for meetings altogether and instead can conduct their business by means of written resolutions. These resolutions perform the same function as the equivalent resolutions at a General Meeting.

Most companies do still hold General Meetings, and public companies are required to hold an Annual General Meeting (AGM). A key issue at the AGM is likely to be finances, as this meeting gives the shareholders the chance to see the annual accounts. The meeting may also present an opportunity for members to remove a director or, indeed, challenge the board more generally over pay and performance, as happened in the 'shareholder spring' (see the **Shareholders/members** section).

There may be issues that need to be decided between the AGMs, and the directors have a general power to call such a meeting. Members also have the right to call such a meeting but only if together they hold more than 10% of the company's shareholding. They might do this, for example, to allow consideration of a resolution to remove a director. Finally, both members and directors can apply for the court to exercise its power to call a meeting.

Legal action by shareholders

▶ **COMPLEXITY** ▶ **INTERNAL/EXTERNAL** The limited internal control which can be exercised by shareholders is supplemented to some extent by the legal action they can take. Shareholders' rights in this regard have been extended dramatically by the 2006 Act. Any member can now bring an action where there has been negligence, breach of duty, or breach of trust by a director. However, any member wishing to bring an action in this way must first obtain permission from the court.

---

[2] The full text of the report is available at <http://lehmanreport.jenner.com>

> *Stop and Think*
>
> So far in this section we have looked at the different types of business organizations and the law surrounding them. Imagine you were starting up a new business with a group of friends which involved making high-quality chocolates.
>
> Which form of business organization would you adopt?
>
> Explain the reasons for your decision.
>
> Would your answer differ if you were merely seeking to open a small shop with your spouse to sell such chocolates?
>
> In answering these questions you can, if you wish, refer back to your answer to the question posed about Cadbury and LG in Mini-Case 5.2.

What is the company for?

Having considered the company's structure we need now to consider the purpose of a company and in whose interests it is run. The answer to this question is fundamental to our understanding of the way that a company might act in any given situation (see also Chapter 1).

STAKEHOLDERS There is a whole series of individuals and organizations who might have an influence on the decisions that a company makes, referred to as stakeholders (see Chapter 1). How does a company balance all of those interests before deciding what to do?

Some guidance is given in s172 of the Companies Act 2006. It is instructive to read this in full.

1. A director of a company must act in the way he considers, in good faith, would be most likely to promote the success of the company for the benefit of its members as a whole, and in doing so have regard (amongst other matters) to—

   a. the likely consequences of any decision in the long term,

   b. the interests of the company's employees,

   c. the need to foster the company's business relationships with suppliers, customers and others,

   d. the impact of the company's operations on the community and the environment,

   e. the desirability of the company maintaining a reputation for high standards of business conduct, and

   f. the need to act fairly as between members of the company.

When the section was framed it was said to embody the notion of 'enlightened shareholder value'. This notion recognizes that whilst the core duty of directors is to ensure the success of the company, for the benefit of its members, they have to take into account a series of other factors. However, there has been some scepticism expressed as to the effectiveness of this provision given that it doesn't confer a right to legal action on those stakeholders mentioned in the section (see Lynch 2012).

Certainly, where the courts have considered the section they have reached the view that it merely restates the existing law. At the same time, most commentators have seen this section as ensuring that directors put the interests of the shareholders first (see, for example, Alcock 2009) albeit that they have to take into account broader factors.

The practical importance of this is the impact it has on the way that companies act on a day-to-day basis. Shareholders are investors and so their main motivation is in a suitable return on their investment. As Lord Goldsmith, then Attorney General, said when discussing s172 before a parliamentary committee, for a commercial company, success will normally mean long-term increase in value ... For most people who invest in companies, there is no doubt about it – money, that is what they want.

(*Lords Grand Committee* 6 February 2006, Column GC256)

Indeed, some institutional investors have by law to secure a good return. Thus, in *Cowan* v *Scargill*, Megarry VC made it clear that in a pension fund 'a power of investment ... must be exercised so as to yield the best return for the beneficiaries' and that trustees (the people who run pension funds) 'must put to one side their own personal interest and views' (1985 Ch. 270, p. 287). If we consider that in 2001 occupational pension funds accounted for £800 billion of assets we can see how important this decision was (HM Treasury 2001, p. 5).

In order to satisfy the shareholders a company must have the maximization of profit at the core of its activities. However, as s172 suggests the profit motive does not necessarily mean that it is in the best interests of the company to act unethically or not be alive to social issues.

As we have pointed out in other chapters, such behaviour can result in damaging consumer boycotts as, for example, with the campaigns against companies who traded in South Africa during the apartheid era. More recently, there have been campaigns in Britain against Starbucks and other companies who were paying little or no corporation tax. Indeed some campaigning bodies, such as The Campaign Against the Arms Trade, seek to persuade investors to sell their holdings in companies who they believe are guilty of unethical behaviour.

However, given that the core purpose of companies is to maximize the return for investors there is a limit on the level of social responsibility that a company can exercise. Indeed, some have argued that the law governing companies, in placing primacy on shareholders' interests, acts to prohibit ethical behaviour.

In his critique of the corporation Bakan points to the 'best interests of the corporation' principle. The principle was most notably outlined in the American case of *Dodge* v *Ford*, although s172 of the Companies Act 2006 is a variant of it. The principle determines that 'managers and directors have a legal duty to put shareholders' interests above all others and no legal authority to serve any other interests' (Bakan 2005, p. 36). According to Bakan this means that corporate social responsibility is illegal unless in some way it benefits the company.

If this is the case then is the answer simply to change the legal structure of companies and to regulate them in a way that forces them to pursue social rather than economic goals?

> **Stop and Think**
>
> In this section we have considered the legal structure of a company and how that might impact on its behaviour.
>
> What issues and personalities do you think a company should take into account when making decisions? Should the wording of s172 be amended to put other interests on an equal footing with those of shareholders?

◼ How far should the law intervene–regulation v deregulation

Deregulation?

⟩⟩ **VALUES** ⟩⟩ **INTERACTION** Deregulation involves reducing or removing the 'burden' that regulation places on business. It is based on the idea that businesses should have more freedom to run their own affairs and to compete freely in the market.

Freer competition can encourage efficiency. A negative example of this comes with the EU's Common Agricultural Policy (see Chapter 13). Under this policy, the EU effectively pays subsidies to farmers through a mechanism called the Single Farm Payment. This is backed up by tariffs which help block imports of goods from outside the EU. As a result, not only is there no incentive for farmers to increase their productivity but prices for consumers are set at an artificially high level.

It is also argued that deregulation, particularly of labour laws, encourages flexibility and therefore can act to reduce costs. These costs can be substantial. Thus, in May 2005 the UK government measured the administrative burden on business at £13.7 billion annually. (Cabinet Office 2006, p. 8).

This issue is central to any argument in favour of a lighter regulatory touch as reducing costs means increased competitiveness. This does not only mean competitiveness for individual companies but nation-states as well, who can encourage inward investment by promoting the business friendly environment that they offer.

The International Finance Corporation and World Bank in their annual *Doing Business* reports provide indices of these sorts of policies (see **<www.doingbusiness.org>**). Countries are ranked according to a variety of measures relating to regulation. Clearly in a globalized and increasingly competitive world economy this imposes pressures on countries to offer the most 'competitive' and business-friendly conditions. Indeed, in the *2013 Doing Business* report, a correlation was drawn between greater levels of foreign direct investment and 'regulatory quality' (International Bank for Reconstruction and Development and World Bank, pp. 47-50) (see Chapter 11).

The benefits of deregulation can arise in a more indirect fashion. In its *Annual Report for 2006*, the Better Regulation Commission argued that '[t]ying people up in red tape makes innovative thinking all but impossible' (p. 10). However, it did not use that as a justification for complete deregulation but rather regulating in a different way.

The arguments for relaxing the burdens of regulation are therefore primarily economic. Those in favour of regulation are more multifaceted although they still have an economic dimension.

Regulation?

The case for regulation was summed up rather neatly by Sir Brendan Barber (the then General Secretary of the British Trades Union Congress) who pointed out that:

> everyone is protected by regulations every day. At work we are protected from exploitation. When shopping we are protected from shoddy deals. And as citizens we are protected from toxic pollution, fire-trap buildings and dangerous vehicles. Law, including regulation, is the difference between anarchy and civilisation.
>
> (TUC 2006)

There are therefore different strands to the arguments advanced by those in favour of regulation. Primarily these are defensive, being largely concerned with protection of employees, consumers, and the environment. However, they are underpinned by a positive ideological argument that emphasizes the social benefits of regulation.

The argument in favour of protecting employees can take various different forms. From a strictly economic point of view a workforce that feels vulnerable is likely to plan its spending accordingly. Workers who feel that they could lose their jobs tomorrow are less likely to make long term or expensive purchases such as houses, cars, or holidays.

The strictly economic argument can intersect with those of a more social nature as can be seen if we look at the issue of health and safety at work. The Health and Safety Executive

Mini-Case 5.4 Asbestos

Asbestos is a mineral which was used widely in Britain until the 1980s because of its heat resistant qualities. There are three main types of asbestos: blue, brown, and white.

As a result of the potentially fatal consequences of exposure to asbestos the use of blue and brown asbestos in Britain was banned in 1985. A similar ban was placed on the use of white asbestos in 1999. Despite the ban in Britain asbestos is still used in many countries throughout the world.

Inhalation of asbestos fibres can cause a number of diseases, particularly lung cancer, asbestosis, mesothelioma, or pleural plaques. The Health and Safety Executive reported that around 4,500 cancer deaths each year in the UK are due to past exposure to asbestos, with mesothelioma accounting for 2,347 deaths in 2010 alone. It is estimated that in the UK the number of deaths from mesothelioma will continue to rise until 2016 (Health and Safety Executive 2009, p. 2).

The reasons why the figures are growing despite the ban are twofold. Firstly, there is a time lag between exposure to asbestos and the onset of symptoms. This can be anything between 15 and 60 years. Secondly, there is still a vast amount of asbestos that was fitted in buildings that has yet to be removed.

Not surprisingly there has been extensive litigation relating to exposure to asbestos. In England, one of the more important recent cases related to pleural plaques, which is a form of scarring to the lungs. The case went up to the House of Lords, which at the time (2007) was the highest court in England. The Law Lords rejected the claim for compensation. The importance of this decision can be seen when we look at the cost of asbestos litigation. We noted above the likely increase in the number of asbestos related deaths. It was estimated in 2004 that the rise in claims that could result would see an increase in costs to British insurers and the state of up to £20 billion (Dyer and Jones 2005).

However, as has already been suggested, the economic argument may not be the most fundamental in deciding when and how far the law should intervene. In the case concerning pleural plaques, the victims obtained judgement in their favour in the High Court. After this decision one of their lawyers, Ian McFall, commented, 'This is good law, which puts people before profits' (Dyer and Jones 2005), suggesting a deeper moral and philosophical argument for intervention.

Since the case was heard, the government has announced a scheme to compensate those who had started claims related to pleural plaques before the Law Lords decision. They did not, as they could have done, overturn the court's decision and allow such claims in the future. This did provoke some criticism (see, for example, Lazenby 2010) and bills were presented which would have taken such a step. Indeed, the Scottish Parliament enacted legislation allowing compensation for sufferers of pleural plaques. The Act was challenged in the courts by UK insurance companies but the challenge was rejected.

Questions

1. Do you agree that law which puts people before profits is good law?

2. Assume that you do agree; should this be the criterion for deciding what the law is in every situation?

---

has estimated that workplace accidents and work-related ill health costs the British economy as much as £13.4 billion a year (Health and Safety Executive 2012, p. 2). Coupled with that economic cost is the social cost in terms of pain, grief, and suffering. A stark example of this comes when we look at the effect of exposure to asbestos (see Mini-Case 5.4).

Alongside the economic and social arguments there may be political reasons for intervention. In recent years, awareness of the need to protect the environment has increased resulting in legislation such as the Pollution Prevention and Control Act 1999 which implemented an EU directive on pollution control. The Act provides for a system of permits underpinned by a number of offences which are designed to regulate the activities of potentially polluting companies.

Whilst such legislation could be said to inhibit business freedom it does fit neatly with the ideas of democracy and social solidarity which underpin the case in favour of regulation. This is that if a company's behaviour is detrimental to the lives of a country's citizens and communities the electorate should have the power, through their representatives, to control that company (Bakan 2005). The Bhopal disaster which took place in India in 1984 provides an instructive example.

In this incident there was a chemical leak from the factory of American corporation Union Carbide. The leak resulted in the death of more than twenty thousand people and the injury of many thousands more. After several years the company reached a multimillion dollar settlement of the lawsuit that arose out of the disaster.

However, controversy still surrounds the incident and led to the resignation of Meredith Alexander from the Commission for a Sustainable London in the lead up to the 2012 Olympics. Her resignation arose out of sponsorship of the games by Dow Chemicals who took over the assets and liabilities of Union Carbide. However, Dow deny any responsibility and argue that Union Carbide's assets and liabilities in India were taken over by a third party.

There are, therefore, a number of political and economic arguments in favour of intervention. Indeed, greater regulation is not necessarily inimical to business success. As we have seen, the political and moral argument that economic gains should be enjoyed by all potentially has the economic benefit of greater consumption.

In fact, the argument that there should be some level of regulation is not as controversial as it may seem. The EU regulates how companies compete with each other and even the World Trade Organization (WTO), which has free trade philosophy at its core, supervises the Agreement on Trade Related Aspects of Intellectual Property (TRIPS).

The agreement was entered into as manufacturers, particularly from developed countries, were increasingly concerned by the billion dollar trade in pirated products which was affecting their profitability. The regulations oblige WTO members to grant and enforce rights to property which is the product of intellectual activity such as new inventions.

There is therefore not a completely free market. The state has to intervene in order to correct the distortions that can arise from the market and create the conditions in which businesses can flourish. As the Better Regulation Commission say, 'We would all be rather disappointed if basic protections such as a clean environment … and a good education for our children were not fulfilled' (Annual Report 2006, p. 12). The issue therefore is not regulation v deregulation but rather what level and what type of regulation is acceptable.

Alternatives to regulation?

It is important to recognize that the process of regulation is not simply carried out by the state through legislation. In their document 'Reducing Regulation Made Simple' the Better Regulation Executive set out a number of alternatives to what they called 'command and control' regulation (Better Regulation Executive 2010). These included self-regulation and co-regulation and broader mechanisms such as economic instruments, information, and education. Indeed, businesses may sometimes judge it better to regulate themselves through their own codes of conduct and trade associations, or use other such measures as a way of fending off more stringent regulation by government.

However, it may not always be possible and desirable to use one of the alternatives to regulation. In such situations the law will intervene. The process of law-making is a balancing act between different competing interests and value systems. The level and type of legal intervention is therefore very much a result of the political process.

❯❯ **INTERACTION** Businesses do have a role to play in this as, whilst they do not have votes, they can still influence legislators both directly and indirectly (see Chapter 11). This influence can be used in both a positive and a negative way. Businesses may therefore press for laws to be removed as well as passed in order to protect their position.

One area where businesses clearly would like their influence to be felt, given its direct effect on their operation, is employment law. This is also an area where views informed by differing ideologies have a practical impact. To illustrate this, in our end-of-chapter case study we will look at one particular aspect of employment law which has excited some controversy; the Working Time Directive (see Chapter 12 for related discussion of work–life balance).

■ Looking ahead

Some of the major changes that are taking place within the legal environment concern the role of lawyers and the way that people access justice. Indeed, one of the major commentators on the legal profession, Professor Richard Susskind, published a book called *The End of Lawyers?* in 2008 (Susskind 2008). Although his latest work is more optimistically entitled *Tomorrow's Lawyers*, Susskind is still predicting major change. Whilst it is not possible to discuss his views in detail here, it is instructive to consider the three major drivers for change that he identifies: the 'more for less' challenge, liberalization, and information technology (Susskind 2013).

Broadly, the first of these issues relates to individuals and organizations having to deal with more regulation but with less resources to pay for lawyers to assist them. There are a variety of solutions to a problem like this but perhaps the most radical is to suggest that lawyers should be taken out of the process altogether. Thus the insurance company, Aviva, produced a report suggesting £1.5 billion could be saved by a series of reforms to personal injury claims. Central to their report was the proposal that claimants should contact insurers directly rather than go through intermediaries such as lawyers (Aviva 2013).

The other two drivers for change have similarly pointed to lawyers playing a less prominent role in the delivery of legal services than is currently the case. In the last edition of this book, this section considered the impact of the Legal Services Act 2007. Amongst other things, the Act allows a more liberal attitude to the ownership of law firms, with non lawyers now being able to own law firms or to deliver legal services as part of their broader business. The effects of this are starting to be seen in various ways. Most notably in England, the Co-operative—a multi-faceted organization more known for its retail, banking, and travel arms—has started to provide legal services. It has managed to do so with some success, generating £33 million of revenue and breaking even in its first year (Baksi 2013).

The success of the Co-operative mirrors that of Slater and Gordon, an Australian law firm who took advantage of similar legislation to float on the stock exchange. Since that time the firm has expanded and now has a national presence in England, through its acquisition of Russell, Jones and Walker.

Inward investment in law firms has run parallel with the greater use of new technology, Susskind's third driver for change. This has taken a number of different forms but the two most noteworthy for our discussion are the opportunities this opens for individuals to undertake legal work themselves and the increased use of outsourcing. A good example of the former is LegalZoom (see **<www.legalzoom.com>**). This is an online service which allows clients to prepare legal documents themselves at a cheaper rate than if they had used a lawyer. The business is expanding, with a 29% increase in revenues in 2011 (legalfutures 2011) which formed the basis for an international expansion in 2012.

More significant is the move to greater outsourcing of legal services. This is where law firms send some of their work outside of their firm, largely because it is cheaper to do so. This is a growing phenomenon with the global market estimated to be increasing at 28% annually and worth $2.4 billion in 2012 (Lacity and Willcocks 2012). Initially, such outsourcing had concerned 'back office' functions but, given the expertise of lawyers in the outsourcing industry, increasingly this involves higher-end legal work (see legalfutures 2012).

These changes are not without their critics or their problems as illustrated by the remarks of Sir Alan Ward, one of England's most senior judges, when he referred in a recent case (*Wright* v *Michael Wright Supplies Ltd and another*) to the chaos brought about by unrepresented parties putting forward their defences or claims. Indeed, most commentators suggest that as law is a knowledge based industry the public still needs interpretation and guidance through the 'legal maze' (Boon 2010, Kirgis 2010). Legalzoom therefore offer access to a lawyer alongside their other services and their entrance to the UK market was carried out in partnership with Quality Solicitors—a network of law firms formed in response to the changes brought about by the Legal Services Act. In fact, it has been argued that giving people greater knowledge of the law will in fact encourage greater use of lawyers (Kirgis 2010).

There are clearly deeper considerations at play with such developments. Traditionally, the relationship between a lawyer and their client is one of trust, where information is confidential and the work that is done is tailored, as far as possible, to the need of that individual client. This is reinforced by the ethical codes which govern the way that lawyers work.

Changing the nature of such relationships may harm the interests of clients, as their lawyers will have less loyalty to them. We have already seen how outside investment can have an impact on the way a company acts. Concern therefore has been expressed that law firms will move from prioritizing the interests of clients to putting the interests of outside investors first. It is feared that this will lower the quality of legal work with commercial pressures pushing firms to employ less well-qualified advisors.

It is clear that the drivers for change outlined by Susskind will have an impact on the way that lawyers work and interact with their clients. What remains to be seen is how far this will disrupt existing practices or in fact help to facilitate them.

Summary

- The law is not a monolithic entity. It is therefore formed in different ways. This is not surprising given the range of activities that are covered by the law.

- The law cannot be seen in isolation and in particular is closely linked to the political environment. The law has therefore been influenced by the process of globalization which is considered elsewhere in this book. Law is therefore increasingly made at an international level rather than within the nation-state. A good example of this is the European Union whose actions and decisions are a central part of the legal environment of business.

- The law also determines the different structures a business can adopt. For companies, in particular, their structure does much to determine their decision-making process. Some commentators argue that, as a result, a company's underlying dynamic is the mere pursuit of profit to the exclusion of social responsibility.

- The law does not exist in a vacuum and therefore is strongly influenced by the prevailing values within society. These values reflect different competing interests. This diversity of views and interests is partly played out in arguments over how much legal intervention there should be, particularly in areas which affect business activity. However, there is always a level of regulation and on occasions that may be helpful to business.

Case Study: The Working Time Directive

The Working Time Directive was adopted by the member states within the European Union in 1993. As its name suggests it sought to protect workers by limiting hours of work and prescribing minimum rest and holiday periods.

The United Kingdom did not put in place the necessary regulations enacting the directive until 1998 and only did so after losing a court case on the issue (*United Kingdom of Great Britain and Northern Ireland* v *Council of the European Union* (1996) ECR I-05755). Even when it did put the necessary regulations in place, it kept an opt-out so that individuals could agree not to be subject to the 48 hours maximum working week allowed for under the directive.

The use of the opt-out by the UK and other countries has been controversial. Indeed, the European Parliament has voted on more than one occasion to remove it. However, negotiations over the removal of the opt-out were unsuccessful and it is therefore still in place.

The central core of the business argument over this issue is one of flexibility. Thus John Cridland, deputy director-general of the CBI (a representative group for employers) argued, '[t]hose who have argued for the ending of the opt out simply do not understand the realities of the modern work place. The ability for individuals to opt out ... is a vital part of the UK's flexible labour market' (Laitner and Taylor 2006).

Specifically, the CBI feels that the opt-out provides 'the most economic and efficient means for tackling upturns in labour demand' (House of Lords European Committee 2004, p. 13). Thus the opt-out could help deal with skills and labour shortages. In addition, there are certain areas where work that was started would have to be finished (ironically one of these areas is safety maintenance). The CBI goes on to argue 'that labour market flexibility made the UK an attractive place to do business' (House of Lords European Committee 2004, p. 13).

Not surprisingly the TUC advances quite a different view which is strongly in favour of ending the opt-out. There are several strands to their argument. In general, they are critical of what they call the UK's long hours culture. Specifically, they feel that working long hours is bad for people's health. In particular, they point to increased risk of 'heart disease, chronic headache, irritable bowel syndrome, diabetes, stress and accidents at work' (TUC 2004). At the same time they argue that long hours are actually indicative of economic inefficiency, being a symptom of poor productivity and bad management (House of Lords European Committee 2004, p. 14 and TUC 2004).

In addition, the TUC points to abuse by employers of the opt-out clause. Under the regulations workers have to agree to work over an average of 48 hours a week over a 17 week period. However, the TUC argue that employers are forcing workers into such agreements by a variety of methods such as making this part of their contract or handbook or just by straight bullying.

Whilst there is research to suggest that in fact many workers do long hours of their own volition (see the Chartered Institute of Personnel and Development survey 'Living to Work?' October 2003, p. 11; see also Chapter 10), the 'Labour Force Survey' suggests that most full time employees wanted to work fewer hours. That being said, for many this is subject to there being no resulting cut in pay (Department of Trade and Industry 2004, p. 16).

However, finance is not the only reason for working long hours, with the amount of work that people have to do and the expectation of employers also being important factors (Department of Trade and Industry 2004, p. 16). Not surprisingly, therefore, there is evidence to suggest that the vast majority of employers support the opt-out and feel their efficiency would suffer if it were removed (House of Lords European Committee 2004, p. 13).

Despite this, the figures seem to suggest that the proportion of the population working more than 48 hours a week has gradually declined since the regulations were introduced in 1998. In evidence to the House of Lords European Committee in 2004 the DTI suggested that the proportion had fallen from 23.3% of full time employees in spring 1998 to 20.4% in spring 2003 (House of Lords European Committee 2004, p. 15) although, as we see below, this figure does fluctuate. The regulations would therefore seem to have had some effect. However, it would be too simplistic to attribute all of this reduction to them.

As we saw at the very start of the chapter our behaviour is influenced by many other factors than the laws that we live under. For many companies therefore the effect of legislation may be determined by broader factors such as the competitive conditions that they operate under (Edwards et al. 2004) or the effectiveness of the enforcement (Stephen et al. 2009). Specifically, in relation to working time there is evidence to suggest that, at least initially, the proportion of people working long hours in Britain fell during the recession which started during 2008 (Philpott 2010). However, it should be noted that this figure rose again quite quickly.

The Working Time Directive may therefore be irrelevant in most workplaces where the norm is to work much less than 48 hours a week. Indeed, in 2012 full time employees in the UK worked a mean average of 39.1 hours a week (Office for National Statistics 2012).

The relationships within firms may also have an impact on how individuals react. Thus a firm with a recognized trade union in place is more likely to be in consultation with the workforce over pay and conditions, although this is done in a collective sense with the relationship being mediated through trade union representatives (Kersley et al. 2005). Union organization is much weaker in smaller firms (Kersley et al. 2005 pp. 13 and 14) where the relationship between employee and employer may be more direct. The relevance of this for the Working Time Directive is that there is evidence that '[e]mployees tended to work more than 48 hours a week with greater frequency … in workplaces without a recognised union' (Kersley et al. 2005, p. 28).

It is important therefore to consider the law and its impact in a broader sense. It is clearly an important factor in determining how businesses operate but cannot be seen in isolation. The competing interests and influences that help to create the law also determine how it is implemented. Consideration of the law is therefore not simply a technical issue but something that brings together many of the themes that run throughout this book.

Questions

1. **Explain whether you think people's working hours should be regulated.**

2. **Should employers and employees not be free to agree between themselves the terms and conditions of their relationship?**

Review and discussion questions

1. Outline the different sources of the law in the UK. In what areas can business have an influence on what the law is?

2. How does the law of the European Union affect businesses? Do you think its impact has been positive or negative?

3. Describe the different legal structures that a business can adopt. What are the advantages and disadvantages of the different structures?

4. How far should decisions made about legislation be influenced by ideological considerations?

5. Summarize the arguments for and against legal intervention. Could the different viewpoints be reconciled through greater degrees of self-regulation?

Assignments

1. Consider again the chapters which have looked at the different belief systems which might potentially have an impact on law-making.

   Outline the influence that these belief systems, both religious and ideological, should have on the law.

2. Commenting on the takeover of Cadbury by Kraft, David Cumming, Head of UK equities at Standard Life—one of Cadbury's shareholders—said, 'It's sad that Cadbury is gone, but business is business.'[3]

   Using the Cadbury takeover as an example, comment on whether business should just be business or whether companies can and should take into account broader concerns.

3. Is regulation that prevents events from happening in the first place the best way to change how businesses operate, or do the alternatives to regulation offer better mechanisms for doing this?

Further reading

The law is forever changing and therefore care should be taken when reading any book on the law as its contents may be out of date. It is also the case that law books can prove to be something of a struggle, even for lawyers, as they are necessarily very technical. With this in mind, the books recommended below are geared towards those who are not experts in the law and give you an overview of the relevant areas.

---

[3] <www.news.bbc.co.uk/1/hi/8467007.stm>

Oxford Dictionary of the Law 8th Edition (2013) (Oxford: Oxford University Press). *Law, like many other subjects, has its own language. You may well find in your reading that you come across a term you are unfamiliar with. If so, this is the book for you.*

Holland, J. and Webb, J. (2010) *Learning Legal Rules 7th Edition* (Oxford: Oxford University Press). *This book provides a good starting point for studying and applying the law. If nothing else you should read chapter 1 which gives a good overview of the basic structure and sources of the law. At the time of writing a new edition of this book was due to be published.*

Davies, K. (2007) *Understanding European Union Law 3rd Edition* (Abingdon: Routledge). *European Law can be very difficult to grasp. This book provides a simple and helpful overview of the main issues. Again, a new edition of this text is due.*

Riches, S. and Allen, V. (2011) *Keenan and Riches' Business Law 10th Edition* (Harlow: Pearson Education). *This covers all the central elements of business law. It therefore looks at the different types of business organization as well as broader legal issues affecting businesses such as the formation of contracts and employing labour.*

Griffiths, J. A. G. (1997) *The Politics of the Judiciary 5th Edition* (London: Fontana). *A seminal text on the role of the judiciary. Whilst not specifically related to business it does give an insight into a central element of the legal system.*

Bakan, J. (2005) *The Corporation* (London: Constable) *(see also the film of the same name). A critique of the company as an institution written by a Canadian law professor. Bakan argues that the legal structure of a company makes it act in a way that puts profit before social considerations.*

online resource centre

Test your understanding of this chapter with online questions and answers, explore the subject further through web exercises, and use the web links to provide a quick resource for further research. Go to the Online Resource Centre at <www.oxfordtextbooks.co.uk/orc/wetherly_otter/2>

Useful websites

<www.companieshouse.gov.uk>
Companies House incorporates companies and collects and stores all the information they are expected to file on incorporation and annually.

<www.legislation.gov.uk>
Has the full text of all UK legislation since 1987.

<www.europa.eu>
The European Union website which gives plenty of information on the institutions and working of the EU.

<www.cbi.org.uk>
Confederation of British Industry.

<www.britishchambers.org.uk>
The website for the British Chambers of Commerce.

<www.bis.gov.uk>
The website for the Department of Business, Innovation & Skills which contains a wealth of information that is helpful to businesses.

<www.tuc.org.uk>
The website for the main employee organization in the UK. Has a wealth of material relating to all aspects of employment and regulation.

<www.legalzoom.com>
A website that offers a glimpse of how legal services might operate in the future.

References

Alcock, A. (2009) 'An accidental change to directors' duties?', *Company Lawyer* 30(12) 362-68.

Aviva (2013) 'Road to Reform: Reducing Motor Premiums by Reforming the Personal Injury Claims Process' (accessed 1 April 2013) <www.aviva.com/data/report-library/Road_to_Reform_Reducing_motor_premiums_by_reforming_the_personal_injury_claims_process.pdf>

Bakan, J. (2004) *The Corporation* (London: Constable).

Baksi, C. 'Probate work helps Co-op ABS break even in year one', *Law Gazette* 21 March 2013 (accessed 1st April 2013) <http://www.lawgazette.co.uk/news/probate-work-helps-co-op-abs-break-even-year-one>

Better Regulation Commission (2006) *Annual Report for 2006* (accessed 12 April 2007) <www.brc.gov.uk/downloads/07/2006_annual_report.pdf>

Better Regulation Executive (2010) 'Reducing Regulation Made Simple' (accessed 25 March 2013) <https://www.gov.uk/government/uploads/system/uploads/attachment_data/file/31626/10-1155-reducing-regulation-made-simple.pdf>

Boon, A. (2010) 'Armageddon for the Legal Profession?' *Legal Profession Jotwell*, 21 May (accessed 4 April 2013) <www.legalpro.jotwell.com/2010/05/>

Cabinet Office (2006) 'Simplification Plans—A summary' (accessed 12 April 2007) <www.cabinetoffice.gov.uk/regulation/documents/simplification/summary.pdf>

Chartered Institute Of Personnel and Development (2003) 'Living to Work?' (accessed 12 April 2007) <www.cipd.co.uk/NR/rdonlyres/348BBDDC-5D2F-470E-B674-92D5E7741D24/0/livingtowork2003.pdf>

Chee, F. Y. (2012) 'EU imposes record $1.9 billion cartel fine on Philips, five others' *Reuters*, 5 December (accessed 1 March 2013) http://uk.reuters.com/article/2012/12/05/us-eu-cartel-crt-idUSBRE8B40EK20121205>

Cohen, G. A. (1978) *Karl Marx's Theory of History A Defence* (Oxford: Clarendon Press).

Department for Constitutional Affairs (2005) 'The Future of Legal Services: Putting Consumers First' Cm 6679 (accessed 10 May 2010) <www.dca.gov.uk/legalsys/folwp.pdf>

Department of Trade And Industry (2004) 'Working time—widening the debate: a preliminary consultation on long hours working in the UK and the application and operation of the working time opt out' (accessed 12 April 2007) <www.dti.gov.uk/files/file11782.pdf>

Dyer, C. and Jones, R. (2005) 'Workers win test case in asbestos claim', *The Guardian* 16 February 2005 (accessed 12 April 2007) <http://business.guardian.co.uk/story/0,1415567,00.html>

Edwards, P., Ram, M. and Black, J. (2004) 'Why Does Employment Legislation Not Damage Small Firms?' *Journal of Law and Society* 31 (2), 245–265.

Financial Reporting Council (2012) *The UK Corporate Governance Code* (London: Financial Reporting Council) (accessed 4 April 2013) <http://www.frc.org.uk/Our-Work/Publications/Corporate-Governance/UK-Corporate-Governance-Code-September-2012.aspx>

Harris, M. (2012) 'Chicago Confidential: Lehman Brothers bankruptcy examiner believes lessons not heeded', *The Chicago Tribune*, 28 October (accessed 3 April 2013) <http://articles.chicagotribune.com/2012-10-28/business/ct-biz-1028-confidential-valukas-20121028_1_anton-valukas-lehman-brothers-balance-sheet/2#sthash.HiZS3M0o.dpuf>

HM Treasury (2001) 'Institutional Investment in the UK: A Review' (accessed 12 April 2007) <www.hm-treasury.gov.uk/media/2F9/02/31.pdf>

HM Treasury 'Budget Report 2006' (accessed 12 April 2007) <www.hm-treasury.gov.uk./media/20E/EA/bud06_ch3_192.pdf>

Health and Safety Executive (2012) 'Costs to Britain of Workplace Accidents and Work—Related Ill Health: 2010/11 update' (accessed 22 March 2013) <http://www.hse.gov.uk/statistics/pdf/cost-to-britain.pdf>

Health and Safety Executive (2009) 'Health and Safety Annual Statistics Report 2011/12' (accessed 22 March 2013) <www.hse.gov.uk/statistics/overall/hssh1112.pdf>

House of Commons Business, Innovation and Skills Committee (2010) 'Mergers, acquisition and takeovers: the takeover of Cadbury by Kraft', HC 234 (accessed 10 May 2010) <http://www.publications.parliament.uk/pa/cm/cmbis.htm>

House of Lords European Committee (2004) 'The Working Time Directive: A response to the European Commission's review', HL paper 67 (accessed 12 April 2007) <www.publications.parliament.uk/pa/ld200304/ldselect/ldeucom/67/67.pdf>

Inman, P. (2010) 'Unions call for 'Cadbury law' to protect British industry', *The Guardian*, 6 April 2010 (accessed 8 April 2010) <http://www.guardian.co.uk/business/2010/apr/06/unions-cadbury-law-kraft-takeover>

Kersley, B., Alpin, C., Forth, J., Bryson, A., Bewley, H., Dix, G., and Oxenbridge, S. 'Inside the workplace: First findings from the 2004 Workplace Employment Relations Survey' (accessed 12 April 2007) www.dti.gov.uk/files/file11423.pdf>

Kirgis, P. F. (2010) 'The Knowledge Guild: The Legal Profession in an Age of Technological Change—Review of Richard Susskind, "The End of Lawyers? Rethinking the Nature of Legal Services"' *St John's Legal Studies Research Paper No 1656910* (accessed 4 December 2012) <http://papers.ssrn.com/sol3/papers.cfm?abstract_id=1656910>

Lacity, M. and Willcocks, L. (2012) 'Legal Process Outsourcing: LPO Provider Landscape' (accessed 1 April 2013) <http://www.outsourcingunit.org/publications/LPOprovider.pdf>

Laitner, S. and Taylor, A., (2006) 'Move to scrap work hours opt-out foiled', *The Financial Times*, 8 November.

Lazenby, P. (2010) 'Asbestos: Straw upholds an injustice', *The Guardian*, 1 March (accessed 9 April 2010) <http://www.guardian.co.uk/commentisfree/2010/mar/01/jack-straw-asbestos-ruling>

Legal Futures (2012) 'LegalZoom gears up for UK entry with $120 m IPO', 14 May (accessed 4 December 2012) <http://www.legalfutures.co.uk/latest-news/legalzoom-gears-up-for-uk-entry-with-120m-ipo>

Legal Futures (2012) 'LPOs set to take on high-value work and "compete directly with law firms"' (accessed 1 April 2013) <http://www.legalfutures.co.uk/latest-news/lpos-set-take-high-value-work-compete-directly-law-firms>

Lords Grand Committee, 6 February 2006, Column GC256 (accessed 16 March 2013) <http://www.publications.parliament.uk/pa/ld200506/ldhansrd/vo060206/text/60206-29.htm>

Lynch, E. (2012) 'Legislative Comment Section 172: a groundbreaking reform of director's duties, or the emperor's new clothes?' *Company Lawyer* 33(7) pp. 196–203.

Office for National Statistics (2012) *'Annual Survey of Hours and Earnings 2012 Provisional Results'* (accessed 27 March 2013) <http://www.ons.gov.uk/ons/dcp171778_286243.pdf>

Office for National Statistics (2009) 'United Kingdom Balance of Payments: The Pink Book' 2009 edition (accessed 8 May 2010) <**www.statistics.gov.uk/downloads/theme_economy/PB09.pdf**>

Philpott, J. (2010) 'Working Hours in the Recession' (accessed 4 April 2013) <**http://www.cipd.co.uk/binaries/WORK_AUDIT_Factfile_Aug10.pdf**>

Powers, C. M. (2010) 'The Changing Role of Chaebol', *Stanford Journal of East Asian Affairs* 10(2) pp. 105–116.

Sibun, J. (2010) 'Cadbury takeover: a crafty bit of business or an overpriced confection?' *The Daily Telegraph*, 20 January (accessed 10 May 2010) <**http://www.telegraph.co.uk/finance/newsbysector/retailandconsumer/7031633/Cadbury-takeover-a-crafty-bit-of-business-or-an-overpriced-confection.html**>

Stephen, F., Urbano, D., and van Hemmen, S. (2009) 'The responsiveness of entrepreneurs to working time regulations', *Small Business Economics* 32, pp. 259–76.

Susskind, R. (2008) *The End of Lawyers? Rethinking the nature of legal services* (Oxford: Oxford University Press).

Susskind, R. (2013) *Tomorrow's Lawyers: An introduction to your future* (Oxford: Oxford University Press).

Thompson, J. (2010) 'Kraft to close Cadbury factory near Bristol' *The Independent*, 10 February (accessed 10 May 2010) <**http://www.independent.co.uk/news/business/news/kraft-to-close-cadbury-factory-near-bristol-1894520.html**>

TUC (2004) Press release 'Time to end long hours working', 30 March (accessed 12 April 2007) <**www.tuc.org.uk/work_life/tuc-7840-f0.cfm**>

TUC (2006) Press release 'TUC comment on red tape review', 11 December (accessed 12 April 2007) <**www.tuc.org.uk/law/tuc-12771-f0.cfm**>

International Finance Corporation and World Bank (2013) *Doing Business 2013 Smarter Regulations for Small and Medium-Sized Enterprises* (Washington: International Bank for Reconstruction and Development/World Bank) (accessed 4 April 2013) <**http://www.doingbusiness.org/reports/global-reports/doing-business-2013**>

Case law

Cowan v *Scargill and Others* (1985) Ch. 270.

Dodge v *Ford Motor Company* 204 Mich. 459 (1919)

NV Algemene Transporten Expeditie Onderneming van Gend en Loos v *Nederlandse Administratie der Belastingen* Case 26/62, [1963] ECR 1

Salomon v *Salomon* (1897) AC 22

Wright v *Michael Wright Supplies Ltd and another* [2013] EWCA Civ 234

Chapter 6
The social and cultural environment

Paul Wetherly

Learning objectives

When you have completed this chapter you will be able to:

- Explain the nature of the social and cultural environments, and their importance for business.
- Analyse demographic trends and the implications of an ageing population for business.
- Explain what is meant by the term multiculturalism and examine the impact of immigration on business and society.
- Analyse class differences and patterns of inequality in Britain, and relate these issues to business responsibility.
- Examine the extent of social mobility in Britain and explain the implications for business.

THEMES

The following themes of the book are especially relevant to this chapter

⟫ DIVERSITY OF BUSINESS

This chapter deals with aspects of diversity in British society, e.g. age, ethnicity, and social class. We also examine how far this diversity is reflected in business and find evidence of an 'ethnic penalty' in the labour market.

⟫ INTERNAL/EXTERNAL

The issues examined in this chapter have an important internal dimension in respect of organization culture and business decisions. For example, growing inequality in UK society has been attributed in part to a culture of greed in boardrooms.

⟫ COMPLEXITY OF THE ENVIRONMENT

This chapter demonstrates the complexity of the business environment by showing that it is not just economic but also has important social and cultural dimensions.

⟫ VARIETY OF SPATIAL LEVELS

This chapter focuses mainly on the UK but aspects of social life and social trends are influenced by the growing interconnectedness of societies as a result of globalization, e.g. migration.

⟫ DYNAMIC ENVIRONMENT

This chapter identifies key social trends, showing how many aspects of social and cultural life are different today than in the past.

⟫ **INTERACTION** BETWEEN BUSINESS AND THE ENVIRONMENT

Business not only has to respond to changes in the social and cultural environment but also shapes social change, e.g. migration responds to labour market conditions.

⟫ **STAKEHOLDERS**

Analysing the social environment also involves identifying a range of stakeholder groups with differing interests in relation to business, e.g. sections of the population defined by social class, ethnicity, and age.

⟫ **VALUES**

Modern societies are pluralistic or 'cosmopolitan', characterized by diversity of lifestyles and values.

▦ Introduction: what is the social and cultural environment?

⟫ **INTERACTION** ⟫ **DYNAMIC** In this chapter we will examine some key aspects of society and culture in order to understand how these interact with business—business activity is influenced by the socio-cultural setting in which it takes place, but also shapes that setting. British society has a growing and ageing population, with a particular racial and ethnic (multicultural) mix that continues to be shaped by immigration, and has a distinctive class structure and pattern of inequality. In analysing the social-cultural environment of business it is important to recognize that society and culture are not homogeneous or fixed. Rather social and cultural change is a hallmark of modern societies and, again, business can be seen as both driving these changes and having to respond to them.

▦ Demographic trends—a growing and ageing population

In this section and the subsequent one we will focus on the following dimensions of the UK population and demographic change:

- population size
- population structure (by age, sex, and ethnicity).

The UK population is growing, and the rate of increase has been rising. According to the 2011 census estimate it reached 63.2 million—its highest ever level, and an increase of 4.1 million (nearly 7%) over the decade since 2001. This was much higher than the increase in the previous decade to 2001 (2.9%), and was the highest decennial increase of the century from 1911. Over the course of that century the UK population increased by 50% (Office for National Statistics 2012).

Population change (growth or decline) is determined by the combined effects of:

- natural change resulting from birth and **death rates** (i.e. the number of births/deaths per 1,000 of the population)
- net migration (i.e. the difference between inward and outward migration flows).

(Table 6.1). Ageing of the population can be seen clearly by the shift outwards of the pyramid in all five-year age groups above 65 years between 2001 and 2011. Increased life expectancy is revealed by a falling death rate (Table 6.1), because within each age band more people survive into the next. For example, a larger proportion of people in their 70s live on into their 80s, so the death rate among 70- to 79-year-olds declines.

》 DYNAMIC The ageing of the UK population can be seen by comparing the age structure in 1971 with that projected for 2021 (Table 6.3). In 1971 10.5% of males were aged 65 and above, whereas this is projected to rise to 18.8% in 2026. For females the figures are 15.9% and 21.9% respectively, reflecting higher life expectancy than for males. The table also shows that over this period the number aged 65 and above has been catching up the number aged under 16—there were more females aged over 65 than under 16 by 2011. The increase in the number of people aged 85 and over (the 'oldest old') is particularly notable—by 2026 it is projected that there will be nearly five times as many people in this age group compared to 1971 (compared to a near doubling of the number aged 65 and over). Ageing over this period reflects both increased longevity and previous 'baby booms'. Figure 6.3 shows the effects of peaks in the birth rate in the late 1940s and early 1960s in the bulges in the 45–49 and 60–64 age bands, and projected ageing occurs as these cohorts move up the pyramid.

It is not certain whether this trend will continue in the future as it depends on the balance between factors that have a positive or adverse effect on life expectancy. For example, high rates of child obesity and the implications for health later in life have raised fears that today's children may have a shorter life expectancy than their parents. However, it has been estimated that 'life expectancy is increasing so fast that half the babies born in the UK in 2007 will live to be at least 103' (Boseley 2009).

》 SPATIAL LEVEL Figures 6.4 and 6.5 compare the UK with other EU member states and show that population ageing is an international phenomenon. Although the percentage of the population aged 65 and over in the UK is projected to rise from 17% to 23% between 2010 and

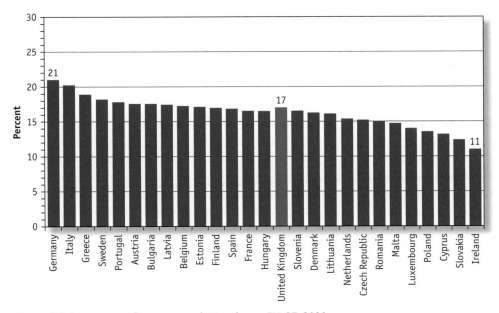

Figure 6.4 Percentage of persons aged 65 and over, EU-27, 2010

Source: Office for National Statistics, 2012b.

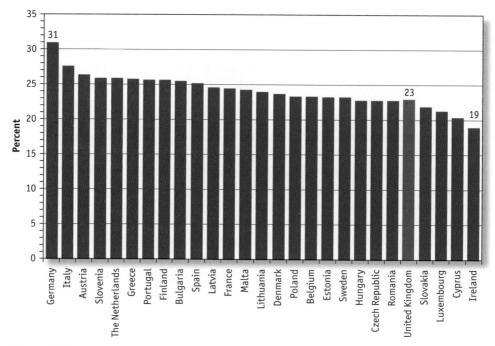

Figure 6.5 Percentage of population aged 65 and over, EU-27, 2035
Source: Office for National Statistics, 2012b.

2035, other countries are projected to experience a greater rise, with the effect that the UK will become one of the least aged societies among EU members by 2035. Whereas in 2010 twelve countries were less aged than the UK, by 2035 there will be just four. Germany is shown as the most aged society in both years, with the proportion aged 65 and over projected to increase to 31% in 2035 (Office for National Statistics 2012b).

Population ageing is also a global phenomenon, not confined to the rich countries such as the EU27 but affecting nearly every country, and happening fastest in poor countries. 'In 2012, people aged 60 or over represent almost 11.5 per cent of our total global population of 7 billion. By 2050, the proportion is projected to nearly double to 22 per cent' (United Nations Population Fund 2012).

Implications of ageing for business and society

▶▶ **VALUES** It is obvious that increased average life expectancy is a 'good thing' since almost everybody would prefer to live a longer life. Yet the ageing of the population is often portrayed as presenting a challenge for the economy and society, even a crisis. For example, in recent years in the UK there has been much discussion of a pensions crisis and a crisis of care for the elderly, and these concerns are also expressed at a global level (United Nations Population Fund 2012). Ageing of the population seems to be, at best, a mixed blessing. To understand this it helps to think about increased life expectancy in terms of 'work–life' balance or, more particularly, the balance between working life and 'non-work life'. (The issue of work–life balance is examined in more detail in Chapter 12.) All societies have to find ways of allocating resources to support the non-working population (or the periods in individuals' lives when they are not working, including old age) from the output produced by the working population. Increased life expectancy presents a challenge to society because it increases the *number* of elderly and the *ratio* of elderly to those of working age. This implies that more

Mini-Case 6.2 Ethnic penalties in the UK labour market

The first black chief executive of a leading UK company was appointed in 2009. At the time there was only one other black director of a FTSE 100 company. This is an instance of a more general pattern of disadvantages experienced by non-white ethnic minorities in the labour market, or 'ethnic penalties'. Research for the Department for Work and Pensions (DWP) showed that:

a number of ethnic minority groups, notably Pakistani, Bangladeshi, Black Caribbean and Black African men continue to experience higher unemployment rates, greater concentrations in routine and semi-routine work and lower hourly earnings.

(Heath and Cheung 2006)

There is a clear pattern of occupational segregation in the private sector—just as ethnic minorities are overrepresented in routine and semi-routine occupations they are underrepresented in professional and managerial occupations. In contrast, ethnic penalties tend to be 'markedly lower' in the public sector. These differentials could not be explained in terms of educational attainment or other factors, and therefore:

unequal treatment on grounds of race or colour is likely to be a major factor underlying the pattern of ethnic penalties.

(Heath and Cheung 2006)

To test the claim that unequal treatment, i.e. discrimination, is a major cause of observed ethnic penalties a method

sometimes described as the 'CV test' has been used. Research for the DWP involved submitting three applications (CVs) which were alike except for the ethnic identity of the applicant (indicated by the use of distinctive English, Asian, or African names) to each of 987 job vacancies in a variety of occupational categories. In each of the 987 cases there was one application with a white name and two with ethnic minority names. Differential success in securing an invitation to interview provides a measure of discrimination on ethnic grounds.

One or more of the three applicants received a positive response in 155 of the 987 cases. Among these the success rate for ethnic minority applications was 39% compared to 68% for white applicants. 'So, the net discrimination in favour of white names over equivalent applications from ethnic minority candidates was 29 per cent' (Wood 2009).

Comparing the overall success rates for the 987 applications with a white name and the 1,974 applications with an ethnic minority name, the research showed that:

16 applications from ethnic minority applicants had to be sent for a successful outcome ... compared with nine white. That is, 74 per cent more applications from ethnic minority candidates needed to be sent for the same level of success.

(Wood 2009)

▓ Class structure

The meaning of class

⟫ **VALUES** The existence of different classes is often seen as an important, and undesirable, feature of British society. What is seen as undesirable about a class system is that it involves a hierarchy: some people are in higher positions in society and some in lower positions. Some people are 'better off' (enjoy a higher standard of living) than others, or simply 'better' (enjoy a higher social status). Class may be a key source of social division and conflict, and a major barrier to individuals realizing their potential. However, class is a controversial concept, and some people argue that class differences are natural and desirable. For example, class differences may be seen as reflecting differences between individuals in terms of talent and effort. Others claim that the importance of class has declined, or even that it is no longer useful to look at society in this way.

In British society people are familiar with the language of class, and most, if asked, could define their own class position. The most familiar terms are 'working', 'middle', and 'upper' class, though finer distinctions are often made such as 'lower-middle' and 'upper-middle' (but see BBC 2013 for a revised approach). But what do these terms mean? What criteria can we use to distinguish between, say, the working class and the middle class? How are class distinctions related to business?

It is common to see class distinctions in terms of aspects of behaviour, for example, accent, manners, and lifestyle. It can be argued that British people are highly sensitive to these behavioural markers of class, such as whether a person speaks with a 'posh' or 'common' accent. However, these behavioural differences may be seen as outward expressions of more basic determinants of class, relating especially to economic factors such as income and economic role. Income seems to provide a straightforward way of defining class: on the whole the middle class is better off than the working class, and the upper class is at the top of the income scale. Income is correlated with behavioural differences to some extent, partly due to the obvious point that higher incomes afford more expensive lifestyles.

》 STAKEHOLDERS Income is closely related to economic position and role, because income is generated primarily by business activity and each person's share is determined by the role they play in business. There are two ways of relating class differences to the business system: the first sees the basic class distinction in capitalist economies as between employers and employees, and the second defines class position in terms of a person's occupation.

Capitalism and class

Capitalism is based on private ownership of business, and the vast majority of people depend for their livelihood on the wage or salary they earn as employees through selling their labour or ability to work to an employer in the labour market. Some have seen this employer–employee relationship as a basic form of class division that is characteristic of capitalist economies. Employers make up a **business class (capitalist class)**, while the very large group of employees constitute the working class. In this view the economic role that defines class position is ownership and control (or not) of business. This is also a distinction in terms of income: profit (business class) versus wage/salary (working class). The importance of this class division is that it may be seen as a perpetual source of tension and conflict because the interests of the two classes are opposed: the profit motive of the business class leads to pressure to hold down wage costs and increase effort and productivity, and members of the working class will resist this pressure. Thus industrial relations are inherently prone to conflict. Some difficulties with this view of class are:

》 STAKEHOLDERS

- It can be argued that employers and employees, far from being in conflict, share a basic interest as stakeholders in the success of the business. Employees have a stake in competitiveness and profitability to ensure their own job security. These two views can be reconciled by arguing that employees' interests do tend to bring them into conflict with employers, but that this conflict is played out within limits imposed by the need to secure the survival of the business.

- Identifying the business class is not straightforward. In the modern economy private ownership of business means, to a large extent, ownership of shares by insurance companies and pension funds and other financial institutions. Indirectly, this seems to mean that the millions of policy holders who, for example, contribute to pension schemes as employees have an ownership stake in business. In addition, the people who run large corporations on a day-to-day basis are not shareholders but directors and senior managers who are, in effect, salaried employees of the business (though very highly paid ones). Finally, the world of 'big business' is far removed from those who own and manage small and medium-sized enterprises (SMEs) or work on their own account, so we might not think of the chief executives of, say, the few major building contractors as belonging in the same class as the proprietors of the numerous 'small-time' outfits in the SME sector. The business class today, then, seems to be comprised mainly of executives at the most senior levels within corporate hierarchies, together with wealthy individuals who continue to play a significant role in ownership of business, and spokespersons for business in organizations such as trade associations, employers' organizations, and business think-tanks.

• Although earning a wage or salary is something that all employees share in common, to refer to them all as 'working class' seems to overlook differences between occupations in terms of skill, status, and income. It can be argued that it makes more sense to see employees as constituting different classes—such as 'working' and 'middle'—according to occupation.

The occupational order

The occupational order provides a snapshot of the character of the economy at a particular time, a framework for identifying processes of change, and also provides a way of thinking about class. Occupation is the common currency of class—we tend to define a person's class in terms of the type of job they do. Social classes (or 'socio-economic' or 'occupational' classes) are identified by grouping occupations together in broad categories. Although there is a very large number of individual job titles, the logic of this approach is that broad groups of occupations are alike in some way and distinct from other groups.

▶ DYNAMIC The occupational order is dynamic. During the last century the UK experienced a transformation of the occupational order, so that the types of jobs that people are engaged in today, the skills that they are required to exercise, and the distribution of people between those jobs, are very different from early in the 20th century. As we will see, these changes have been interpreted by some as involving a transformation of the class structure—a decline of the working class and expansion of the middle class.

Table 6.5 shows the changing occupational class structure during the last century. Here occupations are divided into eight broad categories or occupational classes, including employers

Table 6.5 Occupational class in Great Britain, 1911–91 (%)

	1911	1931	1951	1971	1991
Higher professions	1.0	1.1	1.9	3.3	5.3
Lower professions	3.1	3.5	4.7	7.8	13.9
Employers & proprietors	6.7	6.7	5.0	4.2	3.3
Managers & administrators	3.4	3.7	5.5	6.8	15.1
Clerical workers	4.5	6.7	10.4	13.9	15.4
Foremen, supervisors	1.3	1.5	2.6	3.9	3.8
Sales	5.4	6.5	5.7	5.5	5.6
Manual workers	74.6	70.3	64.2	54.7	37.7
Skilled manual	30.6	26.7	24.9	21.6	14.4
Semi-skilled manual	34.4	28.8	27.2	20.6	17.6
Unskilled manual	9.6	14.8	12.0	12.5	5.7
Total in employment (000s)	18,347	21,029	22,514	25,021	24,746

Source: Adapted from Gallie 2000, p. 288, Table 8.4.

and proprietors. The class of manual occupations is further divided into three subgroups on the basis of level of skill. A major transformation was the decline by half in the share of manual (or 'blue collar') workers within the workforce, from approximately three in four in 1911 to three in eight in 1991. You can see that this decline accelerated in the second half of the century. Early in the last century manual workers constituted the vast bulk of the workforce, but by its close had become a minority. At the same time there was expansion of all other (non-manual or 'white collar') occupations (except employers and proprietors). The shares of the professions, managers and administrators, and clerical workers have increased by factors of between 3.4 (clerical) and 5.3 (higher professions). The actual numbers, within an expanding workforce, have increased by larger factors. For example, the number of people employed in the higher professions increased by a factor of 7.14, from 184,000 to 1,314,000 (1911–91). 'In short, there was a change from an occupational structure heavily dominated by manual work to one where there was a fairly even division between three broad categories: professional/managerial work, intermediary occupations and manual work' (Gallie 2000, p. 289). This occupational shift can also be understood in terms of:

- The shift of the industrial structure from *manufacturing* to *services*. The dominance of manual work in the first half of the century reflected the importance of manufacturing and primary industries (e.g. mining) within the economy (although manual jobs are not confined to manufacturing). The declining share (and number) of manual workers in the second half mirrored the process of manufacturing decline. Conversely, the growing non-manual occupations were predominantly in (though not confined to) the expanding service sector.

- The growth of non-manual jobs (particularly professional occupations) is explained partly by the growth of the **welfare state** in the period after the Second World War (post 1945).

- There is a *gendered* dimension to occupational change. The expansion of non-manual service occupations has been a major source of increased female participation in the workforce. This is particularly marked in the feminization of clerical occupations. In fact clerical occupations switched from being male dominated at the start of the century to being female dominated at its end. It is interesting to note that as clerical work has become more feminized there has been a decline of its relative pay and status. It can be argued that this reflects the undervaluation of 'women's work' in our society.

- In general, the shift in the occupational structure is associated with a process of **upskilling** of the workforce, meaning a rise in the average level of skill required. Although this average conceals ups and downs, with some occupations experiencing deskilling, upskilling is the predominant trend. Gallie reports that in 1992, 63% of all employees reported that the level of skill required to do their job had increased during the last five years.

- The transformation of the occupational order during the 20th century has been interpreted as an overhaul of the **class structure** of British society, involving a decline of the working class and expansion of the middle class. This interpretation stems from a definition of the working class as comprising all those in manual occupations and the middle class as being made up of non-manual workers. In this view, Britain's social structure has changed from one that was overwhelmingly working class to one in which the middle class predominates.

Since 2001 official statistics have been published using the National Statistics Socio-economic Classification (NS-SEC), based on the Standard Occupational Classification 2000 (SOC 2000). This classification differs from that used in Table 6.5, particularly in not distinguishing manual and non-manual occupations. Table 6.6 shows the class structure for the period 2001–12 based on NS-SEC. The table shows continued expansion of managerial

Table 6.6 All in employment by socio-economic classification (NS-SEC) (%)

	2001 (Q2)	2012 (Q2)
1. Higher managerial & professional	13.2	15.6
2. Lower managerial & professional	26.4	27.9
3. Intermediate occupations	13.1	14.0
4. Small employers & own account workers	9.2	107
5. Lower supervisory & technical	11.3	8.2
6. Semi-routine occupations	15.4	13.7
7. Routine occupations	11.6	10.0

Source: Office for National Statistics (no date) 'Table 19: All in employment by socio-economic classification (NS-SEC)' and EMP11: Employment by socio-economic classification (20 February 2013).

and professional occupations (classes 1 and 2), accounting for 43.5% of employment by 2012. At the same time there has been decline in the share (and number) of people employed in occupations at the bottom end (classes 5, 6, and 7). Routine occupations (class 7) now make up 10% of the total. This is consistent with the trend of upskilling observed in the last century.

Relevance of the class structure to business

》 DYNAMIC 》 VALUES

- The changing class structure (whether understood in terms of ownership or the occupational order) is driven largely by the dynamic operation of the business system, influenced by state intervention.

》 INTERNAL/EXTERNAL

- Class distinctions are closely bound up with the nature of the employment relationship and managerial strategies. 'Working class' occupations tend to be characterized by a 'labour contract' whereas 'middle class' occupations tend to be characterized by a 'service relationship' (ONS 2012e). Managerial and professional occupations (in particular class 1) are characterized by a 'service relationship' in which employees enjoy not only higher salaries in return for a 'service' rendered to the employer, but also a high level of discretion and control in their work based on trust, job security, and opportunities for career advancement (Table 6.6). At the other end of the scale, class 7 (routine occupations) is characterized by a 'labour contract' in which a wage is paid on the basis of hours worked or level of output. In a labour contract, employees perform routine tasks with little discretion, are subject to managerial authority rather than controlling their own work, and have less job security and little opportunity for advancement. These features are typical to a lesser degree of occupations in classes 5 and 6. Thus, the workforce tends towards a dichotomy between these two types of employment relationship, with intermediate forms characterizing class 3. The nature of the employment relationship involves managerial choice. This will be guided by efficiency considerations, but it also raises questions about how employees should be treated.

- The degree of social mobility has implications for competitiveness and economic performance. A low level of social mobility not only means that individuals from working class backgrounds may not have the opportunity to realize their talents and improve their standard of living but also suggests that business is missing out on a pool of untapped talent (see the end of chapter case study).

❱ **INTERNAL/EXTERNAL**

- Class is a useful concept for understanding attitudes to work and conflict in the employment relationship. Working class occupations and a labour contract type of employment relationship have been associated with conflictual 'us and them' attitudes and the development of trade unions to represent employees' interests in the workplace.

- Class is a useful concept for understanding the behaviour of consumers because of the link between class, income and lifestyle. In this way class can be used as a way of analysing different market segments.

Stop and Think

....

What is the meaning of the term 'social class'? How would you define your own class position? What criteria do you use to define your own class position?

▧ Inequality

❱ **VALUES** The question of class is closely connected with the issue of inequality in society because of the link between class, occupation and income. As in relation to class, there are sharply divided opinions on the question of inequality: some see inequality as natural and desirable, while others see it as one of the most damaging social problems within modern societies (and as a problem between societies in terms of the gap between rich and poor nations). Most debate does not take the form of inequality *versus* equality, but concerns the degree of inequality that is felt to be acceptable. Should we accept whatever pattern of income distribution the market throws up? Is it sufficient to ensure that there are equal opportunities in the market? Or should we seek to narrow the gap between rich and poor?

Equality of opportunity versus equality of outcome

An important distinction within this debate is between equality of *opportunity* and **equality of outcome**. Some argue that what matters is that people should have the same opportunities to get on in life and earn as much as they can, if that is what they want to do. As long as opportunities are equal it is fair enough, in this view, if some get ahead and others fall behind. This view of a meritocratic society is supported by the Milburn report on fair access to the professions, *Unleashing Aspiration*. Others argue that we should still be concerned about the outcome, to ensure that some don't get left too far behind or that some don't pull too far ahead. The first view is consistent with having laws to ensure equal opportunities through education and by prohibiting discrimination (e.g. the Sex Discrimination Act, Race Relations Act, Disability Discrimination Act). The second view suggests the need for government to do more than this, such as using the tax and benefit system to redistribute income or using the law to set minimum and even maximum wages and salaries. However, these two concepts of equality are closely related, as argued by the Milburn report:

> It is no coincidence that countries such as Australia, Japan, Sweden and the Netherlands, which are the most socially fluid in the world, are also among the most equal. The fact that the UK remains such a persistently unequal society is in large part the reason why social mobility is lower than in other less unequal nations. Greater equality and more mobility are two sides of the same coin.
>
> (Panel on Fair Access to the Professions 2009)

The earnings distribution

Inequality in terms of earnings can be analysed by dividing the earnings distribution into ten bands each containing 10% of earners (deciles). A measure of the dispersal of earnings can be obtained by comparing the top and bottom bands or deciles. A tenth of full-time employees earned less than £282 per week in 2012, while a tenth earned more than £999 per week (Figure 6.6). This gives a ratio of the highest to the lowest decile for gross weekly earnings of 3.5, which has been stable since 1997. In other words, the person at the 90th percentile in the distribution earned 3.5 times as much as the person at the 10th percentile.

This measure doesn't tell us about earnings above and below these cut-off points in the distribution, nor does it show what occupations are involved. Another approach is to identify the highest and lowest paid occupations. Figure 6.7 and Table 6.7 show median gross weekly earnings for full-time employees in occupational groups in April 2012. The highest earnings were for Managers and Senior Officials at £738 (46% higher than the median weekly earnings for all employees at £506) and the lowest were for Sales and Customer Service occupations at £323 (36% lower than the median). Looking at particular occupations (four-digit SOC 2010) rather than broad occupational groups, 'in April 2012 the highest paid ... occupation for full-time employees was aircraft pilots and flight engineers, with median gross weekly earnings of £1,559. ...The next highest paid occupation was chief executives and senior officials, with median gross weekly earnings of £1,547 per week. At £245 per week, leisure and theme park attendants were the lowest paid of all full-time employees on adult rates of pay, followed by hairdressers and barbers at £246' (Office for National Statistics, 2013a, p.18). Thus, the ratio of median weekly earnings between chief executives and senior officials at the top and leisure and theme park attendants at the bottom was more than 6.

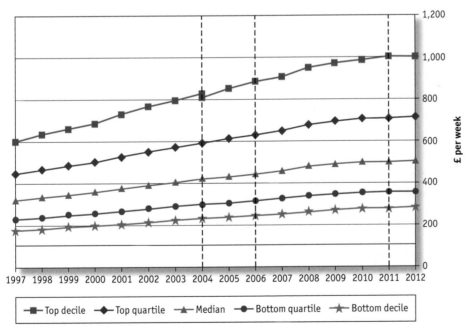

Figure 6.6 Distribution of full-time gross weekly earnings, UK, April 1997 to 2012

Source: Office for National Statistics 2013a.

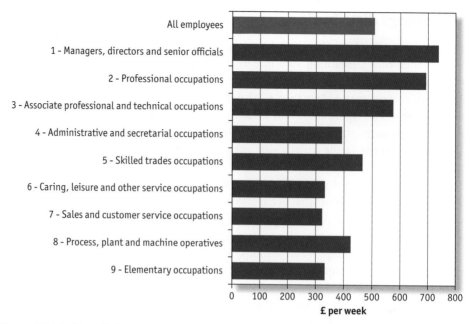

Figure 6.7 Median full-time gross weekly earnings by major occupation group, UK, April 2012 (Standard Occupational Classification 2010)

Source: Adapted from data from the Office for National Statistics licensed under the Open Government Licence v.1.0.

Table 6.7 Median full-time gross weekly earnings by major occupation group, UK, April 2012 (Standard Occupational Classification 2010)

	£ per week
All employees	**505.9**
1 - Managers, directors and senior officials	738.4
2 - Professional occupations	694.3
3 - Associate professional and technical occupations	575.0
4 - Administrative and secretarial occupations	393.1
5 - Skilled trades occupations	465.7
6 - Caring, leisure and other service occupations	332.7
7 - Sales and customer service occupations	323.3
8 - Process, plant and machine operatives	426.4
9 - Elementary occupations	333.0

Source: Adapted from data from the Office for National Statistics licensed under the Open Government Licence v.1.0.

Executive pay

However, this ratio still understates the gap between the highest and lowest earners by a wide margin, particularly because the median figure for directors' earnings conceals the range of earnings above this point. In recent years the growth of executive pay and the gap between the very highest earners and the rest of society has become a focus of political debate in the UK and elsewhere. In 2009 a survey of executive pay by *The Guardian* newspaper showed that the then Chief Executive of Tesco, Terry Leahy, was paid more than 900 times as much as Tesco's *average* worker. The highest paid CEO in the FTSE 100 was Bart Becht, of Reckitt Benckiser, who received £36.8 million in pay, bonuses, perks, and share incentive schemes. This sum was 1,374 times as much as the average pay of company employees. Only two chief executives of FTSE 100 companies received pay that was less than 20 times the average within the company. The survey showed that the average basic salary (excluding bonuses, perks, and share incentive schemes that can significantly boost total pay) of chief executives of FTSE 100 companies was £791,000. In the year of the survey basic salaries of CEOs increased by 10%, compared to an average of 3.1% for private sector employees. This continued a trend of a widening gap between the pay of top executives and employees. In 2011 the High Pay Commission reported increases in executive pay expressed as a multiple of the average pay of employees in the largest companies since the 1970s. For example, 'in Barclays, top pay [in 2011 was] 75 times that of the average worker. In 1979 it was 14.5. Over that period, the lead executive's pay in Barclays ha[d] risen by 4,899.4%' (High Pay Commission 2011, p. 8). This is not unusual: an estimate of the multiple, based on a sample of FTSE100 companies taking part in a survey in 2011, showed that the average ratio between top and bottom pay was 262:1 (One Society 2011). The Directors' Pay Report 2012/13 produced by Incomes Data Services (IDS) shows that median total earnings of FTSE directors had increased by 10% during the year to £3.2 million (Incomes Data Services 2012). In contrast, IDS reported a whole economy median pay award of 2.5% for the three months to the end of January 2013, below the rate of inflation (IDS 2013).

Stop and Think

Do you think that the 262:1 ratio between top and bottom pay levels in FTSE companies is:

a) too high

b) about right

c) too low.

How did you decide?

What has inequality got to do with business?

There are opposing views on whether (widening) inequality is a social problem and the extent to which business is responsible. In recent years survey evidence has indicated widespread public concern that the gap between rich and poor is too wide, and the question of inequality has moved up the political agenda.

To judge whether income inequality is a problem we need to consider its economic and social impacts. These impacts can be both positive and negative. As we have seen, the main debate is about the degree of inequality that is acceptable. Most people agree, for example, that chief executives should be paid more than their employees in the business, but they are likely to disagree about whether the widening gap can be justified. The debate is often framed in terms of two key principles: efficiency and fairness (or social justice).

Incentives

Inequality can be seen as good for efficiency on the basis that incentives are required to attract talent and motivate performance. In other words the very high rewards of chief executives are needed to attract the best people to perform these important jobs. Having the most talented people running our companies means that they are more likely to be efficient and successful.

This argument has also been used to defend bankers' bonuses in response to widespread public criticism in the context of the financial crisis and economic recession. The high rewards available at the top will motivate others to perform to a high level in order to progress up the career ladder.

The going rate

In effect the scarcity of talent bids up the price of chief executives and of other highly rewarded occupations. For example, medical practitioner is one of the best rewarded occupations and the same logic applies here: high earnings attract talented people into these jobs. Against the accusation that CEOs are 'fat cats' awarding themselves excessive pay, it can be argued that companies have to pay the 'going rate' in a competitive market. Just as football clubs have to pay huge sums in transfer payments and salaries to attract top players such as Wayne Rooney, they also, like all other businesses, have to pay whatever is necessary to recruit the best manager. The alternative is to risk loss of competitiveness and the prospect of sliding down the league table.

The same argument applies at the other end of the scale. In other words, checkout operators are low paid because their wages are also determined by competition in the labour market. Only in this case there is no scarcity to bid up the price, rather a plentiful supply of workers able to do this job holds wages down. Again, companies have to pay the going rate since if one company pays more than its rivals it puts itself at a competitive disadvantage by increasing its costs.

Trickle down

Does the market produce a fair distribution of earnings? For some people the gap between the top and bottom of the earnings distribution seems like an obvious case of unfairness. In fact this seems to be a view that is held widely: a large majority of the British population agrees that 'the gap between those with high incomes and those with low incomes is too large' (British Social Attitudes survey, quoted in Hills 2004, p. 32). This suggests that there may be a trade-off between efficiency and fairness: if we want to promote efficiency through incentives this will involve inequalities in earnings that are perceived as unfair, but reducing such inequalities in the name of fairness may reduce incentives and so damage efficiency.

Against this, it can be argued that efficiency and fairness go hand-in-hand through what is sometimes referred to as the **trickle down** effect. The most important form of this argument says that we all benefit, in the end, from the high rewards of chief executives because we all benefit from successful businesses. For example, it could be argued that employees of Barclays should have no complaint about the lead executive pay being 75 times as much as theirs so long as the leadership of the business ensures their job security. More generally, the argument is that the lowest paid may be better off than they would otherwise have been because the high pay awarded to chief executives generates improved performance of the economy and rising living standards.

Social cohesion

However, even if that is true, many checkout operators and others towards the bottom end of the earnings distribution, though better off than in the past, are still likely to feel a sense of unfairness. This is because people tend to care not only about their absolute level of earnings but also their position relative to others in the hierarchy. In this view inequality is a social problem because being at the bottom of the hierarchy, in a society that celebrates affluence and consumption, is associated with failure and low status. For example, those who can afford luxury cars and other forms of 'conspicuous' consumption are sending out a signal that they are successful whereas an extension of this outlook suggests that those who use public transport must have failed in life. Critics of inequality say that it is difficult to sustain social cohesion—the sense that we are all members of a shared society—in the context of a division between rich and poor and a perception of unfairness.

Morale

▶ **VALUES** This dimension of social cohesion has important implications for business in the sense that employees are encouraged to see themselves as working for the good of the team. This sense of team membership may be undermined by a feeling among employees that executives are taking more than their fair share out of the business and are motivated more by greed than the benefit of the team. Because this feeling may undermine morale and work performance it can be argued that a greater sense of fairness in business is a key ingredient of efficiency.

Greed and social responsibility

▶ **VALUES** That's all very well but it's beside the point if, as was suggested above, companies effectively have no choice but to pay the going rate. Even if they want to be fairer the earnings of chief executives and checkout operators (and all occupations in between) are driven by competitive conditions in the market. However, this view is open to question. It is obviously true that firms operating in competitive markets have to have regard for the going rate for various types of jobs. But this does not mean that firms have no discretion or choice in relation to pay, and therefore no responsibility for the earnings gap. For example, it can be argued that there is not really a highly competitive market driving up the earnings of scarce managerial talent. Rather, it can be argued that major companies operate in effect as a cartel and boardroom pay is pushed up by a small number of remuneration consultants. Further, the growth of boardroom pay may reflect, at least in part, a shift in the culture of business in modern Britain in which, according to critics, greed has replaced the moral restraints that previously maintained a lower ratio of boardroom pay to workforce earnings. Critics also maintain that increases in boardroom pay are often not justified on the basis of excellent performance, but occur despite mediocre or poor performance. Inequality is a reflection of market forces, but it is also a question of corporate social responsibility.

Reputation

If ethical restraints on executive pay have weakened, companies might still be concerned about the risk to reputation posed by public criticism of greed. For example, the Wall Street bank Goldman Sachs identified 'negative publicity' arising from the financial crisis and bonus payments as a risk factor in its annual report in 2010. Public criticism takes up management time, can adversely affect the morale and performance of employees whose sense of working for a good employer is undermined, could damage relations with clients who are keen to maintain their own ethical reputations, and could encourage greater political and regulatory scrutiny.

Stop and Think
....
Is there a trade-off between efficiency and fairness in business, or do the two go hand-in-hand?

◼ Looking ahead

As we have seen, population growth is projected to continue in the future at a faster rate in the UK than in the rest of Europe. However, projections are not predictions and there is uncertainty concerning all dimensions of population increase—the birth rate, life expectancy, and net migration.

Ageing of the population is a long-term and largely predictable trend that will continue to influence political and business agendas. However, health concerns, particularly around obesity, have led to some predictions of falling life expectancy.

Immigration can be quite volatile and therefore difficult to predict. In the last decade immigration from the A8 countries, particularly Poland, far exceeded initial expectations. However, more recently the flow of migrants from these countries has reduced. There could be a flow of immigration from Romania and Bulgaria from 2014, though this is difficult to predict. Immigration has become a source of political controversy, and the Coalition government has set reducing immigration as a key policy objective.

Britain is still learning how to operate successfully as a multicultural society. Sensitivities relating to different values and lifestyles, such as the wearing of religious symbols, will continue to pose challenges for politics and business.

The occupational order and class structure will continue to alter as a result of economic change. In particular, globalization will continue to make it difficult to sustain low skill jobs in manufacturing in the UK.

Income inequality has widened markedly in the UK since the 1970s and this trend is continuing. Determined political action to reduce inequality seems unlikely in the foreseeable future. However, there will continue to be controversy over executive pay and business will have to respond to criticism on this issue.

◼ Summary

- Business activity takes place within a social and cultural context, which it both shapes and has to respond to.

- The UK population is increasing, and growth is expected to continue to the middle of the century. In recent years immigration, notably from Eastern Europe, was the principal driver of population increase but natural increase has again become the main factor.

- The UK has an ageing population, an effect of the combination of falling death rates and falling birth rates.

- Immigration to the UK, particularly during the last 50 years, has created a multicultural or **cosmopolitan society**.

- Class is an important feature of British society. There are different ways of conceptualizing the class structure—a common approach is to define class in terms of occupation. Changes in the class structure are driven by economic change. In the 20th century the major transformation involved the decline of manual occupations. This experience has stimulated a debate about the decline of the working class.

- Britain has experienced a widening of income inequality since the 1970s.

Case Study Social mobility—Is Britain a mobile society? How do we compare to other rich countries?

How far does class position limit opportunities in life? In particular, what are the chances of children from 'working class' backgrounds gaining entry to 'middle class' occupations? 'Social mobility is about breaking the transmission of disadvantage from one generation to the next. When a society is mobile it gives each individual, regardless of background, an equal chance of progressing in terms of income or occupation' (Milburn 2012, p.1). In the last century there appeared to be a good deal of upward mobility due to the expanding non-manual occupations recruiting employees from working class backgrounds (there was more room in the middle and at the top). However, the general picture is one in which social mobility is restricted and limited in range. In other words, the chances of working class children entering middle-class professions are not good.

Adding together the data on social mobility of men from a number of generations spanning much of the last century, Heath and Payne show that sons of working class fathers were likely to follow in their footsteps. For example 70% of sons whose fathers were semi-skilled or unskilled manual workers ('lower working class') either remained in the same class (38%) or moved up only into the 'higher working class', including skilled manual workers (32%). Only 18% made it into the 'higher and lower salariat' of professionals and managers (roughly equivalent to classes 1 and 2 in Table 6.6). Conversely, 69% of sons whose fathers were in the highest class (the higher salariat) themselves remained in that class (46%) or the lower salariat (23%) (Heath and Payne 2000, pp. 262–5). The odds of a child making it into the middle class as opposed to ending up in the working class are much better for a middle class child than one from the working class. The ratio of these odds across modern societies (i.e. not just in Britain) has been calculated to be 15:1 (Aldridge 2004). These findings indicate that class background exercises a strong influence on life chances or opportunities in terms of the labour market.

Breaking open the closed-shop society?

In recent years the problem of a low rate of social mobility in the UK has become a focus of renewed debate, including the publication of the Milburn report, a major government-sponsored report focused on fair access to the professions (Panel on Fair Access to the Professions 2009). The report argues that the professions have come to play an increasingly important role in the UK economy over the last century, and will continue to do so in the context of the growth of highly professionalized knowledge-based services.

Whereas only one in 14 jobs was professional in 1911, this had increased to more than one in three by 2001. This growth facilitated social mobility in the 20th century as children from poorer backgrounds moved up into professional occupations. However, despite this, social mobility has historically been lower in the UK than in many other countries, and access to professional occupations remains socially exclusive. In other words, there is not an equal chance of access to professional occupations for people from across the whole of society and from different class backgrounds. Rather, the professions tend to recruit people from wealthy and privileged backgrounds. For example, more than 50% of chief executive officers (CEOs) of companies attended independent schools, even though only 7% of the population as a whole attend the independent sector. In other words, going to an independent school appears to afford a much greater chance of becoming a CEO or other professional. Furthermore,

the professions have become more, not less, socially exclusive over time. Despite a sharp growth in professional employment opportunities over recent decades, access to the professions is becoming the preserve of those from a smaller and smaller part of the social spectrum. … If action is not taken to reverse the historical trend, the typical professional of the future will be growing up in a family better off than seven in ten of all families in the UK.

(Panel on Fair Access to the Professions 2009)

The report makes clear that this is not just a problem of fairness. It is in the interests of the professions, and the wider economy, to draw on a wider pool of talent to ensure that the best people are recruited. It can also be argued that professions need to reflect the diversity of the society they serve in order to do so effectively.

In a subsequent 'progress report', Milburn (2012) states that the professions will account for over 80% of new jobs in Britain over the next decade, and 46% of all employment in the UK by 2020. Thus the professions 'hold the key to improving social mobility', but because of slow progress in ensuring fair access 'Britain risks squandering the social mobility dividend that the growth in professional employment offers our country' (Milburn 2012, p. 1). One of the barriers to fair access identified by Milburn is the increasing importance of internships, which are often arranged informally using personal contacts rather than through an open process. Further, 'unpaid internships clearly disadvantage those from less affluent backgrounds who cannot afford to work for free for any length of time' (Milburn 2012, p. 5). Milburn recommends that internships 'should be subject to similar rules to other parts of the labour market. That means introducing proper, transparent and fair processes for selection and reasonable terms of employment, including remuneration for internships' (2012, p. 5).

Another way to look at social mobility is within a generation rather than between generations (intra- as opposed to inter-generational mobility). Here the question is the extent to which people move up or down the occupational order or earnings distribution within their working lives. To measure this a study by the Resolution Foundation looked at movements within the earnings distribution for a group of individuals during the 1990s who were in their early 30s at the start of the decade, and for a comparable group in the 2000s. For this purpose individuals are allocated to decile or quintile groups within the earnings distribution at the start and finish of the decades being studied. The results showed that around two-fifths stayed in the same quintile in the earnings distribution in each decade—their relative position was stable. This means that more than half experienced movement up or down the distribution. But such movement is predominantly short-range (one or two deciles) with limited impact on living conditions or place in the 'pecking order'. Conversely, long-range mobility is infrequent. The study also shows that mobility is higher for those in the middle of the distribution, and more limited for those at the top or bottom. In other words, those at the top or bottom are likely to stay there or only move a short distance up or down. For example, 'in the 1990s, less than 3 per cent of people who started the decade in the lowest quintile were in the top earning

quintile by the end of the decade' (Resolution Foundation 2011, p. 3).

Barriers to social mobility, or fair access to professional and managerial occupations, is not just an issue for the UK economy. That is because inequality tends to mean that the sons and daughters of better-off parents have advantages in life that are not enjoyed by those from poorer backgrounds. Thus, an OECD study shows that 'the relationship between parental or socio-economic background and offspring educational and wage outcomes is positive and significant in practically all countries for which evidence is available' (Causa and Johansson 2010, p. 1). However, the strength of this relationship varies between countries, being tighter or looser. The OECD study finds that 'low mobility across generations, as measured by a close link between parents' and children's earnings, is particularly pronounced in the United Kingdom, Italy, the United States and France, while mobility is higher in the Nordic countries, Australia and Canada' (Causa and Johansson 2010, p. 3). In the UK about 50% of the economic advantage enjoyed by high-earning parents compared to low earners is passed on to the next generation, compared to less than 20% in Norway and Finland. In other words, there is a high level of intergenerational persistence of earnings differentials in the UK, or low social mobility, compared to other rich countries.

Questions

1. **What is social mobility? How is it measured?**
2. **Would it be a good thing if more CEOs of major UK companies were educated in state schools?**

Review and discussion questions

1. What are the implications of population ageing for business? You should think about different types of business, and distinguish opportunities and threats.

2. Is immigration good for Britain's economy and society? You should identify the implications for different stakeholders.

3. 'Class is still a key feature of British society and has important implications for business'. Discuss this statement.

4. Is fairness or social justice an issue that business should be concerned about? Or should it be concerned only with efficiency and profitability?

Assignments

1. Identify key points to complete the 'society' quadrant of a PEST analysis in relation to a specific business or industry.

2. Identify key arguments that could be used from a trade union perspective to criticize recent trends in boardroom pay, and arguments that might be used from a business perspective to defend these trends.

3. Search the Office for National Statistics (ONS) website to find data on migration to and from the UK and prepare a report on recent trends and projections.

Further reading

Bagilhole, B. (2009) *Understanding Equal Opportunities and Diversity: the Social Differentiations and Intersections of Inequality* (Bristol: Policy Press).

Boswell, C. (2011) *Migration and Mobility in the European Union* (Basingstoke: Palgrave Macmillan).

United Nations Population Fund (2012) *Ageing in the Twenty-First Century: A Celebration and A Challenge.* <http://www.helpage.org/resources/ageing-in-the-21st-century-a-celebration-and-a-challenge/>

Hills, J., Sefton, T., and Stewart, K. (2009) *Towards a more Equal Society? Poverty, Inequality and Policy since 1997* (Bristol: Policy Press).

National Equality Panel (2010) 'An anatomy of economic inequality in the UK', Government Equalities Office (<**http://www.equalities.gov.uk/national_equality_panel/publications.aspx**>).

Giddens, A. (2009) *Sociology* (Cambridge: Polity Press).

online resource centre

Test your understanding of this chapter with online questions and answers, explore the subject further through web exercises, and use the web links to provide a quick resource for further research. Go to the Online Resource Centre at <**www.oxfordtextbooks.co.uk/orc/wetherly_otter/2**>

Useful websites

<**www.statistics.gov.uk**>
Office for National Statistics

<http://www.ifs.org.uk/>
Institute for Fiscal Studies (IFS)

<http://www.dwp.gov.uk/>
Department for Work and Pensions

<http://www.equalityhumanrights.com/>
Equality and Human Rights Commission (EHRC)

Population Ageing Across the United Kingdom and EU-27 - Animated Video Podcast (YouTube): <**http://www.ons.gov.uk/ons/rel/mortality-ageing/focus-on-older-people/population-ageing-in-the-united-kingdom-and-europe/population-aqeing-across-the-uk-and-eu-27--animated-video-podcast--utube-.html**>

References

Aldridge, S. (2004) *Life Chances and Social Mobility: an Overview of the Evidence*, Cabinet Office. <**www.cabinetoffice.gov.uk**>

BBC (2013) 'Huge survey reveals seven social classes in UK', <**http://www.bbc.co.uk/news/uk-22007058**>

Boseley, S. (2009) 'Great expectations: today's babies are likely to live to 100, doctors predict', *The Guardian*, 2 October 2009.

Causa, O. and Johansson, A. (2010) *Intergenerational Social Mobility in OECD Countries* (OECD). <**http://www.oecd.org/eco/growth/49849281.pdf**>

Gallie, D. (2000) 'The labour force', in Halsey, A. H. (ed.) *Twentieth Century British Social Trends* (Basingstoke: Palgrave).

Guillemard, A-M. (2001) 'Work or retirement at career's end?', in Giddens, A. (ed.) *The Global Third Way Debate* (Cambridge: Polity Press).

Heath, A. and Cheung, S. Y. (2006) *Ethnic penalties in the labour market: Employers and discrimination*, Department for Work and Pensions, Research Report No. 341.

Heath, A. and Payne, C. (2000) 'Social mobility', in Halsey, A. H. (ed.) *Twentieth Century British Social Trends* (Cambridge: Palgrave).

High Pay Commission (2011) *Cheques With Balances: why Tackling High Pay is in the National Interest.* <**http://highpaycentre.org/img/Cheques_with_Balances.pdf**>

Hills, J. (2004) *Inequality and the State* (Oxford: Oxford University Press).

Incomes Data Services (2012) 'News Release: Salary and bonus growth for FTSE bosses comes to a halt—but earnings still up 10%', 6 November 2012 <http://www.incomesdata.co.uk/news/press-releases.aspx>

Incomes Data Services (2013) 'News Release—Median pay award rises but stays behind Inflation', 21 February 2013 <http://www.incomesdata.co.uk/news/press-releases.aspx>

Milburn, A. (2012) *Fair Access to Professional Careers: A Progress Report by the Independent Reviewer on Social Mobility and Child Poverty.* <https://www.gov.uk/government/uploads/system/uploads/attachment_data/file/61090/IR_FairAccess_acc2.pdf>

Office for National Statistics (2011) *National Population Projections, 2010-Based Statistical Bulletin*, <http://www.ons.gov.uk/ons/rel/npp/national-population-projections/2010-based-projections/stb-2010-based-npp-principal-and-key-variants.html>

Office for National Statistics (2012) 2011 *Census: Population Estimates for the United Kingdom, 27 March 2011*, <http://www.ons.gov.uk/ons/rel/census/2011-census/population-and-household-estimates-for-the-united-kingdom/stb-2011-census--population-estimates-for-the-united-kingdom.html>

Office for National Statistics (2012a) *Measuring National Wellbeing, Social Trends 42—Population*, <http://www.ons.gov.uk/ons/rel/social-trends-rd/social-trends/social-trends-42---population/art-social-trends-42---population.html>

Office for National Statistics (2012b) *Population Ageing in the United Kingdom, its Constituent Countries and the European Union*, <http://www.ons.gov.uk/ons/rel/mortality-ageing/focus-on-older-people/population-ageing-in-the-united-kingdom-and-europe/rpt-age-uk-eu.html>

Office for National Statistics (2012c) *Pension Trends—Chapter 2: Population change 2012 edition*, <http://www.ons.gov.uk/ons/rel/pensions/pension-trends/chapter-2--population-change--2012-edition-/index.html>

Office for National Statistics (2012d) 2011 *Census: Key Statistics for England and Wales, March 2011*, <http://www.ons.gov.uk/ons/dcp171778_290685.pdf>

Office for National Statistics (2012e) *Patterns of Social Mobility by NS-SEC: England and Wales 1981-2001*, <http://www.ons.gov.uk/ons/search/index.html?newquery=Patterns+of+Social+Mobility+by+NS-SEC%3A+England+and+Wales+1981-2001>

Office for National Statistics (2013) *Pension Trends—Chapter 4 : The labour market and retirement, 2013 edition*, <http://www.ons.gov.uk/ons/rel/pensions/pension-trends/chapter-4--the-labour-market-and-retirement--2013-edition/art-pt2013ch4.html>

Office for National Statistics (2013a) *Patterns of Pay: Results from the Annual Survey of Hours and Earnings, 1997 to 2012*, <http://www.ons.gov.uk/ons/dcp171766_300035.pdf>

Office for National Statistics (no date) 'Table 19: All in employment by socio-economic classification (NS-SEC)', <www.statistics.gov.uk>

Office for National Statistics (2013) 'EMP 11: Employment by socio-economic classification', 20 February, <http://www.ons.gov.uk/ons/search/index.html?newquery=All+in+employment+by+socio-economic+classification+%28NS-SEC%29>

One Society (2011) 'A third of a percent: The gulf between employees' pay and chief executives' pay and the adverse impacts on UK plc.', <http://www.onesociety.org.uk/wp-content/uploads/2011/09/AThirdOfAPercent_OneSociety_29Sept2011_Final.pdf>

Panel on Fair Access to the Professions (2009) 'Unleashing Aspiration' (London: Cabinet Office).

The Pensions Commission (2004) 'Pensions: Challenges and Choices'. The First Report of the Pensions Commission, <www.pensionscommission.org.uk>

Resolution Foundation (2011) *Moving on up? Social mobility in the 1990s and 2000s Summary*, <http://www.resolution-foundation.org/media/media/downloads/Social_Mobility_Summary.pdf>

Wood, M. et al. (2009) *A Test for Racial Discrimination in Recruitment Practice in British cities, Research Report No 607*, Department for Work and Pensions..

United Nations Population Fund (2012) *Ageing in the Twenty-First Century: A Celebration and A Challenge*, <http://www.helpage.org/resources/ageing-in-the-21st-century-a-celebration-and-a-challenge/>

United Nations (2012) *World Population Prospects: The 2012 Revision*, <http://esa.un.org/wpp/>

Chapter 7

Can the marketplace be ethical? Corporate responsibility

Simon Robinson

Learning objectives

When you have completed this chapter you will be able to:

- Clarify the definitions of **corporate responsibility (CR)**, **corporate citizenship** and **business ethics**.

- Examine and assess the free market views of the market and CR, and how these relate to ethics.

- Examine and assess the stakeholder view of business and bring out the implications for CR practice.

- Make a case for CR in business.

- Develop and use a framework for corporate social responsibility that connects to the practicalities of business.

THEMES

The following themes of the book are especially relevant to this chapter

》 DIVERSITY OF BUSINESS

CR applies across the wide diversity of business, from small and medium enterprises to global corporations.

》 COMPLEXITY OF THE ENVIRONMENT

The case study on Caterpillar at the end of this chapter shows the complexity of the business environment. This is the context in which CR has to be worked out. It shows that responses to CR cannot be simplistic and demands the development of an effective CR decision-making process. This process is not about asserting or prescribing predetermined views of CR but about finding appropriate responses through planning.

》 VARIETY OF SPATIAL LEVELS

The business environment operates internally, locally, regionally, nationally, and at the global level. The operation of CR will be examined in this context.

》 DYNAMIC ENVIRONMENT

The constantly changing environment leads to new CR challenges. Effective CR policy looks to respond to that dynamic environment by ensuring that business managers reflect on their operational practices, including regular reporting on how the business responds to that environment.

》 INTERACTION BETWEEN BUSINESS AND THE ENVIRONMENT

This chapter shows the rise of corporate citizenship, in which business sees itself as part of a wider community, with mutual and shared responsibilities. In this model, business not only shares responsibilities for the wider social and physical environment but also contributes to the development of ethical meaning in that environment.

》 STAKEHOLDERS

Awareness of stakeholders, their needs and responsibilities, forms the basis of how corporate social responsibility is determined. This chapter focuses on the need to negotiate responsibility with stakeholders.

》 VALUES

Any business embodies values and purpose. These form the basis of any CR policy. Regular audits reflect on how these values are embodied in practice.

▓ Introduction

Chapter 2 introduced us to the debates about the ability of the free market to produce economic efficiency, and this was further explored in Chapter 4 when we considered the ideological divide between left and right. It is clear that attitudes to business depend on where people are located along this ideological spectrum. Put simply, for those on the right, business makes the world go round. It is business (and especially the private sector) that creates the wealth on which all of society depends. For those on the left, businesses (private) are simply out for themselves and will put profits before people, ignoring their wider responsibilities. Any notion of corporate responsibility (CR) is a contradiction in terms. Corporations only recognize their economic self-interest.

Advocates of the free market argue that in acting out of self-interest businesses are able to realize the common good provided that there is competition and freedom. Critics argue that, in fact, the free market allows business to acquire the power to restrict competition and to exploit consumers and employees. They argue that this will require close government supervision, regulation, or direct control and that there is a need for a vibrant 'third sector' of voluntary groups and **non-governmental organizations (NGOs)**.

There has been a growth in social activism from this sector, highlighting what is seen as corporate irresponsibility and there have been many examples of this indeed. The explosion of a chemical plant run by the American owned Union Carbide in Bhopal, India in 1984, caused a huge loss of life and a continuing genetic legacy of birth defects. It is argued that the company did not face up to its responsibilities (see **<www.bhopal.org/whathappened.html>** for an example of this view and **<www.bhopal.com>** for the company's defence of its actions).

The environmental movement has been particularly vocal in its condemnation of what it sees as the cavalier approach taken by corporations to the environment. For example:

- Shell's record, highlighted by the Brent Spar case (Entine 2002), is still under intense scrutiny by a range of environmental groups.
- Another oil company, Exxon, has been attacked as trying to deny that global warming is a problem by funding 'climate change denial' scientists and using its money to influence politicians not to pass legislation to curb oil consumption.

what is right by looking at consequences. The action that maximizes the best consequences for the most people or groups is seen to be good.

Both these theories have their problems. In the first, there can be no absolute principles, principles that do not have an exception. The second theory is not so much a theory as a means of calculation. It does not say anything about what the good is that should be maximized. Increasingly then, business ethics has focused on the idea of 'virtue ethics'. Building on the ethics of Aristotle, this argues that ethics is not so much about determining what is right or wrong, but rather about building a good character. The character is informed and sustained by the stories of the community, which embody the virtues. The virtues are learned through practice, and good character will lead to good ethical practice. At the centre of this are virtues such as integrity and courage. Business ethics systematically works through these and other ethical theories in relation to practice.

CR is a critical aspect of business ethics, focusing on how the moral responsibility of business is worked out in relation to internal and external stakeholders.

Stop and Think

Consider the following dilemma that illustrates the two approaches to ethical thinking.

Suppose that there is a promotion round within a business and the best person for the job in accordance with the selection criteria is someone who is not well regarded by colleagues. Is there a duty to appoint this person even though it will cause resentment within the workgroup? Or should this duty be disregarded because it is better to disappoint this one person and keep many others happy?

▨ Justifying CR

In this section we will examine two alternative perspectives on CR: free market theory and **stakeholder theory**. We will reflect on these perspectives with the help of a scenario involving a computer game (Mini-Case 7.2). In this case there is a fundamental question about whether the computer game company should have any sense of responsibility beyond signing the contract and ensuring work for the ninety employees.

❱❱ **VALUES** There are two broad perspectives that seek an answer to this question and we deal with these in the following two sections.

The free market view of CR

Milton Friedman is often seen as one of the foremost modern advocates of the free market. In relation to the debate about CR his argument is simple (Friedman 1983). The role of business is the creation of wealth and thus the prime responsibility of business is to make a profit for its owners, usually the shareholders. In this, the executive director acts as an agent serving the interests of 'his principal', i.e. the owners. The interest of the principal is profit maximization, and involvement in any activities in the community outside this sphere would be a violation of trust and thus morally wrong. Friedman does not argue against the social involvement of the company as such, rather simply that the company, and the owners especially, can decide to do what they think is fit. There is no moral or legal obligation on the company to be more socially involved, and the company can follow its own ends, so long as they are legal.

Mini-Case 7.2 Computer games

Following the success of a computer game based upon a scenario set in the frozen north the computer software development company was commissioned by the client company to develop a second game. This time the client wanted increased shock value, the inclusion of the death of young children. As an added incentive, if the computer company agreed to this there would be rapid release of monies outstanding from the first game. The manager of the software firm and his engineering staff were uneasy about this request—though initially a little unsure why they felt this unease. They felt there may be wider issues about how such games affect players and about how their firm might be perceived.

As a result of discussions with his staff, the manager decided that it was important to clarify the situation. He wrote to his client's legal department and asked if they would confirm in writing that the company wished him to develop a second game and that it was their intention that this should involve increased horror and the death of children. No such confirmation was received—and the money owed to the software development company was rapidly released.

Questions

1. Why do you think the legal department responded in this way?

2. There were two businesses involved in this case. Does the responsibility of each of them differ, and if so why?

3. Who are the important people in this case that might be affected by the decisions of these two companies?

If the company executive does decide to get involved in a community project Friedman argues that this is not an obligation but rather a means of achieving the company aims, such as improving the image and reputation of the company and thus contributing to improving profits.

For Friedman, pursuing such responsibility would involve costs that would have to be passed on to the customer, possibly to the shareholder in reduced dividends, and to the employee in reduced wages. Not only is this unfair, it also constitutes a form of taxation without representation and is therefore undemocratic. Moreover, it is both unwise, because it invests too much power in the company executives, and futile, because it is likely that the costs imposed by this approach will lead to a reduction in economic efficiency.

Finally, he argues that the executive is not the best person to be involved in making decisions about social involvement. S/he is neither qualified, nor mandated, to pursue social goals. It is social administrators that understand the needs of the local area and who can determine local priorities. Such a task is better suited to local government and social concern groups, whose roles and accountability are directly related to these tasks. For business to enter this field would lead to a confusion of roles and a raising of false expectations.

According to the free market argument, the social responsibility of the computing firm in Mini-Case 7.2 should have been to take the new contract. To take it would be within the law, and it would fulfil the interests of the owner and the employees. The law would have been responsible for placing an over-18 restriction on any major horror content. In turn, it would then be the responsibility of the individual who buys the game to deal with any negative effects, or the responsibility of parents to monitor what their under-18 children are doing. The computer

---

Stop and Think

Is there one core purpose of business? If so, how does that relate to any other role of business?

Is there one purpose generic to all business or do different businesses have different purposes?

Make a list of all the possible purposes of your business or university. How might a public organization, such as a university, differ from a business?

firm could also say that it had no wider responsibility, and that such responsibility to wider society lay with the commissioning company.

There are a number of criticisms of this free market view. Firstly, seeing profit maximization as the exclusive purpose of business is simplistic. Managers may have several different purposes each of equal importance: care for shareholders, clients, the physical environment, and so on. Shareholders may want profits but they could be concerned for the environment or for the community in which they live. Our different value worlds are connected. This can only be tested in dialogue with each group of shareholders, and in light of the nature of the business and its effects on society.

Secondly, there is an assumption that the ethical worlds of social concern and business are quite separate. The initial response of the computer firm's employees shows that this is not the case. They were all very concerned about being involved in such a project. Much of that worry related to their personal sense of responsibility and, also, the firm's reputation.

Thirdly, it is difficult to predetermine what the responsibility of the business person or the business should be, any more than it is possible to be precise about the responsibility of, for instance, local or national government. In practice, there are broad responsibilities but these are continuously being debated and negotiated.

■ Stakeholder theory and CR

❱ **DIVERSITY** ❱ **DYNAMIC** ❱ **STAKEHOLDERS** The computer firm case was, of course, deceptively complex. Firstly, there were two companies involved each of whom was a stakeholder in the other's business. For the commissioning company this was a minor, but potentially lucrative, relationship. For the computer firm this was a potentially critical deal that would help to keep them alive. Secondly, each company had some very different stakeholders, with different and sometimes conflicting values. The commissioning company, for instance, had a strong line in family entertainment. The game, however, was targeted at late adolescents. This could potentially spoil the company's family image. We do not know precisely why the legal department responded in the way they did, but it can be assumed that they did not want to affect the reputation of the commissioning company. In recent times, there has been also an increase in customers from different cultures, including the Muslim world, with a strong family ethic. Again, this would seem to be an important argument against involving gratuitous horror.

Up to this point, responsibility to any possible customers would seem to coincide with self-interest. There is little point in trying to sell to one group in a way that would actually affect the company's reputation with other potential customers. It may, of course, be that there are wider responsibilities to children and families. What is the effect of violent games on younger people? Research is inconclusive about this. The precautionary principle might well apply here then. If you are not sure what negative effect your project might have on children or wider society, or how that might reinforce other negative social changes, the precautionary principle suggests that the firm exercise precaution and not become involved in gratuitous horror. Alternatively, it might be possible for such a company to be involved in developing further research around this area. At the very least, there are questions about what the responsibility of the company might be.

For the computer games company these questions are a little different. There are responsibilities to the owner and the employees. However, as computer engineers, many employees were part of a wider professional body of engineers. That profession is itself a stakeholder in the sense that any decision made by a computer firm might affect the standing of computer engineers in wider society. Recent work on the responsibility of engineers stresses the importance of maintaining the integrity of the profession. The profession itself has a real concern about the effects of any computer games on the wider society.

Reflecting on the different stakeholders reveals the complex and dynamic nature of any situation, and it is often not possible to simplistically divide the interests of the shareholders and the wider stakeholders. Does stakeholder theory then act as the basis for determining CR?

A stakeholder was initially defined in terms of those groups which were critical to the survival of the business, including employees, customers, lenders, and suppliers (Sternberg 2000, p. 49). This has been further developed to 'any individual or group who can affect or is affected by the actions, decisions, policies, practices or goals of the organization' (Carroll and Buchholtz 2000). This widens stakeholders to government, the community, and beyond. For multinational corporations this becomes even more complex.

It is possible to identify different versions of stakeholder theory (SHT), as argued by Heath and Norman (2004). They include:

- strategic SHT: a theory that attention to the needs of stakeholders will lead to better outcomes for the business
- SHT of governance: a theory about how stakeholder groups should be involved in oversight of management, e.g. placing stakeholders on the board
- deontic SHT: a theory that analyses the legitimate rights and needs of the different stakeholders and uses this data to develop company policies.

It is possible, however, to see all these theories as simply aspects of the larger stakeholder view.

Sternberg (2000, pp. 49 ff) argues against basing CR on stakeholder theory on the following grounds:

- to be responsible to someone we have to be accountable to them but it is not at all clear to which stakeholders a company is accountable
- it is likely that the interests of stakeholders conflict. How does the firm resolve this?

However, stakeholder theorists argue that it is perfectly possible to be accountable to shareholders and also recognize a shared responsibility for wider stakeholders, including the environment, that has to be worked out in practice. It is not a question of a polarized model of stakeholders versus shareholders but one of identifying shared interests and finding ways of responding to them.

Carroll suggests a way of getting over that polarized approach which involves four areas: economic, ethical, legal, and philanthropic (1991, p. 41). He argues that these different responsibilities are set in consecutive layers within a company, with CR involving addressing all four layers one after another.

Corporations have an economic responsibility towards their shareholders to be profitable and provide reasonable returns on shareholders' investments. Economic and financial gain is the primary objective of a corporation in a business sense and is the foundation upon which all the other responsibilities rest (see Chapter 1).

However, at the same time businesses are expected to comply with the laws and regulations as the ground rules and legal framework under which they must operate. A company's legal responsibilities are seen as coexisting with economic responsibilities as fundamental precepts of the free enterprise system (see Chapters 5 and 11).

Ethical responsibilities within a corporation ensure that the organization performs in a manner consistent with expectations of ethics in society. Good corporate citizenship is defined as doing what is expected morally and ethically, and it is important to recognize and respect new or evolving ethical trends adopted by society. It must be noted that the corporate integrity and ethical behaviour of a company go beyond mere compliance with laws and regulations and entail the obligation to do what is right and fair, and to avoid harm.

Finally, Carroll suggests that philanthropic responsibilities include corporate actions that are in response to society's expectation that businesses be good corporate citizens, involved in activities or programmes to promote human welfare or goodwill. Philanthropy, 'love of fellow humans', is highly desired by society, however it is not ultimately necessary (Carroll 1991, p. 44).

Carroll's view is comprehensive and usefully brings together different views of CR. However, we are still left with some difficult questions. Firstly, while the primary aim of a business may not be promoting human welfare, if there is evidence that parts of the business are abusing the human rights of its workers, then this is most directly the concern of the business. Secondly, if businesses are operating in social and political contexts where corruption or repression exist should the business simply go along with this? It could be argued that businesses should actively promote democracy in, for example, areas of economic and political transition. Such considerations bring together concern for the 'common good', based in business ethics, and the focus on the triple bottom line. The triple bottom line places social and environmental needs alongside financial, and seeks to develop adequate ways of reporting on all three aspects of the firm's practice (Carroll 1991, p. 47) (see below on audit and further in Chapter 8).

This takes the complexity of the business environment even further, and leads to more developments in CR, seeing business as itself a stakeholder in wider society and, thus, more accountable in terms of corporate citizenship. Feminist ethics, in particular, point to a web of stakeholder relations that stress connectivity, interdependence, power sharing, collective action, and conflict resolution. Business is a part of society and its identity is established through how it relates to society, not least in its conduct with those who are affected by, and affect, it. This is further stressed by Heath and Norman (2004). Learning lessons from disasters such as the Enron case, they argue that the real problems emerge from managers who keep their actions secret from the shareholders. Hence, the shareholders are not able to be part of a conversation about values, purposes, and ways in which a business is run. They argue that when business is not transparent, responsibility is easily lost at all levels. Responsibility is worked out through dialogue between all stakeholders and shareholders. Only such dialogue can determine a creative and feasible response, and what the possibilities and limits of any CR might be. This would mean that CR has to work hard at developing a culture of critical dialogue within and beyond the company.

How would this view help the computer games company? It would take them into dialogue, a dialogue that they at least began, by trying to clarify just what the commissioning company meant. If the dialogue had continued it might have led the games company to explore whether the use of horror, or the death of children, in a computing game was necessarily wrong. It is possible to see these as being used in the context of a game with a moral framework where those who kill the children, or allow that to happen, can be brought to book. Hence, it might be possible to take the contract and develop a game based in a broader ethical context, thus contributing to a wider social responsibility.

> *Stop and Think*
>
> ⋯⋯⋯⋯⋯⋯⋯⋯⋯⋯⋯⋯⋯⋯⋯⋯⋯⋯⋯⋯⋯⋯⋯⋯⋯⋯⋯⋯⋯⋯⋯⋯
>
> In the light of the discussion on CR, how would you have responded to the request of the commissioning company?
>
> Imagine that you are on the board of the computer games firm. Because of this problem you have been asked to draw up a CR policy. What would be the main things you would include?

▣ The nature of responsibility and motivations for pursuing a CR policy

▶▶ **VALUES** ▶▶ **DIVERSITY** ▶▶ **COMPLEXITY** ▶▶ **DYNAMIC** Reflection on the computer games case also helps to reveal the nature of responsibility. Robinson (2009) outlines a threefold view of responsibility made up of:

- agency
- accountability
- liability.

The first of these is about taking responsibility for values and purpose, and how these relate to practice. The computer games company took time to work through what it believed about its responsibility and what effect any actions might have inside and outside the business. This demands critical thinking about what values and ideas are held by the corporation and awareness of effects on the physical and social environment.

The second is about accounting to particular groups. These are most often defined in terms of contractual relationships or roles within and outside the firm. This requires clear criteria about expectations and good monitoring of practice.

The third goes beyond contract to a sense of proactive moral responsibility for wider projects, including care for the environment and the community. This places the firm as one amongst many other groups in society, sharing responsibility for the social and physical environments now and in the future. This involves working through how responsibility might be effectively shared in any situation.

The three elements are interconnected. Any firm, for instance, may develop a partnership to respond to need in a local area. At this point the firm becomes accountable to its partners for practising a wider responsibility for the local environment.

The so-called 'credit crunch' was characterized precisely by a lack of responsibility in each of these areas. First, there was often a lack of clarity and even understanding about the nature of the financial instruments used to generate profits. In the period leading up to the credit crunch this was exemplified by the sale of Green Tree Finance to Conseco (Robinson 2010). Green Tree had increased their profits through subprime mortgages on mobile homes. Conseco focused in insurance and had little experience or understanding of the mortgage market. Nonetheless, the firm increased this new side of their business, leading directly to bankruptcy. Typically, the dynamic of the credit crunch businesses was to avoid any critical dialogue about the nature of the products and their effects.

Second, the firms involved had little sense of their accountability to any of the stakeholders. In the subprime mortgage firms, for instance, there was no accountability to the clients, leading in some cases to thirty year mortgages being taken out on properties that did not have that life expectancy. Even accountability to the shareholders was questionable. Shareholders were told that the sale of mortgage debts was risk-free, something that had not been effectively assessed.

Third, there was a lack of awareness of any responsibility for the wider community. The thinking of leaders was insulated. Merrill Lynch and WaMu, for instance, built large portfolios of mortgage-related securities that were based on the assumption that housing markets were localized, and thus that failure in one area would not affect other areas. The credit crunch showed that markets were interconnected, linking Kansas to Shanghai, and thus that leaders need to take responsibility for being aware of the possible effects of any practice. Most strikingly, the banks and finance companies did not evince any responsibility for the finance industry as a whole, the industry they brought to its knees.

In the light of all this, it can be seen that motivations for fulfilling CR in practice can reasonably be mixed, including:

- self-interest
- mutual interest
- shared responsibility.

Self-interest

In the computer games case it is clear that both companies saw that it was not in their interest to be associated with a request for more violence. It could easily have affected their reputation in other areas of the market, leading to loss of trust by customers and in the market as a whole. In the long term, this also helps in avoiding stringent regulative legislation.

Mutual interest

Whilst the software firm did not address the immediate worries about the effect of horror games on the players, it is clear that they felt it was in everyone's interest to be aware of this issue. Business has a moral obligation to solve social problems that it has caused or perpetuated. It also has great power that it can use to solve problems. It has even greater power if it works in partnership.

Shared responsibility

This involves a shared sense of obligation, such that the good of the whole is of concern for all. The business sees itself as part of that whole and, thus, has a commitment to work out social responsibility in context. This moves CR into the perspective of corporate citizenship.

In the computer game case this stage was not reached, largely because there was no full debate or dialogue within the game firm about values or responsibility, and not at all between them and the client. Shared responsibility demands a framework of dialogue and partnership that will lead to the most effective CR response. CR then becomes an interactive and learning process, based in core values, working to develop a response in each context through partnership and dialogue.

Sethi and Post (1989) characterize such shared responsibility as:

- social obligation
- social responsibility
- social responsiveness.

Palazzo and Richter (2005) suggest a parallel view with the headings:

- instrumental
- transactional
- transformational.

It is possible to argue that the business which develops CR because it has to, or because of self-interest, is not 'genuinely' ethical. The term 'greenwashing' is often used for companies who develop environmental policies just to be seen as trustworthy. However, it is worth noting that many ethical theories involve self-interest and that few ethical decisions do not contain such self-interest. To deny the interest of the corporation would be to deny the interest of a key part of the local or global community.

An overview of CR policy and process using Petrobras as a case study

A good example of CR in practice is that of Petrobras, styled as the fourth most reputable company in the world, according to the Reputation Institute (<**www.reputationinstitute.com**>). Petrobras's approach involves several elements:

▶ INTERNAL/EXTERNAL ▶ STAKEHOLDERS

- A holistic approach that sees CR as engaging all stakeholders, internal and external
- The inclusion of stakeholders in dialogue and planning—Petrobras is concerned to enable staff and external stakeholders to develop as global citizens
- A transparent framework that includes monitoring and regular reporting
- Staff development that seeks to communicate core standards across the group, particularly important in light of the transnational nature of the group
- Finally, a CR policy that is grounded in reflection on purpose, values, and in standards of conduct, including a concern for staff development, integration, reporting, record keeping, and effective monitoring and auditing.

In all of this CR is not separate from governance, human resources, marketing, and so on but is developed as central to the culture and decision-making of the organization.

The process and practice of CR

▶ COMPLEXITY ▶ STAKEHOLDERS ▶ VALUES As noted above, CR is not something that can be determined beforehand and simply applied to any situation. The appropriate CR response can only be worked out in the particular situation. Hence, the company needs to have a process or method for working out CR in complex and dynamic situations.

Robinson et al. (2007) have suggested a fourfold approach to this involving:

- data gathering, ensuring the development of awareness of the situation in which the firm operates and the effects of the firm on the social and physical environment
- value clarification and management

Mini-Case 7.3 Petrobras' corporate social responsibility policy

To Petrobras, social responsibility is a mechanism of integrated, ethical, and transparent management of its business and activities and of its relationships with all of its stakeholders, driving human rights and citizenship, respecting human and cultural diversity, not allowing discrimination, degrading work, child and slave labour, contributing to sustainable development and to reduce social inequality.

1. **Corporate Performance** Make sure Petrobras System's corporate governance is committed to ethics and transparency in its relationship with its stakeholders.

2. **Integrated Management** Ensure integrated Social Responsibility management at the Petrobras System.

3. **Sustainable Development** Carry out Petrobras System's business and activities with social responsibility, implementing its commitments pursuant to the principles set forth by the UN's Global Compact and contributing to sustainable development.

4. **Human Rights** Respect and support internationally acknowledged human rights, guiding Petrobras System's

actions based on the promotion of the principles of decent work and non-discrimination.

5. **Diversity** Respect the human and cultural diversity of its workforce and that of the countries where it has operations.

6. **Labour Principles** Support the eradication of child, slave, and degrading work in Petrobras System's productive chain.

7. **Workforce Commitment** Commit the workforce to Petrobras System's Social Responsibility Policy. (<http://www2.petrobras.com.br/portal/frame.asp?pagina=/ResponsabilidadeSocial/ingles/index.asp&lang=en&area=rsa>).

Question

How effective a CR policy do you think this is? How would you improve it?

- responsibility negotiation and planning
- monitoring and auditing such that profit can be balanced with concern for the social and physical environment.

Data gathering

⟫ **DIVERSITY** ⟫ **COMPLEXITY** ⟫ **DYNAMIC** ⟫ **INTERACTION** ⟫ **STAKEHOLDERS**

This involves developing an awareness and appreciation of all issues and stakeholders in any situation. Often this requires the perspectives of more than one group, because any situation might be very complex, and any one group will have a partial perception of the situation. When this is not done, major controversies can be sparked about what the actual data is, with polarized thinking and judgement based on negative perceptions of the other stakeholders. A good example of this is a report from War on Want in 2007 into the operations of transnational mining corporations (see Mini-Case 7.4). How might an effective CR policy in this instance have avoided what then happened? Both War on Want and mining corporations such as Anglo American have a concern for social responsibility. However, neither the NGOs or the transnationals took into account the fact that data is rarely value-free, and is often heavily affected by the perceptions of the values and motives of the different groups, leading to lack of clarity about what the data involves.

Many major global industries now have as part of their CR policy a commitment to dialogue with relevant NGOs (Entine 2002). This underlines the importance of identifying and working with stakeholders at the earliest stage. Complex situations can demand an awareness of how the company relates not simply to the immediate situation but to broader aspects, such as the supply chain, and how subsidiaries do business. A good example of that is British American Tobacco's (BAT) involvement in Malawi (see Mini-Case 7.5).

Mini-Case 7.4 War on Want: Anglo American the Alternative Report

In August 2007 the respected NGO War on Want published a report (<http://www.waronwant.org/component/content/article/14777>) which alleged that Anglo American, amongst other transnational corporations, were involved in a number of activities that went against stated CR policies. The report noted 'devastating effects' on the host communities, including collusion with governments to evict families and tribes to make room for mining operations.

Ten days later Anglo American published a response (13 August 2007, <http://www.angloamerican.com/media/releases/2007pr/2007-08-09>), in which it asserted that the accusation about its involvement in the various cases was groundless. They provided specific refutations, including clarification about the exact relationship of Anglo American to various companies and governments. In particular, they argued that none of the allegations had been checked with the company itself, leading to a corruption of the data. One example of that was the allegation that in 2004 paramilitaries had violently subdued a village whose people were protesting against the proposed building of a railway. In fact the railway had been built over a decade earlier.

The result of this exchange was two very different views of the truth, and an increasing lack of trust. Neither side necessarily disputed that some wrong things had happened, but the exact narrative was not clear.

Question

As CR director of Anglo American how would you have handled this report?

The very fact of the global controversy surrounding BAT shows the importance of developing a proactive awareness of all aspects of the supply chain. In a global context this can be very difficult to achieve. Hence, the need to work with all relevant stakeholders. Analysing just what the responsibility of business might be, and developing an effective response that balances all the interests and needs, can be complex. The complexities surrounding child labour, for instance, are spelled out in a UK Department for International Development report entitled, *Helping not Hurting Children* (DFID 1999, see <http://www.new-ag.info/00-5/pov.html>). Central to the awareness of the situation is a clear grasp of accountability, to whom is the

Mini-Case 7.5 Tobacco poison surrounds child workers

15 November 2009 *Sunday Times*
Dan McDougall

A *Sunday Times* investigation in the southern African state of Malawi has uncovered an environmental travesty that is being inflicted by the tobacco industry on some of the continent's poorest people.

Downstream from the tobacco processing plants that dominate the outskirts of Lilongwe, the Malawian capital, rivers run yellow and green from industrial outflow—water used for bathing by villagers who have no other option.

Even more alarming, however, is that in a community already plagued by Aids, cholera, malnutrition and one of the highest infant mortality rates in the world, toxic tobacco waste is being dumped by contractors in open landfill sites where hundreds of children are picking through the remnants.<http://www.thesundaytimes.co.uk/sto/news/world_news/article190548.ece>

This article cited a recent report by a UK-based charity, Plan International, which estimated that close to 2.5m women and children are working in conditions of semi-slavery in the tobacco industry and being paid as little as £160 a year.

The report claimed that children forced to work as tobacco pickers in Malawi are exposed to nicotine levels equivalent to smoking 50 cigarettes a day. Child labourers as young as five, it alleged, were suffering severe health problems from a daily absorption of up to 54 milligrams of nicotine through their skin.

This case raises questions about awareness of the environmental effect of products, the supply and effect chain, the employment of adults and children, and even the role of governments and how the corporation should respond.

Question

As CR director of British American Tobacco how would you respond?

of business and their related values was made even more complex because of the engineering firm's perspective that there seemed to be several different 'clients', companies and government organizations. The subsequent Presidential Commission noted how, amongst other things, this led to a sense in which responsibility was not fully shared by the different companies.

Ultimately, of course, the explosion adversely affected all the key stakeholders and focused on the ethics of 'whistleblowing' (the practice of an employee within a business informing someone outside of the organization about any potential malpractices they have come across). This underlined that an effective whistleblowing system was in the interest of all stakeholders and thus should be a key part of any CR policy.

Stop and Think
....
What are the problems with whistleblowing?

Responsibility negotiation and planning

❱ **STAKEHOLDERS** ❱ **SPATIAL LEVELS** ❱ **INTERACTION** Responsibility negotiation is the third element in deciding what a particular CSR response might be. Firstly, this involves identifying the stakeholders in any situation. Secondly, there is an analysis of the stakeholders in terms of power and responsibility. This enables a full appreciation of constraints and resources in the situation, and leads to an awareness of creative possibilities. Thirdly, responsibility can be negotiated. This does not simply look to the development of goods for all stakeholders, but accepts the need for mutual responsibility and enables its embodiment. Hence, it facilitates a maximization of resources for social responsibility through collaboration.

In this process, several things can be achieved:

- the further development of the ethical identity of the company
- the development of trust and of a sense of shared values with the stakeholders
- reflection on appropriate levels of responsibility
- reflection on how the power of the company can both respond to the effects that they have on the physical and social environment and how they might enable other stakeholders who have little power to fulfil their responsibility.

Mini-Case 7.7 Anglo American and HIV AIDs

Part of Anglo American CSR involves funding the care of employees and their families who have HIV AIDs (Anglo American 2005). However, it could be said that this takes away responsibility for health that properly resides with the local health organizations. It could also be argued that it sets up inequity of care in relation to other HIV AIDs sufferers in the area who do not have good support from under-funded medical resources. It is an open question then as to whether a company should take such responsibility.

Anglo American's response has been to develop a community partnership with local healthcare groups, both in care and in developing public health education around HIV AIDS. This fulfils responsibility to workforce, the wider community, and also enables local healthcare groups to fulfil their responsibility.(<**http://www.timesonline.co.uk/tol/news/world/africa/article6917289.ece**>)

Question

Does the company have a responsibility or obligation to act in this way?

Similar questions emerge with the issue of human rights. Nike, for instance, were faced by human rights abuses by contractors in developing countries who made their running shoes (<**http://www.nytimes.com/1998/05/13/business/international-business-nike-pledges-to-end-child-labor-and-apply-us-rules-abroad.html**>). Their response was to set out a code of practice for all involved in that industry, partly to ensure that CR was not seen as the responsibility of one company. The question remains how a company might respond to a culture that relies on the income from questionable labour or a country that consciously abuses human rights. The answer to the first might be to maintain relations with these groups and to seek to influence the workplace conditions. The answer to the second should involve negotiation with the governments and where necessary, reserving the right to stand out against governments who abuse human rights in relation to the company's work.

Stop and Think
....
How does your company or university negotiate responsibility in terms of CR?

Audit

▶▶ **DIVERSITY** ▶▶ **COMPLEXITY** ▶▶ **INTERACTION** ▶▶ **STAKEHOLDERS** If the development of CR policy and practice is a learning experience then a core part of that has to be reporting. This is the fourth element. Petrobras produce an annual report with external independent assurance. This report enables Petrobras to see how well policy objectives are being embodied, to manage the direct and indirect effects of the business, and to integrate CR into products and services.

Anglo American's report (2005) emphasizes responses to environmental and social challenges. The company base their report in the Global Reporting Initiative. This involves 'triple bottom line' auditing of the financial, environmental and societal dimensions of the corporation, underlining their interconnectedness. It aims to elevate social and economic reporting to the same level as the financial.

The environmental section includes information on:

- total material use
- direct energy use
- indirect energy use
- total water use
- impacts on **biodiversity**
- greenhouse gas emissions
- ozone-depleting emissions
- total amount of waste
- environmental impact of products.

Anglo American accept that such reporting has been relatively recent for them and that it will develop further. They report fines and legal actions taken against them (73% down from 2004), and environmental incidents (level two incidents up by 5%), alongside reference to awards and effective partnerships. On energy efficiency, the 2005 report gives a summary of work across their different companies. This includes an aim of 10% reduction in carbon intensity over ten

Mini-Case 7.8 Anglo American and water

eMalahleni is one of the fastest growing urban areas in South Africa. It is a municipality of 510,000 people in a water-stressed region in the north-east of the country, and has faced considerable difficulties in meeting increased demand for drinking water. Years of mining in the area disrupted natural water cycles. Water that would otherwise flow into rivers was leaked into mines, where coal deposits made it acidic, hampering mining activity and leading to pollution of local water supplies. At the same time, growing demand from local communities and industry was draining supplies from local reservoirs.

Anglo American worked closely with the local community and other project partners, investing almost US$100 million in a water reclamation plant to treat underground water from its mining operations in the Witbank coalfield, converting waste water from the mines to drinking water standards. The plant currently supplies around twelve per cent of the city's water. It has created 700 temporary and 57 permanent jobs, and is also helping to provide affordable housing.

http://www.angloamerican.com/development/case-studies/environment/water_for_adaption.aspx

Question

As the company CSR officer, what arguments would you have used to persuade your CEO to spend the time and money on this project?

---

years. On air quality, sulphur dioxide emissions were decreased by 43% in one company. On water, there is a sustained attempt to preserve fresh water and neutralize acidic waste water. The section on biodiversity lists work where companies have been involved in land steward-ship and reclamation projects.

Reporting of this nature serves to establish benchmarks for performance, but also seeks to engage the imaginations of the different stakeholders through narrative. A good example of this comes from Anglo American (see Mini-Case 7.8), focusing on the creativity of different groups working together to share responsibility.

Another approach to auditing is the Business in the Community (BiTC) Corporate Responsibility Index. Companies involved in this, such as Shaftsbury plc., complete an extensive index questionnaire and the results are published in the BiTC index. It provides a way to assess and compare progress across companies.

Perhaps the most famous case study of accusations of corporate irresponsibility concerns Nestlé and its alleged marketing and distribution practices for the selling of infant formula (baby milk powder) in the developing world. While this is a relatively old case the adverse reaction persists, and for many social activists Nestlé is still one of the faces of corporate mal-practice (see e.g. **www.babymilkaction.org**).

■ **Looking ahead—beyond the triple bottom line**

The rise of CR has been impressive over the past two decades. However, disasters still occur. Banking and the finance industry ushered in the credit crunch of 2008/9 (Tett 2009). In the search for a risk-free industry, business practices developed that allowed the sale of mortgages to customers who could not sustain payment. The debt was then sold on, leading to the loss of a massive number of homes and the near collapse of the banking and finance industries. There was no evidence of a sense of responsibility for the customer, the industry or profession, the global market, or the global economic environment. In addition to these failures to be either accountable to key stakeholders or be morally liable for wider environments there was also the failure of the industry to even understand what some of the products were, and therefore what effect they might have. This provides a reminder that CR is more than simply the development of codes and policies, and more than the monitoring of the triple bottom line. The failure of the credit crunch was as much a failure to take responsibility for critical thinking about ideas, purpose, and practice, as it was a failure of awareness. That provides corporate responsibility with a fourth bottom line, regular reflection on the identity, purpose, and meaning of the corporation.

This demands careful attention to the ethos and integrity of the organization (Brown 2005), bringing us back to the idea of virtues. Does the corporation articulate and stand by its values in practice? At another level it involves developing the sense of responsibility in the members of the corporation, enabling them to critically engage values and practice, thus owning both. This reaches ultimate expression in companies such as John Lewis, where employees are genuine members of the Partnership (Robinson 2002a). They share responsibility and power for values, practice, and relationships with community and the environment, expressed in genuine workplace democracy. This philosophy can extend to other stakeholders developing and practising their own responsibility. This will see the development of more CR partnerships, not least between NGOs and transnational corporations. In a global context the pressure from NGOs and the modern media will force global business to keep reflecting on values and responsibility in practice. This will become ever more complex as business relates to cultures such as China where there is a very different view of the role of business and of responsibility. Together this will take CR increasingly into corporate global citizenship.

All of this goes to the heart of a business ethics that is based not in following rules but in organizational and personal engagement. Hence, work on ethics and responsibility is often connected to governance and leadership on the one hand (Robinson and Dowson 2012), and personal ethical dilemmas on the other (summed up in whistleblowing cases such as the Challenger, where the exercise of courage and wisdom was central). Responsibility, in other words, cannot be summed up in terms of tools to solve discrete ethical problems. On the contrary, these 'problems', arising from factors such as personal gain, competition, conflicts of interest and values (with underlying polarization of values), and scarcity of resources, are an ongoing part of any business, requiring the ongoing practice of responsibility.

■ Summary

This chapter has suggested that CR has moved on from a limited model, largely to do with philanthropy, to one that takes into account the stakeholder network of the business environment. Business still has to make a profit but can see itself as a corporate citizen, sharing responsibilities with other groups in society. These responsibilities have to be carefully negotiated to achieve the best result for stakeholders and the business itself. In all this it is argued that in the global context companies have moved beyond a threshold, accepting 'the fact that, beyond profits there is a political, social and environmental dimension to their activities that cannot be ignored. They have moved beyond compliance' (GRLI 2005, p. 20). This involves:

- An increasing sense of the company as corporate citizen. Faced by environmental and social issues that are greater than any particular interest, there is a position of shared responsibility from which CR begins.

- An awareness and appreciation of the complex and dynamic business environment, including values, issues, and stakeholders connected to the company's business.

- Business being responsive to a social and physical environment that is constantly dynamic. This means that CR can only be worked out interactively, negotiating responsibility with the different stakeholders. This includes awareness of and responsiveness to human rights in all aspects of the value chain, from suppliers to consumers. This makes CR developmental and transformative.

- Codes of practice and mission statements will help the core values of CR to be embedded. However, the ongoing learning process also requires that outcomes be audited.

Case Study: Caterpillar

According to the UN, a total of 4,170 Palestinian homes were destroyed by the Israeli army between September 2000 and December 2004 (War on Want 2004, p. 4). Other sources suggest the effect of such demolition since 1967 has been to make 70,000 people homeless (ibid. p. 5). The Caterpillar D9 was the main bulldozer used by the Israeli army to demolish homes and destroy farm land in the Palestinian territories. This sustained action was justified by the Israeli government as punitive action against the family homes of Palestinians engaged, or suspected of engagement, in armed activities against Israel. The claim was that this involved hiding terrorist in the homes. War on Want (p. 6) questioned the evidence for this claim. Regardless of that issue, the practice breaches Article 53 of the Fourth Geneva Convention (to which Israel is a party): Any destruction by the Occupying Power of real or personal property belonging individually or collectively to private persons, or to the State, or to other public authorities, or to social or cooperative organizations, is prohibited, except where such destruction is rendered absolutely necessary by military operations. (<http://<http://www.icrc.org/ihl.nsf /385ec082b509e76c41256739003e636d/6756482d86146 898c125641e004aa3c5>, accessed 29 June 2012).

The worst example of such actions was the Battle of Jenin in April 2002. Jenin was a densely populated refugee camp of over 14,000 people. Eyewitness accounts claim that house demolitions continued after the end of the action (War on Want 2004, p. 13), leading to the flattening of an entire district including the camp. People were unable to escape from houses because of the crossfire and many were buried alive, including ill and disabled people. Following the death of the activist Rachel Corrie at one of the Palestinian sites being cleared (<rachelcorriefoundation.org/>) the argument has increasingly focused on legal issues, with lawsuits filed by the Corrie family in the US and Israel. The thrust of the lawsuits is to hold the different parties accountable for their actions. US

companies that aid and profit from violations of human rights can be held responsible under US law (<www.guardian.co.uk/ world/2010/mar/10/rachel-corrie-civil-case-israel>).

Whose responsibility?

Can Caterpillar be held to be responsible in some way for the use to which the Israeli government puts its product?

Con

One argument suggests that no company can be held responsible for how a government uses its product. Think of the analogy of the sale of a kitchen knife. No company or individual who sells kitchen knives can be held responsible for customers using these to kill someone. A second argument used by Caterpillar, is that the product itself was designed for earth removal not as an instrument of war. The latter would have to be licensed by the home government. Modifications to the D9 occurred after the sale. Hence, the responsibility for the destruction of the Palestinian homes lies purely with the Israeli government (parallel to Friedman's argument noted in section, 'The free market view of CR', above).

Supporting this is a pragmatic argument that if Caterpillar accepted responsibility for these acts they would be open to legal liability, with associated financial loss. This would endanger the sustainability of the firm and the profits of shareholders.

Pro

The argument by analogy above is only partial. Whilst it is true that the knife seller cannot be held responsible for what a person does with the knife, a different sense of responsibility emerges if the buyer has made it clear that he or she intends to use the product for an unethical or illegal purpose or if there has been a record of this happening. If the seller knows what negative use the product is being put to, even if this was not the intention of the design or sale of the product, then he or she shares responsibility for the eventual end, and thus responsibility for refusing to sell.

The argument that the killer would have got a knife from someone else does not diminish the shared and proactive responsibility.

▶ **STAKEHOLDERS** The argument so far might be seen as too simplistic, and the customer might want to redefine the end to which the product was put. Hence, the Israeli government might argue that this was not a violation of human rights, or an act of murder, but justified in the light of the defence of the Israeli people, to whom it is responsible. Here moral responsibility moves to the terrorists who have intentionally involved families and their houses.

Exercising critical agency, the responsibility to test arguments, the firm could test their customer's assertion. But can it actually make a judgement about justice and human rights, and should it? For a disinterested judgement the firm might involve an appropriate international agency, such as the United Nations, to determine the exact nature of the actions in question. The UN has a strong record in enabling multinational corporations to engage governments in human rights issues, providing judgment on the nature of any abuses and positive ways of influencing behaviour (see e.g. <http://198.170.85.29/Ruggie-protect-respect-remedy-framework.pdf>).

Stop and Think Excerpts from the Caterpillar Global Code of Practice
....

Commitment

The Power of Responsibility

We Protect the Health and Safety of Others and Ourselves As a company, we strive to contribute toward a global environment in which all people can work safely and live healthy, productive lives, now and in the future.....

We actively promote safe practices throughout our value chain—from suppliers to end users. We are committed to providing our customers with products and services that are safe and reliable in the marketplace. ....

We Are Pro-Active Members of Our Communities As individuals and as a company, we contribute significant time and resources to promoting the health, welfare and economic stability of our communities around the world......

We believe that our success should also contribute to the quality of life in, and the prosperity and sustainability of, communities where we work and live. *As a company and as individuals, we hold ourselves to the highest standard of integrity and ethical behaviour... If we do any less, we put Caterpillar's name and our reputation for integrity at risk.*

Other stakeholders with concerns include the shareholders (see <http://www.ekklesia.co.uk/node/8595>), the wider industry, and members of the firm itself. This would also involve critical reflection on the vision and values of the firm and any code (see <www.cat.com/Code-of-Conduct>, see below).

Far from simple 'stakeholder management' this draws all stakeholders into creative dialogue about ethical meaning and responsible practice, involving shared responsibility.

Questions

As the head of CR you have to give a report to the board to frame Caterpillar's response.

1. What options would you place before them?

2. How would you assess the risks of each of these options?

3. How would your recommended choice of option be informed by the Global Code above?

4. Compare that Code with the UN guidelines on business and human rights noted above. What are the differences in the two approaches to responsibility?

5. What response would you recommend to the board in relation to the attacks from NGOs?

(See <http://electronicintifada.net/content/photostory-israeli-bulldozer-driver-murders-american-peace-activist/4449> for some material about Rachel Corrie the activist.)

Review and discussion questions

1. How would you define the nature and limits of CR?

2. What are the arguments for and against CR?

3. What part do NGOs play in the development of CR?

4. How far do the models of CR noted above apply to small and medium size businesses?

5. Is it possible for an industry that causes harm, such as the tobacco industry, to have a policy of corporate responsibility?

Assignments

1. If you are in work find out if your employer has a CR policy. What are the differences and similarities with Petrobras's policy?

   OR

   If you are a full-time student, find out what the CR policy of your educational institution is and compare it with the Petrobras policy.

2. Write a new CR policy for your educational institution or place of work, including:

- the vision, ethos, and values of the institution
- the different areas within the institution that need policies
- suggestions about how to motivate the staff, and develop ethos and transparency
- suggestions about how to monitor practice.

3. Imagine that you are starting up a small business. How would you build concerns about CR into that process? See the BiTC small business page (<http://www.bitc.org.uk/sites/default/files/res_bus_checkup_small_bus_fact_sheet_260213.pdf>).

Further reading

To pursue the cross-cultural trends in CR read:

Werther, B. and Chandler, D. (2006) *Strategic Corporate Social Responsibility: Stakeholders in a Global Environment* (London: Sage).

To pursue CR and the Global and developmental agenda read:

Crane, A. and Matten, D. (2010) *Business Ethics: Managing corporate citizenship and sustainability in the age of globalization* (Oxford: Oxford University Press).

Hopkins, M. (2006) *Corporate Social Responsibility and International Development: Is Business the Solution?* (London: Earthscan).

To pursue underlying ethical ideas and cases read:

Robinson, S. and Dowson, P. (2012) *Business Ethics in Practice* (London: CIPD).

online resource centre

Test your understanding of this chapter with online questions and answers, explore the subject further through web exercises, and use the web links to provide a quick resource for further research. Go to the Online Resource Centre at **<www.oxfordtextbooks.co.uk/orc/wetherly_otter/2>**

Useful websites

Business in the Community
<**www.bitc.org.uk**>

Codes of ethics for different professions (Centre for Study of Ethics in the Professions, Illinois Institute of Technology)
<**http://ethics.iit.edu/research/codes-ethics-collection**>

Computing Professionals for Social Responsibility
<**www.cpsr.org**>

Corporate Responsibility
<**www.corporate-responsibility.org**>

Corporate Watch
<**www.corporatewatch.org.uk/?lid=2670**>

Enterprise and CSR
<**http://ec.europa.eu/enterprise/policies/sustainable-business/corporate-social-responsibility/index_en.htm#content**>

Global footprints
<**www.globalfootprints.org**>

Green Globe 21 (sustainability for travel and tourism)
<**www.greenglobe21.com**>

Institute for Global Ethics
<www.globalethics.org>

International Business Ethics Institute (IBEI)
<www.business-ethics.org>

Scientists for Global Responsibility—Ethical Careers Guide
<http://www.sgr.org.uk/projects/ethical-careers>

The Institute of Science in Society—Science, Society, Sustainability
<www.i-sis.org.uk>

References

Andriof, J. and McIntosh, M. (eds) (2001) *Perspectives on Corporate Citizenship* (London: Greenleaf Publishing).

Anglo American Report to Society (2005) <**www.angloamerican.co.uk/**>

Bauman, Z. (1985) *Modernity and the Holocaust* (London: Polity).

Carroll, A. B. (1991) 'The pyramid of corporate social responsibility: towards the moral management of organizational stakeholders', *Business Horizons*, July–Aug., pp. 39–48, 40.

Carroll, A. B. and Buchholtz, A. K. (2000) *Business and Society—Ethics and Stakeholder Management* (London: Thompson).

Carroll, A. B. and Shabana, K. M. (2010) 'The Business Case for Corporate Social Responsibility: A Review of Concepts, Research and Practice', *International Journal of Management Reviews*, 12, 1, pp. 85–105.

Entine, J. (2002) 'Shell, Greenpeace and Brent Spar: the politics of dialogue', in Megone, C. and Robinson, S. (eds), *Case Histories In Business Ethics* (London: Routledge), pp. 59–95.

European Commission (2001) *'Green Paper: Promoting a European Framework for Corporate Social Responsibility'*, Brussels. 18.07.2001, Com(2001) 366 final <**http://eur-lex.europa.eu/LexUriServ/site/en/com/2001/com2001_0366en01.pdf**>

Friedman, M. (1983) 'The social responsibility of business is to increase its profits', in Donaldson, T. and Werhane, P. (eds) *Ethical Issues in Business* (New York: Prentice-Hall), pp. 239–43.

GRLI (2005) *Call for Engagement* <**http://www.grli.org/index.php/component/docman/cat_view/13-source-documents**>

Gregory, A. and Tafra, M. (2004) 'Corporate social responsibility: New context, new approaches, new applications: A comparative study of CSR in a Croatian and a UK company', paper given at International Public Relations Research Symposium, Bled 2004. <**www.bledcom**>

Heath, J. and Norman, W. (2004) 'Stakeholder theory, corporate governance and public management: what can the history of state-run enterprises teach us in the post-Enron era?', *Journal of Business Ethics*, 53(3), pp. 247–65.

Jonas, H. (1984) *The Imperative of Responsibility* (Chicago: Chicago University Press).

Moeller, K. and Erdal, T. (2003) *Corporate Responsibility Towards Society: A Local Perspective* (Brussels: European Foundation for the Improvement of Living and Working Conditions). <**http://edz.bib.uni-mannheim.de/www-edz/pdf/ef/03/ef0327en.pdf**>

Otter, D. (2011) 'The Ecological Environment', in Hamilton, L. and Webster, P. (eds), *The International Business Environment* (Oxford: Oxford University Press).

Palazzo, G. and Richter, U. (2005) 'CSR business as usual? The case of the tobacco industry', *Journal of Business Ethics*, 6(4), pp. 387–401.

Robinson, S. (2010) *Leadership Ethics* (Oxford: Peter Lang).

Robinson, S. (2009) 'The Nature of Responsibility in a Professional Setting', *Journal of Business Ethics*, 88, pp. 11–19.

Robinson, S. (2008) 'Fethullah Gülen and Responsibility', lecture given at the conference 'Islam in the age of global challenges: alternative perspectives of the Gülen movement', hosted by the Rumi Forum at Georgetown University, Washington DC.

Robinson, S. Dixon, R. and Moodley, K. (2007) *Engineering, Business and Professional Ethics* (London: Heinemann Butterworth).

Robinson, S. (2002a) 'John Lewis Partnership', in Megone, C. and Robinson S. (eds.), *Case Histories In Business Ethics* (London: Routledge), pp. 131–40.

Robinson, S. (2002b) 'Nestle baby milk substitute and international marketing', in Megone, C. and Robinson S. (eds), *Case Histories In Business Ethics* (London: Routledge), pp. 141–58.

Sethi, S. and Post, J. (1989) 'Public consequences of private actions: the marketing of infant formula in less developed countries', in Iannone, P. (ed.) *Contemporary Moral Controversy in Business* (Oxford: Oxford University Press), pp. 474–87.

Sternberg, E. (2000) *Just Business* (Oxford: Oxford University Press).

Tett, G. (2009) *Fool's Gold* (London: Little Brown).

Zadek, S. (2001) *The Civil Corporation: the New Economy of Corporate Citizenship* (London: Earthscan Publications).

Chapter 8

The natural environment: global warming, pollution, resource depletion, and sustainable development

Eamonn Judge

Learning objectives

When you have completed this chapter you will be able to:

- Understand the importance of current key issues in the natural environment as they impact on business, especially, global warming, pollution, and resource depletion.
- Understand the meaning of sustainable development in relation to business.
- Outline the influences leading to changes in the significance of sustainable development.
- Identify alternative views about sustainable development as it relates to business.
- Examine links between the external environment of a business in relation to sustainable development and the internal strategic response of business.

THEMES

The following themes of the book are especially relevant to this chapter

》 INTERNAL/EXTERNAL

It is clear that business activity imposes external costs on the natural environment and this will require firms to change their internal production processes.

》 COMPLEXITY OF THE ENVIRONMENT

Businesses are asked to take responsibility for their activities which are allegedly having a serious effect on the global natural environment yet our knowledge of these effects is the outcome of very complex research and most people struggle to understand the science behind this research. Furthermore, not all observers are equally agreed about their causes.

》 VARIETY OF SPATIAL LEVELS

Environmental impacts range from the global to local levels and are crucial to our understanding of issues associated with sustainable development.

》 INTERACTION BETWEEN BUSINESS AND THE ENVIRONMENT

This chapter is centrally involved with this key theme of the book. Business in its myriad activities has a major impact on the natural environment, but this impact can strike back at business.

》 STAKEHOLDERS

A wide range of stakeholders can be directly and indirectly affected by a firm's impact on the environment. These may be local sufferers, or sufferers in another country. Firms are not islands, but parts of complex supply chains, and other firms forwards or backwards in the supply chain may be part of an environmental problem with which a firm is directly, if often unknowingly, involved.

》 VALUES

Sustainable development raises complex ethical issues precisely because the main contributors to the problems of environment and resources are not necessarily those who suffer from them. Environmental damage today can store up problems for the future and so firms are forced to consider directly their ethical stance in relation to present day equity issues as well as the future impact on equity of decisions taken today.

Introduction: the natural environment of business

The natural environment of business is a term which covers a series of fairly obvious categories such as climate and weather conditions, natural resources, and topography. These may affect a firm on a purely local level, or there may be global implications.

Historical context

Up to about 1800 human influence on the global environment was limited: the globe was sparsely populated and still largely in its natural state, and no matter what disasters happened in one particular local area, civilizations prospered elsewhere.

》 COMPLEXITY Chapter 3 discussed the changes that occurred from about 1800 in the UK with the Industrial Revolution. Rapid population growth, urbanization, and industrialization, along with colonization and empire building created spectacular wealth and poverty. Despite massive changes, with a growing world economy interrupted by world wars and depressions up to 1945, there was still a perception until the 1970s that the undesirable 'side effects' of such rapid economic development were 'local'. Since then, the global environmental impact of business (and other actors) has been a major concern.

》 SPATIAL LEVELS This was highlighted by environmental disasters in the 1980s: the Union Carbide disaster (1984) at Bhopal, India, the world's worst ever industrial accident (see Chapters 7 and 10); the Chernobyl (Ukraine) disaster (1986); and the EXXON Valdez oil spill off Alaska (1989). One could regard these disasters' effects as localized, yet they were generated by globalized processes of economic development. However, a more pervasive phenomenon from the 1980s onwards was argued to be the melting of the polar ice caps, with effects on sea levels and climatic patterns, while hurricanes became more frequent.

Moving from history to the present day

Studies in the 1980s by the United Nations culminated in the Brundtland Report (WCED 1987). This advocated long-term strategies to counter the threat posed by these trends. It used, but did not invent, the term sustainable development (this was coined by the World Conservation Union in 1980, but it did not define it). It advocated the exploration of the complex relationships between people, resources, environment, and development as being essential to the development of sound strategies of cooperation and mutual trust within the world community.

The Brundtland Report projected the most well-known definition of sustainable development:

development which meets the needs of the present without compromising the ability of future generations to meet their own needs.

This definition was apt, but it was a 'lowest common denominator' definition which everyone
could agree with. More practical steps were needed, and this happened with the UN Conference on Environment and Development at Rio de Janeiro in 1992, the 'Rio Summit' or 'Earth
Summit'. Before we consider this, let us outline the nature of the problems in more detail, to
see how business helps generate them, but also suffers from them.

The current global environmental problem and business, and the international response

Global warming

Global warming is not the only issue, but possibly the best known. Global warming describes
the effect of 'greenhouse gases' (GHGs). These gases (mainly carbon dioxide (CO_2), but consisting also of methane, and other gases) are generated by burning fossil fuels (coal, oil, natural gas, etc.) for space heating, electricity, industrial processes, and transport. But natural
processes also generate GHGs; waste from farm animals produces much methane. Work by
the World Resources Institute (**<www.wri.org>**) indicates that CO_2 is 77% of the total and
methane is 15%. But methane is 43 times worse in global warming terms than CO_2, and is not
mentioned nearly as much. Figure 8.1 illustrates the rapid growth of CO_2 emissions since 1900.

》 COMPLEXITY They are called GHGs because of their action. They collect in the upper
atmosphere and prevent solar heat being reflected back into space. This heat collects, so it is
like a greenhouse. The immediate effect, over many years (see Figure 8.2) but only recently
noticeable, is argued to be the melting of the polar ice caps which will cause rising sea levels to
flood low lying coastal regions, e.g. Bangladesh. The possible consequences for business and
the economy are obvious. But climate change is also serious: warm areas get cold, wet areas become dry, and agriculture suffers, especially in poorer countries. Unpredictable and disastrous
weather phenomena, it is suggested, will emerge.

These changes produce enormous economic costs. Disasters are costly, but the threat of
disaster increases insurance costs. The UK insurance industry estimates that a four degree
increase in global temperature could result in the cost of extreme inland floods rising by 30%
to £5.4 billion. Threats to business are paralleled by political instability. Water resources can
become scarce, and the possibility of conflict between countries which share river systems
increases. Though we talk of sea levels rising, in fact, usable water is scarce, and various types
of business activities accentuate the problem (see Mini-Case 8.1).

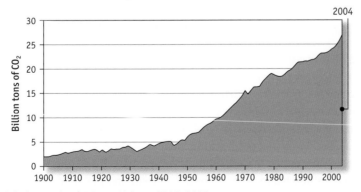

Figure 8.1 Global growth of CO_2 emissions, 1900–2000
Source: World Resources Institute, **<www.wri.org>**

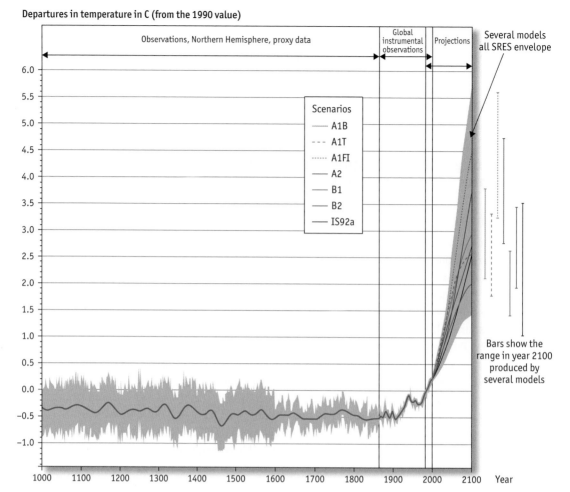

Figure 8.2 Increase in the surface temperature of the Earth from AD 1000 to AD 2100

Source: Intergovernmental Panel on Climate Change (IPCC), <www.ipcc.ch>

Pollution and resource depletion

▶ **INTERACTION** Burning fossil fuels produces acid rain. Sulphur dioxide in the smoke from coal burning power stations combines with atmospheric moisture, making sulphuric acid. This falls as rain, maybe far away, destroys forest and agricultural areas because the soil is too acidic. This damages both food production and tourism. Equally, motor exhausts cause photochemical smog which is a health hazard. People die of respiratory failure, and in cities such as Los Angeles, industrial plants close down if pollution rises too high. Also, certain gases produced by industrial processes (especially Chloro-fluoro carbons or CFCs) accumulate at a height of 15–50km. This destroys the ozone layer in the upper atmosphere, and allows in ultraviolet radiation from outer space. The ozone layer above the polar ice caps is already much depleted. Excessive exposure to ultraviolet radiation leads to increased blindness and skin cancer. In addition it aggravates the global warming process.

Growing crops that require excessive fertilizers and irrigation degrades soil quality and exhausts water supplies. Industrial production generates waste products polluting air, water and land, and ultimately degrading the agricultural resource base. Rivers run to the sea, and liquid run off from land fertilizers and other chemicals concentrates pollutants in the food chain, as they are absorbed by marine life and then eaten by humans, with consequent health problems.

Mini-Case 8.1 Water, water everywhere, and not a drop to drink?

VALUES Most water is sea (97.5%), and, of the remaining 2.5%, 70% is in the polar ice caps, and only 30% (or only 0.7% of global water) is usable from rivers, lakes, underground water, etc. (Climate Institute 2009). This is unequally available. Minimum daily personal requirements for consumption and sanitary needs are 50 litres. Where water is scarce, much less than that might be available. Consumption in the European Union is 200 litres, and in the US 500 litres. The real problem, however, is not personal consumption, but the water to grow products. Water to grow a kilogram of potatoes is 1,000 litres. A kilogram of beef requires 42,500 litres. And it takes 25 bathtubs to produce 250 grams of cotton for a shirt. This might not seem problematic until one appreciates where some products are grown. Thus, for example, American farmers are subsidized to grow cotton in areas requiring irrigation (see Chapter 10). This cotton is sold on world markets below production cost, bankrupting cotton producers in developing countries.

Many major rivers are declining, not just because climate change reduces rainfall, but because of water abstraction for irrigation (Pacific Institute 2009). The Rio Grande between the US and Mexico has declined over 20–25 years to almost a dribble, and the gushing river of cowboy films is just a memory. Where this occurs in politically dangerous areas in Africa, the Middle East, and Asia, there is a war risk (WEF 2010). As population and production increase the problem gets worse. Countries like the US are in fact exporting water (embodied in products as 'virtual water') from areas where it is scarce, while common sense suggests that products should be grown where the natural conditions are optimal without needing scarce water.

Even a bunch of flowers from your local supermarket is problematic. Flower companies in areas like Kenya which export to the UK are accused of stealing water illegally at night from rivers, and hence endangering the livelihoods of local farmers who have inadequate water for their crops.

It is an indication of the complexity of analytical issues in the global environment that some revision of the accepted views (IPCC 2007) on climate change and drought has been necessary. Recent research (Sheffield et al. 2012) shows that with the use of superior drought modelling methods it can be concluded that worldwide drought has actually changed very little since 1950. However, the authors stress they are not arguing that climate change is not happening. But climate change is not the only issue of sustainable development. Water availability remains a problem because it is overall scarce, vis-à-vis increasing population globally combined with unwise usage practices across wide areas.

Question

Why does the relative scarcity of water mean we need to carefully consider the equity issues surrounding its distribution?

Equally, fish stocks decline not only through over-fishing but because the sea is polluted. This problem is aggravated by direct waste dumping at sea.

VALUES The ecology of regions is delicately balanced. Habitat destruction may eliminate species (for instance, logging in rain forests of Amazonia or Southeast Asia which feeds raw materials to the furniture industries) which may have unpredictable effects. Equally, the long-term migration of species as climate changes brings new flora and fauna which can destroy native species. Even more unpredictable is its effects on genetic diversity, by the introduction of genetically modified organisms (GMOs) and plants. These are often associated not just with attempts to design disease-free and improved plant varieties, but are feared by some to represent attempts by multinational companies to take patents on seed varieties on which they have a monopoly.

Apart from water, oil is a major problem, but emerging nations, like China and India, exacerbate the problem. Their high populations have rapidly increasing car ownership: in 2009 China produced 10 million cars, and is now the world's largest producer. It was predicted that by 2030 China alone will consume 99 million barrels of oil daily, but current world production is only 75 million barrels. There has been much debate about when peak oil production will be reached. The widely accepted forecast from the International Energy Agency was that the peak would occur after 2030, but the UK Energy Research Council predicted in late 2009 that the peak would occur as early as 2020, which would cause soaring oil prices and recourse to more polluting fuels.

Mini-Case 8.2   Beyond muscle power: the basis of modern economies and issues of sustainable development

Economic growth scarcely existed before 1750. Up to that time economies were in a relatively steady state, and the ability to produce anything depended largely on muscle power, human or animal, and on natural energy sources such as wind and water power. Prior to 1750, most populations lived on the edge of existence. Recent research (Gordon 2012) suggests that, for the 400 years prior to 1700, there was no growth in GDP per capita in the UK.

After 1750 the Industrial Revolution produced unprecedented increases in output, spreading around the globe. A key element of this was the steam engine, using unlimited energy from coal. The ability to transcend the limits of muscle power, and other crude forms of energy, was a substantial part of the basis for the modern global economy. After coal and steam power came electricity, and then the internal combustion engine, using oil. These cheap energy sources all allowed quantum leaps in our productivity, plus rapid change in the location of industry and population. Finally, we have the revolution of high speed communications and computing.

Perhaps the world then became a victim of its own success. First, we had worries from the 1920s about oil supplies, which came and went regularly up to the present day. And then we had the issue of global warming, which was argued to be caused by the carbon dioxide generated by combustion of coal, oil and gas. The need to reduce carbon dioxide emissions arguably provided an impetus for us to economize on oil and gas, the reserves of which were going to run out if we did not economize, and switch to renewable energy sources (wind turbines, wave power, hydroelectricity, etc). The way to economize was to increase the price by various taxes, though the price was leaping anyway. Alternative energy sources, such as wind turbines, needed to be subsidized until they became economically viable, and energy companies in UK had to charge customers more to pay for the subsidies. The result, controversially, has been rapid increases in household energy bills, though a basic component of this is actually the increase in the cost of energy rather than the taxes and subsidies. More broadly, critics suggested that the direction of energy policy was likely to drive our economies back to the Stone Ages and muscle power by making energy so expensive.

The elephant in the room in the midst of this debate was shale oil and gas. It was true that easily accessible oil/gas was a diminishing resource, and the threats that reserves might be exhausted in the foreseeable future seemed unarguable. But we have been aware for many years that in many regions there were geological strata permeated with vast deposits of oil and gas. The problem was that there was no practicable method of extracting the energy from the earth. However, the fairly recently developed technique of 'fracking', which involved pumping water at very high pressure into these strata and pushing the oil/gas deposits to the surface where they could be gathered, was widely introduced in US.

This technique was criticized by environmental groups who said that the fracking technique caused earthquakes and polluted groundwater. But development of shale oil and gas has thrust ahead in US and totally transformed its energy position, being almost self-sufficient in gas and oil, and also its general manufacturing position (American Chemistry Council, 2011). The cost of gas has halved in the US, and the cost of vital inputs to chemical processes has dropped by up to 70%. Manufacturing in the US is becoming competitive with China, and the US has a cost advantage over countries such as Germany, France, and UK. Manufacturing is pulling back from these and other countries to the US, 'reshoring' as it is called (Boston Consulting Group 2012).

A strange aspect of this transformation of the American energy position, apart from the economic benefits, is that it has been accompanied by significant falls in American CO_2 emissions. Gas emits less CO_2 than coal, and so although the US is only latterly coming round to participation in Kyoto Treaty targets, its CO_2 emissions are falling while those of the UK and similar countries are falling only marginally or are still increasing. Also, while countries like the UK have scarcely less rich shale gas/oil reserves than US, many objections are raised against their exploitation. But, nevertheless the UK government in January 2013 gave the go ahead for the resumption of exploratory drilling in the shale strata around Blackpool.

This illustrates both the fundamental significance of energy availability for sustaining the basis of the economy, while presenting an environmental sustainability threat, and the way in which forecasts about energy availability can be overtaken by events and completely change the perspective of the future.

Questions

Critics say the transformation of the American energy situation may be exaggerated because once the most isolated oil/gas reserves in a large country are exhausted, the exploitation of reserves nearer to population centres will run up against the same constraints which are pointed out in this country, in terms of potential geological shocks and pollution of water resources. Assess the view that hopes of a transformed energy future for the UK are premature, due to these constraints.

One problem with these predictions is the unpredictable. The worry that oil will become scarce is not new. We examine this in Mini-Case 8.2.

Thus, while global warming captures most attention, there is a range of other linked effects which relate to issues of sustainable development. Our discussions of water and oil shortages lead quickly to food shortages, which are also related to global population growth. Again nothing is simple: half the food produced globally, about two billion tons, is simply wasted through various types of mismanagement plus the desire of supermarkets for cosmetically perfect vegetables (Fox 2013). We may now consider the international responses to these issues.

International responses: the 'Earth Summit' and after

The UN Conference on Environment and Development at Rio de Janeiro, the 'Earth Summit', changed the international legal framework for environmental issues. It created an 'Earth Charter', or an environmental bill of rights which set out the principles for economic and environmental behaviour of peoples and nations. Several agreements emanated from the Conference, in particular:

- the Rio Declaration
- Agenda 21
- UN Framework Convention on Climate Change.

The Rio Declaration

This covered many issues relating to the mutual environmental behaviour of nations. Overall, it aimed to establish;

> a new and equitable global partnership through the creation of new levels of cooperation among States, key sectors of society, and people.

> (Ison et al. 2002, p. 109)

However, the declaration could be described as 'soft law', that is, it lacked an enforcement or compliance system.

Agenda 21–Global programme of action on sustainable development

Agenda 21 is:

> a comprehensive plan of action to be taken globally, nationally and locally by organizations of the United Nations System, Governments and Major Groups in every area in which humans impact on the environment.

> (<http://sustainabledevelopment.un.org/content/documents/Agenda21.pdf>)

Again, it had no legal sanctions, but lots of commitment:

> Perhaps the most important impact of Agenda 21 has been at the local level where Agenda 21 officers have been able to try out practical ideas which seek to implement sustainable development on the ground.

> (Ison et al. 2002, p. 111)

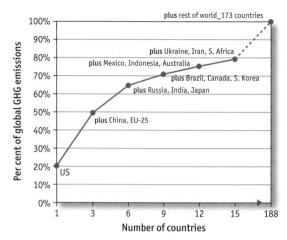

Figure 8.3 The main contributors to GHG emission

Source: World Resources Institute at <**www.wri.org**>

UN Framework Convention on Climate Change

❱❱ **COMPLEXITY** ❱❱ **VALUES** This convention was directly concerned with the problem of global warming, and led to the 1997 **Kyoto Protocol**. Here the developed countries committed to reducing 1990 emission levels of six GHGs by 5% by 2012. It introduced emissions trading, whereby countries which were having difficulty meeting their emissions reduction targets could buy emissions allowances from other countries with spare capacity. The Kyoto Protocol was a significant initiative. But the US, producing 25% of global GHGs, refused to sign the protocol, and still refused up to the election of President Obama in 2008, after which US attitudes started to change in the lead up to the December 2009 Copenhagen Conference. Thus, global warming is generated by few countries, but many, mainly the poorest, suffer from it (see Figure 8.3). This is an enormous injustice.

A related issue is lack of universal agreement on global warming. While it is argued that most scientific opinion suggests global warming is fact, evidenced in tornadoes, glaciers melting, and so on, other key experts disagree with this view. But even if you are of the majority opinion, suggestions of what to do are not simple. If you look at Mini-Case 8.2 you can see the difficulty.

It is true that the research underpinning conclusions about global warming is at the frontiers of science, but the weight of 'officially accepted' scientific opinion seems to be on the side of its current reality and future imminence. We must now consider how these arguments have been taken forward up to the present day.

From Rio 1992 to Doha 2012

❱❱ **SPATIAL LEVELS** The two decades since Rio 1992 have been punctuated by a series of conferences which sought to cement a binding climate change agreement. What was hoped to be the 'clincher' took place in Doha (Qatar) in 2012. This was preceded by conferences in Johannesburg (2002), Bali (2007), and Copenhagen (2009). The conferences basically focused on replacing the Kyoto Protocol, and their themes were: the target limit on global warming (2°C agreed at Copenhagen); how to finance measures to achieve this in developing countries; and how to get the main CO_2 emitters (the US, Russia, China, and India) to agree to sign up to it. But the 2°C target is based on one specific view of the underlying science. How sure can we be? This issue is explored further in Mini-Case 8.3.

Mini-Case 8.3   Even when we think we know, what do we do?

The dominant scientific opinion on many issues has often run counter to what subsequently turned out to be the case.

Critics of those who argue climate change is generated by human activity say that a similar failure of the conventional wisdom (the 'scientific consensus') is occurring (Booker 2009). However, the fact remains that the consensus seems to be that anthropogenic global warming is the most probable possibility (Hulme 2009). But, it is important to remember that scientific hypotheses are not tested by majority voting: all hypotheses are provisional; and can be, and frequently are, displaced by a better one (Popper 1963).

Despite the doubts expressed in some quarters, some analysts have said that the forecasts on which views about global warming are based are substantially correct (e.g. Frame and Stone, 2012). Silver (2012) in his general study of issues in forecasting was also of this view, but qualified his conclusions by saying that we were still not very far into the one hundred year period covered by the IPCC forecasts, and much could happen to stop the forecasts coming to fruition (a few major volcanic eruptions occasionally could have a significant cooling effect).

While one might agree with this view, there can still be much argument about many of the responses to it. Some scientists say that focusing on single issues like CO_2 reduction will not necessarily produce the desired results, because the complexity of the physical systems is too great to make reliable predictions. (Thus, the idea that once the global atmosphere warms up by 2C, runaway uncontrollable warming will occur is a prediction of the forecasting models being used. But critics say that this is because the models are based on positive feedback mechanisms, whereas in nature it is more usual to observe negative feedback, or a damping down of oscillations). This problem of predictions becomes even worse when issues become politicized (Giddens 2009). Then global warming becomes one of a range of issues that influence the seesaw movement of international relations. Reducing American GHG emissions involves great economic costs, while stopping the growth of Chinese and Indian emissions will reduce their economic growth. Who will give way? (As we saw in Mini-Case 8.2 solutions, at least for the US, may suddenly appear!) Behind this is power politics, with nations jockeying for position across a range of issues, only one of which is sustainable development. Another root of the issue is corruption: some poor nations which need international funding for their participation in carbon dioxide reduction strategies are, alas, also amongst the most corrupt governments in the world. The unspoken fear is that money provided would simply disappear.

The issues around global warming are prodigiously difficult and controversial, and they present policy-makers with major issues on how to respond directly, and also how to balance them with other policy areas. But there can be little doubt about the existence of shorter term climatic variations which are argued to produce major problems alongside issues of resource shortages of water, food, oil and so on, and pollution and environmental degradation.

Question

Look back at Figure 8.2. This well-known graph is referred to as the 'Hockey Stick'. This is meant to reflect about 900 years of broadly stable world surface temperatures, followed by the Industrial Revolution, leading to rocketing temperatures from now onwards if we do not control them. This graph is controversial. Do an internet search for 'Hockey Stick graph' and explore sites which seem to argue in favour of the validity of the graph and, also, those that criticize it. What are your impressions about this debate?

After Copenhagen there was Cancun (2010), then Durban (2011). All these conferences were marked by failure to agree on most of the main issues, though from 2009 the US started to become involved. The Doha Climate Change Conference (Nov-Dec 2012) was billed as a last chance to come up with an agreement to rescue the Kyoto Treaty from oblivion. It failed to come up with such an agreement, except to keep talking and to come back in 2015 for another attempt. But the Doha Conference marked more than 20 years since the Rio Conference in June 1992. What had actually been achieved after such a long period? The view of some critics is that the whole process has been a failure of epic proportions (Fleming and Jones 2013, p. 2).

Helm (2012) notes that use of coal over this period has risen from 25 per cent to 30 per cent of energy use, significantly because of new generating capacity in the booming Chinese economy. The UK and European countries congratulate themselves on reducing emissions, but are focusing, says Helm, on the wrong variable, namely carbon production, rather than carbon consumption. That is, the shift of production to China means that carbon is being produced there in the process of producing goods which are consumed here (and which, formerly, were produced here). And, the emissions reductions obtained from current renewable energy policies, such as subsidized wind turbines, involve the most expensive ways of reducing emissions known to man.

He concludes, therefore, that we must focus on carbon consumption, and tax imports of it. And, we should move from coal to gas in a transition which is now possible with the availability of lower carbon shale gas reserves.

■ The application of sustainable development frameworks to environmental issues

Conventional frameworks for dealing with environmental issues

》 **VALUES** 》 **INTERNAL/EXTERNAL** Before the idea of sustainable development evolved, conventional, or classical, economics saw pollution and environmental problems as 'side effects' of the production/consumption process. The approach of conventional economics was not to ignore environmental costs, but to keep them in balance with the societal costs and benefits of economic activity. Hence, such side effects were called 'externalities' and were considered to be 'divergences between private and social costs' (these were explored in Chapter 2). Externalities can be positive or negative, but in the cases we are considering they are usually negative. That is, social costs are greater than private costs, and social costs can be reduced to acceptable levels by instituting taxes to equate social marginal cost with social marginal benefit. A classical example of this is the use of road pricing to reduce traffic congestion. Economists refer to this as 'internalizing the externality' and it is popularly referred to as 'making the polluter pay'. Such ideas have existed for many years, and have been implemented on a small scale in UK cities, like Cambridge and Durham, and on a larger scale in cities like Singapore. The successful introduction of the London congestion charge in February 2003 is probably the largest example to date.

Road congestion is an easy example of the use of the conventional economic approach to controlling an environmental problem. Despite the practical implementation, the situation is simpler in that most of the problem consists of road users imposing costs on other road users. But other types of environmental goods can be more difficult. Unlike road traffic, the perpetrators are most often not sufferers. It may also be difficult to identify who actually are the perpetrators and sufferers. Also, you can only impose charges if it is possible to establish ownership of, or property rights in, the thing that is being charged for (such as road space). The problem is that many environmental goods have badly defined property rights. Who owns the atmosphere? Who owns the oceans? But even if we can establish ownership, it may still be hard to quantify the environmental costs that have to be charged for, and then establish practical charging systems. Nevertheless, as we have indicated already, it is not impossible, and the Kyoto Protocol has already instituted the idea of 'emissions trading' (see Mini-Case 8.4).

Mini-Case 8.4 Carbon trading or 'funny money'?

The principle of **emissions trading** is simple. It keeps the level of a pollutant (in this case CO_2) at a target level by putting a price on it. Producers get permits which allow them to emit a certain amount of carbon, and they use these permits to cover their own emissions, or else invest in clean technologies which allow them to sell some of the permits to another company which has exceeded its permit quota. This creates a market in the permits. The problem is that once you set the overall total and allocate permits you are merely keeping within that total, shifting the total around between those who are buying and those who are selling permits. Thus, the total does not decrease by definition, though it could in principle be organized to do so over a period, and this would be the intention of Kyoto (Hulme 2009).

After the establishment of the Kyoto Protocol, the European Union instituted an Emissions Trading Scheme (ETS) (European Commission 2009). Each member state set a cap on the carbon emissions that would be allowed and issued permits accordingly. The first round of the scheme during 2005–7 had mixed results. The caps were set too high in some countries (but not high enough in Britain), and several countries produced much lower emissions than they estimated. Hence, prices collapsed. But there is inevitably a learning process, and it was hoped that the 2008–12 round could be run with tighter limits. However, the ETS suffered a setback at the end of 2009 after the European Court overturned European Commission caps on the amount of carbon Poland and Estonia are permitted to emit between 2008 and 2012 (causing the price of carbon to dip 2.5%) because they appealed against the financial burdens entailed. This could mean similar rulings being made on other countries' emissions caps with adverse consequences for the cap-and-trade scheme.

Potentially, the effect of ETS on companies is remarkable. Their possible liabilities for purchase of permits have to be indicated on their balance sheets, and investors are very keen to know what a company's emissions position is. The Stern Review, a major government report about the threats facing us from climate change, raised the possibility that emissions may be taxed in the UK and this could have a very significant effect on the stock market. Climate change, it argues, may cost us 20% of world GDP if it is not checked, and taxing emissions is just one specific aspect of the general message of the Stern Review: the polluter must pay (HM Treasury 2006). This view was reflected in the passing of the Climate Change Act on 26 November 2008. But at a European level, some uncertainty was introduced by the 2009 court decision. Other difficulties have accumulated. In late November 2012 the US Congress passed a law forbidding US airlines from paying any carbon dioxide emission charges for flights to/from the EU, as the EU was seeking to extend the emissions trading scheme to airline emissions.

A more general worry as emissions trading becomes more widespread is how, in the light of the financial crisis, to avoid the scheme becoming the basis of another scandal (Giddens 2009). The downturn in the world economy, with low gas and coal prices, has meant that the permits issued are too numerous to sustain a reasonable trading price. On 30 November 2012—in the midst of the Doha conference—it was reported that the price of carbon had dropped to 5.89 euros per tonne, when many analysts consider a minimum price of at least 20 euros is necessary to convince industry and utilities to adopt cleaner forms of energy over coal and gas (Chestney 2012).

Question

What are the problems of attempting to levy taxes on polluters?

■ The concept of sustainable development (SD)

Definitions of sustainable development

As well as the Brundtland definition already discussed, there are over 70 other definitions of sustainable development. The Brundtland definition is intuitively graspable and we can point to two key ideas:

- **Inter-generational equity** (IRGE): that is, fairness between generations, or, being as fair to our grandchildren as we are to ourselves.

- **Intra-generational equity** (IAGE): that is, fairness between different interest groups in the same generation.

It is common to talk about the two ideas from the point of view of what is called 'weak' and 'strong' sustainability:

- Weak sustainability (WS): to achieve IRGE we should aim to pass on to future generations a constant 'aggregate capital stock' (AGS), though its composition may change; to achieve IAGE we should aim to compensate the poor and disadvantaged by support programmes.
- Strong sustainability (SS): to achieve IRGE, the idea of AGS does not apply: losses of environmental capital must be replaced; to achieve IAGE, we still compensate, but we also emphasize the collective value of ecosystems and environment.

But whether we go for strong or weak definitions we need to consider how we measure them.

Development of sustainable development initiatives

▶ **VALUES** The key issue here is how to value environmental goods. There are problems which are well known in using conventional GDP measures with environmental goods. An increase in GDP can be consistent with an increase in environmental degradation.

Expenditures to reduce degradation are regarded in economic accounting terms as an increase in welfare because they increase GDP, rather than being a cost which actually reduces welfare. Hence, alternative measures which reflect this have been devised, for instance, the Index of Sustainable Economic Welfare (ISEW) devised by the Stockholm Environmental Institute in 1994. Thus:

$$ISEW = \text{Personal consumption} + \text{non-defensive public expenditure}$$
$$- \text{defensive private expenditures} + \text{capital formation}$$
$$- \text{costs of environmental degradation}$$
$$+ \text{services from domestic labour} - \text{depreciation of natural capital}$$

In a conventional GDP measure, the first two negative quantities would be positive, while the last two items, one negative and one positive, would not appear in the equation at all. Thus, in the UK since the 1970s GDP has increased annually, but ISEW has declined.

Stop and Think

....

Think of two concrete examples each for (a) and (b) which probably:

a) increase GDP but reduce ISEW

b) reduce GDP but increase ISEW.

From here the development of environmental indicators is a key step. The UK government published its first set of indicators of sustainable development in 1996, and these have been updated since, and form the basis for evaluating the progress being made towards both national and international sustainability targets. The current version is from 2009 (DEFRA 2009). Many indicators are defined at national, regional, and local level. A subset of 20 key indicators apply to the whole of the UK in relation to the four priority areas outlined in the 2005 UK Government Sustainable Development Strategy (DEFRA 2005), namely, sustainable consumption and production, climate change and energy, protection of natural resources and environmental enhancement, and the creation of sustainable communities and a fairer world. The indicators include such as GHG emissions, resource use, waste generation, bird populations, fish stocks, ecological impacts of air pollution, and river quality. Very few items get a 'tick' in the latest summary assessment, and resource use gets a big black cross against it.

Once we can quantify the main things that need to be influenced, the next step is to consider how we influence them.

Types of approaches for dealing with environmental problems

As suggested already, while we talk about the global dimension of environmental problems, many of the responses to them are implemented at a local level. So we often hear the phrase: 'Think globally, act locally'. It is common to classify policy responses into either 'market based' or 'non-market based'.

'Market based' policy measures

⟩ **VALUES** A first approach is by processes of bargaining and negotiation. If property rights in the environmental goods—air, water, or whatever—can be assigned to some party, this is possible. The question, of course, is who will they be assigned to? Equity and ethics suggest that 'the polluter pays'. But if there are too many polluters or sufferers, bargaining is difficult, and it may be impossible to set up any scheme. In this case, the alternative may be a tax.

With environmental taxes, the polluter pays a tax related to the environmental damage. This creates an incentive to reduce the damage, for instance as in the case of a carbon tax. The problem here is that it may be hard to estimate the correct tax level, so that if it is set too high, society loses out because the polluter cuts back production too much, whereas if it is set too low, there is insufficient reduction in the environmental damage.

'Non-market based' policy measures

Here government establishes standards for things like air quality, water quality, chemical processes, waste incineration, and so on. The polluter then decides how to meet standards, adopting the least costly approach. A regulatory body may be appointed to monitor compliance and to take action for breaches of standards. Regulatory systems can be rather blunt instruments. Different firms may be more easily placed to achieve the targets, and might be encouraged to overachieve if some form of trading solution were possible, whereas if the target is easy to achieve, the company can sit back and do little. Equally, if the targets are set too stringently, firms may incur unnecessary costs to meet them.

We may also include, under non-market based measures, the use of public exhortation, persuasion, and education in environmental matters. This may include direct measures which encourage people to do more by giving them a little encouragement to make a start, especially if regulation is going to eventually make things a requirement. A good example here is the campaign to encourage people to start using energy saving light bulbs. There is a lot to do in informing both the public and business about the nature of environmental problems, to facilitate the introduction of appropriate policy measures.

Policy frameworks

⟩ **SPATIAL LEVELS** This section considers what has actually been done in policy terms for the UK and the European Union. Up to the 1970s environmental regulation in the UK was piecemeal, with several inspectorates working independently in relation to land, air, water, and nuclear power. From the 1970s there were attempts to unify the various areas of environmental regulation and, from the 1980s, in the light of developments outlined at the start of the chapter, environmental policy ceased being a national concern and took on progressively a European and then global dimension. The attempts to unify or integrate the various areas of environmental regulation led in 1990 to the Environmental Protection Act which gave legislative backing to the idea of Integrated Pollution Control (IPC), looking to control pollution across media (land, water, air, etc.). This embodied in environmental regulation the principle of requiring the implementation of the Best Available Technique Not Entailing Excessive Cost (BATNEEC), whatever the process. This gave explicit recognition to the economic dimension in what had, up to then, been the principle of the Best Practicable Means (BPM). Following the Environment Act 1996, all the functions of the different environmental agencies were incorporated for the first time into the Environment Agency.

In the 1970s, changes at UK level took place in parallel to Europe-wide and subsequently international initiatives, as the cross-boundary dimensions of environmental processes expanded with growth in the European and global economy.

▪ Sustainable development and business

❯ **VALUES** Business is one of the significant contributors to environmental problems, yet, simultaneously, it provides us with our livelihoods. The need to focus environmental measures so as not to impose excessive economic costs on society as compared with the reduction in environmental costs has also emerged in discussion. Overall we need to maintain high/stable economic growth within acceptable environmental limits. Thus, this section considers sustainable development issues within the context of the internal operations of a business. It will become quickly apparent that this presents not only challenges to a business in terms of how it can reduce its environmental impact, but also opportunities, in terms of the way in which these challenges collectively also present business opportunities in helping businesses to meet the challenges facing them. It also raises the issue of the responsibilities of businesses in terms of considering their activities in ethical terms, which is explored in detail in Chapter 7.

Defining sustainability in relation to business

The following definition of sustainable business conveniently places it in parallel with the Brundtland definition:

> Sustainable business … means taking the goal of sustainability, living and working in such a way that human society will be possible for generations to come, and translating that into the changes required of an individual organization—changes which maintain the organizations capacity for producing human benefits, including the profitability needed for survival, while optimising the environmental balance of its operations.

> (Crosbie and Knight 1995, p. 15)

Another way of expressing this idea of sustainable business is the 'triple bottom line'. While an enterprise is normally judged by its profit and loss account, or 'bottom line', the 'triple bottom line' adds in social and environmental criteria, shortened into 'people, planet, profit'. The idea was set out by Elkington (1997).

❯ **SPATIAL LEVELS** There is almost no aspect of the operations of the average business which does not have an impact on the natural environment. We can usefully employ here the format of Hutchinson and Hutchinson (1997) in terms of looking at four aspects of a business: its site history; the production processes it employs; its product and the communications processes surrounding it; and the external environment of the business. These fit into the well established framework of what is generally called environmental and ecological auditing, and the processes developed from about the mid-1980s in the US. This was further boosted after the 1992 'Earth Summit', and not long after in 1995 the European Union devised an Environmental Management and Auditing System (EMAS). In the same year the International Standardization Organization (ISO) set up a committee to develop an environmental management system for global application. It established ISO 14001. While EMAS applies to the EU, and is especially prevalent in German-speaking countries, ISO 14001 is applied worldwide. The EU has adapted its system so that those firms which have ISO 14001 can achieve EMAS by a series of modifications to ISO 14001.

The audit is a broad way of looking at the operations of a company or organization to sketch out how sustainability issues reach into every part of its operations. Each of the four aspects mentioned above can be broken down into several sub-aspects, and many of them are whole areas of research by themselves. One aspect of the fourth area (external environment) will be taken to provide the main case study of the chapter, namely on sustainable transport for a large business. But once we have considered each of the four aspects, we shall look at a difficult issue. What do these issues actually mean to a business and government in practice?

Site history

All sorts of dangers may lie hidden in a site, and once a company buys it, it buys all the associated risks. Insurance companies may refuse to insure if they suspect hidden risks. There may, perhaps, be concealed noxious substances which could be disturbed and released into the atmosphere during construction or production. An 'Environmental Impact Assessment' (EIA) would be necessary, which is one aspect of an eco-audit. An EIA involves gathering all the information that exists on the site, and developing an assessment of the environmental issues and risks pertaining to past activity on the site, and the relationship of this to any proposed expansion of existing activities, or initiation of completely new activities.

The production process

This concerns the actual production process, particularly energy use and waste generation, plus the product life cycle. Companies waste about 30% of their energy (mainly in buildings). Thus:

> Electricity and gas metering in business appears to be chaotic. Many businesses have estimated metering, and most are unable to be really sure what energy they actually use, unless they have an energy saving programme in place. This situation is untenable.

> (Sustainable Development Commission 2005, p. 31)

It has been calculated that a 20% reduction in energy costs is equivalent to a 5% increase in sales. So helping the environment can be good business.

Reducing total energy use is only one aspect. The sources of energy can also be examined to encourage recycling of energy and the use of renewable energy (e.g. wind and solar power). This can also represent business opportunities in terms of developing new ideas and techniques. The whole area of micro power generation has started to mushroom as new designs of small wind-powered turbines which can be attached to buildings come on the market (but note that wind power can be variable and back-up is needed).

Apart from wasting energy, firms may produce substantial waste in the production process. Dealing with waste after generation to minimize impact (for instance, ensuring that companies hired to take waste away do not dump it illegally) is an obvious first requirement, but even more useful are efforts at minimizing the waste generated in the first place.

❯ **INTERNAL/EXTERNAL** Looking at energy use and waste generation leads to the whole product in terms of a **life cycle assessment** (LCA). A LCA examines all environmental impacts associated with the life of a product from raw material extraction, to pre-production processes, to actual production, and through to distribution and final disposal of the used product. This is easily said, but for many products each of these stages involves quite significant environmental impacts, apart from the production process itself. For instance, furniture industries need to ensure that scarce timbers illegally gathered from threatened tropical forests are not being used by them. Equally, so many harmless looking products wear out and have to be disposed of, and they often contain poisonous components which leak into the atmosphere, the earth or water systems: fridge mountains, PC mountains, old cars, and so on. So there are regular calls to put a tax on such items to pay for their eventual disposal.

Product and communications

The environmental features of a company's production activities can be exploited for its own wider advantage. This may be in terms of protecting itself from the wider public consequences of unforeseen environmental crises, promoting its products, or promoting the image of the company in terms of not only its financial reporting, but also its environmental reporting.

▶ **STAKEHOLDERS** In terms of crisis management and risk assessment we have already referred to environmental disasters, but these can also be public relations disasters which damage the wider image of the company by affecting adversely its product brands and stock market standing. Environmental disasters are nearly always unexpected, yet require immediate company responses to restore confidence and minimize damage to its reputation. When disasters occur there may be attempts to conceal information. However, openness and transparency is the best policy, and companies should prepare for unlikely but possible eventualities, by carrying out risk assessments of what could happen, and making reaction plans ready in case something does go wrong.

▶ **VALUES** Disasters apart, the daily operations of the company may be an asset to be exploited. Companies which have ensured that they source their inputs from other companies which have employed environmentally desirable methods, have produced their products to the highest environmental standards, and have ensured that waste products can be disposed of in the most environmentally efficient way, have a story to tell, or sell, in their marketing activities. This is called **green marketing**, and it is a story to tell not only to consumers and customers, but also to staff, shareholders, investors, the media, and regulatory authorities. However, it has to be a believable and honest story. Consumers and the media soon spot exaggerated or false claims which are intended to boost sales or public image. Such claims are often called **greenwash** (see Mini-Case 8.5).

Product design, packaging, and eco-labelling also present opportunities for environmental gains. Materials can be saved in production and packaging. Packaging can be used not only to provide useful environmental guidance on the product, but also information on safe disposal of the used product and packaging (eco-labelling). Clearly, some of these features will have an obvious benefit to the company, in terms of saving raw materials and the use of energy. But others will have benefits further down the line reducing transport costs, and landfill or incineration costs. Moreover, the opportunity exists, by doing this, to portray the company in the best possible light.

Stop and Think

Think of three examples where a company uses claims about the environmental dimension of its products or activities in a genuine way, and three examples where false or exaggerated claims are made.

Finally, there is environmental reporting. Companies are required to produce annual reports setting out their accounts and financial position. While there is not the same legal requirement for a corporate environmental report (CER), the environmental threats which companies now face both at home and abroad mean that a CER can be almost as important to judging the health of a company, and whether it is a safe investment prospect, as its annual financial statement. Hence a transparent annual CER is produced by major companies. These set out the environmental policies and targets of the company, the systems in place to achieve them, and progress towards achievement.

The external environment

Here we consider two aspects of the external environment of the company which are important to the theme of this chapter, but which seem to get little coverage in the many textbooks that now exist on 'corporate environmental management'. The external environment will here refer to the links which a company maintains with other firms, customers, and organizations to produce its goods and services. The first aspect of these links we call the supply chain, and the second aspect will be the environmental management of the transport demands generated by the activities of the firm or organization.

And yes, you, the reader, are closely implicated here. As a student using this book at an educational institution, you are involved in the activity of an organization which may be one of the largest employers and generators of income in the region you live in. You may be one thousands of students moving back and forth from home to institution, and between sections of it, and generating your own part of the massive environmental footprint of your institution. Hence, in contrast to many texts on the theme of this chapter, we mark out transport as a key aspect (see end of chapter Case Study).

We highlighted the nature of supply chains in Chapter 3. Regarding its environmental management, any company or organization is only one link in the long process which leads to someone somewhere getting a product or service they need. A tree felled in a forest in Scandinavia leads by a long intervening set of operations—raw materials processing, transport, warehousing and storage, further intermediate manufacturing, further transport and storage, final processing, transfer to retail distributors—to a box of matches purchased from a corner shop. A company examining its environmental profile will need to look at not only its own internal operations and processes, but at the supply chain as a whole, to see where changes can be made which will improve the overall environmental performance of the chain.

⟫ DYNAMIC In relation to environmental transport strategies, transport is one of the most important factors in the whole global environmental problem, yet it is one of the most intractable, and getting worse. It is forecast that by 2020, 'transport is likely to account for more than half of global oil demand and roughly one fourth of global energy-related CO_2 emissions' (International Energy Agency 2001).

The demand for cars and commercial vehicles is growing much faster than technological improvements in engines can reduce CO_2 emissions, especially in Central and Eastern Europe, and developing countries like China and India. The demand for air transport is growing rapidly too. Also, it is not just a growth in numbers: road transport (and air transport to a lesser extent) is a very flexible form of transport which reduces the constraints on location, and leads to not only more journeys but longer journeys.

Reducing the environmental footprint of the transport activities of a business raises conflicts to the extent that critics argue it may raise costs and reduce economic growth. It is often argued that investment in transport infrastructure boosts the rate of economic growth generally, and that it is crucial for improving the economic prospects of declining or peripheral regions.

However, if the forecasts of the effects of unrestricted growth in GHGs are borne out, and to which transport is a major contributor, it can be argued that the effects on economic growth of global warming will be much more disastrous than the effects of cutting back transport growth in the first place. This was the basic message of the Stern Review (HM Treasury 2006).

Thus, a company or organization seeking to reduce the demands it places on transport systems and energy related requirements will need to consider the a range of factors and devote considerable effort to developing 'company travel plans', or 'green transport strategies', which look at several or all of these factors, and for which much government advice has been published (DfT 2005). Let us examine these factors:

- *Choice of mode*: In many cases the choices available in the mode of transport a company uses to receive and forward goods may be restricted by site characteristics, the type and value of the goods, and the urgency of receipt and despatch. But it is clear that different modes have different environmental characteristics regarding energy use and emissions, and companies may be able to adjust their practices accordingly.

- *Storage and packaging for transport*: For large companies the demand for warehousing and storage facilities, and for facilities to pack up and dispatch goods, can be massive. Inventories are dead money, and companies try to minimize them. One way is to have **just in time** production methods, so that component suppliers are organized in the supply chain to bring in deliveries just before they are needed. Thus, transport substitutes for storage. This is accentuated in the activities of companies like large supermarket chains, such as Tesco and ASDA. These companies need to keep their stores supplied around the clock. Cash tills connect directly to the computerized inventory systems to indicate instantly the demand around the country for any product. Economies of scale combined with an efficient motorway system encourage the concentration of warehousing and distribution systems into large logistics centres serving the whole country from a few major bases. This substitution of transport for storage facilities generates energy use. And it also leads to situations where goods which could be obtained locally are shipped from the other end of the country.

- *Input sources and product destinations*: This means that companies seeking to minimize their environmental footprint in transport terms need to consider where they get their inputs from, and where they send them to. As just indicated, it is surprising how many resources are spent shifting goods around the country to places where they already are, and generating GHGs in the process.

Stop and Think

Think of as many examples as you can of situations where goods which are available locally are shipped in from a distance. Can you think of reasons why this might have occurred in each instance?

- *Employee travel patterns and alternatives to travel*: Journeys to work, school, or college constitute a major proportion of daily travel. Growing car use and declining public transport are key features of this phenomenon. The drive to reverse the use of the car and to encourage us to use more environmentally friendly modes like public transport, cycling, or walking has been going on for many years as a way of reducing the peak hour problem. But growing recognition of the GHG problem has sharpened this drive. Companies also need to ask if travel is necessary in the first place. This applies especially to travel on company business. Is it always necessary to drive? Can public transport be used? Can an employee work at home and not travel to work? Can telephone/video conferencing be used to avoid travel?

❯❯ INTERNAL/EXTERNAL

- *Other factors—site access, health and safety, noise, and so on*: Increased car ownership means more workers drive to work. Insufficient parking space may be available. Larger delivery vehicles may have difficulty approaching and manoeuvering around within the site. Problems of noise, inhalation of toxic fumes, visual intrusion, etc. become an on-site as well as off-site problem. Dealing with these problems can be considered an internal issue, not related to sustainability issues, but they do relate back. Take parking. If employees drive to work and you have the land, why not pave it over? But land is expensive, and there may be more productive uses for it. Moreover, paving land has a significant impact on water resource problems, as it reduces the area into which water can soak to build up ground water reserves, and the rain runs into drains and to the sea.

❯❯ STAKEHOLDERS

- *Company travel plans*: Unlike the local transport plans which UK local authorities produce, these plans (also called **green transport plans**) are for a company or organization. But they do relate to local transport plans, and are usually developed in close consultation with the local authority and public transport operators, and also with other employers facing the same issues. Studies show that even limited travel plans can achieve 3–5% reductions in the number of employees travelling to work alone by car, and more ambitious plans which include such measures as public transport discounts and parking restrictions on site can achieve 15–30% reductions, or even more, within two to four years. Environmental sense is good economic sense. Research shows that it typically costs a firm £300–£500 per year to maintain a car parking space, but to operate a travel plan costs only £47 a year per full-time employee (see end of chapter Case Study).

▪ The significance of sustainable development for business

❯❯ **VALUES** The previous sections have indicated how a business may review its operations and interpret them in a sustainable development context. But would they all want to? Would it not reduce their profits?

Critics accuse some companies of being against sustainable development measures. The oil company EXXON has been accused of funding pressure groups that cast doubt on the scientific basis of predictions of global warming. Other companies are accused of using their sustainable development or 'green' initiatives as a way of advertising but without any serious basis to them, while others are accused of using them to cover up other undesirable aspects of their business ('greenwash'). For instance, Tesco has been accused of doing this to cover up the hold it has developed on the food and convenience goods business, driving many small operators out who might have sourced goods from the local market area, and been actually much more sustainable than Tesco in their operations.

Equally, the suggestion is made that many companies may see sustainable development initiatives as expensive frills which interfere with making profits, and they only engage in them to the extent that it generates good publicity and promotes the image of their products generally.

No doubt this may be so in some cases. A much stronger and more recent version of this view, in the more general context of **corporate social responsibility** (CSR), is that the logic of corporate capitalism in terms of profit seeking means that the 'win, win' idea of pursuing the triple bottom line in sustainable business is inherently delusory and simply serves as a means of deflecting criticism away from the more questionable practices of large corporate organizations (Fleming and Jones 2013). We explore this in Mini-Case 8.5.

It is, of course, easy to pick out individual companies like Starbucks and point to inconsistencies between what they do in one area of their operations, and what they do in another. It then makes it easy for critics to say that sustainable business is all 'greenwash' to cover up a massive rip-off of the taxpayer. But the techniques of transfer pricing which allow companies to switch revenues from a high tax to a low tax jurisdiction have been known about and debated for decades. It is not illegal, though most would say it is unethical. But companies only have to obey the law. Tax evasion is illegal, but tax avoidance is not (Shaxson 2012). But tax avoidance is conspicuously absent from discussions of CSR. Why?

A more difficult issue for writers like Fleming and Jones (2013) to show is that on balance most companies behave like Starbucks. This would be almost impossible to show, as we simply do not have the internal evidence to assess the true scale of 'greenwash'. But unless one is a believer in global conspiracies, there is mounting substantial evidence that companies are taking

Mini-Case 8.5 Putting your money where your mouth is: Starbucks, sustainable development, and taxes

Large corporations stress their responsibilities in the area of CSR, of which sustainable business is but one aspect. Starbucks is an international corporation with chains of coffee shops around the world (55,000 retail outlets in 55 countries in 2011). Its UK turnover was nearly £400 million in 2011. On the home page of its website <http://www.starbucks.com/> as of May 2013 there were a number of key headings, of which one was 'Responsibility'. If you were to have clicked on the six subheadings that then appeared, you would have noted that they told a great story about Starbucks running a sustainable business. Here are some of the quotes:

We have taken a holistic approach to ethically sourcing the highest quality coffee, tea and cocoa.

When it comes to environmental sustainability, our experience has proven the power of collaboration.

Starbucks is committed to helping communities thrive in the places where we do business.

These searches would clearly have generated signals in the mind of the reader. The same site contained their *Global Responsibility Report*. The current report is from 2011 (released in March 2012). It tells an impressive tale of sustainable business, community involvement, and ethical sourcing in every imaginable aspect of the business.

A controversial issue which emerged in 2012 was the fact that, despite its great turnover in the UK, Starbucks had paid no tax to Her Majesty's Revenue and Customs for five years. In December 2012 it was taken to task by the Parliamentary Public Accounts Committee, and the outcome was that it volunteered to pay £20 million in tax for the next two years. Starbucks was not doing anything illegal. It has good accountants, and, like all international corporations, it has clever arrangements in place to shift funds around the world so that it only pays minimal, if not actually minute, levels of tax. It is legal, but is it ethical? Is Starbucks really running a sustainable business if it is sucking funds out of the UK which could make a major contribution to the country's own sustainability efforts? Are the Global Responsibility Reports all 'greenwash' as Fleming and Jones (2013) no doubt would claim?

Question

Google and Amazon were also taken to task by the Public Accounts Committee about their tax payments. Study their websites and assess the extent to which they make similar promises as regarding their responsibility to sustainability.

more and more notice of sustainable development issues, both because of straight issues of survival, and because they realize it makes good business sense and presents business opportunities. And, the fact that they do it because they see it is advantageous does not devalue their activities or motivations. The whole basis of the market economy is self-interest, where individual actions for one's own benefit redound to the common good. Sustainable business may be seen as being driven not only by enlightened self-interest, but also by the realization that companies should be doing this anyway in the light of an overall evaluation of their activities.

≫ **SPATIAL LEVELS** Companies with global operations, such as the banks, HSBC and Standard Chartered, are highly conscious of the risks that global warming presents. Apart from increased insurance premiums, they face the risk that many of their global operations may simply be submerged by rising sea levels. Equally, looking at current operations from a sustainability point of view actually starts to indicate that there may be a lot of money to save. And the business opportunities which are possible by responding to global warming have been estimated to be about £500 billion, so there is much for the enterprising company to go for.

Many companies have determined to become carbon neutral in their operations. BSkyB was the first company in the FTSE100 to become carbon neutral in 2006. By 2011 there were six companies in the FTSE who were carbon neutral (Carbon Retirement 2011). This may not appear a large number, but one has to consider how long it takes to become carbon neutral. Thus, Marks and Spencer (Smithers 2012) reported in June 2012 that it was the first major UK retailer to meet its sustainability targets, becoming carbon neutral after a five year effort.

We may also look dispassionately at what government is doing. One would get the impression from the foregoing discussion that government at all levels is working hard to promote sustainable development. The UK government and the European Union have numerous measures to promote it, and there are many international agreements. However, we should consider many aspects of the discussion in a wider perspective that merges into considerations addressed in other chapters of this book. Many environmental objectives and measures conflict with measures and objectives in other parts of the economy. It is said that politics is the art of the possible, and governments try to stay in power by seeming to satisfy as many as possible of the conflicting objectives of as many pressure groups and stakeholders in society as possible. Thus, the best possible gloss will be put on every aspect of government activity. A sharp observer needs to watch out for 'greenwash' not only from companies, but from government too.

The difficult part

While one can list all the aspects of a company's operations that may be focused on to improve its sustainability characteristics, the difficult part is to actually bring about a holistic change where the company as a whole works in this direction, rather than sustainability managers located outside operational functions trying to bring about change, or enthusiasts in different parts of the company working in isolation simply doing the best they can. Thus, sustainable businesses trying to operate a 'triple bottom line' are run by people, people who have to learn to work together to achieve sustainable working across the company. How does this happen?

It might be suggested that this is where the ideas of Senge (Senge et al. 1994) and the **learning organization** could be applied. A learning organization is said to be a company that facilitates the learning of its members and continuously transforms itself. The idea has been widely promoted and discussed as a theoretical concept in general business circles, but as Smith (2001) noted: 'while there has been a lot of talk about learning organizations it is very difficult to identify real-life examples', while Caldwell (2011) refers to its 'failures to deliver a practical guide to organizational learning'. It is hard in fact to find any example of the application of this approach in integrating sustainability initiatives into the fabric of business organizations, though it has been explored in a higher education context (e.g. Glantz and Kelman 2010, Atkinson-Palombo and Gebremichael 2012). What one might call 'how to do it' manuals written for practising managers are of a much more pragmatic flavour, and go through all aspects of the operations of a company to indicate how the company may 'green' its operations (e.g. Weybricht 2009, Olson 2010). In fact, they follow very closely, though in much greater detail, the necessarily brief outline in the sections above on sustainable business, though adding the treatment of issues in leadership, training, and internal cultural change. What is interesting is that, though these sources refer to examples from particular companies on particular aspects, they are devoid of complete examples of the application of the guides as a whole to individual companies, and evaluations thereof. This, no doubt, reflects the fact that we are in a very new area, and research results are probably in the pipeline and will come out in a fragmentary way (e.g. Xu Yan 2011). We would anticipate reporting further on this in subsequent editions of this book.

Stop and Think

Bearing in mind the discussion in this section, can you think of ways in which a company could embed sustainable thinking across the whole of its workforce, rather than just make piecemeal progress in limited aspects of its operations?

■ Looking ahead

The global environmental crisis makes progress with sustainable development policies an immediate priority, yet progress seems to be slow. Many still disagree with arguments about global warming, though few disagree with the existence of other issues in sustainable development such as pollution and resource scarcity. But even where people agree on the existence of all issues, including global warming, they may feel that policies suggested in response are wrong, or even disastrous. Where will we be in another five or ten years? Much depends on a variety of imponderable factors. Clearly, if we carry on as we are the future looks gloomy. Climate change (man induced or not), along with environmental degradation and exhaustion of key resources, especially oil, may suggest periods of future global instability.

On the other hand, some changes have taken place which promise to improve the prospects for achieving sustainable development. The change of policy direction in the US, which produces about a quarter of global warming emissions, is one such positive aspect, and the US, via the shale oil/gas revolution, has done more to reduce, almost by accident, its CO_2 emissions than the UK or EU, where they are constant or have actually increased slightly. In contrast, the continuing growth of China and India threatens to wipe out any gains from change in the US, unless all can be persuaded to sign up to international agreements. However, developing nations will only do this if compensated by developed ones, but, in a post-credit crunch period, can it be afforded? Here, progress after the December 2012 Doha Conference will be important. The twenty years post-Rio 1992 have been declared a massive failure. How long can we go on having conference after conference? Will the next conference in 2015 produce anything? We seem to be on the threshold of both technical change, which may produce rapid change in many areas such as the evolution of cheaper non-polluting power sources (such as shale oil/gas); and of political change, where public attitudes are changing cumulatively, making many environmental measures more publicly acceptable. We have, of course, to hope that this is the scenario which actually occurs.

◼ Summary

- Until the last two hundred years man made very little impact on this planet. But since about 1800 cumulative processes have led to a situation where in the last 30–40 years we see ourselves faced with a variety of disasters induced by climate change, and threats to economic, social, and political stability, through to resource shortages and environmental pollution.

- The idea and strategy of sustainable development is put forward as a way of ensuring that we collectively live within the constraints of our resources, and the capacity of the environment to absorb the effects of our presence on the planet.

- Sustainable development involves cooperative action at global, national, and local level. Governments at all levels may set frameworks of laws and regulations involving a variety of market and non-market tools to keep the impact of our activities on the environment within acceptable limits.

- Business in all its forms is a central part of this process; being a major source of the problems in the first place but also a major contributor to solving them; and, as well, a major beneficiary in many ways from having them solved.

In conclusion:

- Business activity is a major contributor to global environmental problems (though not everyone agrees with this).

- And global environmental problems are a major threat to business activity.

- But global environmental problems are also a potential opportunity for business.

- Concepts of sustainable development provide a framework for global thinking and local action.

- Most areas of business activity can be reframed in the light of these concepts to make a contribution to sustainable development, while at the same time in most cases actually improving its economic efficiency.

Case Study: Sustainable transport for a large business: the case of Leeds Metropolitan University

There were 2,496,645 students in UK higher education in 2011/12. A high percentage live away from home, or come from abroad, and they are heavy consumers of transport. There were 179,040 full-time and part-time academic staff (2008/09), plus many administrative and support staff. Higher education is a large foreign currency earner. It is big business. But some universities are massive, and equate with very large corporations both in their financial turnover and in the environmental footprint generated by their transport activities.

Thus, you the reader, and every student in the UK, are directly and intimately connected with this chapter's theme and you have your part to play.

Leeds Metropolitan University is a good example, being one of the largest universities in the country, with 29,000 students (<**http://www.leedsmet.ac.uk/about/facts-and-figures.htm**>). Its turnover is about £170 million per annum, and it contributes about £350 million to the regional economy (year ending 31 July 2011). Its economic impact is far larger than its turnover, as the student body is a significant proportion of the total population of the city, and they are all consumers and spenders. The University has two major campuses. One of the campuses is on the edge of the city centre, while the Headingley campus is five miles north from the city centre on an outstanding parkland site, plus there is an intermediate small campus at Headingley Stadium.

The central campus has always had restricted parking facilities, and staff pay for spaces. The suburban campus has more parking spaces and free parking before 2007 was an attraction for students with cars. The central and suburban campuses lie on one of the most congested traffic arteries in the city. The area between the Leeds campuses is densely populated with Victorian houses subdivided into student

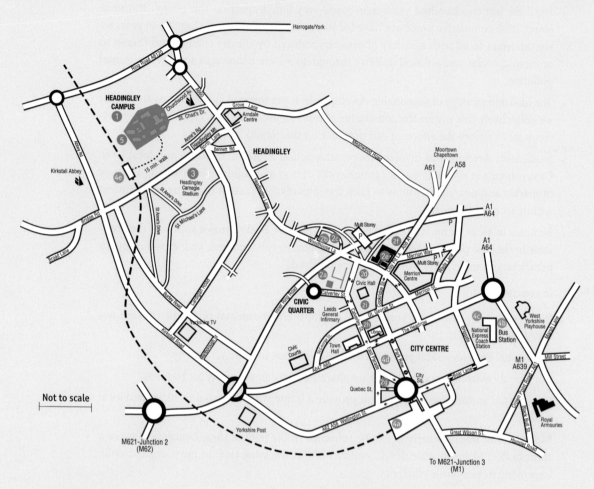

1	Headingley Campus		2h	Electric Press Building
2	Civic Quarter		3	Headingley Carnegie Stadium & The Carnegie Stand
2a	Calverley Street			
2b	Broadcasting Place – Humanities Building		4	Travel
2c	Broadcasting Place – Arts Building		4a	Leeds City Train Station
2c	The Rose Bowl		4b	Leeds City Bus Station
2d	Queen Square		4c	National Express
	The Northern Terrace			Coach Station
	Queen Square Court		4d	Infirmary Street bus stop
2e	Hepworth Point		4e	Headingley Train Station
2f	Cloth Hall Court			
2g	Old School Board		5	Carnegie Village

Figure 8.4 Location of main university facilities in Leeds

Note: Central area 'Civic Quarter' sites are 1a to 1h; suburban site or Headingley campus is 2; and student residences are 3a to 3j.

Source: <www.leedsmet.ac.uk>

flats. The relationship of the University in the city to the overall problems of daily urban traffic congestion and long term sustainability are obvious.

▶ **STAKEHOLDERS** The University works closely with the City Council, and with transport operators, to progress its various planned developments. It is required to develop a 'green transport plan', to show that its plans are within a sustainable development framework. The University has developed its environmental transport strategy since 1999, and published its first 10-year plan in 2002. This had targets, *inter alia*, relating to increasing the level of walking, cycling, and public transport use, and reducing single occupant car use from 45.5% to 30% for staff, and 25% to 12% for students. The new Transport Strategy document for 2012–15 reviewed progress up to 2012. Over this period staff single occupancy vehicle (SOV) travel to the University as a whole reduced from 46% in 2000 to 35% in 2011 and student SOV travel from 24% to 10% over the same period. So overall, this was a remarkable achievement. However, there was a significant difference between the campuses. More staff travelled by non-car modes to the City Campus (73% staff and 89% students) than the Headingley Campus (37% staff and 83% students). This is easily explained in terms of the difference between the two campuses in relation to access to public transport, and the availability of cheap parking. Though from August 2007 parking at Headingley has been charged for, and annual passes for staff are allocated according to a transparent eligibility procedure with annual charges related to income (currently 1% of income), it is still not that expensive compared to the city centre (no passes are available for students, barring those disabled).

Thus the University recognizes it still has progress to make at the Headingley Campus. In this respect, there is no mention in the report of the take-up of parking permits by staff working at the Headingley Campus, or of the proportion that drive to work there who do not have a permit (the data exists but is not easy to extract). Clearly, 1% of income for a permit is not an insignificant sum if you can avoid it.

It would be useful to know the split between drivers with/without permits, as it is relevant to problems that the University initially had with the residents of the surrounding streets after the permit system was introduced (previously, much more space was available on campus, but you will not encourage public transport use if you have a lot of available parking space: this applies everywhere, especially in city centres). The residents complained that their streets were clogged with parked staff cars, ruining their environment. The ability of staff and students to avoid the cost of a parking permit (or pay and display charges) by parking in

the surrounding streets meant that targets for the Headingley Campus would be achieved only if something could be done to change this. This required the University to engage with the surrounding residents' associations, and with the City Council. In the case of the former, there were problems in getting a consistent view of what residents wanted (there were several associations involved), while it had to negotiate with the City Council about getting 'residents' only' parking schemes introduced. This is not an easy matter, as the problem is prevalent across the city, and introducing new restricted areas has to go through extended consultation and management processes. Also, it is very expensive to introduce new zones, and the University had to pay the city to extend residents' parking schemes. But the streets near the campus are now relatively free of parked cars and the residents are satisfied.

The problem, of course, is that this may only push the problem further away. Rules of thumb suggest motorists will park up to half a mile walking distance, possibly more, from their intended destination if they have to. At one level this diffuses the problem over a wider area, so that it may be hard to know what the precise effect of the policy has been, and how long it will take for the Headingley Campus to catch up with the City Campus on the use of non-car modes.

Finally, note that any green transport plan will include reference to a wide range of policies, e.g. bus services, cycle facilities, goods movements, etc., but in a short case study the issue of parking and permits has been highlighted as it provides the material for the following useful discussion points.

Questions

1. Compare the Leeds Met situation with your own university/ college. Has your institution got a green transport plan? If not, do you think it should?

2. Ask your classmates how they access the campus, and whether they would consider changing their travel behaviour if they currently drive. If not, why not?

3. Do you think that it is wrong to charge employees for parking on a business property? Surely this is an expense which should be absorbed by the business or organization?

4. How would you assess a proposal to allocate passes by a balloting process, with everyone, staff and students, having an equal chance of getting one?

5. How would you suggest dealing with local residents around any university/college who claim that its green transport plan ruins their environment? Is it just something they should put up with? Do you think the outcome at the Headingley campus was successful?

Review and discussion questions

1. It is sometimes argued that climate change has positive aspects for business, e.g. melting polar ice caps reduces transport distances for some sea voyages. Consider what other positive aspects of climate change there might be for business, and how they compare to the costs of climate change.

2. How would you respond to someone who argued that business had no real interest in becoming more environmentally responsible and that only compulsion by government would bring about change in business practices?

3. There are still groups who argue that the changes associated with what is described as 'global warming' fall within the range of natural variation, and policies to change business practices to counter its effects will impose needless costs on the economy and yet not make any difference to what is happening. What would you say in response to such arguments?

4. 'Market' approaches to environmental regulation are increasingly preferred to 'non-market' approaches and are gaining more public acceptability in areas like paying for road use. But do you feel that the public will accept the idea of paying for the amount of rubbish each household produces? What problems do you foresee in implementing such a policy?

5. What would you say if you heard someone express the view that global environmental problems are too complex and too far away for individuals and businesses to have any influence on them?

Assignments

1. Look at the environmental policies of your own university or college, or one near you. Does the institution you have chosen seem to be addressing the issues raised in this chapter?

2. This is the third edition of this chapter. The previous two editions are available to inspect in the online resources. Knowledge changes quickly in the three years between each edition. Compare this edition with the previous two editions, and assess what the main changes have been.

3. Visit the website of a FTSE100 company of your choice and study critically its environmental profile. (See the list of FTSE100 companies at **<www.moneyextra.com/stocks/ftse100>**. Choose a company and type its name in the Google, Yahoo, or other search engine.) Each company has a lot of environment-related information on its site. Does it convince you?

Further reading

Blair, A. and Hitchcock, D. (2001) *Environment and Business* (London: Routledge). *Provides a useful contextualization of environmental issues in business, and will allow many aspects of this chapter to be explored in greater depth.*

Ison, S., Peake, S. and Wall, S. (2002) *Environmental Issues and Policies* (London: Prentice Hall). *A rigorous but readable background to many of the technical, theoretical, and policy issues discussed in this chapter.*

Olson, E. G. (2009) *Better Green Business: Handbook for Environmentally Responsible and Profitable Business Practices* (Wharton School Publishing). *Emphasis on strategic overview of incorporating the environmental dimension into business practices.*

Weybrecht, G. (2010) *The Sustainable MBA: The Manager's Guide to Green Business* (London: John Wiley). *Strong focus on translating ideas of sustainability into everyday business practices.*

online resource centre

Test your understanding of this chapter with online questions and answers, explore the subject further through web exercises, and use the web links to provide a quick resource for further research. Go to the Online Resource Centre at <www.oxfordtextbooks.co.uk/orc/wetherly_otter/2>

Useful websites

The following suggestions are a tiny proportion of even the most useful sites. Generally, surf with care, and consider whether promoters of a site have an axe to grind.

The quality daily newspapers:
<www.guardian.co.uk>
<www.times.co.uk>
<www.telegraph.co.uk>
<www.independent.co.uk>

Government departments and related organizations:
<www.defra.gov.uk>
DEFRA (Department of Environment, Food and Rural Affairs)

<www.dft.gov.uk>
The Department for Transport

<www.parliament.uk/commons/>
House of Commons Environment, Transport and Regional Affairs Committee.

UK local authority sites all have the same address format, e.g. Leeds City Council is
<www.leeds.gov.uk>

European sites:
<www.europa.eu>
European Union general site

<www.eea.dk/>
European Environment Agency

<http://ue.eu.intcomm/dg11/index_en.htm>
European Union Environment Directorate

Various United Nations sites:
<www.oneworld.org/uned-uk>
UN Commission for Environment and Development

<www.un.org/esa/sustdev/csd.htm>
UN Commission for Sustainable Development

<http://unep.frw.uva.nl>
UN Environment Programme (UNEP)

Environmental pressure groups, e.g.:
<www.foe.org.uk>
Friends of the Earth

<www.greenpeace.org.uk>
Greenpeace

Other environmental websites:
<www.wri.org>
The World Resources Institute.

<www.ieep.org.uk>
Institute for European Environmental Policy

References

American Chemistry Council (2011) *Shale Gas and New Petrochemicals Investment: Benefits for the Economy, Jobs, and US Manufacturing*, at: <http://americanchemistry.com/ACC-Shale-Report>

Atkinson-Palombo, C. and Gebremichael, M. (2012) 'Creating a Learning Organization to Promote Sustainable Water Resources Management in Ethiopia', *Journal of Sustainability Education*, 19 March 19 2012, at: <http://www.jsedimensions.org/wordpress/content/creating-a-learning-organization-to-promote-sustainable-water-resources-management-in-ethiopia_2012_03/>

Booker, C. (2009) *The Real Global Warming Disaster: Is The Obsession With 'Climate Change' Turning Out To Be The Most Costly Scientific Blunder In History?* (London: Continuum).

Boston Consulting Group (2012) 'Rising U.S. Exports–Plus Reshoring–Could Help Create up to 5 Million Jobs by 2020', 21 September 2012, at: <http://www.bcg.com/media/PressReleaseDetails.aspx?id=tcm:12-116389>

Caldwell, R. (2011) 'Leadership and Learning: A Critical Reexamination of Senge's Learning Organization', *Systemic Practice and Action Research*, Vol. 18, No. 4.

Carbon Retirement (2011) *The State of Voluntary Carbon Offsetting in the FTSE100*, 17 April 2011, at: <http://www.carbon-retirement.com/sites/default/files/The%20State%20of%20Voluntary%20Carbon%20Offsetting%20in%20the%20FTSE%20100.pdf>

Chestney, N. (2012) 'EU climate fight hit by new record low carbon price', Reuters, 30 November 2012, at: <http://uk.reuters.com/article/2012/11/30/us-carbon-price-idUKBRE8AT0U020121130>

Climate Institute (2009) 'Water and Climate Change', at: <http://www.climate.org/topics/water.html>

Crosbie, L. and Knight, K. (1995) *Strategy for Sustainable Business: Environmental Opportunity and Strategic Choice* (Maidenhead: McGraw-Hill).

DEFRA (2005) 'Securing the Future: UK Government Sustainable Development Strategy', at: <http://www.defra.gov.uk/sustainable/government/publications/uk-strategy/>

DEFRA (2009) 'Sustainable Development Indicators in your Pocket 2009', at: <http://www.defra.gov.uk/sustainable/government/progress/data-resources/sdiyp.htm>

DfT (2005) 'Making Travel Plans Work: Lessons from UK Case Studies', Department for Transport, at: <http://www.dft.gov.uk/pgr/sustainable/travelplans/work/>

Elkington, J. (1997) *Cannibals with Forks: the Triple Bottom Line of 21st Century Business* (Oxford: Capstone).

European Commission (2009) 'EU Action Against Climate Change: The EU Emissions Trading Scheme', at: <http://ec.europa.eu/environment/climat/pdf/brochures/ets_en.pdf>

Fleming, P. and Jones, M. T. (2013) *The End of Corporate Social Responsibility: Crisis and Critique* (London: Sage).

Fox, T. (2013) 'Global Food: Waste Not, Want Not', Institute of Mechanical Engineers, January 2013, at: <www.imeche.org>

Frame, D. J. and Stone, D. A. (2012) 'Assessment of the first consensus prediction on climate change', *Nature Climate Change*, 9 Dec 2012, at: <http://www.nature.com/nclimate/archive/issue.html?year=2012&month=12>

Glantz, M. H. and Kelman, I. (2010) 'Universities as Learning Organisations for Sustainability? The Task of Climate Protection', Ch.15, pp.179–192, in Filho, W. L., *Universities and Climate Change: Introducing Climate Change to University Programmes* (Heidelberg: Springer).

Giddens, A. (2009) *Politics of Climate Change* (London: Polity Press).

Gordon, R. J. (2012) 'Is US economic growth over? Faltering innovation confronts the six headwinds', Policy Insight No. 63, September 2012, Centre for Economic Policy Research, at: <http://www.cepr.org/active/publications/policy_insights/viewpi.php?pino=63>

Gray, L. (2010) 'Toxic threat from "green" light bulbs left at tips', *Daily Telegraph*, 3 April 2010, p. 13.

Gray, L. (2010) 'Landfill bills are piling up', *Daily Telegraph*, 3 April 2010, p. 13.

Helm, D. (2012) *The Carbon Crunch: How We're Getting Climate Change Wrong – and How to Fix It* (Newhaven and London: Yale University Press).

HMRC (2009) 'A general guide to landfill tax, Notice LFT1', HM Revenue and Customs, at: <http://customs.hmrc.gov.uk/channelsPortalWebApp/channelsPortalWebApp.portal?_nfpb=true&_pageLabel=pageExcise_ShowContent&propertyType=document&id=HMCE_CL_000509#downloadopt>

HM Treasury (2006) 'The Economics of Climate Change: the Stern Review', at: <www.hm-treasury.gov.uk>

Hulme, M. (2009) *Why We Disagree About Climate Change: Understanding Controversy, Inaction, and Opportunity* (Cambridge: Cambridge University Press).

Hutchinson, A. and Hutchinson, F. (1997) *Environmental Business Management: Sustainable Development in the New Millennium* (Maidenhead: McGraw-Hill).

International Energy Agency (2001) *Towards a Sustainable Energy Future* (Paris: OECD).

IPCC (2007) *Climate Change 2007: Synthesis Report* (Fourth Assessment Report of the Intergovernmental Panel on Climate Change, (Pachauri, R. K. and Reisinger, A. (eds)) (Geneva: IPCC).

Ison, S. Peake, S. and Wall, S. (2002) *Environmental Issues and Policies* (London: Prentice Hall).

Kuhn, T. (1962) *The Structure of Scientific Revolutions* (Chicago: University of Chicago Press).

Laurance, J. (2008) 'Energy saving light bulbs can emit enough UV radiation to damage skin', *The Independent*, 10 October.

The Lighting Association (2007) 'Energy Saving Light Bulbs: The Facts Not Fiction', 22 March 2007, at: <http://www.lightingassociation.com/pdf/LA_PR_0708_EE_Bulbs.pdf>

Olson, E. G. (2009) *Better Green Business: Handbook for Environmentally Responsible and Profitable Business Practices* (Wharton School Publishing/Pearson).

Pacific Institute (2009) 'Water Scarcity and Climate Change: Growing Risks for Businesses & Investors', February 2009 at: <http://www.pacinst.org/reports/business_water_climate/full_report.pdf>

Popper, K. (1963) *Conjectures and Refutations: the Growth of Scientific Knowledge* (London: Routledge).

Ramchurn, R. (2012) 'Phase out of incandescent lamps meets stiff resistance', *Architects Journal*, 6 November, at: <http://www.architectsjournal.co.uk/specification/phase-out-of-incandescent-lamps-meets-stiff-resistance/8637235.article>

Senge, P. M. Kleiner, A. Roberts, C., Ross R. B., Smith, B. J. (1994) *The Fifth Discipline Fieldbook* (New York: Currency Doubleday).

Shaxson, N. (2012) *Treasure Islands: Tax Havens and the Men Who Stole the World* (London: Vintage).

Sheffield, S. Wood, E. F., Roderick, M. L. (2012) 'Little change in global drought over the past 60 years', *Nature*, 15 November, 491, pp. 435–438.

Silver, N. (2012) *The Signal and the Noise: The Art and Science of Prediction* (London: Allen Lane/Penguin).

Smith, M. K. (2001, 2007) 'The learning organization: principles, theory and practice', *The Encyclopedia of Informal Education*, <http://www.infed.org/biblio/learning-organization.htm>

Smithers, R. (2012) 'M&S becomes "carbon neutral"', *The Guardian*, 7 June.

Sustainable Development Commission (2005) Climate Change Programme Review: the Submission of the Sustainable Development Commission to HM Government.

UKauthority.com (2010) 'Chip spy in the bin or rewards for rubbish?', UKauthority.com (news and information service for local government), 5 March, at: <http://www.ukauthority.com/NewsArticle/tabid/64/Default.aspx?id=2732>

WCED (1987) *Our Common Future*, UN World Commission on Environment and Development (Oxford: Oxford University Press).

WEF (2010) 'Global Risks 2010: A Global Risk Network Report', World Economic Forum, January, at: <http://www.weforum.org/pdf/globalrisk/globalrisks2010.pdf>

Weybrecht, G. (2010) *The Sustainable MBA: The Manager's Guide to Green Business* (London: John Wiley).

Xu Yan (2011) 'The relationship between carbon accounting systems and organisational learning', unpublished MCM Dissertation, Lincoln University, New Zealand, at: <http://researcharchive.lincoln.ac.nz/dspace/bitstream/10182/4443/3/yan_mcm.pdf>

PART TWO
ISSUES

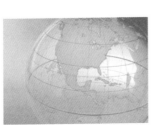

Chapter 9
Growth versus austerity: the macroeconomy in a globalizing world

John Meehan and Chris Mulhearn

Learning objectives

When you have completed this chapter you will be able to:

- Explain what is meant by the terms macroeconomics and macroeconomic policy.
- Describe the three main objectives of macroeconomic policy and explain their importance.
- Explain the importance of macroeconomic stability.
- Explain the two sides of the stabilization policy debate.
- Explain how the UK's macroeconomic policy framework has been informed by the continuing debate over stabilization policy.
- Explain how domestic macroeconomic policy is influenced and constrained by policy perspectives at the global level.

THEMES

The following themes of the book are especially relevant to this chapter

》 COMPLEXITY OF THE ENVIRONMENT

Economies are complex entities—they are the product of millions of decisions taken every day by businesses, governments, and individuals. Macroeconomics is an attempt to render this complexity more manageable.

》 DYNAMIC ENVIRONMENT

Macroeconomic thinking is itself an evolving phenomenon. Macroeconomic priorities change over time and therefore so too do the policies that governments pursue at the macroeconomic level.

▤ Introduction: the economy, macroeconomic policy, and globalization

》 SPATIAL LEVELS In Chapter 2 we saw that it is convenient to think of the business environment as operating at microeconomic and macroeconomic levels.

Microeconomics focuses on issues at the level of the individual—the individual consumer, the individual firm or public sector organization, the individual market and so on. Typical questions here ask:

- What motivates consumer decisions to buy or not buy goods and services in a market?
- What steps should a firm take to ensure profit maximization?
- What factors explain the presence of many or few firms or even one firm in a particular industry?

In this chapter our interest is in macroeconomics.

Macroeconomics is concerned with the behaviour and performance of the economy as a whole. Here, rather than looking at individual consumers, business organizations, and markets, we focus simultaneously on *all* consumers, firms, and organizations in *all* the markets that together compose a national economy. What are the principal features of interest in the macroeconomy? To an extent, these are simply the aggregations of the things we find relevant at the microeconomic level. For example, the micro issue of the output of goods and services of an individual firm or industry becomes, at the macro level, the output of all firms and industries. Similarly, an interest in the rate of change of the price of a particular product becomes an interpretation of the rate of change of all prices taken together—something conceptualized as the macroeconomic phenomenon of inflation.

Macroeconomic policy is concerned with the attempts of policy-makers to influence broad economic conditions in order to improve the performance of the whole economy. All governments practice macroeconomic policy-making; however, the extent and form in which they do so are controversial. There are continuing debates about whether governments actually need to do very much at the macroeconomic level and, indeed, about whether they are actually capable of engineering the positive economic outcomes they desire.

Before reviewing some of these debates we first need to establish what exactly it is that governments, business, workers, and other economic agents actually want from the economy. There is some degree of consensus here and we can in fact identify a number of macroeconomic policy objectives. Broadly, when these are *consistently* attained it is safe to say that we have a well-functioning business environment.

The objectives of macroeconomic policy

❯❯ COMPLEXITY It is possible to identify three main macroeconomic policy objectives. These are:

- a stable and satisfactory rate of economic growth
- a high and stable level of employment, and a consistently low level of unemployment
- a low and stable rate of inflation.

Before discussing each of these objectives in some detail, it is worth noting a common theme across all three—the notion of macroeconomic stability. This is particularly important in a business context. It should be intuitively evident that increased uncertainty in the economy makes business, organizational, and, indeed, personal decision-making more difficult processes. In the corporate world, decisions regarding output levels, recruitment, investment, diversification, acquisitions, and so on, carry more risk when decision-makers have less reliable information about general economic prospects. It would, for example, be more questionable for a firm to embark on a major investment project when the medium-term prospects for the economy are unclear than it would when economic growth, growth in consumer demand and inflation are settled at satisfactory rates for the foreseeable future. The implication is that uncertainty in the business environment tends to inhibit business activity—firms become hesitant about investment and expansion—and this in turn may provoke a vicious circle of deepening macroeconomic malaise. Overall then, while it is important to achieve specific macroeconomic policy objectives per se, it is just as important that this happens in a general climate of economic stability.

Macroeconomic objective 1: a stable and satisfactory rate of economic growth

Economic growth is the most basic measure of a country's economic performance. It measures the percentage rate of increase, year-on-year, in the value of the output of goods and services of countries like China, the UK, Vietnam, Zambia, or any other. We use value or price because this reflects the estimate of worth people freely put on the goods and services they buy. The total value of all goods and services produced by an economy each year is known as its gross domestic product, or GDP.

Table 9.1 shows that from 2005 to 2007 the UK's GDP growth rate hovered between 2.2% and 2.9%. This means that on average in each of these three years the UK produced about 2.6% more goods and services than it did in the previous year—more houses, cappuccinos, medical and educational services, music downloads, cinema attendances, and so on. Note that over the same period the UK's performance was actually bettered by each of China, Vietnam, and Zambia, where growth respectively averaged 11.7%, 8.4%, and 5.9% per year. During the financial crisis that began in 2008 and subsequent recession, UK growth slowed dramatically to 0.5% in 2008 before turning sharply negative in 2009 at an estimated −4.4%. In 2009 the UK was actually producing *fewer* goods and services than it had in the previous year—recording its worst growth performance since the Great Depression of the 1930s. In 2008/09 Chinese, Vietnamese, and Zambian growth each slowed but continued to remain well above UK levels. More recently, each of these three countries appears to have recovered from the low point marked by the financial crisis. The UK, on the other hand, after a revival in output in 2010 experienced sluggish growth in 2011 and an entirely flat economy in 2012 with growth at zero.

But these comparisons are only half the story. Table 9.2 shows that, in per capita terms, the UK is a long way ahead of the other three economies. Per capita GDP is simply total GDP

Table 9.1 Real percentage GDP growth for selected countries, 2005–12

Country	2005	2006	2007	2008	2009	2010	2011	2012 (est.)
China	10.4	11.6	13.0	9.0	6.5	10.4	9.2	7.8
UK	2.2	2.9	2.6	0.5	−4.4	1.8	0.8	0.0
Vietnam	8.4	8.2	8.5	6.2	4.6	6.8	5.9	5.1
Zambia	5.3	6.2	6.3	5.8	4.5	7.6	6.6	6.5

Source: International Monetary Fund; UK Treasury.

Mini-Case 9.1 Macroeconomic stability and its relevance to students at university

We will see shortly that until the financial crisis in 2008 the British economy had grown at a relatively stable and satisfactory rate, especially when compared to its performance during the 1970s and 1980s. This was a positive thing for people—such as students and school leavers—who were about to enter the labour market. When the economy slumped the job prospects of new entrants to the labour market were dimmed as employers—depressed by a climate of uncertainty—shelved recruitment plans. Student readers of this book will be aware that the decision to stay in education carries some notable opportunity costs. Students must contribute significantly to their education in terms of tuition fees, living costs, and earnings forgone while at university.

Such costs are worth incurring when set against potentially higher earnings in the future. But in the presence of economic instability, self-investment on this scale may appear a riskier proposition than when the economy is growing steadily and producing new jobs. So, economic stability is good for students: it makes the future a little more certain and helps them make more informed and better choices. However, even in a recession, it still makes sense to invest in one's own skills.

Question

Why, despite the economic downturn, was there a surge in applications to UK universities in 2009?

divided by the population among which it is 'shared'. In fact, expressed in dollars (to make comparisons easy), GDP or national income per person in the UK crept up from $32,305 in 2005 to $36,253 by 2008, before falling back slightly to $34,874 in the recession of 2009 and recovering thereafter to $36,728 in 2012. In China in 2012, per capita GDP was $9,146; in Vietnam $3,545; and in Zambia $1,701. This means that although the UK has been growing more slowly than the other economies, this 'modest' growth performance still translates each year into a lot more goods and services produced per person.

These data provide an important clue as to why we are interested in economic growth. Simply, the maintenance of a satisfactory growth rate over a sustained period means that a country is generating the potential to significantly raise its standard of living. And this—ultimately—is what a society wants: to generate high material living standards for its inhabitants. The UK enjoys a comparatively high standard of living because it is one of the world's biggest producers of goods and services, and it has a relatively modest population size; it produces, and earns, a lot per head. (The UK's population is 61 million, compared to China's 1.3 billion; Vietnam's 87 million; and Zambia's 12 million).

Can economies that are poorer than the UK catch up? At its recent growth rate it would take Vietnam more than 50 years to surpass the UK's *present* level of overall output, and because of

Table 9.2 GDP per capita expressed in dollars, selected countries, 2005-12

Country	2005	2006	2007	2008	2009	2010	2011	2012
China	4,102	4,747	5,548	6,185	6,781	7,553	8,387	9,146
UK	32,305	34,019	36,047	36,253	34,874	35,731	36,522	36,728
Vietnam	2,143	2,364	2,607	2,800	2,939	3,143	3,359	3,545
Zambia	1,130	1,211	1,291	1,361	1,425	1,517	1,611	1,701

(Some data are estimated.)

Source: International Monetary Fund.

its larger population even then its per capita income would not match that presently achieved by the UK. And the UK will itself continue to grow in the future meaning that the prospects for Vietnam to close on European-style prosperity levels must reside in the very distant future. Comparisons with China are equally interesting.

China is now the world's second largest economy behind the United States. Its GDP in absolute terms is about four times larger than the UK's: that is, it produces much more in goods and services than the UK. On the other hand its population is about *twenty* times bigger, which accounts for the UK's much higher per capita GDP—the UK produces almost one quarter as much but with only one twentieth of the people. Again, with consistent double digit growth rates, China may eventually close the GDP per capita 'gap' between itself and countries such as the UK but it will take a long time to do so. Why exactly is the UK so far ahead? One crucial factor among many others is that the UK's modern growth period began around 1750—so the UK has been engaged in the industrialized growth process for much longer than any of the comparator economies discussed here. We will return to the factors that influence long-term growth shortly.

Although GDP is relatively straightforward to understand as the sum total of the value of goods and services an economy produces, there are two additional points to make about it at this stage. First, to avoid the problem of double counting, we refer here only to **final or finished goods and services**. Think about the physical components of the book you are reading: essentially paper, glue, and ink. If we included the price of the book as a GDP item and then also include the price paid by the publisher for each of the paper, glue, and ink, we would be counting all these components twice—once on their own as raw materials and then again in the final good—the book itself. To avoid artificially inflating the GDP total in this way, we count only *final* goods and services.

Second, consider what would happen to GDP if most prices in the economy were rising rapidly. The market price of books would also be rising and so would their 'contribution' to GDP—we would end up with a bigger total; note this would be the case even if the output quantity of books in the economy remained the same. For this reason we are interested in **real GDP**. You will notice that in Table 9.1 the GDP figures are given in real terms. This means that the figures have been adjusted to strip out the effects of continually rising prices or inflation. Increases in real GDP tell us that output is definitely rising—we have *more* goods and services. Increases in GDP solely generated by higher prices for a given quantity of goods and services— what is known as **money GDP**—do not indicate that there has been any improvement in economic performance as we don't have more output.

Stop and Think
....

When you work are you interested in whether any increase in your earnings is a real or money increase? You should be able to see that money increases may not leave you better off and could even leave you worse off. Real increases always leave you better off. If prices on average are rising by 3% and your money wages also rise but only by 2%, your real wages—meaning what you can afford to buy—have fallen by 1%. You earn more money but you can't buy as much as you did before. On the other hand, a real increase, above 3%, leaves you unambiguously better off. The lesson here is that it's not the amount of money we have that counts but the quantity of goods and services into which money can be turned.

Long-term growth

Before we discuss in more detail economic growth as an objective of macroeconomic policy, let us briefly review the growth performance of the UK economy. Figure 9.1 depicts the long-term growth in real GDP since 1948. One thing is immediately clear—over this long period the UK has indeed tended to produce more and more output, to the extent that we are now a trillion (a thousand billion) pound income economy, a milestone of prosperity reached in the mid-1990s. Is the broad upward trajectory of GDP a testament to the competence of macroeconomic policy as practised by governments over the past 60-odd years? Unfortunately, the answer to this question is no. In the longer term, capitalist economies tend to grow because of certain innate properties that have relatively little to do with the characteristically shorter-term time horizons of many governments. Long-term growth in these economies is predicated on rising productivity as discussed in Chapter 3. This chapter highlighted the combination of factors that are necessary if productivity growth is to be maintained.

Productivity refers to the quantity of goods and services that people produce in a given time period. Referring back to our country comparisons, it is clear that the UK is much more productive than China, Vietnam, or Zambia: it has a per capita GDP much higher than any of these countries. So what explains the UK's relatively high productivity?

There are five main factors determining a country's capacity to efficiently produce:

- its investment in physical capital
- its investment in human capital
- its application of new technologies
- its endowments in natural resources
- its level of institutional sophistication and institutional reliability.

Physical capital is the tools and equipment used in factories, offices, shops, hospitals, schools, transport systems, and so on. Physical capital makes the people who use it more productive.

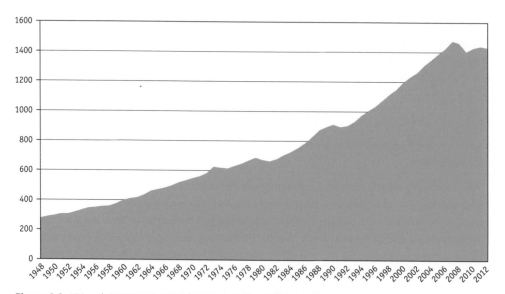

Figure 9.1 UK real GDP 1948–2012 (2012 est.), £bn, 2005 prices
Source: ONS, 2012.

It follows that the more we invest in advanced machinery or computing systems or intelligently designed buildings, the more productive our economy becomes.

Human capital is the skill and knowledge accumulated by people that can be deployed in an economic setting. As you progress through the course you are presently studying you are investing in your own human capital. This is personally beneficial because, in the future, it increases your earning potential. Human capital increases the range of tasks of which we are all capable. So, employers pay highly qualified people more because they are likely to be more productive than the less qualified.

The application of new technologies entails taking advances in human knowledge and using them in an economic setting. A good modern example is the diffusion of information and communication technologies—most obviously mobile phones and the Internet—throughout very many aspects of economic life. These devices have revolutionized the quantity and quality of opportunities for human interaction and information gathering, creating wholly new kinds of activity and forms of business on a worldwide scale. Note that new technology is not precisely the same thing as physical or human capital. Presently, genetic engineering holds out the possibility that it may transform the productive potential of activities such as agriculture, animal farming, and medicine. Only if the potential of this new technology is fulfilled will we then see investment spilling out into related forms of physical and human capital.

Fourthly, some countries enjoy prosperity and satisfactory rates of economic growth because they are able to produce particular goods or services in large quantities given their natural resource endowments. The obvious example here is oil, which has transformed the economic trajectories of many of the economies that possess it. In a similar manner, the possession of a good climate and attractive landscape enables countries to efficiently produce tourist services.

Finally, the institutional frameworks of economies are important: the stability of their political systems and legal and financial frameworks, for example. These provide the necessary setting within which economies develop and grow. The importance of reliable institutions was amply demonstrated during the financial crisis. There is little doubt that the world's banking system was in serious trouble with customers losing confidence in the banks and the banks losing confidence in one other. Had matters deteriorated further the threat to the integrity of whole economies would have quickly become evident. We rather take our financial systems for granted but think what might happen if ATMs froze and banks simply closed their doors because they lacked money to meet their obligations: how could what we think of as normal life carry on?

So, the UK is a high-productivity economy in comparison to China, Vietnam, and Zambia because it scores highly on most, in fact probably all, of the above characteristics and has done so for a very long time. The UK is fortunate enough to be able to invest heavily and consistently in physical and human capital, it is a technologically sophisticated society, it also possesses a valuable natural resource in North Sea oil, and, finally, despite recent travails, its institutional framework is sophisticated and usually reliable. It is this combination that explains the long-term pattern of growth depicted in Figure 9.1.

Short-term growth

⟫ DYNAMIC Figure 9.2 depicts recent short-term UK GDP performance. The bars indicate growth each quarter. The UK's brush with a so-called double-dip recession is clearly evident. The technical definition of recession is two successive quarters of negative growth, so the UK was in recession from Q2 2008–Q2 2009. But at the end of 2011 and the first half of 2012 two quarters of negative growth were separated by a quarter of zero growth. A poor performance certainly but not quite a recession. The recent plight of the UK economy may be contrasted

Stop and Think From long-term to short-term growth

Look again carefully for a moment at Figure 9.1. Notice that the GDP curve is not very smooth in places. When is it bumpiest? Answer: roughly between 1974 and 1993, and then again, dramatically, since 2008. During the 1974–93 period, the curve both rises above its long-term trend and falls below it exhibiting variations in short-term growth rates around the long-term trend. Now, while governments cannot really claim much credit for long-term growth, they can significantly influence the pattern of growth in the short term. This is what many governments were trying desperately to do as a result of the anticipated impact of the financial crisis. Whether or not they should attempt to do this is a highly controversial matter in macroeconomics and one we explore in some detail below.

with the long period up to 2007 when the economy enjoyed a reasonably steady rate of growth. Indeed, for the period 1993–2007 UK growth averaged almost 3% per annum—the most sustained run since records began (glance back to Figure 9.1 to see this performance in a longer-term setting).

So, if an objective of macroeconomic policy is that economic growth should be stable and satisfactory, then this objective was being attained up until the financial crisis. But while growth at around 3% for more than a decade is certainly stable why exactly is it satisfactory? If China, Vietnam, and Zambia can enjoy the kind of rates indicated in Table 9.1, why cannot the UK do the same? After all, if growth is the key to living standards, higher growth would mean still higher living standards for UK citizens. The point here is that the trend line in Figure 9.1 approximates **potential GDP**, that is, the real GDP associated with the full employment of all the economy's resources. Look carefully again at Figure 9.1. Notice the steepness of the curve in the late 1980s. Here the UK expanded beyond this long-run potential with a growth rate

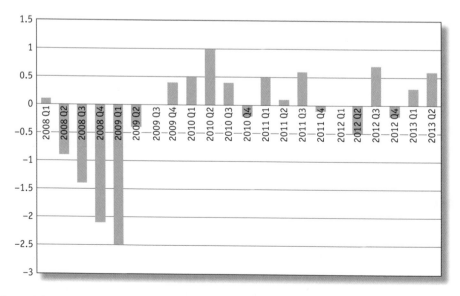

Figure 9.2 UK Real GDP 2008–13, by quarter, per cent
Source: Data from ONS.

between 1985 and 1988 of 4.3%; in other words it used its resources very intensively for a short time but found this impossible to sustain.

One last issue here—if the UK's potential GDP growth rate is somewhere around 3%, how do poorer countries often manage to sustain much higher and, as in China's case, sometimes double-digit rates? The answer is that their relatively low levels of development mean they have both under-utilized resources and much greater scope for catch-up in productivity improvements.

Macroeconomic objective 2: a high and stable level of employment, and a consistently low level of unemployment

There are strong connections between economic growth, employment, and unemployment. When the economy grows consistently near potential GDP its resources—including labour—are close to being fully utilized; there is, in other words, near-full employment. Conversely, in periods of slow growth or outright recession resources are under-utilized and higher levels of unemployment emerge as a policy problem.

Before we consider the actual path of employment and unemployment in the UK, let us reflect on the structure of the UK's labour force. The UK government divides the working-age population into two main categories:

- the economically active = the employed + those unemployed people actively seeking work, and
- the economically inactive—those of working age, not seeking work and therefore excluded from the unemployment figures.

Members of this last group would include, for example, people engaged in full-time care of their own children, early retirees, and lottery winners who've walked away from their jobs.

We are now in a position to define the unemployment and employment rates. The unemployment rate is the proportion of the economically active population (i.e. those in employment or actively seeking work) that do not have jobs. The unemployment rate is calculated as follows:

unemployment rate = (number of unemployed/number economically active) × 100.

The employment rate is the proportion of the working-age population that is in employment. It is calculated as follows:

employment rate = (number of people employed/working-age population) × 100.

Figures 9.3 and 9.4, when read in conjunction with Figure 9.2, illustrate the dynamic relationship between economic growth and the labour market. As growth starts its precipitous fall early in 2008 (see the quarterly data in Figure 9.2) unemployment rapidly increases from a little over 5% to close to 8% in 2012 (see Figure 9.3). Over roughly the same period the employment rate departs from its peak of 73% and falls to a little over 71% (see Figure 9.4).

But why do we desire high rates of employment? We know that economic growth is desirable as it is an effective means of securing rising living standards. The same reasoning applies in the case of employment. The greater the proportion of the economically active population that is able to secure employment, the greater the number of goods and services that can be produced and the better off the UK plc becomes.

The issue of unemployment is slightly more complex as here there are social as well as economic difficulties. We will deal with the economic difficulties first. Any introductory economics textbook tells us that economics explores the choices that all societies have to make in

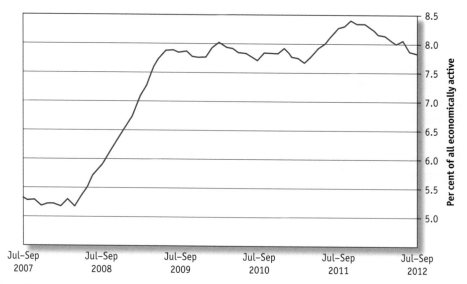

Figure 9.3 UK unemployment rate (aged 16+) 2007–12, seasonally adjusted
Source: ONS, 2012.

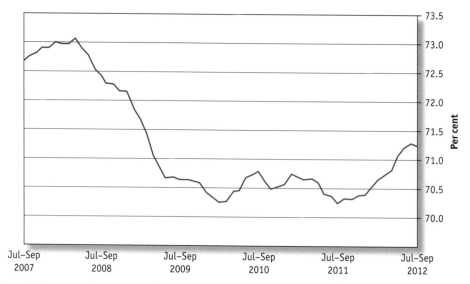

Figure 9.4 UK employment rate (aged 16–64) 2007–12, seasonally adjusted
Source: ONS, 2012.

matching the scarce resources they possess to the limitless wants of their populations. No matter how materially wealthy it becomes, no society can escape difficult decisions about which wants to meet and which to leave unfulfilled. What is left understood here is that societies try to use all the resources they have; waste is not really on anyone's agenda. Yet this is actually what unemployment amounts to—a waste of what is arguably society's most precious resource: its economically active people. And it gets worse. It costs nothing to leave coal or oil reserves in the ground; nor do these reserves decay or disappear if we neglect them. The same cannot be said for labour. In a modern, civilized society unemployed people are supported through the tax and benefits system. Those in work pay tax and a proportion of this money is transferred to the unemployed—thus it actually costs society as a whole to waste resources in this way. Also lost are the direct taxes (i.e. income tax and national insurance contributions) the unemployed themselves would have contributed were they in jobs, as well as lost indirect taxes (i.e. VAT) associated with a fall in expenditure by the unemployed. Moreover, the longer people are unemployed the more likely it is that they will find their skills outdated and their human capital eroded, even to the point at which they may become so disillusioned as to stop seeking work entirely, thus joining the economically inactive.

▶ **STAKEHOLDERS** ▶ **VALUES** The social difficulties that unemployment brings are of two kinds. First, those experienced by the unemployed themselves and their families. Despite the social security systems in the advanced economies, unemployment is associated with low incomes and poverty. Lack of money leads to other problems: for example, unemployed people and their families tend to suffer poor health and lower than average levels of educational attainment. More generally, the effect of unemployment—especially if it is prolonged—is to economically disenfranchise sections of the population. Such social exclusion may carry a range of wider consequences: political and ethnic tensions and rising crime have all been associated with high levels of unemployment.

▶ **DYNAMIC** ▶ **COMPLEXITY** Finally, let us think about policy objectives in the area of employment and unemployment. It would be simple to assume that the government's preference would be for everyone who is economically active to be in work—in other words, the unemployment rate would be zero. This is a nice idea, but impossible in a practical sense. Why? Consider Figure 9.5. This illustrates the dynamism and complexity of the macroeconomic

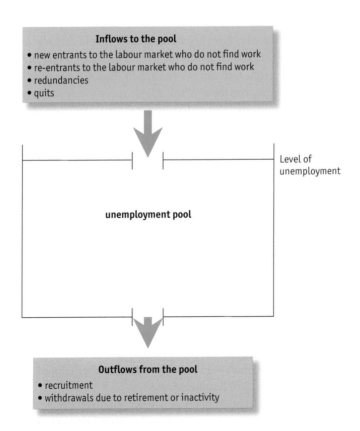

Figure 9.5 The unemployment pool

labour market, with unemployment conceptualized as a pool of unemployed labour. The rate of unemployment will reflect the depth of the pool and the force of the flows into and out of it.

Taking inflows first, the pool deepens as new entrants join the labour market from school or college but do not immediately find work. Similarly, re-entrants to the labour market who have been economically inactive but now want to work again will deepen the pool if they do not go straight into a job. People who leave employment involuntarily through redundancy and those who choose to leave their jobs will also cause the pool to deepen. In both cases we assume that there is a determination to stay in the labour market and find new work.

Now outflows. Unemployed people who find work will cause the pool to become shallower, as will those who decide to end a period of unemployment by ceasing to look for work (they become economically inactive), or permanently retire.

Think for a moment about what will happen to the pool in a period of decelerating economic growth or recession. The forces generating inflows gather momentum. Fewer new entrants and re-entrants to the labour market will immediately find work; more firms are likely to be making workers redundant, and people who voluntarily quit jobs are less likely to quickly find new ones. On the other hand, recession minimizes recruitment and stems outflows—overall then, the pool deepens and the unemployment rate climbs.

> ### Stop and Think
>
> What happens to the unemployment pool's inflows and outflows and the unemployment rate when growth is stable and satisfactory?

Your answer to this question may have been that inflows should dwindle and that outflows should increase, perhaps to the point at which the pool is drained completely and unemployment is indeed zero. But in truth, zero can never happen. Figure 9.5 suggests that the labour market is a fairly complex entity but there is still a little more to say about it. We can in fact identify two categories of unemployment that in a modern and innovative economy can never be entirely eliminated. These are frictional (or search) and structural (or mismatch) unemployment.

Frictional or search unemployment arises when people find themselves, for any number of reasons, temporarily between jobs without leaving the labour market. There are now around 29 million people in work in the UK. It is surely unreasonable to expect that every single one of these people will either continue in their present job or move seamlessly into another without experiencing a single period of unemployment. At the same time, the fortunes of individual business organizations will vary. Some will lay off staff, others will be recruiting new employees; some organizations will close entirely, while new ones will be created. In this environment of change and displacement some frictional unemployment is naturally to be expected.

Structural or mismatch unemployment is also a consequence of economic evolution, and results from a mismatch between the skills or location of existing job vacancies and the present skills or location of the unemployed. It reflects the fact that over time whole industries decay and disappear, casting the people who have skills and experience attuned to those industries economically adrift. These people are said to be structurally unemployed in as much as the entire industry in which they worked has disappeared.

Not too long ago Britain had large numbers of people employed in coal mining. Now there are relatively few miners as we rely more on imported coal and alternative sources of energy. The scrapping of the coal industry was a serious problem for people whose human capital was effectively tied to that industry. Redundant miners cannot overnight become teachers or engineers. Until unemployed people can be retrained there will be a mismatch between their skills and the skills required to fill job vacancies.

But as some industries die, new ones are born. A decade ago, mobile phones were relatively rare, now they saturate our societies, creating many new job opportunities, perhaps for retrained ex-miners. Structural unemployment is simply a reflection of this kind of industrial change. It is not pleasant, particularly when it is geographically concentrated in particular places as mining was, but in a market economy it is to some extent inevitable.

Given these complications, what is the employment/unemployment macroeconomic policy objective? Reflecting the complexity and dynamism of the labour market, there is often no particular target for the unemployment rate. Rather, for many governments, there is an ambition to ensure that those economically active people looking for work are able to find it.

Macroeconomic objective 3: a low and stable rate of inflation

Inflation is a process of continually rising prices. The inflation rate is the average rate of change of the prices of goods and services in the economy over a given period. For example, in March 2013 the inflation rate in the UK was 2.8%. This means that the prices in the UK were then, on average, rising by 2.8% per year. Inflation in the UK is measured by the consumer prices index (CPI) which reveals changes in the cost of a representative basket of goods and services—a range of items that most people buy.

A low and stable rate of inflation is desirable for a number of reasons. For the most part these have to do with the fact that we live in economies that rely heavily on markets to allocate resources. In Chapter 2 we saw how markets are coordinated by price signals. The movements of prices provide incentives to producers and consumers to behave in particular ways. For example, higher prices may signal the possibility of greater profit to producers and encourage them to expand output. On the other hand, consumers may respond to higher prices by contracting demand. But what defines a good signal? One important property is stability. Think what would happen to traffic flows if traffic signals were to have their timings randomly set. You pull up at a stop light and you're unsure if you're going to be stuck there for one minute, three minutes, or even ten. The same is true for all other drivers. Our guess is that this would soon result in gridlock and accidents as people jumped traffic lights and made bad driving decisions. Traffic signals do a good job when they're predictable and people feel they can rely on them. In markets, price signals are also better if they're reliable and people feel they can use them to make informed choices—this happens when inflation is low and stable.

》 INTERACTION We can in fact identify a number of specific costs of inflation. The first of these—in keeping with our example above—has to do with uncertainty. Consumers and producers make decisions in markets by taking account of **relative prices**, that is the price of one good or service compared to another. When inflation is low and stable, relative prices are easy to read and consumers can make informed choices about whether to buy this or that good, taking price into account. Similarly, producers have good indicators of which markets offer better prospects for investment, and which are best left alone. In the presence of high and, therefore, increasingly variable inflation, such clarity is lost. The general process of inflation across all goods and services masks relative price movements between particular goods and services leading to poorer decision-making. Thus, in a low-inflation environment, if the price of outdoor-wear clothing starts to rise, this is a signal for firms like Timberland to invest more. But in a high-inflation environment poor old Timberland just can't tell if this is a definite signal from the rugged outdoor types populating this market that they want more kit, or just

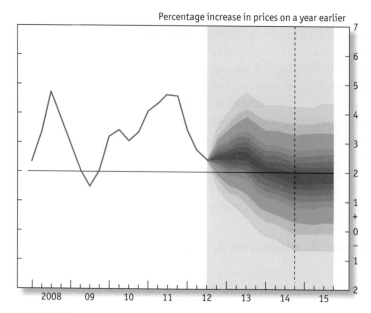

Figure 9.6 UK CPI Inflation

Source: Bank of England *Inflation Report* November 2012.

part of the background noise of general inflation. Replicate Timberland's uncertainty across the whole economy and an inflation-induced recipe for some very poorly informed decision-making begins to emerge.

⟩⟩ **VALUES** Inflation can also arbitrarily redistribute income and wealth between different groups in society, abstracting from what might be deserved or socially desired. For example, in a low-inflation environment, borrowers find the real values of their debts are largely maintained and they must pay them off as expected. But in the presence of high inflation the real values of debts are quickly eroded as prices and money wages surge upwards—an unlooked for but hardly merited bonus for borrowers. Savers find themselves in the opposite position. A pensioner may have saved over a working life to provide for his or her retirement but a sudden surge in inflation could rapidly reduce the real value of what has been saved, with no further opportunity to start again. These arbitrary changes are unhelpful in a market economy where it is expected that reward should bear at least some relation to effort or sacrifice.

The British government has established an annual target of 2% for UK inflation. Figure 9.6 depicts recent UK inflation performance, and the evidence is that the actual inflation performance is a little above target. The shaded area of the figure contains an inflation projection in which the intensity of the shading reflects variation in the probability of outcome.

▨ **The case for stabilizing the economy**

⟩⟩ **VALUES** One of the big unresolved questions in macroeconomics is whether or not policy-makers should try to stabilize the levels of output and employment in the economy. There really is no agreement here and we introduced the broad competing perspectives regarding this question in Chapter 2. Some economists—following the tradition established in the 1930s by the famous British economist John Maynard Keynes—suppose that capitalist economies often behave erratically. If they are caught up in some unforeseen circumstances—an economic shock—they can move into devastating recessions from which it may take some time to recover. The implication these economists draw is that, because economies tend not to recover spontaneously or quickly, it is up to governments to help them get back into shape using particular macroeconomic tools in fairly expansive ways. This could mean decisive stabilization policy measures to counteract the sharp deceleration in growth in 2008–09.

However, a second set of economists, broadly in the neoclassical school and including the late American economist Milton Friedman, is deeply suspicious of this argument. People like Friedman argue that capitalist economies, while they can slide into recession, have well-developed and relatively fast-acting powers of recovery. This means that there is no need for governments to excessively meddle in the economy—it can take care of itself. Moreover, in this view, while government intervention does little or nothing for output and employment in the long run, it does have the very dangerous side effect of increasing the money supply and hence potentially fuelling inflation. For this reason this group of economists is referred to as 'monetarists'. The implication of their argument is that, if the economy is mostly but not exclusively left to itself, one should expect a GDP growth path similar to that in Figure 9.1, but without any substantial or lengthy deviations away from potential GDP.

To fully understand the basis of the differences between these two groups it is necessary to consider their contrasting views about what can be reasonably done with the two major tools of macroeconomic policy: **fiscal policy** and **monetary policy**. We also need to review a little economic history to see how these tools have been used—with mixed results—in the more distant and recent past. We will begin with brief definitions of fiscal and monetary policy.

Fiscal policy involves government expenditure and taxation. As taxation is government income, fiscal policy is the balance between government income and expenditure. For example, expansionary fiscal policy involves governments spending more than they raise in taxation.

Monetary policy is implemented chiefly through the setting of interest rates, which, in the UK, are controlled by the Monetary Policy Committee of the Bank of England. More recently it has also encompassed what for some economists is the highly controversial process of *quantitative easing*—a rather benign phrase for the (electronic) printing of money by the authorities.

⏩ **SPATIAL LEVELS** The story of modern macroeconomics really begins with the work of Keynes and, in particular, with his 1936 book, *The General Theory of Employment, Interest, and Money*. In this volume, and elsewhere, Keynes provided the first comprehensive explanation of how recessions can occur, how they can persist, and what governments can do to help economies recover from them. Keynes's work was developed first in the 1920s in response to extremely sluggish British growth throughout this decade; however, it gained a new relevance from 1929 when not just one economy but the whole world slid into a depression of unprecedented proportions. This became known as the Great Depression.

Keynes's explanation of the Great Depression and, indeed, of recessions generally was relatively simple. He argued that the level of activity in an economy was determined by the prevailing level of **aggregate demand**, that is, the total level of demand for all goods and services. In Keynes's view it was relatively easy for aggregate demand to fall, and once it did there was nothing in the economy which would prompt its early recovery: an economy in recession would very likely stay in recession. Take an economy that is enjoying steady growth with low unemployment. If, for some reason, businesses become generally pessimistic about the future, they will tend to reduce investment—cutting their own spending until a time when economic prospects have improved. But, because *many* businesses act in this way, the results for the economy and everyone in it are catastrophic. As investment falls, firms are doing two things. First, they are reducing the business that they do with each other—cancelling or not renewing orders for materials and equipment. Second, they are shelving recruitment plans and some will be laying off employees. You will agree that things do not look good, but potentially this is just the start. The process becomes a reciprocally confirming one. Business confidence was low and businesses reacted as they thought appropriate. But now, as orders dry up and unemployment begins to rise, it's clear they were right—things *are* bad. Demand in the economy now falls even further—firms buy less and less from each other and rising unemployment means that consumer demand is weakening considerably. At some point, this downward spiral will slow but it may be very a long time before any recovery happens. In the United States during the Great Depression, for example, real GDP fell by 28% and unemployment increased to 25%. For a time there, it looked like capitalism itself was collapsing.

❯❯ COMPLEXITY ❯ STAKEHOLDERS In Keynes's view, the correct way to understand what was going on in such circumstances was to appreciate the importance of aggregate demand. It is the fall in demand which triggers and feeds economic decline. Eventually, the process will come to a halt but, critically, there is no natural recovery mechanism. If aggregate demand eventually falls by, say, a quarter, firms will have no incentive to produce more output than can be bought by this lower level of demand, and they will require many fewer workers than before as they are now producing much less. We illustrate the process in Figure 9.7. In panel a) of the figure, the economy is operating at potential GDP (1) and the output of goods and services (2) is bought by consumers and firms (3), meaning that the current level of aggregate demand (4) is sufficient to maintain the economy at potential GDP. However, in panel b) of Figure 9.7, an adverse shock hits the economy and consumers and firms begin to buy less output (1). This means that aggregate demand is falling (2). Accordingly, firms begin to revise their output plans (3), and lay off workers (4). Output in the economy begins to fall (5). Finally, in panel c) it is evident that the process has spiralled down to a sustainable level. Here, firms have fully revised their output decisions (1), and output has stabilized at a lower level (2). We know that this position is stable and sustainable because consumers and firms buy all this output (3), which means that aggregate demand is once again sufficient to maintain GDP (4), but now at a level below its potential. The economy is mired in recession: GDP has fallen and unemployment has risen and, most important, there is nothing on the horizon that will change things anytime soon.

From a Keynesian perspective then, economies are fragile things, prone to crises of confidence. Aggregate demand is the key to improving matters, but how can demand be revived given, in Keynes's phrase, 'the halting, wavering mood' of business? His solution was relatively simple. If there was no natural force in the economy capable of generating a recovery in aggregate demand and business confidence, one would have to be created. Keynes proposed that governments should themselves step in and raise demand using expansionary fiscal and monetary policy. Over time this would rejuvenate business confidence and reverse the depressive processes outlined in Figure 9.7, bringing the economy back close to potential GDP and full employment.

As noted, one form of expansionary fiscal policy involves the government spending more than it receives in taxes; financed by borrowing. The new spending might be on, for example, new schools, roads or hospitals. In many ways its actual form is less important than the fact that it is happening. Once the process has started business takes heart and begins to plan once again for expansion. Of course, some firms benefit quickly and directly—those building the schools, roads, and hospitals. But others will also respond as employment and consumer demand begins to revive. In effect, the government needs only to initiate economic revival—it is not required to make good the entire aggregate-demand 'gap' on its own. Moreover, as either a supplement or alternative to spending more itself, the government can decide to cut taxes

a) The economy at potential GDP—aggregate demand is sufficient to buy capacity output

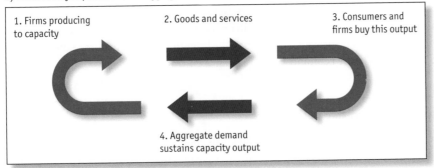

1. Firms producing to capacity

2. Goods and services

3. Consumers and firms buy this output

4. Aggregate demand sustains capacity output

b) Firms have lost confidence—orders are reduced and aggregate demand is falling

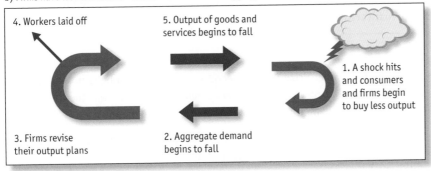

4. Workers laid off

5. Output of goods and services begins to fall

1. A shock hits and consumers and firms begin to buy less output

3. Firms revise their output plans

2. Aggregate demand begins to fall

c) The economy in recession—lower aggregate demand sustains lower output, and there is no mechanism that will prompt an improvement in conditions

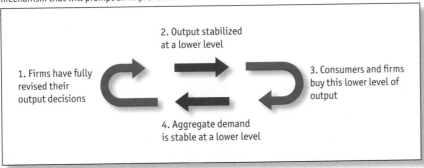

2. Output stabilized at a lower level

1. Firms have fully revised their output decisions

3. Consumers and firms buy this lower level of output

4. Aggregate demand is stable at a lower level

Figure 9.7 A demand-driven economic collapse

leaving businesses and individual taxpayers with more disposable income. This is also a means of prompting an increase in aggregate demand.

Expansionary monetary policy might also be used as a tool of recovery. Were the government to engineer a reduction in interest rates, firms and consumers may respond to the availability of cheaper finance by investing and spending more freely. However, Keynes was less sure that this approach would work as quickly and directly when compared to fiscal expansion. Lower interest rates would in all likelihood, prompt business and individuals to spend more, but if the government increased its spending there was no possible doubt that aggregate demand would rise.

As noted, in response to the 2008–9 recession, the UK authorities engaged in so-called quantitative easing, a euphemism for the printing of money. This unprecedented step was taken because UK interest rates had already been pushed down to the historically low level of 0.5% and as interest rates cannot be less than zero there was little room to reduce them further. The authorities injected £375 billion into the British economy principally by buying government and other bonds held by private sector firms; the intention was to encourage these institutions to add to demand in the economy by increasing their own spending.

Stop and Think Spending and interest rates

Why might business organizations and individuals choose to increase spending as interest rates come down? The answer is that interest rates indicate the cost of borrowing. With lower interest rates all forms of borrowing become cheaper and therefore economic agents are encouraged to both borrow and spend more. Why might the stimulant effect of lower interest rates be reduced as they approach zero?

According to the late Nobel Prize-winning economist Franco Modigliani, what Keynes had outlined in the *General Theory of Employment, Interest and Money* was the following 'need/can/should' case for stabilizing the levels of output and employment:

- Governments *need* to stabilize the economy—capitalist economies have a tendency to slip easily into recession; they are inherently unstable.
- Governments *can* stabilize the economy—they have the requisite fiscal and monetary tools.
- Governments *should* therefore stabilize the economy—there is no case for them not to do so.

Following the end of the Second World War in 1945, Keynesianism came to dominate macroeconomic policy-making in the capitalist economies and stabilization policy was widely practised, to apparently good effect. The period from 1945 until the early 1970s became known as the post-war boom during which, in practically all of the western industrial economies, GDP expanded at unprecedented and sustained rates and, as a corollary, employment rates increased and unemployment remained low and stable. Table 9.3 shows average annual growth rates for the so-called G7—the world's leading industrial nations—since 1870. The sub-period from 1950–73 clearly stands in a class by itself in terms of the growth rates collectively achieved by these economies, with particularly strong performances in continental Europe and Japan.

Table 9.3 GDP growth rates for the G7, 1870–2010, per cent

Country	1870–1913	1913–1950	1950–1973	1973–1998	1998–2010
France	1.63	1.15	5.05	2.10	1.73
Germany	2.83	0.30	5.68	1.76	0.92
Italy	1.94	1.49	5.64	2.28	0.67
UK	1.90	1.19	2.93	2.00	2.01
USA	3.94	2.84	3.93	2.99	2.26
Canada	4.02	2.94	4.98	2.80	2.54
Japan	2.44	2.21	9.29	2.97	0.55

Sources: Snowdon and Vane 2005, adapted from Maddison 2001; IMF.

Questioning the need to stabilize output and employment

❯❯ DYNAMIC Unfortunately, the post-war boom petered out in the early 1970s and the effectiveness of stabilization policy began to be disputed. This was not just because, as Table 9.3 indicates, growth was much slower in the period 1973–98 for all of the G7, but also because of the appearance of a new macroeconomic problem—inflation. This had never really been much of a cause for concern during the post-war boom when policy-makers' minds were quite firmly focused on the need to avoid anything like another Great Depression. However, from the beginning of the 1970s inflation became a worldwide phenomenon. It caused serious difficulties both for economies generally and for Keynesian economics in particular. Figure 9.8 illustrates the acceleration of inflation in the G5 economies. Particularly noteworthy are rates close to 25% in Japan and the UK in the mid-1970s.

The surge in inflation was, in the view of monetarist economists, actually caused by the over-ambitious employment targets of Keynesian stabilization measures. Furthermore, the monetarists also argued that—despite the evidence provided by the post-war boom— stabilization policy was actually ineffective as a means to maintain economies at potential GDP and full employment. The work of Milton Friedman was extremely influential here and we now need to reflect on the Friedman-led monetarist counter-revolution in macroeconomics.

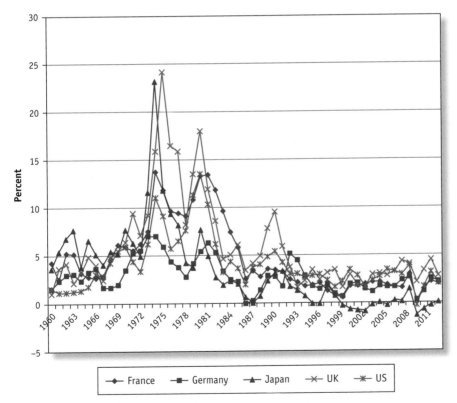

Figure 9.8 G5 inflation 1960-2012 (2012 est.)

Source: Data from IMF, 2012.

Mini-Case 9.2 Japan: from boom to bust

After the Second World War, against all expectations, the Japanese economy enjoyed an 'economic miracle' so much so that by the 1980s it had become the second largest economy in the world and many businesses sought to copy Japanese techniques of production.

So when in the early 1990s the Japanese economy plunged into a recession that was to linger for more than 10 years there was universal surprise. The years 2004 and 2005 began to see a gradual, if tentative recovery, unfortunately ended by the world recession of 2008–9.

The reason for the so-called 'lost decade' of the 1990s was the end of a speculative 'bubble' that had seen land prices surging and stock market prices booming. When this bubble burst, the banks, which had incautiously issued large numbers of loans, were owed vast sums that could not be repaid. The resultant economic shock meant that unemployment began to rise and prices fall. This further cut aggregate demand as consumers stopped spending in the anticipation that prices would *continue* to fall.

Faced with these mounting problems the government embarked on a Keynesian expansion programme by hugely increasing government spending (at one point government debt rose to 130% of GDP), and by reducing interest rates to nearly zero per cent.

Questions

1. What was the Japanese government trying to achieve by this combination of expansionary fiscal and monetary policy?

2. Given the extent of this stabilization programme would you have expected Japan to have recovered from the recession sooner than it did?

In the 1950s and 1960s Keynes's ideas had been highly influential in policy terms because they seemed to provide a policy solution to the devastating problem of depression. Similarly, in the 1970s, Friedman's arguments gained currency because they too addressed a burning economic issue, albeit a different one. Friedman revived and restated an old quantity theory of money tradition in economics. Broadly, this held that inflation is 'always and everywhere a monetary phenomenon in the sense that it can be produced only by a more rapid increase in the quantity of money than in output'. In other words, inflation is caused by too much money chasing too few goods. Two things followed from the relationship between the quantity of money supplied and inflation. First, to reduce the rate of inflation to a desired level, it was necessary to commensurately reduce the rate of growth of the money supply (measured, for example, by the Bank of England's definition of **narrow money** which includes notes and coins in circulation and reserve balances held by commercial banks and building societies at the Bank of England). Second, because government controlled the money supply, the rate of inflation an economy experienced was both its choice and responsibility.

Stop and Think

....

Most of us as children have heard an exasperated response from parents: *'money doesn't grow on trees you know, so you can't have a new bike/pony/PlayStation'*. But what if, magically, it did, would we all be better off? Would you get your PlayStation? Well, no, all that would happen is that money would be rapidly devalued because of its abundance and this would happen via high and rising inflation. Too much money would be chasing too few goods. PlayStations would cost thousands, then millions, then billions; but probably somewhere along the way we'd all lose faith in increasingly worthless notes.

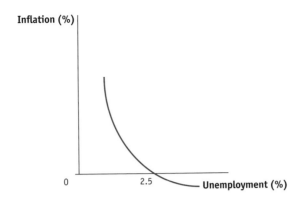

Figure 9.9 The Phillips Curve

To understand Friedman's interpretation of what governments could and could not do in the economy we need to introduce a concept known as the Phillips curve, named after its originator, A. W. Phillips, whose pioneering study was published in 1958. The Phillips curve describes the nature of the statistical relationship between the rate of change of money wages and unemployment in the UK for the period 1861–1957. Remarkably, the relationship appeared to be a stable one. This allowed economists to infer a similar relationship between price inflation and unemployment as depicted by the curve in Figure 9.9. Keynesians supposed that the Phillips curve provided a choice for policy-makers—they could select from a menu of possible combinations of inflation and unemployment. Most Keynesians at the time viewed inflation as a **demand–pull inflation** phenomenon, in that inflation is caused by an excess demand for goods and services when the economy is at or above full employment. We can now understand the policy-makers' choice as provided by the Phillips curve. Policy-makers could—using aggregate demand management—squeeze inflation out of the economy entirely if demand was sufficiently suppressed but at the cost of some higher level of unemployment. In Figure 9.9 this possibility is illustrated by a combination of zero inflation and 2.5% unemployment. On the other hand, lower levels of unemployment are obtainable through expansionary fiscal and monetary policy but at the cost of higher inflation. Thus, in Figure 9.8, as unemployment falls below 2.5% the rate of inflation increases.

For a time it appeared that the Phillips curve fitted snugly into the Keynesian orthodoxy and people like Friedman, with alternative views of how the economy worked, struggled to be heard. However, all that began to change from the early 1970s when two things happened. One was the surge in worldwide inflation seen in Figure 9.8; the second was the re-emergence of unemployment in many economies, as depicted for the G5 in Figure 9.10. Together these became known as **stagflation**—a combination of economic **stag**nation and in**flation**. Stagflation was a real problem for Keynesian economics and its 'either inflation or unemployment, but not both' Phillips curve view of the world. This is where Friedman was able to seize his opportunity. He had to hand an explanation of stagflation and a set of policy measures to deal with it.

From stabilization policy to controlling inflation

We have already covered the essence of Friedman's understanding of the worldwide inflation shock of the 1970s. Because inflation in Friedman's view is always the product of an over-expansion of an economy's supply of money (so that *too much money is chasing too few goods*), the inflation rate, good or not so good, is always the choice of government. The very high inflation of the 1970s was, therefore, the fault of the world's governments that had for too

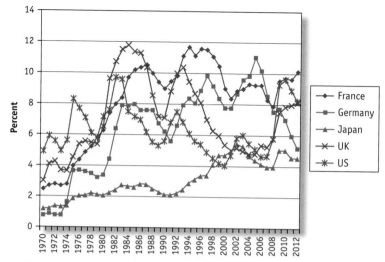

Figure 9.10 G5 unemployment 1970–2012 (2012 est.)
Source: Data from IMF, 2012.

long followed the traditional Keynesian policy prescription of spending their way out of any threatened downturn.

Friedman's interpretation of the stagnation (high unemployment) element of the 1970s recession revived another tradition in economics. Friedman considered unemployment to be a *microeconomic* rather than a macroeconomic phenomenon. What counted was not the level of aggregate demand in an economy but the way in which the labour market functioned. If the labour market was competitive it would, like any other market, tend towards a market-clearing equilibrium at which the demand for labour and its supply were closely aligned. But if the labour market was uncompetitive then unemployment could easily result. For example, if wages were set permanently above the market-clearing equilibrium because of the monopoly power of trade unions there would be a greater supply of labour than demand for it: in other words, there would be some persistent unemployment. Wages might also be pushed above their market-clearing equilibrium by forms of government intervention in the labour market such as the setting of minimum wages or the generosity of the government itself as a major employer. Alternatively, the government could also adversely affect labour market conditions by, for example, paying unemployment-related benefits at a level that discouraged workers from taking jobs.

Friedman summarized the outcomes of these and other dimensions of poor labour market competitiveness in a new concept: *the natural rate of unemployment*. The natural rate of unemployment was not natural in the common-sense meaning of the word, in that it implied unemployment was permanent or immutable; rather, the natural rate in an economy was commensurate with the level of competitiveness in the economy's labour market in any particular period. Better competitiveness would mean falling unemployment and vice versa. Note too that the solution to unemployment is not the macroeconomic policy of demand management but a spectrum of microeconomic polices designed to make the labour market work more efficiently.

Let us now return to Modigliani's 'need/can/should' framework for the interpretation of government policy to stabilize the levels of output and employment in the economy (see the section 'The case for stabilizing the economy'). How does Friedman's work fit in here? The Keynesian view suggested that governments need to intervene, they can intervene,

Mini-Case 9.3 Reducing the natural rate of unemployment in France

Figure 9.10 indicates that the rate of unemployment in France has been relatively high when compared to most other members of the G5 since the early 1990s. One widely acknowledged reason is the poor performance of the French labour market which the French authorities themselves recognize is beset with a number of weaknesses that undermine its competitiveness. Their response in recent years has been to implement a series of labour market reforms which have included:

* measures to extend the length of the working week

* the reform of industrial relations so that collective bargaining takes place more at the level of the individual firm rather than nationally

* reform of the benefits system to make payments to the unemployed dependent on active job hunting

* measures to make it easier for small firms to fire workers.

The authorities have also been urged to reduce the relatively high French national minimum wage.

Monetarists would argue that taken together these labour market reforms should begin to reduce the natural rate of unemployment in France.

Question

Look again at Figure 9.10. Note the very rapidly increasing rates of unemployment in France, the UK, and the US from 2008 as the recession begins to bite. What would Keynesian economists claim about the causes of this increase?

and therefore they should. Friedman's conclusion about stabilization policy is precisely the opposite:

* Governments *don't need* to stabilize the economy—capitalist economies are inherently stable, all governments should so in macro terms is control inflation.

* Governments *cannot* stabilize the economy—macroeconomic policy is ineffective in tackling unemployment and stimulating output in the long run; reducing the natural rate of unemployment is a task for microeconomic policy.

* Governments *should not* therefore try to stabilize the economy—there is no case for them to do so.

▓ Domestic macroeconomic policy in a globalized world

By the 1980s Friedman's thinking had largely won the day and his ideas were widely adopted by both national governments and international financial institutions (IFIs) such as the World Bank, International Monetary Fund, and World Trade Organization. This neoclassical resurgence was rebranded 'neoliberalism' and became an influential policy driver in the acceleration of globalization in the 1980s and 1990s.

Economic globalization in the form of trade openness, capital market liberalization, and increased flows of foreign direct investment (FDI), is seen by many commentators as constraining the domestic macroeconomic policy choices of nation states (Keohane and Nye 1977, Strange 1996, Yergin and Stanislaw 2002, Wolf 2004). By contrast, proponents of the free market neoliberal school claim that economic globalization promotes growth, raises living standards and encourages developing country governments to improve infrastructure and governance to attract capital flows (Bhagwati 1998 and 2004, T. L. Friedman 2005). It is, therefore, necessary to consider the wider global context of macroeconomic policy to better understand the extent to which national governments are free to pursue locally desirable policies.

Let us begin this part of our discussion by examining how globalization impacts on the pursuit of the three objectives of domestic macroeconomic policy considered earlier.

Globalization's impact on domestic growth policy

Economic globalization in the form of trade openness, capital market liberalization, and foreign direct investment (FDI), impacts on the government's objective of satisfactory and stable economic growth in a several ways. First, we will examine the specific claim of globalization's proponents that trade openness is positively associated with growth. Based on the theory of comparative advantage, this argument suggests an international division of labour, arising from globalization, enhances overall growth due to a more efficient allocation of resources. The international division of labour refers to geographical patterns of specialization in economic activity; for example, manufacturing may be concentrated in Southeast Asia but research and development may be concentrated in Western Europe and the US. The relationship between trade openness and growth is hotly debated by economists. Some suggest it is not supported by real world experience (Rodrik and Rodriguez 2001), while others suggest difficulties in doing reliable comparative studies mean the question remains unresolved (Billmeier and Nannicini 2007). However, what is clear is that politicians and their policy advisors have accepted the relationship as valid and so have sought to embrace trade openness (and other aspects of economic globalization) as a means to encourage growth. For example, a recent report by the UK Department of Business, Innovation & Skills stated:

> long-term evidence from a broad sample of OECD countries indicates that an increase of 10% in trade exposure was associated with a 4% increase in output per working-age person.

(BIS/DFID Trade Policy Unit 2011)

Secondly, we come to a more difficult effect of economic globalization on domestic macroeconomic policy. Specifically, the extent to which a country has embraced economic globalization will influence its exposure to exogenous shocks affecting the rate and stability of domestic growth. That is to say, the more engaged in trade, the freer the movement of international capital into and out of a country and the more reliant a country is on attracting FDI to support industrial development, the more likely it is to be adversely impacted by downturns in the global economy.

So, to what extent is the UK economy exposed to these influences? According to World Bank data, the UK economy is very open to trade in both goods and services. The World Bank measures trade openness in goods by the combined value of merchandise imports and exports expressed as a percentage of GDP. On this measure, in 2011, the UK stood at 45.6%, Germany 76.4%, and France 47.3%. By contrast, trade in services as a percentage of GDP was significantly higher for the UK (19.5%) than Germany (15.7%) and France (15.0%). Overall, these figures illustrate high levels of openness to trade in both goods and services for the UK and other leading EU member states.

By comparison, corresponding figures for merchandise trade as a percentage of GDP for the US (24.8%), Japan (28.6%), Brazil (19.9%), and Australia (37.5%) suggest the UK and its fellow EU members are significantly more open than some of their key trading partners. In terms of FDI flows, the UK has traditionally been a favoured destination for those looking to invest in the EU. Following the onset of the global recession, there was a 40% fall in FDI flows globally between 2007-9 (from a record high of $2 trillion in 2007). In 2010, the UK saw its inward

FDI similarly fall by 50% to £46 billion, meaning it fell from third (after the US and France) to seventh in the global league table of recipients (UNCTAD 2012).

What these figures confirm is that the UK government's macroeconomic policy objectives are tightly linked to fluctuations in the global economy, a fact well documented as a result of the global recession. Following sharp downturns in trade and FDI after 2007, global output contracted in 2009 for the first time in 60 years (UNCTAD 2012). Over the same period, UK real GDP has declined markedly as illustrated in Figure 9.1.

Globalization's impact on the pursuit of a high and stable level of employment

In the two decades following World War Two, fiscal policy was the favoured tool for managing aggregate demand to influence the level of employment. This approach, as we have seen, was based on Keynes's influential analysis of why recessions occur and persist. As Keynes pointed out, while both fiscal and monetary policy can be used to affect the level of aggregate demand in pursuit of higher levels of employment, fiscal policy has a more direct effect. This is because changes to government spending plans are in the direct control of governments, whereas using interest rates to stimulate spending and investment relies on the reactions of business owners and consumers—that are not guaranteed.

With the resurgence of free market thinking in the 1970s and 1980s, the macroeconomic policy prescriptions associated with neoliberalism replaced Keynesian thinking to become the dominant influence on the domestic policies of many countries including the UK. Harvard economist Dani Rodrik has summarized the so-called 'Washington Consensus' as involving the following policies:

1. Fiscal discipline (i.e. Balanced budgets)
2. Reorientation of public expenditures
3. Tax reform (e.g. Lower taxes on individuals and companies)
4. Financial liberalization (e.g. Free movement of capital)
5. Competitive exchange rates (free floating exchange rates)
6. Trade liberalization (e.g. Reduction of trade tariffs)
7. Openness to Foreign Direct Investment (FDI)
8. Privatization of state owned assets (e.g. Public utilities)
9. Deregulation of commercial activities
10. Secure Property Rights (e.g. Patent protection).

(*Source:* Rodrik 2006)

The first of the policies identified by Rodrik (fiscal discipline) can be seen as a foundation of 'austerity' packages in many EU countries including Portugal, Ireland, Greece, Spain, and the UK. This emphasis on balanced budgets signals a move away from using fiscal policy (e.g. a budget deficit) to stimulate aggregate demand and raise the level of employment. Under neoliberalism, fiscal policy is viewed as misguided state interference in the operation of markets. If we study the list of policies identified by Rodrik, we see that many of them share a bias against state involvement in the economy and a faith in the efficiency of free markets.

Many commentators have been very critical of the neoliberal policies. One of the criticisms has been whether a 'one size fits all' policy agenda can meet the needs of diverse individual countries whose problems and institutional contexts might better be served by bespoke solutions. In fact, former World Bank chief economist Joseph Stiglitz has gone so far as to condemn the Washington Consensus as serving narrow sectional interests to the detriment of whole societies and democracy in general:

> the net effect of the policies set by the Washington Consensus has all too often been to benefit the few at the expense of the many, the well-off at the expense of the poor. In many cases, commercial interests and values have superseded concern for the environment, democracy, human rights, and social justice.

(Stiglitz 2003)

In terms of the domestic macroeconomic policy objective of high and stable employment, it can be seen that the influence of the global neoliberal consensus, upon which much global economic policy (formulated by the World Bank, International Monetary Fund, and World Trade Organization) has been based, has served to shape domestic policy by severely curtailing the available policy options and latitude for discretionary fiscal policy in particular.

Globalization's impact on achieving a low and stable rate of inflation

Economic globalization has been accompanied by a pronounced downward trend in inflation rates globally since 1980 (measured by consumer prices). This is illustrated in Table 9.4.

The causal factors behind this trend may be less related to effective domestic policies at the national level than contributory factors at the global level.

First, economic globalization impacts consumer prices due to imports of cheap manufactured goods. This stems from the integration of low-wage countries into the global economy, resulting in an enhanced division of labour and, consequently, better exploitation of comparative advantage. This effect is compounded due to rising import penetration as domestically produced goods are substituted for cheaper imported ones.

Second, the integration of low-wage economies intensifies international competitive pressures. Countries heavily engaged in international trade, like the UK and others in the EU, are in competition for export orders and so have strong incentives to keep their domestic prices competitive by controlling relative rates of inflation. This is because rising import costs will translate to higher prices for UK manufactures making them hard to sell both in the UK and to our export markets. Fortunately, intensifying competition also provides strong incentives to improve productivity which, in turn, supports the effort to maintain competitive prices.

The effect of this increased competition is seen in the loss of market share by most advanced economies due to growing exports from emerging economies. Countries such as the Czech Republic, South Korea, Mexico, Poland, and China—among many others—have all seen their

Table 9.4 Change in consumer prices for selected years, per cent

	1980	1985	1990	1995	2000	2005	2010	2015
World	17.4	15.0	27.7	14.5	4.6	3.8	3.7	3.4
Advanced economies	13.0	5.4	5.2	2.6	2.3	2.3	1.5	1.8
Emerging & developing economies	28.4	41.5	98.4	39.1	8.6	5.8	6.1	4.9

Source: IMF.

shares of global exports rise. For example, China's share of world exports has increased four-fold from 2.6% to 10.0% between 1995 and 2010. China has now overtaken Germany to become the world's largest goods exporter (UN 2011).

Finally, the available pool of workers has greatly increased due to the emergence of low wage countries such as China, Vietnam, Indonesia, India, Bangladesh, etc. This creates opportunities for outsourcing production to low wage economies.

Global influences on domestic macroeconomic policy

It is important to be aware that the relationship between globalization and domestic macro-economic policy is complex. Different countries are susceptible to different forms of global economic influence, to varying degrees, at different times. The factors which give rise to these differential impacts include:

- Whether the country under consideration is developing or developed. This is due to differences in perceived risks affecting investment attractiveness and hence capital costs.
- The extent of integration into the global economy (in terms of openness to flows of goods, services, people, and money) will determine susceptibility to fluctuations in the global economy.
- The size of a nation's economy is important because smaller economies tend to be more trade dependent than those with large domestic markets and, therefore, have to align themselves more to global conditions.
- The specific arrangement of domestic institutions may imply embedded commitments to welfare spending, education, and healthcare which moderate external influences on policy choices.

It should be apparent from the above points that discussing the impact of economic globalization on domestic policy macroeconomic choices is not as simple as listing the ways it might support or constrain such choices. Any given factor may have a positive or negative effect depending on the country in question, its stage of development, openness to (and dependence on) trade, exposure to international capital markets, and dependence on FDI flows.

■ Looking ahead

The global economy is at a critical juncture. The immediate need to rescue the global financial system from collapse resulted in enormous emergency government injections of cash into the banking system and attempts to build a global coordinated response. It seemed clear that a narrow Washington Consensus approach to domestic and global economic policy was broken and there was a recognition that government action was needed at both the global and domestic levels.

In the event, the process of building a post-Washington Consensus has been slow, and different approaches have been taken to restoring domestic macroeconomic stability. In the US a moderate Keynesian expansion has been employed, and there is room for optimism that growth will be restored. In Japan, against all expectation, a bold expansion programme dubbed Abenomics (named after the Prime Minister Shinzo Abe) has buoyed business confidence but the outcome is uncertain. In Europe, the prospects for growth are not good. Effective action has now been taken to ensure that there are enough central funds to relieve any speculative pressures on those countries with the biggest deficits, but the austerity measures that they have to enact are proving to be very challenging. While there is global growth as a result of the continued growth in emerging markets, progress on banking reforms has been limited and a global agreement to achieve macroeconomic stability has yet to be reached.

■ Summary

- Macroeconomic stability is a desirable thing but there has been a lengthy and continuing debate in economics about how to best secure it.

- The main aims of macroeconomic policy are to produce an environment that promotes stable and satisfactory growth, high and stable employment and low unemployment, and a stable and low rate of inflation.

- Economists once urged governments to actively and consistently employ the Keynesian tools of fiscal and monetary policy to keep economic growth and employment on track. This approach has enjoyed a pronounced comeback as a result of the recent crisis.

- The inflationary experiences of the 1970s and 1980s suggested a different, less hands-on approach was needed. It was argued that government intervention to reduce unemployment could only work in the short run and was the cause of the inflation.

- Recently, in many of the world's economies, a somewhat eclectic approach to the economy—one that draws on both interventionist and non-interventionist traditions—has given way to Keynesian-inspired strategies to deal with the fallout from the 2008–9 crisis.

Case Study: Austerity in and out of the euro area, a necessity or a choice?

Many of the world's governments reacted to the recession that followed the financial crisis by increasing spending. They briefly forgot—or conveniently put aside—the strictures of the Washington Consensus and embraced old-style Keynesian fiscal measures that supported aggregate demand in their economies. Simply, they spent their way out of recession. More recently, those same governments have once again changed their policy emphasis. Now the priority is to reduce the level of government debt that Keynesian policies necessarily ran up.

As we have characterized it here, this new era of austerity—in the sense that morally strict governments try to live within their means by tightly controlling expenditure—is an *optional* path: one that has been chosen. While this might be true for some governments, it is not true for others that have, in effect, become predisposed to austerity. And it is not just governments; whole societies have fallen into this position. How? Why? The answer is that they are all members of the euro area.

There is a strong economic case for the euro. Because the 17 members of the euro area all use the same currency they are likely, in the future, to trade more intensively with one another.

As more trade generates additional demand for goods and services and allows participant economies to realize economies of scale across the whole continent, there should be a fillip to euro area growth. In addition, because there are no longer any nominal exchange rates inside the euro area there is no longer any risk posed by the tendency for exchange rates to shift in a dramatic and potentially destabilizing way. The euro in France is the same as the euro in Germany. The French franc can never again slide or climb against the German mark. Both have gone, forever. The absence of an internal exchange rate risk makes trade, investment, and decisions about where to work much easier. And, again, the pay-off comes in the shape of more of these transactions in the euro area and consequently more growth and prosperity.

But the case against the euro area may also appear compelling, especially to those on whom it has the greatest impact: the citizens of countries such as Greece, Ireland, Portugal, and Spain. The dimensions of the continuing crisis in these places are simply staggering. Figure 9.11 depicts economic growth in the four countries since the launch of the euro in 1999 (Greece joined the euro area in 2001). Notice

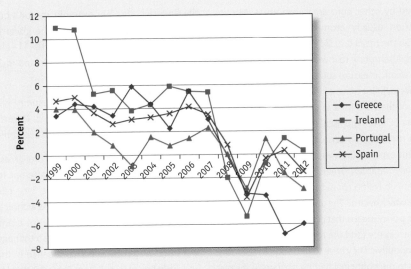

Figure 9.11 Economic growth in selected euro area countries 1999–2012
Source: Data from IMF, 2012.

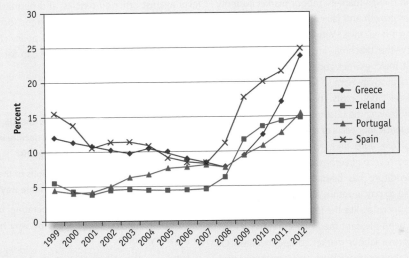

Figure 9.12 Unemployment in selected euro area countries 1999–2012
Source: Data from IMF, 2012.

that prior to 2008 for all these countries, with the exception perhaps of Portugal, growth was relatively stable and satisfactory. Since 2008 it has been neither; Ireland is barely growing and Greece, Portugal, and Spain are presently mired in recession. The plight of the Greek economy, contracting sharply for four consecutive years, looks particularly worrying. Figure 9.12 shows the consequences for unemployment of this poor performance. Unemployment in Ireland and Portugal has reached 15%, but in Greece and Spain roughly one in every four people is unemployed. Economic stagnation of such proportions has raised important political questions in

all these countries, prompting government instability, mass demonstrations, riots and even deaths.

The urgent question is what to do about these appalling economic performances. Unfortunately, euro area membership means there can be only one answer: austerity. The principle cost of euro area membership is the permanent surrender of monetary sovereignty. This means that interest rates are no longer set by individual economies in their own interests but by the European Central Bank (ECB) on behalf of all euro member states. The key problem here is what happens when particular countries get into economic difficulties that are not shared by other euro area economies. Macroeconomic stagnation usually prompts a macroeconomic policy response. On the monetary side this may involve lowering interest rates, attempting to lower the exchange rate, or some other more exotic measure such as quantitative easing (the printing of money). But none of these measures is available to members of the euro area as monetary policy is the sole preserve of the ECB. On the fiscal side too there are constraints. Euro area membership carries with it the obligation to keep government expenditure within certain limits and, in any case, the heavily indebted Greek, Irish, Portuguese, and Spanish governments have no room for manoeuvre here.

What then is the way forward? The unavailability of the tools of macroeconomic policy means that *microeconomic* measures must take the strain. Greece (and the rest) must become more internationally competitive. They have to find ways to sell more goods and services to their principal trading partners in the rest of Europe. The only way this can happen is through their labour markets. Greek citizens must be prepared to accept lower wages and work longer hours to make the things they produce more competitive in foreign markets. Labour market austerity is the path to better growth and falling unemployment. One key issue is how long this will take. Were the Greeks to still have their own currency—the drachma—interest rates in Greece could be quickly cut, making Greek goods cheaper for foreigners. But four years of austerity have so far ground out an estimated 15% fall in Greek labour costs. This is possibly about half of what is necessary, leaving the uncomfortable question: can Greece cope with *another* four years of austerity?

The problems of the euro area's peripheral economies are compounded by severe government indebtedness, and slashing state expenditure has been the price that some economies have had to pay in return for financial help from other EU states and agencies, like the International Monetary Fund. This has not been pleasant medicine but it has added to pressures to improve labour market competitiveness. Of course, it is not just the peripheral euro area economies that have seen their government debts piling up in the wake of the financial crisis. For example, the UK's budgetary position deteriorated to the extent that the government needed to borrow almost £150 billion in 2010–11—about 10% of GDP. The new coalition government, elected in 2010, declared in its first budget that,

The most urgent task facing this country is to implement an accelerated plan to reduce the deficit. Reducing the deficit is a necessary precondition for sustained economic growth.

So there has been austerity too in the UK as the government has cut public expenditure in an attempt to almost entirely eliminate the budget deficit over a five-year period. But notice that austerity in Britain remains a choice. The authorities might have done things differently, for example, by reducing expenditure over a longer period so that aggregate demand, and firms' and consumers' confidence in the economy, held up a little better (recall from Table 9.1 that UK growth continues to disappoint). The UK government also retains monetary autonomy, allowing UK interest rates to be kept at a record low of 0.5% since 2009, keeping the pound at a competitive level against other currencies, and permitting the injection of £375 billion into the economy in the form of quantitative easing. Macroeconomic policy and policy choice exist in the UK in a way that they never again can for members of the euro area.

Questions

1. **Within a single country such as the US, how would the government be able to react to a decline in the competiveness of one of its own internal regions?**

2. **Why have the governing institutions of the EU not found it so easy to support Greece in the same way?**

3. **If the UK economy is not operating under the same constraints as the Greek economy why has it chosen the austerity route?**

4. **What are the advantages and disadvantages to a business when faced with an external environment of austerity?**

Review and discussion questions

1. What do we mean by economic growth?

2. Why is it desirable that the economy should be stable?

3. Explain why inflation became viewed as the central macroeconomic problem from the mid-1970s onwards.

4. Why is the Great Depression central to an understanding of the development of macroeconomic thinking and policy?

5. Why do we have independent central banks?

6. What implications has the 2008–9 recession had for macroeconomic theory and policy?

7. In what ways might globalization constrain the macroeconomic policy freedoms of national governments?

8. What is the case against joining the euro area?

Assignments

1. Take a recent interest rate decision by the Bank of England (summaries available from the Bank of England website). Explain the primary macroeconomic policy concern behind the decision—is it that inflationary pressures in the economy need to be addressed, or is there a more important concern about the prospects for economic growth on the Bank's agenda?

2. Compare growth rates, unemployment rates, and inflation rates for the United States, Japan, China, and Germany over the past decade (figures from the IMF—see list of useful websites below). Which countries are doing particularly well and particularly badly? Look at one or two OECD country reports to find out a little about the macroeconomic policies of these economies.

3. Look at the annual reports of some major UK firms. What do these reports suggest about the importance of the UK macroeconomic climate to the performance of firms?

Further reading

Mulhearn, C. and Vane, H. R. (2011) *Economics for Business 2nd edition* (Basingstoke: Palgrave Macmillan).

An introduction to economics for business by one of authors of the present chapter.

online resource centre

Test your understanding of this chapter with online questions and answers, explore the subject further through web exercises, and use the web links to provide a quick resource for further research. Go to the Online Resource Centre at <www.oxfordtextbooks.co.uk/orc/wetherly_otter/2>

Useful websites

<www.hm-treasury.gov.uk>
This is a key website which contains a wealth of information about the UK economy and its economic policy.

<www.bankofengland.co.uk>
Useful for researching the UK economy, especially monetary policy.

<www.imf.org>
The International Monetary Fund is a vast source of economic information on individual countries. It offers a particularly good interactive free data set.

<www.worldbank.org>
Although its primary focus is on developing countries, this site also allows you to access economic data and analysis for many economies.

References

Bhagwati, J. (2004) *In Defence of Globalization* (Oxford: Oxford University Press).

Billmeier, A. and Nannicini, T. (2007) 'Trade Openness and Growth: Pursuing Empirical Glasnost', *IMF Working paper* WP/07/156.

Friedman, T. L. (2005) *The World Is Flat* (New York: Farrar, Straus and Girou).

Keohane, R. O. and Nye, J. S. (1977) *Power and Interdependence: World Politics in Transition* (Boston: Little, Brown, and Company).

Maddison, A. (2001) *The World Economy in Millennial Perspective* (Paris: OECD).

Rodriguez, F. and Rodrik, D. (2001) 'Trade Policy and Economic Growth: A Skeptic's Guide to the Cross-National Evidence', in

Macroeconomics Annual 2000, eds Bernanke, B. and Kenneth S. Rogoff (Cambridge, MA: MIT Press for NBER).

Rodrik, D. (2006) 'Goodbye Washington Consensus, Hello Washington Confusion? A Review of the World Bank's Economic Growth in the 1990s: Learning from a Decade of Reform', *Journal of Economic Literature*, 44(4), pp. 973–987.

Snowdon, B. and Vane, H. R. (2005) *Modern Macroeconomics* (Cheltenham: Edward Elgar).

Stiglitz, J. (2003) *Globalization and Its Discontents* (New York: W. W. Norton & Co.).

Strange, S. (1996) *The Retreat of the State: The Diffusion of Power in the World Economy* (Cambridge: Cambridge University Press).

UK Department for Business, Innovation & Skills (2011) Economic Openness and Economic Prosperity, *Trade and Investment Analytical Papers*, No. 2, BIS/DFID Trade Policy Unit.

United Nations Conference on Trade and Development (2012) *Trade and Development Report 2012* (Geneva: UNCTAD).

Wolf, Martin (2004) *Why Globalization Works* (New Haven, CT: Yale University Press).

Yergin, D. and Stanislaw, J. (2002) *The Commanding Heights: The Battle for the World Economy* (New York: Simon & Schuster).

Sources

Data from National Statistics website: <**www.statistics.gov.uk**>. Crown copyright material is reproduced with permission of the Controller Office of Public Sector Information (OPSI).

Data from IMF International Financial Statistics ('consumer prices, per cent change over previous year, calculated from indices').

HM Treasury website: <**www.hm-treasury.gov.uk**>. Crown copyright material is reproduced with permission of the Controller Office of Public Sector Information (OPSI).

Chapter 10

Globalization of business: Good or bad?

Dorron Otter

Learning objectives

When you have completed this chapter you will be able to:

- Explain the meaning of globalization.
- Outline the sources that are leading to changes in the scope of globalization.
- Identify the range of competing views as to the nature of globalization.
- Explore the ethical dilemmas that arise out of global business activity.

THEMES

The following themes of the book are especially relevant to this chapter

》 INTERNAL/EXTERNAL

While globalization can be seen as a force that happens 'out there' it is business that both drives this process forward and which in turn has to adopt its internal strategic response to it.

》 VARIETY OF SPATIAL LEVELS

Globalization adds the supranational level to the focus on business activity. This is the defining characteristic of globalization, emphasizing the inter-linkages across the spatial levels from local through to global.

》 DYNAMIC ENVIRONMENT

The nature of the global environment has changed over time and is now rapidly being shaped by a combination of the need for the developed countries of the world to emerge from the problems caused by the financial crisis from 2008 onwards and the rapid growth in the emerging markets of the world.

》 VALUES

Put simply, 'Is globalization good or bad'? It is important to recognize the range of views that are expressed when seeking to investigate the impact of the transformations brought about by the shift in the spatial level of globalization.

There is an increasing interest in the role of global ethics to address issues associated with globalization. While operating across national boundaries presents business with huge opportunities, what are their responsibilities to the countries in which they operate, especially when operating across cultures with differing ethical norms?

■ Introduction: the impact of globalization on the business environment

Globalization raises a series of questions that need to be explored: What is globalization? When did it start? Is it increasing and in what way? Is globalization good or bad? Who and what does globalization affect? What are the challenges that globalization poses? In relation to business, though, we need to consider the strategic response of businesses to the 'challenge of globalization'.

❱❱ **VALUES** There are two central questions that dominate the debate about globalization. While it is clear that globalization can potentially give rise to an increase in prosperity, there are severe doubts as to whether this process will be fair to all, both in the present and to those in the future. We will see that there are a variety of perspectives about the impact of globalization and that the role of ethics in relation to globalization needs to be explored.

❱❱ **SPATIAL LEVELS** Secondly, we have seen in Chapter 2 that for markets to work they need to both be supported by and regulated by states. Since globalization occurs across national boundaries this means that we need to consider the global system of rules and regulations that may be needed. Even before the global recession that started in 2008, there were many people who were arguing that the world lacks robust global governance arrangements to ensure that globalization is a smooth process which will bring greater prosperity for all people and all countries.

Mini-Case 10.1   Death by US chocolate?

On 19 January 2010 the board of the British company Cadbury finally recommended to its shareholders that it should accept a £11.6 billion takeover bid from Kraft. This takeover bid had, at first, been resisted but in the end the board justified its decision to sell out to the US food group as 'the price of globalization' (<www.ft.com/indepth/cadbury-kraft>).

Other commentators recalling the similar fate that had befallen other British chocolate firms, like Rowntrees and Terry's of York, seemed to express a heartfelt feeling of loss in terms of national sentiment. All of these companies had their roots in a form of capitalism based on a religious conviction that business should have a strong local focus and both civic and social responsibility.

It wasn't only the Cadbury board and these wider stakeholders that had been opposed to the takeover. Trades unions were anxious about the effect on their members' employment conditions and the then Labour government was concerned given the number of other foreign takeovers and mergers that had been taking place. In response to this there were calls to strengthen the powers of the takeover panel.

While Kraft had given assurances that it would keep open a plant near Bristol threatened with closure by the previous board, it withdrew these shortly after the merger took place and announced the loss of 200 jobs.

In 2013 at a discussion at the University of Birmingham held to reflect on the legacy of this takeover, Sir Dominic Cadbury, another former chairman argued:

Strategic decisions are influenced by the interests of the country of ownership. Takeovers frequently result in pressure for short-term financial returns; long-term investment in corporate social responsibility is more difficult for subsidiary companies of foreign national corporations to justify, and finally, there will always be a change in corporate culture, which may not necessarily be negative but will certainly be different.

For other commentators the only stakeholders that mattered were the shareholders of the company and, since a significant proportion of these were now seasoned City investors, such as hedge funds and other institutional investors, all that mattered was if the takeover was good for business as measured by profitability (Moeller 2012).

By 2012 it had become clear that the acquisition of Cadbury had been the final part of a strategy by Kraft to split its large global business into two distinct groups. One was a grocery business centred around its strong US brands retaining the Kraft name and, the other, a global snacks and confectionery business using the strong brands that it had now accumulated across the world and then using its global marketing reach to expand the sales of these brands (such as Cadbury's Dairy Milk). This new company is called Mondelez International.

(*Sources:* Wood 2012, University of Birmingham 2013, Moeller 2012)

Questions

1. Why might globalization be good in the case of this merger? For whom might it be good?

2. Why was there resistance to this merger?

3. Why, if the British government was anxious about the takeover, was it not in a position to prevent it from happening?

What is globalization?

There are six main aspects of globalization.

International trade and the creation of the global marketplace

≫ DYNAMIC ≫ SPATIAL LEVELS Globalization at its simplest can be seen as the increase over time of international trade (referred to as *merchandise trade*) and services, and often this is how it is described. With trade comes an increase in the amount of markets across national borders.

Trade itself is a vital feature of economic activity within countries or regions. Without trade, businesses would not be able to benefit from the ability to specialize and the associated benefits of an efficient division of labour. With international trade we are moving trade to a different spatial level. The central question then is, does moving trade to the international level change its nature? It is clear that earlier civilizations across the globe were involved in widespread trading within regions. However, what is different about the modern era is that trade was expanding rapidly as capitalism was fuelling the industrial revolutions in Europe and North America and thus any understanding of globalization must encompass an understanding of the nature of capitalism on a world scale.

Mini-Case 10.2 Banana wars

Historically, the European Union has implemented preferential trade agreements with many countries in Africa, the Caribbean, and the Pacific (ACP trade agreements). This was in recognition of former colonial links and the agreements were designed to help ACP countries boost their economies through trade. These agreements took the form of lowering tariffs on the exports of the ACP countries in relation to competitor countries thus increasing the demand for these ACP products within the EU.

One of these agreements concerned trade in bananas which for many countries, for example, the Cameroons, the

Ivory Coast, the Windward Islands, and Jamaica, provided a main source of export earnings.

However, these agreements had been the source of a protracted trade dispute within the World Trade Organization. Production of bananas for exports is heavily concentrated; just five countries account for 83% of all exports, four of which are in Latin America (Ecuador, Colombia, Costa Rica, and Guatemala) and the other one is the Philippines. Yet, more than 80% of the production is controlled by the large US multinational companies of Fyffes, Chiquita, Dole, and Del Monte. They complained that these ACP agreements broke free trade rules and the agreement ended in 2009 with tariffs on Latin American bananas being progressively reduced to zero by 2017.

(*Sources:* BBC News 2009, Cassidy 2009, UNCTAD 2012a)

1. Why might poor developing countries seek to gain preferential agreements with richer countries?

2. How will the ending of this preferential trade agreement affect banana producers and suppliers across the globe and consumers within the EU?

3. What are the benefits and potential drawbacks to the stakeholders in the banana producing countries of having their industries dominated by the multinational companies?

Globally organized production and investment flows

Businesses have recognized the advantages of organizing production across national boundaries to take advantage of lower costs and the specialist benefits of different geographical locations. This can involve placing production facilities abroad, or splitting the stages of production or other functions of the business, to take advantage of lower costs or be nearer to foreign markets.

Allied to this is the increase in the amount and nature of investment that takes place across borders. This can be in the form of foreign direct investment as well as through financial flows of money and portfolio investment.

After 1945 there was widespread talk of a new international division of labour. This meant that with the freeing up of financial markets businesses in the developed nations would begin to set up production in new markets where resources were cheapest. In particular, this would help the developing world.

Much attention in the literature is paid to the rise of the multinational corporation. Often the term transnational corporation is used to convey the fact that such corporations work across national boundaries.

There has been a big increase in these investment flows, especially in the 1990s. From 1980 to 2002 the world flow of inward investment increased from less than $50 billion a year to $1.2 trillion in 2000. Despite a drop, from 2000–3, inward FDI recovered sharply reaching $2 trillion. The global financial crisis saw this drop and in 2012 the total stood at $1.5 trillion which was 23% below the 2007 peak. It is expected that by 2014 this will stand at $1.8 trillion (World Investment Report 2012).

As well as flows in FDI the recent explosion in investment has come from the rise of stocks and shares flowing across national boundaries. The international financial system has seen unprecedented growth in the last quarter of a century. In particular, the role of the IMF and the need for stronger global governance of financial markets has come under intense scrutiny as individual nations have suffered severe financial instability and debt burden, and where the very integration of these financial markets has meant that such crises can spread quickly to other countries.

Migration

A major feature of the development of trade and investment has been the movements of people across both internal national and international borders. Such movements have had profound effects both on the countries and regions the migrants leave from as well as those they go to.

Often attention is focused on the problems of immigration without an appreciation of the global forces which shape migration and the enormous contributions that migration makes to the growth of business activity both in the private and public sector. An important aspect of the industrialization process within all countries is that, as the towns grow people will move away from rural areas into the urban ones. Globalization offers people in less developed areas the possibility of moving across national frontiers to developed countries.

Communication flows

Globalization has been greatly influenced by the speed with which communications have improved in the world, both in terms of transport and telecommunications.

》 VALUES

Cultural flows

This intermingling of people, and the accompanying rise in communication networks, has brought into focus the question of how cultures combine. It is clear that globalization has brought together people with different cultural beliefs. The challenge for business is how to deal with this and, also, to recognize the potential ethical problems that inter-cultural interactions can create.

》 DYNAMIC

Rapid technological change

There is no doubt that technological change has helped fuel the rapid rise in global economic activity, especially in relation to communication and transport. Mini-Case 3.3 in Chapter 3 examines the impact of containerization as one example. Transport costs have fallen and worldwide travel has increased exponentially. The rise of the Internet and the global telecommunications revolution, in general, has created a new environment which encourages global business activity.

▦ **The growth of globalization**

》 DYNAMIC The World Bank profiles research that depicts three waves of globalization (World Bank 2004). The first wave was in the late 19th century with the rapid increase in the industrialization of the main 'western' nations (mainly Western Europe, the US, and Canada). There was a big expansion in the growth of world trade as measured by the ratio of merchandise exports (trade in physical goods) to world GDP. This expansion was propelled by the development of what Eric Hobsbawm refers to as 'The Age of Empire' (Hobsbawm 1987). Colonial powers imported commodities in the form of primary resources from their colonies and then manufactured these into commodities for sale in their home markets as well as for export back into their overseas possessions. Allied to this was an outflow of investment to the poorer countries and there were mass migrations. However, there were tensions between the main industrial powers with domestic firms keen to exploit the opportunities within their own 'empires' but hostile to competition from outside. This competitive rivalry between the countries in Western Europe provided the conditions that precipitated the First World War.

The period between the First and Second World Wars was marked by a high degree of instability for the industrial countries with many experiencing severe economic problems. One response to these national problems was pressure by domestic firms to keep out foreign competition by continuing to erect barriers to prevent international trade. In response to the decision by the US to erect tariffs, its trading partners followed suit. This represented a 'retreat' from globalization. There was a fall in the proportion of trade to world income from 22% in 1913 to 9% during the 1930s with a marked slowdown in the growth of the world economy.

The third wave of globalization occurred in certain parts of the world after 1945 and picked up universal speed from the late 1970s onwards (see Chapter 2). This was driven by the belief that trade liberalization (the opening of countries' borders to trade and investment by removal of trade barriers) was 'the engine' for the growth of economies.

As we shall see, the global recession that started in 2008 has again highlighted that the process of increasing globalization is far from inevitable or smooth.

■ Perspectives on globalization

❱ VALUES Globalization and its effects provoke intense disagreement. The arguments about globalization have been around ever since scholars began to examine the worldwide expansion of markets. Not surprisingly, the different perspectives that we outlined in Chapter 2, when applied to the growth of international economic activity, came up with different conclusions. For neoclassical/neoliberal critics globalization will be a universally good thing as it will deliver the benefits of free market capitalism to all across the globe. For Marxist and socialist writers, given the huge social, economic, and political differences between countries and groups within countries, it is unlikely that globalization will benefit all but, rather, only the rich elites and businesses. Structuralist and institutionalist commentators focus on the need to ensure that the right institutional frameworks are put in place so that the potential of globalization can be achieved and its dangers minimized.

What unites all three perspectives is that globalization has occurred through the expansion of capitalism on a world scale. What divides them are their views as to the nature of this spatial change and its effects.

Neoclassical/neoliberal views

Chapters 2 and 3 show how Adam Smith highlighted the benefits to an economy of market liberalization and trade, and the intimate relationship between trade, development, and growth. If trade was so important in expanding markets, and therefore allowing greater specialization and increased productivity at the domestic level, it was easy for Smith to show why international trade would be so beneficial.

1. It provides a source of external funding that boosts the amount of money available to fuel trade internally.
2. It enables further room for the expansion of markets on an international scale.

To give a simple illustration of Smith's argument in favour of trade, imagine two countries, A and B; and two goods, wool and wine. For this, Smith uses the concept of **absolute advantage**.

If country A has an absolute advantage in producing wool and country B an absolute advantage in producing wine, then it makes sense for country A to specialize in wool and country B in wine. Overall production of both wine and wool will rise as each country is able to benefit from the advantages of specialization and, provided that these gains from trade are shared equitably, both countries will gain.

By the 19th century the sheer success of the first wave of industrialized countries was astonishing and across a whole range of commodities these countries experienced huge rises in productivity. Neither was this confined to industrial goods, but the industrialization of agriculture began to see big efficiency gains here. This economic success enabled such countries to both expand and, in the process, benefit from a huge economic expansion into overseas markets both to obtain cheap resources and to find new markets to fully exploit economies of scale.

This then posed a problem for trade theorists. If, for example, Britain was better than India at producing a whole host of commodities, what benefit would the less productive areas of the world get from opening their borders to trade? Wouldn't trade simply benefit the advanced countries at the expense of the growth and development of the less advanced ones?

Ricardo and comparative advantage

David Ricardo, writing in the 19th century, refined Smith's theory by arguing that, even if country A is better than country B at producing both commodities, it still makes sense for A to specialize in one and B the other. If A specializes in the commodity in which it has the greater comparative advantage and B in the one in which it has the smallest comparative disadvantage then there will still be overall gains in production. Ricardo still used units of input in relation to output produced as his measure of advantage.

In the world of the 19th century it was easy to argue that the industrialized nations should specialize in manufactures (secondary commodities) and the colonies in raw materials and natural resources (primary commodities). It is still the case today that many countries are heavily reliant for much of their export earnings on only one or two primary commodities.

In the 20th century this theory was refined further by two economists Hecksher and Ohlin, who argued that advantage was related to the cost of a unit of input in relation to output and that the 'factor endowments' of countries could differ. In countries where resources of a certain type were abundant, then the costs of those resources would be low. On a world scale developing countries were abundant in labour, especially in the rural areas, and so it made sense for them to specialize in primary commodities; while in the advanced industrial countries the shortage of labour but abundance of capital meant they should specialize in secondary goods. Thus was born the idea of 'an international division of labour'.

This belief in the combination of free markets and free trade dominates classical thinking and its modern day neoclassical writers. Given the theory of comparative advantage, there is every reason for specialization and trade to occur on a world scale. Moreover, as well as these static gains from specialization there are also further dynamic gains that can be achieved.

Trade not only potentially increases the amount of goods that can be produced but also encourages increases in productivity through economies of scale. Trade openness forces domestic companies to become more efficient because of the competitive threat and provides great opportunities to seek new markets. Flows of inward investment bring in much needed technical know-how and can also reduce costs. Outward flows of FDI enable firms to take advantage of market opportunities and cheaper resources and provide invaluable technical improvements to the host countries. There is clear evidence that countries which experience high growth rates are also those which are open to trade and investment.

The World Trade Organization offers a summary of the case for open trade (see <**www.wto. org/english/thewto_e/whatis_e/tif_e/fact3_e.htm**>).

> **Stop and Think**
> ....
> What are the benefits of trade and investment to an economy?

However, as we saw in Chapter 2, after 1945 both developed and developing countries chose to intervene in markets and to engage in trade protection policies. The crisis years of the 1970s provided the ideal conditions for the 'rediscovery' of neoclassical thinking. This was given expression in the political system with the coming to power of governments advocating these free market policies, especially in the US with Ronald Reagan and in the UK with Margaret Thatcher, and the securing of positions by neoclassical policy-makers within the two key supranational organizations of the World Bank and the IMF. From the late 1970s there was a discernible shift in the ideas coming from a range of national and supranational bodies, and perhaps this was encapsulated in 1995 with the World Trade Organization replacing GATT.

The 1989 *World Development Report* commented that:

> global integration in the flow of goods, services, capital and labor also brings enormous benefits. It promotes competition and efficiency, and it gives poor countries access to basic knowledge in medicine, science and engineering.

(World Bank 1989)

John Williamson sought to encapsulate neoclassical views in what could be seen as a menu for globalization and he coined the term the **Washington Consensus** to capture this (Williamson 1990). The World Bank in the report above characterized this approach as 'the market friendly approach'. For many it is these views that embody the term globalization.

The Washington Consensus can be seen as a 'wish list' of free market policies that Williamson argued would create the ideal environment in which countries would prosper and grow. The actual policies that comprised the Washington Consensus were summarized in Chapter 9. Where governments had directly controlled industries the call was for these not to be privatized and government activity should be directed at providing minimum social security safety nets and supporting education and health provision. Governments should aim to reduce spending so that they no longer run long-term budget deficits. In order to create the climate for entrepreneurship, tax breaks should be directed at those on high earnings and there should be deregulation especially in relation to finance markets.

While these policies were primarily aimed at establishing a free market domestically, equally important was the need for countries to achieve closer integration with the global economy. This would be achieved through allowing exchange rates to find their market levels, through encouraging an increase in both inward and outward flows of FDI, and, of course, through rapid trade liberalization.

A significant feature of this consensus was the belief that, not only were such policies appropriate for developed countries, but they were equally possible for the developing world. There was strong support for these polices as being the base on which the fast growing Southeast Asian Tiger economies has been built (discussed later in this chapter) and, when many Latin American countries began to suffer economic problems in the late 1980s and needed IMF support, this was granted only on condition that they adopt these polices through what was termed 'structural adjustment policies'.

The dramatic collapse of the Soviet Union and its former satellite Eastern European countries from 1989 only reinforced the view that there was only one way to progress and that was the 'road to the market'.

Socialist/Marxist views: globalization is bad—the dependency tradition

We saw in Chapter 2 that the person most associated with radical views of capitalism was Karl Marx. For Marx, 19th century capitalism posed what he saw as a central 'contradiction'. He was in total agreement with Smith that capitalism led to unprecedented growth but he argued that there was a fatal flaw. The social system of capitalism is very unequal, and access to resources and political power is concentrated in the hands of the few. Owners of capital are able to exploit their advantage. The source of this growth was the ability of capitalists to exploit their labourers and as growth and wealth increased the conditions of the workers would deteriorate. This is a central Marxist idea: that growth, rather than being combined and even, can be combined and uneven, providing the conditions for a socialist revolution where the workers would seize control of the economy and run things in the interests of the whole of society, not for the rich elites. However, such a revolution would only occur after a long period of capitalist expansion which would have succeeded in industrializing the economy.

Later on in his life he began to argue that world capitalism might lead to even greater problems for the workers in the less advanced areas because of their even weaker position as subjects of an imperial master. It was this central idea that began to provide the background for later radical writers to argue that capitalism on a world scale works differently in different parts of the global economy. This they referred to as **imperialism**. A world system had been developed that linked together the spatial levels of the economy and society in such a way as to lead to big divisions in the levels of income and wealth.

Imperial rivalry between nations had moved on from competitive rivalry between firms within the same nations. In order to obtain global competitive advantage, individual nations sought to protect their own large monopoly firms by imposing tariffs in home markets, but aggressively supporting their expansion in existing colonies and in newly acquired colonies with military support as required. It was inevitable then that war between the imperial powers would break out, as happened with the outbreak of the First World War in 1914.

We have seen in Chapter 2 and again in Chapter 9 that the inter-war period was one of unprecedented problems for the world economy, and throughout the world Marxist views about the instability of capitalism and its tendency to increase poverty amongst the many appeared to be true. It is certainly the case that the colonial powers were increasingly finding the strains of controlling their empires difficult.

After the Second World War a period of political decolonization occurred, but for many writers, primarily associated with the **dependency** tradition, the economic, political, and social structures that the postcolonial societies have inherited from the colonial past are so entrenched, that exposure to the world system will lead to their continuing to suffer exploitation.

One line of analysis points to the vastly unequal societies that exist in many Third World contexts. In many of these societies tiny elites control much of the business activities of the country and run these in their own interest often in collusion with foreign multinationals or foreign commercial interests. The legacy of **colonialism** left many economies with an economy that was geared to exporting primary commodities to the world market, and where the huge profits that were gained simply lined the pockets of the rich elites who owned these industries. In the dependency school this class of owners is referred to as being 'comprador capitalists'. A lot of this money was then invested abroad so stunting the widening of the industrial base of these countries.

Another strand of the dependency tradition points out that the system of world trade is anything other than free and often the trade rules are clearly discriminatory. The power of the leading countries is such that they dominate the supranational governing bodies and frame the rules in their own favour.

Structuralist writers—globalization could be good if ...

After the Second World War a new discipline of 'development economics' was born out of the belief that indeed the situation of the former colonies, or less developed countries (LDCs), as they now came to be called, was different, and that they could not pursue exactly the same path as the developed countries. Amartya Sen, Nobel Prize winner for Economics in 1998, characterized the nature of the task for these countries not as 'industrialization' but as 'late industrialization'. LDCs faced an already developed capitalist world and so in order to be fully integrated might need time to catch up and a different set of policies to do so. In other words the structure of the world economy meant that there wasn't a 'level playing field' between the developed and developing world, to use a more recent phrase. Furthermore, it was argued that the institutions and structures that are needed for the development of a market system were not yet present in many developing countries. These would need to be constructed before the integration of these economies into the world system. This led many countries to develop a set of distinctive non-market policies in order to rapidly industrialize their economies.

At the heart of this process was the government which sought to control and direct agriculture so that agricultural revenues could be used as a source of investment in industry. Many countries looked to the government to either own or at least have a substantial role in developing the industrial base and often this base revolved around key industries such as steel, iron and transport. Rather than engaging in export led expansion, import substituting industrialization (ISI) policies were implemented whereby domestic industries could be built up protected by a range of tariff and non-tariff barriers. Where countries allowed private enterprise to develop this was still controlled by the use of industrial licences provided by the government. To raise additional revenue for investment and to enable the buying in of foreign technology, countries used their natural resource commodities to raise foreign exchange but, in order to maximize the revenue streams, exchange rates were often overvalued and strict controls were kept on capital accounts to prevent money leaving the country.

The relative advantages and disadvantages of these models are still debated today but what is clear is that they were developed in response to genuine structural weaknesses in developing countries. Countries reliant on primary commodities tend to suffer from short term volatility in prices as well as a long run tendency of falling commodity prices. We explored the importance of price elasticity and income elasticity in Chapter 2. In the 1950s the Prebisch–Singer hypothesis was developed to explain the problem faced by primary goods exporters. Many developing countries do have a strength in terms of their economic base in that they can specialize in producing primary food commodities such as cotton, coffee, fish, and bananas; precious minerals such as diamonds; and rare earth metals increasingly in demand for use in a range of IT devices. As supply of these increases, given the nature of the highly inelastic demands for these goods, ironically, prices for the commodities can tumble putting pressure on the revenues of the producers.

This structural weakness means that there is a tendency for the growth of monopoly power in the industries which are producing the most valuable commodities as powerful players emerge through takeovers and mergers (or other means more or less lawful) so that they can exert control over the supply of the goods and hence control prices. These monopolies tend to be dominated by small groups of powerful nationals, closely connected with multinational corporate interests.

As well as this in terms of more basic primary foodstuffs as global incomes increase, the proportion of income spent on these declines as people spend proportionately more on manufactured goods and services. It is precisely to protect their own farmers from these harsh market forces that countries in the developed world intervene in agricultural markets so heavily through price support mechanisms, subsidies, and tariffs to keep out foreign imports. This makes it impossible for small scale food producers in the developing world to export and thus use trade as an engine of growth.

In relation to farmers, they may lack the necessary access to credit or information that enables them to take advantage of free markets. Joseph Stiglitz, Nobel Laureate for Economics in 2001, was awarded this prize for his work on market imperfections. People in markets have 'asymmetric' information; they do not each have access to all the information needed to make the best choice for them. In agricultural markets buyers can often control the market price by restricting supply and they have power to drive harder bargains because of their buying power. There may also be 'missing' markets. Farmers might not have access to credit or distribution facilities that would enable them to sell direct to markets but need to use intermediaries (see end of chapter case study).

While structuralist critics today would not necessarily agree with the precise way in which the problems above were addressed and that undoubted policy mistakes were made, they still argue that if the business environment is to be constructed in such a way as to allow globalization to bring about an inclusive growth and development then these structural weaknesses did need to be tackled.

Mini-Case 10.3 Cotton

Wool and then cotton sourced from what we now call the developing world but manufactured in textile mills played a hugely significant role in providing the profits that fuelled the British industrial revolution, so couldn't the same be the case for those countries with a competitive advantage in producing cotton, the most common raw material for the world textile industry today?

Around 15 million people in West Africa are dependent on cotton for their livelihoods. Cotton producers face fierce competition from across the world. The power of global markets does ensure that only the most competitive cotton farmers will survive and in turn guarantees cheap prices for consumers.

However, is this market fair? Cotton farmers face the collective buying power of very large multinational retailers who can afford to shop around for the cheapest supplies as well as the high levels of subsidy given to the cotton sectors in many developed countries, including the US government to its 2,000 cotton farmers (Fairtrade Foundation 2010). It is estimated that up to 5 million cotton farmers have gone out of a business as result of these subsidies. In 2003 the 'Cotton Four' (Benin, Chad, Mali, and Burkino Faso, which are very poor countries) requested that the Doha Trade round eliminate such subsidies and in 2004 the WTO declared that US cotton subsidies were indeed illegal, but despite this no agreement has yet been made to remove these and the Doha Trade talks have stalled (Beattie 2011). The Doha Trade round begun in November 2001 was meant to be the latest round of global trade talks to address, in particular, the problems faced by developing countries in relation to trade in general. But for many development activists, the WTO has simply failed to do this (Walker 2011). The negotiations have floundered as a result of differences between the US, the EU, and developing countries in relation to agriculture, industrial tariffs and non-tariff barriers, services, and trade remedies. Developing countries have sought to pressure the US and EU to remove agricultural subsidies and lower tariffs on the manufactured goods that they produce. The US and the EU have refused to budge on the issue of the support that they give for their farmers and have tried to gain access to the industrial and service sectors of the developing countries (Ferguson 2011). (*Sources:* Fairtrade Foundation 2010, Walker 2011, Beattie 2011, Ferguson 2011)

Question

What structures might prevent cotton producers in the developing world from achieving a high profit on their sales?

Structuralist writers argue that globalization can be made to work provided that the right economic and political structures are put in place. Here the challenge for policy-makers is to build the right type of internal and external environment in which businesses both at the national and international level can grow. For writers such as Stiglitz and Rodrik, the world described by the Washington Consensus is not realistic in the context of developing countries. Firstly, such a list does not consider the speed and order (or sequencing) with which countries should try to achieve these goals and, secondly and of crucial importance, the structures that might be needed to support these policy reforms are not there. In terms of speed and sequencing, this will very much depend on the unique circumstances of individual national business environments and it is not possible to have a 'one size fits all' approach.

Even before the 2008 global financial crisis there was a growing belief that, while the original Washington Consensus might describe where policy-makers would like the economic environments to end up, there was a need to recognize that in order to achieve this a raft of supporting structures needed to be put in place first, and that the precise routes taken in designing an appropriate economic environment for each country will be different.

Mini-Case 10.4   The developing Brazilian business environment

Brazil has always been the focus of much attention in relation to the nature of its business environment and as a role model for other developing countries. With a population of 196.6 million, it is Latin America's most populous country and is the 5th largest country in the world both in terms of area and population size. It is also the B in the BRICS (see Chapter 2) and in recent years its rapid economic growth had made it the 6th largest economy in the world ahead of the UK, although in 2012 a slowdown in its growth put it back into 7th place. As the host of the football World Cup Final in 2014 and the Olympic Games in 2016 it will continue to attract global attention.

Brazil is a country of great contrasts in terms of its rural and urban environments, the income gaps between its people and the nature of its economy with global highly competitive world class companies in services, manufacturing, and primary commodity production alongside inefficient protected industries and low productivity agriculture.

What is marked about the Brazilian business environment however, is this diversity. During the 1920s and 1930s Brazil was isolated from world trade as a result of the protectionist policies that were in place globally. It embarked on a policy of ISI and in the 1950s and 1960s this policy continued and also saw a high degree of state intervention in the running of the economy. It was also characterized by a lack of democracy as until the 1980s Brazil was subject to military rule. By the 1980s the Brazilian economy had been restructured away from a reliance on primary commodity goods towards a more highly diversified economy but faced a number of severe problems in relation to enormous income and wealth disparities, high debt, high inflation, and stagnant growth.

From the 1990s in tune with the Washington Consensus agenda, Brazil did embark on a programme of privatizations (albeit with the state often retaining control in the form of a golden share) and did seek to unilaterally reduce tariff barriers and other forms of trade protections as well as engaging in multilateral trade negotiations through the WTO. It entered into regional trading agreements such as MERCOSUR (a free trade area comprising Argentina, Paraguay, and Uruguay) and a range of bilateral agreements with its major trading partners who, in order of importance in terms of exports are the US, Argentina, China, and the EU. However, it still retains a relatively high level of trade protection measures.

In the 21st century Brazil experienced high rates of economic growth and export growth performance was high with over 50% of exports being in manufactured goods albeit with a high proportion of this being in mining ores and processed foods. This has been partly due to the boom in commodity prices until 2008 and to the high growth rates in China. Growth rates have suffered in the light of the global recession. There is a lively debate concerning the need to undertake both internal and external institutional reforms to make it easier to develop businesses in Brazil. In 2013 the World Bank ranked Brazil as being at 130 in its 'Doing Business' league table and Brazil is ranked at the bottom of the G20 nations in terms of trade openness.

Across the political divide there has been agreement about the need to address the social inequalities, and tax rates have increased to pay for social reforms. While inequality has been moderated, Brazil is still one of the most unequal countries in the world and criticisms have been made that too much of the welfare spending has been concentrated on the top 20% of income earners. One area that has proved difficult to reform has been land ownership and, given Brazil's reliance on natural resources, there are concerns that growth cannot be sustainable. (*Sources:* Todaro and Smith 2011, World Bank (2013a), World Bank (2013b), Rohter 2012, Canuto et al. 2013)

Questions

1. Why, if Brazil has a comparative advantage in natural resource commodities, has it not simply relied on a policy of export promotion of these commodities?

2. What problems were created by Brazil's model of ISI and large governmental control of industry?

3. Why does Brazil have such a high degree of income inequality?

4. What are the strengths/weaknesses of the structure of the Brazilian business environment?

◼ The 2008 global crisis and the end of the Washington Consensus

In practice, up until 2008 it had been difficult to resolve the arguments about the impact of globalization as all views can select data to 'prove' their case.

Average global income levels are rising across the world largely as a result of the rise of the Southeast Asian economies and the BRICS. Even in parts of Africa, which for so long has lagged far behind the rest of the world, economic growth has begun to rise. However, relative income inequality has been rising both within countries and between countries and for many critics this growing inequality represents a real challenge for the continuing growth of economies, not least because of the danger of social unrest. Such unrest can be seen in the protests of many terrorist groups across the world that feel a keen sense of injustice.

Paradoxically, as living standards on average across the world have been rising there is still the persistence of crushing absolute poverty. Collier has referred to this as being the 'Bottom Billion' (Collier 2007). It is to address this that the United Nations developed the Millennium Development Goals (MDGs) as a framework to monitor global progress on eliminating poverty. Only 3 of the 8 goals has been realized prior to the deadline of 2015. Others point to the global problems of the debt crisis, global climate change, the global Aids pandemic and other pandemics, and mass migrations. Free trade, it is argued, is not Fair Trade, with primary goods producers vulnerable and with the rigged rules caused by the power of the western dominated IMF, World Bank, WTO, and MNCs. In many parts of the world corruption is rife and serves only to line the pockets of the few.

Throughout the 1990s and into the new millennium there were many voices that expressed 'discontent' with a globalization based on neoliberal/neoclassical policies (Stiglitz 2003). Where countries moved too rapidly to adopt these policies (so-called 'shock therapy') output collapsed and many people fell through poorly provided social nets and ended up facing severe problems. In the rush to privatize and deregulate there was evidence of poor procedures for corporate governance and in too many cases outright corruption.

In relation to the impact of globalization it was argued that too many countries attempted to liberalize their financial markets too quickly and by allowing exchange rates to float freely exposed fragile economies to severe exchange rate fluctuations.

The 1997 Asian financial crisis appeared to provide evidence for this structuralist view as did the internal political upheavals in many of the countries of the former Soviet Union as well as Russia itself.

Prior to 1997, the Thai government on the back of years of sustained economic growth as a result of trade orientated policies sought to attract global capital investment by liberalizing its external capital accounts. This now meant that capital was free to move both in and out of Thailand without restrictions. The booming Thai economy attracted huge inflows of '**hot money**' which are flows of money driven by the speculative hopes that there are big returns to be made by investing in that country. The demand for the Thai currency, the Bhat, thus rose and so therefore did its exchange rate. This now meant that the price of Thai exports, which of course was the base of the underlying strength of the Thai economy, now rose such that the demand for Thai goods began to fall. The Thai government had been hoping to use the inflows of capital investment to boost the long term growth of the economy but in response to the short term falls in the profits of Thai exporters, short term confidence in the Thai economy faltered and this then caused a dramatic outflow of capital leading to a sudden depreciation in the value of the Bhat which caused widespread recession. This recession in Thailand had widespread effects across the region given the interlinked nature of the Southeast Asian economies.

In the former Soviet Union the 'shock therapy' of rapid market liberalization led to an unprecedented 40% fall in output in the early 1990s provoking political upheaval and a deterioration in health and well-being. Of particular concern in Russia was the privatization programme which resulted in the ownership of immensely valuable natural resource industries becoming very concentrated in the hands of a very small oligarchy. In the Middle East the 'Arab Spring' has been the result of a feeling by many that they have left behind by economic progress.

In Latin America despite some evidence of success, dissatisfaction began to emerge and resulted in the development of a 'Santiago Consensus' which argued for greater attention to be paid to inequality and social justice as well as access to education and, importantly, action to be taken to protect countries from global instability.

As we saw in Chapters 2 and 9, these twin problems were brought together when the excessive risk taking of the banking sector, in part fuelled by the desire to earn more from higher and higher bonuses, precipitated the financial crisis that first occurred in the US in 2007 and which then led to the global recession from 2008 onwards.

Writing in *The Nation* Stiglitz commented,

> This is not only the worst global economic downturn of the post-World War II era; it is the first serious downturn of the modern era of globalization.

(Stiglitz 2009)

For Stiglitz, the greatest challenge at the global level is to address the weakness of the international financial regulatory system that would leave countries exposed to external shocks. It was also clear that both within and between countries there was a great increase in the gap between those at the top of the earnings ladder and the vast majority of other people. His argument is not that globalization is harmful but that if it is based on a narrow view of the ability of free markets to deliver then there will be problems. In 2010 the UN sponsored *Stiglitz Report* sought to identify the best way of reforming the global economic system (Stiglitz 2010).

For Rodrik, as well as the free market policies as outlined in the original Washington Consensus, what was needed is an 'augmented Washington Consensus' to show the need for greater attention to be paid to the supporting structures. In order to ensure that businesses behave responsibly, especially in countries where perhaps democratic structures and media scrutiny are less developed then it is important to have robust and transparent corporate governance procedures in place and measures to root out corruption. Even before the financial crisis of 2008, Rodrik and Stiglitz were arguing for the need for stricter adherence to financial codes and standards underpinned by strong central banks freed from political interference. There was a recognition of the need for countries to regulate their capital accounts and exchange rates to avoid short term instability. At the social level it was argued that the benefits of growth would need to be more equitably shared through the provision of social safety nets and targeted poverty reduction policies (Rodrik 2004).

Sen argued for the need for countries to invest heavily in the social and physical infrastructure in such things as education, health, transport, food supply, and sanitation provision.

> The overall achievements of the market are deeply contingent on political and social arrangements.

> (Sen 1999, p. 142)

Stiglitz, in particular, has highlighted the problems that can occur if there is insufficient financial regulation and too liberal a policy regarding the movements of capital across borders and we will explore this further below. In his most recent book, Rodrik argues that until such domestic reforms have taken place and there is sufficient attention paid to the global institutional framework to ensure that the gains from globalization are more equally shared globalization will not work for everyone (Rodrik 2011).

For Acemoglu and Robinson (whose work on economic growth we highlighted in Chapter 3) it is precisely the institutional nature of many poor countries that explains their poverty but to explain why a country develops the particular institutions that it has we need to explore the nature of the political environment. Whilst the rich countries of the world have been able to develop 'inclusive' institutions that have enabled growth to occur and to be more broadly spread across the population, poor countries have developed 'extractive' institutions through which wealth is accrued by powerful controlling elites who enrich themselves and ensure that the business environment is run in their own interest. For Acemoglu and Robinson,

> while economic institutions are critical for determining whether a country is poor or prosperous, it is politics and political institutions that determine what economic institutions a country has.

> (Acemoglu and Robinson 2013)

Without political change, the fruits of globalization can simply be extracted by small controlling elites and lead to high degrees of inequality and corruption.

Such views have now moved to the centre of global economic policy-making. Meeting in London in 2009, the G20 was unanimous in its agreement that, if globalization was to deliver its benefits, there would need to be greater attention paid to supporting structures and the need for policy coordination.

> The old Washington consensus is over. Today we have reached a new consensus that we take global action together to deal with the problems we face, that we will do what is necessary to restore growth and jobs, that we will take essential action to rebuild confidence and trust in our financial system and to prevent a crisis such as this ever happening again.

> (Gordon Brown 2009)

That this was a G20 as opposed to a G8 summit was in itself significant as it heralded a shift in the balance of power between the rich developed and the now fast growing developing countries. In September 2010 at Pittsburg the G20 was officially recognized as the premier forum for international economic cooperation.

In order to build an inclusive world economy it is now recognized that, important as markets are, they need to be supported by effective global institutions to regulate trade and finance, and this requires international cooperation.

> We start from the belief that prosperity is indivisible; that growth, to be sustained, has to be shared; and that our global plan for recovery must have at its heart the needs and jobs of hard-working

families, not just in developed countries but in emerging markets and the poorest countries of the world too; and must reflect the interests, not just of today's population, but of future generations too. We believe that the only sure foundation for sustainable globalisation and rising prosperity for all is an open world economy based on market principles, effective regulation, and strong global institutions

(Official communiqué issued at the close of the London G20 Summit April 2009, Source: <www.londonsummit.gov.uk/resources/en/news/15766232/communique-020409>)

However, despite this rhetoric there has been little real progress in terms of global agreement as the developed countries each try to restore their own economies as a result of the 2008 crisis and, in terms of the World Trade Talks, the Doha Development Round is still to be concluded. (See <http://www.wto.org/english/tratop_e/dda_e/dda_e.htm> for information on their progress.)

■ Globalization and the newly industrialized countries

In the 1970s, the Southeast Asian economies of South Korea, Thailand, Malaysia, the Philippines, Hong Kong, Taiwan, and others experienced remarkable rates of economic growth. Characterized as the **newly industrialized countries** (NICs), their success has provoked intense debates as to why they have grown so fast. In recent years attention has been focused on the rise of the BRICS countries, as discussed in Chapter 2.

For neoclassical economists, the NICs and BRICS have shown the success of market liberalization and the triumph of their view of the world. Far from turning their backs on the global economy, these countries have embraced extensive opening up to world trade. In these countries trade truly has been the engine of growth.

However for structuralists, while it is the case that the NICs have used trade, this was not the only thing that they did and we need to consider the structural changes that they made *before* they felt able to benefit from trade openness. For Sen, it was important for these countries to have the social infrastructure in place before external openness. For Stiglitz, the road to the market has to be a gradual one and in particular cannot begin until the state has taken action to reduce poverty. For Rodrik, the role of the state in controlling which industries to build up was crucial as was the order in which market reforms are made. It is also important that the state puts in place the necessary institutions to control the possibility of fraud and corruption. Rodrik argues that there is a 'globalization paradox' in that if globalization is to deliver for all then there need to be international rules and national economies need to be able to retain controls over their capital accounts and exchange rates and determine their own social conditions (Rodrik 2011).

Dependency writers and activists have always been concerned about the nature of the type of development that has occurred in developing countries that have increasingly been exposed to globalization. Even in the supposed successful newly industrialized countries it is argued that they have been characterized as being examples of 'crony capitalism' with small elites dominating businesses and government. Corruption has been rife and there has been a widening in income gaps which has helped fuel ethnic and religious tension. In response to this, repressive governments have sought to control their people through denial of human rights. Another major highlight of the development in all these areas has been the environmental damage that has been created.

Mini-Case 10.5 Why has China grown so fast?

China, as the fastest growing economy in the world, is the prime example of how its particular road to the market has been carefully managed by the state. The Chinese themselves refer to their system as 'socialism but with Chinese characteristics'.

After the declaration of the Chinese Republic in 1947 China attempted to build its economy based on a system of state planning, rapid industrialization and collectivization of agriculture. The failure of the 'Great Leap Forward' between 1958 and 1961 showed the problems of relying on state planning and suppressing markets and for a time Mao Zedong, China's leader, came under criticism from fellow party members, one of whom was Deng Xiaoping. There were calls for the introduction of market reforms and, in order to defeat what he saw as being 'revisionist' forces, Mao launched the Cultural Revolution which lasted from 1966 to 1976. Essentially this was intended to achieve a wholesale cultural transformation of society to instil in people a respect for working for the common good rather than for achieving individual success. It also allowed for a widespread purge of all those people who Mao believed posed a threat to his position. One of those who suffered from these purges was again Deng Xiaoping.

On Mao's death in 1976 a party struggle broke out between those who defended the Cultural Revolution and those who criticized the economic decline that it had produced. By 1979 the latter group had won power under the leadership of Deng Xiaoping. Since 1979, China has embarked on an opening up and liberalization of its economy. China's strategy has been to allow the development of private enterprises geared to producing light industrial goods and consumer goods for export utilizing its skilled and well educated but cheap labour force. The ensuing transformation in its business environment has brought about a dramatic change in Chinese economic performance and allowed it to reach unprecedented rates of economic growth. Over 300 million people have been lifted out of poverty and there is now a large and growing middle class of urban professionals.

China's success could be seen as a vindication of the neoclassical view that free markets and openness to trade are the essential ingredients for success but, for structuralists, China shows the importance of paying attention to the institutional framework in which market reforms can be embedded (see Rodrik and Stiglitz). There is still a high degree of state control of the financial system, capital controls, and the Chinese currency (the RMB) is not convertible—the exchange rate is controlled by the government. Land in China remains in the ownership of the state, although farmers are able to sell surpluses above that produced for the state in the marketplace. The Communist Party retains a tight grip on all national, regional, and local governance structures and there remain tight social controls, the most prominent of which are the one child per family policy and the 'hukou' system of controlling internal migration.

For some critics such as Hutton and Acemoglu and Robinson, while this system has worked well in allowing China to fully exploit its comparative advantage in cheap labour, it will not continue to deliver as the economy grows and the increasingly restless middle classes desire more and more consumer goods. This will require a restructuring of the economy to allow more production for the domestic market and, in turn, this will require the development of a more dynamic range of businesses free from state regulation.

The 2008 financial crisis and the ensuing drop in demand for Chinese goods brought about by the global recession has encouraged the Chinese leadership to re-orientate the economy to target the domestic market. In 2013 the new party leadership of Xi Jinping, as President, and Li Keqiang laid out a vision for the next decade in order to realize what Xi has called the 'Chinese dream'. In this strategy he acknowledged the huge success of the previous years but also indicated that there have been problems in the Chinese model of development and that there is a need to pay attention to structural reform.

In particular, there is concern at the huge rise in income inequality, the rising gap between urban and rural incomes, corruption amongst state bureaucrats, and the rising levels of pollution in the urban areas.

(*Sources*: China Daily 2013, Hutton 2008, Acemoglu et al. 2013)

Questions

1. What is meant by the term 'socialism with Chinese characteristics'?

2. What are the problems that the Chinese party leadership feel need to be addressed?

Global ethics for the global business?

VALUES Any discussion of the impact of globalization must also encompass an analysis of the way in which global business activity itself impacts on the global environment and this must involve a discussion of ethics. For many the impact of globalization calls for a new way of thinking about business ethics that requires us to develop a framework to especially look at global ethics.

There is no argument that globalization can be seen as an increase in international activity of business but the question is whether this is simply an increase in quantity of these activities or that globalization represents a qualitative change. In other words, to what extent does globalization transform the nature of the impact of business activity and behaviour? Some commentators have chosen to argue that the use of the term globalization in relation to business as opposed to internationalization is an acceptance that indeed there has been a transformation in the qualitative nature of business activity across national frontiers.

> Implicit in the term 'globalization' rather than the term 'internationalization' is the idea that we are moving beyond the era of growing ties between nations and are beginning to contemplate something beyond the existing conception of the nation-state. But this change needs to be reflected in all levels of our thought.
>
> (Singer 2002)

Singer argues that globalization raises a new set of ethical questions that need to be considered once business operates across national boundaries. According to Singer, attitudes to justice are formed in relation to what people feel a fair society would be within their own national boundaries. In other words, that if people were to consider how to make the worst off richer it is only the worst off in their own societies that they may consider. Given the huge inequalities across societies, Singer argues that a just system defined within a national context can simply ignore the reality of injustices across national frontiers.

Stop and Think

If you were a global manager seeking to locate abroad and considering employment conditions:

Should you pay the local wage even if it is very low and workers complain it is barely enough for them and their families to live a decent life?

What if local health and safety standards are below the minimum standard in your home market but comply with local laws?

What is your responsibility if you use subcontractors who are employing child labour?

Employment practices

To what extent is it ethical for global firms to operate different employment practices across national boundaries? There will be differences in labour market conditions across nations but when does this become 'exploitation'? The Ethical Trading Initiative is an alliance of business, trade unions and voluntary groups that attempts to address these issues (<**http://www.ethicaltrade.org/about-eti**>).

In May 2013 a Bangladeshi textile factory which supplied many western retail outlets collapsed killing over 1,000 workers. The factory managers had been warned by employees that there were dangerous cracks appearing but, allegedly, had threatened to sack any anxious workers who might have refused to turn up for work (BBC News Asia).

While there are clear international laws forbidding the use of child labour, what if a western buyer purchases such goods from local manufacturers? Is this firm being unethical? If the people were not employed, what would they do? What responsibilities should businesses have to try to help these appalling social conditions?

Neither is this simply seen as a problem of the rich world exploiting the Third World. In the former, great disquiet has been expressed about the **outsourcing** of many activities and the effects on the domestic economy.

Many manufacturing, and increasingly service, activities are being outsourced to take advantage of lower costs. This has brought accusations of greed and exploitation, and yet outsourcing brings jobs and investment to developing countries. It is clear that far from resisting such outsourcing moves, developing countries positively welcome them, not least for providing the opportunity for local entrepreneurs to innovate and, in time, develop home-grown enterprises.

Whilst it is the case that wages are lower, compared to local wage rates they are much higher. Not only does this allow the incomes of the workers involved to rise but it provides a much needed boost to local markets through increased purchasing power.

For advocates of outsourcing this is a clear example of the principle of comparative advantage—taking advantage of the different skill levels in workforces around the world—but which will lead, in time, to a convergence of incomes, as higher incomes will help provide the taxes to boost the education systems in the developing world.

Human rights

Many countries do not have full protection of human rights and this presents dilemmas for companies. Is it acceptable for companies to operate in such countries even if they try to treat their employees fairly without trying to pressure the governments for change? What is 'fair' within a national context might not seem so in a global sense. How certain are companies that they are not lowering costs by taking advantage of poor human rights or even by their own actions undermining these?

Environment

⫸ **SPATIAL** We can here look at two spatial levels. Many countries do not have high levels of environmental legislation and so it is possible for businesses to benefit from not having to worry about costly environmental compliance. There are numerous examples of the effects of global business on local environments. One particularly devastating example was the explosion of the Union Carbide factory in Bhopal (see Mini-Case 10.6).

Global business itself is a major contributor to possible climate change through the impact of transport systems. Air travel is now the fastest rising contributor to carbon emissions, but shipping also is a major ingredient and all aspects of international trade have severe environmental effects. At the top of all this is the global energy industry which is responsible for the majority of greenhouse gases.

Last but not least there is the worry that growth might be achieved in the poorer countries of the world, not through the development of inclusive institutions that enable prosperity to be achieved by sustainable development but through the extractive institutions that simply exploit the natural resource environment and the majority of the people. Collier has warned of the dangers of a prosperity based on a 'plundered planet' (Collier 2011).

In 2013 Kofi Annan, the former Secretary General of the UN, introduced the annual Africa Progress Report which focused precisely on the need for African countries to address the problems

Mini-Case 10.6 The Bhopal disaster

On 2 December 1984 a Union Carbide plant in Bhopal, India began to leak a deadly gas, Methylisocyanite (MIC).

It is estimated that 8,000 local inhabitants lost their lives that night and that the long term consequences of the leak have resulted in the deaths of over 20,000 people and that over 100,000 people have suffered long term ill health. This remains the worst industrial disaster of all time.

The plant was operated by Union Carbide-India, which was controlled by the American Union Carbide Corporation. Union Carbide itself (now part of Dow Chemicals) although acknowledging that this was indeed a 'terrible tragedy', claims the explosion must have been the result of deliberate sabotage and it feels that it acted in a responsible way to compensate and help clean up the environment (see <www.bhopal.com/irs.htm>).

For critics this was a disaster waiting to happen as there was inadequate provision for safety at the plant. In the aftermath it is argued that Union Carbide's response to the tragedy was to offer too little in terms of compensation and support for the victims and that there was complicity from Indian civil servants in attempting to down play the long term effects (<www.bhopal.net>).

Question

What are the difficulties in allocating responsibility for safety failures across multinational companies?

of losing so many revenues from resource extraction to corruption and tax evasion. In the case of the Democratic Republic of the Congo, it is estimated that twice the annual budgets spent on education and health are lost to the government through tax evasion (Africa Progress Report 2013).

Abuse of market power

What responsibilities do companies have when selling their products in global markets? Tobacco companies have moved sales to the developing world as health concerns and litigation increase in the developed world. Pharmaceutical companies are accused of profiteering from selling drugs at high prices in the developing world and denying desperate people access to the medicines they need by abusive use of copyright.

Attitudes to graft and corruption

Global business will be exposed to environments where corruption and graft might be prevalent. Operating across national legal systems can exacerbate the degree to which corruption and graft are possible and harder to police or detect.

▪ Looking ahead

While the first decade of the 21st century started with a great sense of optimism about the prospects of growth across the global economy, it ended with the gloom and despondency of the global recession. There is now widespread recognition of the structural weaknesses both at the global level and at the national level in many developing countries. It would appear that there is general agreement about the need to take concerted global action to create the necessary international and financial architecture required and all the talk now is of the need to build an inclusive world economy. However, in response to the crisis individual countries are primarily seeking to address their own problems in their own way and the global action along the lines of that suggested by the Stiglitz Report seem unlikely.

There is recognition in much of the developed world of the need to help to reduce the debts of many of the poorest countries and to ally this support to gaining a commitment in these countries of the need for greater transparency and democracy. At the supranational level there is a rebalancing of power with many less developed countries joining together to counter the huge bargaining power of the developed world.

The growth of the BRICS will continue to absorb much attention. East and South Asia are now the new growth poles in the global economy, but Latin America has grown as well, and there has been strong growth in some African countries.

However, the history of globalization shows that this cannot be taken for granted and there can be contradictory tendencies. There is widespread reluctance in the financial sector toward regulations and curbs on bonuses, and without global cooperation it is easy for the international financial system to avoid any particular national system of regulation.

At current rates of growth, Africa will not achieve the millennium development goals and there are still huge tensions to be resolved especially between the developed and developing world. In 2012 the Secretary General of the UN established the High Level Panel of Eminent Persons chaired by the presidents of Indonesia and Liberia and the British Prime Minister to develop the post-2015 Millennium Development Goals and this reported in May 2013.

There are still real obstacles that lie in the path of greater trade integration and there is the possibility that the world could fragment into regional trading agreements if agreements on a world scale cannot be achieved (see Chapter 13).

▥ **Summary**

- Globalization links together all the spatial levels of business activity. It has grown as a result of the expansion of capitalism on a worldwide scale.

- There are competing views as to the effects of this expansion. For neoclassical/neoliberal writers, globalization is good in that it will enable worldwide prosperity to grow and the gap between developed and undeveloped countries to decrease. For radical writers globalization is bad in that it will actually increase inequality both within and between countries and this will lead to instability and conflict. For structuralist writers globalization can be a force for the good if policy-makers put in place the institutions both at national and supranational levels to correct market imperfections and ensure good governance.

- Linking the strategic response of firms to globalization and its impact are the ethical dimensions of global activity. Analysis of the impact of globalization does involve the application of global ethics across the range of global issues.

Case Study: Is trade the engine of growth?

Many of the poorest countries in the world are endowed with a range of natural mineral and agricultural resources which are potentially very valuable on global markets. However, all too often their exports are very dependent on a very narrow range of these commodities and there is a range of problems that they face when seeking to exploit the potential of these commodities. It is argued that all too often the 'blessing' of the resource endowment can then become a 'resource curse'.

For all such basic commodities ranging from coal, oil, copper, raw earth metals, and foodstuffs (such as coffee, tea, bananas and peanuts) we can distinguish between the 'downstream' business of production where producers

Less developed countries and commodity production

	Low value	Downstream
Farming/extraction		
Distribution		
Processing	↓	↓
Brand development		
Marketing		
Distribution		
Selling		
	High value	Upstream

struggle to gain adequate incomes and the 'upstream' commercial activities where profits are high.

In the case of coffee, coffee producers have to face fluctuations in prices which makes planning for the future and decisions about investing difficult. On top of this is the constant uncertainty posed by climatic factors and the threat of plant disease. In 2012/3 Central America suffered one the worst outbreaks of coffee leaf rust in recorded history. PROMECAFFE (a body comprising the coffee authorities of Guatemala, El Salvador, Honduras, Costa Rica, Panama, the Dominican Republic, and Jamaica) reported that this resulted in a loss of $548 million and 441,000 direct job losses across the region (ICO 2013).

The upstream end of the coffee market is dominated by four coffee roasters: Kraft, Nestlé, Procter & Gamble, and Sara Lee, each having coffee brands worth US$1 billion or more in annual sales. If we add in the German company, Tchibo, they buy almost half the world's coffee beans each year. The coffee processors and retailers add value to their products by processing and constantly seeking to establish strong brands through ever more sophisticated marketing and product development. This modern form of food production is often referred to as 'agribusiness'. Agribusiness involves a food chain whereby the food producers or farmers are often in fierce competition. On the other hand, upstream food is processed and branded by a relatively few food companies. These companies spend huge sums in developing new types of food products which are then vigorously marketed. These products are then sold and the structure of the food retailing industry is dominated by a few very large supermarket chains. In the last twenty years there has been a big increase in the demand for coffee in the developed world as incomes have risen and tastes have changed. There has also been the rise of the large global coffee shops such as Starbucks, Costa Coffee, and Café Nero although as markets become mature the rate of growth has been slowing. However, this is now being compensated for by the fast rise in the growth of coffee shops in countries such as China and India.

While potentially profits on the selling of coffee at the upstream end of the process are very high, the incomes of many coffee farmers are very low and in many cases farmers struggle to stay in business. This same problem can be seen in a wide range of natural commodity markets and has provoked a lively debate as to how LDCs with a dependence on a narrow range of resource commodities can best capture the value from these and at the same time restructure and diversify their economies to avoid an over-reliant dependence on these commodities.

The structuralist approach requires a look at the structural problems at the downstream end of the value chain. There may be a lack of basic infrastructure such as roads or transport to local markets, or support to develop technology. Lack of credit or information about prices leaves farmers open to possible exploitation by moneylenders or the ability of buyers to drive down prices. At the global level the market failure is also a manifestation of the problems of the simple belief in the principle of comparative advantage. The concentration of economic activity in a narrow range of commodities has not been natural, but has been as a result of the creation of the historical imprint of colonization or in more recent times the encouragement by the international institutions to specialize in such agricultural products. In some cases this has led to oversupply as a result of global competition. The logic of the market would be for such farmers to diversify into something else, but this will require support from the government in terms of education and training or in terms of ensuring the availability of credit. What is needed then is for countries to seek ways of capturing the value of their commodities as well as seeking ways to diversify their economies and this will require a range of domestic and global structural reforms (UNCTAD 2012b).

Coffee initiatives such as Fair Trade have allowed farmers to retain more of the value of their produce. Indeed, some upstream producers have successfully applied for Fair Trade status to be applied to their brands. At the global level the ICO seeks to maintain cooperation between producers to stabilize prices and raise incomes. Many MNCs are keen to be seen to be operating ethically and according to global ethical codes. One example of this is the Extractive Industries Transparency Initiative which aims to ensure that there is transparency of payments from natural mining resources (see <www.eiti.org>).

Dependency writers argue that all too often the export sectors are controlled either by multinational interests or 'comprador capitalists' so that even where profits are generated they do not get redistributed to the wider population. In recent years attention has been focused on the rising tendency for foreign interests in the form of MNCs, hedge funds, and even countries to acquire valuable agricultural land in the poorest places of the world. This could be justified as a way of bringing in much needed investment but for radical critics it is simply a 'land-grab' (Pearce 2012).

It is clear, then that in order for globalization to work for LDCs there is more that needs to be done than to simply seek to exploit their comparative advantages from trade and in some cases an over-reliance on trade can be detrimental to the development of these countries. In order for trade to deliver, it is vital to pay attention to the broader domestic and global conditions in which trade takes place and to ensure that global trade policy is aligned with the overall domestic economic strategy of a country.

Questions

1. Why is it argued that the 'free market' in coffee is not fair?

2. Why do the coffee roasters have different market power than the farmers?

3. What are the 'structural' weaknesses that affect coffee farmers?

4. Describe the steps involved in the conversion of coffee from bean to finished product.

5. Why are countries which have a dependence on a narrow range of export commodities in a vulnerable position?

6. What types of structural reform are needed if such countries are to be able to benefit from globalization?

Review and discussion questions

1. What are the strengths, weaknesses, opportunities, and threats presented to an individual country by globalization? How might such a SWOT analysis differ between a developed and a developing country?

2. What is 'outsourcing'? Which stakeholders are affected by this and how would we decide if such a tendency is to be welcomed?

3. What are the advantages and disadvantages of international trade?

4. In what ways can the global marketplace not be 'ethical' and what are the obstacles that might prevent it being so?

Assignments

1. Using the British confectionery market as an example, analyse the impact of globalization on the range of stakeholders involved.

2. Visit the website of the G20 and summarize the main findings and predictions about the current state of the global environment and the prospects for global economic growth.

3. Choose three NICs and compare and contrast the way in which they have taken advantage of globalization.

Further reading

Acemoglu, D. and Robinson, J. A. (2013) *Why Nations Fail: The Origins of Power, Prosperity and Poverty* (London: Profile Books). *An accessible and highly readable book which argues that in order to understand how nations grow (or don't grow) depends crucially on developing the most appropriate set of institutions.*

Bhagwati, J. (2007) *In Defense of Globalization* (Oxford: Oxford University Press). *A passionate rebuttal of the arguments of the critics of globalization who argue that it works against the interests of the poor.*

Rodrik, D. (2011) *The Globalization Paradox: Democracy and the Future of the World Economy* (New York: W.W. Norton). *This book explores the potential paradox of globalization and outlines the type of national and global policy responses that are needed so that globalization can ensure inclusive growth.*

Stiglitz, J. (2010) *Freefall and the Sinking of the Global Economy* (London: Allen Lane). *An analysis of the current global economic crisis from an ex-chief economist of the World Bank. He argues that this has been the result of too much faith being invested in free markets and that the balance between state and markets should be restored.*

Stiglitz, J. (2002) *Globalization and its Discontents* (London: Penguin). *In theory, globalization should improve living standards for all, but the way in which globalization is managed, especially at the global level, needs to be reformed and he is particularly critical of the role of the IMF and World Bank in promoting free markets without putting in place the rules and regulations to ensure fairness.*

Friedman, T. (2006) *The World is Flat* (London: Penguin). *This book came to be seen as the classic exposition of how businesses can benefit from a globalized world.*

Test your understanding of this chapter with online questions and answers, explore the subject further through web exercises, and use the web links to provide a quick resource for further research. Go to the Online Resource Centre at
<www.oxfordtextbooks.co.uk/orc/wetherly_otter/2>

Useful websites

The following websites contain a host of information presenting the view from the official supranational organizations and a wealth of statistical data:
<www.worldbank.org>
<www.imf.org>
<www.unctad.org>
<www.wto.org>

This site publishes postings from some of the most prominent global commentators:
<www.project-syndicate.org>

The following websites offer a critical view of the challenges of globalization:
<www.globalisationanddevelopment.com>
<www.globalwitness.org>
<www.globalwatch.org>
<www.eiti.org>
<www.ethicaltrade.org>
<www.globalethics.org>
<www.oxfam.org>
<www.worldwatch.org>

References

Africa Progress Report (2013) 'Equity in Extractives' (accessed 12 May 2013) <www.africaprogresspanel.org/en/publications/africa-progress-report-2013-holding/>

Acemoglu. D. and Robinson, J.A. (2013) Why Nations Fail—The Origins of Power, Prosperity and Poverty (London: Profile Books).

BBC News Asia (2013) 'Bangladesh factory collapse death toll passes 1000' (accessed on 12 May 2013).

BBC News (2009) 'EU cuts tariffs in a bid to end Banana Wars' (accessed 2 April 2013) <http://news.bbc.co.uk/1/hi/business/8391752.stm>

Beattie, A. (2011) 'Hope Fails for Accord at Doha Talks', The Financial Times (accessed on 8 April 2013) <www.ft.com/intl/cms/s/0/becebdda-9ce7-11e0-8678-00144feabdc0.html#axzz2Q3VYfsIB>

Brown, Gordon, (2009), Closing speech at the London G20 Summit in April 2009, this speech can be accessed via Ebsco Host Connection at <http://connection.ebscohost.com/c/speeches/45565733/g20-summit-london>

Canuto, O., Cavallari, M., Guilherme Reis, J. (2013) 'Brazilian Exports Climbing Down a Competitiveness Cliff', Policy Research Working Paper 6302, The World Bank Poverty Reduction and Economic Management Network (accessed on 12 April 2013) <www-wds.worldbank.org/servlet/WDSContentServer/WDSP/IB/2013/01/07/000158349_20130107091437/Rendered/PDF/wps6302.pdf>

Cassidy, N. (2009) 'Banana Wars: The Fruits of World Trade' (accessed 2 April 2013) <http://news.bbc.co.uk/1/hi/business/8413979.stm>

China Daily (2013) '"Chinese Dream" is Xi's Vision', China Daily, 18 March.

Collier, P. (2007) The Bottom Billion (Oxford: Oxford University Press).

Fairtrade Foundation (2010) 'The Great Cotton Stitch Up' (accessed on 4th April 2013) <www.fairtrade.org.uk/includes/documents/cm_docs/2010/f/2_ft_cotton_policy_report_2010_loresv2.pdf>

Ferguson, I. (2011) 'World Trade Organization Negotiations: The Doha Development Agenda', in CRS Report for Congress (Congressional Research Service) (accessed on 8 April 2013) <www.fas.org/sgp/crs/misc/RL32060.pdf>

Hobsbawm, E. (1987) The Age of Empire (London: Abacus).

Hutton, W. (2008) The Writing on the Wall—China and the West in the 21st Century (London: Hachette Digital).

ICO (2013) 'Coffee Market Report March 2013' (accessed 6 April 2013) <www.ico.org/documents/cy2012-13/cmr-0313-e.pdf>

Moeller, S. (2012) 'Case Study Kraft's takeover of Cadbury', The Financial Times (accessed 4 April 2013) <www.ft.com/intl/cms/s/0/1cb06d30-332f-11e1-a51e-00144feabdc0.html#axzz2Oc6O0txU>

Pearce, F. (2012) The Land Grabbers: The New Fight over Who Owns the Earth (London: Transworld Publishers).

Rodrik, D. (2011) The Globalization Paradox: Democracy and the Future of the World Economy (New York: W.W. Norton).

Rodrik, D. (2004) 'Growth Strategies', Department of Economics, Johannes Kepler University of Linz (accessed 5 May 2013) <www.econ.jku.at/papers/2003/wp0317.pdf>

Rohter, L. (2012) *Brazil on the Rise* (Basingstoke: Palgrave Macmillan).

Sen, A. (1999) *Development as Freedom* (Oxford: Oxford University Press).

Singer, P. (2002) *One World—the Ethics of Globalization* (New Haven: Yale University Press).

Stiglitz, J. (2010) *The Stiglitz Report: Reforming the International Financial and Monetary Systems in the Wake of the Recent Global Crisis* (New York: The New Press).

Stiglitz, J. (2009) 'A Global Recovery for a Global Recession', *The Nation*, 24 June.

Stiglitz, J. (2003) *Globalization and its Discontents* (London: Penguin).

Todaro, M. P. and Smith, S. C. (2011) *Economic Development*, Chapter 1, Case Study 1 (Harlow: Pearson).

UNCTAD (2012a) 'Infocomm, Commodity Profile Banana' (accessed 2 April 2013) <**www.unctad.info/en/Infocomm/AACP-Products/COMMODITY-PROFILE—Banana/**>

UNCTAD (2012b) *Enabling the Graduation of LDCs: Enhancing the Role of Commodities and Improving Agricultural Productivity* (New York: United Nations) (accessed 10 April 2013) <**www.unctad.org/en/PublicationsLibrary/aldc2012d1_en.pdf**>)

University of Birmingham (2013) 'Kraft—Cadbury Takeover: Does National Ownership Matter' (accessed 4 April 2013) <**www.birmingham.ac.uk/news/latest/2013/01/Jan-30-KraftCadbury-Takeover-Does-National-Ownership-Matter.aspx**>

Walker, A. (2011) 'How the WTO has failed developing nations on Poverty Matters Blog', *The Guardian* (accessed on 10 April 2013) <**www.guardian.co.uk/global-development/poverty-matters/2011/nov/14/wto-fails-developing-countries**>

Williamson, J. (2000) 'What Washington Means by Policy Reform', in Williamson, J. (ed.) *Latin American Adjustment: How Much Has Happened?* (Peterson Institute for International Economics) (accessed 12 May 2013) <**www.iie.com/publications/papers/paper.cfm?researchid=486**>

Wood (2012) 'Nervous Cadbury settles in with a new owner as Kraft splits itself into two', *The Guardian* (accessed 4 April 2013) <**www.guardian.co.uk/business/2012/nov/04/nervous-cadbury-another-new-owner-mondelez**>

World Bank (1989) *Annual Development Report* (Washington DC: World Bank).

World Bank (2004) 'Globalization, International Trade, and Migration', in *Beyond Economic Growth: An Introduction to Sustainable Development* XII, p. 1 (World Bank Group) (accessed 12 May 2013) <**www.worldbank.org/depweb/english/beyond/global/chapter12.html**>

World Bank (2013a) *Brazil Overview* (accessed on 2 April 2013) <**www.worldbank.org/en/country/brazil/overview**>

World Bank (2013b) *Ease of Doing Business in Brazil* (accessed on 2 April 2013) <**www.doingbusiness.org/data/exploreeconomies/brazil/**>

Chapter 11
Does business have too much power?

Paul Wetherly

Learning objectives

When you have completed this chapter you will be able to:

- Understand the concept of power and how it relates to business and the market.
- Understand the reasons for the participation of business as an actor in the political arena.
- Understand the political process as a play of interests and power involving interaction between business, government, labour, and **civil society organizations**.
- Recognize and assess the effectiveness of methods used by business and other groups to influence government decisions.
- Evaluate evidence from case studies and examples relating to the political influence of business.

THEMES

The following themes of the book are especially relevant to this chapter

➤ **DIVERSITY** OF BUSINESS

Business participates in the political process through companies representing their own interests and/or through associations representing collective business interests. There may be important differences of political values and interests within the business community.

➤ **COMPLEXITY** OF THE ENVIRONMENT

Corporate power needs to be understood not just in relation to the political process but in the economy and society as well.

➤ **VARIETY** OF SPATIAL LEVELS

Globalization has altered the relationship between business and government, arguably enhancing the power of the former.

➤ **DYNAMIC** ENVIRONMENT

Business influence in the political process is not constant but varies over time—it has ups and downs.

➤ **INTERACTION** BETWEEN BUSINESS AND THE ENVIRONMENT

Business is involved in a relationship with a range of stakeholders that seek to influence decisions. A particularly important relationship is with government. Because it is affected by government decisions, business has an interest in influencing these decisions to its own advantage.

> **STAKEHOLDERS**

The range of actors in the political process with which business has to contend can be understood as stakeholders.

> **VALUES**

The values and interests of business have to compete with those of other groups in society.

▥ Introduction

Our broad definition of business (Chapter 1) highlighted that the essential business activity is production of goods and services to meet the needs and wants of consumers. In the private sector business has been defined in terms of private ownership, competition, and the profit motive—private sector businesses operate in a competitive market in which they produce commodities for sale in order to realize a profit.

This chapter will examine another aspect of the business environment and of business behaviour and performance—the exercise of power. We will look at who has power in a market or capitalist system, with a particular focus on a globalizing world and the operations of large multinational corporations (MNCs). This involves looking at the market not simply as a system of voluntary exchange (buying and selling) but also in terms of relationships of power. A key question is: does business have too much power (or too little)?

▥ What is power? What's it got to do with business?

When we think about who has power in modern Britain we might think first of government and the political process (Chapter 4)—political power. UK governments exercise power through their capacity, within the parliamentary system, to make and enforce rules or laws that can affect all aspects of our lives and the future of the country, including laws governing business and economic life. Although national governments remain the key locus of political power in this form, they operate within a framework of multi-level governance. For UK governments the most important aspect of this is membership of the EU with its law-making capacity. A conventional view is that power is in the hands of elected politicians such as members of national legislatures (e.g. UK MPs) or of the European Parliament (MEPs), Prime Ministers and Presidents, or officials such as members of the European Commission. However, power is more complicated than this view suggests.

- First, in a democracy, power and sovereignty are supposed to be in the hands of 'the people' and politicians are elected by us to serve our interests. Through elections we get to choose who is 'in power' and we can get rid of them if we don't think they are doing a good job (Chapter 4).

- Second, there are limits to government power and it cannot always enforce its decisions or achieve its objectives. Passing a law is one thing, but compliance and enforcement are different matters. A law can be quite widely flouted and difficult to enforce, such as the UK ban on using hand-held mobile phones while driving. People may be able to exploit legal 'loopholes' enabling them to obey the letter of the law but defy its spirit or intention, as with tax avoidance. Governments have limited resources and limited knowledge, so sometimes they cannot carry out policies that they favour or their policies do not work. Austerity measures favoured by European governments were justified by the arguments that they were required to reduce government deficits and debts (the cupboard was empty) and that they would lead to economic recovery. Critics argued that austerity wasn't necessary because governments could create more resources through borrowing, and that it didn't work because the 'knowledge' about the economy on which it was based was faulty.

- Third, although we might refer to the Prime Minister as 'running the country', it is clear that power is also exercised in other ways in society and by other organizations or groups, including business. This means that governments may face pressure from other groups and have to negotiate with them, may have to deal with resistance to their policies, and may find it advantageous to cooperate with other organizations in order to achieve their objectives.

Mini-Case 11.1   The world's most powerful people

SPATIAL LEVEL Who do you think are the most powerful people in the world today? How would you rank business leaders in relation to leaders of governments?

Forbes magazine produces a regular list of the world's most powerful people—those 'who truly run the world' (*Forbes* 2012). Its 2012 list contains just 71 names from an estimated global population of 7.1 billion (i.e. a tiny elite comprising one very powerful person for every 100 million people on the planet). Of course, there are very many other people who exercise power in some form which seems inconsequential on a global scale but which can impinge on our daily lives. US President Barack Obama might be the most powerful person in the world, making decisions that have national and global consequences, but if you work as a barrista in a Starbucks outlet you might feel that your manager exercises more immediate power in your day-to-day life.

The top 20 from Forbes' list are shown in Table 11.1. Of these, 14 are politicians and officials from the government sector as might be expected, but 4 of the 20 most powerful people are from the corporate sector. Within the complete list 28 (two-fifths) are from the corporate sector, including many familiar global brands such as Walmart, Google, Exxon Mobil, News Corp, Amazon, Apple, Goldman Sachs, Toyota and Microsoft.

The list is not definitive and the method used may be open to question, but the table amply makes the point that power is in the hands of business as well as government, and therefore that the relationship between business and government is one that involves power.

Power can be understood in terms of being able to make decisions that affect what happens. These decisions will usually involve being able to command the actions of other people carrying out these decisions, and the consequences of the decisions may affect many people. The Forbes study uses a four-dimensional concept of power, as follows:

1. *power over lots of people* e.g. 'Michael Duke, CEO of Wal-Mart Stores, employs two million people'

2. *financial resources* e.g. GDP (government sector), a company's assets and revenues (corporate sector)

3. *power exercised in multiple spheres* e.g. 'New York Mayor Michael Bloomberg has power because he's a politician, because he's a billionaire, because he's a media magnate, and because he's a major philanthropist.'

4. *active exercise of power* i.e. not just having the capacity to exercise power but actually doing so (*Forbes* 2012).

This view of power emphasizes wealth as the key resource that can be translated into power, and also highlights being able to command other people's actions (power over people). Thus, wealthy individuals tend to be powerful compared to those without wealth, as shown by the presence on the list of Bloomberg and Gates. But although personal wealth can be a source of power, the list shows that the most powerful people exercise power not in their personal capacity but through the positions they occupy within institutions. In other words, it is institutions in the government and corporate sectors that are powerful. Barack Obama is only the most powerful person during his term of office, after which he might depart the political scene and drop out of the list (though ex-President Bill Clinton is still active politically and figures at number 50).

The list shows that corporations are intrinsically powerful entities, meaning that they exercise power as part-and-parcel of their normal commercial activities. For example, Walmart exercises power over people as an employer of two million workers. Of course, Michael Duke does not directly tell people

Table 11.1 The most powerful people in the world

Rank	Name / title	Organization
1	Barack Obama / President	United States
2	Angela Merkel / Chancellor	Germany
3	Vladimir Putin / President	Russia
4	Bill Gates / Co-Chair	Bill & Melinda Gates Foundation
5	Pope Benedict XVI / Pope	Roman Catholic Church
6	Ben Bernanke / Chairman	Federal Reserve, United States
7	Abdullah bin Abdul Aziz al Saud / King	Saudi Arabia
8	Mario Draghi / President	European Central Bank
9	Xi Jinping / General Secretary	Communist Party, China
10	David Cameron / Prime Minister	United Kingdom
11	Carlos Slim Helu & family / Honorary Chairman	América Móvil
12	Sonia Gandhi / President	Indian National Congress, India
13	Li Keqiang / Vice Premier	China
14	Francois Hollande / President	France
15	Warren Buffett / CEO	Berkshire Hathaway
16	Michael Bloomberg / Mayor	New York City, United States
17	Michael Duke / CEO	Wal-Mart Stores
18	Dilma Rousseff / President	Brazil
19	Manmohan Singh / Prime Minister	India
20	Sergey Brin / Cofounder, Director Of Special Projects	Google

Source: Forbes 2012.

stacking shelves in Asda stores in the UK what to do on a daily basis, but he is at the peak of a managerial hierarchy which connects him with managers in those stores. Corporations might also be able to exercise power over other stakeholders such as suppliers and consumers through contractual relationships. In all of these cases an important aspect of power exercised by corporations is bargaining power. But bargaining power is two-way, and sometimes corporations have to respond to power exercised by their stakeholders.

Power is an intrinsic aspect of normal corporate behaviour, but corporations can also seek to exercise power in other spheres, particularly in relation to government.

> **Stop and Think**
>
> How is wealth translated into power? Does this alter the idea that power is exercised by voters through democratic elections?

Corporate power

The market can be understood not just as a system of production and exchange but also as a framework of economic power. Because the market is based on private ownership it places power in the hands of businesses which are able to make decisions about the use of resources. The exercise of power by business is certainly an important matter of public interest and concern because its consequences are far-reaching, affecting individuals, communities, and whole societies. For example, in 2013 the biopharmaceutical firm AstraZeneca announced that it would transfer its research activities from Alderley Park in Cheshire to a new research and development centre in Cambridge. This was a commercial decision but, at the same time, an exercise of the power to decide the location of investment and employment. There would be a loss of seven hundred jobs, many employees would be required to move, and there would be a significant impact on the local economy and community in Cheshire (BBC 2013). Due to its consequential nature, Luger likens corporate power to a form of 'private government', suggesting that business decisions have an impact on society that rivals that of government. Luger defines 'corporate power' as multi-faceted, encompassing a range of decisions:

> the power over what is produced, how these products are distributed, how work is organized, which skills workers need to develop, which advertising images are used to shape consumer consciousness, what kind of technology is developed, and what kinds of pollutants are created. Corporate power shapes the distribution of income, the conditions and location of employment, and thus the future of communities and nations.
>
> (Luger 2000, p. 3)

As well as using resources to decide what happens, such as deciding what is produced and where, at which locations to open or close plants, Luger's definition also refers to the capacity to influence or control the behaviour of others, specifically in relation to employees and consumers. The employment relationship is one of authority in which the employer's 'right to manage' is utilized in order to ensure labour productivity and business profitability, including 'how work is organized' and the skills exercised by employees. In relation to consumers, Luger suggests that a type of power exercised by business is the capacity to influence or shape consumer preferences through persuasive advertising.

▦ Political power and corporate power

▶ INTERACTION ▶ STAKEHOLDERS Thus in a modern society like Britain there are two distinct but related frameworks for distributing power: the political system (democracy) and the economic system (the market). Political power, exercised by government, involves centralized collective decisions made on behalf of the whole society and ostensibly in the public interest. The government can, subject to parliamentary approval, make and enforce laws that are binding on all members of society, but it can also make decisions about the allocation of resources by public sector organizations and through decisions about taxation and public spending. For example, in January 2013 the UK government announced the proposed route of the second phase of the high-speed rail project (HS2) linking Birmingham with Manchester and Leeds (the earlier phase 1 proposal was to link London and Birmingham). Subject to the necessary legislation being enacted by Parliament, this involved the power to spend public (i.e. taxpayers') money on the construction of the railway and to override objections to the route from thousands of affected residents, councils, and other organizations in the name of the national interest (BBC 2013a).

Corporate power, by contrast, involves decentralized private decisions in the interests of specific businesses and their owners. These decisions are decentralized in that, although corporate power 'shapes the location of employment' and individual corporations, such as AstraZeneca, can make decisions that affect thousands of employees, the overall spatial pattern of employment within the economy is the outcome of separate decisions by a large number of firms. Thus, a contrast between government power and corporate power is that in the former it is relatively easy to pinpoint who is in charge of government. We can say that responsibility for political decisions in the UK rests with the Prime Minister and members of the Cabinet. In the world of business, on the other hand, although we can easily identify large and powerful corporations and CEOs (such as Michael Duke and Walmart), no one is in overall charge (Kay 2004). Not even the largest companies are able to control what happens in particular markets since decisions are made in conditions of uncertainty in which competition determines which experiments are successful or unsuccessful—a process described by Kay as 'disciplined pluralism'. For example, it is impossible to predict the future of the car and what type of fuel system will replace the internal combustion engine. No single company, however large, is able to control this. However, Luger emphasizes that the whole framework of corporate power has consequences for society that are as important as those of government decisions.

Another important contrast concerns the accountability of government power and corporate power. Whereas, in a democracy, political power is in the hands of 'the people' through elections, we do not get to choose who is 'in power' in business and, unlike politicians, if we don't think business leaders are doing a good job we cannot kick them out. HS2 was subject to public consultation and can only go ahead after approval in Parliament by representatives elected by the people, whereas there was no such public consultation or democratic authority for AstraZeneca's relocation to Cambridge. If democracy is such a good thing, why isn't it extended to the world of business? Traditionally, this lack of accountability has been an important basis of criticism of the capitalist system. Public ownership or government regulation of the private sector have been advocated as ways of effecting some degree of public democratic input to business decisions.

However, two responses can be made to this critique. First, the electorates of capitalist economies like Britain have not supported left-wing schemes of large-scale public ownership and economic planning. Indeed since the 1980s there has been a reversal, through privatization, of the limited measures of public ownership that had established the 'mixed economy' in the decades after the Second World War. Thus it can be argued that, although business leaders are not democratically elected and accountable, as a society we have, through the democratic process, chosen an economic system based on private ownership. In other words, if we didn't think business leaders were doing a good job we could take action to change their behaviour through the democratic process. This takes us to the second point, that arguably what matters to us most is how business performs in terms of efficiency and providing customers with what they want. Thus, Kay argues that business has won legitimacy for the exercise of economic power through success. 'We accept, even welcome, the authority of Sainsbury and Tesco in delivering our groceries because of the manifest effectiveness with which they have done this in the past. In ensuring food safety, consumers now have more trust in supermarkets, which are competing to retain their reputation, than they have in government' (Kay 2004, p. 40).

Kay's argument that the economic power of business is legitimized by success means that it is conditional on performance and therefore can be precarious and open to challenge. This is illustrated by the financial crisis and ensuing economic recession stemming from the manifest ineffectiveness of the banking system to serve the needs of the economy. The financial sector, concentrated in London, plays an important role in the UK economy and, in recent decades, was encouraged as a key driver of economic growth and prosperity. Its competitive success was seen as vital to the future of the UK as a nation, and it won legitimacy through this apparent success. However, the financial crisis from 2008 precipitated a reappraisal and the emergence of the view that the banks had become too big and too powerful. It turned out that the future they led us into involved the deepest economic recession since the 1930s. In contrast to the supermarkets, the banks have *lost* legitimacy for the exercise of economic power through *failure*. Because of this government power was used to intervene in the banking system, including measures of (temporary) public ownership, and proposals for reform and more effective regulation of the banks moved up the political agenda. Thus, among other proposals, in 2013 the UK government announced its intention to legislate to require banks to 'ring fence' their high street banking activities so as to avoid the possibility of collapse due to future bad decisions in their risky investment (or 'casino') banking activities, with powers to break up banks that don't comply.

> **Stop and Think**
>
> What do you understand by the terms 'political power' and 'corporate power'? In what ways are they different or similar?

According to Kay, that Tesco is a powerful company and its chief executive is a powerful businessman are matters that we are sensible not to worry about so long as we are happy with Tesco's effectiveness in delivering our groceries (and a wide range of non-food products and services). Yet the success of the supermarkets is not as clear-cut as Kay suggests. For example, in 2013 supermarkets in the UK were caught up in a scandal caused by horsemeat being found in products labelled as containing beef. More generally, the benefits to consumers are not straightforward, and in any case this is a rather limited criterion for judging success as there is a wider set of issues in terms of which the way supermarkets wield their economic power may be questioned (Simms 2007).

Mini-Case 11.2 Should we welcome or worry about the power of supermarkets?

▶ **VALUES** Yes, they are good at delivering our groceries, but .... Many questions have been raised about the power and impact of supermarkets in modern society, including the following:

1. The supermarket sector in the UK is dominated by just four very large companies. In oligopolistic markets consumers have fewer options to 'shop around' and this usually means that competitive pressure is reduced and the market power of sellers is increased.

2. Although supermarkets do engage in price competition, their claims can be misleading and it is difficult for consumers to make price comparisons, especially in relation to the whole shopping basket.

3. The low prices offered to consumers may be achieved by the capacity of supermarkets to exercise market power in relation to suppliers, forcing down prices paid to farmers in the UK and imposing stringent quality standards.

4. The low prices offered to consumers may be achieved by sourcing products overseas where farmers may be paid very low prices or people have to work for very low wages, sometimes in sweatshop conditions.

5. The growth and diversification of the supermarkets has been at the cost of closure or decline of specialist retailers, such as bookshops, and contributed to the reduction of the diversity and distinctive character of local high streets.

6. Supermarkets use their political and legal clout to win planning battles against local opposition to the opening of new stores.

7. Supermarkets are part of the problem of the marketing and sale of products with adverse social and health impacts, such as cheap alcohol and foods high in sugar, salt, and fat.

8. Supermarkets have damaging environmental impacts through the 'air miles' involved in sourcing food and other products from overseas, and store locations that require most shoppers to travel by car.

9. Some supermarket jobs, such as checkout operators, are among the lowest paid occupations in the UK economy.

Do you agree that consumers get a good deal from supermarkets? Do you agree with Kay that the economic power exercised by supermarkets is legitimated or justified by the good deal that customers get?

■ Stakeholders and the 'play of power'

▶ STAKEHOLDERS From Mini-Case 11.2 we can see that the power exercised by supermarkets involves relationships with a range of stakeholders, defined as individuals, groups, and organizations that are affected by and therefore have a 'stake' in business decisions and behaviour. Because business decisions can have far-reaching economic and social consequences the number and range of stakeholders can be very large, including:

- shareholders
- managers
- employees
- suppliers
- customers
- competitors
- local community/wider society
- government.

The idea of a 'play of power' is used to indicate that power is not exercised in a one-way direction, and that the outcome depends on the resources and actions of the stakeholders involved. In this chapter we will look at corporate power using this stakeholder framework in terms of:

▶ COMPLEXITY

- Relations with direct stakeholders—shareholders, customers, suppliers, employees—which can be characterized in terms of bargaining power.
- Relations with indirect stakeholders in the form of civil society organizations (CSOs) or 'pressure groups' that seek to influence business decisions in relation to their own interests or some wider public good as they see it.
- Relations with government through the participation of business as an actor in the political arena.

Bargaining power

In markets economic actors—individuals and organizations—attempt to realize their interests through exchange relationships. These relationships of voluntary exchange involve the direct or primary stakeholders in business—customers, suppliers, and employees—and yield mutual benefit on the basis of a price that is acceptable to both buyer and seller. In principle each party is better off after the exchange. However, this idea of voluntarism tends to mask the extent to which an exchange relationship intrinsically involves some degree of bargaining power. Bargaining power refers to the ability of buyer or seller to alter the terms of exchange in their own favour—to bid the price up or down, or to get more or give less. Bargaining power depends largely on the number of buyers and sellers (market structure)—your bargaining power is maximized if you are the only seller (monopolist) or buyer (monopsonist).

Consumer sovereignty?

In competitive markets it is the ability and willingness of consumers to 'shop around' that disciplines firms so that they have to produce what consumers are willing to buy and cannot sell above a market price that is determined by the downward pressure of competition. 'Consumer sovereignty' is secured through 'exit' power, as consumers punish firms that attempt to raise their prices by going elsewhere. Conversely, in oligopolistic markets dominated by a small number of large firms the possibility arises of firms refraining from competition and engaging in price-fixing, in this way exercising bargaining power over consumers who have no option to shop around. The power of government, in the form of competition law, provides a mechanism to deter, investigate, and punish such collusion and to ensure that consumers benefit from fair competition (Office of Fair Trading 2009). In other words, the balance of bargaining power between consumers and businesses is tilted in favour of consumers by government power. Regulation is used to prevent abuse of power by business and protect consumers. For example, in 2007 an investigation by the Office of Fair Trading (OFT) concluded that supermarkets broke competition laws by fixing the price of dairy products at the cost of consumers. In 2013 the OFT imposed fines on the vehicle manufacturer Mercedes-Benz and three commercial vehicle dealers for market rigging, in other words, refraining from competition through market sharing and price coordination (Office of Fair Trading 2013).

In a market bargaining power can also be based on differences in information or knowledge. Consumers are generally at a disadvantage because they have limited information about goods or services and rely on what businesses tell them. This creates the risk of consumers being taken advantage of through mis-selling, where they are persuaded by the seller to buy products that the seller knows are not appropriate to their needs. For example, in 2013 the regulator Ofgem (Office of Gas and Electricity Markets) imposed a fine of £10.5m on energy supplier SSE for 'prolonged and extensive misselling'. Ofgem found that 'SSE consistently failed, over a prolonged period of time, to conduct its sales activities in a way that would provide clear and accurate information on prices and potential savings to enable customers to make an informed decision about whether to switch suppliers' (Ofgem 2013). Ofgem is another example of the use of government power to alter the balance of power between consumers and business, through creation of a regulator whose 'priority is protecting and making a positive difference for all energy consumers'.

The Sale of Goods Act, enforced by the OFT, gives consumers rights when they buy goods from a business and provides protection against firms taking advantage of their lack of knowledge or information. Under the Act any contract involves 'implied terms' that the goods are of reasonable quality, fit for purpose, safe, and as described (see OFT website: **<http://oft.gov. uk/business-advice/soga/#.UWZ_XrXWZjU>**).

》 INTERACTION Large companies also use advertising and branding strategies to influence consumer preferences and build up customer loyalty or, as Luger puts it, 'to shape consumer consciousness'. The claim here is that advertising is a form of corporate power through which business is able to instil in consumers wants that they would not otherwise have. This is an important form of corporate power since it brings into question the idea of consumer sovereignty—that consumers are ultimately in charge in markets. The claim that businesses respond to independently formed consumer preferences is opposed by the claim that consumer preferences are shaped by businesses. Rather than consumers stimulating supply to satisfy their demand, firms stimulate demand to satisfy their supply. Instead of businesses serving consumers, consumers serve businesses. In reality, each of these views is probably too simplistic: consumers are not mere dupes of corporate advertising but neither are they unaffected by it.

Advertising is principally intended to persuade us to buy a particular product or brand—to buy a Samsung rather than an Apple iPhone or Corona rather than San Miguel—but it may have a larger social and economic significance. It can be argued that advertising plays a key role in creating and sustaining a **consumerist** or materialist culture in which success and well-being are associated with increased consumption. By continually stimulating new wants, advertising provides business with ever-expanding markets—making more and more money by selling more and more products. This can be seen as a good thing, just as a way of describing the dynamism of the market that has produced prosperity in the rich economies and is now lifting millions of people out of poverty in developing countries. And greater material prosperity may be seen as a basic human desire or preference rather than something that is created by business. But the pursuit of happiness through increased consumption might be self-defeating, particularly in societies that are already rich, since always wanting more is a recipe for dissatisfaction and means happiness is always out of reach. It has also been argued that GDP per head (i.e. average income and material standard of living) is a poor measure of happiness or well-being, and that the pursuit of ever more economic growth is ecologically unsustainable.

Advertising primarily targets consumers in terms of purchasing decisions intended to fulfil our wants or desires. In so far as it is successful in shaping those wants and desires it leads us to question how far consumers are really in charge of markets. But apart from this contested idea of 'consumer sovereignty' which operates through millions of independent purchasing decisions, consumers may exercise power in markets in a more deliberate and organized way through ethical consumerism or consumer activism. This involves consumers seeking to use the power that their purchasing decisions give them to influence business behaviour in order to achieve ethical outcomes. Whereas the conventional idea of consumer sovereignty is essentially concerned with the responsiveness of markets to the self-interest of consumers, consumer activism is concerned with using purchasing power for a wider group or public interest. For example, Nescafé might use advertising to persuade consumers of the superior taste of its coffee, but consumers might be more interested in supporting the Fairtrade movement to ensure a decent price is paid to producers. We will examine ethical consumerism later in the chapter.

Mini-Case 11.3 Is advertising a form of corporate power?

Governments in the UK have moved to restrict advertising of cigarettes as part of public health campaigns to reduce smoking. In 2012 a ban on the display of cigarettes in supermarkets was introduced in England. This followed bans in other countries including Canada and Ireland. These moves are based on the belief that such advertising has a persuasive purpose and effect in encouraging people to take up smoking (especially young people) or increase their consumption. In other words, advertising is seen as a form of corporate power through which corporations can shape consumer preferences and behaviour. In response to this tobacco companies have asserted that consumers make up their own minds whether and how much to smoke and that the purpose and effect of advertising is to persuade consumers to switch brands. Essentially, advertising does not grow the market and has no negative public health effects. People smoke because they want to and not because tobacco companies persuade them to.

Question

Who do you think is right in this debate?

Industrial relations

It can be argued that market competition does generally provide a good deal for consumers, but that this is achieved by bargaining power being exerted back along the supply chain (buyer power) in relation to suppliers and employees (Reich 2008). The primary relationship between business and labour (or employers and employees) can be seen as a market relationship of contract or exchange—buying and selling—in which a wage or salary is the price paid in exchange for the employee's ability to perform a certain role or range of duties. However, unlike many other acts of exchange, that between employer and employee involves an ongoing relationship—the performance of the business depends on how effectively the two sides work together or collaborate. The relationship can be characterized as a 'wage–effort bargain', meaning how much pay employees receive in return for how much effort they have to put in. This bargain is critical for both parties as it determines the livelihoods of employees and the profitability of business. Each party will try to strike the best bargain that it can, and the outcome will depend on their relative bargaining strengths.

▶ **COMPLEXITY** This varies between different labour markets, and over time according to shifts in the economic environment and the legislative framework governing industrial relations. Employees have greater bargaining power when they command skills that are in relatively short supply, whereas unskilled workers have weak bargaining power with employers because they are much easier to replace. Historically, the principal motivation for the development of trade unions was the desire to enhance what was perceived as the generally weak bargaining position of employees in relation to employers by bargaining as a group, i.e. on a collective basis. And the development of trade unions was quickly followed by the attempt to gain political representation so as to influence labour law.

▶ **DYNAMIC** In the post-war decades high employment, economic growth, and a favourable political environment combined to enhance the bargaining power of trade unions in the UK economy. However, trade union power has undoubtedly declined in the UK since the 1970s due to a number of interrelated factors, including:

- Economic change, particularly deindustrialization involving loss of jobs in highly unionized industries.

- Political change involving an ideological shift towards support for 'free markets' and the 'right to manage', expressed in legislative changes designed to weaken trade unions. The idea that trade union power had to be weakened as a condition of improved economic performance was a central plank of the approach of the Conservative governments in the UK in the 1980s.

- Increasing competition in global markets leading to a squeeze on employees (Reich 2008).

There has been a steady decline in trade union membership: 26% of UK employees (6.4 million) were trade union members in 2011, down from 32.4% in 1995. Trade union membership accounts for a higher proportion of employees in the public sector (56.5%) than in the private sector (14.1%). Although we might think of union membership mainly in terms of lower paid jobs, it is actually highest in professional occupations (45.4%) (Brownlie 2012). Although trade unionism has declined since the 1970s, trade unions remain important features of the economic and political landscape in modern Britain.

There is no agreement about what the balance of power *should* be in relations between employers and trade unions, and it has been claimed at various times in relation to one side or the other that it has too much power. Conservative governments under Prime Minister Thatcher thought the unions had too much power in the 1970s, but critics argue the pendulum has swung too far the other way. Business organizations such as the Confederation of British Industry (CBI) and Institute of Directors (IoD) will naturally take a different view of this matter than the representative body for the trade unions, the Trades Union Congress (TUC). This simply reflects the conflicting interests in the wage–effort bargain. But it is also a debate about different models of a capitalist economy and the meaning of business success.

We can broadly distinguish between two models and ideas of business success by asking whether power ought to be exercised by managers in an essentially top-down fashion over the workforce, or employees ought to be seen as partners in the business. These two approaches are exemplified by the United States and Germany, with the UK being identified closely with the American model (Bronk 2000). The top-down approach is expressed in the idea of the 'right to manage': in this view decision-making is the prerogative of managers and employees are essentially hired to carry out instructions. This can also be expressed in an 'us and them' style of employee relations that emphasizes the conflicting interests of employers and employees and is characterized by low trust. The idea here is that managers represent the interests of owners to whom they are properly responsible, and that business success relies on their talented stewardship. In contrast, the German model sees employers and employees as 'social partners' and corporate governance involves 'co-determination' or power-sharing, in the form of a system of works councils and employee participation on boards. This involves a more collaborative style of employee relations that emphasizes the shared interests of employers and employees and is characterized by high trust.

Buyer power in the supply chain

Bargaining power between businesses operates in the supply chain as the power of buyers or sellers. For example, it has been argued that supermarkets are able to offer low prices to consumers by 'squeezing' suppliers, who in turn pass these pressures on to their own employees as low wages. The suppliers have to comply with the demands of supermarkets because of their 'buyer power': farmers might be dependent on their contract with a supermarket, but the supermarket can fairly easily switch suppliers. For example, the National Farmers' Union (NFU) has claimed that some British agricultural produce is being 'endangered' by price promotions which are passed on to suppliers as supermarkets are determined to retain their profit margins. This can mean that prices paid to producers do not cover production costs. Supermarkets are also criticized for fining producers when customers complain, even if it is not the farmer's fault (Insley 2012). In order to tackle these and other practices and protect suppliers, the Competition Commission introduced a Groceries Supplies Code of Practice (GSCOP) which came into force in 2010. The provisions of the code had to be incorporated into contracts between supermarkets and their suppliers, and it encompassed all retailers with annual groceries sales exceeding £1 billion (i.e. including all the major supermarkets). The aim of the code was 'to ensure that suppliers do not have costs imposed on them unexpectedly or unfairly by retailers' (Competition Commission 2009). In 2012 the UK government brought forward the Groceries Code Adjudicator Bill with the primary purpose of creating 'a Groceries Code Adjudicator with the role of enforcing the Groceries Code and encouraging compliance with it' (see **<www.parliament.uk>**; Butler 2013).

Engagement with civil society organizations

》 INTERACTION Business also has to engage with a range of indirect stakeholders in the community and wider society which may seek to influence business decisions and behaviour. There is a large number and diverse range of groups and organizations in society (sometimes referred to as 'civil society organizations' or CSOs. They are non-market and non-governmental) representing different interests and causes—including charities, voluntary organizations, professional associations, campaigning groups, and think tanks—which from time to time engage with business in pursuit of their aims.

These aims might be tied to the interests of their members, such as trade unions or professional associations. This can also include groups formed to express the opposition of members of a local community to a proposed new supermarket or other business (sometimes referred to as NIMBY groups because they make the demand 'Not In My Back Yard'). For example, in 2012 Costa Coffee announced that they would not go ahead with plans to open a coffee shop in the Devon town of Totnes, despite having acquired planning permission for the development, in the face of strong opposition from the local community and existing traders. The aims of CSOs can also be related to a wider public interest, such as campaigns seeking to influence supermarkets in relation to fair trade or environmental concerns, or against large businesses seen as acting immorally by avoiding corporation tax. Civil society organizations might be supportive or critical of business, and sometimes they are established or supported by businesses to represent their interests.

Mini-Case 11.4 Ethical consumerism

❯❯ **VALUES** Ethical consumerism can be defined as:

personal allocation of funds, including consumption and investment, where choice has been informed by a particular issue—be it human rights, social justice, the environment or animal welfare.

(The Ethical Consumerism Report 2008)

Thus, whereas consumer behaviour might normally be understood in terms of personal wants and self-interest, ethical consumerism or consumer activism seeks to harness the purchasing power of consumers to make a difference in relation to an issue of ethical concern. This does not mean ignoring self-interest, but trying to balance it with the interests of others, and may involve being willing to pay a higher price. For example, when people decide to purchase Fairtrade products, such as bananas or coffee, they do so out of regard for the interests of the farmers who produce these crops in developing countries—the whole point being to improve their incomes and help them to escape poverty. In choosing Fairtrade products there is an implied criticism of big business for giving farmers a raw deal. In other words, consumers may be motivated by a desire to do something *for* the world's poor and, at the same time, to take action *against* big business.

Ethical consumerism can be essentially an individual act, but it is often linked to a wider campaign or movement. The point of a campaign or movement is to mobilize a large number of consumers in a process of collective action so as to bring effective pressure on business to alter its behaviour, such as through an organized consumer boycott, or to provide custom for businesses which are seen as ethical. Campaigning organizations have been important in raising awareness of specific ethical issues or products, and the idea of ethical consumerism more generally. For example, the Fairtrade Foundation was established in 1992 by a range of existing CSOs including Christian Aid, Oxfam, and the World Development Movement. The Foundation licences use of the FAIRTRADE Mark as a consumer guarantee on products, works to raise public awareness, and 'through demonstration of alternatives to conventional trade and other forms of advocacy, ... empowers citizens to campaign for an international trade system based on justice and fairness' (<http://www.fairtrade.org.uk/>).

Ethical consumerism appears to be a growing phenomenon in the UK, as shown by continued growth in sales of Fairtrade products so that it might be described as mainstream. For products such as tea, coffee, chocolate, and bananas, Fairtrade accounts for a substantial market share (e.g. a third of all bananas sold). However, 'Fairtrade still has a long way to go, accounting for as little as 1.5% of the overall UK food and drink market' in 2012 (Smithers 2013). More generally, in 2009 a survey in Britain showed that, when choosing a purchase, around three quarters (74%) of consumers think it is 'very' (26%) or 'fairly'(48%) important that a company shows a high degree of social responsibility. This showed a decline from the previous year when the overall figure was 83%, of which 43% thought a high degree of social responsibility is very important. This sharp decline in the proportion holding social responsibility to be very important suggests that ethical purchasing had been squeezed by recession in this period. In 2012 the 'very important' response rate remained at around a quarter. However, the survey shows that a large majority of consumers claim that the degree of social responsibility that they perceive a company demonstrates influences their purchasing decision, and this suggests a level of ethical concern that business needs to take account of. Seeming to reflect this, the same survey shows that a majority (57%) of business leaders agree companies will continue to invest in corporate responsibility despite a tougher economic environment (Ipsos MORI 2009).

> *Stop and Think*
>
> ⋯⋯⋯⋯⋯⋯⋯⋯⋯⋯⋯⋯⋯⋯⋯⋯⋯⋯⋯
>
> Ethical consumerism—do you do it? Does it work?
>
> Have you ever made decisions about spending based on ethical grounds? Were your decisions part of an organized campaign, such as a consumer boycott?
>
> Do you feel that ethical consumerism, such as on environmental grounds, is an effective way of putting pressure on companies and bringing about change? Or are consumers likely to be conned by corporate 'greenwash'?
>
> What do your thoughts on these questions say about corporate power?

Business in the political arena

⟫ INTERACTION ⟫ COMPLEXITY In addition to bargaining power exercised in the economic domain and engagement with CSOs, businesses are also active participants in the political process. In a democracy it is legitimate for business to engage in the political process, like other groups, in order to influence decisions to its own advantage. This may be the most important manifestation of corporate power since, as we have seen, governments can alter the rules within which markets operate and therefore the power relationships between businesses and other stakeholders. Thus, business will look to government (at the national level but increasingly also in relation to the EU) to provide a favourable environment for profit-making through the law and public policy. This might include macroeconomic policies to control inflation, the provision of an efficient transport infrastructure to enable the movement of goods, favourable trade rules and agreements, the reduction of taxation and regulations that are felt to be burdensome, and so on. However, a range of other groups compete to influence government in pursuit of their own interests and values, for example campaigning against road building or airport expansion, or to introduce new regulations on business to protect the environment. We can understand this competition to exert influence or control over political decisions by identifying three principal groups or interests: business, labour, and civil society organizations, as depicted in Figure 11.1.

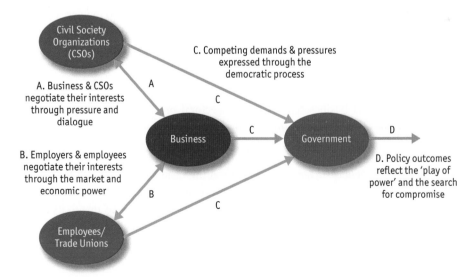

Figure 11.1 The interactions between business, labour, CSOs, and government

Thus, as we have seen, employers and employees negotiate their interests through the market and bargaining power (interaction B in Figure 11.1). However, this economic relationship is governed by law and public policy. For example, labour law determines the individual and collective rights of employees. This means that each party has an interest in trying to shape political decisions so as to alter the economic relationship to its own advantage. For example, trade unions will bargain with employers to try to win higher wages for their members, but they might supplement this with a political campaign to secure a statutory minimum wage as in the UK (see Chapter 1). In other words, we can see how the economic interests of business and labour in the market find expression in political action. Similarly, civil society organizations, such as environmental pressure groups, which target businesses directly through methods such as public relations campaigns or consumer boycotts (interaction A in Figure 11.1) may put pressure on government to introduce laws or policies that will induce or compel a change in business behaviour.

Thus, competing demands and pressures expressed through the democratic process (C in Figure 11.1) can be related largely to interests generated in, or affected by, the operation of markets. Government can be used to alter the distribution of resources and income, and more generally of costs and benefits, that would otherwise result from the operation of the market. Business is an actor in the political arena, and participates in a play of power involving government, trade unions, and a range of CSOs.

Stop and Think
....
To what extent are political debates and conflicts based on economic interests and values?

Does business enjoy a privileged position in the political process?

The political process can be seen in terms of a 'play of interests and power'. In other words, political actors—business, trade unions, and civil society organizations—compete with each other to exercise power in the political process, to ensure that their interests are represented effectively, and to influence political decisions to their advantage. Political decisions may involve reaching a compromise between groups with different interests and values, perhaps based on a view of what's in the national interest, but often the outcome is bound to involve winners and losers. In this competitive political process it can be argued that business enjoys a privileged position because it has certain advantages over other groups in getting its voice heard and influencing decisions (Lindblom 1980). The claim that democratic politics is characterized by business dominance is based on two ideas:

- the advantages that business enjoys in the electoral process and the representation of group interests—*business as a political actor*
- the crucial importance of business decisions for society as a whole—*control without trying*.

Viewing business as a *political actor* means looking at the various ways in which business, individually or collectively, can decide to participate in the political process at various levels in order to influence decisions. It may be able to exert 'disproportionate influence' due to its control of key resources such as organization, knowledge, and finance. To understand this claim we need to examine the two broad processes or channels of influence on government in a democracy:

- the electoral process
- the representation of group interests.

The right of all citizens to vote in regular elections for a choice of candidates is a key component of democracy, allowing the people to choose who will represent them in Parliament and govern them. In elections the main players are political parties that compete for votes on the basis of ideologically based programmes for government. The business community does not organize its own political party but it is normally the case that one or more party is closely identified with and supported by business interests, so this is an important vehicle for business to have a voice in political debate, to be represented in the legislature, and to have a business friendly party elected to government. One of the prime ways in which business can support a business friendly party and help it to get elected is through financial support to maintain the party machine and, particularly, to run the election campaign. The worlds of business and politics may also be intertwined through shared social backgrounds, informal networks, and individuals from business going into politics and government.

In the UK the Conservative party is clearly identified as the main party of business, while the Labour party was originally established to represent primarily the interests of organized labour, i.e. the trade unions. This shows vividly how the major stakeholders—employers and employees—historically created and supported political parties to represent their interests and improve their bargaining power in the market. However, it is fair to say that all the main parties in the UK today are keen to advertise a pro-business stance, so party competition does not take the form of a simple bifurcation of employers' party versus workers' party. Labour feels it cannot get elected just as a representative of workers' interests since many people are not members of trade unions and may feel little sympathy with them, and because the party has to demonstrate that it is competent to manage the economy and this would be difficult if it were seen as hostile to business. On the other hand, the Conservatives cannot succeed electorally just by representing business interests since this would align the party too narrowly with the wealthy and powerful in society, and because many people do not trust business and expect governments to confront businesses that do not act in a socially responsible way.

Mini-Case 11.5 Funding of the main political parties: can money buy political influence?

Companies are an important source of funding for political parties, and the Conservative party is the main beneficiary of donations from companies. Political parties are only required by law to report donations above £7,500 to the party HQ and above £1,500 to the party's accounting units (constituency parties). The main sources of reported donations to political parties are individuals, trade unions, and companies. In the year of the last UK general election, 2010, nearly half of accepted donations to all parties came from individuals (49%), while companies contributed 22% and trade unions 21%. The Conservatives were by far the most successful party in terms of attracting funding, receiving 53% of all donations (£32m), compared to 33% for Labour (£20m).

Table 11.2 shows that in the last quarter of 2012 the Conservatives were again the most successful party in terms of reported donations. The table shows a clear difference between the two main parties in the main sources of donations. Two-thirds of donations to the Conservative party are made by

Table 11.2 Sources of donations (per cent) accepted by main political parties during quarter 4 of 2012 (Oct., Nov., and Dec.)

	Conservative Party	Labour Party
Companies	23	3
Individuals	66	12
Trade Unions	0	72
Other	11	13
Total donations reported	£3.31m	£2.59m

Source: The Electoral Commission 2013.

individuals, with nearly one quarter coming from companies. In contrast, Labour received virtually no corporate donations and only 12% of donations came from individuals. The Labour party relies mainly on trade unions for donations (72%), whereas the Conservatives received no donations from this source. The Conservative party received more than ten times more in donations from companies than Labour. Of the total company donations to all UK political parties in this period 73% went to the Conservatives and only 6.7% to Labour.

Behind these overall proportions there is a high degree of reliance by the Conservatives on one particular business sector. In 2010 more than half (50.8%) of donations to the Conservative party came from companies and individuals connected to the financial services industry (i.e. 'the City'), up from 25% in 2005. A large proportion came from a small number of very wealthy individuals: '57 individuals from the financial services sector made a donation of more than £50,000 each' during the year (Mathiason and Bessaoud 2011). Thus, the figure for donations by 'companies' in Table 11.2 underestimates the extent of business support for the party since 'individuals' includes those with business interests.

Why do companies and wealthy individuals in business make donations to the Conservative party? Why do trade unions make donations to the Labour party? One answer is that businesses and trade unions support the party that they perceive best represents their interests. However, there is a concern that 'he who pays the piper calls the tune', in other words that money buys political influence. In this view the parties' policies may be adapted to suit the interests of donors. For example, it seems reasonable to speculate that donations to the Conservatives from the City may have been motivated by a desire to exert influence over policy in order to fend off calls for tougher regulation in the context of the financial crisis and widespread public anger at the banks. The argument that donations allow influence seems compelling since, even though a direct connection between donations and policy decisions is difficult to prove, political parties which are dependent on donations may be reluctant to 'bite the hand that feeds them'.

Question

Is the reliance of political parties on donations a matter of concern?

▶ **VALUES** In a democracy such as Britain elections are usually seen as the principal form of political representation, through the election of representatives to Parliament (MPs) and, indirectly, the formation of the government. However, a healthy democracy also depends on a range of civil rights or liberties including freedoms of speech, association, and assembly. These rights are important because democracy must allow the expression of opinions and beliefs through dialogue, debate, and argument. What is more, once a government has been elected that is not the end of the political process since individuals and organizations are able to pursue their political aims by seeking to influence government decisions. Thus, business seeks to ensure its voice is heard and taken into account in political decisions not only through elections but also by engaging with and influencing the government of the day. In this endeavour business is one among a very large number of groups or interests in society competing for the attention of government and trying to influence political decisions.

These may be referred to generically as 'pressure groups', and their key roles can be described as:

- interest aggregation, and
- interest articulation.

In other words, groups exist because individuals or organizations come together to pursue shared interests (aggregation) and they express these interests in the form of political demands or pressure on government (articulation).

The representation of business interests

▶ **DIVERSITY** Business interests can be represented individually and/or collectively, and relations between business and government can be, accordingly, decentralized or centralized. Essentially, individual businesses can choose to represent their own interests through direct dealings with government and legislators. This is feasible especially for large companies with in-house resources that can be utilized in the political arena. From a business perspective this political engagement is just a normal part of business behaviour. However, companies may also employ specialist lobbying or public relations organizations for this purpose. They may also be represented through business associations whose rationale is to speak on behalf of collective business interests, which can be those of companies within a particular industry or on an economy-wide basis. Among the most important of these in the UK are:

》 DIVERSITY

- Professional associations such as the Chartered Institute of Personnel and Development (CIPD) or Chartered Management Institute (CMI)
- Trade associations representing the interests of firms in a particular industry or sector, such as the Society of Motor Manufacturers and Traders (SMMT), the British Retail Consortium (BRC), or the British Bankers' Association (BBA)
- Chambers of Commerce representing business at a local level
- Institute of Directors (IoD) representing business leaders
- Confederation of British Industry (CBI) representing the business community at a national level (often referred to as a 'peak' organization).

》 SPATIAL LEVELS Chambers of Commerce also have a national organization which operates at the UK and European levels, while the CBI also maintains offices in Brussels and Washington. Businesses may also join ad hoc coalitions to represent specific shared interests, such as in relation to a specific government policy.

The representation of business interests typically involves a mixture of individual and collective mechanisms, but there is considerable variation between countries in this mix and it is possible to think of a spectrum from highly decentralized to highly centralized systems. In highly decentralized systems the individual corporation is the dominant actor, whereas in highly centralized systems trade associations and **peak organizations** play a more important role. In the UK trade associations and the CBI do enjoy close relations with government (both Labour and Conservative), but on the whole relations between business and government are more towards the decentralized end of the spectrum. In this respect the UK is closer to the US where:

> business representation … is … conducted in a manner that is very decentralized and fragmented. It is the individual enterprise, not the trade association or peak organization, that is paramount.
>
> (Wilson 2003, p. 44)

Mini-Case 11.6　The Confederation of British Industry (CBI)

The CBI was created in the 1960s and is recognized as the principal peak association representing business interests in the UK. Its website states:

The CBI's mission is to help create and sustain the conditions in which businesses in the United Kingdom can compete and prosper for the benefit of all. We are the premier lobbying organization for UK business on national and international issues. We work with the UK government, international legislators and policy-makers to help UK businesses compete effectively.

Working on over 80 policy issues that directly affect business at any given time, the CBI is second-to-none at achieving wins

for business. Members can use the CBI to reinforce their own efforts to bring about change in the legislative and regulatory framework within which they must operate. …

The CBI is…of crucial importance to the entire business community because it can mobilise business opinion and successfully bring influence to bear on government. Such is the strength of the CBI's reputation that government frequently approaches the CBI for advice and opinion.

No other business organization has such an extensive network of contacts with government ministers, MPs, civil servants, opinion formers and the media. …

The CBI enjoys strong support because it gets the results for business at home and abroad.

(<www.cbi.org.uk/>)

However, the balance between companies using the CBI to bring about change in the legislative and regulatory framework and relying on their own efforts is tipped in favour of the latter.

In a survey of British companies in the 1990s 68% of respondents reported direct contact with government, compared to 46% through a trade association and only 24% through the CBI (Mitchell, discussed in Wilson 2003, p. 73).

As Wilson comments, 'In Britain as in the United States, authority resides in the individual company and not the trade association or the peak association (CBI)' (Wilson 2003, p. 70).

Question

The CBI claims that it works for the 'benefit of all' and achieves 'wins for business'. Are these two compatible?

Control without trying?

STAKEHOLDERS Lindblom has argued that business occupies a privileged position in policy-making, one that is unmatched by any other group or interest including organized labour. This privileged position arises from the fact that private business makes decisions about the allocation of resources on which the well-being of all individuals in society depends (see the definition of corporate power earlier in the chapter).

INTERACTION Lindblom notes that these decisions 'matter to all members of society … [and] loom as momentous as the decisions of most government officials … No one can say that … [they] … are too inconsequential to be labelled public policy' (1980, p. 72). No other group in society makes decisions that matter to everybody in the same way. Lindblom's argument is that government is dependent on these decisions taken by private business to ensure a healthy economy which voters expect government to deliver. The problem for governments is that they 'cannot positively command business managers to perform their functions' and therefore must 'develop and maintain business profitability through supporting policies'. Thus, dependence by government on decisions taken in the private sector translates into a consistent bias in policy-making in favour of business interests. Governments must pursue policies that maintain business confidence to ensure that business continues to invest, create jobs, and generate growth, so as to ensure voter satisfaction. Lindblom refers to this as 'control without trying' since it does not rely on businesses actually doing anything to influence government (Lindblom 1980, pp. 72–4).

For example, there was no 'bankers' party' contesting the UK general election (although we saw earlier that organizations and individuals from the City were prominent among donors to the Conservative Party). However, 'control without trying' can be illustrated in two ways in relation to financial markets and institutions. First, the bank 'bailouts' required to prevent them going bankrupt during the financial crisis were justified by the argument that banks were 'too big to fail'. In other words, governments felt compelled to rescue the banks because of the key role they play in the functioning of the economy and the catastrophic consequences of allowing large interconnected banks to go out of business. The bailouts contributed to the mushrooming of government debt, and dealing with the debt became a key preoccupation of government economic policy leading to the era of austerity. The UK government justified its tough austerity programme of public spending cuts and tax rises on the grounds of the need to maintain the confidence of financial markets, particularly as expressed by the AAA rating conferred by credit rating agencies. If this confidence were to weaken, it was argued, the government would only be able to borrow at higher interest rates with damaging economic consequences. In both cases the interests of financial institutions and markets can be seen as automatically influencing government, thus representing a form of control over policy by financial interests 'without trying'.

> *Stop and Think*
>
> Does the fact that 'many of the functions performed by business … are essential to society' justify its privileged position in policy-making?

■ The consequences of globalization

》 SPATIAL LEVELS Lindblom's analysis of the privileged position of business in policy-making was made in the 1970s. Since that time an ideological shift in politics in the UK and elsewhere towards 'market optimism' has arguably reinforced this position. At the same time it can be argued that economic globalization has made it even more necessary for governments to give businesses what they need.

》 COMPLEXITY Globalization is a complex phenomenon with many dimensions—political, social, and cultural as well as economic. In broad terms it refers to the increasing tendency of economic and other relationships to become 'stretched' across borders so that the nations and regions of the world become more interconnected and interdependent. Globalization has been facilitated by technological changes—particularly in the fields of transport and communication—that have made, for example, the movement of people between countries both cheaper and quicker (see Chapter 10). Economic globalization itself has a number of dimensions, among the most important of which are:

- the growth and spread of international trade
- the growth of MNCs that own or control production facilities in more than one country
- the increasing integration of global financial markets.

It has been argued that one important consequence of economic globalization is to increase the power of corporations in relation to governments—what Hertz has referred to as a 'power shift' (Hertz 2001). It has done so by increasing the 'exit options' available to business. This means that MNCs can search the world for the most favourable locations for their production activities. To the extent that **locational advantage** is connected with political decisions, governments are under increased pressure to ensure that decisions are favourable to business in order to attract inward investment by MNCs and prevent production and jobs moving elsewhere. For example, MNCs might be expected to favour deregulated (or 'flexible') labour markets where unions are relatively weak, taxation rates are low, and policies are in place to benefit business such as the provision of training and infrastructure. In other words, globalization accentuates what Lindblom refers to as the privileged position of business in policy-making. For example:

> Automobile manufacturers can switch the production of new models of cars relatively easily between different countries: Ford and GM, for example, have plants in Britain, Germany, France, Spain and Belgium and naturally consider which country will give the highest tax concessions, lowest taxes, least cumbersome regulations and most disciplined workforce in making decisions on car production. The automobiles produced in any one of these countries can be shipped without restriction or tariffs to any other member country; under WTO rules, the automobiles can also be shipped worldwide with only minimal duty being levied.
>
> (Wilson 2003, p. 17)

It has been argued that globalization will produce a **race to the bottom** as governments reduce taxes on business and avoid or remove regulations that are perceived as onerous for business.

For example, governments may feel that making it easier to hire and fire workers will help to attract inward investment.

However, in some cases there appears to be very little that government can do in the way of offering effective inducements to business to invest. A case in point is the shift of car production not just, as Wilson discusses, between Western European countries but to central and Eastern Europe, including the new accession states, and Asia. It appears that governments in the rich countries, such as the UK, can do little to offset the low-cost advantage gained by car makers from shifting production. 'Labour costs in Poland, the Czech Republic and Slovakia can be less than a fifth of those in countries such as Germany' (Gow 2006).

> *Stop and Think*
>
> What is meant by a 'race to the bottom'? Why is this sometimes seen as a consequence of globalization?

The ups and downs of business influence over policy-making

DYNAMIC The extent of the 'power shift' from government to business as a result of globalization is disputed. Although MNCs do have increased 'exit options', as shown by the car industry, business is not 'footloose' in the sense of being able to go easily wherever it pleases. The dependence of business on government to provide key inputs such as skills and infrastructure can lock businesses in to particular countries to some extent and give governments some leverage over their activities. More generally, economic globalization is itself not just an outcome of technological drivers but also of government decisions, such as to liberalize trade and capital flows. This means that governments remain, to some extent, in control of the process of globalization.

INTERACTION **SPATIAL LEVELS** It can be argued that economic globalization has increased the power of business in relation to trade unions and civil society organizations (CSOs) or pressure groups. Trade unions have been left behind by globalization because they don't operate effectively on an international scale. However, globalization has brought with it the rise of effective global pressure groups and protest movements. In particular, the Internet has enabled groups to mobilize international campaigns against business. Well known examples of successful campaigns are those against Nike (sweatshops) and Shell (pollution), both of which mobilized consumer boycotts.

Business influence—'nothing special' or 'unique'?

To argue that business influence is 'nothing special' is to claim that power is fragmented and dispersed and that many other groups, such as trade unions and pressure groups, are equally well placed to influence government. Against this, the view that business influence is 'unique' points to the many advantages enjoyed by business in the competition for influence, including resources, contacts, and the dependence of government on business decisions. However, these two views might not be as polarized as appears at first sight. The first approach does not say that business never exercises a decisive influence over government policy. Rather it says that business involvement in political battles is more a case of 'win some, lose some'. On the other hand, the business dominance approach does not say that business wins all political battles. Indeed it recognizes that 'the precise extent of business control appears to wax and wane' (Lindblom 1980, p. 82). But the business dominance approach does argue that business influence is special in that, on the whole, it is unmatched by any other group or interest in society.

Stop and Think

Do you agree that the political influence of business is 'nothing special', or that it is unique?

Does it matter if there is a bias in favour of business interests in the policy-making process? Does this mean that democracy isn't working properly? Or is it healthy for government to attach so much weight to maintaining business confidence?

Is business influence in the political process a good thing?

▶ **VALUES** You can see that the answer to the question of how much political influence is enjoyed by business is disputed. There is also disagreement over whether business *should* have a dominant voice in the political process. How you answer this question will depend on whether you think that the private interests of business corporations and the business community in general are aligned with the wider public interest, or that there are unavoidable conflicts. It will also depend on whether you believe that business is solely motivated by profit or can be relied on to balance this with concern for the common good.

In the 1950s the president of General Motors famously claimed that 'what was good for the country was good for General Motors and vice versa', a statement that is often translated as 'What's good for General Motors is good for the country.' In this vein it can be argued that we all have a stake in successful business and therefore business should be the most powerful influence on government. Government needs to manage the economy successfully and, in order to do so, needs to take heed of business interests and views.

On the other hand, Luger argues that business does have 'inordinate' influence and that this influence is undesirable. In this view business interests may often conflict with the common good. An example in Luger's analysis is the resistance of the car makers to tighter regulation of vehicle emissions. Therefore, business influence in policy-making needs to be checked so that corporate interests can be balanced with, and sometimes subordinated to, those of other groups.

This is not to say that there are no cases in which businesses use their political influence to press for policy change in the wider public interest. For example, some leading UK businesses have publicly called on government to introduce tighter restrictions on CO_2 emissions from industry, and some business leaders have expressed concerns about excessive boardroom pay.

Looking ahead

As we have, seen the power of business is subject to change—it has 'ups' and 'downs'—and this makes it difficult to predict. However, we have also seen that corporate power is structural in the sense that it is built into the operation of a market system—a market is both a framework of exchange and of power. This means that we can say that the interaction of corporate power and political power will remain a fundamental issue. If we follow the arguments of Lindblom and Luger (see the end of chapter case study), we can predict that business will continue to exercise power that is not matched by other groups or interests.

We can expect that in 5 or 10 years' time the Forbes list of the world's most powerful people will look very much the same. It will continue to be dominated by business and political elites, though the specific names may change as companies and states rise and fall.

It has been argued that economic globalization has resulted in a power shift from government to business in recent decades. As globalization is an ongoing process that is transforming modern societies, this will continue to pose challenges for governments in regulating business behaviour and managing their economies. It also seems likely that the broad pro-business consensus in western societies will continue. In the last century socialist political parties presented a challenge to the power of business, but in the absence of a revival of such parties there is little likelihood of government power in Europe being used to counter the position of business significantly.

However, some factors point in the other direction. We have seen evidence of the political influence of the financial sector in the UK, but the financial crisis has led to an emphasis on the need to 'rebalance' the economy away from financial activities and interests.

Business will continue to operate in the context of a more sceptical public, meaning that it has to work hard to retain public trust, particularly in relation to ethical issues such as climate change. Business will continue to face demands for greater corporate social responsibility and have to engage with civil society organizations, which may become more active.

▧ Summary

- The market system can be understood as a framework for distributing power as well as a system of exchange.
- Corporate power is based on ownership of economic resources. Business decisions are highly consequential for the rest of society.
- Corporate power is exercised as bargaining power in relation to direct stakeholders, through engagement with CSOs, and in the political arena.
- Relations between business and government may be conducted in a centralized way through business associations such as the CBI, or in a decentralized fashion in which individual companies are the key actors.
- Business has to compete with other groups in society for the attention of government.
- The effectiveness of business in the political arena matters to business but it also matters to the rest of society. The question here is whether business interests are aligned with the common good. Is what is good for General Motors good for the country?

Case Study: The political influence of the car industry

It is difficult to overstate the importance of the car industry in modern societies and economies. Its development in the last century was at the heart of the economic growth of the leading industrial capitalist economies, notably the United States, Western Europe, and, in the latter part of the century, rapidly developing countries such as Japan.

Luger has studied the long-term political influence of the US car industry between 1916 and 1996. The importance of this approach is that, while business influence is likely to vary from time to time and issue to issue, a long-term study reveals the overall pattern. Is business revealed, on the whole, to be a dominant influence on government, or a rather weak one? Luger's study shows that industry influence has varied over time. Up to the late 1980s three periods are identified: the first, up to the late 1960s, is one of business dominance over government policy; the second period, until the late 1970s, involved 'bargaining and compromise' between business and government and resulted in the expansion of regulation; and, the final period to 1988 'was a time of resurgence and triumph of industry over government' (Luger 2000, p. 14). However, Luger's overall finding is that the US car industry's political influence is evident in each period and, overall, gives it an 'inordinate impact on public policy' (Luger 2000, p. 1). In other words, the car industry does not always get its own way in relation to government, and there are periods when government has introduced regulations opposed by the industry. Yet, over the long term, the industry has been very effective in getting its own way and its power has exceeded that of any other group in society. How has this influence been exerted?

In general terms the answer is that business has control over resources that is unrivalled by any other group, and it is able to convert this control into political influence. As Luger states, 'the resources available to the large corporation give it leverage over ... government that is often unmatched' (Luger 2000, p. 3). Put simply: money equals power. This means that individuals and organizations, like businesses, that control large amounts of wealth tend to have more political influence than the rest. As an example of this Luger states that 'in 1997 [it was] estimated that the industry spent over $100 million a year to influence government .... In contrast, the entire 1996 budget of the main public interest group devoted to auto safety, the Center for Auto Safety, was approximately $600,000' (Luger 2000, p. 184). But this answer is too simple, for in democracies the basic form of political influence is through the vote, and all democracies have rules designed to limit the influence of money in politics. The mechanisms of influence identified by Luger are more complex and subtle, including the following:

- Lobbying—through in-house lobbyists based at the heart of government in Washington, contact between top managers and senior officials in government, and the hiring of specialist lobbyists and PR firms (Luger 2000, p. 183).

- As well as acting on their own behalf firms also rely on business groups and associations to represent their (shared) interests. These associations operate at industry level (e.g. trade associations) and in relation to the business community as a whole (e.g. Chambers of Commerce) (Luger 2000, p. 183).

- Industry is able to finance technical research to back up its political positions and arguments (Luger 2000, p. 183), e.g. through sympathetic foundations and 'think tanks'.

- Businesses make donations to political parties, particularly in the form of election campaign contributions (Luger 2000,

p. 184). The point is to help parties and/or candidates that are perceived to be sympathetic to business interests to get elected.

- Businesses hire former politicians or government officials to gain inside knowledge of the political process and access to decision-makers (Luger 2000, p. 184). There is also movement in the other direction—from industry into government.

- In addition to these efforts by business to influence politics, Luger also refers to 'the industry's privileged economic position'. This means that business may not have to do anything to get government to take heed of its interests 'because economic growth and political stability can hinge on a healthy auto industry' (Luger 2000, pp. 184–5). (The idea of a 'privileged position' was examined in more detail earlier in this chapter.)

- Large corporations and industries may also derive political influence from activities that are ostensibly non-political and commercial, notably advertising. The marketing of cars in ways that connect with core cultural values—as essential to personal freedom and as expressions of identity and status—has, as well as selling cars, 'provided the auto makers with a reservoir of latent public support' (Luger 2000, p. 182).

These mechanisms have afforded the car industry in America a degree of political influence unrivalled by other groups. This does not mean that other groups can never win political battles with the car industry. As we have seen, Luger identifies the 1970s as a period in which the industry was forced to make compromises over issues such as pollution and fuel economy. Nor does it mean that all industries exercise comparable influence. There may be characteristics of the car industry that boost its political influence—particularly its size and economic importance. Finally, there may be some special features of the US political system that facilitate business influence. In other national contexts there may be a different balance between business and other interests in the political process. However, Luger's study of the US car industry provides an interesting and important case of business political influence.

A second chance for General Motors

GM seemed to exemplify the power of the car industry as the biggest company in America, and the assertion that what is good for GM is also good for the country. This proposition was tested in 2009 when the company, along with Chrysler, went into bankruptcy. This was not a sudden event but the culmination of a long process of the company, along with the other giant US car makers, failing to keep up with international competitors. In this sense the companies making decisions that they thought were best for them turned out not to be good for America, and especially not good for Detroit, because they resulted in industrial decline. 'When faced with stiff competition from imports from Germany, Japan and then Korea from the 1960s, GM did not respond in the most natural, if difficult, way it should have—producing better cars than those of its competitors. Instead it tried to take the easy way out' (Chang 2011, p. 194). One of things it did was to use its political clout by lobbying the US government 'to impose import quotas on foreign, especially Japanese, cars and force open competitors' home markets' (Chang 2011, p. 194). In June 2009 GM became the biggest bankruptcy in US manufacturing history. Bankruptcy is a normal part of the operation of a market, and is consistent with a healthy performance of the economy as a whole. In the US there is a strong commitment to free markets and minimal government. However, the collapse of GM, because of its size and interconnections with other firms and industries, would have had catastrophic economic consequences spreading far beyond the direct job losses in the company. In effect, and like the banks which had to be rescued in the financial crisis, GM was 'too big to fail'. Thus 'the US government

took over the company and, after an extensive restructuring, launched it as a new entity. In the process it spent a staggering $57.6 billion of taxpayers' money' (Chang 2011, p. 194). The GM case illustrates the two forms of business political influence identified by Lindblom: business as a political actor (lobbying government for protection against imports) and control without trying (the rescue of the company as it was too big to fail).

Questions

1. Review your understanding of how the automobile industry is able to exercise political influence.

2. Are there any specific characteristics of the car industry that help to enhance its political influence?

3. What other groups or interests in society might oppose the car industry and counteract its influence?

4. How does the rescue of GM by the US government illustrate the privileged position of business?

Review and discussion questions

1. Examine the nature of corporate power and how it is exercised within a stakeholder framework.

2. Analyse the claim that business occupies a privileged position in policy-making, and that this has been enhanced as a consequence of globalization.

3. Explain how civil society organizations can bring pressure to bear on business to change its behaviour.

4. Do you believe that business has too much or too little power in modern Britain?

Assignments

1. Produce a short report into the role of lobbying in the UK system of government. Your report should include:

   * A definition of lobbying
   * An indication of the pros and cons of lobbying, i.e. how it contributes to democratic decision-making and why it is seen as a cause for concern.

   Use the following sources:
   House of Commons Political and Constitutional Reform Committee , Second Report: Introducing a statutory register of lobbyists <http://www.publications.parliament.uk/pa/cm201213/cmselect/cmpolcon/153/15302.htm>
   Commercial Lobbyists (Registration and Code of Conduct) Bill (HC Bill 39) <http://www.publications.parliament.uk/pa/bills/cbill/2012-2013/0039/cbill_2012-20130039_en_2.htm#l1g4>
   Mathiason, N. (2013) 'Government's new lobbying proposals slated by MPs', Bureau of Investigative Journalism. <http://www.thebureauinvestigates.com/2012/07/13/government-new-lobbying-proposals-slated-by-mps/>

2. In 2013 Starbucks, Amazon, and other multinational corporations were investigated by the House of Commons Public Accounts Committee in connection with tax avoidance. These companies have been targeted by campaigning groups, such as UK Uncut, to expose their activities and pressure them into paying more tax. Investigate this issue and produce a report describing the tactics used by UK Uncut and other groups and the responses made by Starbucks and other companies. Reflect on the implications of your research for understanding corporate power.

3. Compile a brief report on ethical consumerism. Your report should include the following elements:

   * the meaning of ethical consumerism
   * an analysis of trends and projections in ethical consumerism
   * an outline of the methods used to promote ethical consumerism by campaigning organizations
   * an analysis of the response to ethical consumerism by a large supermarket or retailer.

Further reading

Wilson (2003) *is an introduction to business and politics. It uses a comparative approach and considers the implications of globalization for the relationship between business and government. Also see Grant (1993).*

Moran (2009) *analyses the relationship between business and government, comparing the UK and US.*

Bakan (2005) *and* Hertz (2001) *provide critical perspectives on the power of the modern corporation.*

Peston (2008) *is an investigation of the financial crisis and economic recession that analyses the power of business.*

Kay (2004) *argues that the power exercised by business in markets depends on the social and cultural institutions in which markets are embedded.*

Reich (2008) *examines the relationship between the market and democracy, and argues that as capitalism has triumphed democracy has weakened.*

online resource centre

Test your understanding of this chapter with online questions and answers, explore the subject further through web exercises, and use the web links to provide a quick resource for further research. Go to the Online Resource Centre at <www.oxfordtextbooks.co.uk/orc/wetherly_otter/2>

Useful websites

Find out about the role of business associations by going to the websites for:

Confederation of British Industry

Chambers of Commerce

<http://www.iod.com/>
Institute of Directors

<http://www.bis.gov.uk/About/who-we-are/bcb>
Business council for Britain

For campaigning and investigative organizations try out:

The Center for Public Integrity

Transparency International

The Bureau of Investigative Journalism
<http://www.thebureauinvestigates.com/>

UK Uncut
<http://www.ukuncut.org.uk/>

References

Ashley, J. (2006) 'A local consumer rebellion that carries a political lesson', *The Guardian*, 3 July.

BBCD (2103) 'AstraZeneca axes 700 jobs in Cambridge move', 18 March 2013. (<http://www.bbc.co.uk/news/uk-england-21833207>)

BBC (2013a) 'HS2 ruling 'a victory' despite unlawful compensation move', 15 March 2013 (<http://www.bbc.co.uk/news/uk-21795755>)

Bakan, J. (2005) *The Corporation: the Pathological Pursuit of Profit and Power* (London: Free Press).

Bronk, R. (2000) 'Which model of capitalism?', *OECD Observer*, No. 221/222, Summer 2000. (<http://www.oecdobserver.org/news/archivestory.php/aid/345/Which_model_of_capitalism_.html>)

Brownlie, N. (2012) *Trade Union Membership 2011* (Department for Business, Innovation & Skills). (<https://www.gov.uk/government/uploads/system/uploads/attachment_data/file/32192/12-p77-trade-union-membership-2011.pdf>)

Butler, S. (2013) 'Supermarkets watchdog gets ready to "sort out the bullies"', in *The Guardian*, 31 March 2013. (<http://www.guardian.co.uk/business/2013/mar/31/supermarkets-watchdog-ready-sort-out-bullies?INTCMP=ILCNETTXT3487>)

Competition Commission (2009) 'News Release: CC publishes code of practice and ombudsman recommendation', 4 August 2009. (<http://www.competition-commission.org.uk/assets/competitioncommission/docs/pdf/non-inquiry/press_rel/2009/aug/pdf/36-09>)

Electoral Commission, The (2013) 'Quarter 4: 2012', 20 February 2013. (<http://www.electoralcommission.org.uk/party-finance/party-finance-analysis/party-funding/party-finance-analysis-Q4-2012>)

Forbes (2012) 'The World's Most Powerful People', Forbes, 5 December 2012. (<http://www.forbes.com/sites/davidewalt/2012/12/05/the-worlds-most-powerful-people/>)

Gow, D. (2006) 'Fears for UK car plants as factories shift east', The Guardian, 2 March 2006.

Hertz, N. (2001) The Silent Takeover: Global Capitalism and the Death of Democracy (London: William Heinemann).

Insley, J. (2013) 'British farmers wilting as supermarkets pile on the promotions', The Observer, 12 August 2013. (<http://www.guardian.co.uk/business/2012/aug/12/farmers-wilt-under-supermarket-promotions>)

Ipsos MORI (2009) 'Ethical purchasing squeezed by recession, but companies will continue to invest in company responsibility (CR)', Ipsos MORI Reputation Centre, 28 October 2009. (<http://www.ipsos-mori.com/researchpublications/researcharchive/2505/Ethical-purchasing-squeezed-by-recession-but-companies-will-continue-to-invest-in-company-responsibility-CR.aspx>)

Kay, J. (2004) The Truth About Markets (Harmondsworth: Penguin).

Lindblom, C. E. (1980) The Policy Making Process (Harlow: Prentice-Hall).

Luger, S. (2000) Corporate Power, American Democracy, and the Automobile Industry (Cambridge: Cambridge University Press).

Mathiason, N., and Bessaoud, Y. (2011) 'Tory Party funding from City doubles under Cameron', The Bureau of Investigative Journalism, 8 February 2011. (<http://www.thebureauinvestigates.com/2011/02/08/city-financing-of-the-conservative-party-doubles-under-cameron/>)

Moran, M. (2009) Business, Politics and Society: an Anglo-American comparison (Oxford: Oxford University Press).

Office of Fair Trading (2009) Quick Guide to Competition Law Compliance. (<http://oft.gov.uk/shared_oft/ca-and-cartels/competition-awareness-compliance/quick-guide.pdf>)

Office of Fair Trading (2013) 'OFT issues five infringement decisions in the distribution of Mercedes-Benz commercial vehicles investigation'. (<http://oft.gov.uk/news-and-updates/press/2013/30-13#.UWZ6DbXWZjU>)

Ofgem (2013) 'Press release: OFGEM fines SSE £10.5million for misselling'. (<http://www.ofgem.gov.uk/media/pressrel/Documents1/SSE%20Press%20Release.pdf>)

Peston, R. (2008) Who Runs Britain? (London: Hodder and Stoughton).

Reich, R. (2008) Supercapitalism (Cambridge: Icon Books).

Simms, A. (2007) Tescopoly: How one Shop came out on Top and Why it Matters (Constable).

Smithers, R. (2013) 'Growing taste for Fairtrade shows it's Britain's cup of tea', in The Guardian, 2 March 2013. (<http://www.guardian.co.uk/money/2013/mar/02/fairtrade-taste-growing-britain?INTCMP=SRCH>)

Wilson, G. K. (2003) Business and Politics (Basingstoke: Palgrave).

Chapter 12
Are opportunities in business equal?

Stephen Taylor and Paul Wetherly

Learning objectives

When you have completed this chapter you will be able to:

- Explain what is meant by 'equal opportunity' and 'work–life balance', and understand how they are related.
- Identify developments in the business environment which are driving the equal opportunity and work–life balance agenda in business and politics, and the conflicting values, interests, and pressures involved.
- Assess how far progress has been made in achieving equal opportunity in business and work–life balance in the UK and elsewhere in the world.
- Describe key aspects of government policy and the evolving legal framework.
- Examine the range of policies and practices developed by employers in relation to equal opportunity and work–life balance.

THEMES

The following themes of the book are especially relevant to this chapter.

▶ **DIVERSITY** OF BUSINESS

The shift towards equality of opportunity and, more recently, work–life balance affects the whole business community, though not all firms and sectors respond to this agenda in the same way. Managerial approaches and workplace cultures vary as do the specific market conditions and pressures that firms face. In general, public sector organizations have been at the forefront of developments compared with the private sector, partly reflecting the idea that the public sector should act as a good employer. However, measures are also increasingly being taken by small and large companies seeking to gain a reputation for being 'employers of choice'.

▶ **INTERNAL/EXTERNAL**

Changes in the external environment are driving the equal opportunity and work–life balance agenda, especially the increased female employment rate. Competitive pressures in labour and product markets influence the business response, sometimes pulling in different directions. Implementing equal opportunity and work–life balance policies requires internal changes within organizations in relation to managing the internal labour market, such as the introduction of more flexible patterns of working. It may be important to confront barriers to change embedded in the workplace culture, such as sexist attitudes or a long hours culture.

⏩ COMPLEXITY OF THE ENVIRONMENT

Political, economic, social, and technological factors have all influenced the shift towards equal opportunity and work–life balance. For example, the changing position of women in society and the weakening of traditional ideas of gender roles; competitive pressures in product and labour markets; technological developments enabling more flexible patters of work; and government policy at national and European levels.

⏩ VARIETY OF SPATIAL LEVELS

The significance of the equal opportunity and work–life balance agenda varies considerably across the world. In general terms this agenda is characteristic of advanced western economies but is less developed or has little support in poor and developing countries. There is a close link between equal opportunity and 'western' ideas such as freedom; and work–life balance issues gain support in societies in which women participate in the labour force in large numbers and where prosperity allows a growing concern with quality-of-life (or post-material) issues. Among the rich economies there are important differences in the extent to which equal opportunity and work–life balance policies have been implemented, reflecting differing national cultures and approaches to economic life. For example, there are marked variations in average annual work hours. This chapter focuses on developments in the UK but draws attention to the influence of EU law.

⏩ DYNAMIC ENVIRONMENT

Equality of opportunity appeared on the business and political agenda in the 1970s, and work–life balance has become a prominent issue more recently (although much earlier antecedents can be traced for both issues). They are expressions of a changing society. Even during this relatively short period the terms of debate have shifted. For example, the equal opportunity agenda has been extended to tackle a wider range of forms of discrimination, such as on grounds of age, sexual orientation and disability. The work–life balance agenda is now seen not just in terms of women balancing work and care of dependent children but also the desire among men to have more time for family life. These issues appear likely to remain on the agenda for the foreseeable future. However, this is not inevitable and social and economic change can produce counter pressures. For example, when labour market conditions loosen (i.e. skill shortages are eased) as a result of recessions or changes in an economy's structure, a major reason for businesses adopting work–life balance policies becomes weaker. Moreover, governments also sometimes come under pressure to deregulate in this area so as to promote international competitiveness and economic growth.

⏩ INTERACTION BETWEEN BUSINESS AND THE ENVIRONMENT

The rise of the equal opportunity and work–life balance agenda is an excellent example of organizational practice being influenced by developments in the business environment. Social, economic, demographic, competitive, and regulatory trends have all played a part. The response on the part of employers demonstrates how some organizations have sought to turn the situation to their advantage by developing a positive reputation in key labour markets. At the same time the very process of business development and economic growth has played an important part in creating the social conditions in which equal opportunity and work–life balance issues have come to the fore, by drawing women into the labour market and creating affluent societies in which quality of life issues become more prominent.

⏩ STAKEHOLDERS

The development of the equal opportunity and work–life balance agenda primarily relates to the employer–employee relationship and hence to the stake that employees have in organizations, and to responses by business to shifts in social values and to competitive pressures in labour and product markets. However, governments have also been major stakeholders through their power to establish a framework of legal rights and duties. Government intervention has mainly been shaped by objectives of fairness and efficiency, but it may also be seen as recognizing that there are advantages to be gained for the wider communities in which organizations are based.

》 VALUES

While most attention focuses on the business case for equal opportunity and practices which promote work–life balance, there are major ethical and political issues to be considered too. It can be argued that organizations should not move in this direction purely because of business imperative, but simply because it is right to do so. The same debate is relevant to the regulatory agenda. Irrespective of the role the promotion of work–life balance plays in the meeting of economic objectives, there is a straightforward case for such developments rooted in social justice and the enhancement of the quality of life.

Introduction

This chapter deals with two related issues concerned with the nature of the employer–employee relationship and the way work is organized: work–life balance, and equality of opportunity. The chapter focuses primarily on the UK and EU, but these issues are important in other western societies to varying degrees, driven by affluence and changing attitudes to gender. In developing parts of the world these issues generally have less prominence but can be expected to move up the agenda. Balancing work and life healthily and ensuring equal opportunities are important for people everywhere.

These issues are important for business because the way businesses deal with them can affect their competitiveness and profitability, and because they reflect important shifts in social attitudes to work and concerning the purpose of business and how its contribution to society is judged. There is, of course, a possible tension here between the business need for profitability and the demand for business to demonstrate wider social benefits. For example, the drive for competitiveness and profitability can lead to longer working hours, but this may conflict with a desire on the part of employees to limit the demands that work makes on their time in order to fulfil commitments outside of work and enjoy a fuller family life. How this tension is managed and getting the balance right is a key challenge for business today.

》 STAKEHOLDERS The issues of work–life balance and equality of opportunity are often presented as though they are primarily of concern to women. However, although much of the focus of this chapter will be on the position of women, it is important to recognize that these are not just 'women's issues'. Work–life balance is also an issue for male employees, and the demand for equality of opportunity in business is made by, or on behalf of, a range of groups that are recognized as being disadvantaged on the basis of age, race, sexuality, or other grounds (see Chapter 5).

Some preliminary definitions

Before going on to analyse these issues in detail, it will help to start with some preliminary definitions. In one way the idea of **work–life balance** is odd since it suggests a distinction whereas work is actually part of life. However, it concerns the way in which the time and energy committed to paid employment is balanced with the time and energy available to us outside of work, or to put it slightly differently, the way in which paid employment is balanced with all the other relationships and activities that make up our lives—our family and social lives and our leisure interests. The basic thought is that a good work–life balance is an important ingredient of individual well-being or happiness and therefore of a good society. It is, therefore, one of the ways in which the performance of business might be judged. Of course, the question of what constitutes a good balance between work and life can be answered in different ways:

❯❯ DYNAMIC

- Attitudes to work and work–life balance are likely to change over time within any particular society, and also vary between societies or cultures. For example, average working hours in the United States are very high by international standards.

- Within any society or culture, whatever the prevailing norm, people might disagree about the desirable balance between work and life. Different attitudes are linked closely to the occupational hierarchy. People in some professional jobs, such as academics or doctors, might regard work as a central life interest, be prepared to devote long hours to it, and not make a sharp separation between work and non-work life. Individuals in low- or unskilled jobs are more likely to regard work as a means to an end rather than as an activity that is intrinsically rewarding and what they really want to do with their lives. In this case working long hours is more likely to be a response to economic necessity. (The contrast between these cases is sometimes made in the rather stark terms of 'living to work' versus 'working to live'). Attitudes within society may also vary between men and women, particularly where they reflect the influence of traditional ideas of differentiated gender roles in which males are seen as the primary 'breadwinners' while women are expected to assume the main burden of domestic responsibilities. We will examine the impact of such 'sexist' assumptions on work–life balance and equality of opportunity later in the chapter. Finally, in modern multicultural societies attitudes to work may vary between ethnic groups or communities.

❯❯ VALUES

- Different views of what constitutes a 'good' or 'reasonable' work–life balance may be a source of tension or conflict, as already indicated, between employers and employees. Here employers face competing pressures. On the one hand in order to recruit and retain staff employers may need to offer a more favourable work–life balance. They may also want to be 'good employers' because of their own ethical standpoint (see Chapter 7). On the other hand, market pressures from competitors or customers may feed through into demands for longer working hours and/or more intensive working.

It seems clear, then, that a good work–life balance means different things to different people. From this it might be concluded that it is not a very helpful term for business since it does not offer any clear guidance on what businesses should do. However, the proper conclusion is that work–life balance will always have to be negotiated, and that the terms of negotiation will change as circumstances and attitudes alter.

Stop and Think

What do you understand by the term 'work–life balance'? How far do you think a desire on the part of employees to achieve a better work–life balance will bring them into conflict with employers?

❱❱ VALUES

Equality of opportunity can be seen as one of the core values of western societies, related to ideas such as freedom and individualism (see Chapter 4). The basic idea here is that individuals should be, as far as possible, free to live as they choose and, in particular, should have equal opportunities to use their talents and energies in the way that they see fit to get on in life and achieve the goals and aspirations that they set for themselves. This doesn't mean that we all do or should have the *same* goals and aspirations. On the contrary, the value of freedom is associated with the idea that individuals make different choices about how they want to live their lives. For example, some people might think of a good life in terms of earning as much money as they can, while others think in terms of doing good for others (or we might have different ideas about how we balance these goals). The point is that, as individuals, what matters to us varies.

However, the idea of equality of opportunity is quite complex and involves two types of question: What kinds of opportunities are we concerned with, and, how can we make them equal? Although we could think of endless kinds of opportunities in terms of different goals or aspirations, the discussion tends to focus on a more limited range of opportunities that are recognized as being important for everybody. High among these are education and employment. Education is important for everybody no matter what kind of life they choose to live, and therefore it is generally accepted that everybody should have the same opportunity to benefit from education to a certain standard. Employment opportunities are important for a number of reasons:

- For most people in capitalist societies paid employment is the primary source of livelihood. In other words, the principal extrinsic benefit of employment is the wage or salary earned.

- Employment is an important source of social status and self-respect.

- Paid work can bring a range of intrinsic benefits such as social contact and job satisfaction.

Thus, paid work is highly valued in society and recognized to be important for everybody so that it would be wrong if some people have a greater opportunity than others to work or to attain particular positions within the occupational hierarchy. For example, women should have the same opportunity as men to become company directors.

But what does it mean for men and women to have the same or equal opportunity to become a company director? How can we make opportunities equal? As we will see, this question can be answered in different ways, and this means that there can be strong disagreements between people who are in favour of equal opportunity. A generally accepted limited conception of equal opportunity is meritocratic. This means essentially that appointment to positions in the occupational hierarchy should be determined by the talents of the applicants and how well they match up to the employee specification. In other words, employers should choose or discriminate between applicants only on these grounds. That would seem to be the best way to choose between candidates since the employer presumably wants the best person for the job. But the point here is that if the employer were to choose on other grounds, such as having a preference for men over women for particular jobs, it would constitute unfair discrimination. Thus, ensuring equal opportunity for men and women in the labour market requires that sexual discrimination is prohibited. Unfair discrimination on grounds of gender has now been outlawed in most industrialized countries. In the UK this has been the case since 1975 when the Sex Discrimination Act was passed.

▶ STAKEHOLDERS Unfair sexual discrimination is a barrier to women doing the kinds of jobs they want to do as an aspect of the kinds of lives they choose to lead. But we can see why it can be argued that removing this barrier is not enough to ensure equal opportunity, and more has to be done. This is because there may be barriers or constraints that make it harder for women to apply for jobs in the first place. And here we can see the connection between work–life balance and equal opportunity. Mothers may want to balance the time and energy they commit to paid employment with the time and energy they need to devote to caring for dependent children. For some mothers full-time employment may not enable them to achieve this balance, and they may require other working arrangements such as part-time, flexi-time, or term-time employment. It can be argued that if such working patterns are not made available by business, or if only low-skilled and low paid work is available on these terms, women with young children do not enjoy the same employment opportunities as men. Increasingly, as we enjoy longer life expectancy, middle-aged people are finding they must devote more time to caring for elderly parents. Here too there is a tendency for women to bear the lion's share of the burden.

Of course there is another side to this issue, which is to point out that women are disadvantaged in relation to men only in so far as it is usually women that accept prime responsibility for childcare and eldercare. The constraint or barrier that women face can be described in terms of the domestic division of labour. This means that opportunities for women in the labour market are tied up with men's choices in relation to work–life balance too, and specifically their choices as fathers in relation to childcare responsibilities.

Stop and Think

What is a meritocratic conception of equality of opportunity? Why is it rational for businesses to be equal opportunity employers in this sense? Is a meritocratic approach enough to ensure that women really do have the same opportunities in business as men?

■ Why has equality of opportunity moved up the agenda?

▶ VALUES Attitudes towards women and their place in society have shifted considerably in Britain and other societies in recent decades—within the space of one lifetime. In the middle of the last century a widely held view could be summed up in the phrase: 'A woman's place is in the home', referring to a division of labour (that may have been thought of as 'natural') in which men worked to earn a family wage while women stayed at home as mothers and 'housewives'. It was entirely usual up until the 1970s for employers to have separate pay scales for their male and female employees and very common for women to leave their jobs altogether when their first child was born. By the turn of the century this view had been replaced by support for the idea of equal opportunity—that women should have the same opportunities (and rights) to engage in paid employment as men. Moreover, it had become fully accepted that employers should keep jobs open for women to return to after a period of paid maternity leave. In other words, during the 20th century, many traditional ideas or norms about the nature of 'masculinity' and 'femininity' were increasingly questioned and challenged. They have now very largely been replaced by a wholly different set of social values.

》 DYNAMIC At the same time there has been increasing recognition of the need to extend the principle of equality of opportunity to other groups who are perceived to suffer disadvantage in education, employment, and other areas of life. In the 1970s the focus of campaigning and legal reform was on race and sex, but in the succeeding decades the equal opportunity agenda has been extended. In the UK, the Equality and Human Rights Commission (EHRC) has statutory responsibility to protect, enforce, and promote equality across nine 'protected' grounds—age, disability, gender, race, religion and belief, pregnancy and maternity, marriage and civil partnership, sexual orientation, and gender reassignment.

This is a remarkable process of social change. Forms of discrimination that were regarded by many as natural or acceptable a generation ago are now prohibited in law. The series of legal enactments may be seen as both reflecting and promoting the changing values and attitudes within modern society. Although prejudicial and discriminatory attitudes and behaviours may have receded, changes in the law have been required because:

a) the law is a powerful *public statement* of values and gives authoritative expression to the principle that discrimination is unacceptable, and

b) law enables *enforcement* of non-discriminatory behaviour and thus protection of vulnerable and disadvantaged groups.

Timeline of equal opportunity—key Acts and regulations

1970	Equal Pay Act	To prevent discrimination, as regards terms and conditions of employment, between men and women.
1975	Sex Discrimination Act	To render unlawful certain kinds of sex discrimination and discrimination on the ground of marriage, etc.
1976	Race Relations Act	To make fresh provision with respect to discrimination on racial grounds and relations between people of different racial groups, etc.
1995	Disability Discrimination Act	To make it unlawful to discriminate against disabled persons in connection with employment, etc.
1998	Human Rights Act	Enshrined rights and freedoms under the European Convention on Human Rights in UK law.
2001	Special Educational Needs and Disability Act	Amends the Education Act 1996 to make further provision against discrimination on grounds of disability in schools and other educational establishments.
2003	Employment Equality (Religion or Belief) Regulations	To prevent discrimination on the grounds of religious or philosophical beliefs, etc.
2003	Employment Equality (Sexual Orientation) Regulations	To prevent discrimination on grounds of sexual orientation, etc.
2005	Disability Discrimination Act	Amends the 1995 DDA, e.g. extends the definition of disability and introduces a public sector disability duty, etc.
2006	Employment Equality (Age) Regulations	To prevent discrimination on the ground of age, etc.
2006	Equality Act	Established the EHRC, etc.

2006	Racial and Religious Hatred Act	To make provision about offences involving stirring up hatred against persons on racial or religious grounds.
2010	The Equality Act*	• replaces previous anti-discrimination laws with a single Act, including most of those listed above. • establishes a Single Public Sector Equality Duty covering 8 protected characteristics. The protected characteristics are: • Age • Disability • Gender reassignment • Pregnancy and maternity • Race • Religion and belief • Sex • Sexual orientation.

* For further information go to the EHRC website: <**http://www.equalityhumanrights.com/legal-and-policy/equality-act/what-is-the-equality-act/**> and see Equality Act 2010: guidance at <**https://www.gov.uk/equality-act-2010-guidance**>

In other words, government action in the form of making and enforcing law is necessary because experience shows that discrimination will otherwise persist—the market will not eliminate the problem if left to itself. However, passing a law does not by itself solve a social problem. To be effective a law must introduce measures that are appropriate and adequate, and there has to be compliance. Has the law been effective in realizing the goal of equality of opportunity between men and women in business?

A woman's place?

The shift away from the traditional idea that a woman's place is in the home is reflected in the changing sexual composition of the labour market resulting from a long-term trend of increasing economic activity among women, narrowing the gap with men.[1] In the UK in 2011 a higher proportion of working-age men than women were in employment, but the gap was among the smallest on record as a result of convergence of employment rates. Between 1971 and 2011 the employment rate for men fell from 92% to 76%, while for women it rose from 53% to 66% (Spence 2011, p. 6). Overall economic activity rates, which include self-employed persons, were 83.5% for men in 2012 and 71.2% for women. Similarly, a higher proportion of all those in employment are men than women, but the gap has been narrowing. Of a total of 29.6 million in employment in 2012, 53% (15.9 million) were men and 47% (13.4 million) were women.

》 DYNAMIC Yet this apparent evidence of a trend towards equalizing opportunities between men and women conceals some marked and persistent differences in male and female experiences of paid work. These differences can be analysed in terms of:

- the distinction between traditional and flexible patterns of working
- the types of jobs that men and women do (occupational segregation)
- the amount that men and women, on average, are paid.

---

[1] The labour market is made up of the population aged 16 years and over, divided into three main groups: employed, unemployed (which together comprise the economically active, or the 'labour force'), and the economically inactive (including those looking after a home, retirees (the largest proportion), and those unable to work due to long-term sickness or disability).

Flexible work

Flexible work includes temporary and part-time work, and is often contrasted with 'traditional' full-time, 'permanent' (i.e. of indefinite duration) jobs. In the UK there has been a long-term rise in the share of part-time jobs, though this has stabilized in the last decade. Of the total of full- and part-time employees taken together in 2012 the share of part-time was 27% (up from 25% in 1998). Table 12.1 shows that although the number of men working part-time has increased more rapidly than the number of women, it remains the case that women are much more likely than men to work part-time. For example, female part-time employees make up over 43% of the total of full- and part-time female employees, whereas the corresponding share for men is 13%. In other words part-time employment is a common experience for women but remains rare among men.

Looked at another way (Table 12.2), of 8 million part-time employees in 2012 over 70% were women.

Flexibility and parenthood

So far we have considered men and women in general, but another way we can examine how far their participation in the labour force differs is in terms of parenthood. If we look more closely at increased female economic activity it is particularly noticeable among mothers with dependent children (age 0–18 years). Between 1975 and 2010 this increased from half to 67%. However, 'the presence of a dependent child in the family continues to have a major effect on the economic activity of women of working age' (ONS 2009, p. 47), in contrast with men. Men of working age with dependent children are more likely to be in employment in each age group between 16 and 64 than men without dependent children. In contrast, women of working age with dependent children are less likely to be in employment. For example, 89% of women in the 25–34 age group without dependent children are in employment, as against 61% of those with dependent children, whereas for men in this age group having dependent children makes virtually no difference to the employment rate. This contrast does seem to reflect the 'traditional' idea of the male 'breadwinner'. The gap in the employment rate between women with and those without dependent children is greatest in the 16–24 and 25–34 age groups, and this is consistent with the employment rate being correlated with the age of the youngest dependent child. For example, 63% of married or cohabiting mothers whose youngest child is under 5 are in employment and this rises to 82% where the youngest child is 16–18 (the corresponding figures are lower for lone mothers). In other words, mothers are more likely at all ages than

Table 12.1 Employees in employment*, by employment status and sex, UK (No. = Million)

	1998						2012					
	Men		Women		All		Men		Women		All	
	No.	%	No.	%	No.	%	No.	%	No.	%	No.	%
Full-time employees	11.0	91.7	6.2	55.8	17.3	74.9	13.8	86.8	7.8	56.9	21.6	73.0
Part-time employees	1.0	8.3	4.9	44.2	5.8	25.1	2.1	13.2	5.9	43.1	8.0	27.0
All employees	12.0	100	11.1	100	23.1	100	15.9	100	13.7	100	29.6	100

* The category of employees constitutes the majority of economically active but excludes self-employed, others in employment, and unemployed.

Source: Derived from ONS (2009a, p. 47, Table 4.2) and Statistical Bulletin (2013).

Table 12.2 Employment status of employees in UK by sex, 2012

		Million	%
Full-time	Men	13.8	63.8
	Women	7.8	36.2
	All	21.6	100
Part-time	Men	2.1	26.2
	Women	5.9	73.7
	All	8.0	100

Source: Derived from ONS, *Social Trends 39*, p. 47, Table 4.2.

fathers to be looking after children (and less likely to be in employment), and mothers with younger children are more likely to be looking after them and less likely to be in employment than mothers of older children. The employment rate of mothers increases as they and their children get older (ONS 2009b, p. 48, Table 4.3 and p. 50, Table 4.6).

We have also seen that women are more likely to work part time than men, and we can now add that working part time is closely associated with motherhood. In 2011, 37% of working women with dependent children worked part time, whereas the figure for working women with no dependent children was 30% (EHRC 2013). By contrast, having dependent children makes it *less* likely that men work part time. In 2011 just 6% of working fathers worked part time, whereas the figure for working men with no dependent children was 13% (EHRC 2013).

Occupational segregation

Occupational segregation refers to the fact that men and women are not equally represented throughout the labour force, and this is another persisting difference in the experience of work that may be seen as part of the pattern of disadvantage faced by women. There are two dimensions of occupational segregation, and evidence for both can be gained from Table 12.3. Horizontal segregation refers to the fact that men are more likely than women to work in certain occupations, and women are more likely than men to be found in others. To some extent this pattern reflects persisting cultural norms concerning 'women's work' and 'men's work'. Some of the female dominated occupations reflect the household tasks for which women have traditionally been primarily responsible (e.g. caring, cleaning, and catering). Vertical segregation refers to the greater representation of men at more senior levels in the occupational hierarchy, such as in managerial and professional roles. The phenomenon of segregation is sometimes referred to by saying that women are 'under-represented' in certain types of work and in senior positions, but both of these terms must be treated with some caution. 'Segregation' may suggest deliberate exclusion of women but, while this may be part of the story, there may be other factors at work. 'Under-representation' implies some desired or appropriate level of representation which is not being achieved, but there may be different views of what that level is. For example, what level of female representation would be appropriate on the boards of major companies (see Mini-Case 12.1)?

Table 12.3 shows the projected extent for the UK of 'horizontal' segregation in 2015 (UK Commission for Employment and Skills 2012). There are some occupations in which men and women are equally (or nearly equally) likely to be represented (professional, associate professional and technical, elementary), although closer inspection would reveal differences within these broad categories. For example, within 'professionals', schoolteachers are predominantly

Table 12.3 UK employment by sex and occupation, 2015 (% and (rank))

	Males	Females
Managers and senior officials	13.0 (4)	8.0 (7)
Professional	19.1 (1)	21.1 (1)
Associate prof. and technical	14.2 (3)	12.3 (4)
Administrative and secretarial	4.6 (8)	18.7 (2)
Skilled trades	18.3 (2)	2.8 (8)
Caring, leisure and other service	3.3 (9)	15.6 (3)
Sales and customer service	5.5 (7)	11.4 (5)
Process, plant, and machine operatives	10.1(6)	1.2 (9)
Elementary	11.8 (5)	8.9 (6)
All occupations	100	100

Source: UK Commission for Employment and Skills 2012, p.85-85 Tables 4.2 & 4.3.

women. There are three occupational groups in which women are more likely to work than men (administrative and secretarial, personal service, sales, and customer service). Nearly one in five women work in administrative and secretarial occupations compared to less than one in 20 men. Looked at another way, of 3.5 million in employment in this occupational group, in 2015 nearly four out of five (78%) are likely to be women. A similar gap is apparent in personal service occupations. Conversely, men predominate in skilled trades, this being the second highest ranked occupation for men (18.3%) and the second lowest for women (2.8%): skilled trades are virtually a male preserve.

Table 12.3 also shows a pattern of vertical segregation, in which women are less likely than men to be found in managerial positions. Nearly one in eight men is a manager or senior official compared to less than one in ten women. This 'under-representation' of women is often referred to as the glass ceiling, meaning that women face a barrier to their progression to the most senior positions in organizations. Vertical segregation is most pronounced at the very top: only 6.1% of executive directors of the UK's top 100 companies are women (Davies 2013).

> *Stop and Think*
>
> Do you find it surprising that only 6.1% of executive directors of the UK's top one hundred companies are women? Is it plausible that women have equal opportunities with men when so few at the top are female? Do you think that the figure should be greater than 6.1%? How much greater?

■ **The gender pay gap**

Across the world there is a gender pay gap which has narrowed over time, but which remains substantial. In the UK the gender pay gap based on median hourly earnings for all employees decreased from 22% in 2008 to 19.7% in 2012. The median hourly earnings of women in part-time work are slightly higher than for men (the pay gap is negative, at -5.2%, but for full-time work it is 9.6%). The overall gap is larger because the median hourly earnings for part-time work are so much lower than for full-time work and, as we have seen, most part-time employees are female. Here work–life balance and equal opportunity issues are bound together. Women who work part-time to balance employment with care of dependent children are disadvantaged by the scarcity of well-paid part-time jobs.

The gender pay gap can be explained largely by occupational segregation: the occupational areas in which women are clustered are low paid compared to those occupations where women are under-represented. The 'pay gap' and 'opportunity gap' are closely related. This does not necessarily mean that the jobs women do are less skilled—it may be that these jobs are undervalued and the skills involved unfairly less rewarded than skills exercised in some jobs done by men (Women and Work Commission 2006).

Comparing weekly or annual earnings shows a bigger gender pay gap because men, on average, work longer hours and are more likely to receive overtime pay and bonuses. In the financial year 2011–12 median earnings for men working full time in the UK were £546 per week, whereas for women the figure was only £449 (ONS 2012). Thus, the gender gap has narrowed but remains at 17.8%. Differences in bonus payments may be found to be discriminatory. For example, in 2010 an employment tribunal found in favour of 4,000 female workers employed by Birmingham City Council who were excluded from bonuses from which men in the same pay-graded jobs benefited (Pidd 2010).

The Equal Opportunities Commission (EOC) used ONS data to estimate a lifetime earnings gap of around £330,000 for the average woman working full time compared to full-time men (EOC 26 October 2006a).

Mini-Case 12.1   Women in the City and on boards

A report by the Equality and Human Rights Commission (EHRC, 2009) examined the extent of sex discrimination and the gender pay gap in the financial services sector. It found that although 'men and women make up almost equal proportions of employees within the sector' (p. 9), there is a persistent pattern of occupational segregation and a related marked pay gap. These problems are more marked in the financial services sector than in the economy as a whole.

Gender pay gap

The overall gender pay gap is 55% based on mean full-time gross annual earnings, and 'there is evidence of gender bias in the distribution of bonuses and performance-related pay' (p. 10).

Occupational segregation

Woman are concentrated in the lower-paid jobs, and underrepresented in revenue-generating functions for which basic and performance-related pay are much higher. Hence the opportunity- and pay-gaps are closely related. 'Men occupy two-thirds of managerial and senior jobs and nearly three-quarters of professional jobs' (p. 11).

Work culture

▶ INTERNAL/EXTERNAL Some important aspects of work culture are seen to disadvantage women. Client networking activities play an important role in the sector and tend to be male-oriented, serving to 'exclude women (such as a focus on male-dominated sports) or even demean women (such as socializing at lap-dancing clubs or hostess bars)' (p. 12). The characteristic long-hours culture is an obstacle to improved work–life balance and disadvantages employees trying to balance work and family responsibilities, particularly women. Furthermore, requests for flexible working for senior employees are not regarded positively and may involve demotion, and women taking maternity leave are disadvantaged by reallocation of their clients and other negative consequences.

The EHRC put forward a number of recommendations to improve the opportunities for women in the financial service sector on the basis not only of fairness but also the benefits to business. Trevor Phillips, chair of EHRC, argues that through such improvement 'financial firms have the chance to boost morale, bring on new talent, and maximize the potential of their existing employees' (quoted in *The Guardian* 7 September 2009).

Similar arguments have been made in favour of greater female representation on the boards of directors of large companies. In 2011 Lord Davies published the findings of an independent review into *Women on Boards*. This showed that in 2010 only 12.5% (1 in 8) of directors of FTSE100 companies were women and eighteen companies had no female board members. Davies recommended that these companies should be aiming for a minimum of 25% female board member representation by 2015. According to the report:

The business case for gender diversity on boards has four key dimensions:

- Improving performance
- Accessing the widest talent pool
- Being more responsive to the market
- Achieving better corporate governance (Davies, 2011)

Davies commented, 'This is not ... just about promoting equal opportunities but it is about improving business performance. There is growing evidence to show that diverse boards are better boards, delivering financial out-performance and stock market growth'. The voluntary approach advocated by Davies led to progress towards the 2015 target: by March 2013 women made up 17.3% of all directorships in FTSE100 companies (Department for Business, Innovation & Skills 2011, 2013).

Stop and Think

Some people argue that when a woman chooses to be a stay-at-home mother, this 'choice' simply reflects the way girls are socialized. In this view, males and females are equally capable of performing high-flying roles in the City and would be equally likely to choose this path if it weren't for their upbringing or other factors. Do you agree?

Mini-Case 12.2 Can opportunities ever be equal?

The idea of equal opportunity is that men and women, on average, should have the same chances of, say, becoming the chief executive of a FTSE 100 company, or of pursuing careers in management at all levels. What individuals make of their lives should depend on their talents, choices, and efforts, not on artificial barriers such as sexual discrimination. We might expect that equal opportunities will lead to roughly equal representation of men and women in management, or at least that representation at this level will reflect the balance between males and females within the workforce. Should we expect 50% of managers to be women? If so, British business is clearly a long way short of the mark. However, this outcome should only be expected if men and women have, on average, the same talents and make the same choices. It can be argued that part of the 'under-representation' of women in management is a reflection of women having, as a group, different attitudes to work and careers than men. In particular, if a proportion of women choose home (i.e. being a stay-at-home mother looking after young children) over career then we would

expect men, on average, to be more successful in their careers than women.

'Mummy, I *want* to be a housewife' (Hakim 1996).

VALUES Hakim's research suggests that some women choose to prioritize 'home' over 'career', and that these choices go some way to explain occupational segregation and pay differences: 'sex differentials in employment experience ... are ... due to personal choice as much as to sex discrimination'. She claims that there is a polarization of the female population between 'career women' and 'home-centred women'.

This research suggests that we need to distinguish between support for the principle of equal opportunity and approval of working wives/mothers among women, and the personal choices of many women about their own lives.

However, this argument is controversial because, it can be argued, we need to consider the pressures and constraints that influence women's 'choices'. These choices might be explained by cultural norms concerning femininity or by the refusal of men to take on a fair share of childcare and household chores.

Why is work–life balance moving up the agenda?

Several distinct reasons can be identified for the increased interest in work–life balance issues on the part of employees, employers, trade unions, government, and commentators. Here we focus on three sets of developments that have particular relevance in the UK: major social changes, the intensification of work, and labour market trends.

Social trends

▶ **DYNAMIC** ▶ **VALUES** We have seen that equality of opportunity and work–life balance are closely related issues. As female economic activity has increased and 'old-fashioned' ideas that a woman's place is in the home and a man's role is to be the family 'breadwinner' have weakened, demands for greater equality of opportunity and improved work–life balance have moved up the agenda. Work–life balance was initially framed largely as a women's issue but is increasingly recognized as an issue for men too, because women sharing the same opportunities as men in work depends both on the way that paid work is organized and the way both men and women balance work and domestic responsibilities, and because there is increased desire among men to be more involved in childcare.

Population ageing (see Chapter 6) is also of relevance in this context because of the increased likelihood in the future that employees of working age will have elderly relatives to care for. Already 12% of the working population have such responsibilities. As more and more people live into their nineties and beyond, this percentage will grow.

The intensification of work

Increased interest in work–life balance issues can be explained partly by evidence of increased hours and intensity of work. Due to the lack of reliable statistics, there is some disagreement between analysts about the extent to which the numbers of hours worked have increased or decreased in recent years. In the UK, after several decades in which full-time workers worked fewer hours on average each year, the trend appears to have reversed in recent years although the rise in part-time working suggests that some people are undertaking rather fewer hours of paid work than they did in the past (Philpott 2010). What can be stated with some confidence, however, is that UK employees perceive that they are working more rather than fewer hours each year, the same being true of employees in many other countries (see Green 2006, pp. 45–6 and Walsh 2009, pp. 490–2).

In the UK around 30% of men and 10% of women claim to work in excess of 50 hours a week, while substantially more people than previously report working unpaid overtime on a regular basis. Moreover, as Green (2006, p. 46) points out there is no question that the average number of hours worked each week by the adult members of each household *in combination* has risen substantially in recent years, due to the rapid rise in the number of dual-earner households since the 1970s. Thus, considerably more time is now spent 'at work' (i.e. paid work) than was the case 20 years ago (see Berthoud 2007).

In addition, surveys carried out in the UK show that people believe that the speed at which they are required to work and the effort that they are required to expend in order to get their work done has increased a great deal since the 1980s. The 2004 Workplace Employment Relations Survey (Kersley et al. 2006, p. 101) found that 76% of employees agreed with the statement 'my job requires that I work very hard', while 40% agreed that 'I never seem to have enough time to get my work done'. In both cases, however, the numbers are highest in the case of managers and professional staff. A similar trend towards increased intensification of work is reported by studies undertaken across Europe and in the US and Australia (Green 2006, pp. 58–61).

Stop and Think

In their study of how work–life balance issues are perceived by different stakeholders in different countries Gambles et al. (2006) found many examples of people who said that they chose to work long hours and that they were not compelled to do so by their employers. CIPD (2006) found that UK employees who choose not to take all their annual leave are more likely than those who do to be engaged with their work, to rate their own performance highly and to stay with their current organizations than those who do.

Why do you think that such a sizeable proportion of people actively want to work hard and would resist attempts to force them to work fewer hours?

Labour market trends

⟫ **DYNAMIC** A third factor which puts pressure on employers to improve work–life balance is a tightening of the labour market (see IRS 2002; Caligiuri and Givelekian 2008), due in part to long-term demographic trends (see Chapter 6). Despite the low levels of economic growth experienced in most industrialized countries since 2008 and concerns about unemployment and underemployment, skills shortages remain common. The Chartered Institute of Personnel and Development (CIPD) (2012a, pp. 11) reported that 82% of organizations in the UK had difficulties filling vacancies, particularly in managerial and professional jobs. Previous CIPD surveys have demonstrated that employers, in part, respond to such situations by increasing flexible working opportunities.

When faced with skills shortages employers put in place different kinds of strategies, including: reducing the need for skills through restructuring; investing in staff development; and trying to attract skilled workers through recruitment campaigns or by paying higher wages. However, increasingly employers are seeking to achieve longer-term solutions by positioning themselves in the labour market as 'employers of choice' through offering a better work–life balance. This is not enough on its own because employees also seek job security, interesting work, and influence over how their jobs are performed, as well as good terms and conditions when they are deciding who to work for (see Taylor 2001). But for an increasing number of us, finding a job which allows us to combine a rewarding career with a full and satisfying home life is a major priority. Employers who can provide such employment are far better placed to compete for scarce staff than those who cannot.

▪ Government initiatives

Governments and opposition parties have shown an increased interest in legislating to help provide work–life balance for a number of reasons:

⟫ **VALUES**

- Such policies are seen by progressive thinkers as being socially just or fair.
- They are popular among voters, media commentators, and bodies such as trade unions which provide political funding.

- 'Family-friendly regulation' can contribute to the achievement of wider economic policy objectives.

In the UK over the past decade these factors have all played a role in shaping an extensive programme of government action in this field, and European directives have also been important drivers. What is more, a number of further new rights are planned for the future.

Governments, like employers, are right to be concerned about the impact of skills shortages. This is because they can act as a constraint on economic growth and fuel wage inflation, and undermine the government's own ability to deliver improvements in the quality of public services. Initiatives in the regulation of employment have played a significant part in the government response, the aim being to encourage as many people as possible to put their skills at the disposal of the economy by undertaking paid work. It is important to remember that there are, at any one time, millions of people of working age in the UK (nearly 8 million in 2013) who are 'economically inactive', neither working nor claiming jobseeker's allowance. The major categories are: retired people under the age of 65, parents of young children, full-time students, and people with long-term health problems. In order to attract as many as possible into work (and in some cases off welfare at the same time), the government has created legislation that makes it easier for them to combine work with other activities. It also aims to use legislation to make the prospect of working more attractive in general terms. Some policy initiatives have been general in their effect, while others have been targeted at providing assistance to particular groups, such as parents of young children. The major examples are the following:

Working Time Regulations

》 SPATIAL LEVEL The Working Time Regulations 1998 gave effect in UK law to the European Working Time Directive. This remains a matter of political controversy because it is so much less rigorously enforced in the UK than in other EU countries. Nonetheless it is important in that it provides workers with an opportunity to complain to the health and safety authorities or to an Employment Tribunal when they are obliged to work more than 48 hours a week against their will on a regular basis. The Working Time Regulations also: provide for a minimum of four weeks' paid holiday a year in addition to bank holidays; regulate the number of hours that can be worked overnight; and, seek to ensure that every worker has a

---

Mini-Case 12.3 CIPD research

In 2012 the Chartered Institute of Personnel and Development (CIPD) carried out a major survey of employer and employee attitudes towards flexible working and work–life balance initiatives. The survey was based on a sample of 1,000 UK-based employers and 2,000 employees from across the different industrial sectors.

Some of the key findings were as follows:

- 96% of employers offered some form of flexible working to their employees, including all the larger organisations included in the sample.
- A very common form of flexible working practice is flexi-time, 50% of employers offered such an arrangement.
- 33% of employers offered term-time contracts.

- A further 44% offered compressed hours systems.
- 20% of employees claimed to work from home on a regular basis.
- Employees who have flexible working arrangements are more likely than those who don't to state that they are emotionally engaged and satisfied with their work. They are also more likely to have a positive view of their organization and are less likely to want to quit.
- Yet only 37% of employees either agree or strongly agree that their organization provides them with sufficient support to help them manage their work–life balance.

(*Source:* CIPD 2012b)

break of at least 20 minutes every six hours, a break of 11 hours in any one 24-hour period and 24 hours of rest in any seven day period. Specific additional protection is given under the regulations to young workers under the age of 18.

Stop and Think

In France in 2000 the then government introduced the so-called 'Loi Aubery' (named after the employment minister of the time). This limited all employees, with one or two exceptions, to a maximum working week of 35 hours. It was introduced primarily as a means of reducing unemployment by seeking to ensure that what work was available was shared around more evenly. It proved very controversial, many economists claiming that it served to slow economic growth and hence caused unemployment to be higher than it otherwise would be. In 2008 it was repealed.

What is your view of laws such as this which require employers to limit the number of hours people work? Would you like to see such a law introduced across Europe?

Part-time workers regulations

A further EU directive seeks to protect part-time workers from unfair treatment by making it unlawful to discriminate against them vis-à-vis equivalent full-time workers. The relevant UK legislation is contained in the Part-Time Workers (Prevention of Less Favourable Treatment) Regulations 2000. Among the rights conferred by this legislation:

- Part-time workers who believe that they are being treated less favourably than a comparable full-time colleague can write to their employers asking for an explanation, which must be given in writing within 14 days.
- Where the explanation given by the employer is considered unsatisfactory, the part-time worker may ask an Employment Tribunal to require the employer to affirm the right to equal treatment.
- Employers are required to review their terms and conditions and to give part-timers pro rata rights with those of comparable full-timers. However, no inspectorate has been created to enforce this.

Time off for family emergencies

The right to 'time off for dependants' also has a European origin, the relevant UK legislation being found in the Employment Rights Act 1996 (as amended by the Employment Relations Act 1999). The right is to a reasonable amount of time off during working hours for urgent family reasons, such as: to provide assistance when a dependant falls ill, gives birth, or is injured; to make arrangements for the provision of care for a dependant who is ill or injured; or on the death of a dependant. The right is only to unpaid time off and employers must be informed of the intention to take the leave 'as soon as is reasonably practicable'.

Maternity and paternity leave

In the UK female employees who become pregnant have long had a right to take a period of maternity leave and to return to their jobs some months after the baby is born. This right was first established in 1974, and for employees with more than six months' service 15 weeks before the baby is due, there has always been an additional right to receive statutory maternity pay (SMP) during at least some of the period of leave. The legislation is now found in the Employment Rights Act 1996, amendments having been made several times in this area. In recent years rights in this field have steadily been extended, a new set of regulations being introduced every two or three years—notably via the Employment Act 2002 and the Work and Families Act 2006. Over time it is expected that all employees who have babies will be entitled to take a full year's leave and to receive SMP throughout that period.

Since 2003 fathers of new babies have had the right to take two weeks' paid paternity leave soon after a birth. In 2011 fathers' rights were much extended with the introduction of new regulations that permit mothers to 'pass on' a portion of their maternity leave (including some paid weeks) to the father of a new baby, allowing the mother to return to work 20 weeks after the birth. In the future a further major extension of paternity rights is planned. From April 2015 the distinction between maternity and paternity leave will be largely done away with. Instead, both parents will be able to split a period of 'parental leave' between them, some paid and some unpaid, as they see fit. This will allow both parents to take paid leave concurrently for several weeks after a new baby is born.

Adoption leave

Adoption leave is also available under the same set of regulations to both of an adopted child's new parents. One parent is entitled to take a full year's leave (equivalent to maternity leave), while the other is entitled to take a two-week period of leave (equivalent to paternity leave). Here too much greater flexibility is being planned for adoptions that take place after April 2015.

Parental leave

This comprises a right to take 18 weeks of unpaid leave in addition to any standard contractual holiday entitlement following the birth or adoption of a child. It originates in the EU and was given effect in the UK via the Maternity & Parental Leave etc. Regulations 1999. As matters stand, the leave must be taken within the first six years of a child's life (except in the case of later adoptions). The right currently applies only to employees who have completed a year's service at the time of the birth.

The right to request flexible working

These regulations, originally introduced as part of the Employment Act 2002, go some way to meeting the demands of campaigners that parents with child-rearing responsibilities should be able to work part-time as a right, but fall short of this position by some margin. The regulations set out quite a complex procedure requiring a parent or someone with caring responsibility for a disabled adult to write formally asking for a one-off change in terms and conditions, together with an explanation as to how his or her request could be accommodated. Any changes made as a result of the request are therefore contractual and permanent. There is no right to demand a year's part-time work followed by a return to full-time working. From April 2014 it is likely that this right will be extended to all employees, irrespective of their domestic responsibilities.

The employer can turn the request down if it believes there is a good business reason for doing so, such as: burden of additional costs, detrimental effect on ability to meet customer demand, inability to reorganize work among existing staff or to recruit additional staff.

An appeal mechanism for those who are turned down must be made available by employers, appeals being heard within 14 days of the request being received. Only one application can be made per person per year. Complaints can be made to an employment tribunal on the grounds that a request was rejected out of hand without a meeting, that an appeal hearing was denied, or the employer was too slow in dealing with the matter.

> ### Stop and Think
>
> When people decide to have children they should accept the responsibilities as parents that this brings with it. They should not expect that their employer, or colleagues, will have to make adjustments, such as covering time off for family emergencies, to accommodate these responsibilities. Do you agree with this negative view of work–life balance?

Stress checks

Since 2003 the Health and Safety Executive (HSE) has added concern about stress-related illnesses to the list of factors their inspectors check when visiting employer premises. To support this initiative the HSE has published detailed guidance on the systematic management of stress at work which indicates clearly that employers are expected to carry out stress-oriented risk assessments alongside their assessments relating to physical injury. They identify six 'key areas of work' that they wish to see 'properly managed', these being: demands, control, support, relationships, role, and change. They really serve as a checklist of factors to consider when assessing risk. In principle this means that employers can now face criminal proceedings and be fined if they knowingly allow someone to become ill due to excessive work-related stress. Moreover they could be fined simply for wilfully failing to include stress-related factors in their risk assessments.

■ Employer initiatives

⟫ INTERNAL/EXTERNAL Employers are obliged, as a minimum, to have in place policies which give effect to the legal rights described above. However, many in practice go a great deal further in helping to provide their employees with the opportunity to achieve a reasonable work–life balance. The following are the most common approaches used:

- The right to move from a full-time to a part-time contract. Often two part-time employees are able to occupy one position on a job-sharing basis.
- Term-time working arrangements allow parents to take unpaid leave during school holidays and to return to their jobs once term starts again. The employer typically replaces them during the holidays with university students who are looking for temporary work during their vacations.
- Compressed hours arrangements permit people a degree of flexibility over the days on which they work. They are employed on full-time contracts but work longer shifts on fewer days. For example, someone might work four ten-hour shifts instead of five eight-hour shifts each week.

- Flexi-time schemes allow people to vary their hours on a day-to-day basis, typically around core times of 10am–12pm and 2pm–4pm. Those who work for more than their contracted hours over the course of a month can then ask to take a 'flexi-day' or flexi-afternoon' off by way of compensation.

- Homeworking policies permit people to base themselves at home for part or even all the working week.

- Sabbaticals permit people who have completed a defined period of continuous service to take a period of several weeks or months as unpaid leave and to return to the same job or a similar job at the end.

- Crèches are often provided by larger organizations to give parents of children who are below school age access to subsidized childcare facilities. After school clubs and school holiday clubs are sometimes provided for older children to attend while their parents are working.

- Childcare vouchers are often provided as a benefit by organizations which are too small to provide in-house crèche facilities.

- Employee Assistance Programmes (EAPs) have long been provided (or funded) by larger American corporations, as well as some UK organizations. They provide confidential advice to employees about practical matters such as finance and counselling services to people who are feeling over-stressed. Advice about achieving a better work–life balance forms an important part of their work.

All the available evidence suggests substantial growth, albeit from a small base, of these types of initiative in recent years. The 2004 Workplace Employee Relations Survey (see Kersley et al. 2006) reported significant increases in the proportion of UK workplaces having flexible working arrangements in place since an earlier survey in 1998. Job-sharing, flexi-time, annualized hours, and term-time working all saw big increases in this period alongside schemes which allow full-timers to switch to part-time contracts. More recent research undertaken by the Chartered Institute of Personnel and Development (CIPD 2012b) demonstrates that the use of such approaches continues to grow, with almost all UK employers now choosing to provide some form of flexible working options to their staff.

However, researchers who have examined in detail what happens when employers introduce policies of this kind have reported mixed findings as to their practical impact. Gambles et al. (2006, p. 5), for example, find that their effect tends to be limited in practice, even when a package of measures is introduced and promoted actively by managers as being aimed at improving the work–life balance for employees. This appears to occur because having policies in place does not shift attitudes. The culture of many organizations remains one in which commitment to one's work is seen as a necessity if one's career is to develop, and in which commitment is demonstrated by a willingness to work long hours and to volunteer for additional responsibility. Workplace cultures of this type are very common and are often labelled 'macho'. The ability to cope with pressure is admired, while work–life balance policies are seen as being introduced for political reasons. Taking them up is judged as being the action of a 'wimp'. By contrast, Walsh (2009, pp. 498–9) and Caligiuri and Givelekian (2008, pp. 23–9) report a range of studies which have found positive benefits for organizations to result from the introduction of work–life balance initiatives. The major examples are as follows:

- reduced staff turnover
- reduced absenteeism

- improved job satisfaction rates
- improved productivity
- improved levels of employee commitment.

The extent to which positive effects of this kind are observable varies depending on the type of initiative. Allowing people to exercise a measure of control over their own work schedules (i.e. flexi-time) appears to have the most positive effect. This is an unsurprising finding given the amount of published research that demonstrates how appreciative employees are when they are given more autonomy and freedom to organize when, where, and how they carry out their own work.

▶ VALUES For many organizations more is therefore needed than a set of policies. If people are genuinely to attain a better work–life balance, without suffering in career or earnings terms, attitudes need to change. The only way to achieve this is for organizations to promote the benefits of work–life balance relentlessly over a sustained period and to take steps to change their prevalent cultural norms.

■ Summary—Does it matter? Is business responsible?

▶ VALUES This chapter has examined two related issues that have moved up business and political agendas in recent years—equal opportunity and work–life balance. We have also identified the range of factors and pressures that have contributed to the increasing prominence of these issues, and the principal stakeholders involved—employees, employers, and policy-makers. In large part these issues have become more prominent because they are linked to demands for greater freedom of choice, fairness, and improved quality of life and happiness. In other words they can be seen as reflecting new demands on business and new ways of judging its performance. The core purposes of business—competitiveness and profitability—are not enough, for we want good employers who offer equality of opportunity and better work–life balance. Looked at in this way it is easy to see business as the 'villain' of the piece, forced to change by pressure from employees and legislation. There are certainly strong grounds for arguing that the shift towards equal opportunity and work–life balance would not have occurred, or, at least, would have occurred more slowly, if business and the market had been left to their own devices. For example, the rationale for sex discrimination legislation is that women have faced discrimination in the workplace from some employers and would, without the law, continue to do so. If there was no discrimination, the law would not be necessary. Indeed, as we have seen, it has been claimed that still today 'institutionalized gender discrimination' is prevalent in the financial services sector. Similarly, the extensive programme of government action establishing employee rights to improve work–life balance would not be necessary if this outcome would be produced by business and the market left to themselves.

However, it is necessary to understand the conflicting pressures that confront business and the limits of business responsibility. On the face of it discrimination is irrational from a business point of view since a focus on competitiveness and profitability requires that the best people are recruited regardless of sex or other irrelevant criteria (including age, ethnicity, etc.). Yet the possibility of young women taking maternity leave might be seen as a risk to the business and result in discrimination, so that unfair discrimination appears to be rational business behaviour. Similarly, policies to improve work–life balance can be seen as a burden on business in a competitive environment which has tended to increase the hours and intensity of work.

Thus, firms will be reluctant to accept increased cost and/or reduced flexibility that may put them at a disadvantage in a competitive market. On the other hand, we have seen that market pressures can encourage business to embrace the equal opportunity and work–life balance agendas. In particular the need to be able to recruit and retain the best employees, especially in conditions of skills shortages, can lead businesses to position themselves as 'employers of choice' through equal opportunity and work–life balance policies. Thus, sustaining competitiveness involves responding to conflicting pressures.

We can see that policies adopted by business do not just reflect the attitudes or values of employers but the need to respond to market pressures. Because these pressures may induce differing responses from business, and because not all firms may strive to position themselves as 'employers of choice' there is a strong case for governments to act by establishing legal rights and duties—to create a 'level playing field' on which businesses compete, and fairness for employees. This does not mean that the issues are settled by the law. Because of the competing values, interests, and pressures involved, equal opportunity and work–life balance policies will continue to be the focus of political argument, with some arguing for the law to go further and others for the burden on business to be reduced.

▶ **INTERNAL/EXTERNAL** We have also seen that there are other pressures and constraints that affect work–life balance and equality of opportunity, and which may be difficult to tackle through the law and business policies, especially workplace culture and values within the wider society. Equal opportunity and work–life balance policies and commitments can be undermined by the persistence of 'macho', 'sexist', or long hours cultures. Workplace cultures are aspects of the internal environment that can be shaped through management policies. However, employers cannot do very much to influence women's and men's career aspirations and choices which might reflect wider social and cultural factors that can act as influences or constraints, such as:

- dominant norms in society concerning 'masculine' and 'feminine' characteristics and behaviours, reflected in ideas about 'men's work' and 'women's work': these ideas can be transmitted in the media, through advertising images, and in films and television programmes
- the different upbringing or 'socialization' of boys and girls in the family and the education system
- the unequal sharing of tasks in the household, with women still expected to take on primary responsibility for childcare and domestic chores and to fit paid work around these responsibilities
- workplace cultures that value long hours.

▶ **COMPLEXITY** Thus, equal opportunity and work–life balance are complicated issues, influenced by a range of economic, political, and social-cultural factors. How they are resolved matters both for employees and employers. For employees:

- Equality of opportunity matters as a question of fairness because employment is a valued opportunity in society, not only in terms of income but also status, social contact, and job satisfaction.
- Work can be a central life interest for some people, although many jobs are not of this nature. But whether 'living to work' or 'working to live', work is not all that matters in life. A good work–life balance allowing individuals time and energy to commit to other activities and relationships is an important ingredient of individual well-being.

- Equality of opportunity and work–life balance are closely related issues because women sharing the same opportunities as men in work depends both on the way that paid work is organized and the way that both men and women balance work and domestic responsibilities.

These issues are important for business because:

- Being an equal opportunity employer and enabling employees to enjoy a healthy work–life balance can be seen as a key question of business ethics. In other words, it is a question of the right thing to do.

- By doing the right thing businesses can show that they are in tune with changing social attitudes, or even pioneering change. This can have positive reputational effects for business.

- A commitment to equal opportunity and work–life balance can assist recruitment, staff morale, and retention.

- Equal opportunity aligns with efficiency, while the effects on reputation and on recruitment and retention of staff also make a strong business case. However, employers may perceive that equal opportunity and work–life balance policies can have a negative impact on the running of the business and damage competitiveness and profitability. The way employees would like work to be organized might not be consistent with the needs of the business. In that case the challenge for business is to strike the right balance.

■ Looking ahead

》 DYNAMIC This chapter has shown that the nature and meaning of work are not fixed but subject to debate, negotiation, and transformation. Within living memory work has been associated strongly with the notion of a male 'breadwinner', involving full-time jobs of indefinite duration, with a continuous working life. For many people work was a fixture around which other dimensions of life had to be organized. Of course the reality of work has always been more diverse and complex than these associations suggest, but they have been weakened or broken down by increasing acceptance of equality of opportunity and the, more recent, growth of interest in work–life balance. We now live in a society where it is taken for granted by many that men and women ought to have the same opportunities in the labour market, and where it is an increasing expectation that the way work is organized ought to enable a better balance with other aspects of life. Looking ahead, we can expect there to be an ongoing debate about the nature of work, reflecting shifting values, lifestyles, and economic pressures. For example, our notion of a retirement age at which working life ends is breaking down in the context of an ageing population in which people are both expected to work longer and may wish to do so but on a more flexible basis. In other words, a different work–life balance will be part of the way society copes with an ageing population.

Commitments to equality of opportunity and work–life balance can be seen to reflect deep-rooted social trends in terms of values and lifestyles in affluent societies, such as the challenge to 'sexism' and the increasing prominence of 'post-material' or quality of life concerns. Therefore they are likely to continue to influence government policy and business practice in the future. However, these changes are not uncontested and the pace of change will be influenced by economic and political pressures and constraints. The economic outlook has altered fundamentally since 2008 and for the next five years, and more, will be dominated by government attempts to reduce its debt, during which time unemployment is likely to remain high even as the economy recovers from the recession. It is possible, therefore, that problems of recruitment and skills-shortages will fall down the corporate HR agenda. Employees fearing the possibility of redundancy are less well-placed to press for further concessions in this area, while those who are already out of work and looking for jobs are typically happy to accept whatever opportunities to earn are provided, even if it does afford them a poorer work–life balance than they were used to in the past. In such circumstances the maintenance of profitability and hence business survival tends to become the overwhelming imperative for organizations, and this may be at the expense of initiatives such as those we have been describing, especially to the extent that they were adopted on purely pragmatic grounds in the first place. Similarly, concerns have been expressed that in a difficult economic climate it is often women who are more vulnerable to redundancy. Over the longer term, however, the demographic and wider social trends we have identified in this chapter will continue to drive the equal opportunities and work–life balance agendas forward. As indicated in this chapter, we are only in the early stages of achieving improvements in work–life balance where legislation and business policy needs to be supported by cultural change. Even though the equal opportunity agenda is well established it can be argued that progress has been limited and there is still a long way to go.

Case Study: McDonald's restaurants

McDonald's is the biggest restaurant chain in the world, operating over 30,000 restaurants in 118 countries. The company estimates that it serves over 58 million customers every day. In the UK the chain operates over 1,200 restaurants, many of which are managed by franchisees. It has continued to grow steadily throughout the last decade and now employs 90,000 people, 95% of whom work in its restaurants.

In the early 2000s McDonald's suffered from a reputation as a poor employer. It was widely caricatured as being somewhere that people would not want to work if they could avoid doing so, a commonly held view being that pretty well anyone could get a job 'flipping burgers' at McDonald's. The term 'McJob' started to be used widely to indicate poor quality employment, and in 2003 found its way into the Oxford English Dictionary defined as follows:

an unstimulating, low-paid job with few prospects, especially one created by the expansion of the service sector.

The organization's reputation took a further knock in 2004 with the release of Morgan Spurlock's film 'Supersize Me' and from negative press stories relating to legal action taken by the company in the so-called McLibel case. When people were asked in an opinion survey in 2004 whether or not they thought that McDonald's was a good employer, fewer than 20% said 'yes'.

Since 2004 McDonald's has embarked on a sustained programme of reputation building designed to decontaminate its image as an employer. All kinds of initiatives have been launched with this end in mind, ranging from the introduction of a staff discount scheme to private healthcare for employees who have completed three years' service. Millions have also been invested in training and career development schemes which enable McDonald's employees to study for a wide range of qualifications while working. In all these areas the company is able to offer its staff a great deal more than almost all its competitors.

A major stand of the reputation-building project has been the introduction of a range of flexible working arrangements, many of which go further than those offered by any large employer in the UK. Promoting work-life balance was identified as being a key potential source of competitive advantage in the labour market, mainly because it was an aspect of working for McDonald's that staff said they appreciated most when surveyed. The economics of the fast food industry mean that rates of pay can never be high, so other aspects of the reward package have to be competitive if the company is to attract and retain people who it can rely on to deliver a high quality service. Moreover, of course, the long opening hours operated by McDonald's restaurants, many of which are now open 24 hours a day, mean that there is a need for staff to work unusual shift patterns.

David Fairhurst (2007), head of HR for the company's European operations makes a distinction between 'inflexible flexibility' and 'flexible flexibility'. The former comprises arrangements which assist people who have very specific requirements in terms of the hours that they work. In order to combine working with their domestic responsibilities, they are unable to commit to any shifts outside quite specific times each day, being unavailable, for example, at the weekend or in the evenings. By contrast, 'flexible flexibility' is about helping people to combine working with meeting unpredictable domestic responsibilities. What they want is the ability to work as and when they are able to, perhaps chopping and changing their shift patterns at short notice week by week.

McDonald's offers its staff a wide range of flexible working options aimed at meeting the needs of both 'inflexible flexible' and 'flexible flexible' staff. Some of the more cutting-edge examples are as follows:

- The company has pioneered the use of term-time and school hours contracts in the UK, in the process providing job opportunities for parents of dependent children, and single parents in particular. Their hours of work are fixed to coincide with the hours that their children's schools operate. The company then employs college and university students to work the same shifts out of school hours.
- The company's McTime system allows staff to access holiday and work schedules online using home computers, mobile phones or the PCs that are now present in all restaurant staff rooms. This enables staff to book themselves in for any unassigned shifts without the need to go through a manager. It also enables staff to swap shifts at short notice.
- In 2006 McDonald's introduced family contracts. These enable members of the same family to decide among themselves who is going to work which shift. As long as a qualified employee turns up for work, it is for the family and not the restaurant manager to decide who exactly that is.
- In 2008 the family contract scheme was extended to groups of friends. The same principle applies. The group is assigned shifts each week, deciding for itself which individual member will work which one.

- The company's McPassport programme operates across Europe. It allows trained restaurant staff to work in any participating McDonald's restaurant in any European country. The scheme permits younger staff in particular to travel while working, moving on from city to city.
- The company is unusual in allowing quite senior staff, as well as all its office-based administrative employees, to work part time or via job-share arrangements.

Staff surveys undertaken by McDonald's demonstrate that these forms of flexible working are greatly appreciated by its employees and that they have contributed greatly to the reduction in overall staff turnover that the company achieved between 2004 and 2010 (from 80% to 37%). The early turnover rate (i.e. the proportion of new staff leaving within 90 days of starting) fell even more dramatically from 24% to 2.4%. McDonald's has also found itself to be in far greater demand as an employer in the UK. It now receives between 3,000 and 4,000 applications from would-be employees every day, of which fewer than 1 in 15 are ultimately successful. This enables the company to be very selective in who it employs, which has in turn led to a substantial increase in the customer service ratings recorded by 'mystery shoppers' who judge restaurants on their cleanliness, quality and the time they take to serve food. Negative scores have more than halved since 2005.

(*Sources:* Sparrow et al. 2010, Taylor 2012)

Questions

1. What features of employment in McDonald's make it possible for the company to offer more flexible working options than most employers are able to?

2. To what extent and in what ways can developments in the company's business environment explain the decision to enhance flexible working opportunities after 2004?

3. How useful do you find the distinction between 'inflexible flexibility' and 'flexible flexibility' when thinking about ways of achieving work–life balance?

4. What further steps could the company take to enhance the work–life balance of its employees?

Review and discussion questions

1. Using relevant evidence, examine how far women have achieved equality of opportunity in the labour market. To what extent is the evidence, such as relating to the gender pay gap, open to different interpretations?

2. Studies of differences in attitudes between older and younger people have shown that demand for effective work–life balance is strongest among people who are in their twenties and who are now entering the labour market. Why do you think this is apparently more of a priority for the generations born in the 1980s and 1990s than it was for their parents and grandparents?

3. To what extent do you agree with the view that employer commitment to work–life balance initiatives is mainly a

product of prevailing labour market conditions and that it will weaken in the context of persistent unemployment as the economy recovers from recession?

4. Is fairness or social justice an issue that business should be concerned about? Or should it be concerned only with efficiency and profitability?

Assignments

1. Prepare a report on the implications of The Equality Act 2010 for businesses in both the private and public sectors.

2. Prepare a brief written or verbal presentation on what steps a business should take to be an equal opportunity employer. You should refer to good practice guidance from the Equality and Human Rights Commission (EHRC).

3. Critically assess the work–life balance policies and practices developed by your own organization, or one with which you are familiar. List the major factors in the business environment that have determined how extensive or restricted they are. How is this likely to change in the future, and why?

4. Review the measures introduced by governments and by the EU to date which aim to promote the work–life balance agenda. Make a list of points to indicate to what extent you consider these to be sufficient, and what reforms and new initiatives you would like to see brought forward and why.

Further reading

See References below

online resource centre

Test your understanding of this chapter with online questions and answers, explore the subject further through web exercises, and use the web links to provide a quick resource for further research. Go to the Online Resource Centre at <www.oxfordtextbooks.co.uk/orc/wetherly_otter/2>

Useful websites

<www.statistics.gov.uk>
Office for National Statistics

<www.equalityhumanrights.com>
Equality and Human Rights Commission

<www.womenandequalityunit.gov.uk>
Women & Equality Unit

<www.fawcettsociety.org.uk>
Fawcett Society

<www.cipd.co.uk>
<www.employersforwork-lifebalance.org.uk>
<www.flexibility.co.uk>
<www.pcs.org.uk/WorkLifeBalance/>
<www.tuc.org.uk/work_life/>
<www.unison.org.uk/worklifebalance/>
<www.w-lb.org.uk>

References

Berthoud, R. (2007) *Work-Rich and Work-Poor* (York: The Joseph Rowntree Foundation).

Caligiuri, P. and Givelekian, N. (2008) 'Strategic human resources and work–life balance' in Poelmans S.A.Y. and Caligiuri, P. (eds) *Harmonizing Work, Family & Personal Life* (Cambridge: Cambridge University Press).

Chartered Institute of Personnel & Development (2006), *Working Life: Employee attitudes and engagement, research report* (London: CIPD).

Chartered Institute of Personnel and Development (2012a) *Resourcing and Talent Planning and Turnover, Annual Survey Report* (London: CIPD).

Chartered Institute of Personnel and Development (2012b) *Flexible Working Provision and Uptake, Survey Report* (London: CIPD).

Davies, M. (2011) *Women on Boards* (Department for Business, Innovation & Skills). <http://www.bis.gov.uk//assets/biscore/business-law/docs/w/11-745-women-on-boards.pdf>

Davies, M. (2013) *Women on Boards: April 2013* [second annual review], (Department for Business, Innovation & Skills). <https://www.gov.uk/government/uploads/system/uploads/attachment_data/file/182602/bis-13-p135-women-on-boards-2013.pdf>

Department for Business, Innovation & Skills, (2011) 'Announcement: Women on Boards' <https://www.gov.uk/government/news/women-on-boards>

Department for Business, Innovation & Skills, (2013) 'Press release: Women on boards 2013: Two years on' <https://www.gov.uk/government/news/women-on-boards-2013-two-years-on>

EHRC (2009) 'Financial Services Inquiry: Sex discrimination and gender pay gap report of the Equality and Human Rights Commission' (London: Equality and Human Rights Commission).

EHRC (2013) 'Women, men and part-time work' (London: Equality and Human Rights Commission).

Gambles, R., Lewis, S., And Rapoport, R. (2006) *The Myth of the Work–life Balance: The Challenge of our time for Men, Women, and Societies.* (Chichester: John Wiley & Sons).

Green, F. (2006) *Demanding Work* (New Jersey: Princeton University Press).

IDS (2000a) '24 hour society', *IDS Focus* 93, Spring (London: Incomes Data Services).

IRS (2002) 'Hanging in the balance', *Employment Review*, 766 (London: Industrial Relations Services).

Kersley, B., Alpin, C., Forth, J., Bryson, A., Bewley, H., Dix, G., and Oxenbridge, S. (2006) *Inside the Workplace: Findings from the 2004 Workplace Employment Relations Survey* (Abingdon: Routledge).

Leaker, D. (2009) 'Economic inactivity', *Economic & Labour Market Review* 3.2 (February).

Office for National Statistics (2009a) *Social Trends* 39 (Office for National Statistics). <www.ons.gov.uk>

Office for National Statistics (2009b) *Statistical Bulletin: 2009 Annual Survey of Hours and Earnings* (Office for National Statistics). <www.ons.gov.uk>

Office for National Statistics (2012) *Annual Survey of Hours and Earnings, 2012 Provisional Results* (Office for National Statistics). <http://www.ons.gov.uk/ons/dcp171778_286243.pdf>

Office for National Statistics (2013) *Statistical Bulletin: Employees in Employment 2012* (Office for National Statistics). <www.ons.gov.uk>

Pidd, H. (2010) 'Female Birmingham council workers win £200m equal pay case', *The Guardian,* 28 April 2010.

Philpott, J. (2010) *Working Hours in the Recession* (London: Chartered Institute of Personnel and Development).

Sparrow, P., Balain, S., and Fairhurst, D. (2010) 'McDonald's UK: From corporate reputation to trust-based HR' in Sparrow, P., Hird, M., Hesketh, A. and Cooper, C. (eds) *Leading HR* (Basingstoke, Palgrave).

Spence, A. (2011) 'The Labour Market', *Social Trends* 41, Office for National Statistics.

Taylor, R. (2001) 'The Future of Employment Relations', ESRC Future of Work Seminar Series.

Taylor, S. (2012) 'McDonalds UK: Improving recruitment and retention by enhancing corporate reputation' in Dundon, T. and Wilkinson, A. (eds) *Case Studies in Global Management Strategy, Innovation, and People* (Australia: Tilde Publishing).

UK Commission for Employment and Skills (2012) *Working Futures 2010-2020: Evidence Report 41.*

Walsh, J. (2009) 'Working time and work–life balance' in Wilkinson, A., Bacon, N., Redman, T., and Snell, S. (eds) *The Sage Handbook of Human Resource Management* (London: Sage).

The Women and Work Commission (2006) 'Shaping a Fairer Future', Women and Equality Unit. <www.womenandequalityunit.gov.uk>

Chapter 13

Creating effective trading blocs: What lessons does the European Union provide?

Stratis Koutsoukos and Dorron Otter

Learning objectives

When you have completed this chapter you will be able to:

- Explain the different levels of economic and political integration at the regional level and assess the relative advantages and disadvantages of these.

- Describe the institutional and policy-making framework of the European Union (EU), including the European Parliament, Commission, Council, and Central Bank and their significance and impact to business.

- Analyse the differing forms of economic integration relevant to EU development and issues arising from successive enlargements.

- Explain the recent development of European Monetary Union (EMU) and the impact of the euro on the EU business environment.

THEMES

The following themes are particularly relevant in this chapter

》 INTERNAL/EXTERNAL

There is a very strong case for countries at the same level of economic development and in geographical proximity to push ahead and forge greater levels of integration for the mutual benefit of all. But there are also problems in that greater integration involves close cooperation and, indeed, a pooling of sovereignty that may fit uneasily with the desire to have national independence.

》 COMPLEXITY OF THE ENVIRONMENT

Ironically, trying to create a 'level playing field' where there is open and free competition between members in regional trade groups requires complex political and economic structures with which businesses will need to deal. Regulatory shifts in areas such as competition, agriculture, or financial services policy mean businesses have to constantly re-evaluate their strategies.

》 VARIETY OF SPATIAL LEVELS

Integration can take place at different levels, with each level requiring an appropriate structural framework to support its aims.

⟫ **DYNAMIC** ENVIRONMENT

A key theme in this chapter is the extent to which the movement towards greater regional integration is leading to a deeper or wider integration among the members of these groups and is taking the world towards or away from greater global integration.

■ **Introduction**

⟫ **INTERNAL/EXTERNAL** We explored the contrasting views about the nature of globalization in Chapter 10 and we saw that in reality while it potentially has great benefits, trade across national boundaries, especially when nations are at different stages of development, can be problematic. The major fault line in creating closer global cooperation in relation to trade has been the conflicting interests between the developed and the developing world. And, in the absence of a completion of the last round of world trade negotiations (the Doha 'development' round), there has been an increased focus on the plethora of regional trade associations that exist.

⟫ **SPATIAL** In this chapter we will explore the different types of regional trade agreements that can exist and how the nature of these affects the business environment and, in turn, the implications for business behaviour. The European Union (EU) will be a particular focus.

The themes and issues surrounding the impact of the EU, one of the world's most influential trading blocs, on business activity, strategy, and performance are many and varied. From labour law to immigration law, competition policy and law to environmental policy and law, economic restructuring policies, trade agreements, and many more areas this makes it a unique case study of an economic union and trading bloc.

At the heart of the debates about the current state of affairs in the EU is the political level and the issue of **sovereignty**. Inevitably, by being members of an economic union, individual nation-states have had to accept a transfer of political influence to the governing institutions at the regional level, which we will explore later in this chapter. This has provoked intense disagreements between those who see this as 'ceding', or giving up power or sovereignty over national self-interest, and those who see this as a 'pooling' of power for collective and shared responses in the context of a global world economy facing global challenges (e.g. the environment, financial crisis, conflict resolution).

Chapter 2 examines the debates in relation to how economic policy should be conducted and the experience of the EU shows that in order to build economic cooperation there are political changes that need to occur, which have the potential to create tension across the political divide. For neoliberal critics, the EU's mission is primarily to produce a single free market across the European continent whereas others argue that for this to work effectively there needs to be more integrated political and economic structures to support the market. For many people, while there is a desire to see the widening of free trade within regions, there is a reluctance to accept the need for the deepening of this integration beyond the formation of simple Free Trade Area (FTAs) or the continued use of Preferential Trading Areas (PTAs which normally encompass relationships between developed and developing countries which formerly were conjoined through colonization). For structuralist writers, a deepening integration is vital if there is to be genuine free trade that works in a way that is really inclusive to all parties.

The political battles over sovereignty are illustrated in this chapter through the applied example of the EU engaged in the economic 'haggling' relating to the nature of the 'European Union development project'. Furthermore, working across so many national boundaries involves the assimilation of different business cultures. Whilst a widespread cultural diversity exists within the Union, it is acknowledged that there is a shared lowest common denominator describing the notion of European identity. The prospect of future enlargement, including possible entrants such as Turkey, raises the prospect of introducing Asian cultures into the EU mix, further questioning the nature of a unified concept of a European identity. Others argue that perhaps the biggest cultural export and trademark of Europe inc. is the spread of democracy, respect of law, and inclusion of minority groups.

The global economy and the EU are at a critical stage of their development and this chapter seeks to evaluate business and decision-making in this context and explore the potential lessons that may be learned from the EU experience for other regional trading blocs.

Forms of integration and trade in theory

》 SPATIAL We have seen in Chapter 10 that international trade can potentially be hugely beneficial for individual countries. Trade can take place at three spatial levels: Bilateral Trade occurs when two countries agree preferential trade arrangements between each other, Regional Trade occurs when groups of countries in a particular geographical area develop trade relationships common across all members, and Global Trade relationships which are negotiated through the World Trade Organization (WTO). Given the inability of the WTO process to conclude the latest round of trade negotiations, there is a feeling that in the medium term it is regional trade agreements that will continue to shape the future of the global business environment. For advocates of globalization this tendency for the increased importance of regional trade is seen as regrettable, as it prevents the creation of a genuine global free market and may result in future potential economic and political rivalry and even conflict between big separate power blocs.

Economists distinguish between the static gains from trade that stem from the ability to exploit comparative advantages and the wider dynamic gains from trade such as the ability to exploit larger markets and thus benefit from economies of scale, the exposure to higher levels of competition that opening up trade might create, the opportunities for technology transfer and simply consumers having the benefit of a greater choice of goods and services. However, closer integration may also bring political advantages such as creating closer relationships for peace and security or allowing a greater political voice at global economic and political negotiations. Table 13.1 shows a spectrum of economic linkages encompassing ever closer integration.

A free trade area such as the European Free Trade Area (EFTA) that covers countries Iceland, Norway, Liechtenstein, and Switzerland extends preferential tariff treatment to all

Table 13.1 Different types of economic integration

	No internal trade barriers	Common external tariff	Factor and asset mobility	Common currency	Common economic policy
Free trade area	✓				
Customs union	✓	✓			
Single market	✓	✓	✓		
Monetary union	✓	✓	✓	✓	
Economic union	✓	✓	✓	✓	✓

members (see <http://www.efta.int/>). It is a loose association in which members eliminate trade barriers between themselves but retain their own trade policies with respect to outsiders. Tariffs are taxes that are levied on goods coming into a country and traditionally were a way for nation-states to protect themselves from trade.

A **customs union** is where a joint external trade policy exists with the imposition of a common external tariff (CET) on non-member imports. The customs union shares revenue from this CET as part of the common budget. A customs union creates trade among its members but diverts it from those excluded. While trade might grow substantially, much of this may be internally within the regional bloc. While this might be successful in terms of boosting regional integration it might not actually lead to an increase in world trade overall as it will simply divert trade from non-group members. In some cases these other countries might have had strong historical, cultural or political links with members inside the group and in others might actually prevent future beneficial trading links being established on a bilateral basis. In the UK context, one of the arguments of those who oppose the UK's continuing membership of the EU is precisely that they feel that, in being a member of the EU, British business is prevented from fully pursuing its traditional links with countries with which it had former colonial links or as in the case of the US, one with whom they feel there is a 'special relationship' and will prevent the British economy from developing links with the fast growing emerging economies elsewhere in the world. We profiled one such example in the Banana case study in Chapter 10.

Stop and Think

....

Assume UK footwear manufacturers produce trainers for domestic consumption that retail at £60 per pair. In Spain these shoes can be produced and delivered to the UK for £40 but when the UK imposes a £25 tariff on such imports, Spain cannot compete effectively. If, however, the UK and Spain become part of a customs union and abolish all trade barriers between them, UK shoe imports from Spain will increase to the extent that this replaces expensive UK production and contribute to 'trade creation'.

However, suppose China can produce and ship trainers to the UK for £30 per pair. Before the customs union China sold trainers to the UK for £55 (£30 + £25 tariff) but the tariff reduction only applies to Spain. Thus Spanish trainers also replace UK imports from China. Since China is a lower cost producer than Spain, this part of the increased Spanish exports is 'trade diversion'.

》 DYNAMIC Both a free trade area and a customs union can essentially be seen as being essentially examples of negative integration that simply remove barriers to trade. Higher levels of integration involve positive integration, implying the building of an institutional framework and policy harmonization, as in monetary union. A common or single market abolishes all trade barriers—not just tariffs but non-tariff barriers (NTBs) and mobility restrictions, embracing the free movement of

- Goods: consumers and companies can buy and sell their products anywhere in member states
- People: individuals are free to move and work within the common market
- Capital: seen as facilitating the free movement of people, services, and goods
- Services: encompasses both the freedom to establish a business and the right to offer services in another member state.

The highest order of integration would be to have a Monetary Union and as we shall see, in practice, this has come to be the most controversial aspect of the EU experience. Even with the removal of all the trade barriers as outlined above one major obstacle to trade would be the continued existence of national currencies within the common market. If trade is conducted across national boundaries with different currencies this means that for exporters and importers the actual value of the costs or revenues received will depend on the value of the currency in which they are making or receiving payment compared to the value of their home currency. The problem is that in reality exchange rates are very volatile especially as a result of speculation on the international money markets. This volatility can increase business risk.

> ### Stop and Think
>
> Consider the following example: In September 1999 a UK chemicals company sold £100,000 of chemicals to a Spanish customer which quoted a euro price of €146,000 at an equivalent rate of £1 = €1.46. On the basis that it would receive £100,000 on completion of the sale the UK company was happy to agree to take eventual payment of €146,000. The customer subsequently ordered and paid the agreed amount in euros but in the intervening period the exchange rate had moved to £1 = €1.68 (in other words the value of the pound had strengthened relative to the euro) so the €146,000 only produced £86,904.76, a 'loss' of £13,095.24 on the expected sum.

To avoid this damaging uncertainty which might deter businesses from 'getting their fingers burned' in this way by trading, there is a strong case for fixed rates and ultimately having a common currency. If the logic for greater integration is that it will create more trade then it seems illogical to stop short of full monetary integration and allow a major obstacle to trade to remain. If all countries within the full union had the same currency, then this would mean that national governments would need to coordinate monetary and fiscal policies which would provide a common stable macroeconomic environment across the union. This favourable business environment would encourage trade and greater competition as the costs and prices charged by all firms throughout the region would be subject to greater transparency. In this way, for many proponents of the benefits of monetary union the inevitable consequence of this is that there will need to be a full economic union with close coordination of economic policy. As we shall see, the strength of this argument has propelled many members of the EU to accept the need for a common currency and adopt the euro, including Spain, but not the UK.

However, there are though a range of economic and political arguments that urge caution in the belief that greater integration automatically implies monetary union. A common currency requires cooperation between different countries over macroeconomic policies and such collective action diminishes the individual nation's sovereignty over domestic policy. It can be argued that once the step towards an economic union is taken then this implies a political union. While opponents of this possible move toward political integration may deem this action to be appropriate within an individual country such as the US, it is regarded as inappropriate across separate countries, such as within the EU, and they may resist any attempt to indeed create a 'United States of Europe'.

The decision to do away with individual currencies and adopt a common currency is intimately tied to the arguments over whether it is better for the exchange rate of a country to float freely and be determined by market forces or for governments to intervene and determine the external value of the currency by having 'fixed' exchange rates. The possible adoption of monetary union is the extreme version of this. No longer do you need to swap your currency for that of another's if you wish to trade; by using the same common currency, all businesses across the union would have the certainty of what they would receive through trade and the common currency would have the further advantage of ensuring that prices across all countries and goods and services are immediately transparent. The downside of this, though, is that each country now loses the power to determine the value of its currency externally.

Floating rates offer autonomy to nations (socalled economic sovereignty). If, for example, the UK was to find that as a result of a decline in competitiveness compared to other countries it was seeing its exports declining but that consumers in the UK were still buying imports this would be reflected in an adverse balance of payments. However, under a floating exchange rate regime it could allow its currency to float downwards in value. This drop in the exchange rate would mean that people abroad could now buy goods valued in the weaker pound more cheaply and conversely as consumers in the UK would now have to pay more for imports, the demand for these would fall. The floating exchange rate thus 'disguises' the short-term loss in competitiveness and might allow the government the breathing space to address the underlying competitive weakness. In response to what they hope would be a temporary loss of economic competiveness, governments might use fiscal policy to provide for social security assistance, Keynesian demand management policies to boost the economy, and direct support for ailing industries.

In a fixed rate system or a monetary union this option would not be available to the national government and the country would now face a recessionary situation. Without the ability to allow the currency to depreciate in order to restore macroeconomic stability in the long run, the country would have to undertake draconian microeconomic measures such as cutting wages, welfare benefits and, in return for attracting the short-term borrowing needed to finance the balance of payments deficit, the government would have to accept high levels of interest and commit to reducing public expenditure. The end of chapter case in Chapter 9 illustrates the problems that have been faced by certain members of the EU that signed up to monetary union and we will return to this later in this chapter. However, certainly if a country were to try to 'tough it out alone', relying simply on these microeconomic austerity measures, the result would be severe short-term declines in living standards and jobs until the long-term re-structuring of the economy occurred.

Economists have always warned that, if full monetary union is to be achieved, it would be necessary to ensure that there was a large stability fund at the central or federal level so that when countries find themselves under competitive pressure, funds would be available to help lessen the economic hardship. If there are deficit countries in the Union, then it is likely that such sovereign funds would be available from the surplus countries. Since it is in the strategic interests of surplus countries to restore growth for less competitive regions, then surely it would be beneficial to release these? As a way of ensuring that this was the case, it would be advisable if all members of a monetary union were to pool some of their reserves into a central fund which could be used for precisely this purpose. These funds would then be viewed as a common insurance fund to help in those individual cases of temporary hardship, but in such a way as to benefit the union as a whole. Ultimately, monetary integration would involve full economic union, implying macroeconomic policy coordination and including both fiscal and monetary policy. Members forgo their economic independence and a central federal government would dominate macroeconomic policy-making.

If it were the case that generally all nations in the bloc were at a similar level of development in terms of competitivenesss, then the likelihood of these funds being needed would be small, but as we shall see in the case of the expansion of the EU, this does not seem to have been the case. While careful conditions are placed on countries seeking accession and there have been careful plans in place to ensure that the process to EMU was achieved, it would appear that the safeguards were insufficient and what resulted was an EU that was some way from a full economic union, with members retaining fiscal sovereignty whist simultaneously being tied into a monetary union.

Thus, integration is wide in scope and, while depicted here in economic terms, also requires political will, as progressive interdependence requires the release of ever more sovereignty over domestic decision-making.

◼ Trading blocs in reality

There are a huge number of regional and preferential trading associations and to keep track the WTO maintains a database at **<wto.org/english/tratop_e/region_e/rta_pta_e.htm>**. Often these trading blocs aim to achieve cooperation across a wider range of political, strategic, and cultural objectives than the narrow economic arguments detailed above. The fact that the WTO has to request signatories of the various agreements to permit them to catalogue these deals shows the extent to which it is this regional trade expansion that is driving the global trading environment. The patchwork nature of these individual trading agreements is seen by some critics as an obstacle to the eventual goal of a global free trade system. However, for others it is seen as an inevitable consequence of the economic and political sovereignty problems that too rapid or deep an integration might produce.

We will discuss the European Union in detail later in this chapter. As the most integrated trading bloc, it helps to shed light on the contrasting views about the benefits of integration outlined above (for the official EU view about the European integration see **<http://europa. eu/index_en.htm>**).

In North America NAFTA is an example of a trading bloc which brings together a developing nation, Mexico, with its developed northern partners, the US and Canada (see **<www. nafta-sec-alena.org/>**). This is unusual because, as we saw in Chapter 10, structuralist and dependency critics warn of the potential problems in opening up trade between the developed countries in the 'Global North' and the developing countries in the 'Global South'. They argue that until the appropriate supporting institutions are put in place to ensure that free trade is equitable, greater South-South trading relationships are needed instead of North-South models of trade. Chapter 16 will explore recent developments in relation to China's increasing trade in Africa and the attempts by the BRICS to take the lead role in development away from organizations like the World Bank.

In Latin America in the 1990s there was an attempt to build a free trade area for the Americas (FTAA) which sought to bring together all the Latin American countries, the Caribbean countries, Canada, and the US. However, suspicions amongst many countries that it would be a trading bloc primarily benefiting the US led to its failure. Over the years there have been many expressions of interest for further regional integration, but intra-regional trade is relatively low and progress has been slow. The main trading blocs are: the common market CAN (or the Andean Pact) which includes Columbia, Bolivia, Ecuador, and Peru; and MERCOSUR, which is now a full customs union consisting of Brazil, Argentina, Uruguay, and Venezuela. Paraguay's membership has been suspended as a result of a *coup d'état,* and Bolivia is waiting to join (see **<http://en.mercopress.com/about-mercosur>**).

The main obstacles to greater integration in Latin America have been: a tendency for countries to react to unfavourable external economic shocks, such as the 1997 Asian crisis, by resorting to non-tariff trade restrictions; an unwillingness to implement agreements that could be politically contentious in a national context; and a lack of coordinated macroeconomic policy. Political and ideological differences can often be profound. For another example see Mini-Case 13.1.

In Southeast Asia the ASEAN bloc has expanded quickly and looks to be moving fast towards greater regional integration The way it is developing is in part in a response to the problems faced by the EU. We explore this in detail in the case at the end of this chapter.

In Africa the most notable bloc is the Southern African Development Community (SADC), a free trade area comprising the following countries: Angola, Botswana, Lesotho, Malawi, Mozambique, Namibia, South Africa, Swaziland, Zambia, and Zimbabwe (see <http://www.sadc.int/>).

SADC is trying to deepen its levels of integration though progress is difficult because some members were also members in other African trading groups, such as the East African Community and the Common Market for East and Southern Africa. Since 2008 integration has been made easier by the formation of the African Free Trade Zone, which is seeking to create a free trade area across all three of the existing groups.

In reality, there is a broad range of regional economic blocs, all with different and sometimes overlapping principal objectives. The implications for businesses are profound, as trading within regional blocs requires knowledge of the rules and regulations within each bloc and, if businesses are trading across these regional boundaries, they have to cope with different regulatory frameworks and institutional structures. The rest of this chapter will focus primarily on the issues relating to European integration, which currently is experiencing economic slowdown (blamed by some on the integration process itself). The case at the end of the chapter will profile Southeast Asia, a region that is leading the way in terms of economic growth.

Mini-Case 13.1 The ALBA Regional Economic Bloc

The name of the emerging regional bloc ALBA, *Alianza Bolivarian para los Pueblos de Nuestra América* (in English, the Bolivarian Alliance for the Peoples of Our America) includes 'Peoples of Our America' as a way of stressing that its aims are ideologically different to those of the 'neoliberal' trading relationships in North America, which are seen as 'expansionist and driven by imperialist appetites' (ALBA 2013). ALBA developed from an agreement in 2004 between the oil-rich Venezuela, then led by the charismatic socialist President Hugo Chavez, and Cuba. The agreement involved a barter relationship whereby Cuban medical personnel would be deployed in Venezuela in return for oil—socialist Cuba is renowned for the quality of its health services (Chavez himself was treated in Cuba for the cancer that eventually resulted in his death in 2013). Since 2004 the following countries have joined: Antigua and Barbuda, Bolivia, Dominica, Ecuador, Nicaragua, and St Vincent and the Grenadines.

ALBA's principles distinguish it as an alternative to regional trading relationships in order to avoid the 'resource curse' that we discussed in Chapter 10. It aims to redress the power imbalances between developed and developing countries. In a statement released for its 11th summit meeting in Venezuela, it announced,

[W]e have set the goal to dismantle the neoliberal model and build an alternative model that meets the immediate and *historical demands of our peoples, as well as those of our partners in South-South cooperation mechanisms. We advocate income redistribution, democratization of communications, strengthening of the democratic rights to participation and social inclusion, the fight for equity and gender equality, with particular attention to female heads of households, the empowerment of the youth for them to exercise their full right to education and work, environmental protection, defence of national sovereignty, and unity and integration of the peoples of Latin America and the Caribbean, as well as peace in the region.* (Alba 2013)

Questions

1. What are the reservations that poorer developing nations have in engaging in free trade agreements with developed countries?

2. Look at the details of the ALBA agreements on its website, <www.alba-tcp.org/en/contenido/statement-1st-meeting-alba-tcp-political-parties-progressive-and-revolutionary-movements>. How would you characterize this model of regional integration in relation to the spatial levels of integration we have explored in theory?

The European Union: a deepening, widening, or fragmenting union?

> COMPLEXITY The modern history of Western Europe covers two contrasting periods of the 20th century. The first half was plagued by the horrors of two world wars and national fervour; the second half attempted to build peace through economic and social integration. There has been a lively debate about how best to achieve the latter. At the heart of this debate is the broad ideological divide between those who see the EU as providing a means of expanding the free market and those who believe that structural economic and political interventions are needed. Furthermore, key members have sought different outcomes from participation in the European Economic Community (EEC) and later EU.

For example, Germany and France, for many years the dominant powers, favour a **federalist**, long-term, and politically-integrated Europe. A federalist Europe would mean that the institutions of the EU would have a wider range of power to determine policies which would then become binding on the individual countries. Moreover, France is often perceived as being implicitly protectionist, for example, seeing the EU as a means of giving help to its agricultural sector, with a particular focus on preserving the Common Agricultural Policy. Spain has sought cohesion and funding support for the southern states, while the Italians desire improved governance. The new Central and Eastern Europe accession states see membership as a means to overcome the legacy of centrally planned communist rule and embark on sustained development. The UK has sought a loose union; an anti-federalist, free trade, 'cafeteria' approach in which it could pick and choose policies to suit its needs. The UK is seen as adopting a reluctant and limited participation in European integration (e.g. its reluctance to join the euro; its opt-out from the **Schengen Agreement** (a Union-wide single state agreement for international travel purposes with no internal border controls) and the EU Charter of Fundamental Rights integration). Successive UK governments have argued for the development of an enlarged Europe, focusing on a large single market rather than proceeding with further political and social integration. Thus, although the EU represents a partnership of 28 sovereign nations, it contains a diverse set of countries with differing aspirations that complicate decision-making and consensus (see Table 13.2).

Table 13.2 EU members and future enlargement possibilities

1958	1973	1981	1986	1995	2004	2007	2013	2020+?
Belgium	Denmark	Greece	Portugal	Austria	Cyprus	Bulgaria	Croatia	Turkey
France	Ireland		Spain	Finland	Czech Republic	Romania		Former Yugoslavia
Germany	UK			Sweden	Estonia			Republic of Macedonia
Italy					Hungary			Montenegro
Luxembourg					Latvia			Serbia
Netherlands					Lithuania			Iceland
					Malta			Albania
					Poland			Norway
					Slovakia			
					Slovenia			

The modern EU is based on treaties agreed by member governments and, ultimately, their electorates. Once agreed, the treaties form the 'EU club' rules and the foundation for everything the EU undertakes. In drafting the original Treaty of Rome the EEC was charged with:

Establishing a common market and progressively approximating the economic policies of the Member States, to promote throughout the Community a harmonious development of economic activities, a continuous and balanced expansion, an increase in stability, an accelerated rise in the standard of living and closer relations between the states belonging to it.

(Article 2 of the Treaty of Rome 25 March 1957 (ec.europa.eu/economy_finance/emu_history/ documents/treaties/rometreaty2.pdf))

The key **European treaties** are:

1951	Treaty of Paris—European Coal and Steel Community (ECSC)
1958	Treaties of Rome—European Economic Community (EEC) and European Atomic Energy Community (Euratom)
1986	Single European Act—Single Market creation
1992	Treaty of Maastricht—European Union (EU)
1997	Treaty of Amsterdam—amended EEC treaty and paved way for completion of the Single Market
2001	Treaty of Nice—amended earlier treaties and streamlined the EU's institutional system
2004	Treaty of Rome—Treaty establishing a Constitution for Europe
2009	Treaty of Lisbon—the Reform Treaty establishing the 'rebranded' EU constitution

(The text of these treaties can be found at **<http://europa.eu>**)

Under the treaties, the EU members delegate some national sovereignty to shared institutions representing their collective interest. The treaties represent 'primary' legislation, from which regulations, directives, decisions, opinions, and recommendations are derived.

There are four types of legislative instruments as established by the Treaty of Amsterdam:

1. A **Regulation** has a general application. It is binding in its entirety and directly applicable in all member states.

2. A **Directive** is binding, as to the result to be achieved, upon each member state to which it is addressed, but leaves to the national authorities the choice of form and methods.

3. A **Decision** is binding in its entirety upon those to whom it is addressed.

4. **Opinions** and **Recommendations** have no binding force.

These legislative instruments, and EU policies generally, result from discussions among the **institutional triangle**—the Council of the European Union, the European Parliament, and the European Commission. This institutional triangle only functions effectively with mutual cooperation and trust.

EU expansion and challenges from globalization and terrorism led the member nations to consider revising the EU's rules. Following the initial rejection of the EU Constitution Treaty (Treaty of Rome) in referenda in France, the Netherlands, and Ireland, eight years of intense negotiations and amendments, and the Berlin Declaration of common intent, in 2007 EU leaders came to an agreement. The outcome was the 2009 Treaty of Lisbon which established a Reform Treaty.

This Treaty consolidates and simplifies existing treaties, clarifies the powers of members, and sets out to modernize the EU's institutions and streamline its decision-making. It established the posts of full-time president of the EU Council and an EU 'High Representative' who heads a new European Diplomatic Service. The Reform Treaty also enshrines a Charter of Fundamental Rights which requires national parliaments to check whether proposed laws could be better implemented at national level or EU level, and makes decision-making easier by removing the national veto in areas such as climate change, energy security, and emergency aid. Unanimity will still be required in the areas of tax, foreign policy, defence, and social security. The Reform Treaty also introduces a redistribution of voting weights between member states phased in by 2017, meaning more qualified majority voting decisions (achieved by a 'double majority' of 55% of member states and representing a minimum of 65% of the EU's population).

Stop and Think

Discuss your views about a further EU enlargement post-2020 by identifying the potential new entrants and the arguments for and against their joining.

Enlargement

EU enlargement is not a new concept (see Table 13.2), but in 1993 the European Council set out accession conditions (the 'Copenhagen Criteria'):

- *Political*: stable institutions guaranteeing democracy, the rule of law, respect for and protection of human rights and minorities;

- *Economic*: a functioning market economy and capacity to cope with competitive pressures and market forces within the EU;

- *Aquis Communautaire*: the implementation of EU legislation via an appropriate administrative and judicial structure. It implies the ability to assume the obligations of membership, including meeting the aims of political, economic, and monetary union.

The precise implications of enlargement remain uncertain (see Table 13.3). General political and social benefits are assumed to flow from the extended zone of peace, stability, and

Table 13.3 Economic advantages and disadvantages of enlargement

Advantages	Disadvantages
Market: enlargement increases the internal market, raising demand for EU goods.	*Budget:* enlargement costs for the financial perspective 2000–6 were estimated at 40.8 billion euros.
Economic growth: effective 1.5% rise in GDP among new members raises spending power and job growth.	*Regional policy:* 'statistical effect' on existing structural fund recipients who lose relative to the new members.
Investment: new members offer new FDI opportunities and skilled but cheaper labour.	*Overstated benefits:* many trade and investment effects are due to global forces and restructuring not enlargement.
Allocation effects: encourages competition, trade, and greater consumer choice and reduces barriers in previously protected markets.	*Transition costs:* expense of social, political, and economic changes to meet the Copenhagen criteria and balance of payments deficits resulting from 'catch-up' expenditure.
Accumulation effects: furthers the process of liberalization in progress since the start of the 1990s.	*Uncertain migration:* tensions and costs might arise from widespread migration from the new member states.

Mini-Case 13.2 Turkey and the EU

With a relatively young population of 70 million, an export oriented economy, and a developing information society, Turkey's accession has the potential to increase the size and competitiveness of the single market. The elimination of technical and non-technical barriers to trade and Turkey's adoption of EU legislation and standards are gradually increasing competitiveness and product quality. With a services sector constituting 65% of its GDP, a public procurement market of over 30 billion, and FDI opportunities, Turkey offers huge potential for European firms.

However, Turkey's standard of living is barely half that of Poland, only 45% of Turkish people of working age have a job. The female employment rate is only 25% and educational standards are low. The economy has also suffered from high and variable inflation, erratic growth, and high levels of public debt.

Economic improvement is a necessary, but not sufficient, condition for membership. Turkey must prove it can meet the Copenhagen criteria in terms of the rule of law, democracy, and respect for human rights. If accepted, Turkish entry offers the EU an opportunity to absorb a potentially prosperous, large, and overwhelmingly Muslim country. This could help to reduce tensions in a divided world.

Question

What are the main the benefits and costs of Turkey joining the EU?

---

prosperity which enhances security, offers political reunification of the EU, and links with states to the south and east. Improvements in the quality of life for citizens occur as new members adopt common policies for protecting the environment and fighting crime, drugs, and illegal immigration. New members enrich the EU through increased diversity, the interchange of ideas, and better understanding of other peoples.

In the case of Eastern European countries, there are many who argue that enlargement has been a success (Foxley 2010). Prior to the collapse of the Soviet Union most Eastern European trade had taken place within the Soviet economic bloc, the Council for Mutual Economic Assistance (COMECON). By the 1980s growth rates across the region were low and there was widespread dissatisfaction with the lack of consumer goods. After the demise of Soviet style communism, Eastern European countries quickly sought to strengthen their links to the EU. They endeavoured to develop strong democratic structures, re-orientate their economies, and build the appropriate institutions and structures to bring their living standards up to Western European levels. The convergence criteria acted as a standard to aspire to and, in turn, the EU allowed countries access to the structural and cohesion funds that previously were available for EU members only. In the period from accession until the 2008 crisis, generally, economic growth rates in the former Eastern Europe countries were increasing, as were their exports as a percentage of their GDP (Foxley 2010).

The mere prospect of joining the EU does seem to provide countries with the ability to develop their economic and political systems and enjoy increased growth. Turkey is widely seen as being one of the next generation of countries to follow in the footsteps of the BRICS, and, in part, its recent surge in terms of development has been fuelled by its objective to join the EU (see Mini-Case 13.2).

Institutions and decision-making in the EU

Council of Ministers of the European Union

The Council of Ministers, 'the Council', consists of ministers from each member state, who vary with the subject under discussion. Hence, transport ministers attend transport-related discussions, and so on. It is the champion of national interests, with a European Council President appointed by EU member states for a period of two and a half years (and renewable once as established by the Lisbon Treaty). In 2009 EU leaders chose the Belgian Prime Minister Herman Van Rompuy to be the first permanent Council President, replacing the system where countries take six month turns leading the Council Presidency. European 'summits' involve heads of state, governments of the member states, and the president of the Commission and occur twice yearly. The Council has a decisive role in legislation, co-decision-making with the European Parliament. Following the Amsterdam Treaty, most legislative decisions are taken by qualified majority voting with unanimity required in a few areas.

European Parliament

Following eastern enlargement the European Parliament (EP) has 751 members, elected for a five-year term. It is the champion of the interests of the EU people. Its roles are to: approve the member states' choice of president of the EC and endorse the appointment of commissioners; amend and adopt the community budget; amend and approve legislative proposals in co-decision with the Council; and investigate complaints of maladministration in other institutions. With EU decision-making increasingly in the hands of members of the European Parliament (MEPs), the EP has acquired almost equal legislative powers (boosted by the Lisbon Treaty) with the Council (co-decision procedure including agriculture, energy policy, immigration, and EU funds). It can use its position to delay reports or extract concessions from the Commission or Council. Seats are distributed among countries according to 'degressive proportionality', i.e. MEPs from more populous countries will each represent more people than those from smaller countries. No country has less than six or more than 96 MEPs.

European Commission

The European Commission (EC) is, in effect, the European civil service and the champion of European integration. It is responsible for: initiating and drafting legislative proposals; formulating policy; implementing decisions taken by the Council of Ministers and the EP; administering the EU's various funds; and monitoring law implemented by the member states.

Increasingly, the EC focuses less on legislation and more on encouraging the member states to align their own policies to common guidelines. The commission comprises 27 members (one per member state, a condition reaffirmed by the Lisbon Treaty); a president and 26 commissioners, known as the College of Commissioners, nominated by member states. The whole Commission must be approved by the EP. The main part of the Commission comprises 37 departments, or Directorates-General (DG) responsible for policy areas.

Decision-making in the EU

The Council of Ministers is generally perceived as the most influential decision-making body, tasked with approving EU laws. The EP monitors laws and the other bodies and is gradually assuming a higher profile. The EC proposes new laws for the Council and Parliament to consider. These three institutions work together to formulate policies, the most important of which include:

- enabling businesses and people to trade and work freely (trade, industry policies)
- creating an area of freedom, security and justice across the EU (security policy)
- helping poorer regions (regional policy)

- improving the environment (environmental policy)
- supporting EU agriculture (common agricultural policy)
- giving the EU a stronger global voice (external policy)
- helping nations coordinate their policies to boost growth, stability and employment, and the single currency (macroeconomic and euro policies).

As established by the Treaty of Lisbon, the EU shares sovereignty with member states on a number of areas ('shared competencies' and, in some cases, provides a consultative role in areas of 'limited or supporting EU competencies') and has exclusive sovereignty in some areas defined under the 'exclusive competencies clause' (Table 13.4).

Stop and Think

With reference to the main three EU institutions, where does the balance of power lie and why? How do you think the main EU institutions differ from those governing your country and what are the similarities? Argue the strengths and weaknesses of a shared EU competencies system of governance.

Table 13.4 Dimensions of sovereignty between the EU and member states

Exclusive EU competencies	Shared EU competencies	Supporting or limited EU competencies
The Union has exclusive competence to issue directives and conclude international agreements as stipulated in the EU Treaties and legislative acts.	Shared competence between the EU and member states, however, the latter cannot exercise competence in areas where the Union has done so.	The Union can carry out actions to support, coordinate, or supplement member states' actions.
<ul><li>the customs union</li><li>common commercial (trade) policies</li><li>conservation of marine biological resources (common fisheries policy)</li><li>common market policies</li><li>monetary policy for the member states whose currency is the euro</li></ul>	<ul><li>agriculture and fisheries, excluding the conservation of marine biological resources</li><li>consumer protection</li><li>economic, social, and territorial cohesion (EU Regional Policy)</li><li>environment</li><li>social policy, for the aspects defined in the Lisbon Treaty</li><li>the internal market (inc. competition policy)</li><li>energy</li><li>transport</li><li>external relations</li><li>trans-European networks</li><li>the area of freedom, security, and justice</li><li>common safety concerns in public health matters</li><li>common foreign and security policy</li></ul>	<ul><li>education, youth, sport, and vocational training</li><li>public health policy</li><li>industrial policy</li><li>culture</li><li>tourism</li><li>civil protection (disaster prevention)</li><li>administrative cooperation</li></ul>

Cultural diversity and business implications

❱❱ **DIVERSITY** Chapter 5 showed us that culture is the glue that binds a society together; it is about people and their behaviour stemming from their backgrounds, group affiliation, values, and practices. Cultural traits derive from various factors, such as: language, social organization, the law, religion, education, and political ideology.

Europeans share a common heritage but the integration and administration of an enlarged EU, comprising almost 500 million people of diverse cultures, is an enormous task. At a basic level, there is no single European language and relatively few people can follow a conversation in a language other than their own.

For businesses, such cultural aspects impinge on decisions to take a pan-European perspective, treating Europe as a relatively uniform market, or targeting specific nations or cultural groups. If the latter, the diversity of the EU might suggest groupings such as the following:

• Anglo-Saxon	UK, Ireland
• Baltic	Estonia, Latvia, Lithuania
• Central & Eastern European	Bulgaria, Czech Republic, Hungary, Slovakia, Slovenia, Poland, Romania
• Germanic/N. European	Austria, Belgium, France, Germany, Netherlands, Luxembourg
• Mediterranean	France, Spain, Portugal, Italy, Greece, Cyprus, Malta
• Nordic/Scandinavian	Denmark, Finland, Sweden

> *Stop and Think*
>
> What is a European citizen? What other groupings can there be (history, language, geography, etc.)?
>
> What are the main cultural and globalization challenges facing companies operating in the new Europe?

▮ The euro and business—one step too far or one step short of a full ladder?

❱❱ **DYNAMIC** ❱❱ **INTERACTION** We discussed the macroeconomic aspects of European Monetary Union (EMU) in Chapter 9's end of chapter case study, and we have explored the arguments for and against having a single currency above.

With the advent of the single market programme, it became clear that transaction costs linked to currency conversion, and high risk premiums associated with exchange rate fluctuations, would hinder realization of the internal market potential. Hence, a three-stage approach (Mini-Case 13.3) was formulated for the introduction of a single currency, enshrined in the 1992 Maastricht Treaty. This shows clearly that the theoretical problems of creating monetary union were appreciated, but, for many members of the EU, these dangers could be negated with coordination and careful planning, thus ensuring the prize of a single currency with all the associated benefits.

Central to the introduction of the euro was the need to avoid destabilizing inflation that would undermine competition, confidence, and purchasing power. Accordingly, an independent European Central Bank (ECB) was formed in 1998 tasked with controlling interest rates to effect monetary policy; mainly interpreted as a 'year on year' increase in the Harmonized

Mini-Case 13.3 The stages of European Monetary Union (EMU)

EMU Stage 1: 'Convergence' July 1990

Stage 1 involved measures to progress economic convergence including: consolidation of the single market; the removal of physical, technical, and fiscal barriers; and a stronger **competition policy**.

Nominal criteria were specified for the convergence of participant nations' economies

Price stability: the rate of inflation as measured by the Consumer Price Index was not to exceed that of the best performing three nations by more than 1.5%

Interest rates: long-term interest rate gaps should not exceed that of the best performing member states by more than 2%

Budget deficit: planned or actual government deficit was not to exceed 3% of GDP (at market prices) under normal circumstances

Government debt: not to exceed 60% of GDP (at market prices) unless the ratio is sufficiently falling

Exchange rates: to have maintained membership of the narrow band of the ERM for at least two years without 'severe tensions' (although it should be noted that the ERM effectively collapsed in 1993).

EMU Stage 2: 'Institutional' January 1994–December 1998

Stage 2 was a transitional phase to consolidate convergence. It included the development of the European Monetary Institute (EMI) whose roles were: advisory; to strengthen cooperation between national central banks; and to prepare for the euro. National central banks were to become independent of their governments.

EMU Stage 3: 'Euro' January 1999–February 2002

Stage 3 marked the birth of the single currency with payment transfers but not cash transactions. A dual currency situation occurred with 'no compulsion, no prohibition', namely the euro could be used but there was no compulsion to do so. Eventually, on 1 January 2002 euro bank notes and coins were introduced in 12 nations, and national currencies were withdrawn by 28 February.

Question

Why did the process of finalizing the birth of the euro take so long?

Index of Consumer Prices (HICP) of less than 2%. During 1997 the European Council adopted three supporting resolutions covering:

- economic growth—to ensure that employment was a key objective
- economic coordination—closer ties between members to embrace financial, budgetary, social, and fiscal policies
- the revised Stability and Growth Pact—a commitment to budgetary discipline.

The **Stability and Growth Pact** set legally binding ceilings of 3% GDP on Eurozone members' budget deficits, a breach of which would incur fines of up to 0.5% of GDP. However, the pact was widely considered too rigid for countries struggling to grow. The rules were relaxed but, with hindsight, this was not enough. Critics point out that this was a crucial mistake, as it effectively forced member states to undertake unpopular reforms necessary to structurally re-adjust their economies and make them more competitive. This measure was needed to allow for a stable and sustainable Eurozone but might be impossible to achieve. However, the counter argument holds that such conditions act as a huge incentive for countries, especially the less competitive ones, to improve their economic performance and, thus, can actually speed up convergence.

■ The performance of the euro

On the one hand, the EMU can be seen as representing a remarkable achievement. Only ten years elapsed between the Treaty of Maastricht, which laid the foundations for the single currency, and the 2002 introduction of euro notes and coins in 12 nations. The euro replaced individual currencies that were long-standing instruments, and crucially, symbols of national identities. People now travel and trade across large swathes of Europe using a single currency. In 2011, Estonia became the latest member state to join the Eurozone, bringing the total to 17 out of 28 member states, and approximately 331 million EU citizens using the euro.

However, as we saw in Chapter 9's end of chapter case study, all is not well in the Eurozone, especially in what have come to be called by people seeking to apportion blame, the PIGS countries (Portugal, Ireland/Italy, Greece, and Spain).

It is important to distinguish between cause and effect here, as it is not the euro itself that caused the crisis, nor indeed is it primarily the 'fault' of the PIGS. The roots of the problem lie in the global recession of 2008 which was the result of the irresponsible financial practices and the lack of an effective global regulatory environment. We explored the immediate causes of this in Chapter 2 and the possible global responses in Chapter 10, but it is clear that there has, as yet, not been an effective global response.

Consequently, individual countries have responded to the crisis in different ways. In the US there has been a measure of old-fashioned Keynesian fiscal and monetary expansion and, in the view of structuralist critics, this has both prevented the US from experiencing a collapse and brought the beginnings of the restoration of growth. In Europe the main model adopted has been one of austerity. Here the fault lines of the euro become horribly exposed. The UK and other non-Eurozone countries feel vindicated in their decision not to join the euro as they can exercise their own response. Instead, in the UK, to the frustration of most of the academic economics community and a wide range of economic commentators who would advocate a Keynesian expansionary programme, an austerity programme has been instituted, albeit accompanied by a very large increase in the money supply supported by its ability to borrow short term at very low interest rates.

For the relatively strong countries in the Union, even where growth rates are slowing or even dipping, their good credit ratings mean that they can continue to borrow to offset the worst effects of the recession as they seek to restore their competitive positions. There is also the belief that, while the PIGS may not have caused it, the 2008 crisis simply exposed the fact that they had allowed budget deficits to rise too far and not done enough to restructure their economies to become competitive.

The richer countries within the Eurozone do recognize the danger of a financial crisis being precipitated by the default of a struggling country. And, there have been attempts to ensure there are sufficient funds in place to rescue a country should there be a speculative attack on one. In this the EU central bank has been supported by the IMF. However, essentially, the long term burden to address the large budget deficits does fall on each country and, in return for the funds they are receiving from the IMF and ECB, they are forced to enact deep austerity measures. Currently, as we have seen in Chapter 9, this is creating huge social and political tensions in Greece and Spain in particular.

There are plenty of critics of the policy of the EU, and the Eurozone specifically, and they come from all sides of the economic and political divide. For Keynesian critics, the immediate blame has to be with the EU itself and its austerity policies. While it might be a logical tactic for one country alone to undertake microeconomic adjustment at the macroeconomic level, the reduction in aggregate demand collectively brings everyone down and is, ultimately, self-defeating. What is needed is a fiscal expansion in all countries, which if led by the stronger countries, would restore confidence in the European economy and still allow borrowing to occur at low interest rates.

When it comes to the role of the euro, opponents simply see the current pressures as evidence that the euro is a step too far, and the edifice of European unity is now crumbling. For free market critics, the PIGS may have got themselves into this mess but they cannot do anything else but undertake drastic measures to bring their economies under control now that they are deprived of the ability to use the exchange rate to buffer their economies. For left wing critics, there are strong objections to the loss of democracy as citizens and elected national governments are essentially forced to comply with the conditions attached to the loans.

For those who firmly believe in the long-term benefits of a full economic union, what this situation reveals is that there must be much greater economic and political integration, involving a greater role for an independent central bank with access to larger stability funds contributed by members. Members would have to agree to allow much greater central scrutiny of their government spending plans, and fines for non-compliance would be necessary. It is not that the current situation shows the ultimate and complete failure of the euro project, it is simply that the process towards an effective Eurozone is incomplete. It seems that what is needed is a 'two-speed' Europe, with those who wish to join and remain in the Eurozone agreeing to undertake more overarching political and economic cooperation and those who do not wish to participate remaining part of the negotiations but not signing up to the agreements (see Piris 2012).

◼ Doing business in Europe

❱❱ **INTERNAL/EXTERNAL** Having explored the main external issues that are affecting the European Business environment, in this next section we look at some of the ways in which operating in Europe may affect the internal decisions of businesses.

The Lisbon Summit in 2000 set the following business goals for Europe by 2010 (the Lisbon Agenda):

> that the EU should become the most competitive and dynamic knowledge-based economy in the World, capable of sustained economic growth, with more and better jobs, and greater social cohesion.

The agenda aims to create an effective internal market with an improved infrastructure and more investment in research and development (R&D), leading to a strong industrial base, characterized by an adaptable workforce, free and fair trade, and innovation. To meet these aims the EU requires efficient business-related policies.

Stakeholder management in the EU

❱❱ **STAKEHOLDERS** Decisions made in Brussels affect businesses, consumers, and citizens in many different ways. Often these decisions must reconcile the needs of the various stakeholders through open debate and examination of the opposing and conciliatory arguments. Understanding and compromise are key to delivering decisions acceptable to all. It is crucial for businesses to be involved and have an influence at an early stage in the formulation of EU regulations and legislation.

This has given rise to a large lobbyist body in Brussels, representing large companies, industrial and economic sectors, trade associations, employer and union representatives, consumers, chambers of commerce, city and regional representatives, and think tanks. They all seek to influence and contribute to EU decision-making.

Stop and Think

What drives businesses to pay attention to EU decision-making? Use examples to argue your case.

Competition and industry policy

EU competition policy follows the neoclassical free-market philosophy now prevalent in all member states; a liberal economic vision contrasting with the centrally planned approach previously experienced by the new eastern members. Competition policy follows articles 81 and 82 of the Treaty of Rome and seeks to ensure the internal market is not distorted. Areas which hinder efficiency and competitive forces (e.g. monopoly, oligopoly, cartels, restrictive practices, subsidies, state procurement, and protection) are targeted. EU competition policy has grown in significance, boosted by the Lisbon 2000 economic reform and competitiveness agenda.

There are broadly five components:

Anti-trust agreements prohibit concerted or restricted practices or agreements among firms that limit competition, unless special circumstances exist to promote technical or economic progress. Enforcement of anti-trust legislation has gathered momentum with actions against cartels covering beer, banking, and vitamins.

Anti-trust abuse of a dominant position targets monopoly and oligopoly situations where abuse occurs, such as low pricing to eliminate the competition, discriminatory pricing (the charging of different prices for the same commodity) within or between member states, and limits imposed on production, markets, or technological development to raise prices and/or profits. The main tests are: a market share of 40% or more; the degree of independence from competitors; the ability to eliminate the competition; or a dominant relationship with suppliers or customers. However, prosecutions are rare, partly because many people feel there is a need for large, globally competitive corporations that are EU and national 'champions'.

Mergers can create or strengthen a dominant position which may lead to abuse. A Merger Regulation was adopted in 1989 (No. 4064/89) which established exclusive commission jurisdiction for mergers between firms with a joint global turnover of €5 billion and within the EU of €250 million each, below which national legislation prevails. During the 1990s the EC became more interventionist and accordingly was criticized, for example, for having prohibited the GE/Honeywell merger and having decisions overturned by the Court of Justice (Airtours/First Choice; Schneider Electric/Legrand; and Tetra Laval/Sidel). In 2004 a new Merger Regulation (No. 139/2004) placed greater responsibility on firms to assess the impact of any merger or acquisition.

State aid refers to financial assistance from public funds that distort competition and efficient resource allocation. It applies to subsidies, tax breaks, soft loans, preferential procurement, and guarantees. Article 87 (2,3) of the EC Treaty allows for state aid under circumstances compatible with the internal market, for example, social aid or that given to overcome the effects of natural disasters.

A total ban on state aid is impossible; indeed a fundamental EU tenet is that intervention is necessary for balanced and sustainable economic development. Consequently, a history of state aid support exists, notably rescue subsidies for shipping, car, coal, and steel industries. These subsidies have been substantially reduced and redirected via regional policy. Despite progress, state aid issues remain; indeed they have re-emerged with the accession of former centrally planned economies.

Utilities have been liberalized throughout the EU, boosted by privatization drives and single market reforms. Key sectors are 'network' industries or natural monopolies such as energy, water, postal services, telecommunications, railways, and airlines. For years these public interest monopolies were protected, but technological developments have exposed operating weaknesses. The Commission's liberalization policy based on article 86(3) has created complex packages of directives, restrictive practice, and merger case law to open up these areas.

Competition legislation has a special place in EU policy as it defends the collective interest in economic efficiency secured through the single market. Nevertheless, it faces radical challenges. National competition agencies have grown in stature, with often better analytical and legal bases, and the European Court of Justice has often expressed concern about Directorates-General's competition interpretations. Moreover, member nations are often reluctant to reduce state support for their companies. The test will be whether policy can be flexible enough to meet national concerns and lead to the gains in EU competitiveness and growth required by the Lisbon Agenda.

Industry policy

Competition policy has played a central role in the 'economic EU constitution', in shaping and giving birth to an industrial policy for the EU. The concept of an EU industrial policy in itself has been, and remains, contentious in the EU. Taken literally, industrial policy entails all acts and policies of the state relating to industry. This would include instruments and measures designed to control and influence the performance of firms within particular sectors of the economy as well as passive or active measures (i.e. relating to liberalization of markets or correction of market failure), tasks usually associated with the sovereignty of the national state. Therefore, the original Treaty of Rome did not provide a legal basis for active sectoral policies to be pursued and left industrial policy within the competence of member states. However, with the liberalization of global trade, increased attention was placed on whether member state's national, often protectionist, industrial policies could distort economic competition between states and ultimately harm the ability of the trading bloc to compete globally. Therefore, an EU industrial policy was first introduced in 1991 in the Treaty of the European Union (TEU) Article 3 (1) which states that activities of the Community shall 'strengthen the competitiveness of Community industry'. Under the Treaty the Commission was tasked with the coordination of member states in this matter. Subsequently, the Maastricht 1992 (article 129b); and Amsterdam 1997 (article 157) treaties provided a further basis for solidifying an EU industrial policy. The intention has been to promote structural adjustment, encourage small- and medium-sized companies, and stimulate innovation. Maastricht also emphasized trans-European network developments in areas of transport, telecommunications, and energy.

EU industrial policy is being developed with the principles of an integrated approach across sectors and member states and a non-interventionist ethos. The main strategies applied are, firstly, the creation of a business environment conducive to developing new technologies and entrepreneurial activity. This includes promoting institutional measures such as venture capital provision, a European patent system, and boosting R&D by strengthening links between universities, research organizations, and businesses. Secondly, a key focus has been to provide a framework for pan-EU mergers and takeovers via approval of a takeover directive, seen as critical to cementing the single market and enlargement.

❱❱ **VALUES** However, EU industry policy is a collection of often conflicting programmes. For example, there are diverse views about the benefits of allowing cross-border takeovers, hence debate in the European Parliament has held up the takeover directive. One perspective favours a robust competition policy backed by deregulation to overcome protectionist tendencies that have prevented EU-wide competition. Policies to raise productivity in key technologies (e.g. biotechnology, information technology, and creative industries) (see

Chapter 3) would support this approach. An alternative view emphasizes restructuring the industrial base with less concern for internal EU competition. This approach takes a more global view, arguing that Europe needs large efficient businesses which would be competitive with the US and Far East, such as Airbus Industries in the aviation sector. Such issues are debated at European summits, but there is still reluctance to abandon protectionism as a tool of industrial policy.

For EU business leaders, there is often considerable frustration at the policy hurdles faced. They helped to shape the Lisbon Agenda and communicate their views via trade associations, chambers of commerce, and the thousands of lobbyists in Brussels; yet they struggle to see tangible industrial policy benefits. However, the close connection between competition policy and industry policy is now better understood in the EU, and the value of a coordinated approach within the context of globalized market economies is recognized.

Mini-Case 13.4 Industry and competition policy and the European airlines

EU economic growth requires an efficient and effective air transport system. There are 280 airports but key hubs are dominated by the large-scale, national 'flag carriers': Heathrow (British Airways); Frankfurt (Lufthansa); and Paris CDG (AirFrance/KLM). Overall, the European air travel market has grown rapidly, especially as a result of the expansion of low cost airlines.

There have been various challenges for the EU authorities in relation to industry and competition policy. Flying generates considerable environmental costs. Countries have sought to protect markets, preserving monopoly and market dominance for national airlines. And, local authorities have been under pressure to grant aid to airlines as a way of encouraging them to use regional airports and thereby increase employment in areas experiencing long-term structural unemployment. Often, national politics have also played a key part in attempting to rescue failing carriers.

The industry's cost structure reveals a complex situation with: high fixed costs (planes, facilities); high airport charges (e.g. 20% of Ryanair's operating costs); volatile fuel costs (impact on prices, profits); differing cost structures between flag carriers and low-cost, 'no frills' airlines; and deregulation, liberalization, and privatization driving down fares.

The EU airline market has moved from a highly regulated system, based on bilateral agreements, to a competitive internal market. Prior to 1998, airlines were limited to operating from their national base, which restricted mergers. Now any airline holding a valid EU Air Operators Certificate can operate in any market within the EU. Freedom exists to set fares, open new routes, and determine capacities. Enlargement nations now belong to the 'Open Skies' Treaty which allows point-to-point service and offers opportunities for the low-cost operators.

Rapid consolidation in the European airline industry is now taking place, with the gradual de-regulation in the sector throughout the 1990s and liberalization that allowed for an accelerated growth of low-cost airlines. Incumbents struggle to find a viable response to the aggressive new entrants. The market is now dominated by Europe's three major network carrier groups plus the two major low-cost airlines (Ryanair and EasyJet). The three major network carriers are well positioned, thanks to their range of products and services, tightly knit network of European routes, and high percentage of intercontinental flights; but they are seeing their previously comparatively strong financial position dwindle in the aftermath of the global financial crisis. Meanwhile, Ryanair and EasyJet dominate the low-cost market with more than 50% market share and a superior cost position. Smaller regional and national carriers are not in strong positions. These carriers are in danger of being squeezed out in predatory competition between the big network carriers and the leading low-cost airlines.

Moving ahead, all airlines, whether network, low-cost, smaller national operators, regionals, or independent charter companies, must face the fact that the increasing strength of low-cost carriers has changed the way the European airline industry competes.

One of airlines' preferred strategies has been to explore mergers and acquisitions options. So, a delicate balance has to be struck to provide a supportive environment in which European airlines can operate and prosper in a global market while ensuring that passengers are not exploited.

Questions

1. Why have low-cost airlines grown in significance within the EU?

2. Why is state aid a particular problem in the context of the European airline industry?

■ Looking ahead

In all the current doom and gloom about the low rates of growth in Europe, and in light of the particular problems faced by Greece and other Southern European countries, advocates of the EU project remind us that prior to 2008 huge gains were made across all countries, and that especially the new accession countries in Eastern Europe have been dramatically transformed.

There are undoubted economic benefits derived from the greater trade opportunities and competition that the EU has brought, and it is still the case that the EU provided a role model for other aspiring trading blocs.

Politically, enlargement has been one of the EU's most successful policies and a powerful foreign policy tool. The zone of peace and democracy has been progressively extended and, in this 'democratic' sense, a closer union of member states exists, stretching from the Atlantic to the eastern Mediterranean, from Lapland to Malta.

Given the problems that the WTO is facing in forging ahead with the latest round of trade talks, it is clear that the pattern of world trade is being heavily influenced by regional trade agreements. Across the globe more and more countries want to join such trading blocs. One interesting development is how these blocs relate to each other—something we look at in Chapter 16.

As we will see in the ASEAN case study at the end of this chapter, FTAs can be mutually beneficial even for countries at moderately different levels of development. But it is South–South cooperation that will have the best chances of success. The reservations of structuralist and dependency writers that we saw in Chapter 10 regarding trade between the developed and developing world still remain. If integration is to proceed beyond the FTA level then it is clear that there must be much greater political and economic integration, as well as attention paid to the need for realistic convergence between members. The experience of the EU shows the danger of too rapid an integration, and that some members might not be able to bring their economies up to the levels required to benefit from the free competitive conditions. As the recent experience with the euro shows, the jury is still out on the issue of the feasibility of a full economic union. For many, the only way this could be achieved is through much closer political and economic cooperation in a federal model, but this may be a step too far for some members. On 1 January 2013 the Treaty on Stability, Coordination, and Governance in the European Monetary Union (otherwise known as the Fiscal Compact) came into force to create greater coordination across all members of the Eurozone and non-Eurozone countries that wanted to accept its terms and therefore be able to take part in its ongoing deliberations (for the detail of this see European Council 2013). The UK has refused to sign up to this Treaty.

Britain's history within the EU is marked by hesitancy. In 1973 the UK joined the EEC, then, in 1975, held a referendum on membership. The UK opted out of stage 3 of the European Monetary Union and is not part of the Eurozone. In 1989 it opted out of the social chapter, which lays down minimum social welfare standards, then under a new government subsequently reversed its position. Not surprisingly, the British are nevertheless widely considered 'reluctant Europeans'. Within the UK there is a strong current of opinion that resents the economic and political power 'given up' in order to be part of the EU, and there is a suspicion that countries such as France and Germany are determined to form a 'United States of Europe'. Not only is the prospect of Britain joining the euro now extremely remote, but there are calls for a referendum to decide whether to continue as part of the EU at all. Britain is not alone in having these reservations, but it is very much in a minority. At the very least, there is a view that the Lisbon Treaty needs to be renegotiated and there is every prospect that there will be a two-speed Europe. But how this will hold together remains to be seen.

Summary

- The process of globalization is being heavily influenced by the development of regional trading blocs and there is a range of levels of integration possible within these blocs.

- The EU provides an instructive model in managing integration. The EU involves complex decision-making based on treaties and the 'institutional triangle'. Integration has progressed from removing trade barriers to positive building and harmonization of policies, the most significant of which is the experiment with monetary union and the creation of the Eurozone.

- The euro is a key building block in the Europeanization process, but challenges national sovereignty at a macroeconomic level. This raises strategic questions for firms at the micro-level in terms of markets and pricing, production, and financing. The limited ability of the Eurozone to adjust in order to dampen crises like the Greek debt crisis raises questions about the sustainability of an artificial and incomplete monetary union in Europe.

- Doing business in Europe is strongly influenced by the EU policy environment, especially industry and competition policies. These are influenced by the neoclassical free-market philosophy dominant in member states to enhance the single market and prevent distortion of competitive forces. Key industries such as the utilities, car, telecoms, and airlines have all changed radically under such influences.

- In attempting to become an ever closer union of member states, Europe faces future challenges in implementing the Lisbon Agenda and making a success of enlargement. Efforts to both deepen and widen integration will create tensions among existing members with differing objectives. And it requires businesses to appreciate different scenarios that may impinge on their operating environment, ranging from operating in a two-speed union to the possibility that certain countries might break away.

Case Study: The development of the ASEAN trading bloc

We saw in Chapter 10 that trade has been the most important engine for growth in Southeast Asia, but the way in which these countries developed their trade strategies owed little to the idea of free market orthodoxy. Initially, Japan's model was one of state-led industrialization exploiting its comparative advantage in low cost but skilled labour to export to Europe and the US. With the state and other financial institutions directing investment into designated export activities and fostering technology transfer, Japan was able to move up the value chain—away from low cost labour intensive goods to capital intensive intermediate goods and then to high tech manufacturing goods.

The Association of Southeast Asian nations or ASEAN started in 1967 with a membership of Singapore, Indonesia, Malaysia, the Philippines, and Thailand. It was initially for political co-operation, acting as a bulwark against the many communist countries that they bordered. The Japanese economist Akamatsu published his 'Flying Geese' model of economic development in 1962 (Akamatsu 1962). For Akamatsu, the pattern of regional economic development in areas such as Southeast Asia would resemble the formation of a flock of geese with a lead member pulling all the others forward but with a constant process of leadership rotation. In this model, Japan would provide the initial leadership for the region and, as it developed, it would progressively move up the value chain and directly out source, or vacate, the labour intensive activities to allow countries in the region to exploit their comparative advantages in these areas. Foxley shows that indeed countries such as South Korea, Singapore, Taiwan and Hong Kong did initially become part of a vertically integrated supply chain to enable Japanese business to continue its process of export expansion (Foxley 2010). As we have seen in Chapter 10, the type of industrial policies that each country had developed by concentrating on certain sectors with a large amount of state directed support, enabled them to trade up the value chain, providing room for other countries to follow in their paths, e.g. Indonesia, the Philippines, Thailand, Malaysia and, of course, China which was more recently followed by Vietnam, Laos, and Cambodia. In the process, South Korea, Singapore, Taiwan, and Hong Kong all became economic power houses in their own right.

The ASEAN nations were reluctant to undergo trade liberalization within their bloc, which would increase intra-regional trade, as the prime focus of their economic activity was on exporting to the developed world of North America, Europe, and Japan. However, a number of important changes in the external environment have led to increasing integration and a widening of its present and potential membership. The changes in the orientation of the communist economies, and especially the rise of China with its huge numbers of low-cost workers, has given further impetus to the shifting of comparative advantages in the region and encouraged an acceleration of the ASEAN members' movement towards higher technology manufacturing industries. The 1997 Southeast Asian crisis demonstrated the need for greater cooperation in terms of co-ordinated fiscal and monetary policies to avoid the contagion spreading so rapidly. And, finally, the global recession and ensuing slow growth in the West has shown the Asian economies that there is a need to diversify their trading relationships to avoid over concentration in certain markets. While this might be seen as a negative defensive response which is encouraging closer integration, the sheer speed with which living standards in the region have risen, and the creation of large urban middle class consumers, means that there is now a positive interest in this large and growing intra-regional market.

In 1992 the ASEAN free trade area (AFTA) was established with the intention of phasing out all tariffs between members and in recent years the ASEAN bloc has grown to include: Brunei Darussalam, Lao PDR, Myanmar, Cambodia, and Vietnam (see <www.asean.org>).

Prior to the currency turmoil of the 1997 Southeast Asian financial crisis, ASEAN+3 (APT) was formed to provide a platform for regular meetings between ASEAN and China, Japan, and South Korea in coordinating trade relationships with Europe. But after the crisis it became clear that APT would increasingly be needed to strengthen mutual interests. Two direct examples of this cooperation are the signing of the Chiang Mai Initiative, which provides a forum for currency swaps to build up funds to use in the event of future currency instability, and the creation of the Asian Bonds Market Initiative, which seeks to channel domestic savings into targeted areas of regional investment. APT has also now broadened the areas of cooperation to include a range of political, social, and strategic objectives (see ASEAN 2013).

More recently the ASEAN+6 has developed, adding India, Australia, and New Zealand. All of the +6 countries have already negotiated FTAs with ASEAN, but now the proposal is to create a FTA across all 16 countries which would create a free trade area of 3.6 billion people.

Questions

1. How have the nations of Southeast Asia sought to integrate themselves into the global economy?

2. What role did geographical proximity play in developing trading links?

3. How, prior to the formal development of ASEAN, were the development strategies of their members influenced both domestically and regionally?

4. What have been the external and internal factors that have encouraged the more recent forms of integration for the ASEAN bloc?

Review and discussion questions

1. What are the advantages for a business of being able to operate within a regional trade area?

2. Critically assess the argument that the EU is merely a protectionist trade bloc.

3. Examine whether a single currency is necessary for the efficient working of the European single market.

4. Is the development of regional trading blocs an example of the possible fragmentation of the world trade system or the inevitable consequence of a global business environment consisting of countries at different levels of development and with different historical and cultural determinants?

Assignments

1. a) Imagine that there is going to be a referendum in the UK in 2017 to decide whether the UK should stay or leave the EU. Research into the opposing views and decide which way you would advise British people to vote. Would you be pro or anti advising the UK to stay in?

b) Depending on your answer to the question above imagine that you have been recruited by one of the campaign organizations to help them in their pro or anti campaign by producing a two page campaign leaflet to be distributed to your local business community (for useful research material see the websites below).

2. Write a report which compares and contrasts two of the following trading blocs, in terms of their scope and levels of integration, and identify the likely areas of development in these blocs in the next ten years.

ASEAN
EU
MERCOSUR
NAFTA

Further reading

De Grauwe, P. (2012) *Economics of Monetary Union, 9th edn* (Oxford: Oxford University Press). *A comprehensive evaluation of the costs and benefits of monetary union followed by its present workings covering the ECB, monetary and fiscal policies, and the international role of the euro.*

Johnson, D. and Turner, C. (2010) *International Business: Themes and Issues in the Modern Global Economy* (London: Routledge). *Profiles the context of the international business environment and has chapters on*

the regional dimensions as well as on emerging and developing countries.

World Bank (2012) Doing *Business—Regional Profile: European Union* (**<www.doingbusiness.org/~/media/FPDKM/Doing% 20Business/Documents/Profiles/Regional/DB2012/DB12-European-Union.pdf>**). *The World Bank's assessment of the nature of the EU business environment. This is one of many 'Doing Business' reports, and you can search for all countries and regions on the main site at <www.doingbusiness.org>.*

online resource centre

Test your understanding of this chapter with online questions and answers, explore the subject further through web exercises, and use the web links to provide a quick resource for further research. Go to the Online Resource Centre at <www.oxfordtextbooks.co.uk/orc/wetherly_otter/2>

Useful websites

<http://europa.eu/index_en.htm>
The official home page for the EU

<http://www.efta.int/>
The home page for EFTA

<wto.org/english/tratop_e/region_e/rta_pta_e.htm>
The WTO data base of all RTA's and PTA's

The home page for NAFTA

<http://en.mercopress.com/about-mercosur>
The home page for MERCOSUR

<http://www.sadc.int/>
The home page for SADC

<www.alba-tcp.org/en>
The home page for ALBA

<www.european-voice.com>
A useful source of news and views about the EU

<www.gov.uk/trading-in-the-eu>
An advice site run by the UK government for doing business in Europe

The home page for the Centre for European Reform, a leading EU research think tank

<www.euromove.org.uk>
The home page for the European Movement which campaigns to present the positive case for UK membership

<www.brugesgroup.com>
The home page of the Bruges Group which is an UK all-party think tank which campaigns to stop deeper integration for the UK within the EU

References

Akamatsu, K. (1962) 'A Historical Pattern of Economic Growth in Developing Countries', *Journal of Developing Economies*, March-August, 1 (1) pp. 3-25.

ALBA (2013) Statement of the 1st meeting of the ALBA_TCP political parties progressive and revolutionary movements (accessed 18 May 2013) <**www.alba-tcp.org/en/contenido/statement-1st-meeting-alba-tcp-political-parties-progressive-and-revolutionary-movements**>

ASEAN (2013) 'ASEAN Plus 3 Co-operation' (accessed 19 May 2013) <**www.asean.org/news/item/asean-plus-three-cooperation**>)

Foxley, A. (2010) *Regional Trade Blocs: The Way to the Future?* Carnegie Endowment for International Peace. (accessed on 14 May 2013) <**http://carnegieendowment.org/files/regional_trade_blocs.pdf**>

Piris, J. C. (2012) 'Europe's Two Speed Future', Project Syndicate, 14 December 2012 (accessed on 18 May 2013) <**www.project-syndicate.org/commentary/two-options-for-creating-a-two-speed-europe-by-jean-claude-piris**>

European Council (2013) '"Fiscal Compact" entered into force on 1 January 2013' (accessed 20 May 2013) <**www.european-council.europa.eu/home-page/highlights/fiscal-compact-enters-into-force-on-1-january-2013?lang=en**>)

Chapter 14

The public sector: becoming more business-like in a globalizing world?

Richard Rooke

Learning objectives

When you have completed this chapter you will be able to:

- Characterize the distinctive nature of the public sector with the aim of reviewing both its business opportunities and its political challenges in the present era.

- Appreciate that the 'traditional' public sector and welfare state have been challenged by new political and managerial perspectives—often referred to as **new public management**—although there are newer formulations such as **digital era governance**.

- Assess the new context that recent technology has brought to the public and private sectors and their respective clientele.

- Outline the political, economic, and social pressures which created challenges for the public sector, opening in the mid-1970s and continuing today.

- Identify the range of competing views about the changing political landscape at the many levels of **governance** that impact on **private–public partnerships**.

- Explore the political and ethical dilemmas that arise out of public sector reform through case study work.

THEMES

The following themes of the book are especially relevant to this chapter

▶ **DIVERSITY** OF BUSINESS

The 'public sector' is a diverse collection of organizations, changing over time, and meaning different things in different countries. There is a range of delivery mechanisms for public services: public, private, and voluntary sectors, and combinations of all of these by means of partnerships.

▶ **INTERNAL/EXTERNAL**

This chapter looks at organizational reform within the public sector, driven by changes in the external environment.

▶ **COMPLEXITY** OF THE ENVIRONMENT

The public sector constitutes an important element of the complex environment of business. Public sector reform is visible both in policy-making outcomes and institutional change. The private sector business world now complements public sector services while at the same time

The result is a complex web of factors encouraging, not reducing, interdependency between the public and private sectors on one hand, and presenting new governance issues on the international/transnational stage, on the other.

Stop and Think The public and the private

Can you make a distinction between your public side and your private world? How do you define your terms? Is the definition political, economic, social, or legal? Perhaps it is all four. In your own lives, does it matter who 'controls' you? Does it matter whether the 'boss' or the 'owner' represents a public sector organization or a private company? In thinking this through you are looking, in part, at the present-day debate about how to understand the distinctiveness and connections between the public and private sectors.

》 VALUES 》 INTERNAL/EXTERNAL For convenience, and as a way into our subject, Figure 14.1 illustrates some of the factors or processes affecting public service delivery and its management. You may wish to reflect on the model, even create your own. This diagram indicates the core activity as 'Public Services' and around it the various approaches available,

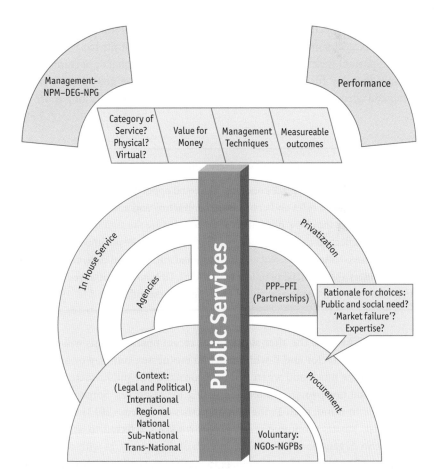

Figure 14.1 Indicative factors surrounding the delivery of public services

to states and businesses alike, in managing the delivery of these services. There are various routes: in-house and regulatory control through agencies, management techniques, and finally contractual arrangements, which can vary from procurement to privatization, to partnerships, even the use of voluntary groups.

In all of this, context matters—and in the diagram (bottom left) this is indicated as both legal and political in nature. This is most important if we are to appreciate how the differing public sectors across the world actually operate. Societies, legally and politically, let alone economically can vary enormously, so no one pattern fits all: context always matters.

⟫ DYNAMIC Of all the factors creating an era of new public service initiatives, and Figure 14.1 is only an indication, for this chapter three innovations are relatively 'new'. They are highlighted in grey in the figure. First, under the (public sector) Management heading, what is conveniently called **new public management** (NPM) techniques, and its critics through **digital era governance** (DEG). Secondly, under the heading of Partnerships, the introduction of **public private partnerships** (PPPs and PFIs). Lastly, there is the heading Performance, under which accountability also falls. The chapter therefore has these elements at its core, although they often overlap.

▪ Management: public sector management in the globalizing era

⟫ VALUES The public sector now acts under new rules and new thinking. This is something that both the public sector and the private sector business community has learnt to appreciate. It is not only important for ethical or workplace concerns, like equal opportunities or tackling discrimination, but also for the financial rules and controls on contracting, procurement, and auditing and accountability in general, let alone the market forces of a more globalized market.

Stop and Think In public service terms are there 'universal values'?

....

It is argued that ethical or workplace concerns, like equal opportunities, or tackling discrimination, but also the financial rules and controls on contracting and auditing seem on the surface self-evident. Yet, across the globe, diversity is as powerful as are the arguments for such apparent universal values. Reflect on the differences that the following make on 'universality': moral and religious differences, cultural differences, constitutional and political differences. Even so, are converging business and financial practices (e.g. BASEL III banking initiatives 2010 rev. 2011), linked to global trade and financial stability, challenging these differences?

⟫ INTERNAL/EXTERNAL The after-shock of the recent financial crisis will mean more regulation of the financial sector and it will impact all businesses, one way or another, although the arguments on how much and when will be a constant. The public sector, often reliant on private sector capital borrowing, is often competing for resources. Some notable cases from our own era come to mind, such as the banking crisis of Cyprus (2013) or Spain (2012), or in the recent past, Japan's economic crisis—controversially referred to as the 'lost decades' (1991–2003)—also Argentina (1999–2002). In each of these cases, as with so many more, the welfare provision of public services altered as the public purse diminished in relation to the forced changes to the political economy. Therefore, the effects of any economic crisis are not limited to finance but spill over across all the sectors in policy terms, and this includes the maintenance of public services.

Why is this important? First, overriding these issues is the importance of the public sector in modern developed societies, not only as a baseline major economic player but also as the principal link to political, executive, and judicial power that confront social needs as well as economic sustainability. In the present global crisis, governments of all persuasions have stepped in to assist the banks with taxpayers' money, brought forward state spending plans to boost the economy, and in some cases, introduced austerity packages.

▶ **STAKEHOLDERS** Moreover, we live in a globalizing world that develops and continues to evolve new forms of regulation, with the World Trade Organization (WTO) being a good example, but also free trade agreements such as that proposed between the US and the EU (2012–13) and possibly the EU and Japan (2013) on the horizon. All of this was designed to encourage economic growth, stabilize trade, and its financial foundation, while at the same time trying to balance social demands in society in such a way as to provide security and stability in political terms. This too influences the delivery of public sector services.

Secondly, successful 'public' infrastructure projects are a major opportunity for private business, especially in the construction industry, and increasingly services such as consulting, health, transport, and managing information services (IT).

Thirdly, no matter the rhetoric about the coming together of the public and private sectors, there remain differences for those who work in the two sectors and especially on the international, global stage because of the diverse contexts in which they operate (see Figure 14.1). This shows itself in differing management approaches and equally deeper, more philosophical arguments about the nature of the business community and its financial structure on one side, and the political representation represented by those in the public political processes on the other.

▶ **COMPLEXITY** Fourthly, public servants have to respond differently to their policy environment compared to private sector employees—even those working in semi-autonomous organizations (which are often semi-detached from ministries) are embraced in the term 'government agencies'. We shall return to the latter in the section: The increasing complexity of public service provision: the voluntary sector, NGPBs, and 'agencification'.

▶ **DIVERSITY** Across the globe, no matter the actual constitutional arrangement, the 'managers' in the public sector have to be aware not only of effectiveness and performance but also of the political agendas that surround them. Political agendas and policy-making are constantly evolving. At best, they seek to create a sense of public involvement in common public services, balancing public interests and the servicing of public goods as circumstances change. For many years, for example, environment policy and recycling of waste has had a low profile amongst politicians, but now, politically, economically, and environmentally, it is of the utmost importance for the future. Priorities move and so does the political agenda.

▶ **VALUES** Bearing in mind there is a relationship between what political masters, public sector managers, and workers provide in policy terms they must be equally sensitive to the electoral or other socio-political systems: compare US models of political behaviour with those of China, or the wider BRIC countries, for example. Inherently there are different possible shifts in political thinking that the electoral or voting system or state decision-making processes imply. These can alter, almost overnight in some cases, the provision and delivery of services both in national and international contexts.

The changing public sector in a global age

❯❯ INTERNAL/EXTERNAL From the 1970s and especially since the 1980s, there have been increased attempts to introduce private business management practice to public policy administration. This has led to the privatization of many services formerly controlled directly by the public sector, and paradoxically, an increase in regulatory, performance-enhanced accountability by the state, or its agencies, of public policy standards: education, health, police, fire, transport, and information technology are notable examples. Equally, this shift in emphasis may appear to apply more to the Anglo-Saxon world, but across the world the arguments from this period still resonate with governments old and new, wide and far.

❯❯ DIVERSITY To understand the arguments we have to dip into the process of reform that is not new but based on 'incremental' change. The argument was, and is, that the tax burden of the state hinders the inherent dynamic of the economy (the market) as a whole. More than this, some argue the public sector often encourages inflexibility and closed in-house management where sectional interests, rather than service to the public, become supreme. In particular, public services are 'producer-led' rather than customer focused. Consequently, the citizen, the customer, the clients, have all been less than well served. Of course, there are those who argue this is not the case. Nevertheless, this has been the reasoning behind a whole raft of reforms and innovations in the public sector across the globe.

Privatization

❯❯ SPATIAL Privatization was the key turning point in creating the future public-private partnerships and new public management. It altered the relationship between the two sectors and changed our 'way of thinking' about providing services. The privatization of public services and the selling-off into the private sector of much of the public housing stock for example in the UK (1980)—one of the prime movers of privatization—had both popular support and wider political ramifications. It spread through further major privatizations such as the ports (1983), British Gas (1986), British Petroleum (1979–87), and British Steel (1988) and beyond, and became an example for other countries to follow.

❯❯ INTERNAL/EXTERNAL This was, arguably, the case in China from 1995, though a single date is probably inaccurate and the process of changing the system, *gaizhi*, covers the wider period 1993–2004 (*The Economist* 2011). This privatization process continues to the present day, although contextually the Chinese case had a political starting point far from some of the initiatives started by 'Western' societies. Similarly, Russia began its own specific process of privatization, or 'de-statism' (*razgosudarstylenic*) with the Yeltsin reforms in 1992 (Intriligator 2001). Global trade brings the various strands together, of course.

❯❯ DIVERSITY The privatization process is not just about 'businesses' such as telecommunications and energy suppliers, but also involves key elements of welfare provision, at least in some countries. Even the famous UK National Health Service (NHS), recently celebrated in the Summer Olympics opening celebration in London (2012), while remaining a service free at the point of delivery, has been subject to new initiatives that move it away from the old model of the state as a complete provider of healthcare paid for by tax. Privatization of some services peripheral to the NHS continues in one form another.

This shift in the nature of socialized healthcare has spread to Spain, where in 2013 new forms of privatization in hospital provision, for example, have been introduced. In the UK over recent years we have seen new public-private initiatives (mixing both private sector involvement and public sector needs) to build hospitals and manage them. Similarly, new schools built by the private sector and to a certain extent even managed by them, have broken the conventional connection between schools and political authorities, raising real issues about the relationship between the sectors. Around the globe, there are countless other examples. No matter the controversies, the creation of regulatory agencies to monitor the 'new' industries followed. It seems there has been a move toward 'consumer-driven' initiatives and in-built market mechanisms—or 'quasi markets'—for public sector services (Bishop et al. 2004).

New public management

▶ **INTERACTION** More broadly, the management of public services came under a wave of new policy directions often referred to as new public management (NPM). This applied to in-house provision through procurement, as well as public-private partnerships (PPPs) and, for larger projects, public finance initiatives (PFIs), and now newer derivatives such as 'cooperation networks' and the inclusion of non-government public bodies (NGOs–NGPBs).

First, what does 'new' public management mean? Has the 'old' welfare state and the centralization of governance through the state dwindled? The simple answer is 'no', or 'not inevitably'; but there have been changes. Globally the period after the 1970s has seen the 'old' assumptions challenged and new ways of providing services adopted.

In particular, the role of the modern state and its established bureaucracy has been the target of much reform. This reform set out to create more effective policy-making and make better use of resources. This reform is the 'new' in the 'new public management' ethos, as opposed to the 'old'.

▶ **INTERNAL/EXTERNAL** Also, and perhaps just as important, the old assumptions about who 'owns' the public sector are being redefined, as we have seen from Chinese and Russian examples of former full-bloodied 'communist' regimes restructuring into forms of 'statist capitalism'.

▶ **VALUES** Nonetheless, the state normally remains legally responsible for providing services based on need (or political pressure defining need) but does not necessarily own the means of provision—the buildings, the people, the 'financing'. This is the essential element of a 'new' era. However, that does not mean that the 'new' is a one-stop global system of management, and variations in public service delivery are the norm, not the exception. This may complicate our meaning of what is NPM, but the essentials remain—new management, new ownership, and new performance accountability.

Stop and Think How do you define the 'new'?

We tend to use the word 'new' easily: a 'new' initiative, a 'new' policy, a 'radically new' way of thinking. Even so, what is the 'new' compared to the old? How do we define it so that our analysis of what is going on is helpful to our organization, our employers, or us?

In this chapter we have talked about the concept of a 'new' public management, though it is closer to the truth to talk about a change in emphasis in policy-making rather than saying something 'new' has been created. The seeds of change lie in the past. 'New' things evolve over time, and in politics as in business, this is often the case. Knowing how to define the 'old' helps to define what the 'new' is today. The new era, post economic crisis, is adding to this evolving pattern of initiatives.

For example, it is important to note that some countries, like Sweden, provided a welfare model much more regulatory in nature, using private sector provision at its core of delivery, when compared to the UK in-house and procurement welfare model.

❱ INTERACTION Does that mean that, as we have previously known it, the state bureaucracy has decreased in importance? The simple answer again is 'no', but there is some truth in the argument that the state and state provision of public services is changing. Government is now more a flexible instrument of regulatory power rather than a simple state-owning power-centered organization. At least in theory.

One of the most recent evolutions has been the increasing use of IT management systems that successive governments have invested in to assist in policy-making. One estimate is that in the UK 1% of GDP is used for this purpose (Dunleavy 2006) and it is growing to such an extent, some argue, that 'NPM' has been superseded by what is called 'DEG', digital era governance—more on this later in this chapter. Nevertheless, at this stage, this implies a future emphasis less on 'management style' and more on rational choices based on the hard evidence of data, which the new digital age offers.

❱ DIVERSITY Other alternatives are also beginning to emerge with many acronyms but, for convenience, we can call them 'new public governance' (NPG). What is most relevant perhaps is how governance in the new era uses a broad range of tools that are both in-house public and private sector orientated, and both created because of the pressure for reform (see Figure 14.1).

■ Partnerships: the public and the private sectors and the building of partnerships

❱ DIVERSITY Traditionally, the divide between the public and the private sectors was described as organizational, ideological and one of different management styles. They performed in response to different political and economic agendas (see also Chapter 1 and Chapter 4). However, nowadays, the economic, policy relationship between public and private has been constantly evolving in relation to what is meant precisely by 'public interest', 'public ownership', 'public services', and the 'public good'. These have all been discussed in previous chapters, but in terms of delivery, decisions often turn on the question of which sector is best placed to provide for public services and why.

Public services

❱ VALUES To the extent that the public sector relies on a public 'ethical' argument (public ownership and public regulatory control) whether due to a perceived 'market failure' of provision (see Mini-Case 14.1) or for more ideological constitutional reasons, it also relies on defining what its 'services' are, in contrast to those of the private sector. In context, and in practice, countries make different choices about how to provide for public services. Therefore, there are traditional differences regarding how services are provided and for what purpose or outcome. This state public sector 'ethos' is sometimes welfare driven and sometimes security focused and, again, there are many variances across the globe.

❱ DYNAMIC Usually, public state services do not charge a price for their individual services or goods. Because of decisions related to the collective social need, it is forms of taxation which mainly finance public services. Provision is based on need, rather than an ability to pay. This 'choice' varies from country to country, as do income streams (see Figure 14.2). In recent years this has changed, in part, with the development of partnerships where private and public sectors jointly share the costs and the risks.

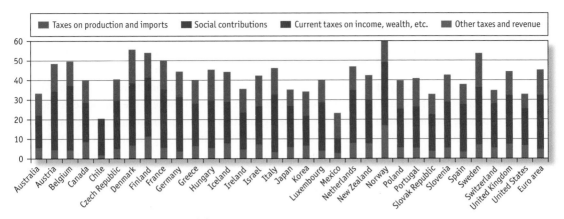

Figure 14.2 Tax rates vary across the globe

Source: Data from OECD, *National accounts at a glance*, 2010, p. 63.

Note:

a) The range of taxes, and the varying types of tax between each country, indicate different choices made within national contexts; and

b) In comparative terms, the overall percentage, and choices they imply, vary considerably.

▶ **COMPLEXITY** These public sector tax choices and their underlying choice of economic models are changing into new financial arrangements where the public and private sectors are connected in new forms of contractual arrangements not used previously. Keeping a weather eye on comparative public sector finance is becoming increasingly important. In practice, this is having an impact on business and public sector provision and some would say, profoundly. Moreover, it is difficult to see a scenario where this will not continue. It is both an opportunity and a challenge for all concerned.

The share of GDP used on PPPs, for example, varies from country to country. From the initial burst of activity in the field over the last decade, there are some signs of slowing in some regions (not least in Europe, see Figure 14.3), in part due to austerity measures, even if

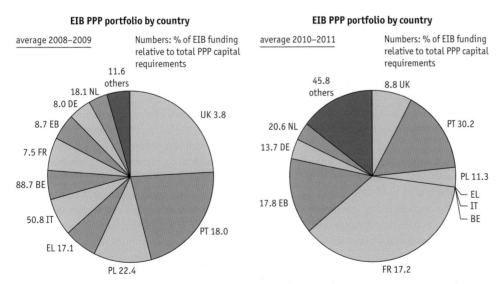

Figure 14.3 Example of regional scope of PPP in the EU (EIB 2012): still a minority concern but growing in importance

Source: Data from European Investment Bank (EIB) ECON Department Economic Studies Division, 2012.

they remain an important innovation in providing for public services, in particular amongst new developing economies. We will investigate this further in a moment, but at this stage it would be good to ask a fundamental question. What creates an argument for a public-private partnership?

On the surface, you would think this is easy to define, but in practice, it has not been so. In broad terms, it could mean any connection or joint venture where the public sector and the private sector work in tandem for a given goal. This has been the reality of the system since the development of states and is not new. The international organizations OECD, the IMF, Standard and Poor, and the European Union (The European Commission and the European Investment Bank) all have slightly different operating definitions of the terms.

❱ DIVERSITY Some public sector work provides in-house control, of course, and remains technically the majority policy method; even if often private firms tender contracts through 'public procurement' (see Chapter 4). For major projects, this is the most used system in developed countries. This system has strict rules and awards are normally tied to agreed and expressed outcomes: this applies to central and local government and international agreements.

Public spending financed the payment for the services and goods under the 'old' system. For some commentators, this was a problem and an inefficient way to handle innovating, modern economies. This has led to a heated debate on how public services should be delivered and paid for. It often comes down to how to 'manage' the notion of social need when confronted by an apparent private sector 'market failure' unwilling to provide appropriate services. What does this mean in practice? See Mini-Case 14.1.

Mini-Case 14.1 The public sector as provider in terms of a 'market failure' for 'deemed necessary' public services: the case for public licensing and taxation for the provision of media (Europe), or not (US)—the case of early television and Google Reader

What if there is a defined social need demanded by the public but there is, for whatever reason, no interest in the private sector to invest in the 'business' as it is deemed unprofitable, or at least, not sufficiently viable? The government, or a public agency, can then step in to use an argument that the market has not been able to provide the service required. Therefore, and in the wider interests of society in general, it needs support from public funds. In such a circumstance, it is deemed that there has been a 'market failure' and this justifies the economic use of taxation or other public means to pay for the service.

This form of argument is not new. With the early introduction of what was innovatory and expensive television technology, most European states from the 1920s opted for 'public broadcasting' rather than private sector investment. This was paid for by taxation, or by enforced household-spend through licensing, and created what we now know as the public broadcasting system (PBS).

Consequently, in the early days of European broadcasting the studios, and most public channels, in a majority of European states became 'public' broadcasters. They were paid for by taxation or licences, with government directly, or indirectly, imposing what they saw as 'standards' on public information for the maintenance of the freedom of speech.

This did not mean the private sector was excluded from the industry: the making of television sets, providing repair and maintenance, and even support services (from aerials to content magazines) were, normally, left to the private sector.

However, this 'European' solution was not used everywhere and, most notably, in the US the private sector development of radio and television was chosen. To this day, this defines the American broadcasting system, and its media network in general. The US has always argued that individual choice and responsibility is often paramount over state or central/federal interference. Consequently, it relies much more heavily on private sector finance and competition as drivers for its media network. The result is much more private sector involvement in the American media-broadcasting environment compared to the European.

Policy choice using the 'market failure' argument varies from country to country. Examples of this type of thinking abound. A more recent case involves Google. Google suggested they would suspend their 'free' Google Reader application, causing complaint. Intriguingly, in the *Financial Times* Izabella Laminska, citing the economics Nobel prize winner Paul Krugman's critical commentary, reported:

Basically, if the monopolist tries to charge a price corresponding to the value intense users place on the good, it won't attract enough low-intensity users to cover its fixed costs; if it charges a low price to bring in the low-intensity user, it fails to capture enough of the surplus of high-intensity users, and again can't cover its fixed costs ... So what's the answer? ... historical examples with these characteristics—like urban transport networks—have been resolved through public provision. It seems hard at this point to envision search and related functions as public utilities, but that's arguably where the logic will eventually lead us. (Laminska 2013)

In effect, the above argument about Google Reader was a 'market failure'. Of course, others would claim that Google Inc. is not a monopoly, and this is a product failure not a market failure. Equally, there are other successful 'Readers', some free and some paid for. Even so, the argument raises questions as to the status and use of 'market failure'.

Whatever the finer arguments about 'market failure', state control, and regulatory patterns, in the present context media companies are increasingly transnational. This means global media companies are now competing, some would say combating, national public service provision in ways not seen before. The market evolves. In Europe, this has meant a bringing together of European public broadcasting regulatory models into a new form of audio-visual control (The Television without Frontiers directive 1997, now superseded by the Audio-Visual Media Service Directive 2009), which is meant to safeguard the older PBS system, but equally encompasses more private sector involvement. Other media players such as the Arab led, Doha based, *Al Jazeera* TV broadcaster (its name means, significantly, 'Freedom' in Arabic) relies on direct forms of state subsidy for gaining access to international markets. They use a variant of 'market failure' thinking, in so much as they argue the international media scene is 'dominated' by western led companies and needs alternative views.

Here, in even such a ubiquitous technology, one can see the divided and differing views of what actually is a 'market failure', and what role the authorities should play in providing for what they may argue are necessary public services even in the field of broadcasting.

(*Sources*: Rooke 2009, Laminska, 2013. See also the full Krugman article: *The New York Times* 2013.)

Questions

1. Is television 'broadcasting' a suitable sector for public sector funding? What are the reasons for and against?

2. Does the digital age alter our perceptions of what is suitable for 'public interest' media products?

3. Can you list the type of media/broadcasting that serves a 'public interest'? Justify your choices.

Public-private partnerships (PPPs)

PPPs involve a departure from what was considered the normal model of a public service. A difficulty is that we do not have agreement on exactly what a 'public sector service' is, as opposed to a 'private sector service'. If one argued that a public service is one paid for by taxation alone, this could discount income from selling services by the public sector. For example, public authorities who gained income from car parks, or DVD rentals at the local library, or the renting of property, would immediately complicate the audit. Moreover, even the old standard 'procurement' process usually included the private sector, in one form or another, much more than often realized.

The 'public-private partnership', it is argued, then becomes an effective policy choice when both the public and private sectors are jointly determined to develop service provision and share responsibility for its effective delivery. The public sector gains, it is said, by new management techniques brought in from the private sector; and the private sector secures financial access to service provision in the public sector.

The public sector creates a contract, or takes out a 'mortgage', for the services offered by the private sector. Penalty clauses or some compensatory measures are usually included in case of failure. The private sector gains because it has greater control of its involvement in service provision. It may also gain financially far more than under the old rules and practices of normal 'public procurement'.

» COMPLEXITY No matter the complications, PPPs have developed at a rapid pace. See Figure 14.3 as an example of the scope of PPP investment by the European Investment Bank (EIB 2012).

» INTERNAL/EXTERNAL » SPATIAL LEVELS Across the globe, there have been interpretations of what a PPP is, both by definition and in operation. Much of the debate centres on who 'owns' what, in what part of the contract, and where economic and service responsibility can be shared (see Mini-Case 14.2).

Mini-Case 14.2 Germany, China, new management, and PPPs

The development of public sector management is often associated with the search for 'effectiveness' in public service policy which has led, in part, to public private partnerships PPPs. To illustrate this Germany and China are good examples of governments where public sector in-house control has been traditionally strong. Even so, they have started to innovate and use private-public partnerships. A brief look at their development allows us to consider the importance of initial start-ups using PPPs in such states and question some of their findings.

Germany: Since the 1980s and especially from the mid-1990s, the German Federal Republic with its intricate democratic balances between the Länder and the Federal State instigated NPM and PPP reform in the delicate area of police services amongst others.

Commentators found a tension between the 'public' operational goals and the 'private' performance contracts and adapted their models of implementation according to the distinct Länder contexts in which they worked. They concluded:

Thus the introduction of NPM reforms implies a comprehensive consideration of the political and historical context of the respective political-administrative system. The varying contexts of Germany's seventeen political-administrative systems explicate why there exists no single NPM reform model, but rather a heterogeneous set of concepts and practices (Ritsert et al. 2009, p. 39).

China: The rapid rise of China as a major, global, economic power is perhaps the story of the 21st century. This does not mean that China is merely economically dynamic but that the changes to its economy have had profound changes on society. A mix of urbanization and new wealth has created many social demands, not least for improved transport systems.

From 2001 China looked to develop public-private partnerships in the transportation sector. Subsequently, serious commentators appeared to be 'positive' about the initiative but they realized that there were bureaucratic and governance issues that needed to be worked out for successful implementation:

It is likely to take some time before legal safeguards against bad practices in PPP are fully in place, but these seem underway. It is likely to take at least as much time for public and private players to establish reliable partnerships guided by mutual trust and reasonableness in negotiating contracts when this becomes necessary. Personal networks (guanxi in Chinese) can oil decision processes and have often benefited management and policy in China; but modernisation will tie them to certain norms of transparency and accountability. That is an intriguing challenge for the awaking giant (De Jong 2008, p. 14); see also for a similar commentary on PPPs in China more generally (Cheng et al. 2009).

Questions

1. Looking at the German example, commentators stress the importance of historical and political arrangements in the creation of NPM. What could they be and why is this significant?

2. Looking at the Chinese example, commentators stress the importance of building 'trust' between the two sectors when building PPPs. Why would this be particularly important in the Chinese business environment?

3. Some argue that the recent financial crisis may change government thinking on 'new public management' and 'public private partnerships'. Thinking through the German and Chinese cases, could there be a change in policy direction for either and if so, why?

Private finance initiative (PFI)

▶ **SPATIAL VALUES** If we are looking for a more prescriptive shape to the PPP idea, the PFI is often cited. It relies on a method sometimes known as a DBFO (**design, build, finance, and operate system**), where the private sector offers a total service 'package' to the public sector provider.

In general terms this means the private sector designs the public service based on outputs and service needs specified by the public sector. It then sometimes builds (for example, a new hospital), arranges finance, contracts with the public sector on agreed limits, and then operates the service. In practice, there are different ways that a PFI is handled (service provision, freestanding finance, and joint ventures) with different payment mechanisms.

▶ **STAKEHOLDERS** The arguments over creating the PFI continue, mainly over price and effectiveness. Creating a PFI can be an exhausting, long negotiated process and includes a form of comparing what might be the better alternative for providing the service. This is called a **public service comparator** (PSC), where an attempt is made to compare the overall estimated cost of a non-PFI scheme and the PFI scheme itself. Having the right data is therefore essential. A point we shall return to shortly in the 'Performance and accountability' section below.

All of this has stimulated debate about the nature of public governance and the 'reform' of the system in the present era. One area where reform was to play a major part was the use of more quantifiable management techniques. This meant creating links between goals and accountabilities, and rational management practices. In many respects, this led to the setting up of professional agencies of government to achieve what were hoped to be PFI improvements leading to:

- a reduction in unit costs and greater efficiency
- improved speed of transactions and improved quality of service to customers
- the greater use of new technology.

These are major claims and much research is now going on to evaluate the new schemes and the thinking behind them. Criticisms of previous PFIs abound but as a policy innovation they persist. The sums involved can be large. Recently in the UK, this led to one agency closing ('Partnerships UK') to be replaced by a supposedly more rigorous organization ('Infrastructure UK') based in the UK Treasury. It involved the re-negotiation of contracts and the 'repayment' of up to £2.5bn (Peston 2012). This has not stopped the process in the UK.

▶ **INTERNAL/EXTERNAL** But is this just a national UK phenomenon? The answer is no. Recently there has been a new 'privatization' of its air and rescue service (2013) where publicly owned government military resources have been replaced by a UK-US company, Bristow, with a PFI ten-year contract (from 2015 to 2025) signed at an estimated £1.6bn. Bristow Group is a transnational company that already provides similar services in the Netherlands, Trinidad and Tobago, Australia, Russia, Brazil, and Canada. No matter the criticism of PFI, these sorts of policy choices are being proposed to public authorities across the globe (see Mini-Case 14.3).

The increasing complexity of public service provision: the voluntary sector, NGPBs, and 'agencification'

▶ **COMPLEXITY** So far, in looking at the development of the public services, and public-private partnerships and their impact on business we have concentrated on statutory bodies.

Mini-Case 14.3 Global variations and influence of governance on public and private sectors: PPP-PFI or Procurement?

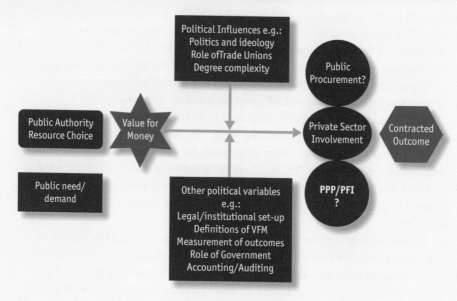

Figure 14.4 Public authority resources choice flowchart

Flow charts are often used to explore resource choices. Figure 14.4 represents a simplified form of choice available for a public authority deciding on the management of a public need. Note how important 'Value for Money', political influence, and other political variables are at the start of the process. They often precede the rationale leading to a decision on procurement, or partnership, and the contracted outcome.

To deepen this view, see an intriguing OECD report (2011) on the subject, covering a variety of different countries using PPP arrangements. The report enumerates many of the variables, such as political and other legal contexts, imposing heavily on the choices made by a public authority. In the end, the various pressures related to public interest, public services, public ownership and definitions of public goods, all come into play (Burger and Hawkesworth 2011, p. 92: note, Figure 14.4 is different to the original; compare with Figures 3a, 3b, and 4 on pp. 37–48 at: <http://www.oecd.org/gov/budgeting/49070709.pdf>).

Although there has always been controversy about just how effective a method PPPs, and later PFIs, are in developing services for the public sector, their impact is large. Recent OECD findings (2006/7) on working with PPPs appear to encourage their use. For a flavour of the arguments, the following citations, taken from a participating company's report (Macquarie 2010) are useful and raise questions:

A major report released by the Organisation for Economic Co-operation and Development (OECD) concludes that the growing need for infrastructure investment will run far beyond the capacity of governments alone to pay for it, and that there is an important role for the private sector to play in funding the development of these essential services. (Macquarie 2010, p. 1)

The report titled 'Infrastructure to 2030' shows that global infrastructure investment needs are growing, with around US$50 trillion required for investment in roads, water, electricity, telecommunications and rail in OECD countries between 2005 and 2030. (Macquarie 2010, p. 1)

This investment will be used to build new infrastructure and to maintain and upgrade existing systems. Pressure will increase with globalisation, economic development and population growth. (Macquarie 2010, p. 1)

Traditionally governments have facilitated infrastructure investment, however this is becoming increasingly challenging as they focus their spending on areas such as health, education and security. As a result, the report suggests that traditional means of funding need to be enhanced by private sector investment. This is already well established in some sectors, such as telecommunications, power generation and railways. (Macquarie 2010, p. 2)

In OECD countries alone, some US$1 trillion of state-owned assets have been sold in recent decades. Considerable scope still remains for further privatizations—for example, it is estimated that around US$3 trillion of infrastructure in the United States is still in public hands. (Macquarie 2010, p. 2)

Then again, you might expect companies involved in these partnerships to argue this way. To balance our approach:

Questions

1. Can you find a weakness in the Macquarie arguments, for example, from those who would argue from a publicly owned, public sector management point of view?

2. The original OECD report was prior to the economic crisis of 2008, but the latest reports from the OECD continue to offer advice and support for the development of PPPs. Is this significant and does this tell us anything about the OECD?

Even so, the modern management of the political environment is now more devolved, not only down to local and regional levels but also up to the international scene.

More than this, modern politics does not work just through statutory bodies but also through three different kinds of category of organization among others:

- statutory
- voluntary
- agencies, which can be statutory or non-governmental.

They all operate with different sets of rules. Again, to understand the political and policy spatial scales is to understand how the national governing system relies on the relationship of the so called 'statutory bodies'—those laid down by official statute—and the other types of organization as indicated above which all link together into civil behaviour. In this way, there is always a sort-of private-public underpinning to how any society actually operates.

The voluntary sector

» SPATIAL LEVELS » VALUES In the eyes of many, the voluntary sector is the key to 'civil society', even 'citizenship', and within a society a major representation of political and specific interests. This arises out of a perception that in some societies the reliance on the voluntary sector is an important element in service provision. The Netherlands and Germany, for example, have large voluntary sectors.

» INTERNAL/EXTERNAL Most governments will encourage the voluntary or 'third' sector, because it is less costly and in some areas more effective than professional organizations or departments. In the UK, the 2002 'Cross-Cutting Review' not only called for the modernization of the voluntary sector but also linked it as much as it could into the new public management agenda. The Cabinet Office of the UK had a designated 'minister of the third sector' who was assisted by what was known as a 'volunteering champion' signalling its importance at the highest levels of government. Similar schemes can be found around the globe.

There are often tax incentives for volunteer and charity groups. There are many umbrella groups bringing the various and disparate groups together to create a collective 'voice'. Again, using the UK as an example, these include quasi-informal organizations, such as Volunteering England or Voluntary News; and more formal groups, such as the National Council for Voluntary Organizations (NCVO, which has been in existence for over ninety years). Although often portrayed as marginal within society, they actually play a key role. This is especially the case when public spending through taxation comes under pressure but the social welfare needs of society remain.

》 DYNAMIC Nor is the sector small. By 2006/7, there were approximately 170,900 voluntary sector organizations with a collective income of over £33.2 billion in the UK as an example. Although statutory investment (mainly from local government) in these organizations represented £12 billion (as a comparison approximately 1% of total central government expenditure), almost 75% of the voluntary sector received no statutory funding (NCVO 2009). In every corner of the globe voluntary organizations play both major and minor roles, and their influence appears to be growing. Even in China, who until recently viewed voluntary organizations critically, there are signs of a nascent growth of charity organizations (Tuttle 2012).

》 STAKEHOLDERS 》 INTERACTION There is of course a potential tension between the 'professional' (sometimes referred to as 'corporatist welfare organizations') and the 'volunteer'. The new political agendas in civil and welfare policies often try to embrace, link and regularize the relationships between the two. Many 'voluntary' sector organizations are embraced in a wider term—non-governmental organizations on non-governmental public bodies (NGOs or NGPBs) such as Oxfam, and Connexions, the young persons' support group related to the umbrella organization National Association of Connexion Partners (NACP 2009). Worldwide there are many such organizations. One definition of NGBPs emphasizes accountability: NGBPs do not refer or account for their actions through formal government procedures. This gives them some independence of action. They can be highly effective and focused in the best of cases.

'Agencification' or distributed governance

SPATIAL LEVELS A full understanding of the modern business environment in public services must include not only the voluntary sector, but also note the growth of agencies—organizations given specific mandates by government, often reporting directly to a ministry but, at the same time, removed from direct departmental procedures (see Figure 14.1). Some fall into the category by legal statute, but some operate more like companies, semi-autonomous from government. Agencies are, therefore, seen as 'independent' bodies free, in part, from political control but with very influential regulatory powers to hand ('agencification'). They can influence state and private sector provision: broadcasters, as we have seen, and universities (private or state) are surrounded by an array of validating or regulatory agencies. This is increasingly the case in many policy areas. Once again, this varies from country to country (see the end of chapter case study). There are academic debates about the general trend of their use globally, as well as their effectiveness.

Stop and Think

.....

Should all citizens get involved with public service, or should we leave it to the 'professionals'? Why not tell citizens it is their right to live in a society, but also their responsibility to do something for it? In some countries voluntary or community service is actively encouraged, such as in the Netherlands. In some societies, citizens are obliged to vote (even if they abstain) as in Belgium. What is the role of a voluntary organization in your native country and how influential is it?

Where we draw the line between 'professional' and 'amateur'—and who decides—is a tricky question, it seems.

Performance and accountability: the importance of data collection and the auditing of public services, its impact on the public-private partnerships, and public service delivery

Essential to the whole process of public service delivery is the question of performance and accountability and, in particular, data and the auditing of accounts and outcomes. Equally important is the degree to which control of the public service, and any associated PPP—PFI, is a share of public sector responsibility on the one side and the private sector on the other. Moreover, in-house procurement based public services nowadays are also assessed and measured for their effectiveness.

>> **INTERNAL/EXTERNAL** This has become more relevant and fitting following the Enron scandal in the US (Turnbull 2002), although there are many more examples around the world. However, the extent of business failures (recently the Lehman bank failure is often cited, Christopoulos et al. 2011) shows just how complex and corrupting accounting practices can be in the private sector business environment and has caused worries in the public sector.

Equally, to believe that the in-house public sector procurement process has been free of financial mismanagement is also plainly false: witness the problems of ministry IT project failure and mismanagement in the UK and elsewhere. Case studies are freely available: training, education, health, pensions, immigration, and defence have all been touched in one way or another over the last few years (noting that we should separate the blatant fraudulent behaviour from the more general mistakes of management).

Quantifying data has become a major industry both in the private and public sectors, assisted by new technologies, enabling the sharing and collating of data. Data, and its new form 'Big Data', and its measurement are essential in policy-making. The old days of so-called arbitrary political judgments, if they ever existed, have gone. Most decision-making in the modern era demands at least some quantifiable and then qualitative judgement which demands gathering data in forms that are usable and comparative. The degree to which this is now the norm would surprise previous generations of administrators.

>> **SPATIAL LEVELS** Government bodies at every level not only collate but also interpret performance management findings. Measuring performance through indicators has become a major aspect of the public sector environment, not least in detecting the effectiveness of a service. Whether a public sector project, a PFI, or a PPP, those involved would do well to ensure they embrace and measure their outcomes, for they will be usesd in evaluation procedures somewhere and in some form, often with political and financial consequences.

Stop and Think

'Lies, damned lies, and statistics' (attributed to Benjamin Disraeli, and Mark Twain and others) How do we make sure that we are using the statistics and data we collect correctly? Is it really possible to be accurate, objective, and effective all at the same time?

Which organizations collecting data can we trust and use? How do we judge them? What criteria do we use to assess the results? Who writes down the criteria?

>> **VALUES** How exactly performance indicators are used fuels controversy and debate. Eventually the business sector will be judged, rightly or wrongly, by its profitability as much as

the effectiveness of the service it provides. In the public sector, by its nature, there will be a demand for interpretative and qualitative judgement based on the social needs that services are designed to meet: in a word 'outcomes', where profitability comes second.

Auditing within the public sector is also of major importance for both the transparency and the reliability of the data that is collected. It often fuels political debate. Most countries will have precise forms of auditing following agreed rules and regulations. They will be both internal and external to the public sector organization and once again, politically, constitutionally, they will perform at many levels.

The private sector is also audited, for example by company reports and accredited approval of accounts. The public sector is similar and its accounts at central and local level are usually agreed and corroborated by independent accountancy. Equally, the public sector is subject to performance indicators, which come in many guises.

As with diverse management levels, you will also find different layers of auditing in the public sector. They influence private involvement in public-private initiatives. These layers often work together but there are differences in how they manage and report findings. In broad terms, there are auditing organizations that usually cover:

Central government

Local government

Regional governance, such as the European Union and African Union

International level

Private sector corporate reporting.

Consequently, some commentators have worried about what is referred to as an 'explosion of governance indicators' from such diverse sources as the World Bank, OECD, IMF, Eurostat, NGO/NGPBs such as Transparency International and Freedom House, all of which fit into a new transnational pattern of global auditing. Of course it remains a 'loose' network, but appears to be pushing states together into a new network of comparators, and by so doing, increases transparently displayed transnational influence (Buduru et al. 2010). One commentator argues quite clearly:

> Currently, we are witnessing a comprehensive change in the theoretical understandings of how coordination is provided in the pursuit of public governance … In the new theories; one of the main questions is how to get a better hold of this new understanding of coordination in processes of public governance…

> (Pedersen et al. 2011, p. 375)

All of which, of course, has now been bundled into what might be called the new conceptualized 'e-era': e-government-; e-governance; e-democracy; e-participation; and even universities offering curriculum based on what is strangely but effectively called 'e-media'. And perhaps inevitably, there is a leading business directory for advertising that brands itself by the name.

New debates: the changing public sector in a digital age–digital era governance (DEG) a new hypothesis?

》 DYNAMIC 》 VALUES The launch of a new public administration model of governance in digital era governance (DEG) (Dunleavy et al. 2006), was a hard-worked, well researched argument that countered the prevailing often persistent acceptance of 'new public management'

(NPM) techniques. In so doing it raised important questions about the changing nature of our contemporary policy-making in a digital era.

Although not strictly targeting the business environment, it can be seen to complement our normal approaches to the present scene, and is beginning to have some traction with contemporary commentators. This includes the broader regulatory managerial context within which policies operate nationally, transnationally (e.g. European Union), or even globally.

No matter the view—be it political governance techniques or changing regulatory patterns—there appears to be a growing consensus that we may be witnessing a real breakdown, or at least a radical new mix, of the 'public-private' for one; and a redefining of the relationship between public and private sectors because of new and technology-related cross platforms, for another. Both are important issues and are indicative of this wider and, what may be called, 'new' debate.

First, the new questions raised by DEG: What are they?

▶ **DYNAMIC** ▶ **INTERNAL/EXTERNAL** Quite powerfully, and at the risk of over simplifying their work, the authors argued that the breaking up (or at least a loosening) of public (state) control of policy development and the increased enhancement of a NPM public-private mix (public-private partnerships, PPP, and private finance initiatives, PFI, for example and all mentioned above) from 1990–2005 and beyond, led to the fragmentation of policy, the 'disaggregation' (or an apparent more chaotic separation) of policies, and unintended consequences.

The authors' claim that this was leading to a disempowering of citizen's (state) control and poorer policy-making. Moreover, it led to the enhancement of private interests over the public, while purporting to use the 'rationality' of access to private sector IT-systems to achieve better public aims within a process of competition; whereas, in practice, it had led to a less holistic, less public interest structure than perhaps first envisaged.

Dunleavy et al., among previous leading exponents, also argued that by 2005/6 NPM had failed or was failing in practice, even if some states were still pursuing its mantra. States had invested in IT systems, often outsourced as was the flavour of the time, thus disaggregating control with, in some cases, extremely high costs for the public.

▶ **STAKEHOLDERS** ▶ **COMPLEXITY** To this was the added problem that the private sector often found it difficult to follow public policy stakeholders' demands, perhaps unaware of the medley of factors that surround public policy, and this led to expensive private sector corrections. This may have enhanced, for example, the major global IT players in the private sector, and inevitably reinforced their global reach (ibid., p. 59) but had it made the public sector policies and their outcomes more effective?

For Dunleavy et al. it had not. What was needed was more aggregated policy development, more holistic ('state smart' we could say) approaches to the digital age and, perhaps surprisingly, IT systems—the new IT developments of the contemporary age—could now allow this to happen. Hence, the powerful Dunleavy et al. comment that NMP was 'intellectually dead' and we needed a new era of digital-driven governance procedures: 'DEG'.

Bearing in mind the date of the work, we can now look back with hindsight and add that the enhancement of private sector involvement was no doubt fuelled by the apparent growth in the relatively easy credit of the period, and led to an argument that the private sector seemed to be the easier path to policy efficiencies rather than the over-bureaucratic formulations of previous (state) involvement. But then again, looking at new initiatives across the globe, is this really the case?

Stop and Think

The public/private divide issue needs to answer the question: does it make any difference whether the individual or the corporation is public or private? Does it answer the big question of who should be in charge? Is a public figure that falsifies any different to a private figure that does the same? Who should govern the process? Is a private sector manager who fails clients and customers any different to a public sector manager who fails the citizens? How do we measure the outcomes, and whether they are working, and do the private/public issues hinder or help our judgement? Does the emergence of a citizen-customer change our thinking about public sector management, partnerships, and performance accountability?

》 INTERACTION Where are we in terms of end-user and new research on governance issues and the use of IT in a converging digital environment? Much is going on and it is fascinating. Who will be 'in charge' of this new digital age? Who collects the data? Who stores it? Who should have access? In a world where most IT providers are private, what is the role of the state and the public sector? These questions raise issues across the board, and across borders, in ways which the previous governance issues did not, even with the creation of PPPs and PFIs. The 'new' digital age demands, it seems, ever more adaptation, not just mitigation. See the Case Study at the end of this chapter and link to the Review and Discussion Questions and the Assignments.

■ Looking ahead

For some, the development of new public management misses the political point and there are battles ahead. For many, the 'credit crunch' has shown the weakness of public-private partnerships and revealed the fundamental flaws of the private sector and the market. The relationship between the public sector and the private sector, for them, remains one of philosophical distinction, even political action. Others argue the opposite.

When the dust has settled over the financial crisis, the questions will remain. How do we pay for and sustain both private sector enterprise, and meet the social demands of the public sector? Regardless of the debate regarding the appropriate balance, it appears the boundaries have changed. It is very difficult to see a world that separates the sectors as in the past.

Looking ahead means a greater focus on questions of performance-accountability, data evaluation, effectiveness, and value for money, and not least their relationship to governance. Of course, the debates will continue and the political world will shift around the existing political and social interests within every society.

The future for the public-private sectors will be one based on statistics and qualitative judgments made even more relevant by the economic pressures on state provision, due to increased public debt, which has increased in some countries dramatically. The research that goes with this, of course, will continue hand-in-hand with the development of the policies. It is, and will be, a fascinating era for modern contemporary societies as each compares themselves with others. The private sector will be involved whether they or others want them to, or not. Knowledge of both sectors was, is, and will be, the key for entrepreneurs and policymakers alike.

Summary

- The degree of interdependencies between countries and regions has created a more global system than hitherto. This has led to policy and economic models that encourage innovation between the public and private sectors. An important part of this movement is the blending, as much as possible, of the private and public sectors into partnerships (PPPs and PFIs for example) which has raised new dilemmas and issues for management, both in the private and the public sectors.

- Governance of public and private partnerships has increasingly come to terms with a multi-polar multi-layered policy environment where external transnationalism is important, as is any domestic or internal relationship established by political constitutional arrangements.

- The public sector of old appears to be on the brink of moving into a new global and digital-related era. Not only is the established order and control through nation-states beginning to alter, but the number of dependencies and political levels through which the public sector works are also: interdependencies at both the macro and micro-level are now deeply entrenched. The levels now include: local, regional, national, European, and international. They all play out in what is becoming a 'global' network of business and political connections unlike previous trading patterns. The new digital age has thrown up not only an important information-led economy but one where the normal frontiers and border controls are no longer barriers. The glaring example is the creation of the World Wide Web and the Internet, collectively referred to as 'cyberspace' (see case study at end of chapter).

- Privatization, marketization, and the new technology have been the spurs for an even more thorough, if evolutionary, process of change. At the same time, there has been a regulatory shift back to ultimate financial responsibility within the public sector and their institutions in times of crisis.

- The most striking aspect of new public sector thinking embraced the terms of 'new public management' and 'digital era governance'. The new management practice tries to shift the management style towards outcomes which are 'citizen-consumer' led. In so doing, there has also been an increased emphasis on transparency and measurement of performance. This is changing the relationship between policy-makers and those who use the services they promote.

- The new era of public-private administration and management is not yet based on a fundamental consensus, and the details of policy development remain contested. Even so, the process of change appears to be unstoppable taking into consideration present political and economic agendas.

Case Study: The information economy and the digital age: cyberspace and cyber-crime and the reaction of agencies through private and public partnerships in the European Union. The way forward?

Is regulation of the Internet a public or a private matter? Law and regulation are a part of the politically judged public sector, but that does not mean that a public service needs to police it alone as the sole stakeholder in such security issues. Who should protect us from cybercrime, for example? Normally police and military in the public sector handle security issues, but because those who operate in cyberspace are normally private companies such as Google or Microsoft or Apple, let alone the criminals and their countless applications they engender (botnets, malware, etc.) who is best placed to secure us from mal practice? If we follow the three main sections of this chapter—**management, partnerships, and**

performance accountability—can we unpick this 'service-product', which touches, one way or another, a vast level of business activity. Does cyberspace and cybercrime reveal a new relationship between the state public sector and private corporations? Does it illustrate a new and technologically driven dilemma?

Underlying the importance of the subject, corporations and states increasingly rely heavily on data transference. They rely on trans-communication cables, satellites, and the latest technology networks to perform literally millions of transactions. The opportunities for creativity, innovation, control of costs, outreaching, and so on, are exponential in nature and practice in this new environment. It also brings risk and security issues, not least in the form of 'cybercrime'.

Background

Cybercrime is becoming a major issue with billions of pounds, euros, dollars, and Chinese Yuan Renminbis (CNY) at stake. There are dissenting voices to this view but they are few. The approaches to the issue often start nationally but nowadays, almost inevitably, most nations will refer up to international, regional such as the European Union, institutions for answers. See Figure 14.1 and Figure 14.4. What should public authorities do? Procure or collaborate with partners? How should outcomes be measured and performance audited? What is the public sector response in a globalizing world?

Organizing the correct management and measuring the data in a world of so much cyberspace activity is fraught with difficulties, and demands new management techniques. The European Union and its institutions have not been idle in this area and are an example of a regional, transnational, multi-state response. It illustrates new management, cross-national public-private partnerships, and performance accountability.

The threat of cybercrime, both public state and private criminal acts, is present at many levels. Of all the 'crimes', not only is it in many ways the 'newest', but by its very technological nature, is the almost perfect example of a cross-national crime, demanding a transnational/international response. As a phenomenon, it goes beyond the normal geographic, political, and institutional borders of nation-states and their control. It is the example of cross-border activity, which threatens security and causes or aids other crime, and impacts both the public and private sectors.

The problem is not small. Recently the UK government assessed the state of cybercrime (HMSO 2011) and the range of activity and financial impact surprised many. These are illustrated by Figures 14.5 and 14.6 below, taken from the governments' (probably underestimated) view.

Extrapolating from these figures to include all the member states of the European Union yields alarming numbers. A recent security estimate put the value of the potential 'cyber-criminal economy' at global corporate losses of around Eur 750 billion (McAfee 2013). A rival company had previously estimated Eur 290 billion (Norton 2011): clearly, the data is only an estimate and probably an underestimate.

It seems clear from initial reports that the governing bodies for both public and private sectors need to respond quickly. Europol, the EU transnational policing agency, in its annual report OCTA (2011) illustrated the inter-connectedness of cybercrime with a wider more threatening 'underworld' of 'EU Criminal Hubs'.

As is the normal contemporary organizational response, the EU, which represents 28 (2013) member states and their public policies, has begun to establish cross-national,

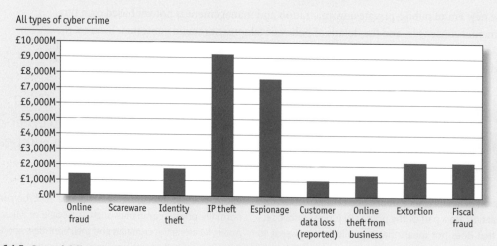

Figure 14.5 Cost of different types of cybercrime in the UK economy
Source: Data from HMSO 2011.

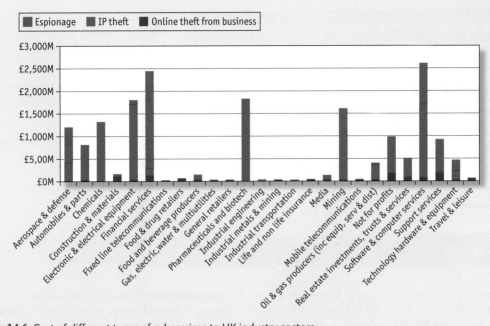

Figure 14.6 Cost of different types of cybercrime to UK industry sectors
Source: Data from HMSO 2011.

transnational **agencies**, relying on the plethora of existing agencies and adding to them in this field. In this case, a dedicated centre has been proposed and agreed by the Justice Ministers of the EU. It will be operational in 2013 as a European Cybercrime Centre within Europol based in the Hague.

In its argument for a transnational mix of public private sector stakeholders working together, Europol has stated:

Investigations into online fraud, child abuse and other crimes regularly involve hundreds of victims at a time, and suspects in many different parts of the world. Operations of this magnitude cannot be successfully concluded by national police forces alone. No crime is as borderless as cybercrime, requiring law enforcement authorities to adopt a coordinated and collaborative approach across borders, together with public and private stakeholders alike. It is here that the European Cybercrime Centre will add significant value. (European Cybercrime Centre (EC3) 2013)

Nonetheless, as with a great deal of cross-border activity, the legal position is always complex and most policing and jurisdiction remains solidly 'nationally sovereign' rather than international. In this area the response of the European Court of Justice, when fully competent , will be profoundly important for the direction the EU it is likely to take on these and similar security and crime issues.

The proposed solutions to the problems of cyberspace and new criminal behaviour has, therefore, been a mix of private-public partnership, transnationalism, multi-layered convergence of policy, research consultation across the sectors, demand for greater performance accountability, and 'agencification'.

Questions

The case above illustrates how fine tuning the institutional responses to cybercrime no longer fits within a narrow 'national' context. The question of mixing the private and public sectors appears a logical and now obvious step forward toward 'new management' procedures even in sensitive policing matters: However, the following questions merit thought:

1. **Does the digital age fundamentally change the public-private relationship in the case above? If so, how?**

2. **Does cybercrime in particular need a national or regional response, or an international regime of control and policing?**

3. **Which courts should form the basis of legal judgements—national, regional, or international?**

4. **Is 'agencification' the answer? Can we trust the regulators?**

5. **Where does public sector influence start and where does it stop?**

6. **Where are the boundaries between public and private?**

Review and discussion questions

1. What is a PPP and how does it normally work?

2. What are the advantages and disadvantages of 'new public management' as compared to 'digital era governance'?

3. To what degree are the changes in the public sector brought about by individual nation-states when compared to the global nature of present day politics, trade, and business development?

4. Are there limits to the partnerships that can be created between the private and public sectors? If so, what are they? Give examples.

5. What are the essential differences in role between the public sector accountability and auditing organizations, and private sector corporate auditing? And, what is their impact on public private partnerships?

6. How has the digital age changed the relationship between public and private sectors, if at all?

Assignments

1. Choose a public sector organization or service that would possibly benefit from a PPP or PFI and develop a business case report arguing for its development. Remember to include in your analysis the benefits and pitfalls on both sides of the public private initiative. Add also a comment on the role of agencies and the voluntary sector.

2. Using data available to you from such sources as the OECD, draw up a comparative table of public sector 'variables' (statistics) that illustrate both the differences and the similarities between states in public sector provision, in either a regional (such as a European Union setting) or a more international comparison.

Further reading

There are two main approaches to reading around the subject; books and their noted authors, and new research work in academic reviews. Among the many excellent authors of books available to you, three might catch your imagination for their depth and clarity. They also contain excellent bibliographies that will help you spin off into your own further research:

Hill M. (2009) *The Public Policy Process*, 5th edn (Harlow: Pearson Longman).

Dye T. R. (2012) *Understanding Public Policy*, 14th edn (Harlow: Pearson Longman).

The work of Roemer J., (2009). See an introductory interview on 'The future of capitalism' at <http://www.yale.edu/macmillanreport/ep22-roemer-051309.html>. He has his critics but, for a stimulating debate on present day public policy and politics, the work has much value. His books include:

Racism, Xenophobia, and Distribution (2007) Harvard University Press and Russell Sage Foundation.

Democracy, Education, and Equality (2006) Cambridge University Press.

Political Competition (2006) Harvard University Press.

Equality of Opportunity (2000) Harvard University Press.

Theories of Distributive Justice (1998) Harvard University Press.

For reviews, much will depend on the sector you want to examine. There are some fascinating journals to explore. This chapter used many as a bibliography, but the following is a list of some of those used to review specifically the latest research and informed the commentary over and above the chosen references:

Accounting, auditing and accountability journal
Eastern economic journal
Economics and management
Financial accountability & management
German policy studies
Governance: an international journal of policy, administration, and institutions
Harvard international law journal online
Information polity
International business research
International journal of business and management
International journal of business and public administration
Journal of business ethics
Network industries quarterly
OECD journal on budgeting
Philosophy and public affairs
Public administration
Public management review

Public performance & management review
Research journal of business management
Review of economic studies

The Australian journal of public administration
The innovation journal: the public sector innovation journal
The journal of finance

online resource centre

Test your understanding of this chapter with online questions and answers, explore the subject further through web exercises, and use the web links to provide a quick resource for further research. Go to the Online Resource Centre at <www.oxfordtextbooks.co.uk/orc/wetherly_otter/2>

Useful websites

This chapter drew together three themes: policy management, public private partnerships, and policy performance and accountability; and under each heading below, there are many online resources available for you to begin research work.

For international case studies use the OECD library for an excellent introduction to specific country 'unit' case studies, OECD, (2010) *Dedicated Public-Private Partnership Units: A Survey of Institutional and Governance Structures*. This is found at the following website and is freely available to read online. It covers Australia, Germany, Korea, South Africa, and the UK. As complementary to this chapter, this is recommended as prime reading:
<http://www.oecd-ilibrary.org/governance/dedicated-public-private-partnership-units_9789264064843-en;jsessionid=167d896hfr7io.x-oecd-live-02>

In addition and as a national example, for a broader range of UK statistical material use: <**www.statistics.gov.uk/**>

For government and governance, a good starting point is <**www.direct.gov.uk/**>

For auditing regimes, look at:
   National Audit Office <**www.nao.org.uk/**>
   Audit Commission <**www.audit-commission.gov.uk/**>
   European: European Court of Auditors <**www.eca.europa.eu/**>
   International: OECD <**http://www.oecd.org/**>

For the wider community of comparative policy work across the globe the OECD and similar organizations are good starting points and so are the equally important national qualitative and statistical archives to be found through national libraries and governments.

References

Allen & Overy (2010) *Global Guide to Public-Private Partnerships*, <http://viewer.zmags.com/publication/5db30be7>

Bank for International Settlements (2010/rev. 2011) *BASEL III: A global regulatory framework for more resilient banks and banking systems*, <http://www.bis.org/publ/bcbs189.pdf>

Bishop, M., Kay, J. and Mayer, C. (eds) (2004) *Privatization and Economic Performance* (Oxford: Oxford University Press).

Buduru B. and Pal, L.A. (2010) 'The globalized state: Measuring and monitoring governance', *European Journal of Cultural Studies* 13: 511.

Burger P. and Hawkesworth, I. (2011) 'How to attain Value for Money: Comparing PPP and Traditional Infrastructure Public Procurement', *OECD Journal on Budgeting*, Volume 2011/1, pp. 37-48.

Cheng, C. and Wang, Z. (2009) 'Public Private Partnerships in China: Making progress in a weak governance environment',

China Policy Institute Briefing Series, Issue 56, December 2009, The University of Nottingham.

Christopoulos, A.G., Mylonakis, J., and Diktapanidis, P. (2011) 'Could Lehman Brothers' Collapse Be Anticipated: An examination using CAMELS Rating system', *International Business Research* Vol.4, No.2, April 2011.

Dunleavy, P., Margetts, H., Bastow, S., and Tinkler J. (2006) *Digital Era Governance: IT Corporations, the State, and e-Government* (Oxford: Oxford University Press).

Dye, T. R. (2012) *Understanding Public Policy*, 14th edn. (Harlow: Pearson Longman).

The Economist (2011) 'Capitalism confined', 3 September 2011.

European Commission (2013) 'Press Release: Commission proposes rules to make government websites accessible for all', accessed December 2012, <http://ec.europa.eu/digital-agenda/en/news/commission-proposes-rules-make-government-websites-accessible-all>

European CyberCrime Centre (EC3), accessed May 2013, <https://www.europol.europa.eu/ec3old>

European Investment Bank (EIB) (2012) *PPPs and their Financing in Europe: Recent Trends and EIB Involvement*, ECON Department, Economic Studies Division, SG/ECON/ES/2012-523/Aka/as September 2012, p. 8.

Europol (2011) *OCTA 2011: EU Organized Crime Threat Assessment*, 6. Annex, p. 50. <https://www.europol.europa.eu/sites/default/files/publications/octa2011.pdf>

Fernando, C. S., May, A. D., Megginson, W. L. (2012) 'The Value of Investment Relationships: Evidence from the collapse of Lehman Brothers', *The Journal of Finance*, Vol. LXVII, No.1, February 2012.

Hill, M. (2009) *The Public Policy Process*, 5th edn (Pearson Longman).

HMSO (2011) *The Cost of Cyber-crime* (Cabinet Office).

Intriligator, M. (1994) 'Privitisation in Russia has led to Criminalisation', *The Australian Economic Review*, 2nd quarter, 1994.

Jong, W. Martin de (2008) 'The effectiveness of public-private partnerships in China's transport infrastructure', *Network Industries Quarterly*, vol. 10, no. 2, 2008. <http://newsletter.epfl.ch/mir/index.php?module=Newspaper&func=viewarticle&np_id=158&np_eid=28&catid=0>

Krugman, P. (2013) 'The Economics of Evil Google', *The New York Times*, 23 March 2013.

Laminska, Izabella (2013) 'What Google Reader tells us about banking and nationalization', *Financial Times*, 25 March 2013.

McAfee cited in European Commission *communication 'Towards a general policy on the fight against cybercrime'*, 2007, accessed March 2013, <http://europa.eu/legislation_summaries/justice_freedom_security/fight_against_organised_crime/l14560_en.htm>

McAfee, *The economic impact of cybercrime and cyber espionage*, report for the Center for Strategic and International Studies, July 2013. <http://www.mcafee.com/us/resources/reports/rp-economic-impact-cybercrime.pdf>

Macquarie Co. Ltd., accessed December 2012 <http://www.macquarie.co.uk/dafiles/Internet/mgl/uk/mfg/docs/infrastructure-oecd-study.pdf>

National Audit Office (2009) *'Defence Committee Inquiry into the Comprehensive Approach: Perspectives of Non-Governmental Organizations on the Comprehensive Approach, a paper prepared by the National Audit Office for the defence committee, October 2009'*

Norton (2011) *Cybercrime Report*. <http://now-static.norton.com/now/en/pu/images/Promotions/2012/cybercrime/assets/downloads/en-us/NCR-DataSheet.pdf>

OECD (2011) 'How to attain Value for Money: Comparing PPP and Traditional Infrastructure Public Procurement', *Journal on Budgeting*, Volume 2011/1, p. 92.

OECD (2010a) *Dedicated Public-Private Partnership Units: A Survey of Institutional and Governance Structures*.

OECD (2010b) *National Accounts at a Glance*.

OECD (2007) *Infrastructure to 2030: Global investment needs*.

Pedersen, A.R., Sehested, K., and Sørensen, E. (2011) 'Emerging Theoretical Understanding of Pluricentric Coordination in Public Governance', *The American Review of Public Administration* 41: 375.

Peston R. (2012) 'PFI becomes less private', BBC, December 2012.

Pollitt, C. and Bouckaert, G. (2011) *Public Management Reform, A Comparative Analysis (3rd edn): new public management, governance, and the neo-Weberian state* (Oxford: Oxford University Press).

Ritsert, R., Pekar, M. (2009) 'New Public Management Reforms in German Police Services', *German Policy Studies*, Vol. 5, No. 2, pp. 17-47.

Rooke, R. (2009) *The European Media in the Digital Age* (Harlow: Pearson Longman).

Turnbull, S. (2002) *A New Way To Govern: Organisations and society after Enron* (New Economics Foundation).

Tuttle, C.T. (2012), 'Productivity in a private charity Interview with the founder and leader of one of China's largest private charity foundations', *International Journal of Productivity & Performance Management*, Vol. 61, Issue 5, pp. 563-577.

The UK Parliament (2006) *Select Committee on Public Accounts Sixty-third report*, accessed April 2013,

Acknowledgements

This new edition chapter would not have been possible without the support of Professor Alison Harcourt and Professor Claudio Radaelli, and the ECPR governance bi-annual conference, Exeter University 2012. Equally, I am grateful for the support on security and social policy issues from the library at, and academic work previously developed for, the Hochschule für Wirtschaft und Recht Berlin (HWR)—the Berlin School of Economics and Law—with the support of Professors Erwin Seyfried and Hans-Gerd Jaschke, noting of course, the judgements and interpretations remain the author's. Lastly, gratitude to the many anonymous reviewers, and the editors, whose commentary was invaluable.

Chapter 15

Small and medium-sized enterprises (SMEs): A larger role in driving economic progress?

Martyn Robertson, Carol Langston, and Alison Price

Learning objectives

When you have completed this chapter, you will be able to:

- Define and appreciate the role of enterprise and entrepreneurship in all its forms.
- Examine how entrepreneurship and enterprise interrelate.
- Assess the important role played by micro businesses and small and medium-sized enterprises (SMEs).
- Analyse the strategic response of entrepreneurs in different market environments
- Outline why entrepreneurship in the UK is encouraged within disadvantaged communities and with under-represented groups.

THEMES

The following themes of the book are especially relevant to this chapter

》 INTERNAL/EXTERNAL

The strategic response of entrepreneurs is very much conditioned by the nature of the external market conditions in which they are attempting to start up.

》 COMPLEXITY OF THE ENVIRONMENT

The economic, political, and social environments are all important for understanding entrepreneurship and enterprise.

》 VARIETY OF SPATIAL LEVELS

Small businesses operate at a variety of spatial scales, from local settings to international markets.

》 DYNAMIC ENVIRONMENT

It is the nature of entrepreneurship that it responds to opportunities that arise as a result of changes in market opportunities; successful entrepreneurs are those who have the skills to cope with change and risk.

⟩⟩ INTERACTION BETWEEN BUSINESS AND ENVIRONMENT

Whilst small businesses are dependent on external market changes, the impact of entrepreneurship is seen as having a vital role to play in boosting the competitiveness of the national economy as a whole.

⟩⟩ STAKEHOLDERS

Whilst small businesses are important and numerous, and ownership can reside with one person, small businesses are not subject to the same pressure as large organizations to achieve shareholder returns for outside investors. However, the remaining stakeholders, namely banks, suppliers, customers, and competitors etc., do have a significant impact.

⟩⟩ VALUES

The values of the entrepreneur impact directly on the way in which the business is conducted.

▥ Introduction

Facing the toughest economic climate Britain has seen since the Second World War, with rising unemployment and constraints on public spending, the whole country is looking to entrepreneurs to bring prosperity and jobs. To do this we must work hard to address the barriers that hold back entrepreneurship – from a lack of confidence to a lack of opportunity.

(Jones 2010)

⟩⟩ DIVERSITY 'Enterprise' and 'entrepreneurship' are key attributes of business, both within the UK and for economic development and wealth creation across the rest of the world.

The purpose of this chapter is to provide an understanding of what **enterprise** means, what it means to be an **entrepreneur**, or **intrapreneur**, and to explore their role within society. This chapter will explain what is meant by key terms. It will also explore the forms of entrepreneur that exist within the UK, appreciating the values that drive entrepreneurs to start different forms of organizations. It will examine how sometimes clear articulation of an entrepreneur's values can be used to form competitive advantage for businesses, using examples such as the origins of The Body Shop and The Co-operative Bank.

⟩⟩ INTERACTION From this initial understanding of enterprise, the chapter will then focus on the importance of starting new businesses, or ventures, for the UK economy or 'UK plc'. This section will explain how SMEs impact on the development of a national economy, and explore 'gaps' in potential —between what could be achieved and what is actually being achieved, particularly within UK universities. Identifying the gaps shows that not all members of society have the same opportunities to start their own business: there is untapped potential for enterprise in the UK, particularly within female, graduate, and Black and Minority Ethnic (BME) communities.

▥ Understanding enterprise and entrepreneurship

⟩⟩ DYNAMIC As Peter Drucker remarked in 1985, 'innovation' and 'enterprise' have become 'buzz words' widely used in the media, and it is therefore necessary to be very precise about the differences between them.

Within business textbooks, the term *enterprise* is often used as a noun, as another word for a firm (e.g. a 'small–medium sized enterprise'—SME), but it can be used as an adjective to describe an individual as being 'enterprising' or innovative.

Being enterprising involves spotting opportunities, creating new ideas, and having the confidence, skills, and capabilities to turn these ideas into working realities, and is inherently risky. Enterprise capability then involves innovative and imaginative thinking, creativity, risk management, and a sense of drive. Enterprise can therefore be broadly understood as 'the application of creative ideas and innovations to practical situations. It combines creativity, ideas development and problem solving with expression, communication and practical action' (QAA 2012, p. 8).

Take the following illustration from Google: Innovators Page and Brin thought about a web-based search engine in 1996 and formed a company Google Inc. in 1998. It was not until they started selling advertising against their search results in 2000 that they started to become successful. Since then they have gone from strength to strength to offer other innovative products or services—such as Google Earth and Street View, Gmail and the Chrome browser, the Android phone (Llewellyn Smith 2009)—and are 'the undisputed global leader in search and online advertising. Its Android software powers three-quarters of the smartphones being shipped' (*Economist* 2012, p. 13).

Enterprise also implies creative solutions and innovation. Schumpeter (1936) introduced the notion of 'creative destruction' within economic theory as entrepreneurs became recognized for their potential to create change (be 'creative') and see new opportunities within the existing environment (even by 'destroying' the existing to create the new). This then becomes one of the hallmarks of capitalism—the relentless pursuit of innovation by entrepreneurs and the inevitable consequence of 'destroying' previous commodities and ways of doing things.

Stop and Think Perspectives on entrepreneurship

An entrepreneur is a person who is willing and able to convert a new idea or invention into a successful innovation.

(Schumpeter 1936)

The notion of taking risks; identifying an opportunity and seeking to develop the idea or innovation; and managing an environment of considerable uncertainty.

(Drucker 1970)

[The] pursuit of opportunity without regard to the resources currently under one's control or influence.

(Timmons 1989, pp. 16–17)

This association of the term enterprise with change and activity should also be recognized as having resource implications. Peter Drucker described true enterprise not as just starting up a business, but as achieving an 'upgrade in yield from resources' (1985, p. 25), that is adding value and gaining competitive advantage.

> *Stop and Think* **The National Council for Graduate Entrepreneurship defines the following concepts:**
>
> **The Enterprise Concept** focuses upon the *development of the enterprising person and the enterprising mindset* through a demonstration of enterprising skills, behaviours and attitudes across a diversity of contexts. These include intuitive decision-making, the capacity to make things happen autonomously, networking, initiative taking, opportunity identification, creative problem solving, strategic thinking, and self-efficacy. The focus is on creating entrepreneurial ways of doing, thinking, feeling, communicating, organizing and learning.
>
> **The Entrepreneurial Concept** focuses upon *the application of these enterprising skills and the entrepreneurial mindset* in setting up a new venture, developing/growing an existing venture or designing an entrepreneurial organization. The context might be business, social enterprise, charitable purpose, non-governmental organisations or public sector bodies. *Entrepreneurship 'makes it happen'.*
>
> **The Innovation Concept** is *the product of the Entrepreneurial Concept.* Innovation is defined as creating and exploiting opportunities for new ways of doing things resulting in better products and services, systems and ways of managing people and organisations. The successful pursuit of innovation is a function of individual enterprising endeavour and entrepreneurial organization capacity. *Entrepreneurship is a necessary pre-condition for Innovation.*
>
> (*Source*: NCGE <**www.ncge.com**> (now NCEE at <**www.ncee.org.uk**>))

What is 'an enterprise' or SME?

▶ **INTERNAL/EXTERNAL** The noun *enterprise* suggests a large or small private sector business, but it can also be a third sector 'social enterprise', like a charity or not-for-profit venture (see Chapter 1), a public enterprise, or even used to describe a project or hobby. This chapter focuses specifically on small and medium-sized enterprises (SMEs).

To determine whether a business is large, small, or very small (a 'micro' business) it is important to know the number of people working in the company (the employees) and the economic activity of the company (turnover or balance sheet). Table 15.1 shows a way of classifying businesses according to size. It must also be appreciated that different sectors require different organizational structures and sizes to deliver their business effectively—i.e. a web design company can be very effective as a micro business with only one expert, the entrepreneur and business owner, working alone.

Table 15.1 European definition of a SME and micro business (2005)

	No. of employees (max. headcount)	Either/or (less than or equal to in euros)	
		Turnover (euros)	Balance sheet total (euros)
Micro business	0–9	2 m	2 m
Small business	10–49	10 m	10 m
Medium-sized business	50–249	50 m	43 m

Source: <**http://europa.eu**>

Who is an entrepreneur?

An *entrepreneur* is defined by the UK Department of Trade and Industry (DTI) as 'anyone who attempts a new business or new venture creation, such as self-employment, a new business organization or social enterprise' (DTI 2004) and can be described as someone who is enterprising (having ideas and making them happen). However, it is important to understand that the term does not necessarily equate to the owner or manager of a private sector business. It could also relate to a public enterprise. As Drucker (1985) suggested, an entrepreneur does not need a profit motive and therefore need not be running a small business (as it is possible to be a *social entrepreneur*, creating a not-for-profit organization or a charity). Also, some business owners do not display the true characteristics of an entrepreneur.

Drucker believes that 'the entrepreneur always searches for change, responds to it and exploits it as an opportunity' (Drucker 1985, p. 25) rather than manages a business. This broader definition accepts that an entrepreneur is more than a manager and allows us to include people that are driven to be creative and entrepreneurial in all areas—this helps define different kinds of entrepreneurs, who all act to create change whilst within a large company or working for the benefit of society.

Defining the entrepreneur as social, serial, or an intrapreneur

A **social entrepreneur** is a specific term for someone who employs business principles and business start-up techniques for societal good and social benefit. Social entrepreneurs 'identify under-utilized resources—people, buildings, equipment—and find ways of putting them to use to satisfy unmet social needs. They innovate welfare services and find new ways of delivering existing services. Social entrepreneurs who deploy entrepreneurial skills for social ends are at work in parts of the traditional public sector, some large private sector corporations, and at the most innovative edge of the voluntary sector (Leadbetter 1997, p. 2).

This 'third' sector (voluntary/not-for-profit/social enterprise) of the economy has grown significantly over the last 25 years (Harding 2006). Of the global adult population, 2.8% are involved in social enterprise activities but this varies considerably around the world, from 0.02% in Malaysia to 7.6% in Argentina, with Terjesen (2011) identifying those individuals or organizations involved in the activity by region. The regions of Africa, US, Caribbean, and Latin America have a greater number of social enterprise activities than the rest of the world. The UK is about average. He reported that males are more likely to start a social venture than the females, however the social entrepreneurship gender gap is not as high as with commercial entrepreneurship.

The Global Entrepreneurship Monitor Report on Social Entrepreneurship (Terjessen et al. 2009) found that there was a scarcity of data and many existing definitions of social entrepreneurship being used around the world. The UK government defines a **social enterprise** as 'a business with primarily social objectives, whose surpluses are principally reinvested for that purpose in the business or community rather than mainly being paid to shareholders or owners' (BIS 2010, p.1). Estimates updated from the Small Business Survey of 2010 reveal that there are approximately 68,000 SME businesses, with employees which fit the UK government definition of social enterprise (BIS 2011a) and that '34% of businesses founded in the last three years [between 2007 and 2010] defined themselves as social enterprises compared to 25% of those founded 10 years or before' (BIS 2011a, p. 15). Though sales turnover amongst 'social enterprise SME employers is lower than for profit SMEs generally' (BIS 2010, p. 3), evidence from Fightback Britain notes that social enterprises are reporting a growth in turnover, 'median annual turnover of social enterprises has grown from £175,000 in their 2009 survey to £240,000' in their 2011 survey (Social Enterprise UK 2011, p. 6). This growth shows that social enterprises are developing and building effective business models in new areas. For example, a key feature of the London 2012 Olympic bid was the commitment to environmental and social principles with a strong focus on a meaningful long-term legacy for communities in the whole country, not just in London. There were many examples of innovative social enterprises being contracted for the running of the Olympics, from catering to new transport solutions (Social Enterprise London 2012).

A 'serial' entrepreneur

》 DYNAMIC Entrepreneurs that start many businesses may be referred to as *serial entrepreneurs*. This can be because their original businesses fail (a third of start-ups close within the first five years, Barclays 2009) and because they learn from each business and take that learning into the next one. This behaviour can also be seen in successful entrepreneurs such as Richard Branson who has taken his innovative vision of business to a range of new markets, including train travel, the soft drinks market, membership gyms, and even healthcare.

What is an 'intrapreneur'?

》 INTERNAL/EXTERNAL 》 DIVERSITY An *intrapreneur* has been defined as 'a person within a large corporation who takes direct responsibility for turning an idea into a profitable finished product through assertive risk-taking and innovation' (*American Heritage Directory* 1992). This term has now been subsumed within the notion of corporate entrepreneurship to define an individual's entrepreneurial behaviour in an established larger organization. There

---

Mini-Case 15.1　Social entrepreneurs beating international homelessness through football!

The Homeless World Cup was co-founded by Mel Young from Scotland and Austrian Harald Schmied, who came up with the idea in 2001 following a conference about homelessness. They both felt there was more they could do to address this global issue and came up with the idea of changing the lives of homeless people around the world through football.

The first Homeless World Cup football tournament was realized in Graz, Austria in 2003, where they hosted 18 nations. Now it has grown to include 72 countries and the tenth Homeless World Cup took place in Mexico City in 2012. The Homeless World Cup website notes that the impact of the event is significant:

players build their self esteem; come off drugs and alcohol; move into homes, jobs, education, training; repair relationships; become social entrepreneurs and coaches and players with pro or semi-pro football teams. The Homeless World Cup project involves over 50,000 homeless people throughout the year.

Global aims:

The Homeless World Cup uses football as a catalyst that helps homeless people change their lives; and to change attitudes of governments, media, public and key influencers toward creating better solutions to homelessness around the world.

These global aims are to be achieved through five main goals:

1. *To build a global brand that stands for the power of football to change lives, to change the world and to end homelessness;*

2. *To work closely with and support our network of 70+ National Partners to catalyse new football programmes and jobs creating social enterprises;*

3. *To hold a world-class, annual international football tournament that continues to demonstrate the power of football to change lives and achieving a significant, lasting local and global impact; and*

4. *To provide a positive vision, address negative attitudes and break down stereotypes, so that people who are homeless receive encouragement and support to change their lives.*

(Source: <www.homelessworldcup.org>)

Question

What are the motivations for social entrepreneurs?

are four identifiable strands: corporate venturing, intrapreneurship, internal markets, and entrepreneurial transformation. Burns (2008, p. 18) states that,

> entrepreneurial management is about the ability to lead and manage this entrepreneurial organization. It involves the development of an entrepreneurial architecture—the network of relational contracts within, or around, an organization, its employees, suppliers, customers and networks—that encourages opportunity, innovation, vision, relationships, new ways of dealing with risk and uncertainty and continuous learning. … Entrepreneurial transformation is about adapting large firms through their leadership, strategies, systems, structures and cultures so that they are able to cope with change and innovation.

What makes an entrepreneur?

There are many authors who have sought to create a list of the most important traits or characteristics that entrepreneurs have and they tend to include some, or all, of the qualities identified by Gibb (1996; 1999) that are listed below:

Entrepreneurial behaviour	Entrepreneurial attributes	Entrepreneurial skills
Opportunity seeking and grasping	Achievement of ambition	Creative problem solving
Taking initiatives to make things happen	Self confidence and self belief	Persuading
Solving problems creatively	Perseverance	Negotiation
Managing autonomously	High internal locus of control	Selling
Taking responsibility for and ownership of things	Action orientation	Proposing
Seeing things through	Preference of learning by doing	Holistically managing business/projects/situations
Networking effectively	Hardworking	Strategic thinking
Putting things together creatively	Determination	Intuitive decision-making under uncertainly
Using judgement to take calculated risks	Creativity	Networking

Mini-Case 15.2 Post-it notes

The most famous example of intrapreneurship is the story of Mr Art Fry who developed a new product for 3M—Post-it notes. This development, now essential for any office, was actually once a 'failed' product, as it was originally a non-sticking glue and created an innovation with no obvious use! However, Art Fry took the non-sticking glue out of the research and development lab, and used it on small strips of paper to mark pages in a hymnbook at church. Being able to label and mark-up sections, week-on-week without harming the book, proved to be the innovation that 3M were looking for. Post-its have now become an essential item for students, workers, and in the home; and 3M have now developed a range of further innovations (brand extensions) from this original concept, securing a major long-term income stream.

(*Source:* <www.3m.com>)

Questions

1. In the light of this example, can you explain the meaning of the maxim 'Innovators learn that it's better to ask for forgiveness than for permission'? Consider this rule in relation to the intrapreneur and their manager.

2. Can you think of other examples of successful intrapreneurship where employees within the business have initiated new product/service developments?

However, *trait theory*—that is, the theory of identifying and understanding the specific human characteristics of an entrepreneur—is complex (Steiner 1979; Chrisman et al. 1998). Counter-theories suggest that the situation or environment (Kuratko and Hodgetts 2001) are equally important factors to consider as natural ability or personality traits.

❱ INTERACTION These two theories address a central question that may be asked in relation to how leaders in general are created—the question as to whether they can be 'made' through environment and education, or whether someone is just 'born' with the attributes, skills, and capability (the traits) to become enterprising (Jack and Anderson 1999). These two different schools of thought are very important to consider, as they have different implications for the way governments may support start-up businesses and create the most conducive environment for them through free trade, regulatory transparency, and a tax system that rewards enterprise (HM Government 2009). The UK government accepts a role in supporting entrepreneurs, having stated their commitment 'to make the UK one of the best places in Europe to start, finance and grow a business' (HM Treasury 2011). However, many feel that governments can only help to create the right environment for enterprise to flourish; they cannot make people into entrepreneurs.[1]

Stop and Think

What are the meanings of the terms 'enterprise' and 'entrepreneur'? Can you identify the different types of entrepreneur and think of real-life examples?

■ Key dimensions in the development of small business

We can identify three key dimensions in the development of small business:

1. Stage of business growth
2. Sector
3. Values.

Stage of growth

Businesses can be said to have several stages from start-up to exit, as listed below.

   A. Idea

   B. Proven Idea

   C. Planning and Development

   D. Ready to Start-Up

   E. Business Growth

   F. Maturity

   G. Exit Strategy

Stages of Business Start Up (Churchill and Lewis 1983)[2]

---

[1] Regulation otherwise known as red tape: The cost of compliance to legislation for SMEs is significant. The Forum for Private Business estimated that small firms were paying out £5.8 bn for regulatory compliance services to external firms (Quick 2012). The average payment of £4,900 per annum for advice on issues such as employment, health and safety and tax was more than double the £2,100 bill in 2009.

[2] Business Start Up © Leeds Met Model of Business Start Up developed by Robertson, M. (2000) from Churchill N. C. & Lewis V. L. (1983), The five stages of Small Business Growth, *Harvard Business Review*, 63(3): May–June, and Stevenson, H. H. Six dimensions of entrepreneurship, in Birley, S. and Muzyka, D. F. (1997) *Mastering Enterprise*, FT Pitman.

These stages show the business development from the original idea (A), to researching and proving the idea (B), and then the planning and development (C), which leads to the final 'start' of the business (D). From this position of actually trading, the business then hopefully enters a phase of expansion ('business growth' (E)) until a point when the business stays relatively static as a small business (possibly as a 'lifestyle' business (F)) or continues to grow (E) until it reaches a major shift in organizational structure and the development of the business—such as being bought up by a larger company, or becoming a franchise. These major changes in a business can be called 'exit strategies' (G) as they can be the way that the entrepreneur that started the business exits the business, having taken it as far as they want to. 'Lifestyle' indicates that the entrepreneur has taken the business as far as he or she wants and now is prepared to reap the rewards to suit their lifestyle. These stages can be depicted in a linear diagram of growth.

Figure 15.1 suggests that business growth is a 'linear' activity, that is, it is always moving forward and has specific separate stages. However, most entrepreneurs experience these stages as more random and are often less able to plan for each stage. It is, however, helpful when thinking about a new venture or business to be aware of these stages as each makes different demands on the business and its staff. This means that the skills of the entrepreneur may need to be developed over time as the needs of the business change.

Any new venture is heavily dependent upon the skills and knowledge of those who are starting it up and recent evidence shows that 'compared with employees, the self-employed need the ability to combine and deploy a wider range of competencies' (UKCES 2011, p. iii) and many self-employed or potential entrepreneurs may have difficulties due to: lack of awareness of their own skills; lack of business experience or training; insufficient 'soft' skills, such as interpersonal skills; and lack of management skills (UKCES 2011, p. iii–iv).[3] There are many checklists and models to help with the assessment of the resources available to start up a business but few consider both personal and physical resources. The MAIR model (Gibb and Ritchie 1982) draws together six elements providing an appreciation of the personal capacity and business development processes required to start up any new venture or project.

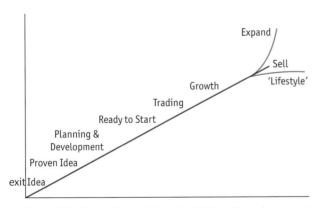

Figure 15.1 Stages of growth from initial idea through start-up to

---

[3] Branson (2012) outlined the key requirements for running a business. Namely: a strong sense of vision, a will to make the business different, a good idea where the product/service will stand out, belief, self-confidence and motivation to make it work, freedom to get on and make it work, good people, a strong customer base, quality service, great value for money, innovative products, theoretical and practical experience of running a business, risk awareness and the ability to identify gaps in the market or where potential customers are poorly served.

Criteria for successful growth of the business from initial idea to exit—the MAIR model.

1. (**M**) motivation and commitment
2. (**A**) abilities and skill
3. (**I**) idea in relation to the market
4. (**R**) resources
5. plan and strategy
6. organization and administration.

The MAIR model presents the personal capacity required to start up—the knowledge, support, skills, and confidence. From its origins, MAIR has been adapted and developed (Hartshorn and Richardson 1993) and is now more relevant for all new start-ups (including university graduates, women, and those from disadvantaged or under-represented areas or groups). Assessing each of these areas within the start-up process allows for planned *capacity building*, defined as 'helping organizations to develop their resources (people, buildings, etc.) so that they are better able to meet their aims. This term is commonly used when an initiative or training programme is likely to increase the ability of the individuals or organizations to improve their performance, or take the lead, in specific economic or business development activities' (DTI 2004).

Stop and Think

Could you start a new business? Write a list of the resources you require.

What skills do you have that would be good for selling, purchasing, negotiating, managing, working with colleagues, or employing staff?

Write a list of things you might need to learn, develop, or buy in from someone else (such as an accountant or a lawyer).

Try the GET TEST to see how entrepreneurial you are: <**http://www.get2test.net/**>

Sector

Within the business environment, specific business sectors have been determined (see Table 15.2) and a business's development and progress may be affected by the performance of the sector as a whole. Table 15.2 shows the classification of industries and sectors derived from the *Financial Times* classification of stock market companies.

Richard Branson (2012) recognized that,

> a successful economy needs a balance of industries ranging from financial through manufacturing, creative and technological. The UK has been very dependent on big business and financial services for many years but to ensure a strong recovery we need to develop a much broader base for the future, including a range of successful small and medium sized businesses.

This section will show that SMEs can be innovative, responsive to changing conditions, and adaptable. The UK economy comprises a wide range of different sectors whose activities, and those of the firms within them, have evolved over time. In common with other advanced economies, there has been a marked shift in the structure of the UK economy away from manufacturing towards services, now accounting for 75% of activity, in particular to knowledge intensive services such as finance, professional, business services, Information and Communication Technologies (ICT) (BIS 2012a).

Table 15.2 Classification of industries and sectors

Aerospace and defence	Healthcare
Agriculture	Horticulture
Automotive and parts	Household
Biotechnology	Information security
Broadcasting and media	Leisure
Building and construction	Marine industries
Chemicals	Medical
Computing and electronics	Materials/metals/minerals
Distribution and transport	Oil and gas
Education	Property services
Energy	Radio and media
Engineering	Retail
Environmental	Software services
Financial	Telecoms
Fisheries	Travel and hotels
Food and drink	Utilities

The Kelley et al. (2012) global report showed industry sector participation at the three development levels. It demonstrated the dominance of consumer orientated businesses (mostly retail) at the factor driven and efficiency stages.[4] Just as important, there were high levels of business services in the innovation driven economies, particularly when compared with the factor driven development level. Business services tended to compete more on knowledge and technology. On the other hand, extractive or transforming businesses were less frequent in the innovation driven economies compared with the other two development levels.

⏩ **DIVERSITY** Each sector makes specific demands on the businesses that operate within it, and it is clear that some sectors are more likely to be conducive to SMEs than others are.

⏩ **INTERACTION** Table 15.3 shows the industry share and number of businesses in the UK private sector, by industry sector, at the start of 2012.

According to BIS (2012) at the start of 2012, there were 907,000 businesses operating in the construction sector.[5] This represents almost a fifth (18.9%) of all UK private sector businesses. A further 666,000 businesses (13.9%) were operating in the professional, scientific, and technical activities sector and 515,000 (10.7%) in the wholesale and retail trade and repair sector.

At the start of 2012, 59.1% of private sector business employment was in SMEs (0–249 employees), although this proportion varied considerably by industry (see Figure 15.2). In the financial and insurance activities sector only 25.3% of employment was in SMEs. However, in the agriculture, forestry and fishing sector virtually all employment (95.4%) was in SMEs (BIS 2012).

Overall, 48.8% of turnover was in SMEs. Again, there were variations by industry (see Figure 15.3), ranging from 25.5% in the arts, entertainment and recreation activities sector to 90.0% in agriculture, forestry and fishing (BIS 2012).

---

[4] These are explained in detail in the 'Strengths and weaknesses of small businesses' section where social and political economic forces come into play.

[5] There were 875,000 in 2011.

Table 15.3 Share of businesses in the UK private sector (and numbers) by industry, start of 2012

	Number of businesses	Share
All industries	**4,794,105**	**100%**
F – Construction	907,480	18.9%
M – Professional, scientific and technical activities	665,625	13.9%
G – Wholesale and retail trade, repair	514,805	10.7%
N – Admin and support service activities	378,735	7.9%
Q – Human health and social work activities	303,540	6.3%
J – Information and communication	289,075	6.0%
H – Transportation and storage	269,945	5.6%
S – Other service activities	268,805	5.6%
P – Education	243,220	5.1%
C – Manufacturing	230,970	4.8%
R – Arts, entertainment & recreation	209,430	4.4%
I – Accommodation and food service activities	166,555	3.5%
A – Agriculture, forestry and fishing	152,085	3.2%
L – Real estate activities	91,810	1.9%
K – Financial and insurance activities	76,380	1.6%
B,D,E – Mining; electricity, gas, water	25,655	0.5%

In the professional, scientific and technical activities sector, the SMEs (99.9% of total) produced around 67% of turnover and provided 77% of the jobs. The SMEs within the agriculture sector dominate on all counts. Within the mining sector, a very high proportion of both turnover and of employment is in large firms. In the transport sector, these figures are above 56%. In both of these sectors, SMEs still account for 99% of the firms. Let us explore aspects

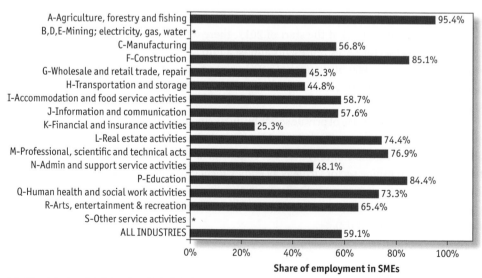

Note: A * symbol replaces data that are deemed to be disclosive.

Figure 15.2 SME share of employment in the UK private sector, by industry, start of 2012

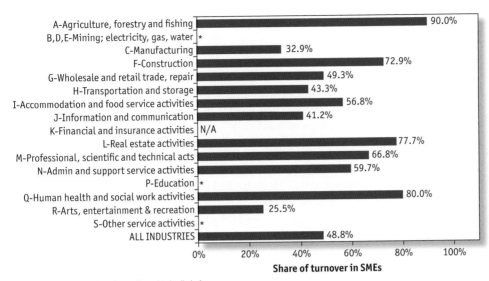

Figure 15.3 SME share of turnover in the UK private sector, by industry, start of 2012

Note: A * symbol replaces data that are deemed to be disclosive.

of the business environment for some of the other sectors and their implications for the future of the business.

General building contractors

Construction, a highly fragmented sector, is an easy sector to enter and leave (defined as churning) because of the nature of the work. It is characterized as being labour intensive with a relatively low level of entry capital required to set up in business. No one firm has a significant share of the market. Entry is also helped by the prevalence of contracting and subcontracting, alliances, and the range of specialist trades in the industry. Of these businesses, 83% were either sole traders or partnerships (BIS 2011).

Restaurants and cafés

This sector is one of the most volatile sectors of the economy. It is characterized by the relative ease of setting up a restaurant business, frequent closures and changes of ownership, and its responsiveness in providing catering services readily where demand arises. It relies heavily on personal service and, as such, its workforce is a key element in its success. So competitive has it become that Britten (2010) states that 'pub goers are more likely to visit their local to eat rather than drink, as the rise of the gastropub calls time on the traditional "boozer".

Retailing and the rise of supermarkets

Chapter 3 showed that the expansion of market share by supermarkets has been at the expense of small firms. The survival of small food retailing firms is likely to be dependent upon meeting local needs through a combination of long or anti-social opening hours and satisfying the attitudes and tastes of their customers (e.g. ethnic, healthy, concerns for the environment, etc.). Similarly, other small businesses such as confectioners, tobacconists, and newsagents (CTN) and off-licences have been severely affected by supermarkets as consumers have adopted a one-stop shopping attitude.

Paphitis (2012) believes that,

> the High Street's been caught in a classic pincer movement. On one side, you've supermarkets that don't sell just packaged food, any more, they sell everything. They've been allowed to replace just about every shop in the High Street. At the same time those in charge of planning have then allowed out of town shopping centres to be built all over the place. It's meant that people have got out of the habit of going to the High Street. For a long time now the High Street has been under pressure from more attractive out of town shopping centres and malls.

The number of independently owned and run petrol forecourts has continued to fall, from 39,958 in 1967 to 8,480 in 2011, as a direct result of fierce competition and expansion by the supermarkets, who now sell over 45% of all motor fuel (PowerSwitch 2012).

The fast moving mobile technology market is changing the way business is undertaken. (Armstrong 2012). With over 50% of the UK and US population owning a smart phones; 310 billion downloads of mobile apps by 2016 generating sales of £47 billion (Gartner 2012); 40% of all retail searches being made from mobile devices has resulted in a 74% conversion rate after visiting a retailer's mobile site or app; Cooper (2012) found that on-line could be up to 4 times cheaper than stores so consumers are switching to internet retailers and by 2015, digital currency will be accepted everywhere from the local corner store to national chains resulting in 17 billion mobile payment transactions; the ability for SMEs to compete in the marketplace will be different and require speed and adaptability.

The Internet has made it feasible for anyone to start and run a successful venture. The rules have been changed because the differences in scale between companies have been minimized and businesses now have greater access to information about new markets and the sales trends in their sector inform their decisions (Bell 2012).

SMEs therefore have to compete and/or embrace internet shopping (which accounts for about 15% of retail spending in the UK), provide good customer service to retain existing shoppers, operate in a niche market, steal market share from others, and consider very new markets.

Technology and knowledge intensive services

Wymenga et al. (2012) found that over the period 2000–2009, knowledge intensive services including finance, professional business services, and ICT grew by 40.8%, contributing 13.4% of total UK growth over this period. This growth resulted from investment in intangible assets such as research and development (R&D), software, and skills so that 'hi-tech' and knowledge intensive firms were able to produce productivity gains, growth in employment, and improved Gross Value Added (GVA). There are almost 46,000 SMEs in high-tech manufacturing (HTM) and more than 4.3 million SMEs offering knowledge intensive services (KIS) in the European Union (EU). These include: SMEs producing pharmaceutical products, electronics, legal and accounting services, as well as scientific R&D and creative industries. They represent more than a fifth (21.1%) of all of the EUs SMEs. While Germany contains the largest number of SMEs in high-tech manufacturing, Italy, the UK, and France have the largest number of knowledge intensive services. As many of the goods and services they produce are more export-oriented, they are more vulnerable to sudden external shocks in the global economy.

Values of enterprise

❱❱ **VALUES** Whilst the stage of the business and the sector will have a major affect upon the business and its staff, it is the values of the entrepreneur that will influence upon the way business is conducted. Every person has a value system or set of values that guide and direct the way that they conduct their activities. While some businesses make their business ethics explicit as a form of competitive advantage (such as **fair trade** or recycled products), the values that underpin all the decision-making in a business indicate the values of the entrepreneur.

Chapter 7 discussed in detail the contemporary arguments about ethics in large complex companies, but how do values affect those businesses starting out? In 2002, a national survey showed that there is a strong perception that those who are successful in business have low morals or ethics (SBS 2002). More recently these results have been changed as SME owners are deemed to have higher value sets than those in large companies (see Hatten 2012, p. 57, Figure 3.2. What is unacceptable conduct?). Obviously, the outcomes of all business activity and decision-making can be judged as positive or negative, but this is because of the values of the people who are engaging in the enterprise, not the act of starting a new venture. Values are therefore an important part of enterprise and have an impact upon small business start-up.

Some well-known entrepreneurs started their businesses because their values do not match existing business practice and they seek to follow a more responsible approach to business. This can create competitive advantage.

Stop and Think

Imagine shopping early one morning, so early that the street is empty, and on the floor, you find either:

a 50p

b £5

c £50

d £500

e £5000.

Do you keep it? (In addition, would the amount make a difference?)

If you had found the money in a wallet or purse, with a name and address, would that make a difference?

Explain any changes in your thinking and try to express the values that you have that would cause you to act (Price 1997).

Now reflect on your learning and thinking in this task. If you were an entrepreneur, how might your values be seen in action in your small business? Would you tell a large customer that they had overpaid you? Would you pay your bills on time?

Recognition of appalling working conditions across the world has resulted in a consumer interest in 'fair trade'. This has resulted in new entrants using their values to enter existing markets, such as Cafédirect successfully entering an apparently saturated market with an ethical new coffee. Penny Newman, the owner who blazed a trail for Cafédirect, took it from a niche market position and placed it into the mainstream, with the fair trade hot drinks brand now sold through most of the major supermarkets (Enterprise Insight 2005). Green & Black's also entered the confectionary market by making a unique selling point of their ethical stance to sourcing cocoa beans, and have since been sold to Cadbury (see discussion of ethical consumerism in Chapter 11).

Mini-Case 15.3 The Co-operative Bank: 'customer-led, ethically guided'

Acting responsibly, honestly and with integrity is a key part of our tradition as a co operative society.

The *Co-operative* Bank, which was founded under cooperative principles in 1844, launched an ethical policy in May 1992, under the following philosophy: 'At the Co-operative Bank, we always remember that it's your money in your account. Our role is simply to take good care of it for you—and not do things with it that you wouldn't do yourself.'

This resulted from a major ethics survey of 30,000 customers in which the majority (84%) of customers who responded believed that it was a good idea for the Co-operative Bank to have a clear ethical policy. Their new policy statement was endorsed by 78% of customers and a further survey in 2001 showed that this support had increased to 97% of customers. The Co-operative Group was voted the UK's most ethical brand in 2008.

<www.co-operativebank.co.uk>

Question

Does it matter to you as a customer whether your bank makes loans to companies that might be considered unethical, such as arms manufacturers?

As with the Body Shop (sold by the late entrepreneur Anita Roddick to large corporate L'Oreal), the values of the entrepreneur can be seen within the activity of the business venture, the way it operates, and the products it sells. The Body Shop publishes its campaign/values report each year at <**http://www.thebodyshop.co.uk/values/index.aspx**>.

Stop and Think

Imagine that you are the owner of a business that has an ethical policy and fair-trading practices and uses these in marketing campaigns as part of its competitive advantage.
Do you still:

a *bluff* when negotiating the purchase of raw ingredients in order to get a good price for yourselves, and therefore offer the best price to your customers?

b *exaggerate* the demand for your product when trying to establish your brand with new retailers?

Is this normal business practice, or unethical practice? Where do you draw the line?
What are your ethics? (Price 1997)

❱ **STAKEHOLDERS** Chapter 7 showed that defining the values of a business can be complex, but customer awareness of business impacts means that it is increasingly becoming an issue. Some customers now include the impact of the business upon the environment, or their treatment of their suppliers (i.e. whether they employ children to work in factories abroad or have different standards of health and safety internationally) within their decision to purchase a product.

Stop and Think

Are businesses like Cafédirect the exception rather than the rule? Do the pressures that small businesses are under make it difficult for them to prioritize ethical issues?

The importance of SMEs within the overall economic activity

The impact of one individual small company could be easily overlooked as not making much contribution to the economy, but as 99% of all businesses within the EU are defined as micro, small, and medium-sized businesses, their impact is huge.

A number of studies, Reynolds et al. (2001) to Kelley et al. (2012), have been undertaken which show the importance of small firms and entrepreneurship. The Global Entrepreneurship Monitor (GEM) has repeatedly stated that small firms are the real driving force behind economic growth.

The GEM model (see Figure 15.4 and Figure 15.5) shows how social and cultural forces impact on the economy and the entrepreneurial conditions that either encourage or dissuade individuals from being enterprising (Kelley et al. 2012). If the conditions are positive then a greater number of opportunities will exist and hence improve economic performance. If there is not a climate for assisting new businesses to start and grow, and there is a lack of new ideas or innovations, then minimal change in the economy will take place and performance will be poor. Entrepreneurial capacity and opportunities affect 'businesses churn' (the difference between businesses starting and ceasing to trade), and result in the business population

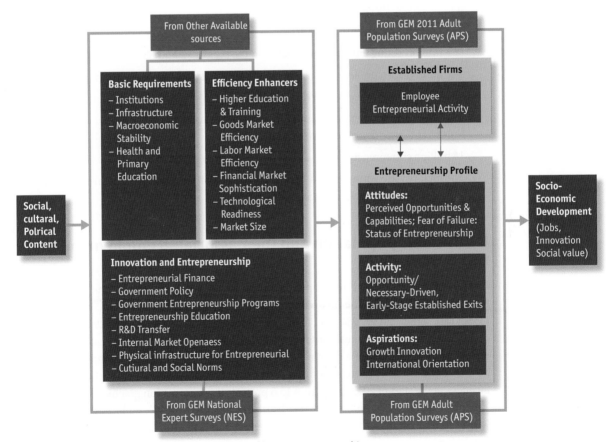

Figure 15.4 The institutional context and its relationship to entrepreneurship

Source: Kelley et al. 2012.

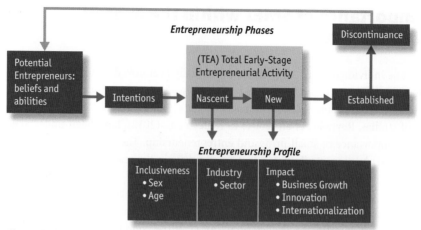

Figure 15.5 The entrepreneurship process and GEM operational definitions

Source: Kelley et al. 2012.

constantly changing. This significantly impacts on SMEs where over a third of the stock of businesses has started in the last three years.

Global GEM 2011 (Kelley et al. 2012), estimated that 388 million entrepreneurs were actively engaged in starting and running new businesses and profiled the estimated early stage entrepreneurs into the following categories:

- 163 million women entrepreneurs
- 165 million young entrepreneurs between the ages of 18 and 35
- 141 million entrepreneurs who expected to create at least five new jobs in the next 5 years
- 65 million entrepreneurs who expected to create 20 or more new jobs in the next 5 years
- 69 million entrepreneurs who offer innovative products and services that are new to customers and have few other competitors
- 18 million entrepreneurs who sell at least 25% of their products and services internationally
- The majority are young to mid-career, from 25 to 44 years old, with the next most prevalent in the 45 to 54-year-old age group.

UK business population and their associated employment and turnover[6]

At the start of 2012, there were approximately 4.8 million businesses in the UK, of which 3.6 million were run as self-employed businesses (74.2%). Small and medium-sized enterprises (SMEs) are significant (99.2% of all firms) and important; they generate £1,529 billion (48.8%) of the combined private annual turnover of £3,132 billion and employ an estimated 14.1 million people, providing 59.1% of employment in the UK. Table 15.4 shows the estimated number of businesses in the UK private sector and their associated employment and turnover, by size of business, at the start of 2012 and Figure 15.6 presents this information graphically (BIS 2012).

Almost all of these enterprises (99.3%) were small (0 to 49 employees). Only 29,750 (0.6%) were medium-sized (50 to 249 employees) and 6,455 (0.1%) were large (250 or more employees).

---

[6] Statistics reproduced with permission from the Department of Business, Innovation & Skills (2012)

Table 15.4 Estimated number of enterprises, employment and turnover by number of employees, UK private sector, start of 2012

	Number		
	Enterprises (/ 1,000)	**Employment (/ 1,000)**	**Turnover[1] (/ £ million)**
All enterprises	4,794	23,893	3,131,549
All employers	1,238	19,991	2,923,744
With no employees[2]	3,557	3,902	207,805
1–9	1,023	3,848	416,162
10–49	178	3,471	454,327
50–249	30	2,909	450,384
250 or more	6	9,763	1,602,870

[1] 'All Industries' turnover figures exclude SIC 2007 Section K (financial intermediation) where turnover is not available on a comparable basis.

[2] 'With no employees' comprises sole proprietorships and partnership comprising only the self-employed owner-manager(s), and companies comprising only an employee director.

Source: BIS 2012.

The number of businesses operating in the UK has increased markedly over recent decades. Estimates indicate that thirty years ago there were fewer than two million firms based in the UK, about 40% of the current total. Growth rates were particularly buoyant in the 1980s (self-employment rates doubled between 1979 and 1990). Since 2000 business stock has increased 40%. In 2000 there were just 3.5 million private sector enterprises operating in the UK, now there are 4.8 million (BIS 2012).

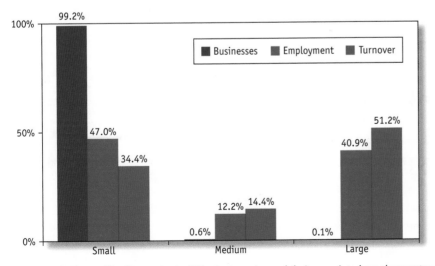

Figure 15.6 Share of businesses in the UK private sector and their associated employment and turnover, by size of business, start of 2012

Source: BIS 2012.

Registered and unregistered businesses

Private sector businesses fall into three different types of legal status: sole proprietorships, run by one self-employed person; partnerships, run by two or more self-employed people; and companies (including public corporations and nationalized bodies) in which the working directors are classed as employees. At the start of 2012, 62.7% of private sector businesses were sole proprietorships, 28.0% were companies and 9.3% were partnerships. The majority of private sector businesses (55.3%) are neither registered for PAYE (tax of employees) nor VAT (sales tax). There were 2,143,000 registered businesses, representing 44.7% of all private sector businesses (BIS 2012).

From the BIS (2012) Report, the business stock figures over the last decade present some significant changes worthy of investigation. Some of these results are shown graphically in Figure 15.7.

- Since 2000, the number of private sector businesses in the UK has increased in each of the last twelve years and by 1.33 million (38.6%). They are at their highest level.

- More specifically, these changes were driven by the increase in the number of businesses without employees, which since 2000 has increased by 51.4% (over 1.2 million). This trend persisted despite the two recent periods of recession.

- Since 2008 those businesses without employees increased by 534,000 (17.7%) to reach 3.56 million in 2012. This could be because of the tough labour market conditions, which may have encouraged people to set up in business, as they are made redundant, for example. The self-employed businesses (74.2% of total businesses) were 16.3% of the total workforce and produced 6.6% of private sector turnover.

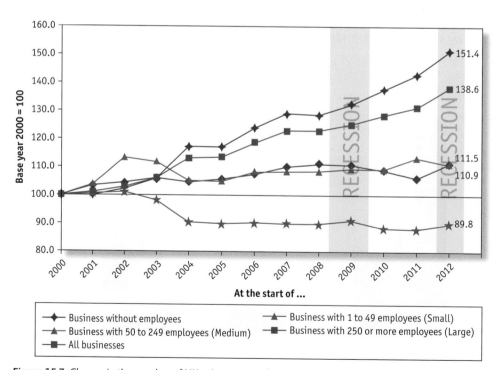

Figure 15.7 Change in the number of UK private sector businesses by size band, 2000–2012 (indexed)

Source: BIS 2012.

- Businesses with employees accounted for over a quarter of all private sector businesses in the UK at the start of 2012 (25.8%, or 1.2 million businesses), 83.7% of private sector employment, and produced 93.4% of private sector turnover.

- The number of large private sector businesses (with 250 or more employees) has decreased by 10.2% over the period, falling from 7,200 at the start of 2000 to 6,500 at the start of 2012.

- Businesses with 1 to 49 employees have progressed to reach over 1.20 million—a rise of 10%.

- A fall in the number of businesses within the manufacturing sector.

- An increase in the number of independent companies from 825,000 to 1.3 million with the number of non-employers increasing by over 70% to 516,000, so that they could benefit from tax saving schemes.

- An increase in the number of sole traders to 3.0 million, but a decline in the number of partnerships from 671,000 to 448,000. It would appear that most of these have converted to independent companies. BIS (2012a) report that despite having a relatively high proportion of firms which grow or contract rapidly, almost 30% of UK firms have experienced static or very low growth over the last three years.

How did this come about? Will the position continue? During the 2008/9 recession and until the 2012 recession there has been a marginal increase in the total number of enterprises. Although turnover and employment levels initially dropped (BIS 2009) they appear to have recovered to the old levels.

Small businesses can, therefore, stimulate competition within a market economy and rejuvenate existing and established markets with a new approach (think about Richard Branson's Virgin).

UK entrepreneurial performance and activity

The UK has an average level of entrepreneurial activity both globally (Reynolds et al. 2001; Levie et al. 2009) and within the EU (Cowling 2003; Levie et al. 2009). In the UK, 9.8% of working age adults expected to start a business within the next 3 years in 2011, compared with 15.8% in the US (Levie et al. 2012).

There has been an apparent rise in entrepreneurial activity in the UK since 2010. However, the gap with the US widened as a result of a sharp rise in the TEA rate[7] in the US: the UK TEA rate was around two thirds (62%) of the US equivalent rate of 12.3% and above that of France (5.7%) and Germany (5.6%) (see Figure 15.8).

The UK's performance and activity was surveyed by Levie et al. (2012) who found that:

- 4.2% of the adult population in the UK were actively trying to start a business (nascent entrepreneurs), compared with 8.3% in the US.

- 3.4% of the UK working age adult population were new business owner-managers (3–42 months old) and they compare favourably with France (1.7%) and Germany (2.4%), although they are lower than in the US (4.3%).

- The proportion of the adult population who owned and managed a business older than 42 months (established business owner-managers) in the UK was 6.5%, similar to Germany (5.6%), higher than in France (2.4%), but lower than in the US where the rate was 9.1%.

---

[7] TEA (total entrepreneurial activity) is the percentage of the population for each country engaged in some form of entrepreneurial activity. With a high TEA activity score there is a greater likelihood of economic development.

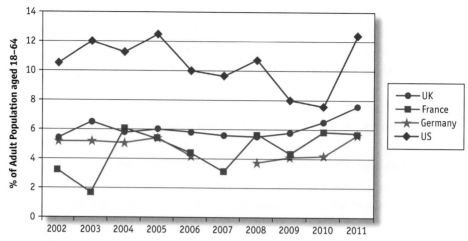

Figure 15.8 Total early stage entrepreneurial activity (TEA) in the UK, France, Germany and the US (2002–2011)

Source: Data from Levie et al. 2012.

If entrepreneurial facilitating conditions are perceived as so important, why has the UK's position remained unchanged? What has the government or business done? The position was well known in 2003 when the Department for Trade and Industry (DTI) issued its 'Strategy for prosperity for all' (DTI 2003) with enterprise at its core. At that time the UK had a persistent productivity gap of at least 20% with its major competitors—France, Germany, and the US—and was just a middle ranking country in terms of GDP per head. Why didn't it improve?

The UK's position is now under threat as the world economy has become intensely competitive; growth in emerging markets and developing economies continues to outstrip that in developed economies. Even so the government, in its document 'Enterprise: Unlocking the UK's Talent' (HM Treasury 2008), has stated that it wants:

> more new and growing businesses and more companies and people acting on enterprising ideas. It is about enabling the enterprise environment on regulation and finance and enabling enterprising people by unlocking talent through culture, knowledge and skills, and improving our ability to innovate: to commercialize new ideas.

Strengths and weaknesses of small businesses

❯ DIVERSITY Competitive advantage is a vital concept within business, and the conditions that it is argued are necessary, both at the national and business levels, are explored in Chapter 3. Competitive advantage is the essence of what makes each business different to another business and should form the basis upon which business operates. This could be the reason why customers use one business, or call upon its services, rather than another. One reason might be that a new business offers something that you cannot get anywhere else (think about new products when they are launched—such as the Apple 'iPad'); or it might just be that they are the nearest place that sells that product.

Whatever the cause, it is important to identify what this advantage is to ensure that it can provide a long-term or 'strategic approach to outperforming other business' (Porter 1980). In some cases, small firms operating in a niche market can achieve this.

⟫ INTERACTION SMEs experience positives and negatives, due to their size and capacity, as to how they operate in the business environment.

Strengths of small businesses may include the following:

- Flexibility in their structure and approach enabling small businesses to respond to changes in the business environment and adapt quickly in the marketplace

- Responsiveness to large firms who sub-contract to them; use of advanced technology and flexible systems ensures a fast turnaround

- Lean organization structure, lack of bureaucracy and low overheads meaning that they deliver on quality and price

- Capability to identify new market opportunities and bring ideas, products, and services to market quicker than their larger competitors

- Geographical dispersion, together with closeness to the customer and understanding of local culture, ensuring the cooperation of their community to support their enterprise.

Weaknesses of small businesses may include the following:

- Difficulty with cash flow

- Lack of ability to influence the business environment

- Lack of appropriate managerial experience and depth in certain specialisms; inability to create functional departments

- Difficulty in providing staff development, training, and career paths

- Generally under-capitalized and not having sufficient resources to keep abreast of changes in market conditions

- Difficulties competing with large firms, e.g. as larger firms are able to benefit from 'economies of scale'

- Legal changes and requirements that are are proportionally more costly and difficult to implement

- Often having to work within short timescales and planning horizons.

Mini-Case 15.4 eBay entrepreneurs

Nearly 70,000 people in the UK are making a living by selling goods on eBay (eBay Survey 2005). Launched in 1995, eBay is a well-known website that brings together buyers and sellers across the world to buy the things they want and sell the things they don't, as they trade directly with each other supported through the eBay site. It was originally started by Pierre Omidyar in September 1995 to help his wife find more items for her collection (hobby). The site now has over 114 million customers worldwide, with 7.4 million in the UK. Up to 2.7 million British items are on sale every day and items worth more than £2 billion were sold on eBay's UK website in 2005.

eBay has also become a low-cost route to business start-up and is providing new opportunities for those who traditionally find many barriers to starting a business (such as those with caring responsibilities for the elderly or children) as they can use the site as a way to run a business from their home or outside core work hours. However, eBay entrepreneurs can also be existing small businesses selling through auctions to boost sales. This provides attractive environments for graduates and young entrepreneurs around the world. In China, it is estimated that 40% of the shops on Taobao.com site are run by college graduates (Ye and Jing 2006).

(*Source:* <www.startups.co.uk>)

Question

What is the competitive advantage of eBay?

The relationship with large firms is not balanced: large firms possess power and exercise significant control, may be late with payments, and generally only use SMEs for small and intermittent purchases and express no loyalty, as price, quality, and delivery are more important. (See also 'Obstacles to business success' in Williams and Cowling 2009.)

Around the world the cultural, political and social forces in play have a different impact on, and contribution to, the nation's economy. This depends upon the stage of development and activity of the state[8] namely:

- factor driven states provide the basic requirements of health, education, and business infrastructure
- efficiency enhancer driven states provide technological readiness, market size, and proper functioning of the market
- innovation and entrepreneurship driven states provide government programmes, training, and regulation and infrastructure.

Factor driven economies such as India, Africa, and Central America (except Mexico), put emphasis on the basic requirements to develop institutions and the infrastructure, health, and primary education. As efficiency driven countries' economies progress, for example in Brazil, Russia, the new EU states, South America, and Mexico, other conditions which require a proper functioning of the market, called efficiency enhancers, come into play (e.g. specific higher education and business training programmes). These factors develop and the markets become more efficient, thus, encouraging entrepreneurship. The innovation and entrepreneurship driven group, countries such as the US, Japan, the UK, and the original EU states, have innovation and entrepreneurial conditions and mechanisms to support the related activity. Sources of finance, education, research, and legislation are normally in place. The dynamic components of entrepreneurial attitudes, activity, and aspirations are then reflected in the country's national economic growth. The economic and geographical groupings are shown in Table 15.5 (Kelley et al. 2011).

◼ Widening participation in entrepreneurship

We have seen in Chapters 6 and 12 that it is important to consider the world of business in terms of equal opportunities and the participation of different groups in the economic life of the country. For example, women are significantly under-represented in UK senior management positions—a problem that is sometimes referred to using the metaphor of the 'glass ceiling'. Here we will look at the representation of women, ethnic minorities, and graduates in small businesses and enterprise.

Female entrepreneurs

In the UK out of the 4.8 million enterprises approximately 700,000 are majority-women-owned businesses (Williams et al. 2009). They generate around £130 billion in turnover.

Women-led businesses tend to be smaller than other businesses. 90% of women-led SME employers are micro businesses, compared to 83% of those not led by women. However, women starting up in business will tend to provide a more immediate contribution to the economy because three times as many women come into self-employment from unemployment compared to men (SBS 2005).

---

[8] See Figure 15.4 The institutional context and its relationship to entrepreneurship.

Table 15.5 GEM economies classified by development level and geographical location, 2010

	Factor-driven	**Efficiency-driven**	**Innovation-driven**
Sub-Saharan Africa	Angola, Ghana, Uganda, Zambia	South Africa	
Middle East/ North Africa	Egypt, Iran, Pakistan, Saudi Arabia, West Bank and Gaza	Tunisia	Israel
Latin America and caribbean	Jamaica, Guatemala, Bolivia	Argentina, Brazil, Chile, Columbia, Costa Rica, Ecuador, Mexico, Peru, Trinidad and Tobago, Uruguay	
Eastern Europe		Bosnia and Herzegovina, Croatia, Hungary, Latvia, Macedonia, Montenegro, Romania, Russia, Turkey	Slovenia
Asia Pacific	Vanuatu	Malaysia, China, Taiwan	Australia, Japan, Republic of Korea
United State, and Western Europe			Belgium, Denmark, Finland, France, Germany, Greece, Iceland, Ireland, Italy, Netherlands, Norway, Portugal, Spain, Sweden, Switzerland, United Kingdom, United States

Source: Data from Kelley et al. 2011.

The gender gap in entrepreneurial activity varies greatly across G7 and BRIC countries. The GEM 2010 Report (Kelley et al. 2011) stated that in 2010, 104 million women in 59 economies—which represent more than 52% of the world's population and 84% of world GDP—started and managed new business ventures. These women entrepreneurs made up between 1.5% and 45.4% of the adult population in their respective economies. Another 83 million women across those regions ran businesses they had launched at least three and a half years before. Together, these 187 million exemplify the contribution that women make to worldwide entrepreneurship and business ownership. Where women do not participate, the economies lose out from the benefits provided by new products and services, additional money, and new jobs.

Levie et al. (2012) stated that in most high-income countries, men are around twice as likely to be entrepreneurially active as women. However, in the US and Germany in 2011, male and female TEA rates were much closer than in the UK and France.

In the UK female early stage entrepreneurial activity is 49% of male activity, (5% compared to 10.2% for men) while established business ownership is just 45% of male ownership. The figures for the USA are 73% and 60% respectively.

(Levie et al. 2012)

Figure 15.9 presents a summary of TEA rates by gender in the UK, France, Germany, and the US in 2011.

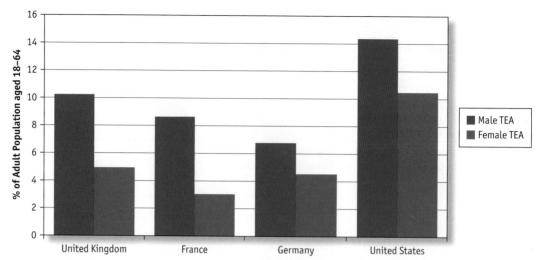

Figure 15.9 Total early stage entrepreneurial activity (TEA) rates by gender in the UK, France, Germany, and the US in 2011

Source: Data from Levie et al. 2012.

Females are under-represented in the self-employed population, at only 26%, even though women account for 44% of all economically active people. Furthermore, they are half as likely to be involved in start-up activity as men (Allen at al. 2007 and Harding 2004). In the US, the Women's Business Act 1988 put in place a long-term infrastructure to support women's enterprise development. (Since then women's business ownership has increased significantly.)

There are some distinctive features of female entrepreneurs. Compared to men, women are not as positive about opportunities for entrepreneurship, are less inclined to start a business, and have a greater fear of failure. Women's fears become even greater in the innovation driven economies. Greene (2008) states that women's business ideas are not 'born global'. Women often articulate local, accessible markets (DTI 2004), and are not encouraged during business advice/support programmes to develop their ideas for future growth.

However, since 2002 perceptions have changed and now closely mirror those of men. Traditionally, the self-employed were mainly men working long hours. Now it appears most of those 'going it alone' in business are female, part-time, and ready to improvise (Stern 2012). Many went into self-employment voluntarily when they realized that without much job security they were better off. Many were laid off and saw no other options. Whilst two thirds of the self-employed are men, 60% of those who have become self-employed since 2008 are women. Not only are women bearing the brunt of mass job shedding but there remains a working world that reveals a culture essentially hostile to family life. One woman summed it up, 'I'm in my late 50s and I don't have a degree. All that's available to me is boring little jobs in offices or supermarkets. Then I thought, why not make a job out of the things I do at home anyway?' The business set up focused on selling quirky vintage finds and shabby chic soft furnishings.

Women face significant barriers to starting a business: access to finance, fear of debt, perceived high risk of running a business, significant time commitments competing with caring responsibilities of parents and children, and finally a lack of self-confidence that the business will be successful (Allen et al. 2007).

Within the sectors, both men and women were more likely to be entrepreneurs in the consumer sector, as opposed to extractive (farming, forestry, fishing, and mining), transforming

Mini-Case 15.5 The Women's Organisation: a social enterprise creating entrepreneurs with clear organizational values

The Women's Organisation (formerly Train 2000) was established in 1996, as a non-profit distributing social enterprise, in order to promote a range of high quality business support services for women. The founder members, drawn from the voluntary, private, and education sectors, recognized that the existing business support provision failed to recognize the specific needs of women seeking self-employment as it was mainly inaccessible and inappropriate. Their vision of an integrated business support service laid the foundations for the way in which services are now delivered, and has enabled it to be recognized as one of the leading women's enterprise development organizations in the UK.

Mission and Objectives: The Women's Organisation (formally Train 2000) seeks to be an innovative organization that provides quality enterprise and employment services for women and influences policy in order to improve the economic position of all women. This mission is achieved in three key ways:

1. Through providing a range of quality, client sensitive enterprise and employment services for women in Merseyside.

2. By influencing local, regional, national and international policy, and practices in the area of women's economic development.

3. By developing and maintaining The Women's Organisation as a sustainable organization able to achieve its mission.

All of The Women's Organisation's activities are underpinned by their organizational values, which are:

To be inclusive, recognizing the needs of individual women and particularly ensuring that we reach and respect the needs of disadvantaged and underrepresented women.

To be innovative, continually improving the way we work and provide services by incorporating new ideas, information and methods.

To work in partnership, adding value to what we do by working with others to build trust, develop mutual understanding and through reciprocal actions develop social capital.

To strive for quality, committing the organisation to improvement and high standards in all aspects of its activities and working environment.

(*Source:* <www.train2000.org.uk>)

Question

Is it only social enterprises that need to consider their underpinning values?

(manufacturing and construction), and business services. Fewer than half the males work in the consumer sector whereas nearly two thirds of women do. Of women entrepreneurs, 48% own a business in the service sector, compared with 36% of male entrepreneurs. Their competitive edge is achieved by offering a product or service unfamiliar to the market. They are more likely than male businesses to be offering a product or service to the market that has been developed in the last year and to use technology in their products or services (Harding et al. 2004). Tracey Powell, who founded Tiger Bay Beverages in 2001, spent two years developing a range of smoothies and juices. 'We needed a unique selling point, and set upon extending the shelf life, to avoid wastage without adding preservatives' (Enterprise Insight 2005).

Women's businesses can often be found in traditional female areas such as retail, catering, and caring professions, which are often lower paid sectors (Allen et al. 2007). These are the sectors where women have traditionally been employed and which they know best; however, this is also an area that lacks investment opportunities and therefore female businesses can be categorized as 'undercapitalized'.

Women entrepreneurs tended to have smaller and less diverse networks than their male counterparts (see Figure 15.10). They were more inclined to seek guidance from family, especially spouses. Men on the other hand, sought the advice of friends as well as business colleagues, and professional advisors.

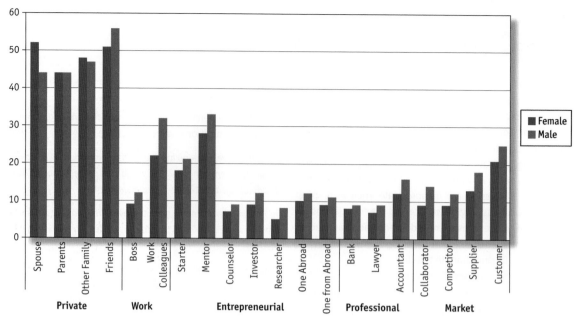

Figure 15.10 Sources of advice for female and male entrepreneurs and business owners in 37 economies, 2009–2010

Source: Data from Levie et al. 2012.

Why fewer women than men start businesses: A summary

There are broad similarities between men and women in their characteristics in starting a business—however; research shows that differences can be seen in:

1. fear of failure (women may feel that the risk they are undertaking by starting a business will impact directly upon those they have direct caring responsibilities for—children or elderly);

2. lower perception of women's skills (support to start-up); and

3. lack of experience (glass ceiling; lack of promotion; and limited opportunities).

There are three key ingredients, which can support any entrepreneur, but particularly women, to develop their potential:

1. creating the right environment: This is creating a focus on women's needs, which may mean providing support to build confidence;

2. encouraging personal growth by recognizing all the assets a female entrepreneur offers and developing them together:

   • Human assets—skills; experiences; know-how; attitude

   • Natural assets—location

   • Financial assets—financial support; money

   • Physical assets—equipment, property; land

   • Social assets—sources of help; knowledge of who can help; networks; family; friends (Ref: Richardson, P. 1998); and

3. an understanding and perspective: An appreciation of the barriers that face women, as well as the aspects that tend to limit female businesses.

(DTI 2003)

Black and minority ethnic (BME) entrepreneurs

BME businesses can appear to be generally dependent upon their local market, and this apparent inability to trade beyond the local area places significant constraints upon their growth. The BME target group is perceived as being hard to reach, socially excluded, and living in areas of multiple deprivations where language and culture are either misrepresented or misunderstood. The traditional links into business through local councils, the Chamber of Commerce, and business support agencies are not normally accessed. Self-employment rates are among the highest in Pakistani, Indian, and Chinese groups and lowest in the Black group (Caribbean and African).

Some ethnic minority groups display higher than average levels of self-employment. There are estimated to be 275,000 BME SMEs in the UK, contributing £20 billion to the UK economy each year. They make up 6% of all SMEs across a diverse range of industries (BIS 2009). The experience of all ethnic minorities is not the same and the self-employment rate of ethnic minority males (11.2%) is lower than for white males (12.4%), and female self-employment among ethnic minorities is lower (3.5%) than among white females (4.5%). However, whilst Chinese (8.7%) and Indian (5.2%) females have higher self-employment rates than white females, Pakistanis (1.9%) do not. The position of the Pakistani female (1.9%) to male (14.2%) ratio is notable. This level represents just 13%, whereas the Chinese (53%),[9] Indian (36%), and white (36%) levels are significantly higher (SBS 2002).

Why is this so? Mascarenhas-Keyes (2006) believes that female BME figures should be treated with some caution as they are unlikely to capture the invisible work undertaken by ethnic minority women, notably the true extent to which women within the South Asian communities participate in business, and their pivotal roles in management (Fielden and Dawe 2005; Phizacklea and Ram 1996). This work indicates broad trends but perhaps does not reveal the unique experiences of entrepreneurship and business ownership among ethnic minority women. The potential contribution of ethnic minority entrepreneurs to the regeneration of inner cities, confirmed by national data, is significant (Deakins and Freel 2003).

Successful BME development has been achieved through specialization available in expanding niche markets. Even though writers have claimed BMEs have the advantages of informal networks to access informal sources of finance and family labour (Deakins and Freel 2003), there is a need to develop an infrastructure to support them and their communities, by promoting and supporting work with young people to build their confidence, and encourage the development of their enterprise and personal leadership skills. The support available for all business start-ups and existing businesses (business planning, assistance and skills, marketing advice, access to funding, legal advice) has to be sensitively delivered to meet the needs of this group.

Graduate entrepreneurs

A view from the UK: the NCEE

The National Centre for Entrepreneurship in Education (NCEE) (formerly trading as the National Council for Graduate Entrepreneurship) was created in 2004.

It has the aims of:

- raising the profile of entrepreneurship in education across the FE and HE sectors;
- stimulating cultural change in institutions to create environments in which entrepreneurial aspiration and endeavour can flourish and is encouraged;

---

[9] These figures are calculated by dividing the female self-employment rates by the male rates.

- institutional capacity building through staff development opportunities for embedding enterprise and entrepreneurship opportunities within the educational experience;
- and supporting the option of starting a business or a new venture as a future life choice amongst students, graduates and staff.

<www.ncee.org.uk>

The entrepreneurial graduate is critical to the success of major economies across the world. In a knowledge economy, the higher-level skills of graduates are essential to the development of new jobs and industries as well as the creation and development of new businesses. Higher education needs to ensure that it supports graduates to be enterprising in their careers, to create intrapreneurs and entrepreneurs of the future. Research in the UK (NCGE 2006) suggests that graduates tend to start businesses in response to interest or a contract from a client (a 'first sale') and this first opportunity is often not planned for, but responded to. From this first bold move, a business often develops and formalizes and the stages of development then unfold. This more complex less distinct approach to business start-up is likely to be the experience of most start-ups, not just graduates, as these phases of start-up can be interlinked.

A view from the UK: graduates given a 'flying start'

Chris Quickfall, a BEng Mechanical Engineering graduate from Northumbria University co-founded Invate with business partner Sheldon Gold in 2006. The company was founded on a desire to improve on the technological support he was offered as a dyslexic learner while at university. Invate Ltd is now a leading assistive-technology supplier and developer based in the North-East and expanding nationally. Through Flying Start, Chris gained industry contacts and knowledge, and found networking with likeminded entrepreneurs boosted his enthusiasm to set up his business.

<www.invate.co.uk>

Nin Castle, a Fashion and Business Studies Degree graduate from the University of Brighton started Goodone with business partner Phoebe Emerson to design and produce high quality, unique clothing, made from new sustainable fibres and up-cycled fabrics. They participated in the NCGE-RSA (the Royal Society for the Encouragement of Arts, Manufactures and Commerce) Flying Start Design Programme, which provided Goodone with initial business support and networking opportunities. Goodone trades online as well as through several stockists nationally and internationally. Phoebe left the company to pursue her own projects, but Goodone continues to grow and gain international recognition in the world of fashion.

<www.goodone.co.uk>

Do you think you could start up? Look at <http://www.flyingstartonline.com/> for help and support.

Family firms are important

The European Commission (2008), acknowledge that family firms are important, because they make an essential contribution to the economy, through the long-term stability they bring, the specific commitment they show to local communities, the responsibility they feel as owners, and the values they stand for. Family businesses make up more than 60% of all European companies, encompassing a vast range of firms of different sizes and from different sectors. Most SMEs (especially micro and small enterprises) are family businesses and a large majority of family companies are SMEs.

Many of the challenges faced by family businesses also concern SMEs in general. However, some affect family firms more specifically, and others are exclusive to them. The European Commission (2008) maintain that some challenges stem from the environment in which those enterprises operate, for example, policy-making are unaware of the specificities of family businesses and their economic and social contribution.[10] Some are related to the family firm's internal matters in balancing the family, ownership, and business aspects within the enterprise; and other issues relate to both the environment and internal matters, for instance, (lack of) entrepreneurship education and family-business-specific management training (European Commission 2008).

▥ **Looking ahead**

Politically how will the various governments cope?

These are challenging times. The world is going through a painful and fundamental readjustment of a model of global growth that was badly broken. The government in 2010 inherited a huge budget deficit which they addressed by making significant cuts in capital spending, infrastructure, and public sector employment, without protecting front line jobs and social services. For example, women in the Northeast bore the brunt of the cuts (O'Hara 2012) and economic conditions for growth were not produced. Even now, public expenditure is still too large in relation to the economy's sustainable tax base, hence the deficit (Smith 2012) with half of Britain's population a burden on the state (Grimston 2012).

The UK Prime Minister acknowledged that, 'the future of our economy depended on a generation of entrepreneurs coming up with ideas, resolving to make them a reality and having the vision to create wealth and jobs. I know how free thinking, inventive and enterprising the British people are so I'm confident about the future' (Cameron 2010). More recently Lord Green (2012), a Trade and Investment Minister, announced that the 'UK Government intended to become a more export orientated economy; rebalancing the economy away from debt fuelled spending to investment. Exports will be crucial towards achieving long term sustainable economic growth.'

Yet has the current government successfully accomplished its goal? Even though there have been tax breaks on investing in new companies and national insurance holidays (Hargrave 2012a) many industrialists and business people want more decisive action to overcome faltering growth, high unemployment levels and poor prospects. They see their salvation in the need to promote the country's entrepreneurial spirit by making it easier to set up business in the UK. Existing costs and rules too often hamper the activities of start-ups and small businesses (Mactaggart 2012). Paphitis is very clear that SMEs will pull the country out of recession yet are receiving no help from the government. He says that, 'Politicians are peddling schemes they claim will fuel a recovery, leaving the SMEs no option but to fend for themselves. As for the High Street, the recession has hit these hard' (Hargrave 2012). Paphitis is clear that a key problem has been the actions of leaders in planning departments and planning authorities. His message is that growth will only come through one's own sheer determination and hard graft, a passion for business and being truly driven to succeed.

---

[10] Such as financial issues related to gift and inheritance tax, access to finance without losing control of the firm, favourable tax treatment of reinvested profits.

Mactaggart (2012) agrees that, 'growth and job creation is going to come primarily from SMEs rather than corporates. However, starting a business demands serious commitment of time, often money, and isn't a route for everyone.'

As explained earlier the 'entrepreneurial environment' refers to the overall economic, socio-cultural, and political factors that influence people's willingness and ability to undertake entrepreneurial activities. It also refers to the availability of assistance and support services that facilitate the start-up and growth process. If entrepreneurship can be encouraged, what is the government's position? Should it provide initiatives to encourage enterprise and, if so, which ones? Should disadvantaged groups be supported to start up?

Will appropriate support, advice and funding be provided?

There is considerable debate about the type of businesses to be supported and to what extent. Should they be community based social enterprises or those driven totally by profit? Some commentators wish to see economic impact, whilst others link performance to social, environmental, intellectual, political, and economic factors. Those seeking economic returns support high impact, high growth, and high technology organizations, whilst community voices support a broad spread ranging from social and low-level service operations to larger economic concerns. The government's role is one of intervening where market failure might exist and the private sector might not invest.

The UK government recognizes the importance of the SME sector and has sought to embrace it within its economic policy (HM Treasury 2011). The Department for Business, Innovation & Skills (BIS) has lead responsibility for small business and enterprise policy and works across Whitehall and key delivery partners to ensure that they understand and respond to the needs of entrepreneurs and small businesses, as well as implementing its new 'Plan for Growth' (HM Treasury 2011). To support this, it has published *Bigger, Better Business: Helping small firms start, grow and prosper* (BIS 2011). Its vision for business growth:

> we will provide: Online business information and tools tailored to each business' needs; a national contact centre to help businesses who cannot find the information they need on the web or who are not connected to the internet; help for start-ups, including, a network of at least 40,000 experienced business mentors offering practical advice; Business Coaching for Growth, backing high growth SMEs to enable them to realise their potential; and tailored action to raise low entrepreneurial activity among key parts of our communities, including women, Black, Asian and Minority Ethnic groups and Service leavers and the new Enterprise Allowance.

> (BIS 2011, p. 4)

Over the last three decades small firms' policy has oscillated from growth to start-up businesses, from specific to generic support, from personal one-to-one support to web-based information, through to gap filling. Several commentators (Storey 1994; Bennett 1996; Curran 2000; Greene et al. 2008; Bridge et al. 2009) have raised concerns about the rationale for the selected provision, quality, appropriateness, evaluation, and impact of small business support. The government sought to intervene where it thought it was appropriate and when it could achieve maximum economic impact. This did not necessarily mean that all parties in the economy were treated equally by the state. It sought to maximize gap filling by targeting certain groups (clusters, deprivation areas, uncompetitive regions) and implementing policy initiatives that supported disadvantaged and under-represented groups and those which addressed social inequality. What is clear now is that important questions needed to be asked and resolved. There is still a need to build an enterprise culture, encourage a more dynamic start-up market, and build the capability for small business growth. There is a recognition that access to finance and support needs to be improved and, as we have seen, that more enterprises in disadvantaged communities need to be encouraged.

The Government profess that they are creating opportunities for businesses to grow and flourish by providing access to finance. Prisk (2012), Minister of State for Business and Enterprise, announced, 'the Enterprise Finance Guarantee (EFG) will be extended to make £2 bn of loan guarantees available to viable small firms through to 2014.' New accredited lenders could also offer EFG funding to SME businesses and that access to finance should come from a range of sources. In late 2011 the government launched a new £50 million Business Angel Co-Investment Fund, supported through the Regional Growth Fund. 'This fund would receive equal or better matched funding from partner business angel investors to establish an overall fund size of over £100 million.'

Even though the effort is there, the commitment by the banks to the government's lending target to small firms, Project Merlin, whereby the high street banks are expected to support small firms, has under-delivered its lending target by £1.1 bn (Hurley 2012). Branson (2012) confirmed that 'getting business funding is difficult. Banks are less willing to lend to SMEs and businesses need to find a way round that.' Perhaps this is one of the reasons why more SME owners are becoming self-financing with personal savings the most likely source of working capital. The majority of businesses therefore are concentrating on their core activities before they venture further afield. Will that be sufficient or will government have to intervene?

In the past, the EU has supplied financial support to under-performing regions to stimulate economic and social activities; however, post economic crisis, national budgets which support entrepreneurship, a potential economic driver to prosperity, have been reviewed. What appears to have happened is that the private sector has been expected to fill the void. Continuous investment in innovation and enhanced skills among the SME workforce and graduates will be required together with a supportive business environment. These elements will be vital to consolidating and enhancing the competitiveness of UK businesses in key sectors and markets at home and overseas. Our future prosperity appears to be in the entrepreneurs' hands.

■ Summary

- The term *enterprise* is used in many ways and can refer to:
  - profit making or a mission to change society
  - an activity or a set of skills
  - a venture or project
  - a small business or SME.
- An *entrepreneur* is an individual who has ideas and makes them happen.
- Enterprise activity (innovation and creativity), when displayed in a large corporation, is described as 'intrapreneurial'.
- A *small business* can be described as 'a business with fewer than 50 employees' (Small Business Service DTI 2004).
- Values can provide a business with competitive advantage, if clear and promoted to the customer, but all business activity can be seen as the result of values.

- The government supports the idea that innovation, creativity, and enterprise can be encouraged and runs social programmes to support under-represented groups to start businesses or social ventures.

- An SME can be thought of as undergoing several stages of development, but the entrepreneur may not recognize them as separate phases.

- Each of these stages calls upon different skills within the entrepreneur and it is important that this is recognized to ensure that the business can grow.

Case Study: The female entrepreneur (interview)

Background:

The company, a digital data and network provider, distributes digital data online, anywhere in the world, with total security and management, and 24/7 support and resilience. It provides leading software and advanced network management solutions that substantially increase efficiency and reduce cost. The female managing director is married and 35 years old.

Her background:

I've got an engineering father and an artist of a mother. My inspiration has been my grandfather, who used to be managing director of Ford Motor Company. I chose a business studies degree, sponsored by the De La Rue Group, security printers. They expected me to work for them six months every year during my placement periods. After graduation, I joined Crossfield Electronics, one of their companies in the printing/publishing division. I went round the world with them and met everyone in the company. I changed jobs every year and after ten years became a director. One of my strengths is marketing. I ran my own business unit and obtained experience of running my own team, sourcing and developing products and meeting sales and profit targets. All of this was supported by the plc.

I left them and worked as a director for Fuji responsible for technology product management and distributors worldwide. Opportunities to develop a distributive managed network for the printing industry culminated in a strategic alliance and joint venture with British Telecom and Cytex. With their financial backing, I was offered a directorship and the opportunity to set up the business. It was exactly what I was looking for. They asked me to write a business plan, decide space, equipment and financial requirements, how many staff, the business objectives, and determine the strategy. I'm used to managing my own domain, taking decisions and seeing the way that I'd like my company to go. I see myself as a leader—an inspirationalist.

Product/market interface:

It's never easy to identify gaps in the marketplace. The hardest thing is being the leader because you spend substantial sums

of money developing the marketplace only to find competitors entering the market and eroding your share and profitability. For three years, we spent substantial sums building the marketplace. My experience is in the digital printing process market, from computer to plate—taking digital data and writing it immediately onto the printing plate. The technology has been around for 15 years. It took ten years for the market to understand the benefits. In order to get ahead and stay ahead of the market you need to be a big company with deep pockets to get a huge return. If you are a small business with minimal backing, it's a big risk. We were too advanced for the market and ran out of money before the market was ready to adopt the product. Customers were not ready for the new technology or concept. Sometimes it's better to be a follower rather than a leader. Perhaps it's better to go into an informed market so that you can differentiate what makes your product offering special. It's a huge effort to create, define, and establish market need.*

Change of direction/triggers for change—management buyout:

At this point the major investors decided not to invest any more money and withdrew all support. I decided to review my position and consider a management buyout using venture capital finance.

Standards within and education of the market is crucial:

Standards and quality are essential within this environment. We have built our product into an industry standard called job definition format—an open interface that can interchange with 72 other vendor products. I chair one of the industry standards committees.

We have customized our software to enable our customers to put their own branding on it. With customized fields we can manage their processes effectively and independently, process more data from all of our customers and allow the customer to track and effect changes to design and content of their material. The printing and publishing industry is focused on speed, costs out, and quality. Removing manual processes and errors is crucial. That's what we do.

Our entry into the market was four years later than our major competitor. We ran a system with central managed servers rather than putting distributed servers on every customer's site. This reduced costs. Central databases are at the heart of our processes. We are now quicker on upgrades, managing our customer solutions, and open to new ideas. Our speed of response gives us competitive edge.

Barriers to success:

As a woman, you are going to hit a lot of walls. You just have to work around them and prove that you are good. It's very challenging in a technology world. They think you are a secretary and you don't know a lot. That kind of attitude makes me so driven that I almost over-prove nearly everything I do. You just carry on doing your job, you do it well and you don't make a big thing of being a woman. You just say I'm a businessperson, and I'm good. Macho doesn't work. Show vulnerability. Play to your strengths—women's skills, use charm. I've had endless help throughout my career and I still get it. Women aren't scared to ask for help so they get people to help them. I've built up a huge support network.

Running the business:

Really believe in what you do. You have to have a passion to do it because it's hard work. You will hit lots of highs and lows. There's a lot of unpredictability in setting up your business. You should surround yourself with good people. Get a good core team in place. People are crucial. It's all to do with reputation and networking. All the staff have a passion for the business and an understanding of the market. They have contacts, which enable us to recruit new staff and reach new customers.

When you are running a small business, everyone has to be prepared to do everything. We were looking for staff that has core skills. The operations team requires technical competence. Our development team is based in Israel and we have sales teams in the USA, Paris, and London. We are looking for people who'll get on in the team and who believe in what they are doing and are hard working. We often have to ask people to go home because we all work round the clock. For the first three years, I worked 20-hour days, six days a week. You can't walk out on it—it's part of you. The management team set the standards, build the culture and set the field for the business. Either new people fit in or they don't. If they don't they go.

A successful business is one where you have the right product in the right market delivered at the right time. It has to have unique selling points. There has to be a significant potential market opportunity. The quality of the staff is important. This company only develops because of the people in it. Ensure you have the right people, the right quality of service and the right product.

Monitoring and control:

We always track the following week by week: our sales forecast, the costs within the business, and cash flow. We are always on target with our costs. Because customers are unpredictable, sales are more difficult—we have a hard and soft sales forecast pipeline. Hard forecasts are customers who have actual proposals where we are 50% certain of closure. We have a weighted forecast to account for unpredictability. We always assume that some customers will have a 40% chance of closure in this month whereas others might be a 100% chance. The weighted average reflects this and revenue is made up from hard and soft forecasts. From this, we set revenue and cost targets. Keep an eye on your cash! Look after it. Get a good accountant or accounting system. If you are not collecting your money in, you're likely to get bad debts.

Venture capitalists' expectations:

A venture capitalist is the majority shareholder, but they have left the management team with a sizeable stake of the business so that we are motivated to run it. Don't ever expect money for nothing. You have to put your life on the line; you have to indemnify the business. You have to put your own money in, whether that's mortgaging your house or your car. They expect a commitment that proves you believe in that business as much as you say you do.

Venture capitalists always discuss their exit. Before they put their money in, they want to know how they will get their money back. They will ask you for the names of your competitors. Would they be interested in buying you out? Are there any other industry players that would be interested in buying your type of technology to complement their own solutions? They are always looking for potential buyers who might have an interest in your type of business. They look at the return on their investment because if they can get a good return going forward they'll keep investing, particularly if they can see significant growth potential. Our venture capitalist was very interested that our technology is transferable—possible to get a quicker return on their money if the core investment was transferable to other sectors.

The future:

In five years time we will be in more countries and moving into other sectors. There's always that sense of adventure and the challenge of making it happen.

Questions

1. What kind of entrepreneur is talking and what qualities does she have?

2. What skill development has taken place during the growth of the business?

3. How has the business chosen to compete and what is its competitive edge?

Review and discussion questions

1. What do you understand by the term 'enterprise'—how do you define it?

2. Explain the difference between being a serial entrepreneur and a small business owner-manager.

3. What is the difference between a micro business and a medium-sized business?

4. What stages of growth might an entrepreneur experience in developing a business?

5. Illustrate, with examples, how an entrepreneur's values can provide competitive advantage to a small business.

6. Are entrepreneurs 'born' with the necessary skills or can they be 'created'? If the latter, then what are the conditions that need to exist to develop an entrepreneurial environment?

Assignments

1. *Skills*: You are thinking about becoming an entrepreneur but need to understand whether you have the skills to start up a business on your own, or whether you should create a team with broader skills. Undertake a self-analysis of your current skills and either devise a personal development plan to gain the additional skills you might need to start a new venture, or indicate the skills you need in additional team member(s).

2. *Supporting new and under-represented groups to start a business*: Conduct some research on your local area, using the Internet to look at a local enterprise support organization site or local government site to find out where areas of need or deprivation are within your region. Suggest some activities that could help people in these areas start their own businesses if they wanted to.

3. *Understanding entrepreneurs*: Find a local entrepreneur to interview, or choose a famous one from the list below and use the Internet to try to understand the following:
What type of entrepreneur are they?
What sector do they work in?
How many businesses or business ideas have they had?
What stage of growth is their business in now?
How have their values impacted upon their business?
Suggestions of entrepreneurs to study include: Stelios Haji-Ioannou; Jamie Oliver; Bill Gates; Alan Sugar; James Dyson; Anita Roddick; and Richard Branson.

Further reading

These books encourage and develop entrepreneurship skills. There are chapters on family and international businesses and on social entrepreneurship. They also have additional mini and long case studies.

Burns, P. (2010) *Entrepreneurship and Small Business: Start-up, Growth and Maturity*, 3rd edn (Basingstoke: Palgrave Macmillan).

Southon, M. and West, C. (2008) *The Beermat Entrepreneur: Turn your Good Idea into a Great Business* (Harlow: Pearson).

Burke, R. (2006) *Small Business Entrepreneur—guide to running a business* (Burke Publishing).

online resource centre   Test your understanding of this chapter with online questions and answers, explore the subject further through web exercises, and use the web links to provide a quick resource for further research. Go to the Online Resource Centre at <www.oxfordtextbooks.co.uk/orc/wetherly_otter/2>

Useful websites

Business in You: <www.businessinyou.bis.gov.uk>
Highlights best advice, resources, and tools available from across government and the world of business, making it easy for SMEs to find out what they need. It includes advice on mentoring, employment, exporting, and access to finance.

British Chambers of Commerce: <http://www.britishchambers.org.uk/>
The British Chambers of Commerce comprise nationally a network of quality-accredited Chambers of Commerce, all uniquely positioned at the heart of every business community in the UK.

Confederation of British Industry:
The CBI is a vital source of expert advice and information, and a forum for the generation of ideas, best practice exchange, and high-powered networking.

Federation of Small Businesses:
The FSB is the largest campaigning pressure group promoting and protecting the interests of the self-employed and owners of small firms.

Forum of Private Business: <www.fpb.co.uk>
The FPB helps its members cope with day-to-day problems by influencing laws and policies affecting businesses and supporting their profitability.

Institute of Directors:
As a worldwide association of members, the Institute of Directors (IoD) provides a network that reaches into every corner of the business community.

National Enterprise Network: <http://www.nationalenterprisenetwork.org/>
The National Enterprise Network is the membership body for those committed to the support and development of enterprise. Members are not-for-profit organizations committed to providing impartial and independent advice, training, and mentoring to start-up and emerging businesses.

Business Link: <https://www.gov.uk/business-support-helpline>
Business Link is the national business advice service.

Chambers of Commerce: <http://www.britishchambers.org.uk/>
Chambers of Commerce is a useful contact to provide information on conferences, exhibitions, registers, publications, training and legal advice.

Companies House: <http://www.companieshouse.gov.uk/>
Companies House is the government agency responsible for company registration in Great Britain.

Department for Business, Innovation and Skills <https://www.gov.uk/government/organisations/department-for-business-innovation-skills>
The Department for Business, Innovation & Skills works with a wide range of individuals, groups and organizations to promote trade, boost innovation and help people to start and grow a business.

Department for Work and Pensions:
This site offers help for unemployed people including support for self-employment.

References

Allen, I. E., Langowitz, N., Elam, A., and Dean, M. (2007) 'Global Entrepreneurship Monitor' (GEM) 2007 Report on Women and Entrepreneurship, (Boston: GEM, Babson).

American Heritage Directory (1992) 3rd edn (Boston: Houghton Mifflin).

Armitstead, L. (2010) 'UK bosses anger over as decade of decline', *Daily Telegraph,* 25 October 2010.

Armstrong S (2012) 'Mobile Business', *Raconteur,* distributed by *The Sunday Times,* London, 2 December 2012.

Barclays (2009) 'Small firms in Britain, 2009: A review by Barclays Local Business' (London: Barclays Bank).

Bell, K. (2012) 'Trust the professionals', *Ingenious Britain,* 8 July 2012, ISSN 2049-7644 (London: Inteligis Group Limited).

Bennett, R. J. (1996) 'SMEs and Public Policy; Present Dilemmas, Future Priorities and the Case of Business Links', presented at the ISBA National Small Firms Policy and Research Conference in Leeds, UK.

Branson, R. (2012) cited in Mactaggart (2012) 'Vision, Excitement and Fun', *Ingenious Britain,* 8 July 2012, ISSN 2049-7644 (London: Intelligis Group Limited).

Bridge, S., O'Neill, K., and Martin, F. (2009), *Understanding Enterprise* (Basingstoke: Palgrave).

Britten, N. (2010) 'Pub pulling diners more than pints', *The Guardian*, 27 November 2010.

Burns, P. (2008) *Corporate Entrepreneurship* (Basingstoke: Palgrave).

BIS (2009) 'SME Business BarometerJune 2009', IFF Research Ltd, August 2009, (London: Department of Business, Innovation & Skills).

BIS (2010) 'Social Enterprise Barometer 2010', IFF Research Ltd, February 2010, URN 10/1076 (London: Department of Business, Innovation & Skills).

BIS (2011) 'Bigger, Better Business: Helping small firms start, grow and prosper', January 2011, URN 11/515, (London: Department of Business, Innovation & Skills).

BIS (2011a) 'BIS Small Business Survey 2010', IFF Research Ltd, April 2011, URN 11/P74 (Sheffield: Department of Business, Innovation & Skills).

BIS (2011b) 'Estimates for Women-led, Minority Ethnic Group (MEG) led and Social Enterprises in the UK', produced by BIS Enterprise Directorate, URN 11/1077 (London: Department of Business, Innovation & Skills).

BIS (2012) 'Business population estimates for the UK and Regions 2012, Statistical Release', 17 October 2012 (London: Department for Business, Innovation & Skills).

BIS (2012a) 'Benchmarking UK Competitiveness in the Global Economy', BIS Economics Paper no. 19 (London: Department for Business, Innovation & Skills).

Cabinet Office (2006) 'Social Enterprise Action Plan 2006'. <**www.cabinetoffice.gov.uk**>

Cameron, D. (2010) Foreword: The future of our economy depends on a new generation of entrepreneur', Global Entrepreneurship Week 2010: UK Impact Report.

Chrisman, J. J., Bauerschmidt, A., and Hofer, C. W. (1998) 'The determinants of new venture performance: an extended model', *Entrepreneurship Theory and Practice*, Fall: 5–30.

Churchill, N. C., and Lewis, V. I. (1983) 'The Five Stages of Small Business Growth', *Harvard Business Review*, May/June.

Cooper, K. (2012) 'Online up to 4 times cheaper than stores', *The Sunday Times*, 16 September 2012.

Cowling, M. (2003) 'The Contribution of the Self-Employed to Employment in the EU', report to the Small Business Service URN 03/539, at <**http://berr.gov.uk/files/file38300.pdf**>

Curran, J. (2000) 'What is the Small Business Policy in the UK for?', *International Small Business journalArticle*, 18 (3): 61–71.

Deakins, D. and Freel, M. (2003) *Entrepreneurship and Small Firms* (Maidenhead: McGraw-Hill Education).

Drucker, P. (1985) *Innovation and Entrepreneurship—Practice and Principles* (Oxford: Butterworth-Heinemann).

DTI (2003) 'A Government Action Plan for Small Business: the Evidence Base', URN 04/517 (London: DTI).

DTI (2004) *The Case for Women's Enterprise* (London: DTI/Prowess).

Economist (2012) 'Battle of the internet giants: Survival of the biggest', *The Economist*, 1 December 2012, p. 13.

Enterprise Insight (2005) 'The Enterprise Report 2005: Making Ideas Happen Summary', <**http://www.mbsportal.bl.uk/secure/subjareas/smlbusentrep/enterprise%20UK/113790enterprise05summary.pdf**>

European Commission (2005) 'The new SME definition: User guide and model declaration', European Commission (Brussels: Enterprise and Industry Publications).

European Commission (2008) 'Overview of family business relevant issues: Research, networks, policy measures and existing studies' (Vienna: European Commision) <**http://ec.europa.eu/enterprise/policies/sme/files/craft/family_business/doc/familybusiness_study_en.pdf**>

Fielden, S. L. and Dawe, A. J. (2005) 'The Experiences of Asian Women Entering Business Start-up in the UK', eScholarID:3b4979 (Cheltenham: Edward Elgar).

Gartner (2012) cited in Armstrong, S. (2012) Mobile Business, *Raconteur*, distributed by *The Sunday Times*, London, 2 December 2012.

Gibb, A. (1996) 'Entrepreneurship and small business management: can we afford to neglect them in the twenty-first century business school?' *British Journal of Management*, 7(4): 309–21.

Gibb, A. (1999) 'Creating an entrepreneurial culture in support of SMEs', *Small Enterprise Development, An International Journal*, 10(4): 27–38.

Gibb, A. and Ritchie, J. (1982) 'Understanding the processes of starting small businesses', *European Journal of Small Business*, 6: 70–80.

Green (2012) A marathon not a sprint, *Ingenious Britain*, 8 July 2012, ISSN 2049-7644 (London: Inteligis Group Limited).

Greene, F.J., Mole, K.F., and Storey, D.J., (2008) *Three Decades of Enterprise Culture* (Basingstoke: Palgrave).

Grimston, J. (2012) 'Half of Britain is burden on state', *The Sunday Times*, London, 17 October 2012.

Harding, R. (2002) *Global Entrepreneurship Monitor 2002* (London: London Business School).

Harding, R. (2004) *Global Entrepreneurship Monitor 2004*, (London: London Business School).

Harding, R., (2006) 'U.K. Social Entrepreneurs: Specialist Summary', Global Entrepreneurship Monitor, <**www.gemconsortium.org/**>.

Harding, R., (2007) 'U.K. Global Entrepreneurship Monitor', Global Entrepreneurship Monitor, <**www.gemconsortium.org/**>.

Harding et al. (2004) *Achieving the Vision: Female Entrepreneurship* (British Chambers of Commerce).

Harding et al. (2008) 'U.K. Global Entrepreneurship Monitor, Focus on Female Entrepreneurs', <**www.gemconsortium.org/**>.

Hargrave, S. (2012) 'Success is down to us alone', *Ingenious Britain*, 8 July 2012, ISSN 2049-7644 (London: Inteligis Group Limited).

Hargrave S (2012a) 'Launching young entrepreneurs', *Ingenious Britain*, 8 July 2012, ISSN 2049-7644 (London: Inteligis Group Limited).

Hartshorn, C. and Richardson, P. (1993) 'Business start up training: the gender dimension', in Allen, S. and Truman, C. (eds), *Women in Business: Perspectives on Women Entrepreneurs* (London: Routledge).

Hatten, T. S. (2012) *Principles of Small Business Management*, *International Edition* (Cengage Learning).

HM Government (2009) 'New Industry, New Jobs: Building Britain's Future' (London: Department for Business, Enterprise, and Regulatory Reform).

HM Treasury (2008) 'Enterprise: Unlocking the UK's talent', (London: HM Treasury).

HM Treasury (2011) 'The Plan for Growth', March 2011 (London: HM Treasury and The Department for Business Innovation and Skills).

Hurley, J. (2012) 'No grey areas for investment firm for student entrepreneurs', *The Guardian*, 14 February 2012.

Jack, S. and Anderson, A. (1999) 'Enterprise education within the enterprise culture', *International journalArticle of Entrepreneurial Behaviour and Research*, 5(3): 110–25.

Jones, P. (2010) 'Foreword: The future of our economy depends on a new generation of entrepreneur', Global Entrepreneurship Week 2010: UK Impact Report.

Kelley, D., Singer, S., and Herrington, M. (2012) 'Global Entrepreneurship Monitor: 2011 Global Report' (Babson, Massachusetts: GEM).

Kelley, D., Brush, C., Green, P., Litovsky, Y. (2011) 'Global Entrepreneurship Monitor: 2010 Report: Women Entrepreneurs Worldwide' (Babson, Massachusetts: GEM).

Kuratko, D.F. and Hodgetts, R.M. (2001) *Entrepreneurship–a Contemporary Approach*, 5th edn (New York: Harcourt College).

Lambert (2010) cited in Armitstead, L. (2010) 'UK bosses anger over as decade of decline', *The Daily Telegraph*, 25 October 2010.

Leadbetter, C. (1997) *The rise of the social entrepreneur* (p. 2), Demos, <http://www.demos.co.uk/publications/socialentrepreneur>

Levie, J. and Hart, M. (2009) 'Global Entrepreneurship Monitor: United Kingdom 2008 Monitoring Report', (Glasgow: GEM and Strathclyde Business School).

Levie, J., and Hart, M. (2012) 'Global Entrepreneurship Monitor: United Kingdom 2008 Monitoring Report', (Glasgow: GEM and Strathclyde Business School).

Llewellyn Smith, C. (2009) 'High points of the decade: Technology', *The Observer*, Review section, p. 4, 27 December 2009.

Mactaggart (2012) 'Vision, Excitement and Fun', *Ingenious Britain*, 8 July 2012, ISSN 2049-7644 (London: Inteligis Group Limited).

Mascarenhas-Keyes, S. (2006) 'Ethnic minority small and medium enterprise in England: diversity and challenges', paper presented at Institute for Small Business and Entrepreneurship Conference, Cardiff.

National Council for Graduate Entrepreneurship (NCGE) (2006) 'Career-Making: Graduating into Self-Employment', Leeds Met Human Resource Development Team (Holden, R., Nabi, N. and Walmsley, A. with Harte, V., Jameson, S., Kyriakidou, N. and Price, A.).

O'Hara, M. (2012) 'Women in north east bear brunt of cuts', *The Guardian*, 24 October 2012.

Paphitis, L. (2012) cited in Hargrave, S. (2012) 'Success is down to us alone', *Ingenious Britain*, 8 July 2012, ISSN 2049-7644, (London: Inteligis Group Limited).

Phizacklea, A. and Ram, M. (1995) 'Ethnic Entrepreneurship in Comparative Perspective', *in: International journalArticle of Entrepreneurial Behaviour and Research*, 1, (1).

PowerSwitch (2012) 'Tracking Societal Changes/Impacts high energy costs', <**www.powerswitch.org.uk/forum/viewtopic.php?t=20294&sid**>

Price, A. (1997) 'Corporate social responsibility', in Boddy, D. and Paton, R. (1998) *Management* (Harlow: Prentice Hall).

Prisk, M. (2012) 'Driving the economy forward', *Ingenious Britain*, 8 July 2012, ISSN 2049-7644 (London: Inteligis Group Limited).

Quality Assurance Agency for Higher Education (2012) *Enterprise and entrepreneurship education: Guidance for higher education providers*, QAA 488 09/2012, p. 8, (Gloucester: Quality Assurance Agency for Higher Education).

Quick, C. (2012) 'Compliance Costs, Accounting and Business', June 2012, p. 44, ISSN 1460-406X (London: ACCA).

Quick, C. (2012a) Slow recovery for lending, Accounting and Business', June 2012, p. 45, ISSN 1460-406X (London: ACCA).

Reynolds, P. et al. (2001) 'Global Entrepreneurship Monitor Report 2001' (London: London Business School).

Reynolds, P. et al. (2002) 'Global Entrepreneurship Monitor, 2002 Executive Report' (London: London Business School).

Robertson, M. (2000) 'Business Start Up © Leeds Met Model of Business Start-up', working paper, Leeds Metropolitan University.

SBS (2002) 'Household Survey of Entrepreneurship' (Sheffield: Small Business Service).

SBS (2005) 'Promoting Female Entrepreneurship' (London: Small Business Service).

Schumpeter, J. A. (1936) *The Theory of Economic Development*, 2nd edn (Cambridge MA: Harvard University Press).

Smith, D. (2012) 'Bungled cuts: time to call an expert axeman', *The Sunday Times*, London, 7 October 2012.

Social Enterprise Coalition (2009) State of Social Enterprise, 2009, at <http://www.socialenterprise.org.uk/uploads/files/2011/12/stateofsocialenterprise2009.pdf>

Social Enterprise London (2012) 'London 2012 Conference– creating a lasting legacy', London, 15 March 2011.

Social Enterprise UK (2011), Fightback Britain: A Report on the State of Social Enterprise Survey 2011 at <http://www. socialenterprise.org.uk/uploads/editor/files/Publications/ Fightback_Britain.pdf>

Steiner, G. A. (1979) *Strategic Planning* (New York: Free Press).

Stern, M. (2012) 'Meet the new self employed', *The Guardian*, work section, 3 March 2012.

Stevenson, H. H. (1997) 'Six dimensions of entrepreneurship' in Birley and Muzyka, *Mastering Enterprise* (Harlow: FT Pitman).

Storey, D. (1994) Understanding the Small Business Sector (London: Routledge).

Timmons, J. A. (1989) *The Entrepreneurial Mind* (Andover, Mass: Brick House Publishing)

Terjesen, S., Lepoutre, J., Justo, R., and Bosma, N. (2009) 'Global Entrepreneurship Monitor: Report on Social Entrepreneurship' <www.gemconsortium.org>, <www.gemconsortium.org/>.

UK Commission for Employment and Skills, Meager, N. et al. (2011) *Skills for self-employment: Evidence Report 31*, August 2011.

Williams, M. and Cowling, M. (2009) 'Annual Small Business Survey 2007/8', Institute for Employment Studies (London: Department for Business, Enterprise, and Regulatory Reform).

Wymenga, P., Spanikova, V., Barker, A., Konings, J., and Canton, E., (2012) *EU SMEs in 2012: at the cross roads* (Rotterdam: Ecorys).

Chapter 16
Conclusion: Looking ahead—managing in a dynamic environment

Dorron Otter and Paul Wetherly

Learning objectives

When you have completed this chapter you will be able to:

- Give a broad overview of the likely future trends in the business environment.
- Integrate the main predictions from the 'Looking ahead' sections of the previous chapters.
- Develop your own views as to the changing nature of the business environment.

THEMES

》 DIVERSITY OF BUSINESS

Businesses are diverse but they share the common problem that the future is uncertain. It is important that all businesses are able to try to minimize this uncertainty by looking ahead.

》 INTERNAL/EXTERNAL

Chapter 1 showed us that it was important for businesses to scan the external environment in order to anticipate change. They need to do this if their internal strategies are to be successful.

》 COMPLEXITY OF THE ENVIRONMENT

Despite the environmental uniqueness of a particular business there are general features of the external environment of which all businesses need to be aware.

》 VARIETY OF SPATIAL LEVELS

Globalization and technology are dramatically altering the distance between the spatial levels.

》 DYNAMIC ENVIRONMENT

The one certain thing that can be said about the future is that it will be uncertain and that change is a dynamic process.

》 INTERACTION BETWEEN BUSINESS AND THE ENVIRONMENT

How will businesses manage future changes and in turn what will be their impact on the future of the business environment?

⟫ STAKEHOLDERS

There is an increasing recognition of the impact that individual business decisions have on wider society and a focus on the responsibility of businesses across the full range of stakeholders.

⟫ VALUES

Our reactions to the impact of changes depend in part on our ethical values.

▉ Introduction

⟫ **COMPLEXITY** ⟫ **DYNAMIC** The one thing that business managers would like to have is certainty but in the fast changing and dynamic external environment this is not possible. Therefore, managers need to be able to make decisions based on what they see as the likely conditions that will prevail in the future. While successful businesses will be the ones that are able to exploit their opportunities, they are also the ones which will be able to assess what the likely impacts from the external environment are going to be and plan to either avoid or minimize these risks if they can. Successful business strategy involves effective risk assessment and planning.

The main thrust of this book has been to show that by a careful examination of underlying political, economic, social, and technological factors we can identify important themes and features of the global business environment which can help us to better understand business behaviour in the present, as well as having a tentative stab at predicting future changes.

This chapter will bring together the main outlines of what is likely to happen within the business environment in the next few years. The structure of the book has been designed so that we would first explore the key themes in the external environment. In Chapters 1 through to 8 we explored the traditional PEST factors of the political, economic, social and technological environments and then also highlighted the legal, ethical, and natural environments which have become so important when analysing business behaviour. We then focused on what we see as being the key issues in the external environment for business, and throughout we have sought to integrate the themes that help to conceptualize the global business environment.

Each chapter ended with a short 'Looking ahead' section where we explored the things that are most likely to develop in the future in each of the key issue areas. This chapter seeks to knit together the common threads in these predictions using the general PEST framework and so look ahead to the future trends in the business environment. Having worked through the rest of the book you should be in a position to develop your own views as to the shape of the business environment in general and how this may impact and be affected by individual areas of business activity.

⟫ **INTERACTION** ⟫ **VALUES** The nature of changes in the business environment is itself often contradictory and uncertain. Change can be achingly slow and sometimes extraordinarily rapid. It is difficult to appreciate the changes that are taking place over a long time when we are most often concentrating on the 'noise' of the here and now. There are contradictions in the evidence that we see and, as Chapter 2 showed, not all people see the same evidence and draw the same conclusions.

Stop and Think

Why is it difficult to make predictions in relation to the business environment?

There is a search in academic life for rational explanations for how change occurs and many of us hope that in the end, no matter how 'messy' the environmental influences might be, we will be able to explain why things have occurred and therefore attempt to predict on this basis why things might occur. Equally, there are analysts who argue that we have to accept that we are all living in an uncertain world where the information we have is imperfect and that change will not be rational and predictable. We have also stressed in the book that while we can identify the individual changes in the business environment, in reality many of these operate at the same time and interrelate in complex ways.

In order to get a better idea of the possible future developments in the business environment it is vital to look back into the past, and we did this in Chapter 2 when exploring the evolution of the global economic environment. While the past is not a reliable guide to the future, history does enable us to learn a lot about ourselves. Indeed, the future global business environment will be dominated by attempts to try to secure the stable path of peace and prosperity that was so difficult to achieve in the 20th century. In order to look ahead to the future we need to look back.

When looking ahead we can take varying positions ranging from outright optimism as to what is likely to happen to dire pessimism. It will be interesting to see where you feel you lie on this continuum.

Stop and Think

What are your hopes and fears as to the nature of the future business environment in which you will live and work?

▦ **Looking ahead: the global political environment**

⟫ INTERNAL/EXTERNAL The growing focus on the dangers of too little regulation in terms of top pay and the bonuses being awarded to traders in the financial sector has become a central concern amongst not just policy-making but across the wider society. We explored the issue of regulation in general in Chapter 5 and looked at the wider issue of the need to curb business power in Chapter 11. The battle lines over the nature of the economic environment are still firmly entrenched. We first explored this in Chapter 1 and then outlined the competing views in more detail in Chapter 2. For structuralist and radical critics, the events of the last five years since the global economic crisis of 2008 have shown the need for economies to construct and develop supporting institutions and structures that can guide markets without succumbing to the instability and social divisions that can sometimes exist.

⟫ SPATIAL While even those who argue for a pro-market approach accept the need for greater regulation of the banks, their views are that the greatest challenges facing business both globally and domestically still lie in the profligacy of governments in borrowing too much and in the imbalance between the size of the public sector in relation to the private. Within the business community there is an acknowledgement that with power comes responsibility, but there is a view that this can be achieved with responsible leadership within companies and there is a distrust of regulation. Here then the focus for political change is not at the government level but in the exercise of corporate responsibility (see Chapters 5, 7, and 11).

The battleground for the competing perspectives is fought over this central political issue of the degree and manner in which governments should intervene in the running of an economy. What is clear is that in capitalist economic systems there is a large role for government across a range of microeconomic and macroeconomic policy areas. In terms of microeconomic management, governments seek to intervene directly and indirectly in markets in a large number of ways. Most clearly many governments take a direct role in the provision of key public services such as health, education, and welfare; although the influence of the neoclassical perspective has been seen in the wave of privatizations that have occurred in many countries, and the recent attempts to introduce market processes into areas once thought the preserve of public policy. This was a major focus of Chapter 14.

Despite these differences in approach, and notwithstanding that the process of economic growth has not been stable, since the middle of the of the 20th century the long-term trend has been for rising prosperity in the more developed countries of the world and, encouragingly, there is fast growth now in many emerging countries. However, with this there has been growing concern expressed about the unsustainability of rapid economic growth and a call for a reassessment of prevailing economic models. This green view of economics has grown rapidly so that now, throughout the political spectrum and increasingly within business itself, there is a call to place sustainable development at the heart of debates about the nature of the economic environment. In relation to climate change, Sir Nicholas Stern, a renowned British economist, referred to this as 'the greatest example of market failure ever seen' (Stern 2006). For environmentalists, our current approaches to managing economies have ignored the rapid rate at which we have been using non-renewable resources and the environmental costs of economic activity.

Approaches to regulation are many and varied, but attempt to devise a system that recognizes the inequalities created by the expansion of capitalism, the problems of operating the market in that context, and the inherent instability of the market itself.

Mini-Case 16.1 profiles some of the likely factors that will affect the future global business environment and the relative significance of their impacts.

Mini-Case 16.1   Governing the global business environment

After the Global Financial Crisis in 2008 and the shifts in economic power with the rise in the BRICS, the forum for global coordination moved from the G8 to the G20. The summits that occur each year have highlighted the changes that have taken place at the domestic and global levels but there is general agreement that this is still a work in progress. In particular, despite the acceptance that there is a structural weakness at the heart of the financial system progress has been slow. Within Europe calls for a Financial Transactions Tax to reduce the temptation to engage in the more risky speculative deals have met with resistance from the UK and from the US banks that operate within the EU. The European Central Bank is also proposing placing a ceiling on the bonuses of bankers but, again, this is being resisted by the UK and US.

In 2013 the agenda for the G20 reflected the structuralist arguments about the need to build inclusive institutions at the domestic and global level. The priorities were:

- Developing financial regulation
- Encouraging multilateral trade
- Energy sustainability
- Growth through investment and employment
- Development for all (focusing on the developing world in terms of food security, infrastructure, development of inclusive financial institutions, education, and moving beyond the 2015 Millennium Goals
- Reform of the international financial system and trade reform
- Fighting corruption (including better coordination to stop MNCs being able to undertake tax avoidance). (G20 2013)

At the annual meeting of the 2013 World Economic Forum (WEF) at Davos, which brought together those people from government, business, and civil society with the most power to alter the business environment, the following were seen as priorities: the need to attain global economic stability, the need to reduce income inequality and attain social cohesion, the growing challenge of climate change, and a need to define the values of business (WEF 2013a). The theme of the meeting was 'Resilient Dynamism'; aptly reflecting the

Table 16.1 Global risk assessment

Likelihood	Impact
Severe income disparity	Systemic financial failure
Chronic government fiscal imbalances	Water supply
Rising green house gasses	Chronic government fiscal imbalances
Threats to water supply	Diffusion of weapons of mass destruction
Mismanagement of ageing populations	Failure of climate change adaptation measures

Source: adapted from WEF 2013b.

cautious optimism that lessons were being learned and progress was being made to improve the external environment, although some very real challenges still lie ahead.

In its analysis of the main global risks the World Economic Forum surveyed business managers, asking them to rate the top 50 risks in terms of likelihood of occurring and severity of the impact on business performance if they were to occur. Table 16.1 lists the top 5 in each category.

The survey also showed the fastest risers in the risk ratings were, in terms of likelihood, the unforeseen consequences of developments in life sciences technologies; and in terms of impact, the unforeseen negative consequences of regulation.

It is clear that, while the 2008 crisis has not sounded the death knell for capitalism, there is an acknowledgement of the need to shape the political environment in which to create the conditions for a dynamic business environment.

Questions

1. Why would the business community be so concerned about the impacts as revealed by the WEF survey?

2. How can businesses respond to these risks?

3. Who is responsible for guarding against these risks?

▪ Challenges for the future global political environment

Looking back then across the themes and issues that have emerged in this book we can highlight five main political challenges that lie ahead.

Global and national governance

▶▶ **DIVERSITY** Firstly, we saw in Chapter 10 that there is a need to develop the institutions and rules that will enable all countries to feel that they are able to share in the benefits of a globalized world. Before the 2008 global recession the focus here had been on the global order as being characterized by sharp income inequality, and on the many parts of the world where war, conflict, and political instability exist.

The impact of the world economic crisis has directly led to a realization that if world economic stability is to be achieved it will require the political cooperation of not only the developed countries in the world but also the new and fast rising developing world. The year 2009 marked the historic turning point in geopolitical decision-making, as the G20 replaced the G8 as the highest level of global intergovernmental economic cooperation (see Chapter 8).

Thus, looking ahead, a major focus will be on the development of supranational political and economic institutions to deal with the twin problems of global inequality and global economic instability (ever present without concerted global policy coordination). We have seen in Chapter 13, though, that this is proving to be problematic. In dealing with the problems of recession, countries in the developed world have moved in different directions in terms of economic policy. In the US there has been a move towards Keynesian demand management although this has been limited. In Europe the austerity route has been chosen and this has meant severe hardship in the PIGS (Portugal, Ireland, Greece and Spain) and caused severe political problems. Governments might be democratically elected but they have little room for economic independence. We will explore these economic challenges below. In all likelihood the revised Stability and Growth Pact will lead to greater coordination within the Eurozone countries, and for those countries aligning themselves to the Fiscal Compact, but will also create a 'two speed Europe'.

It is ironic that the parts of the world with the political and economic institutions generally recognized as being the most conducive to ensuring growth and stability are the ones that are mired in low or no growth, and it is in the emerging economies, where the institutions are not as well as developed, that growth rates, although falling as a result of the global recession, are nevertheless still healthy. However, at the supranational level there is an increased tendency for greater South-South relationships to be developed. There are closer links now within the ASEAN and ASEAN + 3 and + 6 groupings and the BRICS have begun to operate in a concrete policy formulation way, beyond just being an acronym. At the domestic level the rhetoric is all of greater transparency, inclusive growth, and the need to develop more robust institutions as epitomized by the declaration in 2013 of Xi Jinping, the newly elected President of China, that the task for the next 10 years of his tenure would be to build 'the Chinese Dream' (see Chapter 8).

It is no coincidence that the first foreign destination of Xi Jinping after his assumption of power was to visit Africa, where China has been very active in building bilateral trade links. In the poorest parts of the world the necessary prerequisite for economic growth is political change from within and political and economic support from without. Internally, many governments are far from perfect, with abuses of human rights and widespread corruption. The danger here is that while deepening trade relationships are potentially a major catalyst for growth, if the benefits of this growth are extracted by a small elite or filtered away via corrupt deals or disappear into the profits of external business interests, then trade will not be beneficial. What is required is that internal reforms are carried out, and external advice and direct financial support might be needed in the form of infrastructure and capacity building.

Global power of big business

❱❱ VALUES ❱❱ STAKEHOLDERS In the first edition of this book we predicted that:

> The issue of how best to ensure that businesses do not abuse their global market positions and operate in a globally responsible way will be very important.

(Wetherly and Otter 2008)

The lessons from the recent past show that if the increasing private power of global businesses allows them to circumvent the traditional national safeguards for employees, consumers, and the wider stakeholders then there is a need for closer global political regulation.

Chapter 9 presented an optimistic view of the willingness of businesses to engage in genuine social responsibility. But in the years since 2008 the spotlight has fallen on extreme examples of irresponsibility, especially in the bonus culture that developed in the financial sector. Those that preached the virtues of the free market and argued vehemently against government regulation seemed to have no qualms in accepting huge amounts of public money to keep their banks afloat and then still were awarded their bonuses even when their banks had failed. Those that left the industry were able to soften the blows to their reputations with large redundancy payments or, in some cases, very generous pension payments.

We considered this issue of business power and responsibility in Chapter 11. It would not be in any way fair to tar all businesses with this brush and the examples of irresponsibility seem to be particularly prevalent within the very large global corporations. This would have come as no surprise to Adam Smith who warned of the dangers of monopoly power and the need for state regulation. Indeed, one of the most ironic claims made by some in the banking industry was that it was not individual or corporate acts of irresponsibility that were to blame but that it was the fault of the regulators in not anticipating that these things might occur, and they should have put in place effective regulation to stop this. To many this sounded a little like a house burglar blaming the victims of his/her crimes for leaving the doors or windows of the house open, and it would be fair to say that public opinion is not with the banks. This is reflected in the intentions of the policy-making to implement banking reform.

However, it would appear that these words have not been fully translated into actions, not least in the US and UK where the power of the financial sectors are so strong and governments are careful not to do anything that they feel might undermine the competitive advantage of the sector. Critics argue that it is not surprising that this will always tend to come down on the side of less rather than more reform, given the dominance of people with links in the industry who are advising the governments on what to do (for details of the banking reforms in the UK see HM Treasury (2013). For a critical assessment of what needs to be done see Stiglitz (2010); for proposals from the EU see European Commission (2013).

Such irresponsible behaviour has not been confined to the banks and a common feature that unites the alleged cases of wrong doing has been the global nature of the businesses in which they occur, especially amongst corporations headquartered in developed countries. In the case of the banking sector, if regulation in one country is to work then there needs to be a global agreement or else there is the risk of banks simply moving their business elsewhere. A fear for the rest of the business community has to be that the crisis that unfolded in 2008 could easily do so once again. And in the meantime all businesses are affected by the recession that has occurred and, for small businesses in particular, the difficulty of gaining access to credit. It is not surprising then, as revealed in the WEF survey above, that the stability of the financial sector and the wide gap in inequality weigh heavily in the minds of the businesses surveyed.

We profiled the growing attention on tax avoidance in Chapter 1 and here the suspicion is that corporations are able to employ the brightest accountancy graduates to legally circumvent paying taxes in the countries where they are making their money by using offshore tax havens or taking advantage of the fact that different countries operate different tax rates. Companies from Starbucks to Amazon, and in 2013 even Google and Apple, were brought before government scrutiny committees in both the US and UK and accused of tax avoidance on a huge scale. While the defence of the companies is that they always operate within the laws of every jurisdiction in which they operate, the accusation sticks that this is because they are using every available means to find ways of avoiding the taxes. At a time when governments in the developed world are seeking to pay down their deficits and need all the money they can get, looking ahead we will see attempts to develop global coordination to curb such tax avoidance.

▶ **STAKEHOLDERS** In Chapter 10 we profiled how the transnational nature of global businesses can produce a range of difficult ethical issues in relation to human rights, the environment, abuse of market power, and how to deal with regimes that are prone to graft and corruption, and that companies risk being accused of malpractice. Irrespective of the rights and wrongs of the accusations, corporations are ever mindful of the reputational damage that can occur. The rise of the use of social media means that campaign groups can quickly mobilize boycotts or generate adverse publicity so corporations are keen to show that they are responsible citizens (see Mini-Case 16.2).

Mini-Case 16.2 Ethical trading: The Rana Plaza factory collapse

In Chapter 1 we looked at the accusations from War on Want regarding the low wages being paid to Bangladeshi garment workers and in that chapter and again in Chapter 10 we referred to a factory that collapsed as a result of the lack of proper safety inspections. The factory was called the Rana Plaza and the final death toll was 1,126. This case, not surprisingly, attracted a lot of global media attention in part fuelled by the actions of campaigning groups who were able to publicize the names of the global retail outlets which were purchasing textiles from this factory. What subsequently came to light was that, since November 2012, 400 Bangladeshi textile employees had lost their lives in factory fires and within 2 weeks of the Rana Plaza disaster 23 workers lost their lives in yet another factory fire. It then was reported that in Cambodia workers were severely injured when a platform used for breaks had collapsed.

International labour groups and campaign groups together with organizations like the Ethical Trading Initiative had been seeking an industry-wide agreement over building standards in Bangladesh, and the aftermath of Rana Plaza led to prompt action from many global retail brands such as Primark, Mango, H&M, C&A, Tesco, and Marks & Spencer to sign up to the Accord on Fire and Building Safety. War on Want had urged people to use Facebook and Twitter to pressure those companies that had not signed up. Asda/Walmart and Gap declined to sign, preferring instead to stick with and develop their own voluntary agreements.

(*Sources:* <www.wow.org>, <www.laborrights.org>, <www.ethicaltrade.org>)

Question

Why did the majority of the global clothes retailers sourcing clothes in Bangladesh sign up to this accord? What might the reasons be for some not signing?

The need to demonstrate responsible behaviour will continue to be important for business managers. At the WEF summit at Davos, Feike Sijbesma, the CEO and Chair of the Managing Board of Royal DSM, said,

> Businesses have much more power and money than ever before. They can destroy large parts of the planet. If your impact is high, your responsibility is high.

(World Economic Forum 2013a)

With all of these discussions of corporate excess we must not forgot that, given the institutional structure of the business environment, at least the issue of responsibility is easier to highlight and encourage within the context of active democratically accountable governments, free and inquisitive media, and a vigilant civil society to pressurize business to do the right thing. The degree to which such institutions exist elsewhere in the world is patchy and, given the fast emergence of many economies in the developing world, increasing attention will focus on the behaviour of businesses in these settings. The CSR agenda is not confined to western business environments and is, as we have seen in the case of China, at the fore-front of the minds of national policy-makers.

Global climate change

》 INTERACTION The third challenge is that posed by global warming. As discussed in Chapter 8, the process towards gaining global cooperation is difficult. However, at the official government level there is universal agreement that climate change is real and that its causes are anthropogenic. While there is limited concerted global action, at least the annual climate change meetings take place and all governments profess a commitment to reducing their GHGs. Global agreements are still some way off, but individual countries are ever conscious of environmental pressures. There is still a considerable groundswell of pressure from the environmental pressure groups and green issues are widely discussed, although there remains a small but active climate change denial lobby.

Businesses are changing their practices to embed principles of sustainability partly as a result of regulation but also, positively, many can identify a solid business case for these changes in that being green can also cut costs (for case studies in how businesses are responding see <http://www.wbcsd.org/> and <http://www.forumforthefuture.org/>). Of course, even if these positive reasons for addressing sustainability issues did not exist there are the reputational issues involved and while a measure of 'greenwashing' may occur, nevertheless, it is clear that many businesses are now addressing the sustainability agenda.

There will continue to be pressure from environmental groups for governments to impose tighter regulations and incentives to enable a greener business approach but, equally, there will be countervailing arguments that such regulations need to be voluntary. Other approaches try to square the circle by arguing that through 'a new green deal' we can have prosperity with sustainable growth and that we can create a business environment in which 'enough is enough' (Jackson 2009, Dietz and O'Neill 2013).

Moves towards more environmentally friendly ways of operating and the need to plan for mitigation and adaptation to climate change present many opportunities to develop alternative technologies and cater for more alternative lifestyles. Membership of leisure clubs and gyms continues to rise in Europe even despite the recessionary conditions in many countries and the sector employed 400,000 people in 2012 (EHFA 2012). The amount of people taking up cycling either for sport, leisure, or commuting has been steadily rising, and in 2011 the London School of Economics estimated its total worth to the British economy at £3 billion, with growing output for manufacturing and specialist retail outlets (LSE 2011). There is a growing global demand for alternative energies, such as wind and solar, and for energy efficiency measures but here campaigners argue governments need to do more to subsidize their development.

It is clear, though, that the issue of sustainable development will impact on business behaviour and while potentially this could be seen as a threat there are also opportunities for businesses to exploit.

Stop and Think

What changes can businesses make to lessen their 'carbon footprint'? To what extent do you think that there is a business case for making these changes?

Global inequality and political instability

>> SPATIAL LEVELS >> INTERACTION Global income inequality continues to blight the progress of humanity. While there is clearly an ethical case to eradicate global poverty and there is global agreement to move beyond the 2015 MDGs (see Chapter 10), there is also a business case in boosting the incomes of significant numbers of the global population. Across the globe there has been a huge rise in the numbers of middle class consumers and we saw in Chapter 13 that this is leading to a recalibration in the structural balance of the emerging economies as they begin to trade amongst themselves and seek to target their own internal and regional markets. Africa as a continent still contains many of the world's poorest people, but in recent years the growth of its middle classes and economies has been attracting much attention (see Mini-Case 16.3). Businesses within the developed world too are keen to develop links with these emerging markets.

Mini-Case 16.3 The rise of the African middle class

As African economies are growing (7 out of the 10 fastest grow-ing in the world are African) wealth is trickling down, and Africa now has the fastest growing middle class in the world.

(Deloitte and Touche 2013)

While it is still the case that two thirds of the population of Africa live below the poverty line there is a rapidly expanding middle class. The African Development Bank estimates its size to be 331 million, which means that it is roughly equivalent to the numbers of middle class consumers in China and India (African Development Bank 2011).

While historically African trade has been with the former colonial powers and in a narrow range of primary commod-ities, its proportion of global trade has been tiny. However, since China's growth together with that of the other BRICS nations there has been a large expansion of trade with these countries. This has supplanted 'an old and tired order dominated by former colonial powers' (Wallis 2013). Wallis reports that while in colonial times European trade consti-tuted over two thirds of Sub-Saharan trade by 2011 this was only 25%, and there is no doubt that it is China that is the most significant partner with trade having grown from $10.6 billion in 2000 to $229 billion in 2012 and with projections of an annual increase of 25% in the years to come.

China has been accused of simply seeing Africa as a source for vital energy and raw materials to fuel its own manufactur-ing base in the same way as in former colonial times (and, it is argued by dependency writers, as with Western MNCs today). However, of increasing importance to China is the opportu-nity provided by this growing African middle class. Writing in the *South China Morning Post*, Huang argues that Africa is 'one of the world's largest untapped consumer markets' and that '[l]ow quality, cheap textiles, electronics and other products produced for rock bottom prices in China have a ready-made market in impoverished African countries, most of which have poor manufacturing bases of their own' (Huang 2013a).

After his selection as President of China in 2013 Xi Jin-ping highlighted Africa's importance by visiting Tanzania, The Republic of Congo, and then South Africa to attend a BRICS summit. In Tanzania he announced, 'China has and will continue to work alongside African countries to take practi-cal measures to appropriately solve problems in trade and economic co-operation, so that African countries gain more

from that co-operation'. In the same speech he committed China to training 30,000 African professionals, giving scholar-ships to 18,000 students, and increasing technology transfer (Huang 2013b). It is clear that for China its expansion into Africa is part of its strategy to increase its links with other de-veloping countries and promote 'South-South' cooperation.

Western businesses have not targeted these growing markets although there are signs that they are beginning to appreciate the potential. The Deloitte-Touche report argues that in par-ticular there is a growth in the demand for financial services, retailing (especially through shopping mall development), tele-communications, and technology goods as well as housing and infrastructure development. Middle class consumers in Africa are not as prosperous as elsewhere and so targeting these mar-kets would involve different strategies, for example, units need to be sold in smaller quantities or more basic models of goods need to be produced. There is a growing demand for cars and motor bikes but leasing arrangements are more attractive in these markets. Financial services need to be focused on micro-credit type schemes and, importantly, there is evidence that female small scale entrepreneurs could be a dynamic source of growth if they were afforded access to credit.

Last but by no means least, it needs to be remembered that over 60% of Africa's population still live below the poverty line, but this too could represent a business opportunity if creative 'bottom of the pyramid' models are developed. And, in the African context there is clearly demand for education and health services.

(*Sources:* Huang 2013 and 2013b, Wallis 2013, Deloitte and Touche 2013), African Development Bank 2011)

Questions

1. Why has trade between Africa and China and other emerg-ing economies been rising so rapidly and what are the mutual advantages of these trading relationships?

2. Why is Xi Jinping so keen to show that he is aware of po-tential problems in relation to trading relationships and how is he seeking to show that Chinese businesses will help African development?

3. Why might the different characteristics of the African busi-ness environment require different marketing strategies?

While it is clear that there is still a need for aid to help the poorest of the poor, it will be provid-ing the best environment in which poor people can develop their own business activity that is key. Initiatives such as micro-credit in the developing world and the general focus on 'bottom of the pyramid' models of business development see poor people not as passive victims but as potentially active entrepreneurs who will become the burgeoning middle classes of the future.

Political instability continues to affect many parts of the developing world and this makes it difficult for businesses. Nowhere is this more evident than in the uncertainty over energy supplies security, as these vital resources are found in many of these areas.

In Chapters 3 and 10 we did draw the distinction between countries that have been able to develop inclusive institutions—that can both produce economic growth as well as ensuring that its benefits are shared more widely—and those with extractive ones. In such countries high rates of growth are possible benefiting relatively small numbers of people and the likelihood is that they will be trading with richer developed countries. It is the case that while the BRICS have indeed been successful at producing growth, the levels of inequality and the severely distorted social structures that have developed will not be conducive to long run development. Progress has been made in terms of education, health, and infrastructural reforms but the extreme levels of inequality in these countries can give rise to civil unrest and create powerful oligarchies resistant to wider political reform. It is important that across the global environment attention is paid to reducing inequality as a way of ensuring that growth is more equitably shared. Within these environments governments and third sector organizations, both at the national and supranational levels, have a large role to play in lifting people out of poverty.

Looking ahead: the economic environment

DYNAMIC ▶ INTERACTION We have seen that, above all, what businesses would like to experience as regards the external economic environment is certainty and stability and, allied to this, a favourable environment in which there can be dynamic growth. The global economy has clearly not been able to deliver this in the years since 2008.

The global economic recession following 2008 has been a big shock to the economic environment. As we have seen in Chapters 2, 9, and 10 the crisis called for a re-assessment of the Washington Consensus. Initially, it did appear that this resulted in the acceptance that, whilst different countries may develop different ways of implementing market reforms and do things in a different order, essentially it is through states supporting the market mechanism and directly intervening in cases of market failure that economic success can be achieved. Of course, as we have seen, this does not mean that we agree as to how we get there and different national and regional approaches have been adopted.

What the financial crisis has done is to reveal a structural weakness in the banking system and the way in which a crisis here can so quickly affect all businesses and become a global phenomenon. There is now a determination to rein in the power of the banks and a recognition that, if this is to be done, what is needed is global coordination of economic policy and this involves global political cooperation. If banks are to be regulated this needs to be done on a global basis so that they cannot evade one particular country's law given the transnational nature of financial markets. However, there remains intense opposition to these policies from within the financial and wider business community and, as we have seen at the global level, despite a recognition of the need to build a more robust monetary and financial system, this has yet to be effected (Stiglitz 2010).

Trade, development, and growth in a rebalanced global economy

We referred to the cautious optimism of the WEF in 2013 earlier in this chapter but there are many critics who are equally cautious pessimists.

Economies in the developed world have suffered greatly as a result of the recession in terms of falls in output, loss of jobs, business failures, and very large levels of public sector debt. The region that has suffered most has been Europe closely followed by the US. But, of course, while it was in the developed world that the worst falls in economic activity were seen, this had contagion effects on many of the emerging economies whose models were based on export promotion primarily to the West.

We have highlighted the increasing importance of the BRICS and they will continue to lead the world in terms of high growth rates. As exporters, they do depend on the mature economies recovering from recession and while they are likely to grow more slowly, as was pointed out in Chapter 9, this still does mean that in absolute terms consumer demand will increase and this will find its way into export demand. One lesson the global recession has taught the Asian and other emerging economies is the importance of 'recession proofing' themselves from global instability. It is important that they pay attention to boosting domestic demand and that as a group of emerging nations the growth in their own middle classes provides huge potential for South-South trading links.

In Europe, to the frustration of many members of the economic community, the macroeconomic choice has been one of too high a level of austerity but with strong and immediate state support for expanding the money supply to ease credit flows and to prevent banking collapses. We discussed the problems that the PIGS have faced and the problems that they in turn have posed for the wider European Union in Chapter 13. At least for the moment the prospect of one of the PIGS countries either being forced to default on their foreign debts or leave the euro has been relieved by the action of the ECB and the IMF in providing the sovereign funds needed to prevent a crisis in confidence. This still leaves the individual countries to try to reduce their deficits through squeezing public spending, and this is imposing enormous social pressures on their citizens and a loss of political sovereignty as they try to adhere to the conditions that come attached to the loans they receive. In the neoliberal orthodoxy that seems to have persisted in relation to domestic macroeconomic policy, the belief is that if budget deficits can be reduced then this will: restore confidence to the global financial system; increase the availability of credit; lower interest rates across all countries; and then allow the private sector to move in, restoring the dynamism of free market capitalism and bringing economic growth.

For Keynesian economists there needs to be much more government borrowing, not less, especially if targeted on infrastructural programmes. The paradoxical effect of austerity is that if it were just one or two deficit countries restoring competitiveness in this way then this would be a viable strategy, as long as the surplus countries supported them through fiscal transfers. These would be needed to soften the effects on the social conditions and to provide investment funds over and above the immediate funds to service the debts. In Europe's case the surplus countries are unwilling to provide the sums required and with all countries pursuing austerity the result will be falls in aggregate demand and, thus, growth which will simply worsen the budget positions of the weaker countries. In other words, while some of the lessons from the crisis have been learned in theory as regards the need for global cooperation in relation to monetary policy, fiscal policy has gone the other way and the prospects for Europe to grow its way out of its problems are low.

It seems clear that if the economic environment is to stabilize then there will need to be a re-balancing both within the existing power houses of the developed world and between the developing and developed world. There is, however, continued uncertainty about the future of world trade and, in the absence of the completion of the latest round of trade talks, the regional trade agenda has become more important. In 2013 four key proposals were launched, which will have an enormous impact in terms of shaping the global trading system:

- The start of negotiations to develop a free trade area between Japan and the EU
- A proposal to develop a Transatlantic Trade and Investment Partnership to achieve free trade between the US and the EU
- The opening of free trade talks between Japan, South Korea, and China
- A proposal to establish a development bank funded by the BRICS.

▶ **DYNAMIC** Managers within this changing environment need to develop appropriate strategies. Managing in environments where there is a downturn in economic activity require businesses to focus on the core elements of the business that add value. A particular problem is cash flow as credit remains tight and, of course, it is important that cost savings are achieved. What has been surprising about the recession in the US and the EU is that unemployment has not risen as much as would ordinarily have been expected. The main reason for this is that workers have been prepared to accept real cuts in wages and indeed longer hours at work. There has also been an increase in part-time working. It is vital in situations like this that businesses are able to plan for the future and undergo effective risk assessment.

Of course the opening up of trade provides an opportunity to diversify markets and, for firms involved in trade, effective foreign entry strategies need to be undertaken. One important consideration has to be the fit between the business environments of the countries that they might target and, for this, detailed research needs to be completed. National governments provide trade assistance through trade delegations and embassies and supranational bodies, such as the IMF and World Bank, can provide useful advice on how best to conduct business in different countries (see **<www.doingbusiness.org>**).

■ Looking ahead: the social environment

We explored the nature of the social environment in Chapters 6, 11, and 12. In relation to the global business environment three major areas have been highlighted: the rise in affluence in general allied to the widening income gap between people; the implications of increases in migration; and demographic changes. We will see that the way these interact with business differs in different country settings.

Social inequality and relative affluence

▶ **VALUES** ▶ **INTERACTION** Businesses inevitably are affected by changes in the social structure as this will affect the patterns of demand. As affluence increases in much of the developed world, this has enabled businesses to target a range of high value activities and this has affected their marketing and branding strategies. There have been big shifts in the patterns of demand as the proportion of consumption has switched to services and away from basic goods. We have seen that patterns of demand in different countries at different levels of production do call for appropriate products for different levels of purchasing power and different approaches to marketing and market entry strategies.

While it is not the job of business to take responsibility for social inequality, and it is for governments to decide what levels of equality are or are not acceptable, we have seen that management decisions as to how to reward and treat employees do have a social impact, and that business in general does have to recognize its social responsibilities.

We have seen that globally there is disquiet at the growing gaps in inequality within societies but the focus differs depending a country's level of development.

There has been a recent surge in economic research into what people say about what makes them happy. This research harks back to a research paper published by Richard Easterlin (Easterlin 1974). He argued that while people with higher incomes are happier than those on lower ones, as people get richer they do not, in fact, get any happier. What seems more important to people is their relative status. We are not happy if we feel poorer than other groups. This so-called Easterlin Paradox has been interpreted as proving that richer people are happier because they are richer than others, not because of the actual amount that they earn. This then brings into question the role of economic growth in developed societies.

Related to this work on happiness, is the work of Wilkinson and Pickett (2009). In their book *The Spirit Level* they use a range of indicators to show that in affluent societies with high degrees of inequality the quality of life for all people is actually lower.

> Economic growth for so long the great engine of progress has, in the rich countries, largely finished its work. Not only have measures of well-being and happiness ceased to rise with economic growth but as affluent societies have grown richer there have been long-term rises in rates of anxiety, depression and numerous other social problems.

(Wilkinson and Pickett 2009, pp. 5–6)

This ties in with the work of social psychologists such as Oliver James as well as with the views of the green critics we profiled when discussing climate change. For James, in affluent societies 'affluenza' occurs with people constantly feeling that they haven't got enough as they compare themselves always to the groups above themselves (James 2007) (see Mini-Case 16.5). In this view of the world, the recent tendency for the concentration of wealth in the hands of an elite group of super-rich people is problematic as it will raise unrealistic expectations from the middle class and, therefore, place too much strain on resources. If 'enough is to be enough', then one way of moving towards sustainable living and increased well-being is to reduce these income disparities.

We have seen the recognition that governments do wish to curb the culture of excess pay and awards of bonuses, but at the same time there is a reluctance to risk the potential political unpopularity of such overt attempts to cut top pay. As a direct result of the public mood against what is seen as undeserved pay awards, there have been many attempts by shareholders of companies to pressure their boards to show restraint in the face of the global recession.

Mini-Case 16.4   Have you caught the 'affluenza' bug?

As we entered the 21st century there was a rise in interest as to what constituted happiness. The conventional wisdom was that if individuals and, therefore, society were to be richer what was required was for them to become more affluent.

This view has come to be questioned both by social psychologists and by a revival of what is known as 'happiness economics'. It has been argued by some psychologists that as societies become richer there is a rise in the range and level of mental problems reported by people and that people seem to become more insecure and suffer higher stress

levels. The term 'affluenza' has been developed to describe this tendency. It is argued that the symptoms of this 'virus' are seen in people being obsessed with money, wanting to look good in the eyes of others, and wanting to be famous. It causes depression, anxiety, and the need to take comfort in substance abuse.

It is argued that it is not just income that makes us happy but a range of other factors such as levels of education, stable relationships and friends, security in the home and at work, leisure, and fitness.

This has led to calls for the development of new ways of measuring well-being in the belief that in framing growth simply in income terms we were ignoring the real basis of prosperity and, in fact, that this had led to people not noticing the evidence that was to lead to the global economic crisis (see Stiglitz 2009).

> *Stop and Think*
>
> Do you want to earn as much as possible or would you be happy to earn less but have more time and leisure?

Of course, such concerns may only be relevant in the post-materialist developed societies and, even here, we need to be careful as there is a persistent minority of people whose incomes are still well below what can could be seen as constituting an affluent lifestyle.

In the developing world it could be argued that this is the case for the majority of people and there is some way to go before 'affluenza' develops. However, as we have seen, the relative levels of inequality are even more pronounced in many of the fastest growing economies. There is not only a danger that social inequality gives rise to corruption and acts as a barrier to social mobility but there is much less evidence that the fruits of the economic growth are trickling down to the bottom of the pyramid and far too many people are being left behind.

Migration

》DIVERSITY The onward march of globalization will also increase migration. While this will mean that it is important for countries to develop appropriate ways of handling the diversity of communities, businesses need to be mindful that their recruitment policies do not undermine social cohesion by using immigration as a way of driving down wages and in so doing displacing indigenous workers. Immigration brings clear economic benefits to countries, as migrant workers are often very skilled or else are prepared to work more flexibly than indigenous workers. However, unregulated immigration can impose unexpected increases in appropriate welfare provision and fuels ethnic suspicions. The inability to resolve cultural and ethnic differences can lead to tensions, and may provide the ideal environment for this to result in extreme political protests in the form of racist behaviour and actions. It is important in the future that diversity is handled effectively.

Demographic changes

》DIVERSITY 》INTERNAL/EXTERNAL We have seen that in the developed world the improvement in health and living have led to big increases in life expectancy and, while this provides commercial opportunities for business to target the 'grey' market and benefit from the willingness of people to work longer (and thus benefit from their experience), it also means greater consideration must be paid to pension provision. In terms of human resource policies, businesses will need to respond to the demands from their workforces to try to enable flexible working and to recognize that diverse people require diverse approaches to human resource management.

In the developing world the focus has shifted from seeing population as a problem to seeing it as a potential advantage, if people gain access to educational skills and training and if the entrepreneurial dynamism at the bottom of the pyramid can be unleashed. The rise in the middle classes profiled earlier in this chapter, if this can spread to the people at the lower ends of the pyramid, represents a huge opportunity for businesses. In China there is every prospect that the infamous 'one child per family' policy will end in 2015 (Associated Press 2012). What is needed for the emerging economies is to invest in their people as their key resource by directing the wealth generated from economic growth into education, health, housing, and environmental reform in the urban areas and to help raise rural incomes and diversification in rural areas. The main barriers to this would be the social inequality and corruption we have already discussed, and it is not surprising that policy-makers in emerging countries are seeking ways to reduce these.

◾ Looking ahead: the technological environment

⟫ DYNAMIC The revolution based on new technologies has combined with the increase in globalization to create what is, for many commentators, a new paradigm of the 'network age'. In the old industrial age of the 20th century production needed to be vertically integrated (all stages of the production process kept together geographically) because of the high costs of transport and communications. In this new age, it is argued, we will see an increasing horizontal organization of business activity. It is now possible for businesses to organize their activity in functional areas located in different parts of the globe, e.g. research, marketing, education and training, distribution, and production split into separate processes outsourced across the world.

What is likely to be the impact of what has now become called 'disruptive innovation'? Quite clearly the spread of information and communications technology will bring about great benefits in terms of enabling people to gain access to knowledge. This will greatly help in terms of a wide range of activities, from participation in the political process and, therefore, greater transparency, through to access to research and market information. IBM has developed a super-computer that is able to process millions of pieces of medical data to diagnose illnesses and suggest treatments that would be beyond the capabilities of human medical practitioners. The huge amounts of data that we share through our use of digital platforms and social media sites has created enormous amounts of 'Big Data' which can now be analysed and utilized by businesses to target specific products to individuals and, indeed, spot the potential for new ones. We are already well down the line of enabling every home in the developed world to have high speed Internet access, and in developing economies the access to information that the Internet brings is enabling banking to develop and empowering entrepreneurs.

However, as we discussed in Chapter 3 a closer analysis of these growth rates does call for caution over technological flights of fancy. Before the recent economic turmoil growth rates in the US and Europe had been steady rather than spectacular, and where growth rates have been high, such as in Southeast Asia, there have been a host of other factors involved in creating the environment for growth.

⟫ INTERACTION Technology has changed the way in which businesses are organized, especially as a result of the speed with which information, goods, and people can be moved around. Biotechnology and nanotechnology mean that businesses can undertake rapid new product development and seek to build new markets, particularly in the areas of food production and health.

While it is public investment that is vital in providing the educational infrastructure for the knowledge economy, it is the private sector that is primarily responsible for translating this knowledge into product development. Across the developed countries, typically 50–60% of research and development is in private companies, with universities responsible for around 15–20% and public research institutions between 15–20%.

Private research is even higher in the developing world. This means that there is a potential conflict between the desire of the private sector to use technology to establish competitive advantage, and the desire of the public to be both protected from unsafe technologies and to fully benefit from those that will improve the quality of our lives. There is pressure to develop open-source operating systems, and governments have to guard against the creation of monopoly power and bridge the digital divide between developed and developing countries and high and low income groups.

It is no surprise that the main advocates of the view that we are in a qualitatively different disruptive age of technology come from the new digital industries. In the 1980s the 'masters of the universe' were the financial brokers and in the 21st century it is the computer geeks. The digital start-ups that have so rapidly become the behemoths of the modern corporate world are generally headed by unconventional and very young entrepreneurs who feel that they are engaged in truly changing the world (see Mini-Case 16.5) but Marxists would predict that eventually the venture of these bright young things will be snapped up and end up being concentrated in the hands of the few.

Mini-Case 16.5   Will the 'long tail' control the 'head'?

Advocates of the disruptive nature of the digital age see the technology of coding and development of a myriad of applications in millions of bedrooms and small workplaces as heralding the birth of a new age of entrepreneurial dynamism which will transform society, alter the structure of business, and flatten hierarchies as networks spread. In an interview with McKinsey, the global management consultancy firm, Eric Schmidt, Chief Executive of Google, gave precisely this vision but warned that technology would displace workers and that, therefore, in the 'race against the machine' people would need to become educated to engage in the new digital industries or risk losing out (McKinsey & Company 2013).

In March 2013 Nick D'Aloisio, a 17 year old British student, sold his news app to Yahoo for $30 million. His app distilled news stories into small readable chunks that could be viewed on smartphones. He was quoted by Reuters as saying,

If you have a good idea, or you think that there is a gap in the market, just go out and launch it because there are investors across the world right now looking for companies to invest in.

In the same year Facebook bought Instagram for $1 billion and Yahoo bought Tumblr for $1.1 billion. The *Japan Times* reported an emerging trend for young computer engineers,

many of whom had worked for companies like Sony and Panasonic, to develop manufacturing start-ups using readily available and cheap digital technologies such as 3-D printers and CAD software. This trend in part was influenced by the Japanese translation of Chris Andersen's book, *Makers: The New Industrial Revolution* (Nakata 2013). In this book Andersen envisages a world where we will all be able to become designers and use digital technologies to transform our ideas into manufactured products (Andersen 2012).

Questions

1. Why would Facebook and Yahoo pay such large sums of money for businesses that had yet to make any real income?

2. How could the examples in this mini-case be used to justify each of the following?

   a) fears that the digital revolution will simply concentrate wealth into fewer hands

   b) fears of the monopoly control of information

   c) the vision of those who see a future where millions of entrepreneurs will bloom.

We saw in Chapter 3 that there is a fierce debate about whether the digital age is truly a fundamental change in business motivation and strategy. For technology optimists like Andersen, the digital age will create a long tail of many small entrepreneurial businesses which will spread the benefits of their enterprise widely and ensure that wealth is evenly distributed. Newspapers regularly profile a recently self-made digital multi-millionaire (see Mini-Case 16.5). On the other hand, there are voices of dissent. We saw that the evidence for the impact of technology on productivity is limited and that, while undoubtedly the impact of the digital age is truly amazing in terms of the gadgets that arise and the changes in lifestyle and working practices that it enables, fundamentally these are not revolutionary in the way in which electricity and running water were.

Furthermore, the dominance of the digital industry by such huge players as Google, Amazon, Facebook, and Apple mean that the 'Head' seems to dominate in much the same way as with the old technologies, leading to intense concentrations of corporate wealth and power. In 2013 the spotlight on a range of alleged practices was shone on Google (privacy violations, predatory pricing, and tax avoidance with the slogan 'Don't be Evil' held up to scorn) as well as on Amazon and Apple (for tax avoidance).

However, if it is the case that we are at the beginning of the digital age then maybe the gains in productivity are yet to be seen. In Chapter 3 we saw the many ways in which ICT is transforming the way we live and work and the ways in which business can use it across all aspects of the supply chain.

》 COMPLEXITY This chapter has attempted to look forward to spot the main factors that will affect the future business environment. Inevitably this has taken place at a general level but, by using the PEST framework, we have been able to identify some key future developments. In the end of chapter case study we will show how PEST factors will impact on one business in particular.

■ Summary

- Analysis of the underlying political, economic, social, and technological factors helps us to map the important themes and features of the business environment which can act as guide for the future.

- The nature of the business environment is complex and businesses need to be able to analyse the external environment, develop effective risk assessments, and then plan how to deal with these.

Case Study: The football business—the state of play in 2013

》 COMPLEXITY 》 SPATIAL LEVELS In the previous editions of this book we showed how the football business has demonstrated the changing nature of the external environment and its effects on business strategy and structure. We charted football's move away from being an English game with amateur clubs rooted in their local communities. Football has become the most popular global sport played by millions and watched by billions. In the process, a tiny minority of footballers and their teams have become global brands, and the real business of football is about much more than what happens on the field of play. The main reason for this change has been the global television revenues that were made possible through the development of satellite and digital broadcasting, but there is a wide range of other external factors that have played their part.

Changes in the political and economic environment

》 INTERACTION 》 DYNAMIC It has been television and globalization that have enabled elite football to become a global business and it is commercial television's need to earn advertising revenue that has been behind this. Changes in regulatory regimes across the world have allowed the development of commercial TV companies who quickly recognized the power of sport in general, and football in particular, with its global appeal to draw in large audiences.

The manner in which broadcasting rights have been negotiated has rapidly led to a concentration of wealth in the hands of an elite group of clubs who, in turn, are able to diversify their income streams through sponsorship deals (naming rights of stadia, deals with kit manufacturers, corporate logos on shirts) and merchandising of branded goods from clothes to key rings. In the 2011/12 season the top two teams in terms of earnings were the Spanish giants, Real Madrid and FC Barcelona. Real Madrid became the first club in any sport to earn over €500 million in a year (Deloitte 2013).

While the TV industry is regulated by governments, football is not and regulates itself through its own governing bodies, with FIFA at the global level, UEFA at the European level, and through national football associations at the national level.

It is the global reach of football that has powered the huge increases in revenues. The Deloitte report above shows that Real Madrid's revenue was split as follows: 25% gate receipts, 39% broadcasting rights, and 36% commercial revenues. In terms of growth, gate receipts revenue is limited by ground capacity and ticket prices, although many teams are doing all they can to increase stadia size and ticket prices, but the latter is constrained by the desire to be seen to be good corporate citizens.

The price of broadcasting rights, though, is rising exponentially. The English Premier League negotiated a new deal in 2012 which will boost revenues by 70% to over £5 billion over the three years to 2015/16. The bulk of this comes from domestic TV companies and here the heightened competitive environment has led to bidding wars which has resulted in a huge increase in the price paid for the rights. Increasingly, though, overseas networks also are competing for rights to the coverage and this is providing a growing source of revenue (Gibson 2012, Garside et al. 2013).

Similarly, there is seemingly no ceiling to the potential of global merchandising. It is estimated that Manchester United, third in the Money League in 2013, has a fan base of 200 million in China alone. Just think if it were to get each one to pay £1 for a branded item each year! Two examples of commercial expansion in 2013 are a sponsorship deal with a Chinese sports drink manufacturer, and the China Construction Bank paid to have the club branded on its credit cards (Bloomberg 2013).

The ownership of the top football clubs is a contentious issue and most commonly they are owned by wealthy private individuals or groups who made their wealth outside of football and whose primary motivation was the status that came from ownership in itself, irrespective of whether they would make any money from their investment. While at the elite level this is no longer the case, there are still too many examples of financial irresponsibility within football with short term gains being made at the expense of long term financial sustainability.

▶ **STAKEHOLDERS** Politically, there have been questions raised about the effect this pattern of ownership has had on football and all its stakeholders with the escalating effect this has had on transfer fees and the ability of the new superstar footballers to demand large salaries. Within the global governing organizations of football, there are claims that this pattern of ownership distorts fair competition and leads to a closed rich elite which, in the long run, will damage the game. This model of ownership isn't the only one, as in some cases there are clubs where the supporters have more of a voice. To allow these different forms of control to continue and to try and create a more disciplined financial environment, the football authorities are seeking to bring in 'financial fair play' rules (UEFA 2013). These rules are to be introduced in a phased manner with assessment of the degree of compliance taking place in 2013 and 2014.

While it is Europe that dominates world football in the sense of commercial revenues, FIFA is looking to boost football's prospects globally. One way it can do this is through the siting of the high profile World Cup Finals, and it is no surprise that this will take place in Brazil in 2014 and Russia in 2018 (but rather more surprising that it will be in Qatar in 2022).

Changes in the Social Environment

▶ **VALUES** ▶ **STAKEHOLDERS** It has been the rise in the affluence of football supporters that has had the biggest influence in the game, both domestically and globally. Domestically, there has been a change in the income brackets of those that attend the game, and many supporters are keen to buy into the club merchandise by at least buying the team shirt. Globally, the rise in the middle classes has fuelled the TV-watching audiences but even poor people have access to TV sets and are able to be part of the global 'football family', which is how FIFA likes to characterize this support.

For some, the old values of local community have now been lost in this new commercial world. Some supporter groups are trying to counter this by developing more supporter involvement and, in some cases, direct ownership. The social landscape of football has changed.

Changes in the technological environment

▶ **DYNAMIC** Of course, none of the developments above would have been able to come together were it not for the technological advancement of global television through digital and satellite. Broadcasting technology continues to develop with web streaming, HD television, and 3D, but crucially it has given the global audience immediate access to the games and all the celebrity culture that surrounds it.

Questions

1. Is it legitimate for the government to try to intervene in the football business?

2. What have been the main changes in the business environment of football that have caused the developments referred to above?

3. Looking ahead to the future, what are the prospects for the football business?

Review and discussion questions

1. How has the financial crisis of 2008 and ensuing economic recession impacted on the business environment? Do you think these changes will be long lasting?

2. How successful have attempts to coordinate global economic policy been?

3. What are the obstacles that make it difficult for governments to try to reduce income inequalities?

4. As the second decade of the 21st century opens and develops do you think that businesses are becoming more socially responsible?

5. Using a company that you either work in or have knowledge of as an example, what do you think are the key aspects of the external business environment that will impact upon it in the next few years?

Assignments

1. Read the following annual reports (see relevant web links below):

   World Economic Forum's Global Agenda and Global Risks and at least one of the following: UNCTAD Trade and Development Report, IMF World Economic Outlook.

   Write a report that compares and contrasts their views as to the future of the business environment and assess the main likely factors and their impacts on business in general.

2. Write a report which analyses how you see the business environment affecting a business or business sector that you want to profile for a business magazine.

3. You are working as a business analyst for a private consultancy firm and have been asked by the local chamber of commerce to prepare a presentation which profiles an emerging economy which might provide a good place with which local SMEs might want to target as part of their international strategy. Visit the World Bank's Doing Business website and select a country and then show why you feel this would be a good choice and what factors would need to be considered in doing business there. (You could also look at <http://www.ukti.gov.uk/export.html> which is the UK government's site to help British businesses in terms of global expansion.)

online resource centre

Test your understanding of this chapter with online questions and answers, explore the subject further through web exercises, and use the web links to provide a quick resource for further research. Go to the Online Resource Centre at <www.oxfordtextbooks.co.uk/orc/wetherly_otter/2>

Useful websites

<www.bbc.co.uk>
The BBC website is a good source of information both in written archives and in terms of its 'listen again' archives. The best programmes to listen again to are the *In Business* and *Analysis* series which always contain views about the future.

<www.unctad.org>
This is the website of the UN Trade and Development organization, and you will find its annual report here.

<www.worldbank.org>
The World Bank publishes annual reports on the global environment.

<http://www.doingbusiness.org/>
The World Bank's Doing Business website

<http://www.ukti.gov.uk/export.html>
The UK government's site for helping businesses export

<www.imf.org>
See, in particular, the annual World Economic Outlook that can be downloaded from this site.

<www.wef.org>
The website of the World Economic Forum

<www.forumforthefuture.org.uk>
This site profiles and champions the case for sustainable development.

<www.technologyreview.com>
This site is run by MIT in the US, one of the leading technology universities in the world.

<http://www.bis.gov.uk/foresight>
This is the UK government's science and technology programme to research into the future.

<http://steadystate.org/>
A research organization that looks at ways of attaining sustainable growth

<http://www.wbcsd.ch>
This is the site for the World Council for Sustainable Business and on this site you can see case studies of how businesses are dealing with the sustainability agenda.

<www.laborrights.org>
A campaigning group for labour rights across the world

<http://www.waronwant.org/>
The site of War on Want, a charity that campaigns against world poverty

<www.ethicaltrade.org>
An organization that seeks to encourage business to incorporate ethical practice

For local business information look up the web addresses of your local Chambers of Commerce.

References

African Development Bank (2011) *The Middle of the Pyramid: Dynamics of the Middle Classes in Africa* Market Brief, 20 April 2011 (accessed 23 May 2013) <**http://www.afdb.org/fileadmin/uploads/afdb/Documents/Publications/The%20Middle%20of%20the%20Pyramid_The%20Middle%20of%20the%20Pyramid.pdf**>

Andersen, C. (2012) *Makers: The New Industrial Revolution* (New York: Crown Business).

Associated Press (2012) 'China thinktank urges end of China one-child policy', *The Guardian*, 31 October 2012 (accessed 23 May 2013) <**http://www.guardian.co.uk/world/2012/oct/31/china-thinktank-abolition-one-child-policy**>

Bloomberg (2013) 'China's Richest Man Signs Manchester United Sponsor Deal' (accessed 24 May 2013) <**http://www.bloomberg.com/news/2013-01-15/manchester-united-signs-sponsorship-deal-with-wahaha.html**>

Dietz, R. and O'Neill, D. (2013) *Enough is Enough: Building a Sustainable Economy in a World of Finite Resources* (London: Routledge).

Deloitte (2013) *Deloitte Football Money League 2013: Captains of Industry* (accessed 24 May 2013) <**http://www.deloitte.com/assets/Dcom-UnitedKingdom/Local%20Assets/Documents/Industries/Sports%20Business%20Group/uk-sbg-football-money-league-2013.pdf**>

Deloitte and Touche (2013) *The Rise and Rise of the African Middle Class* (accessed 12 March 2013) (<**https://www.deloitte.com/assets/Dcom-SouthAfrica/Local%20Assets/Documents/rise_and_rise.pdf**>)

Easterlin, Richard A. (1974) 'Does Economic Growth Improve the Human Lot?' in David, P. A. and Reder, M. W. (eds) *Nations and Households in Economic Growth: Essays in Honor of Moses Abramovitz* (New York: Academic Press, Inc.).

European Commission (2013) *Reforming the Structure of the EU Banking Sector—Consultation Paper* (accessed 22 May 2013) <**http://ec.europa.eu/internal_market/consultations/2013/banking-structural-reform/docs/consultation-document_en.pdf**>

EHFA (2012) *European Health and Fitness Association Annual Report* (accessed 22 May 2013) <**http://www.ehfa.eu.com/sites/ehfa.eu.com/files/documents/EHFA%20Annual%20Report_2012.pdf**>

G20 (2013) *Priorities of Russia's G20 Presidency in 2013* (accessed 21 May 2013) <**http://www.g20.org/docs/g20_russia/priorities.html**>

Garside et al. (2013) 'BT promises free Premier League football on the TV for the first time', *The Guardian*, May 2013 (accessed 24 May 2013) <**http://www.guardian.co.uk/media/2013/may/09/bt-free-premier-league-football**>

Gibson (2012) 'TV rights set to top £5 billion for first time', *The Guardian*, November 2012 (accessed 24 May 2013) <**http://www.guardian.co.uk/football/2012/nov/12/premier-league-tv-rights-5-bn**>

Huang, C. (2013a) 'Xi's African Quest For Resources', *South China Morning Post*, 26 March 2013.

Hunag, C. (2013b) 'Xi seeks a new bond with Africa', *South China Morning Post*, 26 March 2013.

HM Treasury (2013) *The Independent Commission on Banking: The Financial Services* [Banking Reform Bill] (accessed on 22 May 2013) **<http://www.hm-treasury.gov.uk/fin_stability_regreform_icb.htm>**

Jackson, T. (2009) *Prosperity Without Growth: Economics for a Finite Planet* (London: Earthscan).

James, O. (2007) *Affluenza: How to be Successful and Stay Sane* (London: Vermillion).

LSE (2011) The *British Cycling Economy: Gross Cycling Product Report* (London School of Economics) (accessed on 22 May 2013) **<http://eprints.lse.ac.uk/38063/1/BritishCyclingEconomy.pdf>**

McKinsey & Company (2013) 'Insights and Publication—The impact of Disruptive Technology: A Conversation with Eric Schmidt' (accessed 23 May 2013) **<http://www.mckinsey.com/insights/high_tech_telecoms_internet/the_impact_of_disruptive_technology_a_conversation_with_eric_schmidt>**

Nakata (2013) 'Venture manufacturers on the rise', *Japan Times*, 29 March 2013.

Reuters (2013) 'Pursue Your Dreams Says Teen Phone App Millionaire' (as reported in the *South China Morning Post*, 27 March 2013).

Stiglitz, J. et al. (2009) *Report by the Commission on Economic Performance and Social Progress* (accessed 24 May 2013) **<http://www.stiglitz-sen-fitoussi.fr/documents/rapport_anglais.pdf>**

Stiglitz, J. (2010) *Reforming the International Monetary and Financial Systems in the Wake of the Global Crisis* (New York: New Press).

UEFA (2013) 'Financial fair play' (accessed 24 May 2013) **<http://www.uefa.com/uefa/footballfirst/protectingthegame/financialfairplay/index.html>**

Wallis, W. (2013) 'West pays catch-up in African markets', *Financial Times*, 16 and 17 March 2013.

World Economic Forum (2013a) *Global Agenda: World Economic Forum Annual Meeting Resilient Dynamism* (accessed 21 May 2013) **<http://www3.weforum.org/docs/AM13/WEF_AM13_ExecutiveSummary.pdf>**

World Economic Forum (2013b) *Global Risks 2013* (accessed 21 May 2013) **<http://reports.weforum.org/global-risks-2013/>**

Wetherly, P. and Otter, D. (2008) *The Business Environment*, 2nd edn (Oxford: Oxford University Press).

Wilkinson, R. and Pickett, K. (2009) *The Spirit Level: Why More Equal Societies Almost Always Do Better* (London: Allen Lane).

GLOSSARY

absolute advantage if two countries produce the same range of goods one has an absolute advantage over the other if it can produce greater quantities of the goods using the same amount of resources. Adam Smith showed that where this is the case it is better for each country to specialize in the goods in which it has an absolute advantage so increasing total production. Trade could then occur so that each country would be able to increase the amount of all goods available to it (see also comparative advantage).

acid rain burning fossil fuels releases gases such as sulphur dioxide and nitrogen dioxide into the atmosphere. These gases are transported by prevailing winds, and combine with moisture to produce 'acid rain', devastating natural vegetation and ecological systems.

affluenza the term used to refer to the alleged tendency of people to suffer a range of mental illnesses as a result of striving to increase their incomes so that, paradoxically, higher incomes lower the quality of life.

age structure structure of the population in terms of the proportions in each age band.

ageing population falling death rates (increased longevity) result in a growing number and share of elderly in the population, and increasing average age.

agencification private or public organizations given specific mandates by government, often reporting directly to a ministry but, at the same time, often one-removed from direct governmental procedures. Context and national differences will apply to the specific status of such agencies. The increasing use of agencies has prompted other working-titles, such as 'executive-agencies', and they are often linked to what is known as 'distributed governance'.

Agenda 21 a document about sustainable development formulated at the Rio conference in 1992.

agentification the increasing use of 'professional' agencies rather than civil service based ministries.

aggregate demand the total level of demand for all goods and services in an economy.

allocative efficiency (see efficiency).

alternative scenarios a form of environmental analysis in which alternative possible futures are identified.

apropriate technology the use of technology best suited to the external environment in which business is operating. Most often used to highlight the need for developing countries to adopt 'low-tech' solutions.

basic economic problem scarcity, requiring the allocation of resources between competing wants or needs, the need to minimize resource use and the need to ensure equitable distribution.

best value a term used both legally and managerially to quantify and qualify the 'best value' services available to the public from service providers: this was building on previous recommendations in relation to value for money (see below).

biodiversity the totality of species and life forms on earth.

birth rate the number of births per 1,000 of the population.

bureaucracy the paid (normally) civil servants or officials and their system of public administration.

business often defined narrowly in terms of the private sector, but a broad definition includes the public and 'third' sectors. Business involves the transformation of inputs into outputs to produce goods and services for customers or users.

business class (capitalist class) social group defined by ownership and control of business.

business dominance refers to the claim that business exercises unrivalled influence in politics.

business ethics the systematic study of the theories and practice of ethics applied in business.

capacity building refers to helping organizations to develop their resources (people, buildings, etc.) so that they are better able to meet their aims.

capitalism an economic system in which the means of production are overwhelmingly privately owned and operated for profit; decisions regarding investment of capital are made privately; and where production, distribution, and the prices of goods, services, and labour are affected by the forces of supply and demand in a largely free market.

capitalist class (see business class).

caretaker state refers to the main role of government being the provision of goods and services, rather than the classical role of exercising authority.

central government and local authorities most developed countries have developed public administration systems that often embrace central control and local delivery.

circular flow of income in a simple model of a market system money (or income) flows between firms and households in the form of payments for labour and commodities.

civil disobedience a tactic used by some campaigning organizations involving a willingness to break the law in order to protest a law or business action.

civil society organization (CSO) usually used as another term for pressure group—a voluntary association formed to campaign on specific issues, e.g. Greenpeace.

class social group defined by common characteristics or social position, especially occupation.

class structure a way of classifying the population according to class positions, e.g. working class and middle class.

colonialism the term is most often used in the context of the expansion of European powers across the globe from the Spanish and Portuguese conquests of South America and then the dominance of countries such as Britain, France and Holland in North America, the Far East and Africa. There is a fierce debate as to the effects of colonialism. Refer also to imperialism.

common good what is good for society as a whole, as opposed to purely private interests.

comparative advantage even if one country is better at producing all ranges of commodities compared with another, trade will still lead to overall gains in production. Here the more efficient country should specialize in the goods in which it has the greater comparative advantage and the less efficient country should specialize in the goods in which it has the smallest comparative disadvantage. In this way total production of the two countries would increase and trade will enable both countries to benefit.

competition the existence of competition is seen as being vital if businesses are to behave in an efficient manner. In reality, competition may be prevented by monopoly power and in some cases can be 'destructive'.

competition policy a major policy impacting on the EU business environment which aims to ensure that competition in the single market is not distorted by anti-competitive forces such as monopoly, oligopoly, restrictive practices, or state interference.

compulsory competitive tendering introduced as an administrative mechanism to determine effective competition procedures for public services.

complements these are commodities that we buy as a result of buying another commodity, e.g. if the demand for car transport increases so will the demand for petrol.

comprador capitalists is a term used by writers in the dependency tradition to characterize what they saw as the type of capitalism that would occur in the developing world as a result of trading with the developed world. Rather than a capitalist class growing within a developing country which was based on growing domestic goods and services for domestic needs, globalization would encourage capitalists to have an outward orientation through gearing production to external markets based on a very narrow range of activities which exploited the natural resources of the country.

comprehensive performance assessment (CPA) a means by which to determine the effectiveness of public service provision.

constitution the highest form of law and a device for limiting the power of the state; sets out the rules about making rules.

consumer sovereignty the claim that consumers, not firms, are ultimately in charge of the economic system through their spending decisions. In a free market system it should be the consumer who has the power to decide what should be produced. If there are anxieties that this is not the case and that producers have the power then there needs to be consumer protection.

consumerism an attitude in which consumption is seen as a prime source of personal well-being (see also materialism).

corporate citizenship this term views corporations as members of society with similar rights and responsibilities to citizens.

corporate responsibility (CR) a development of corporate social responsibility which broadens the focus of responsibility to relationships with internal staff and wider industry.

corporate social responsibility (CSR) the practice of corporate responsibility in relation to the stakeholders who form the social context of the business. The term is increasingly less used because of its narrow focus on methods of reporting, narrow stakeholder focus, and lack of integration into governance.

cosmopolitan society a society that is open to a wide range of cultural influences (see also **multiculturalism**).

creative destruction is the term given by Schumpeter for the process by which new inventions and innovations will constantly evolve, with the new replacing the old.

culture refers to the set of values, beliefs and lifestyles that characterize a group or society.

death rate the number of deaths per thousand of the population.

declaration of incompatibility the courts have the power to declare any piece of legislation incompatible with the provisions of the Human Rights Act 1998. This Act brought the European Convention on Human Rights into UK law. The power of the courts is limited as a declaration of incompatibility does not affect the ongoing operation of the law. There is, however, a procedure by which the government can remove the incompatibility following such a declaration.

demand–pull inflation inflation associated with an excess demand for goods and services when the economy is at or above full employment.

democracy (see also **liberal democracy**) a political system in which political power is in the hands of the people: 'rule by the people'.

deontological ethics this theory argues that there are certain core ethical principles that apply in any situation, such as 'It is wrong to kill another person'.

dependency often used to describe the inequality of power and forms of economic domination that characterizes the relations between rich and poor countries. Dependency theory emerged from the work of André Gunder Frank and the United Nations Economic Commission on Latin America under Raul Prebisch. Reacting against theories of development and modernization that contended that poor countries would inevitably follow the stages of western economic development, dependency theorists argued that these countries faced systematic 'underdevelopment' within the world economy.

dependency culture the argument that state benefits can foster dependency on the part of recipients and undermine independence.

design, build, finance and operate system (DBFO) a working system for developing PPP and PFI developments.

destructive competition there are areas of business activity in which unregulated competition could be harmful. Cutting costs could mean endangering health and safety to workers and consumers and so regulation is needed. There are also whole areas of business where it would be better to have only one firm (see **natural monopoly** below).

devolution the sharing or giving up of power from central to local level, e.g. the establishment of a Scottish parliament.

digital era governance the means by which a government governs in all its forms and all its levels in the digital era.

diminishing returns occur when businesses face a capacity constraint. Commonly, this might be a capital or land constraint and as business tries to expand production it will find that its costs rise and productivity falls because it comes up against capacity constraints.

disposable income the amount of income that people can actually spend after all taxes, etc. have been deducted.

distributive efficiency (see **efficiency**).

divisional structure a type of organization structure based on semi-independent operational units or divisions.

dynamic gains from trade are on-going and arise from the additional benefits of trade on top of the gains from specialization. For example, by opening up to trade a country can gain from the exposure of its domestic businesses to foreign competition as well as the ability of its domestic businesses to now sell to larger markets and, thus, benefit from potential economies of scale.

economic growth the process of increasing the output of goods and services produced by the economy or, more strictly, the process of increasing productive capacity.

economies of scale refer to a range of circumstances in which producing and selling greater volumes of output will enable cost reductions to be made. Chapter 3 Mini-Case 3.3 explores how containerization has enabled transport costs to be dramatically reduced.

ecosystem a community of interdependent living organisms, plants and animals, set in the non-living components of their surroundings.

efficiency refers to the way in which the three parts of the economic problem are resolved.

For a business to be efficient in an economic sense it must produce so that: customers get 'value for money' and this will happen if prices equal marginal costs (allocative efficiency); the average cost of each unit of output is minimized so that resources are being used as efficiently as possible (productive efficiency); the distribution of the output is 'fair' and creates equity (distributive efficiency). Deciding on what is equitable is very contentious. In the neoclassical perspective the free market is the best way of achieving this. Structuralist and Marxist critics argue that unregulated markets can lead to exploitation of consumers and employees and create a divided world where there is gross inequity. The Green movement argues that it is the planetary system that is being exploited and that our present prosperity endangers that of future generations.

elasticity of demand price elasticity of demand refers to the responsiveness of demand to changes in price. It determines the effect on a firm's revenue of price changes. Income elasticity of demand is the responsiveness of demand to changes in income.

emissions trading creating a market in carbon dioxide emissions whereby countries and companies receive licences to emit carbon dioxide. If the companies exceed their emission limits they must buy permits from other companies which have reduced their emissions. This creates an incentive to reduce emissions on the part of an individual company.

empirical research the gathering and use of evidence to try and prove the validity of theories.

employee protection is a term used to describe laws whose purpose is to protect the interests of employees in the workplace, such as protection against unfair dismissal.

employer of choice an employing organization which has gained a reputation for being a good employer in the employment market. Employers of choice are characterized by competitive terms and conditions, the provision of developmental opportunities for staff, fair dealing, involving employees in decision-making, interesting work, and an interest in work–life balance.

endogenous change occurs when a variable is affected by other variables within an economic model.

enlargement the EU has grown via several waves of new entrants, although enlargement commonly refers to the 2004 accession of ten new members, largely from Eastern Europe.

enterprise 'making things happen, having ideas and doing something about them, taking advantage of the opportunities to bring about change' (SGE programme 1999: see Chapter 14 References).

'Any attempt at new business or new venture creation, such as self-employment, a new business organization, or the expansion of existing business, by an individual, teams of individuals or established businesses' (Irwin and Wilkinson 2001).

enterprise and entrepreneurship 'enterprise is a set of qualities and competencies that can be employed in different settings, whilst entrepreneurship involves the process of creating and developing new ventures' (Enterprise Insight 2005: 23: see Chapter 14 References).

entrepreneur anyone who attempts a new business or new venture creation, such as self-employment, a new business organization, social enterprise or the expansion of an existing business by an individual, teams of individuals, to established business (DTI 2003: see Chapter 14 References).

environmental analysis the more or less systematic analysis of the business environment to assist business strategy and performance.

environmental and ecological auditing refers to processes that are analogous to financial auditing. Environmental auditing would refer generally to evaluations of processes and situations which have environmental implications to ensure compliance with regulations and implementation of environmental management systems. Ecological auditing refers to the measuring and monitoring of conditions to protect or enhance the natural environment.

environmental footprint in relation to an individual company or organization, its total environmental impact, referring to direct and indirect resource use, generation of waste and effluent, plus any other changes it imposes on the natural environment. For a whole economy, it is the land and sea area needed to provide all the energy, water, transport, food and materials it consumes. Thus, if the population of the whole world lived at the same level as the UK, it would require three worlds to sustain it.

environmental impact assessment (EIA) is the assessment of the possible positive or negative impacts that a proposed project or course of action may have on the environment, covering the environmental, social, and economic impacts.

environmental uniqueness the recognition that each business operates in an environment that is, in some ways, unique to it.

equal opportunity the idea that people from all backgrounds should enjoy the same chances to benefit from valued opportunities, e.g. in education and employment.

equality of outcome equality between people measured in terms of outcomes such as income and wealth.

equilibrium analysis the use of demand and supply diagrams to predict the effects of changes in markets. An essential part of microeconomics.

equity (see efficiency above).

ethical consumerism bringing ethical considerations into spending decisions, e.g. fair trade.

ethnocentrism belief in the superiority of one's own culture over other cultures. In business, this can mean a tendency for many western global businesses to assume that the norm to aspire to is a western cultural model, and that it is western values of individualism and personal aspiration that are embedded in the supra-national bodies.

EU budget the means to fund common policies, balance the gains and losses from integration, promote cohesion and redistribute wealth. Expenditure dominates with substantial sums allocated traditionally to the Common Agricultural Policy (CAP) and increasingly regional policy. Contributions have increased progressively necessitating new resources such as VAT and later GNP-based measures.

euro-centric view focusing on European culture or history to the exclusion of a wider view of the world; implicitly regarding European culture as pre-eminent.

European integration a process of economic association in which progressive integration requires policy harmonization and institutional changes rather than merely the removal of trade barriers.

European Monetary Union a three-stage process involving convergence of participants' economies, the establishment of a common monetary policy run by the European Central Bank, and ultimately the introduction of the single currency, the euro.

European treaties agreed by member states' governments and ratified in their parliaments, these are the legal basis for the EU and its operations, e.g. Treaty of Rome that founded the EEC, Treaty of Maastricht that formed the EU.

executive the branch of government that is concerned with implementing public policy and law.

executive dominance refers to the dominance of Parliament by the executive (government) through control of a parliamentary majority coupled with party discipline.

expert opinion a form of environmental analysis relying on expert views, often using external consultants.

external environment environmental forces that operate in the world outside the organization.

fair trade (or fairtrade) 'is about better prices, decent working conditions, local sustainability, and fair terms of trade for farmers and workers in the developing world. By requiring companies to pay sustainable prices (which must never fall lower than the market price), fairtrade addresses the injustices of conventional trade, which traditionally discriminates against the poorest weakest producers. It enables them to improve their position and have more control over their lives' (Fairtrade Foundation <http://www.fairtrade.org.uk/what_is_fairtrade/faqs.aspx>).

federal state a state in which power is shared constitutionally between the centre and localities (as opposed to a unitary state).

feudalism refers to the type of social system which is characterized by a rigid hierarchy transmitting power and control downwards from an all-powerful monarch, supported by the landowning nobility, down to the mass of property-less peasants. In this system political and economic power is concentrated in the hands of this tiny elite.

final or finished goods and services goods and services purchased by their ultimate users.

final salary pension a form of employer-sponsored occupational pension arrangement. It is the most common type of 'defined benefit pension schemes'. It pays former employees a pension calculated as a percentage of the salary that was being received at the date of retirement or in the final years of work prior to retirement.

fiscal policy measures that alter the level and composition of government expenditure and taxation.

first past the post (FPTP) electoral system used for parliamentary elections in the UK, in which the winning candidate in each constituency needs just to obtain more votes than any other candidate (not necessarily a majority). Criticized by supporters of proportional representation (PR).

five forces Porter's (1980) framework for analysing competitive forces in a market.

flat structure a type of organization structure or principle based on delayering, i.e. stripping out management layers.

food miles the distance food travels between producer and consumer, commonly used to highlight the impact on the environment caused by production of carbon dioxide emissions during transport.

Fordism describes the mass production assembly line techniques pioneered in the automobile industry but then adopted across manufacturing industry in the early to mid 20th century.

foreign direct investment investment of capital by a government, company, or other organization in production and marketing operations that are located in a foreign country.

free market in a strict sense refers to a market that is free of government regulation or intervention. In practice, supporters of the free market advocate minimum government.

freedom (see **liberty**) a key political principle referring to the ability of individuals to decide for themselves how to live their own lives, often linked with arguments in favour of the 'free market'.

frictional or search unemployment arises when people find themselves, for any number of reasons, temporarily between jobs without leaving the labour market.

functional structure a type of organization structure based on functional departments, e.g. finance, marketing, HR.

generalization to make a statement that is intended to be of general application.

generation gap because of cultural change people of different ages exhibit different values and lifestyles.

genetically modified organism (GMO) creation of plants, animals and micro-organisms by unnatural manipulation of genes, perhaps taking DNA from one species and inserting it into another unrelated one. GMOs can spread and cross with naturally-occurring organisms. Proliferation in an unpredictable way may produce unknown consequences. GMOs are a form of genetic pollution.

glass ceiling a metaphor to refer to the under-representation of women in senior positions, especially management, above a certain level of advancement.

global warming the heating up of the earth's atmosphere mainly due to burning fossil fuels, leading to global climate change.

globalization the processes by which it is argued that the world economy has become more integrated. Globalization can be seen as an increase in flows across national boundaries. These include not only economic flows of trade and investment in the form of multinational companies and international finance but also the transmission and mixing of cultural influences, migration and increased communication. The benefits and drawbacks of these processes, and the extent to which they may be controlled or influenced, are the subject of much controversy.

glocalization the process of tailoring products or services to different local markets around the world.

good governance All societies need government in some form, but there may be disagreement about the form of government and its role in society. There is substantial agreement, particularly in the West, that good governance requires democracy.

good society In all societies the need for politics arises from disagreements and conflicts between people over values and interests—different views about the nature of the 'good society'.

governance the means by which a government governs in all its forms and all its levels.

government can refer to the process of governing (see also **governance**), or to those who are in government, the government of the day.

green marketing refers to the marketing of products which can be construed as having favourable environmental characteristics which can be emphasized in the marketing message to make the product more attractive to the consumer. The presumption is that the environmental characteristics highlighted in the message are genuine. Green marketing can cover changes to the product, the production process, the packaging, and the advertising.

green transport plans are produced as a matter of course by public authorities to minimize the environmental impact of the operation of the whole transport system in a town, city, or region, but green transport plans are also produced by organizations such as companies and educational institutions to minimize the environmental impact of the transport activities they generate, whether by workers, customers, or goods delivery/despatch.

greenwash is green marketing used to deceive the consumer into thinking that an organization's products, aims, and/or policies are environmentally friendly when in reality they are not.

Health and Safety Executive (HSE) the government body charged with enforcing health and safety regulations in the UK. Together with local authorities,

HSE inspectors regularly examine premises to check that regulations are being fully complied with.

hierarchical structure a type of organization structure based on layers of authority with power concentrated at the top.

hot money refers to inflows of foreign currency into a country simply as a result of the speculative hope that by buying a country's currency it might appreciate in value and produce a windfall profit.

ideology a set of political belief and values, e.g. liberalism, socialism.

immediate environment refers to those aspects of the business environment that are relevant to day-to-day decision-making and operations, e.g. the behaviour of competitors.

imperialism imperialism is a policy of extending control or authority over foreign entities as a means of acquisition and/or maintenance of empires, either through direct territorial conquest or through indirect methods of exerting control on the politics and/or economy of other countries. The essential feature of the Marxist theories of imperialism, or related theories such as dependency theory, is their focus on the economic relation between countries, rather than the formal political relationship. Imperialism thus consists not necessarily in the direct control of one country by another, but in the economic exploitation of one region by another or of a group by another.

individual freedom What it means to be free and to what extent freedom should be curtailed by laws are highly contested questions. In a basic sense freedom may be defined in terms of 'living as I choose'.

individualism no single meaning, but can refer to the idea that as individuals we make our own choices, as well as to the idea that people tend to behave in a self-interested way.

inflation the process of continually rising prices.

informal economy refers to activities, which can be paid or unpaid, which are not registered with the tax authorities. Informal paid work includes illegal tax evasion such as 'cash-in-hand' payments.

institutional triangle the three decision-making bodies that implement EU laws and policies: the Council of the EU; the European Parliament; and the European Commission.

integration refers to the extent to which people from different ethnic and religious backgrounds participate as members of a common society rather than living separately.

intensification of work the process by which employers place increased pressure on employees to work longer hours and/or to expend greater effort so as to increase productivity.

inter-generational equity refers to the concept of fairness between generations, or, being as fair to our grandchildren as we are to ourselves.

inter-governmental organization (IGO) (also intergovernmentalism) an association of sovereign nation-states usually for the purpose of treaty or common action, e.g. World Trade Organization (WTO).

internal environment this phrase reminds us that managers have to operate within an environment that is constituted by the organization itself, e.g. relations with other colleagues and departments.

intra-generational equity refers to the concept of fairness between different interest groups in the same generation.

intrapreneur an intrapreneur has been defined as 'a person within a large corporation who takes direct responsibility for turning an idea into a profitable finished product through assertive risk-taking and innovation' (*American Heritage Directory*, 3rd edition, 1992: see Chapter 14 References).

invention is the creation of a new product or process of production.

ISO 14001 an international standard of best practice for carrying out environmental management systems audits, policies, etc. It sets out a range of criteria which companies must satisfy to achieve the standard.

joint ventures a commercial undertaking entered into by two or more parties, usually in the short term. Joint ventures are generally governed by the Partnership Act (1890) but they differ from partnerships in that they are limited by time or by activity.

jurisdiction essentially this is the geographical scope within which a court or parliament can exercise its power. The nature of jurisdiction has changed with the rise of globalization particularly in the member states of the European Union.

just in time refers to the organization of production processes to minimize the holding of inventories, which is very expensive. The production process is organized so that parts and raw materials are delivered to the production site as nearly as possible to the time when they are actually required.

Keynesian welfare consensus broad agreement (consensus) between the main political parties and within society (in the 1950s and 1960s) that government should be responsible for managing the economy, especially to secure full employment (Keynesian), and provide a range of welfare services such as health and education (welfare).

Kyoto Protocol an international agreement linked to the United Nations Framework Convention on Climate Change, which committed its signatory parties by setting internationally binding emission reduction targets. It was adopted in Kyoto, Japan, on 11 December 1997 and entered into force on 16 February 2005.

labour market flexibility is when the labour market functions in such a way that labour resources can be utilized on a flexible basis. For example, the use of 'zero-hours' contracts which became a focus of controversy in the UK in 2013. The criticism of such flexibility is that it is beneficial to employers but disadvantageous for employees.

late industrialization after the end of the Second World War, many former colonies (see colonialism) gained their political independence. Amartya Sen argues that in order for these countries to develop they would need to industrialize using a different set of economic policies than that followed by the western capitalist countries.

learning organization one that consciously seeks to manage the learning and development of its workforce. Learning organizations, and the people in them, learn constantly from everything they do. Such an idea is harnessed to the target of making the organization as a whole behave in a sustainable way, rather than it just being the responsibility of the Sustainability Officer or the PR Department.

left wing has no single meaning, but generally refers to an ideological viewpoint that supports greater state involvement in business and society, and greater equality.

liberal democracy is a form of government that combines democratic procedures with forms of individual freedom and equality that have been championed in the liberal political tradition, hence 'liberal + democratic'.

liberty (see freedom).

licence to operate the idea that corporations need to retain a level of public trust and legitimacy.

life cycle assessment is the assessment of the environmental impacts associated with all the stages of a product's life; from raw material extraction through to materials processing, manufacture, distribution, use, repair and maintenance, and disposal or recycling. Such a comprehensive overview improves decision-making.

Lisbon Agenda the Lisbon Summit in 2000 set the goals for the future economic development of the EU to 2010, notably that the EU should become the most competitive and dynamic, knowledge-based economy in the world, capable of sustained economic growth, with more and better jobs, and greater social cohesion.

lobbying a method of political influence through advocacy and persuasion of policy-makers.

locational advantage companies, especially MNCs, have the option to locate their operations in response to potential business advantages, such as cheap labour.

macroeconomics/microeconomics macroeconomics is the study of the economy in terms of the broad aggregates of employment, inflation, economic growth, trade, and the balance of payments as well as levels of inequality. Microeconomics is the study of individual product and resource markets.

macroeconomic policy is action by policy-makers to improve aspects of the performance of the whole economy.

majority-minority city the phenomenon of ethnic or religious groups that are minorities in a national context coming to form a majority in a particular city.

marginality whenever we make a decision we do so 'at the margin', in other words we weigh up the advantages of the next decision to be taken against the disadvantages of not doing it. By studying these marginal costs and benefits we should not only be able to make better decisions but should be able to predict how economic actors are likely to behave.

market a system of voluntary exchange, created by the relationship between buyers and sellers.

market failure whilst markets do mostly work efficiently there are large areas in which they fail to work or else will need government support or control to enable them to do so.

market structure refers to the number and size of sellers in a market, e.g. oligopoly.

materialism an emphasis on material living standards and possessions as a prime source of well being, e.g. that a good life means having more money (see also consumerism).

matrix structure introduces a horizontal principle cutting across departments, e.g. on the basis of project teams.

micro businesses is a term to describe a 'very' small business.

millennium development goals eight goals that all 191 United Nations member states have agreed to try to achieve by the year 2015. The United Nations Millennium Declaration, signed in September 2000, commits the states to:

- eradicate extreme poverty and hunger
- achieve universal primary education
- promote gender equality and empower women
- reduce child mortality
- improve maternal health
- combat HIV/AIDS, malaria and other diseases
- ensure environmental sustainability
- develop a global partnership for development.

minimum wage the national minimum wage (NMW) in the UK imposes a statutory duty on all employers to not pay below a defined minimum.

mixed economy a mix of private and public sectors, e.g. a predominantly capitalist economy with some element of public ownership of industry (nationalization).

money GDP GDP unadjusted for inflation.

monetary policy measures that alter interest rates or the money supply.

money purchase pension a form of employer-sponsored occupational pension scheme, also sometimes called a 'defined contribution scheme'. Employee and employer contributions are made into separate individual pension accounts and then invested. At retirement the money in the account is used to purchase an annuity from an insurance company which pays a weekly or monthly pension for the rest of the retiree's life.

multicultural society a society in which many ethnic and religious communities co-exist, as opposed to a society with a homogeneous culture.

multi-level governance governance takes place on a number of spatial scales—national, sub-national, supra-national.

multinational corporation (MNC) a company that has production facilities in more than one country (i.e. undertakes foreign direct investment) including securing supplies of raw materials, utilizing cheap labour sources, servicing local markets, and bypassing protectionist barriers. Multinationals may be seen as an efficient form of organization, making effective use of the world's resources and transferring technology between countries. On the other hand, some have excessive power, are beyond the control of governments (especially weak governments), and are able to exploit host countries, especially in the Third World, where they are able to operate with low safety levels and inadequate control of pollution.

narrow money refers to notes and coins in circulation and reserve balances held by commercial banks and building societies at the Bank of England.

nation-state refers to the conjunction of a system of political rule (a state) and a population comprising a national community (nation).

National Pensions Saving Scheme (NPSS) a government-sponsored pension fund proposed by the Turner Committee as a means of increasing pension savings in the UK. From 2012 all employers who do not operate an occupational pension scheme will have to contribute a sum equivalent to 3% of their pay-bill into NPSS accounts set up for their staff. A further 4% of pay will be contributed by employees and 1% as a result of tax relief. Membership will be voluntary, but new employees will be automatically enrolled.

national sovereignty the capacity of a nation to govern its own affairs: national self-determination.

natural monopoly in industries where the capital costs are very large it is often sensible to only have one firm operating so that as output expands the capital costs are spread across the output, thus lowering average costs.

natural rate of unemployment the rate of unemployment which reflects the prevailing level of competitiveness of the labour market.

neoclassical endogenous growth theory sees growth as being the result of the constant development of technology. Whilst this is driven by businesses constantly seeking to boost profits, it is also important that there is openness to trade between countries, with technology flowing across frontiers through technology transfer.

neocorporatism a system of political representation in which privileged status is accorded to business and labour, which may be seen as partners with government in formulating and implementing economic policy.

neoliberalism a label given to the revival of classical liberal ideas in the 1980s, often referred to as a free market ideology.

new international division of labour After the end of the Second World War and as many former colonies were gaining independence there was a belief that these developing countries would be able to specialize in labour intensive products and that the developed world would specialize in manufacturing and service activities. A global free trade system would mean that all countries would prosper and grow on the basis of this international division of labour.

New Labour a term coined by Tony Blair to distinguish the modernization of Labour party politics under his leadership, as opposed to 'old Labour'.

new public management (NPM) a general term for new management practices introduced in the public sector since the 1970s.

New Right a label given to the character of right-wing politics in the 1980s especially in the UK and the US. No single meaning but usually refers to a combination of neoliberal and conservative ideas.

newly industrialized countries (NICs) countries which have recently increased the proportion of industrial production in their national income and of industrial exports in their trade. The NICs have been the most rapidly growing part of the world economy in the last quarter of the twentieth century. There is no standard list of NICs: they include the 'East Asian tigers', Hong Kong, South Korea, Singapore and Taiwan, and various other countries including Brazil, China, India, Malaysia, Mexico, South Africa, and Thailand, and their number is growing.

non-democratic refers to a political system that lacks basic democratic rules and procedures, such as: competing parties, regular elections, all adults having the right to vote, freedom of speech, etc. In practice, it is more useful to think of a spectrum of political systems which are more or less democratic than a simple dichotomy between 'democratic' and 'non-democratic'. For example, some states in the EU are more democratic than others.

non-governmental organization (NGO) refers to any non-profit voluntary citizens' group which is organized on a local, national, or international level. Such groups contribute to the wider civil society through direct service to, or advocacy on behalf of, groups in need. Good international examples are Oxfam and Amnesty International.

non-profit objectives goals or aims that are not making or intending to make profit.

occupational segregation a measure of the extent to which males and females are found in different occupational groups.

old Labour a reference to traditional Labour party values and policies such as public ownership and

redistribution of income, often used pejoratively by supporters of New Labour.

opportunity cost scarcity means that choices have to be made about what to produce. If you choose one thing then something else is given up and the opportunity cost is the cost of the next most desirable alternative.

organization culture the values and beliefs of an organization.

organization structure refers to the internal layout of an organization, e.g. in terms of departments and lines of accountability.

organizational design all organizations are subject to processes of conscious design intended to enhance performance, e.g. by changing the organization structure.

outsourcing the buying in of components, sub-assemblies, finished products, and services from outside suppliers rather than by supplying them internally. A firm may decide to buy in rather than supply internally because it lacks the expertise, investment capital, or physical space required to do so. It may also be able to buy in more cheaply or more quickly than manufacturing in-house.

peak organization usually in reference to the CBI and TUC, as organizations which represent the interests of business and labour as a whole.

PEST analysis a form of environmental analysis in which environmental forces are classified as political, economic, social and technological.

pluralism a model or theory which emphasizes the dispersal and fragmentation of political influence among a large number of groups and interests in society.

politics no single definition, but may be seen as the activity that is concerned with determining the rules under which we live in society.

popular sovereignty the idea of popular rule (see also democracy).

portfolio investment the list of holdings in securities owned by an investor or institution. In building up an investment portfolio an institution will have its own investment analysts, while an individual may make use of the services of a merchant bank that offers portfolio management.

positive action measures to recruit from under-represented groups, e.g. through targeted advertising of job opportunities or training.

potential GDP the real GDP associated with the full employment of all an economy's resources.

poverty contested term referring to those who are poor according to some absolute or relative measure. An absolute measure has no regard to average living standards whereas a relative measure defines poverty in relation to the general living standards within the society.

Prebisch–Singer hypothesis the theory predicts that the terms of trade between primary products and manufactured goods tend to deteriorate over time. Developed independently by economists Raul Prebisch and Hans Singer in 1950, the thesis suggests that countries that export primary commodities (such as most developing countries) would be able to import less and less for a given level of exports. Prebisch went on to argue that, for this reason, developing countries should strive to diversify their economies and lessen dependence on primary commodity exports by developing their manufacturing industry. This may initially mean that such countries need to protect their domestic industries from open trade.

precautionary principle the presumption that no new technology should be introduced if there is a potential risk that the costs might outweigh the benefits even if there is no hard evidence that this may be the case.

precedent has more than one usage. In its technical legal sense, it refers to a decision of the court that can be relied upon in later cases. As noted in Chapter 6, if the precedent is found to be authoritative it will normally be followed by courts of similar or lesser standing. In the broader, less technical, sense lawyers will often refer to precedents when drafting legal documents. These precedents are documents that have been used in previous cases which can be adapted to the needs of the current client.

price elasticity of demand measures the 'responsiveness' of demand to changes in price. It is the percentage change in the quantity demanded as a result of a small percentage change in price.

private finance initiatives (PFIs) a fully developed set of rules and regulations governing the relationship between private and public sectors with targeted advice on financing.

private sector consists of all businesses in some form of private ownership.

privatization mainly refers to the transfer of assets from the public sector to the private sector (e.g. the privatization of nationalized industries and the sale of council houses) but can include opening tax-funded services up to competition from private sector businesses, and contracting out.

The fear of monopoly power persuaded many people in the 20th century that many key industries should be directly run by the government. In the UK many such industries were nationalized post-1945. This was reversed by the Conservative governments from 1979 with a wave of privatization which encouraged their private ownership and tried to extend market mechanisms even into areas of the welfare state such as education and health.

process innovation the introduction of new methods in the production process through application of knowledge.

producer-led sometimes put forward as a criticism of public services, i.e. that they are run in the interests of the producers rather than the consumers or users.

product innovation the development of new or improved products through application of knowledge.

production possibility frontier this illustrates the potential combinations of output that a country can attain if it uses its given resources efficiently.

productive efficiency (see efficiency).

productivity measures the rate at which inputs are converted into outputs. Productivity is rising if, for any given level of resource input, output rises. Productivity is also defined as the quantity of goods and services that people produce in a given time period.

profit the excess of total revenue over total costs. Profit is the primary motivation of private sector business.

public finance initiatives the use of public–private partnerships (PPP) for the public sector with a focus on finance.

public interest When we say that government should act in the public interest we mean it should act so as to benefit society as a whole. A 'whistleblower' who exposes corporate wrong-doing might damage the interests of the company but be acting in the public interest. (Also see common good.)

public–private partnerships (PPPs) a fully developed set of rules and regulations governing the relationship between private and public sectors.

public sector the part of the economy that is owned and controlled by the state, including public services.

public service comparator (PSC) an administrative device to ensure that a comparison is made between public and private service costs and effectiveness when considering PPPs and PFIs.

public service ethic the idea that public service managers and employees are, or should be, motivated by the desire to provide a service to the public or contribute to the public good. This is contrasted with the idea that self-interest in the form of making money governs the private sector.

race to the bottom the claim that nation-states are obliged to reduce the 'burden' of regulation and taxation on business in order to attract inward investment.

real GDP GDP adjusted to strip out the effects of inflation.

recession a decline in real GDP that lasts for at least two consecutive quarters of a year.

regional development agencies (RDAs) organizations created by government to aid and focus on regional development.

regional policy a key policy area involving transfers to regions performing below the EU average and facing structural difficulties. It has increased in significance following enlargement.

relative prices the price of one good or service compared to another.

resource depletion the using up once and for all of natural resources which cannot be renewed, e.g. oil.

right to manage refers to the claim that business decisions should be in the hands of managers. An alternative idea is that employees should have more say in the running of business.

right wing has no single meaning, but generally refers to an ideological viewpoint that opposes greater state involvement in business and society, and accepts or supports inequality.

Rio conference or **Rio summit** a global environmental conference held in Rio de Janeiro from 3 to 14 June 1992.

rule of law means that the powers exercised by government are based in law and all citizens are equal before the law.

Schengen Agreement is a European Union-wide single state agreement for international travel purposes with no internal border controls.

secularism a secular society is one in which religion is a weak source of values and beliefs, and has been displaced by science and reason.

separate legal personality this is the legal device by which those who own a company are distinguished from it. Once a company is accepted as being properly formed it has an independent legal identity which gives it separate rights and responsibilities.

separation of powers a constitutional principle referring to the separation of the three main branches of government: legislative, executive, and judicial.

single market the single, common or internal market of the EU involves the abolition of obstacles to trade among members. It embraces the four freedoms covering the movement of goods, people, capital and services.

social cohesion refers to the extent to which society is held together, e.g. by shared values rather than some people feeling marginalized or excluded.

social enterprises 'businesses with primary social objectives whose surpluses are principally reinvested for that purpose in the business or in the community, rather than being driven by the need to maximize profit for shareholders and owners' ('Social Enterprise: a strategy for success' <http://www.dti.gov.uk/ socialenterprise>).

social entrepreneur a specific term for someone who employs business principles and business start-up techniques for societal good and social benefit.

social justice a political principle that is concerned with the fairness of society, particularly in respect of the distribution of income.

social mobility a measure of the chances of people from different backgrounds to attain positions of high status and/or income, e.g. for working-class children to 'move up' into middle-class occupations.

social partners usually in reference to business and labour, as partners in a shared endeavour to secure the health of business and the economy.

social responsibility obligation of an organization towards the welfare and interests of the society in which it operates.

socialism a left-wing political ideology, involving a critique of capitalism and support for state regulation and/or control of business.

sovereign the highest form or source of authority.

sovereignty a term referring to the highest form or source of authority, e.g. parliamentary sovereignty.

spatial level the territorial or geographical scale at which business or other activity takes place, e.g. local, national, global.

Stability and Growth Pact a commitment to budgetary discipline among euro-zone members. It sets a ceiling of 3% GDP on government borrowing, a breach of which could invoke substantial fines (up to 0.5% GDP). Considered too rigid and politically unpopular, its rules were relaxed in March 2005.

stagflation a combination of economic stagnation and inflation.

stakeholder any individual or group that is affected by (and thus has a stake in) business decisions.

stakeholder analysis a form of environmental analysis based on identifying key stakeholders and assessing their interests and potential influence.

stakeholder theory the view that business has many stakeholders. These are groups who have an interest in or are affected by business. Hence, it is argued that business should take these groups into account.

state a narrow definition refers to the capacity to make and enforce rules within a defined territory backed up by coercion. In a broader sense refers to the public sector (see also caretaker state).

static gains from trade occur as a result of the efficiency gains from exploiting relative comparative advantages. These arise as a result of a nation's ability to specialize and trade, and are a 'one-off' gain in terms of boosting living standards amongst trading partners.

statutory maternity pay (SMP) the minimum amount of money that employers are obliged to pay employees while they are taking periods of maternity leave up to and following the birth of a baby.

structural or mismatch unemployment arises when labour is released from declining industries without the skills to be readily absorbed into new or existing industries.

sub-national governance a level of political authority below or within the nation-state e.g. local government.

supply chain the chain of organizations involved in transforming raw materials into goods and services for the end-user.

supra-national governance a level of political authority above the nation-state e.g. the EU.

sustainable development an approach to economic and social development that seeks to strike a balance between the need for economic growth, and equity between social groups and between generations, especially in terms of issues of global resource depletion and global environmental degradation.

SWOT analysis a form of internal–external environmental analysis to identify strengths, weaknesses (internal), opportunities and threats (external).

technology transfer refers to technology flowing across frontiers.

Thatcherism a label given to the ideology of the Thatcher governments in Britain in the 1980s. At one level the term simply recognizes Thatcher's dominance of British politics during this period, but the ideological content is usually referred to as neoliberalism or the New Right.

transnational corporation a firm which has global presence, range of markets, production and/or subsidiaries (see also multinational corporation).

treaty an international agreement between two or more nation-states which becomes binding in law. The most obvious example of this is the Treaty of Rome which founded the European Economic Community, the forerunner of the European Union.

trend extrapolation a form of environmental analysis based on identifying and projecting trends, e.g. sales figures.

trickle down the idea that inequality may benefit the poorest members of society because the high rewards at the top motivate improved economic performance from which all benefit.

triple bottom line refers to the idea that, while an enterprise is normally judged by its profit and loss account ('bottom line'), it should also be judged by social and environmental criteria; also referred to as 'people, planet, profit'.

two-party system Britain is often characterized as a two-party system because the two main parties—Conservative and Labour—have dominated national politics for the last century.

unitary state a state, like the UK, in which power is concentrated at the centre, as opposed to a federal state in which power is shared between different levels of government.

upskilling is a rise in the average level of skill required.

utilitarian ethics this theory argues that something is right when it maximizes the greatest good for the greatest number.

value chain Porter sees the firm as comprising a set of horizontal functions (e.g. procurement, IT, human resources) and vertical operations, both upstream towards the market and downstream towards the sources of the resources, across which it is possible to add value by changing the way things are done (see Porter, 1985, Chapter 3).

value for money (VFM) a legal and managerial term introduced to encourage local and central government to evaluate the provision of public services.

Washington Consensus a set of policies promulgated by many neoliberal economists as a formula for promoting economic growth in many parts of Latin America by introducing various market-oriented economic reforms which are designed to make the target economy more like that of first world countries such as the United States. It was first presented in 1989 by John Williamson, an economist from the Institute for International Economics, an international economic think tank based in Washington, DC. It is so-called because it attempts to summarize the commonly shared themes among policy advice by Washington-based institutions at the time, such as the International Monetary Fund, the World Bank and the US Treasury Department, which were believed to be necessary for the recovery of Latin America from the financial crises of the 1980s.

welfare state refers to the growth of state expenditure on a range of public services such as education, health, housing, social services and income support.